THE Comedy COLLECTION

THE Comedy COLLECTION

CHANCELLOR
PRESS

First published in Great Britain in 1994 by Chancellor Press
an imprint of Reed Consumer Books Limited
Michelin House, 81 Fulham Road, London SW3 6RB
and Auckland, Melbourne, Singapore and Toronto

Compilation: Alex Bennion
Design: Gwyn Lewis

ISBN 1 85152 316 2

A CIP catalogue record for this book is available from
the British Library

Printed in Great Britain by the Bath Press

CONTENTS

☆★☆★☆★☆★☆★☆★☆★☆★☆★☆★☆

Funny Turns

☆★☆★☆★☆★☆★☆★☆★☆★☆★☆★☆★☆★☆

JAMES HERRIOT

I was always apprehensive and ill at ease when I had Mrs Featherstone's problem dog on the table, but this time I felt relaxed and full of confidence. But then I was always like that when I was delirious.

Delirium was only one of the countless peculiar manifestations of Brucellosis. This disease, which causes contagious abortion in cattle, had ruined thousands of good farmers of my generation and was also a constant menace to the veterinary surgeons who had to deliver the premature calves and remove the afterbirths.

Thank heaven, the Brucellosis scheme has now just about eradicated the disease but in the fifties such a thing hadn't been dreamed of and I and my contemporaries wallowed almost daily in the horrible infection.

I remember standing stripped to the waist in cow byres – parturition gowns were still uncommon and the long plastic protective gloves unknown in those days – working away inside infected cows for hours and looking with wry recognition at the leathery placenta and the light-coloured, necrotic cotyledons which told me that I was in contact with millions of the bacteria. And as I swilled myself with disinfectant afterwards, the place was filled with the distinctive acrid odour of abortion.

The effects on many of my fellow vets were wide and varied. One big fat chap faded away to a skeleton with undulant fever and was ill for years, others developed crippling arthritis and some went down with psychiatric conditions. One man wrote in the *Veterinary Record* that as part of his own syndrome he came home one night and decided it would be a good idea to murder his wife. He never got round actually to doing it, but recorded the impulse as an interesting example of what *Brucella abortus* could do to a man.

I used to pat myself on the back and thank God that I was immune. I had been bathing in the infection for years and had never experienced the slightest reaction and as I looked around at some of my suffering friends I was so thankful that I had been spared their ordeal. And after all this time I just knew that such a thing would never happen to me.

That was before I started my funny turns.

This was my family's term for a series of mysterious attacks which came unheralded and then passed off just as quickly. At first I diagnosed them as repeated chills – I was always stripping off in open fields, often in the middle of the night – then I thought I must have a type of flu of short duration. The symptoms were always the same – a feeling of depression, then an ice-cold shiveriness which drove me to my bed where within an hour I shot up a temperature of 105 or 106. Once I had developed this massive fever I felt great: warm and happy, laughing heartily, chatting to myself and finally breaking into song. I couldn't help the singing – I felt so good.

This was a source of great amusement to my children. When I was at the singing stage I could always hear them giggling outside the bedroom door, but I didn't mind – I didn't mind anything.

However, I finally had to find out what was happening to me and a blood test by Dr Allinson dispelled all doubts by showing a nice positive titre to *Brucella abortus*. Reluctantly I had to admit that I had joined the club.

The particular attack when Mrs Featherstone brought her dog to the surgery was on a Saturday. I was driving back from a football match in Sunderland with some of my pals. Our team had won and we were all in high spirits, laughing and joking, and I hardly noticed just when I stopped being the life of the party and went quiet. I did know that when I got to Skeldale House and huddled miserably over the fire, shaking like a man with malaria, that another funny turn was on the way.

Helen took one look, chased me upstairs and began to fill the hot water bottles. Feeling like death I crawled between the sheets and lay, cuddling one bottle, feet on another, while the bed vibrated with my terrific rigor. Helen piled another eiderdown on top of me, turned out the light and left me to it. We both knew what was going to happen.

It wasn't long before the familiar pattern started to set in. Quite soon I began to feel a bit better – warmer, more cheerful – then the warmth mounted and increased and spread through every corner of my being until I was floating along in a delicious languor, utterly at peace, all my troubles dissolved and gone. This, I felt, was heaven. I could stay like this forever, but the warmth developed into a fiery heat when I felt even better; no longer languorous, but powerful, dominant, foolishly and riotously happy.

This was the time when I usually extended a burning arm to pick up my bedside thermometer and stick it under my arm. Ah, yes, there it was, 106, exactly as I thought. I chuckled with satisfaction. Everything was just fine.

Lying there, I was so full of the joys of life that I began to talk aloud, discussing interesting matters with myself, and then my bursting high spirits had to find some further outlet and singing was the natural thing. 'Maxwelltown braes are bonny, where early fa's the dew, and t'was there that Annie Laurie gie'd me her promise true.' I let rip at full volume and never had my voice sounded as rich and rounded.

A few hee-hees sounded from behind the door followed by Jimmy's whisper, 'There he goes' and a muffled laugh from Rosie. The little beggars were there again, but what the hell? 'Gie'd me her promise true, which ne'er forgot will be!' I hit the high notes without a trace of self-consciousness, ignoring the further outburst from beyond the door.

I had a further chat with myself, agreeing wholeheartedly with everything I said, then I thought I'd try my John McCormack impression of 'The Rose of Tralee'. I took a long breath. 'The pale moon was shining above the green mountain.'

'Ha-ha-ha-haaa!' My children were having a great time out there. Then I heard the ringing of the front door bell, moments later feet on the stairs, then a knock on the bedroom door.

Jimmy's head poked into the room. 'Hello, Dad.' His face worked in his effort to stifle his laughter. 'Mrs Featherstone's downstairs with her dog. She says it's urgent and Mum's had to go out for a few minutes.'

'Right-oh, old lad,' I swung my legs from the bed. 'I'll be down immediately.'

My son's eyes widened. 'Are you sure?'

'Absolutely. I'll be down in two ticks. Put her in the consulting room.'

With a final startled glance, Jimmy closed the door and left.

As I pulled on shirt and trousers, the blood thundered in my ears and my face was afire. Normally, the very mention of Mrs Featherstone made me shrink. Rich, middle-aged, imperious, she had plagued me for years with the imaginary ailments of her little poodle, Rollo.

Rollo was an outstandingly healthy little dog. In fact, like many poodles, he was a tough little animal with the characteristic of being able to leap six feet in the air from a standing position as though he were operated by springs, but where he was concerned Mrs Featherstone was a raving hypochondriac. From a commercial point of view, it may seem ideal to have a rich client willing to pay for regular visits with her dog which has nothing the matter with it, but I found it increasingly wearing. Endless sessions of 'Really, Mrs Featherstone, the thing you are pointing out is quite normal' or 'I assure you, Mrs Featherstone, you are worrying needlessly' with the lady drawing herself up and sticking out her chin. 'Are you suggesting, Mr Herriot, that I am dreaming these things? That I cannot believe the evidence of my own eyes? My poor Rollo is suffering and I expect you to do something about it.'

Weak-mindedly I invariably submitted and fobbed her off with some form of placebo which would do the little animal no harm, but the sense of shame was deep. I had to admit that I was overawed by the woman, a jellyfish and a wimp in her presence, allowing her to dismiss my wafflings with a wave of her hand. Why couldn't I assert myself?

However, at this moment, knotting my tie, humming a happy tune as the glittering eyes in the vermilion face glared back at me from the mirror, my past diffidence seemed totally incomprehensible. I was really looking forward to seeing the lady again.

I ran downstairs, snatched a white coat from its hook, trotted along the passage and found Mrs Featherstone standing by the consulting-room table.

Damn, she wasn't a bad-looking woman! Very very nice, in fact. Funny I had never noticed that before. Anyway, there was not the slightest doubt in my mind as to what I had to do. I would grab her, give her a big, smacking kiss and a good long squeeze and all our past misunderstandings would melt away like the morning mist in the sun.

I was advancing on her when I noticed something strange. She had vanished. I was quite sure she had been standing there a second ago. I was blinking around me in bewilderment when I saw that she had ducked behind the table. How wonderful that she, too, was feeling skittish and ready for a game of peek-a-boo.

In a moment her head bobbed up and I greeted it with a merry cry. 'Yoo-hoo, I see you!' I trilled, but it seemed she had merely been stooping to lift her dog which she deposited on the table.

She gave me an odd look. 'Have you been on holiday, Mr Herriot? You have such a high colour.'

'No, no, no, no. I just feel extraordinarily well. In fact, I – '

The lady pursed her lips and brushed off the rest of my sentence impatiently. 'I really am most frightfully worried about poor Rollo.'

At the sound of his name, the poodle, aggressively fit, began to caper around on the table and jump up at my face.

'You are? Oh, what a shame. Tell me all about it.' I suppressed a chuckle.

'Well, we had just started on our evening walk when he coughed quite suddenly.'

'Just one cough?'

'No, two, like this. Hock-hock.'

'Hock, hock, eh?' I was having terrible trouble keeping a serious face. 'And then what happened?'

'Nothing else happened! Isn't that enough? A nasty cough?'

'Well, tell me, do you mean two hocks or one hock-hock?' I could not suppress a giggle, captivated as I was by my wit.

'I mean, Mr Herriot, one very unpleasant and alarming cough.' A dangerous light glinted in the lady's eye.

'Ah yes.' I took out stethoscope and thermometer and began a thorough examination of the patient. Everything, of course, was normal, and I could swear I detected an apologetic glance from Rollo.

And all the time the giggle was struggling steadily to the surface and finally it burst out into a loud 'Ha-ha!'

Mrs Featherstone's eyebrows shot up and she stared at me. 'Why are you laughing?' she enquired in glacial tones. She made the word seem more portentous by drawing it out into a long 'laawfing'.

'Well, really, you see, it's so funny.' I leaned on the table and laughed some more.

'Funny?' Mrs Featherstone's expression was a mixture of horror and disbelief. Her mouth opened soundlessly a few times. 'I fail to see anything *funny* in an animal's suffering.'

Wrapped in my cloak of heat and euphoria, I wagged a finger at her. 'But he's not suffering, that's what's so funny. He never *is* suffering when you bring him in to me.'

'I beg your pardon!'

'It's true, Mrs Featherstone. All Rollo's ailments are imagined by you.' The table shook as another paroxysm seized me.

'How dare you say such a thing!' The lady glared at me down her nose. 'You are being insulting and I really cannot – '

'Hey, just wait a minute. Let me explain.' I wiped a few tears away and took a few gasping breaths. 'Do you remember being worried to death by this habit of Rollo's where he lifts up a hind leg for a few steps, then puts it down again? I told you it was nothing, just a mannerism, but you insisted on my treating him for arthritis?'

'Well, yes, but I was worried.'

'I know, but you wouldn't believe me and he's still doing it. There's nothing wrong with him. Lots of little dogs do it.'

'Well, possibly, but . . .'

'And another thing,' I said between my chuckles, 'there was the time you made me give him sleeping pills because of his terrible nightmares.'

'Yes, and rightly so. He made the most pathetic whimpering sounds while he was sleeping and his paws kept working as though he was running away from something terrible.'

'He was dreaming, Mrs Featherstone! Probably a nice dream about chasing his ball. All dogs have these dreams.'

I took hold of Rollo's head. 'And look here, ha-ha! You must recall your insistence that there were things growing over his eyes. You would never believe me that they were his normal third eyelids, ha-ha-ha! And see, they're still there, aren't they? You can see them now and he's quite happy with them, ha-ha-ha-ha!' I abandoned myself completely and bent over to dig her in the ribs, but she drew back and evaded my finger.

She put her hand over her mouth and continued to stare at me. Her eyebrows had taken up permanent residence high on her forehead. 'You . . . you cannot really mean all this!'

'Oh, but I do, I do. I could go on and on.'

'Well, I don't know what to say. And about his cough tonight?'

'You can take him away,' I said, 'And if there are any more hock-hocks, bring him back tomorrow, but there won't be.' I wiped my streaming face and lifted Rollo from the table.

The lady seemed in a daze as I steered her along the passage to the front door. She kept putting a hand over her mouth and giving me an incredulous sidelong glance, but she remained silent as though stunned.

After I had shown her out I retired to bed and drifted to sleep with the satisfied feeling of having cleared up a problem happily and effortlessly. I had handled the whole thing beautifully.

I didn't feel like that next morning. My latest funny turn was following its usual course. After the elation of the night before, a devastating deflation, lethargy, gloom, despondency and, in this case, the horrid spectre of remorse. As I lay in bed, pulling the sheets round my chin, my recollection of the previous evening was a frightening jumble. I couldn't get any of it sorted out in my mind.

I had been awake only a few moments before the memory hit me. Mrs Featherstone! Oh, my God! What had I said to her? What had I done?

Desperately I tried to bring back the details without success, but the main indisputable fact was that I had laughed, even jeered at her, possibly even pawed at her person. Had I really attempted to embrace her? Had I given her a little cuddle as I walked her down the passage? My mouth opened in a series of soft moans.

Of one thing I could be sure – I had been guilty of the most ghastly impropriety and I had a searing conviction that I would have to pay dearly for it. Certainly she would never set foot in my surgery again. The whole shameful story would get around. She might even report me to the Royal College. I could see the headlines in the *Darrowby and Houlton Times*. VETERINARY SURGEON ON SERIOUS CHARGE, HERRIOT TO APPEAR BEFORE DISCIPLINARY BODY.

Groaning, I huddled deeper, gazing sightlessly at the cup of tea which Helen had placed by my bedside. After my funny turns I always had a day's rest and after that I made a remarkably quick recovery. But this time the mental scars would take a long time to heal. And how about the dire consequences?

I couldn't stand the self-torture any longer. I swallowed my tea, pulled on my clothes and trailed downstairs.

'Feeling better, Jim?' my wife asked brightly as she washed the dishes. 'You'll soon be okay again, you always are. What a strange business it is, but anyway, the kids enjoyed it. I understand you were in excellent voice last night.' She giggled as she reached for the towel.

I thought a gentle stroll in the fresh air would make me feel better, so I set off to walk around the town. I could hardly believe it when I saw Mrs Featherstone approaching a mere hundred yards away. Panic-stricken I scuttled over to the other side of the street, but the lady had spotted me and she crossed over too. And as the expensively tweeded figure bore down on me with purposeful strides I knew there was no escape.

Ah well, I told myself, here it comes. 'Mr Herriot, I thought you might be interested to know that I have placed the matter of Saturday night in the hands of my solicitors. Your behaviour was quite outrageous and I feel it my duty to ensure that defenceless women are protected from you in future. I can scarcely believe that a professional man would act as you did – taking advantage of your situation, betraying the trust placed in you. And as for your incredible callousness in the face of my poor dog's suffering – well, I cannot bear to think of it.'

But it wasn't like that at all. When Mrs Featherstone came up to me she put a hand on my arm. 'Now, Mr Herriot, you did me a service last night.'

'Eh?'

'Yes, you were so understanding. I realize now that I have been foolish about Rollo. I must have been such a nuisance to you.'

'Oh, no, no, no . . .'

'You are kind, but I know I have been unreasonable, troubling you over nothing at inconvenient times and here again I was at your door on a Saturday night.'

'I assure you . . .'

'But instead of being upset, you laughed, and it was so wonderful how you made me see the funny side of my silliness. I feel so ashamed that I always refused to listen to you when you so rightly tried to explain that I was worrying needlessly, and I do hope you can forgive me. From now on, I intend to be a sensible dog owner. And Rollo really is quite healthy, isn't he?'

Waves of relief rolled over me as I looked at the little dog, bright eyed, laughing-faced, leaping almost head high at the sound of his name. 'Well, I'm not too sure. He doesn't look very lively to me.'

'Oh, now you are trying to make me laugh again.' She put her hand over her mouth with the same embarrassed gesture I remembered, then gave me a quizzical look. 'I feel I'm going to laugh a lot more in future.'

I haven't had a funny turn for thirty years. They just gradually disappeared from my life. But when I think of that Saturday night with Mrs Featherstone, I still get an attack of the shivers.

On the Trail

☆★☆★☆★☆★☆★☆★☆★☆★☆★☆★☆★☆★☆★☆★☆

GIOVANNI GUARESCHI

Don Camillo had let himself go a bit in the course of a little sermon with a local background, allowing himself some rather pointed allusions to '*certain people*' and it was thus that on the following evening, when he seized the ropes of the church bells – the bell-ringer having been called away on some pretext – all hell broke out. Some damned soul had tied crackers to the clappers of the bells. No harm done, of course, but there was a shattering din of explosions, enough to give the ringer heart failure.

Don Camillo had not said a word. He had celebrated the evening service in perfect composure, before a crowded congregation from which not one was absent, with Peppone in the front row and every countenance a picture of fervour. It was enough to infuriate a saint, but Don Camillo was no novice in self-control and his audience had gone home disappointed.

As soon as the big doors were closed, Don Camillo snatched up an overcoat and on his way out went to make a hasty genuflection before the altar.

'Don Camillo,' said the Lord, 'put it down.'

'I don't understand,' protested Don Camillo.

'Put it down!'

Don Camillo drew a heavy stick from beneath his coat and laid it in front of the altar.

'Not a pleasant sight, Don Camillo.'

'But, Lord! It isn't even oak; it's only poplar, light and supple . . .' Don Camillo pleaded.

'Go to bed, Don Camillo, and forget about Peppone.'

Don Camillo had raised his arms and had gone to bed with a temperature. And so when on the following evening Peppone's wife made her appearance at the presbytery, he leaped to his feet as though a cracker had gone off under his chair.

'Don Camillo,' began the woman, who was visibly greatly agitated. But Don Camillo interrupted her. 'Get out of my sight, sacrilegious creature!'

'Don Camillo, never mind about that foolishness. At Castellino there is that poor wretch who tried to do in Peppone! They have turned him out!'

Don Camillo lighted a cigar. 'Well, what about it, comrade? I didn't make the amnesty. And in any case, why should you bother about it?'

The woman started to shout. 'I'm bothering because they came to tell Peppone, and Peppone has gone rushing off to Castellino like a lunatic. And he has taken his tommy-gun with him!'

'I see; then you have got concealed arms, have you?'

'Don Camillo, never mind about politics! Can't you understand that Peppone is out to kill? Unless you help me, my man is done for!'

Don Camillo laughed unpleasantly. 'Which will teach him to tie crackers to the clappers of my bells. I shall be pleased to watch him die in gaol! You get out of my house!'

Ten minutes later, Don Camillo, with his skirts tucked up almost to his neck, was pedalling like a lunatic along the road to Castellino astride a racing bicycle belonging to the son of his sacristan.

There was a splendid moon and when he was about four miles from Castellino Don Camillo saw by its light a man sitting on the low parapet of the little bridge that spans the Fossone. He slowed down, since it is always best to be prudent when one travels by night, and halted some ten yards from the bridge, holding in his hand a small object that he happened to have discovered in his pocket.

'My lad,' he inquired, 'have you seen a big man go by on a bicycle in the direction of Castellino?'

'No, Don Camillo,' replied the other quietly.

Don Camillo drew nearer. 'Have you already been to Castellino?' he asked.

'No. I thought it over. It wasn't worth while. Was it my fool of a wife who put you to this trouble?'

'Trouble? Nothing of the kind . . . a little constitutional!'

'Have you any idea what a priest looks like on a racing bicycle?' sniggered Peppone.

Don Camillo came and sat beside him on his wall. 'My son, you must be prepared to see all kinds of things in this world.'

Less than an hour later, Don Camillo was back at the presbytery and went to make his report to the Lord.

'All went well according to Your instructions.'

'Well done, Don Camillo, but would you mind telling me who it was that instructed you to take him by the feet and tumble him into the ditch?'

Don Camillo raised his arms. 'To tell you the truth, I really can't remember exactly. As a matter of fact, he appeared to dislike the sight of a priest on a racing bicycle, so it seemed only kind to prevent him from seeing it any longer.'

'I understand. Has he got back yet?'

'He'll be here soon. Seeing him fall into the ditch, it struck me that as he would be coming home in a rather damp condition he might find the bicycle in his way, so I thought it best to bring it along with me.'

'Very kind of you, I'm sure, Don Camillo,' said the Lord with perfect gravity.

Peppone appeared just before dawn at the door of the presbytery. He was soaked to the skin, and Don Camillo asked if it was raining.

'Fog,' replied Peppone with chattering teeth. 'May I have my bicycle?'

'Why, of course. There it is.'

'Are you sure there wasn't a tommy-gun tied to it?'

Don Camillo raised his arms with a smile. 'A tommy-gun? And what may that be?'

'I,' said Peppone as he turned from the door, 'have made one mistake in my life. I tied crackers to the clappers of your bells. It should have been half a ton of dynamite.'

'*Errare humanum est*,' remarked Don Camillo.

Confessions of a TV Playwright

☆★☆

SIMON GRAY

I became a writer of television plays entirely by accident, before I was in possession of a set or thought of television as anything other than a magic machine that transmitted cricket and football matches into the living rooms of friends; who were thus victim to unexpected visits during, and to deft cultural jokes between, important internationals. I didn't know – wouldn't have been caught dead knowing – who Honor Blackman was; had never in my life clapped eyes on a ballroom dancer, at least in action; and wouldn't have believed that people actually wrote plays *for* television. Now, a mere two and a half years later, I can usually identify by name the second villain in *The Avengers*, feel that my judgement ought to carry weight in the ballroom competitions, and have once or twice been overheard saying a soft goodnight back at the closing-down announcer. I am an addict. The only respect in which I haven't changed is in my ignorance about the nature of television plays, although this ignorance is now a complex and active state.

The first play I did was an adaptation of a short story I had had published in *Voices*. The BBC offered to buy the rights, and my agent was anxious to sell them, but there was never, in the early stages of negotiations, any intention on either side that I should do the adaptation myself. But when the script editor revealed in a slip of the tongue that the rights were worth less than the work of adaptation, I became both thoughtful and bold. I told my agent that I was sure I would soon 'pick it up', my agent presumably told the BBC that I had already picked it up, who courteously but presumably with qualifications agreed that I might at least be allowed to try to pick it up. For the next few days I worked at visualizing the story in television terms. When on the bus or in the bath I would project it on to an imaginary screen; I went to the public library and scrutinized a book with a title like *Writing for Television*; and I struggled to realize a weak recollection of having once seen a television script, while struggling to forget that I had had to put it away from a dizziness induced by phrases like 'boom-in', 'angle right cam', 'angle left cam', and 'tracking shot'. I still have no idea whether these words actually exist in the television vocabulary, but I became frighteningly convinced that they or something like them did, and that it was the merest part of my function to know when they should be employed. I didn't, of course, know what a television camera looked like, but another recollection of certain films suggested that it was sat on by an expert in headphones who drove it backwards and forwards, sideways and in circles, in accordance with this crucial code. So my visualizations became now feeble, now frenzied, and my library pursuit of knowledge became more eccentric (to the point, actually, of reading Gilbert Harding's autobiography; for his was a name I did know), and in other words I did everything that I thought might assist me write the script except arrange to watch a short play on television. I suspect that in those two weeks I did as much genuine research as I had ever done while a registered Ph.D. student, and to approximately the same effect. In the end there was nothing for it but to sit down at the typewriter and begin.

It took me about four hours to produce the script (it was a half-hour play); for my approach, when the chips were down, was simple to the point of imbecility. I eliminated all the prose between the dialogue – of which there was, thankfully, a great deal – and then replaced the prose with terse but masterful instructions. So instead of describing the way in which a character entered a room, I wrote:

> JOHN: (*Opens the door, comes into the room, walks towards the sofa. Stops. Turns. Sits down on the chair.*) Good God are we really . . . etc., etc.

Occasionally and experimentally, as for instance when I couldn't think of anything to go in parenthesis, I wrote in 'close-up', or 'hold camera', or 'track significantly'. When I had done this, I typed the whole out again and, with the confidence of a man who is in possession of thirty neat pages, had them delivered to the BBC. The script editor telephoned the next day to say that everything was fine, although there *was* a problem.

The problem was that the play was to be done 'live'; by which was meant that the play was not to be taped or filmed; which in its turn meant that I would have to think again about continuity; which finally and specifically meant that a man who is in the bath in one scene cannot be expected to appear fully clad and halfway through a cigarette in the next (which I in fact had expected of him) and vice versa (which I had also expected of him). *So*, the script editor said, if I could just think of ways around this problem. I thought of them immediately, for I was not afraid to draw on all the resources that I assumed were at the disposal of so technologically complex an organization as the BBC, only to hear, in amazement bordering on contempt, that these vaunted experts could manage very little in the way of expertise after all.

'You mean you *can't* superimpose water on an actually empty bath in which a nude man is sitting (who have you got for the part, by the way, have you toyed with Gielgud?), *but* cutting off his head so that Gielgud's head *looks as if* it's on the top of his neck – a perfectly simple trick shot I should have thought, actually (what about Olivier?).' At the end of the conversation it was agreed that I would rearrange the scenes; a matter, I was comfortably told, of only a few hours' work.

It was a matter of only a few minutes' work. I moved another scene in between the bath scene and the dressed-with-a-half-smoked-cigarette scene, thus allowing Gielgud or Olivier a full 75 seconds to change into a suit and get into his fag; and I retyped two other pages that had become grubby in transit, and I sent it in again, and it was accepted as the final version. I had written a play for television.

I had never before attended rehearsals for anything, although (again) I had seen enough films to know what authors looked like when they did so. I took my posture from Henry Fonda – an authorial hunch, a humane smile, an air of inner grace. I paused, for a second, before the door behind which the first reading was to take place, checked a minor lesion of confidence, then stilt-walked inside. A number of instantly familiar faces turned towards me, smiled courteously, turned away from me. I found an empty chair and, with flaming cheeks and lowered head, tried to become deaf to my own dialogue. I don't believe that, in the six or seven rehearsals I attended after this, I exchanged more than a few phrases with any of the actors, who were unfailingly but mutely polite, as if there were water between us. The director, on the other hand, warm and loquacious, contrived to use effusion as a means of evasion. I was thus kept isolated, by two contrasting types of charm. It wasn't until I had experienced the same thing in longer plays that I came to realize why this happens. The writer, until he becomes hardened, is acutely embarrassed at hearing his lines said aloud by people who are publicly stuck with them; the actors are acutely embarrassed at possessing voices, faces, even personalities, that they suspect are deeply at odds with the lines they have to say, which they also suspect they haven't understood anyway; the director is hysterically alert to any whiff of conspiracy between the author and the actors. He knows (quite falsely) that the overriding ambition of any author is to direct his own work, and that, foiled in this, his next immediate ambition is to direct the director by taking over the actors. But during rehearsals for that first small play of mine I had only the desire (too modestly held even to pass as an ambition) to be allowed to mingle with actors I had admired in the cinema, and perhaps to pick up pieces of praise from here and there. To have a small part, in fact, in the whole magic process.

Oddly enough I made more real contact with the actors on the night of transmission than I did on the occasions when there was no immediate strain. I was escorted down to the dressing rooms by the script editor, instructed in the etiquette of well-wishing (hugs and kisses for the ladies; powerful hand-clasps and confident smiles for the men) and in each room I found, not an egomaniacal star eagerly awaiting the moment when he or she could hog the cameras, but a diffident, sympathetic and extremely nervous person who would have given a great deal to be somewhere else, about to do something else. Up to this moment I had myself been unimaginatively confident (after all, *they* were professionals, even if I wasn't) but before so much bravely contained panic it was impossible to be anything but sick with fear. I was shown around the set, which had cost some £6,000 to construct, and which seemed an extraordinary chaos. The studio itself was a muddle of trailing cables, abandoned cameras, and meaningless (to me) steel constructions that rose, with sinister imprecision, to a roof so high that it was almost out of sight. Here and there a cool fellow in jeans loitered, negligently. Dumped arbitrarily, or so it appeared, in all this vastness was the set; a clutter of fake rooms, fake offices and fake corridors, the totally fake and yet hideously extravagant realization of those peremptory phrases – 'Goes down a corridor, enters office, proceeds through it to bar' – that I had thrown so casually down on paper. The original story, from which all this had blossomed, had taken a day and a half to write. The television script a few hours. The scene changes a few minutes. My total expense could not have been more than sixpence and the story anyway had never seemed more than a trifling exercise between important literary adventures. And here were the consequences of that cool frivolity. Six thousand pounds of debris, six terrified actors, and a host of ace (judging by that negligence) technicians. I could see only two possible conclusions. Either denunciations from press barons and money chancellors, or universal recognition for a genius whose throwaway jokes, even, had to be brought to the attention of the widest possible public, no expenses spared.

I trudged beside the script editor, up to a little glass box with a television set and two armchairs inside it. This room gave on to a window-lined corridor from which I could take in a descending panorama – by way of the director and his assistants in a kind of science fiction control room immediately beneath – down to the floor of the hangar below. I had, under the pressure of reality, abandoned my Henry Fonda imitation in favour of a country-bumpkin-in-the-big-city bewilderment – a role that on the whole better suits my *fils du peuple* face. I made incomprehensible conversation with the script editor and kept my eyes off the clock.

What started at ten precisely was both agonizing and amazing. By walking a few feet out into the corridor my gaze could rest, first on the director, who sat at the centre of a large desk, with subsidiary directors beside her and a row of television screens, all giving off different pictures, in front of her; then I could shift my gaze down to the muddle of the studio – over the cables, the struts, the blank spaces that surrounded the set; then across to the set itself. There, with cameras aimed at them, the actors were at last at work, live. They bobbed out of balsa-wood doors to reappear in balsa-wood corridors; they whipped around untelevised corners to saunter smoothly into roofless bedrooms; they stood frozen with tension before relaxing into abrupt expressions, emitting easy bursts of laughter that were followed by swift sprints to seemingly arbitrary spots where they froze again, into perhaps postures of rage. I remember particularly the leading actor, sensual in a bath, replete, smiling; then out of the bath, behind a camera, thrashing himself into shirt, trousers, tie, jacket, and a half-smoked cigarette that was passed smoothly to him by a lady in a smock with a script under her arm.

On the other hand, by returning to the glass box, I could watch a polished little piece (I refer only to its visual appearance) in which men and women moved up and down the halls of a modern office block or in and out of the boudoirs of Hampstead Garden Suburb. I could watch this and marvel. Yes, marvel at my own mastery.

When it was all over, at 10.30 precisely, the script editor led me down to the dressing rooms again. This time I needed no instructions. Intoxicated, I embraced the men, shook the ladies warmly by the hands, preened among the experts, who still loitered negligently, and modestly allowed myself to be escorted up to the BBC bar and bought drinks. I deserved them, for had I not peered into the abyss, and seen not simply order, but an order composed of brilliant and witty surfaces, conjured out of it? I rode home in a BBC taxi, my self-esteem burgeoning naturally out of the morrow's headlines. As I glanced out of the windows into the London night, I knew what the nation was talking about. The morrow's papers, which dealt in idiot detail with some Cabinet crisis or foreign war, failed nevertheless to mention my play. I was never mentioned at all in the press, to my knowledge; which was vast, as I was still scanning the television columns ten days later.

But if fame was still deep in the bushes, its scent had reached my nostrils. I made my first move down the trail by hiring a set from a shop in Kilburn, and my second, more important move, when I telephoned the script editor with an idea for a new piece, one that would last for a memorable length of time. The script editor, who had just been transferred to the *Wednesday Play* series, listened attentively, jotted down some details, and telephoned a few days later to say that I could go ahead. Before I had even begun to think properly about the project, I was in receipt of the first half of the fee. It was then, on my way to the bank, that I knew finally that I had jumped from having written a television play to becoming a television playwright. There was nothing in the experience that has not been repeated, with varying degrees of intensity, on every subsequent occasion – the sensation of confidence, a temporary impersonation of the wealthy man, followed by a vertiginous descent into a depression that was marked by a compulsion to telephone the script editor, my new agent, the publishers of my novels. But what distinguished it radically from the previous experience was simply that I did not have thirty pages of dialogue with adaptable passages of prose to start from. I had only the memory of a scrappily written and hastily read account of a murder committed in the 1930s, and the knowledge that this time the result was to be taped. The first draft amounted to about a hundred pages, which seemed to me just right. The script editor, however, explained that by his reckoning my first draft would run to a few minutes under two hours. Could not the normal limits of the *Wednesday Play* be expanded somewhat? I reckoned back at him, to accommodate every pause and pan that I was prepared to burn at the stake for. They could not. A *Wednesday Play* was one and a quarter hours long. Mine was to be a *Wednesday Play*. It was to be one and a quarter hours long. Furthermore, there was no stake to burn at. Only the chance that the play wouldn't be done, the second half of the fee wouldn't be paid, and fame would continue to lurk free in the bushes.

I sent in the second draft, which amounted to some seventy pages, confident that *now* everything was just right. This time it was the director, calling in person at my flat, who explained what was wrong. The problem amounted to a curious legacy from the half-hour live play. Whereas in that piece I had allowed the scenes to follow on in the manner of the original short story, with no worries about the consequent difficulties for the cast, I now made absolutely sure that none of my characters ended a scene without being able to step naturally into the next one, or, if that were impossible, had at least a five-minute break in which to slip out of an overcoat. The result made for a chronological coherence that in no way compensated for the disordered dramatic logic that puzzled everyone who read it. Each scene went on for too long, very little seemed to happen in it, and yet there lay behind it some curious atmosphere, really, of purpose.

There was a tentative suggestion from the director that perhaps I had not thought about the visual freedom of television, a suggestion I indignantly repudiated. But in the course of the ensuing apology and counter-apology I suddenly found myself in possession of two crucial facts. One: in a taped play one could jump from here to there, from now to then, because the production could be stopped and started at will (not quite true, as it happens; there are prescribed major breaks and even prescribed minor breaks; but true enough to make all the difference between live and taped). And two: that one was permitted eight minutes of film that could be incorporated into the tape during performance. I approached the third draft with a sense of freedom that could well have culminated in disaster, but the methods I had already and mistakenly confined myself to held the play in a secure grip. I could change and cut, let things happen as they dramatically ought to happen, without being able to distort the basic structure. And so I completed the third and final draft.

Again my relationships with the actors failed to develop until the play had been performed, and again the director manoeuvred charmingly around me, and again I felt as if I were present as either the poor relation or the bailiff. But this time I did have at least the wit to watch what everybody was doing. At first sight they were merely rehearsing in a large, draughty hall owned, I think, by one of those military groups that people like the Duke of Norfolk are constantly appealing to the nation to keep alive. Photographs of uniformed men, massed together and staring hopelessly, hung about the walls between insignia, paintings of cannon, and hand-written directions to the lavatories and snack bar. The wooden floor was marked at intervals by chalk lines on which the props or their substitutes were placed, and here, oblivious to the cold and to the sad, unused spaces around them, the actors were acting with passion and intelligence, and the director was directing them with passion and intelligence and something more. Crouching over a chart with squares and numbers on it, or crouching a few feet away from the actors, boxing off his vision of them from now one angle, now another; pouncing forwards or leaning sideways, he was clearly practising at once the most secret and the most significant part of his craft. What he was doing, as I found out at the post-performance party, was calculating possible shots for the television screen; being, in fact, the camera.

While I, taking up an inconspicuous position at a convenient distance from the actors, was being a theatre spectator. It never for an instant occurred to me that the whole of what I was seeing was in bulk much more (and in significance much less) than what would finally be taped. This seems to me a crucial point, not only against myself in my naivety but about writing for television in general. The audience of a television play has no choice at all, far less even than a cinema audience has. For the fact that the television screen is very much smaller than the cinema screen means not that the effects are merely smaller, but that they are totally different. All through those rehearsals I behaved like a man in the front stalls, with a view of the stage or screen that was certainly comprehensive but could be made selective. Sometimes, as at a film or a play, I watched one actor's face, sometimes another's; sometimes I focused on a detail – the accidental movement of hands or feet. And it became apparent to me, when I read the script again the other day, that I had written out of the same misconception.

I *saw* the characters in their physical completeness, embracing each other or standing away from each other, and assumed, in my quite potent ignorance, that this would be how the final audience would see them. But of course on the television screen there is room only for either a diminutive version of everything or a larger version of something. It is the director's responsibility (and ultimately the writer's also) to ensure that what fills the screen is what is dramatically most necessary. Which is precisely television's strength, for the continuous act of concentration and exclusion amounts to a positive discipline. A television play, in fact, is not a play done on television. Nor is it a film for the small screen. It has its own laws. And this is after all another way of saying that the medium has created a form, flexible and generous when explored imaginatively, inhibiting and even destructive when accepted grudgingly.

When I sit down to a television play now, I do so in a very different spirit from when effecting that first casual adaptation. I know that I am involved in a different mode of realization, one in which the exchange of dialogue is more likely to be the starting point than the conclusion. But at the same time – as I confessed at the beginning – I know nothing about the real nature of television plays, what it is, for example, that distinguishes the writing of a good one from the writing of a bad one. That secret is as inaccessible as the secret of writing good films, good novels and good stage plays; as inaccessible as the secret behind all art. A familiarity with the possibilities of the medium makes the beginning merely a beginning, just the same. And although the bushes still rustle, and my nostrils still twitch to the scent, there are many days when I would gladly exchange all my experience for that time of innocence, when ballroom dancers danced in a million homes, but did not dance for me.

I should like to make it clear that I do not hold myself responsible for any inaccuracies in this account of my early experiences as a television playwright. I have merely been as faithful as possible to what I now think it probably seemed like.

December

☆★☆★☆★☆★☆★☆★☆★☆★☆★☆

HELENE HANFF

This is the season when there are two kinds of New Yorkers: those who hate-the-holidays and flee them on some cruise ship; and those who look forward to them as passionately as any five-year-old. To a passionate five-year-old like me, Christmas in New York has dazzling advantages. But celebrating it properly in a New York 'studio' apartment – a one-room flat – has disadvantages that would drive any house-owner clear up the wall. We'll take the advantages first.

Christmas in New York begins with the Park Avenue tree-lighting ceremony up at Brick Presbyterian church. I have to explain first of all that our Avenues run through the island from south to north, and are intersected by the Streets which run east to west; and second, Park Avenue gets its name from the strip of green grass and flower beds running down the middle of it from 96th Street to 45th. Well, at Christmas, a small evergreen tree is set up at every second street along the Avenue's green strip, and is decorated only with small white-gold lights. On the appointed day you go up to the church at 94th and Park, to an outdoor carol service; and the minister or somebody pulls a switch and you see the lights come on, on all the little trees, clear down the Avenue for fifty blocks.

That's my signal to go shopping – and Christmas shopping on Fifth Avenue is full of lovely diversions. First you queue up at Lord & Taylor's to see their Christmas windows. This year's windows feature Coming Home for Christmas. One window has a replica of a JFK airport terminal, complete with lifelike passengers, luggage and waiting room. Another has a replica of the George Washington Bridge, with the lights, the traffic – and a hapless driver stuck with a flat tyre. My favourite window has a replica of a New York subway station, complete with crowds, a snack bar and a gent coming down the steps with a Christmas tree over his shoulder.

If you're shopping on a Wednesday, you drop in, at noon, at St Thomas's church – halfway between Saks and Bonwit's – to hear their marvellous men's and boys' choirs do Benjamin Britten's *St Nicholas* or the *Ceremony of Carols*. And of course you stop at Rockefeller Plaza at twilight, for the carol singing under the sixty-five-foot-high Christmas tree.

The free concerts here in December are wonderful altogether. Each week you read the Sunday church notices in *The Times* and make agonizing decisions. Should you chase all the way up to Riverside church at 122nd Street to hear the best *Messiah* in town – or settle for a Bach Christmas oratorio at St Bartholomew's at 49th and Park? And if you do hear Bach at St Bart's this Sunday, will you get the best *Messiah* next Sunday down at Ascension at 10th Street or up at Heavenly Rest at 94th Street?

If you're at an evening concert in midtown you walk home up Park Avenue afterwards. Midtown Park Avenue is lined with skyscraper office towers, set in landscaped plazas; and at Christmas the shrubs in the plazas are strung with tiny white lights, mere pinpricks of light, but thousands of them. You walk home between aisles of ground-level stars with the gold-lit trees running up the middle.

My own tree goes up the Saturday night before Christmas; but I don't have my annual tree-trimming party any more. Which brings us to the problems of a one-room Christmas. In this age of sofa beds, it is my belief that the real reason for the existence of bedrooms is to have a place to put guests' coats. The day of my tree-trimming party I used to carry my entire wardrobe up to a friend's bedroom-apartment, to make room in my double-door closet for twenty-five guests' coats. I'd invite the twenty-five active members of my Democratic Club to the party; and if a few singles said, 'Can I bring somebody?' I said, 'Sure.' I got eight or ten regrets, and invited eight or ten more people from a neighbouring Democratic Club. Well, one year there was a blizzard, everybody who was going away stayed home, and forty-two people came to my party. I ran out of food, forks and floor space, and at midnight the closet rack fell down from the weight of forty-two winter coats, and that was the end of my annual tree-trimming party.

I have eight people and two dogs coming for Christmas dinner and, since studio apartments have small refrigerators, you have to work out the logistics in advance. You make your pies, cranberry sauce and sweet-potato casserole ahead of time and then distribute them around the building in other people's refrigerators, since the turkey, hors-d'oeuvres, vegetables and eggnog bowl are all you'll have room for in yours. On Christmas morning, once your turkey's in the oven, you go and get everything back. And the logistics consist in remembering whether the casserole is in 4-F or 16-B, and did you get the keys to 8-E-up-the-hall, because Shelley and Susan have gone skiing in Vermont for Christmas, with your pies in their freezer.

Duke, the German shepherd, comes to Christmas dinner, Chester, the Old English sheepdog, comes for dessert and coffee, and I haven't filled their Christmas stockings yet. I'm going over to Saks' Dog Shop to see what's new. My high-fashion friend, Arlene, phoned to say she got her presents for the two dogs there.

'It's a canine aftershave called Sniffe. S-n-i-f-f-e. Is that chic?!'

Merry Christmas.

The Unrest-Cure

SAKI

On the rack in the railway carriage immediately opposite Clovis was a solidly wrought travelling bag, with a carefully written label, on which was inscribed, 'J. P. Huddle, The Warren, Tilfield, near Slowborough'. Immediately below the rack sat the human embodiment of the label, a solid, sedate individual, sedately dressed, sedately conversational. Even without his conversation (which was addressed to a friend seated by his side, and touched chiefly on such topics as the backwardness of Roman hyacinths and the prevalence of measles at the Rectory), one could have gauged fairly accurately the temperament and mental outlook of the travelling bag's owner. But he seemed unwilling to leave anything to the imagination of a casual observer, and his talk grew presently personal and introspective.

'I don't know how it is,' he told his friend, 'I'm not much over forty, but I seem to have settled down into a deep groove of elderly middle-age. My sister shows the same tendency. We like everything to be exactly in its accustomed place; we like things to happen exactly at their appointed times; we like everything to be usual, orderly, punctual, methodical, to a hair's breadth, to a minute. It distresses and upsets us if it is not so. For instance, to take a very trifling matter, a thrush has built its nest year after year in the catkin-tree on the lawn; this year, for no obvious reason, it is building in the ivy on the garden wall. We have said very little about it, but I think we both feel that the change is unnecessary, and just a little irritating.'

'Perhaps,' said the friend, 'it is a different thrush.'

'We have suspected that,' said J. P. Huddle, 'and I think it gives us even more cause for annoyance. We don't feel that we want a change of thrush at our time of life; and yet, as I have said, we have scarcely reached an age when these things should make themselves seriously felt.'

'What you want,' said the friend, 'is an Unrest-cure.'

'An Unrest-cure? I've never heard of such a thing.'

'You've heard of Rest-cures for people who've broken down under stress of too much worry and strenuous living; well, you're suffering from overmuch repose and placidity, and you need the opposite kind of treatment.'

'But where would one go for such a thing?'

'Well, you might stand as an Orange candidate for Kilkenny, or do a course of district visiting in one of the Apache quarters of Paris, or give lectures in Berlin to prove that most of Wagner's music was written by Gambetta; and there's always the interior of Morocco to travel in. But, to be really effective, the Unrest-cure ought to be tried in the home. How you would do it I haven't the faintest idea.'

It was at this point in the conversation that Clovis became galvanized into alert attention. After all, his two days' visit to an elderly relative at Slowborough did not promise much excitement. Before the train had stopped he had decorated his sinister shirt-cuff with the inscription, 'J. P. Huddle, The Warren, Tilfield, near Slowborough.'

Two mornings later Mr Huddle broke in on his sister's privacy as she sat reading *Country Life* in the morning room. It was her day and hour and place for reading *Country Life*, and the intrusion was absolutely irregular; but he bore in his hand a telegram, and in that household telegrams were recognized as happening by the hand of God. This particular telegram partook of the nature of a thunderbolt. 'Bishop examining confirmation class in neighbourhood unable stay rectory on account measles invokes your hospitality sending secretary arrange.'

'I scarcely know the Bishop; I've only spoken to him once,' exclaimed J. P. Huddle, with the exculpating air of one who realizes too late the indiscretion of speaking to strange Bishops. Miss Huddle was the first to rally; she disliked thunderbolts as fervently as her brother did, but the womanly instinct in her told her that thunderbolts must be fed.

'We can curry the cold duck,' she said. It was not the appointed day for curry, but the little orange envelope involved a certain departure from rule and custom. Her brother said nothing, but his eyes thanked her for being brave.

'A young gentleman to see you,' announced the parlour-maid.

'The secretary!' murmured the Huddles in unison; they instantly stiffened into a demeanour which proclaimed that, though they held all strangers to be guilty, they were willing to hear anything they might have to say in their defence. The young gentleman, who came into the room with a certain elegant haughtiness, was not at all Huddle's idea of a bishop's secretary; he had not supposed that the episcopal establishment could have afforded such an expensively upholstered article when there were so many other claims on its resources. The face was fleetingly familiar; if he had bestowed more attention on the fellow-traveller sitting opposite him in the railway carriage two days before he might have recognized Clovis in his present visitor.

'You are the Bishop's secretary,' asked Huddle, becoming consciously deferential.

'His confidential secretary,' answered Clovis. 'You may call me Stanislaus; my other name doesn't matter. The Bishop and Colonel Alberti may be here to lunch. I shall be here in any case.'

It sounded rather like the programme of a Royal visit.

'The Bishop is examining a confirmation class in the neighbourhood, isn't he?' asked Miss Huddle.

'Ostensibly,' was the dark reply, followed by a request for a large-scale map of the locality.

Clovis was still immersed in a seemingly profound study of the map when another telegram arrived. It was addressed to 'Prince Stanislaus, care of Huddle, The Warren, etc.' Clovis glanced at the contents and announced: 'The Bishop and Alberti won't be here till late in the afternoon.' Then he returned to his scrutiny of the map.

The luncheon was not a very festive function. The princely secretary ate and drank with fair appetite, but severely discouraged conversation. At the finish of the meal he broke suddenly into a radiant smile, thanked his hostess for a charming repast, and kissed her hand with deferential rapture. Miss Huddle was unable to decide in her mind whether the action savoured of Louis Quatorzian courtliness or the reprehensible Roman attitude towards the Sabine women. It was not her day for having a headache, but she felt that the circumstances excused her, and retired to her room to have as much headache as was possible before the Bishop's arrival. Clovis, having asked the way to the nearest telegraph office, disappeared presently down the carriage drive. Mr Huddle met him in the hall some two hours later, and asked when the Bishop would arrive.

'He is in the library with Alberti,' was the reply.

'But why wasn't I told? I never knew he had come!' exclaimed Huddle.

'No one knows he is here,' said Clovis; 'the quieter we can keep matters the better. And on no account disturb him in the library. Those are his orders.'

'But what is all this mystery about? And who is Alberti? And isn't the Bishop going to have tea?'

'The Bishop is out for blood, not tea.'

'Blood!' gasped Huddle, who did not find that the thunderbolt improved on acquaintance.

'Tonight is going to be a great night in the history of Christendom,' said Clovis. 'We are going to massacre every Jew in the neighbourhood.'

'To massacre the Jews!' said Huddle indignantly. 'Do you mean to tell me there's a general rising against them?'

'No, it's the Bishop's own idea. He's in there arranging all the details now.'

'But – the Bishop is such a tolerant, humane man.'

'That is precisely what will heighten the effect of his action. The sensation will be enormous.'

That at least Huddle could believe.

'He will be hanged!' he exclaimed with conviction.

'A motor is waiting to carry him to the coast, where a steam yacht is in readiness.'

'But there aren't thirty Jews in the whole neighbourhood,' protested Huddle, whose brain, under the repeated shocks of the day, was operating with the uncertainty of a telegraph wire during earthquake disturbances.

'We have twenty-six on our list,' said Clovis, referring to a bundle of notes. 'We shall be able to deal with them all the more thoroughly.'

'Do you mean to tell me that you are meditating violence against a man like Sir Leon Birberry,' stammered Huddle; 'he's one of the most respected men in the country.'

'He's down on our list,' said Clovis carelessly; 'after all, we've got men we can trust to do our job, so we shan't have to rely on local assistance. And we've got some Boy-scouts helping us as auxiliaries.'

'Boy-scouts!'

'Yes; when they understood there was real killing to be done they were even keener than the men.'

'This thing will be a blot on the Twentieth Century!'

'And your house will be the blotting-pad. Have you realized that half the papers of Europe and the United States will publish pictures of it? By the way, I've sent some photographs of you and your sister, that I found in the library, to the *Martin* and *Die Woche*; I hope you don't mind. Also a sketch of the staircase; most of the killing will probably be done on the staircase.'

The emotions that were surging in J. P. Huddle's brain were almost too intense to be disclosed in speech, but he managed to gasp out: 'There aren't any Jews in this house.'

'Not at present,' said Clovis.

'I shall go to the police,' shouted Huddle with sudden energy.

'In the shrubbery,' said Clovis, 'are posted ten men, who have orders to fire on any one who leaves the house without my signal of permission. Another armed picquet is in ambush near the front gate. The Boy-scouts watch the back premises.'

At this moment the cheerful hoot of a motor-horn was heard from the drive. Huddle rushed to the hall door with the feeling of a man half-awakened from a nightmare, and beheld Sir Leon Birberry, who had driven himself over in his car. 'I got your telegram,' he said; 'what's up?'

Telegram? It seemed to be a day of telegrams.

'Come here at once. Urgent. James Huddle,' was the purport of the message displayed before Huddle's bewildered eyes.

'I see it all!' he exclaimed suddenly in a voice shaken with agitation, and with a look of agony in the direction of the shrubbery he hauled the astonished Birberry into the house. Tea had just been laid in the hall, but the now thoroughly panic-stricken Huddle dragged his protesting guest upstairs, and in a few minutes' time the entire household had been summoned to that region of momentary safety. Clovis alone graced the tea-table with his presence; the fanatics in the library were evidently too immersed in their monstrous machinations to dally with the solace of teacup and hot toast. Once the youth rose, in answer to the summons of the front-door bell, and admitted Mr Paul Isaacs, shoemaker and parish councillor, who had also received a pressing invitation to The Warren. With an atrocious assumption of courtesy, which a Borgia could hardly have outdone, the secretary escorted this new captive of his net to the head of the stairway, where his involuntary host awaited him.

And then ensued a long ghastly vigil of watching and waiting. Once or twice Clovis left the house to stroll across to the shrubbery, returning always to the library, for the purpose evidently of making a brief report. Once he took in the letters from the evening postman, and brought them to the top of the stairs with punctilious politeness. After his next absence he came halfway up the stairs to make an announcement.

'The Boy-scouts mistook my signal, and have killed the postman. I've had very little practice in this sort of thing, you see. Another time I shall do better.'

The housemaid, who was engaged to be married to the evening postman, gave way to clamorous grief.

'Remember that your mistress has a headache,' said J. P. Huddle. (Miss Huddle's headache was worse.)

Clovis hastened downstairs, and after a short visit to the library returned with another message:

'The Bishop is sorry to hear that Miss Huddle has a headache. He is issuing orders that as far as possible no firearms shall be used near the house; any killing that is necessary on the premises will be done with cold steel. The Bishop does not see why a man should not be a gentleman as well as a Christian.'

That was the last they saw of Clovis; it was nearly seven o'clock, and his elderly relative liked him to dress for dinner. But, though he had left them for ever, the lurking suggestion of his presence haunted the lower regions of the house during the long hours of the wakeful night, and every creak of the stairway, every rustle of wind through the shrubbery, was fraught with horrible meaning. At about seven the next morning the gardener's boy and the early postman finally convinced the watchers that the Twentieth Century was still unblotted.

'I don't suppose,' mused Clovis, as an early train bore him townwards, 'that they will be in the least grateful for the Unrest-cure.'

A Year in Provence

PETER MAYLE

Our friend the London lawyer, a man steeped in English reserve, was watching what he called the antics of the frogs from the Fin de Siècle café in Cavaillon. It was market day, and the pavement was a human traffic jam, slow-moving, jostling and chaotic.

'Look over there,' he said, as a car stopped in the middle of the street while the driver got out to embrace an acquaintance, 'they're always mauling each other. See that? *Men kissing*. Damned unhealthy, if you ask me.' He snorted into his beer, his sense of propriety outraged by such deviant behaviour, so alien to the respectable Anglo-Saxon.

It had taken me some months to get used to the Provençal delight in physical contact. Like anyone brought up in England, I had absorbed certain social mannerisms. I had learned to keep my distance, to offer a nod instead of a handshake, to ration kissing to female relatives and to confine any public demonstrations of affection to dogs. To be engulfed by a Provençal welcome, as thorough and searching as being frisked by airport security guards, was, at first, a startling experience. Now I enjoyed it, and I was fascinated by the niceties of the social ritual, and the sign language which is an essential part of any Provençal encounter.

When two unencumbered men meet, the least there will be is the conventional handshake. If the hands are full, you will be offered a little finger to shake. If the hands are wet or dirty, you will be offered a forearm or an elbow. Riding a bicycle or driving a car does not excuse you from the obligation to *toucher les cinq sardines*, and so you will see perilous contortions being performed on busy streets as hands grope through car windows and across handlebars to find each other. And this is only at the first and most restrained level of acquaintance. A closer relationship requires more demonstrative acknowledgement.

As our lawyer friend had noticed, men kiss other men. They squeeze shoulders, slap backs, pummel kidneys, pinch cheeks. When a Provençal man is truly pleased to see you, there is a real possibility of coming away from his clutches with superficial bruising.

The risk of bodily damage is less where women are concerned, but an amateur can easily make a social blunder if he miscalculates the required number of kisses. In my early days of discovery, I would plant a single kiss, only to find that the other cheek was being proffered as I was drawing back. Only snobs kiss once, I was told, or those unfortunates who suffer from congenital *froideur*. I then saw what I assumed to be the correct procedure – the triple kiss, left-right-left, so I tried it on a Parisian friend. Wrong again. She told me that triple-kissing was a low Provençal habit, and that two kisses were enough among civilised people. The next time I saw my neighbour's wife, I kissed her twice. '*Non*,' she said, '*trois fois*.'

I now pay close attention to the movement of the female head. If it stops swivelling after two kisses, I am almost sure I've filled my quota, but I stay poised for a third lunge just in case the head should keep moving.

It's a different but equally tricky problem for my wife, who is on the receiving end and has to estimate the number of times she needs to swivel, or indeed if she needs to swivel at all. One morning she heard a bellow in the street, and turned to see Ramon the plasterer advancing on her. He stopped, and wiped his hands ostentatiously on his trousers. My wife anticipated a handshake, and held out her hand. Ramon brushed it aside and kissed her three times with great gusto. You never can tell.

Once the initial greeting is over, conversation can begin. Shopping baskets and packages are put down, dogs are tied to café tables, bicycles and tools are leaned up against the nearest wall. This is necessary, because for any serious and satisfactory discussion both hands must be free to provide visual punctuation, to terminate dangling sentences, to add emphasis or simply to decorate speech which, as it is merely a matter of moving the mouth, is not on its own sufficiently physical for the Provençal. So the hands and the eternally eloquent shoulders are vital to a quiet exchange of views, and in fact it is often possible to follow the gist of a Provençal conversation from a distance, without hearing the words, just by watching expressions and the movements of bodies and hands.

There is a well-defined silent vocabulary, starting with the hand-waggle which had been introduced to us by our builders. They used it only as a disclaimer whenever talking about time or cost, but it is a gesture of almost infinite flexibility. It can describe the state of your health, how you're getting on with your mother-in-law, the progress of your business, your assessment of a restaurant or your predictions about this year's melon crop. When it is a subject of minor importance, the waggle is perfunctory, and is accompanied by a dismissive raising of the eyebrows. More serious matters – politics, the delicate condition of one's liver, the prospects for a local rider in the Tour de France – are addressed with greater intensity. The waggle is in slow motion, with the upper part of the body swaying slightly as the hand rocks, a frown of concentration on the face.

The instrument of warning and argument is the index finger, in one of its three operational positions. Thrust up, rigid and unmoving, beneath your conversational partner's nose, it signals caution – watch out, *attention*, all is not what it seems. Held just below face level and shaken rapidly from side to side like an agitated metronome, it indicates that the other person is woefully ill-informed and totally wrong in what he has just said. The correct opinion is then delivered, and the finger changes from its sideways motion into a series of jabs and prods, either tapping the chest if the unenlightened one is a man or remaining a few discreet centimetres from the bosom in the case of a woman.

Describing a sudden departure needs two hands: the left, fingers held straight, moves upwards from waist level to smack into the palm of the right hand moving downwards – a restricted version of the popular and extremely vulgar bicep crunch. (Seen at its best during midsummer traffic jams, when disputing drivers will leave their cars to allow themselves the freedom of movement necessary for a left-arm uppercut stopped short by the right hand clamping on the bicep.)

At the end of the conversation, there is the promise to stay in touch. The middle three fingers are folded into the palm and the hand is held up to an ear, with the extended thumb and little finger imitating the shape of a telephone. Finally, there is a parting handshake. Packages, dogs and bicycles are gathered up until the whole process starts all over again fifty yards down the street. It's hardly surprising that aerobics never became popular in Provence. People get quite enough physical exercise in the course of a ten-minute chat.

These and other everyday amusements of life in nearby towns and villages were not doing much for our spirit of exploration and adventure. With so many distractions on our doorstep, we were neglecting the more famous parts of Provence, or so we were told by our friends in London. In the knowledgeable and irritating manner of seasoned armchair travellers, they kept pointing out how conveniently placed we were for Nîmes and Arles and Avignon, for the flamingoes of the Camargue and the *bouillabaisse* of Marseille. They seemed surprised and mildly disapproving when we admitted that we stayed close to home, not believing our excuses that we could never find the time to go anywhere, never felt a compulsion to go church-crawling or monument-spotting, didn't want to be tourists. There was one exception to this rooted existence, and one excursion that we were always happy to make. We both loved Aix.

The corkscrew road we take through the mountains is too narrow for trucks and too serpentine for anyone in a hurry. Apart from a single farm building with its ragged herd of goats, there is nothing to see except steep and empty landscapes of grey rock and green scrub oak, polished into high definition by the extraordinary clarity of the light. The road slopes down through the foothills on the south side of the Lubéron before joining up with the amateur Grand Prix that takes place every day on the RN7, the *Nationale Sept* that has eliminated more motorists over the years than is comfortable to think about as one waits for a gap in the traffic.

The road leads in to Aix at the end of the most handsome main street in France. The Cours Mirabeau is beautiful at any time of the year, but at its best between spring and autumn, when the plane trees form a pale green tunnel five hundred yards long. The diffused sunlight, the four fountains along the centre of the Cours' length, the perfect proportions which follow da Vinci's rule to 'let the street be as wide as the height of the houses' – the arrangement of space and trees and architecture is so pleasing that you hardly notice the cars.

Over the years, a nice geographical distinction has evolved between work and more frivolous activities. On the shady side of the street, appropriately, are the banks and insurance companies and property agents and lawyers. On the sunny side are the cafés.

I have liked almost every café that I have ever been to in France, even the ratty little ones in tiny villages where the flies are more plentiful than customers, but I have a soft spot for the sprawling cafés of the Cours Mirabeau, and the softest spot of all for the Deux Garçons. Successive generations of proprietors have put their profits under the mattress and resisted all thoughts of redecoration, which in France usually ends in a welter of plastic and awkward lighting, and the interior looks much the same as it must have looked fifty years ago.

The ceiling is high, and toasted to a caramel colour by the smoke from a million cigarettes. The bar is burnished copper, the tables and chairs gleam with the patina bestowed by countless bottoms and elbows, and the waiters have aprons and flat feet, as all proper waiters should. It is dim and cool, a place for reflection and a quiet drink. And then there is the terrace, where the show takes place.

Aix is a university town, and there is clearly something in the curriculum that attracts pretty students. The terrace of the Deux Garçons is always full of them, and it is my theory that they are there for education rather than refreshment. They are taking a degree course in café deportment, with a syllabus divided into four parts.

One: the arrival

One must always arrive as conspicuously as possible, preferably on the back of a crimson Kawasaki 750 motor cycle driven by a young man in head-to-toe black leather and three-day stubble. It is not done to stand on the pavement and wave him goodbye as he booms off down the Cours to visit his hairdresser. That is for *gauche* little girls from the Auvergne. The sophisticated student is too busy for sentiment. She is concentrating on the next stage.

Two: the entrance

Sunglasses must be kept on until an acquaintance is identified at one of the tables, but one must not appear to be looking for company. Instead, the impression should be that one is heading into the café to make a 'phone call to one's titled Italian admirer, when – *quelle surprise*! – one sees a friend. The sunglasses can then be removed and the hair tossed while one is persuaded to sit down.

Three: ritual kissing

Everyone at the table must be kissed at least twice, often three times, and in special cases four times. Those being kissed should remain seated, allowing the new arrival to bend and swoop around the table, tossing her hair, getting in the way of the waiters and generally making her presence felt.

Four: table manners

Once seated, sunglasses should be put back on to permit the discreet study of one's own reflection in the café windows – not for reasons of narcissism, but to check important details of technique: the way one lights a cigarette, or sucks the straw in a Perrier *menthe*, or nibbles daintily on a sugar lump. If these are satisfactory, the glasses can be adjusted downwards so that they rest charmingly on the end of the nose, and attention can be given to the other occupants of the table.

This performance continues from mid-morning until early evening, and never fails to entertain me. I imagine there must be the occasional break for academic work in between these hectic periods of social study, but I have never seen a textbook darken any of the café tables, nor heard any discussion of higher calculus or political science. The students are totally absorbed in showing form, and the Cours Mirabeau is all the more decorative as a result.

The Futility of Life

☆★☆★☆★☆★☆★☆★☆★☆★☆★☆★☆★☆★☆★☆★☆

PETER COOK AND DUDLEY MOORE

DUD *gives* PETE *a cup of tea.*

DUD Tea's up, Pete.

PETE No, thank you.

DUD What, no tea?

PETE Would you like me to submit a memo? No.

DUD Oh. Have you got the collywobbles or something? You feeling a bit peaky?

PETE No.

DUD I thought perhaps those whelks might be clashing with the éclairs.

PETE They are not, and if they were I would keep it to myself.

DUD I'm not sure that you'd have the option. What's the matter?

PETE No words can convey the merest inkling of my innermost feelings.

DUD On the contrary. What you've just said has conveyed to me in detail the nature of your malaise. You're feeling a bit droopy.

PETE A bit droopy? You're the sort of person who'd have gone up to Joan of Arc as the flames licked round her vitals and said, 'Feeling one degree under? Like a nice cup of tea?'

DUD You know what my mother would say?

PETE No.

DUD 'Somebody has got out of bed the wrong side this morning.'

PETE If your mother said that to me today, I'd smash her in the teeth with the coal scuttle.

DUD Oh, I see. You're feeling a bit temperamental. As Dr Groarke would say – half temper, half mental . . . ha ha.

PETE These glib platitudes are, if anything, exacerbating an already unbearable mood of depression.

DUD If you're depressed, there's no point sitting around feeling sorry for yourself. That won't get the washing-up done.

PETE Dud, your uncanny grasp of domestic trivia is of negligible therapeutic value, and if you tell me to pull myself together or snap out of it, I might well do something rash.

DUD I wouldn't say anything like that. Get a grip on yourself, look on the bright side.

DUD *and* PETE (*together*). Count your blessings.

DUD Ooh, Mr Acid Drop himself. Come on, you'll feel better if you get it off your chest. You can confide in me. I mean, what am I here for?

PETE In your fumbling way you have actually articulated the fundamental question. What are you here for? What am I here for? What is the purpose of life?

DUD The purpose of life? Well, we are here on this earth for a brief sojourn; life is a precious gift; the more we put into it, the more we get out of it; and if on the way I can have spread a little sunshine, then my living shall not be in vain.

PETE Thank you, Patience Strong. Have you ever thought about death? Do you realize that we each must die?

DUD Of course we must die, but not yet. It's only half past four of a Wednesday afternoon.

PETE No-one knows when God in His Almighty Wisdom will choose to vouchsafe His precious gift of Death.

DUD Granted. But chances are He won't be making a pounce at this time of day.

PETE As far as I'm concerned, He can get a bloody move on.

DUD That's morbid. Think of all the good things in life.

PETE Like what?

DUD Just look out the window.

He opens the curtains and closes them rapidly.

Perhaps not.

PETE I think it was rightly said, 'See Dagenham Dye Works and die'.

DUD Yes, but think of all the happy times you've had. That's what I do when I'm feeling below par. This room is filled with joyous memories. Look at this. A certificate proving we've been up the Post Office Tower.

PETE And why did we go up it?

DUD Because it was there, Pete, a challenge.

PETE A brief escape from a life consisting of cups of tea, interminable games of Ludo and the occasional visit to your Aunt Dolly.

DUD Well, what does this remind you of?

He shows PETE *a souvenir programme.*

PETE It reminds me of our dismal visit to the Planetarium.

DUD That was nice, wasn't it? Seeing the sky at night during broad daylight.

PETE And emerging into a cold wind and drizzle, buying a newspaper only to read the headline 'London Airport Disaster – thirty old ladies sucked to death in Jumbo Jet engine.'

DUD But think of the millions of old ladies who weren't sucked to death in a jet engine, who are now happily playing snap up and down the country.

PETE The mental image of millions of old ladies shouting 'Snap' at each other merely confirms my ideas about the futility of life.

DUD What about that time we went to the National Gallery then?

PETE And you spent four hours with your nose up against one of Rubens's more voluptuous nudes.

DUD I was bewitched by the Dutch master's handling of light and shade.

PETE With particular reference to busty substances.

DUD My apparent concentration on this area was due to the fact that I had heard that Rubens had used these busty appurtanences to obliterate an earlier more controversial study of Clapham Common.

PETE Did you perceive any blades of grass peeping through the opulent pink orbs?

DUD No, but I could see the dim outline of Battersea Power Station looming up through her nether regions. I think I've got the postcard somewhere.

PETE Yes, it's up in the bedroom amongst your art collection of 'Spick and Span' and 'Beautiful Britons'.

DUD Actually, I think you borrowed it to use as a bookmark for your copy of *La Vie Parisienne* . . . or was it *Lilliput*, edition number 159? One or other of your nudie books.

PETE I purchased that copy of *La Vie Parisienne* for the very interesting article on marine life by Captain Cousteau.

DUD Strange then that it should always fall open at a page not so much connected with the sea bed as with a scantily clad adagio dancer from the Moulin Rouge.

PETE That must have been caused by the previous owner. I'm not interested in that sort of thing.

DUD No wonder you're depressed. It's not healthy not to be interested in ladies of the opposite sex.

PETE Well I'm not.

DUD I don't believe you. Own up. Spring is here and perhaps disquieting emotions are seething beneath your mackintosh.

PETE Nothing is seething beneath my mackintosh save for a general feeling of despair and futility and boredom with you.

DUD I know. I know what will perk you up. 'Sausages and Mash'.

PETE I'm not hungry.

DUD No, the game, 'Sausages and Mash'. You read a book out loud and put the word 'sausage' for every word beginning with 's' and 'mash' for every word beginning with 'm'. It's very funny.

He gets a book.

Look what happens. 'I mash go down to the sausages again, to the lonely sausage and the sausage. And all I ask is a tall sausage and a sausage to sausage her by . . . ' John Mash.

PETE Bloody stupid.

DUD Bloody sausage, you mean, – I mean you mash. I mash, you mash.

PETE What's this then. 'Sausage sausages sausage sausages on the sausage sausage. The sausages sausage sausages are sausage sausages for sausage.'

DUD Keats?

PETE No, 'She sells sea shells on the sea shore.' We could also waste our time playing 'Fish and Chips.'

DUD I don't know that one.

PETE I'll give you an example. Why don't you fish off, chip chips.

DUD I don't get that one. Fish off?

PETE I'll give you a clue. The 'chips' in 'chips chips' stands for 'chops'.

DUD Oh I see, so it's 'Why don't you fish off chip chops.' Oh, I sausage what you mash.

PETE What?

DUD I see what you mean.

My Father

☆★☆★☆★☆★☆★☆★☆★☆★☆★☆★☆★☆

DAMON RUNYON

My father is a Pioneer.

Of such an institution, Mr N. Webster, who was himself something of a pioneer, says:

'Pioneer. One who goes before, as into the wilderness, preparing the way for others to follow.'

I do not know that this description covers my father's case accurately – it sounds more like a word picture of a Frémont or a Pike, or an irrigation promoter, with little bearing upon a man who was the playmate of the untamed William Hickok, Mr B. Masterson, and such; nevertheless, I have my father's word for it that he is a Pioneer.

His high-heeled boots have left their imprint upon the old cattle trails down Abilene and Dodge City way. I can picture in my mind's eye his small but hardy frame encased in the fringes fashionable at that day, cleaving a path towards the setting sun as he hotly pursued the elusive maverick and furrowed the pine bars of the Red Light and the Pink Dog Cafés of that interesting period with his hard-earned dollars.

I have a deep reverence for my father as a Pioneer, which is not shared by my wife Ellen.

She sees only, in that weatherbeaten little figure, an old gentleman with a tremendous capacity for indenting the cushions in the Brown Palace Hotel, where he foregathers at night with his ancient friends and talks in a loud and querulous tone of voice.

My wife was born in the West at a time when department stores and nickelodeon theatres had crowded out the picturesque landscape to make room for a ragged skyline. Her father is not a Pioneer. He is merely the general superintendent of a railroad and travels in a private car. Her mother is not a Pioneer, either. She is a society leader.

Ellen, therefore, is inured to an atmosphere of labour difficulties and bargain sales, and could hardly be expected to sense the romance of the sunset trail as personified in a mild-looking little man with a stringy goatee, who declines to shake up the furnace on cold days. My father stands in proper awe of Ellen, and while he may raise his voice in a loud 'I – remember – when' down at the Brown Palace, his tone is low and well modulated around my house, where he resides.

Understand, Ellen is not a shrew – far from it. Neither is she inclined to be peckish. She simply came into the world at a time when pioneerism had become a sort of misdemeanour, so far as six-pistols and wild Indians are concerned, and society felt it best to preserve a respectable silence regarding certain early days.

Also, my wife – but this does not go if she hears it – is very obtuse when it comes to an appreciation of the historical value of the notches in my father's gun. I myself know, from rumour and otherwise, that in his day my father was a man of parts, and his aim was esteemed along the border.

The Society of Pioneers decided to hold a reunion one summer, and for the purposes of that gathering they picked the old city of Trinity. There was method in this selection. The average Pioneer, like my father, has daughters-in-law and other womenfolk holding receptions and functions about his family fireside, at which no account is taken of those hoary harbingers of civilization. Trinity is well removed from the social trail and is without reserve regarding the old days.

When my father announced his intention of attending the reunion, my wife offered no objection.

'Just so you ridiculous old men do your pioneering outside the city limits, I'll be satisfied,' she remarked.

So my father, with patient resignation, packed his suitcase full of buckskin clothing and other odds and ends, and betook himself to Trinity, in company with a large number of other old gentlemen whose voices began to touch the highest pitch in the vocal scale as soon as the train moved them beyond the zone of home hostility.

When I returned that evening, I found Ellen in quite a state of mind.

'The Daughters of the Revolution have appointed me a member of a committee to go to Trinity and assist in dedicating a museum to the Spanish explorers,' she announced. 'I am to make a speech.'

Personally, I have always felt that the son of a man who fought at

'Dobe Walls was as good as the great-great-granddaughter of a family who pitchforked Britons in the Lexington road, but I do not say so. I never shall, openly.

'Trinity? That's where father has gone,' I said.

'Well,' Ellen replied tartly, 'those foolish old men haven't anything to do with this museum. This is being done by the Daughters, and as other members of the committee are taking their husbands, you can go with me.'

'It will be quite a surprise to father to see us,' I suggested.

I do not feel called upon to explain that the dedication of the museum might have been arranged to coincide with the Pioneer reunion because of the connecting historical relation of the two events. I, a scion of the 'Dobe Walls, will never gratuitously offend any Daughter of the Revolution.

I did not see my father, but I heard of him as soon as I registered our names at the best hotel in Trinity, and urged the grizzled man doing duty as clerk to give us good rooms.

'Kivingson, hey?' he remarked, scrutinizing the register. 'Any relation to Bill Kivingson?'

'My father's name is William Kivingson,' I replied coldly. My wife sniffed one of the most disdainful sniffs.

'The son of ole Bill Kivingson can have anything I've got,' replied the old man. 'Me'n' Bill are pards; we useter raise hell together around Lamar. . . .'

'Jonas, let us go to our rooms,' interrupted Ellen scornfully.

'Yore old man's around town sum'eres,' called the clerk, as we mounted the stairs.

Trinity is a small but enthusiastic town on the old Santa Fe trail, which preserves many of its old-time traditions and all of its saloons. It was humming with activity. The business houses and the streets were hung with bunting and beaming with hospitality, while grizzled men dotted the landscape freely. It appeared that there were really two celebrations – the Pioneers' reunion and the dedication of the museum, the latter designed by the women as a sort of antidote for the masculine gathering.

I soon discovered that, as the son of Bill Kivingson, I was a man of honour in those parts at that particular time. The clerk at the hotel took care to point me out in my capacity of Bill Kivingson's offspring; and my hand was cordially shaken by ageing men with a violence that threatened my physical well-being.

Ellen was busied with the other members of the committee of the Daughters, arranging the programme for the dedication, and I wandered about the town. My search was not an exhaustive one, as I did not care to encroach upon my father's vacation, and, in addition to my natural feelings, there *are* some places where a bank attaché cannot follow even a Pioneer parent.

As I went about, mingling with the queer crowds, I heard strange and disquieting rumours dealing with the personality and actions of one whom they called 'Still Bill,' who appeared to be a character of some vehemence.

'Still Bill's broke the faro bank over to the Blue Moose,' announced an ancient exfrontiersman as he approached a group of bronzed old men at the hotel office that evening.

'Made 'em turn the box after he took out twenty-six hundred dollars!'

'That Bill's a grey wolf,' replied a tall man with long straight hair. There was admiration in his tone. 'If Still Bill gets to going good, there will be some fun in this burg!'

'He's eyes-going fair enough right now,' replied the bearer of the news. 'I mind the time at Trail City when he cleaned out the whole blame town. It was bustin' the bank started him that time, too.'

'Yes,' put in another, 'I rec'leck how he stood off the marshal and the en-tire pop'lation of Dodge City for two days an' nights.'

'Well,' said the messenger, 'he's got that ol' cap'n'ball pistol – that ole forty-five howitzer – an' he was tunin' up some when I left. He useter be able to singe your eyelashes with that weepon at fifty yards.'

At this point a fat, breathless gentleman who added locomotion with a manzanita cane, hobbled excitedly into the office.

'He's loose!' panted this latest courier, in a quavering voice. 'Ole Still Bill has done ontied himself! He's raisin' hell and puttin' a plug under ear over at the Moose! Like as not he'll come a'-bulgin' down this street pretty quick. I'm goin' home!'

'He useter be a long-winded cuss, too,' said someone. 'I don't reckon at his age, he can hold out more'n two days, but I seen the time when a week wasn't no limit!'

'They's been a-many a-ring-tailed, red-eyed son o' trouble turned loose in these here parts,' quavered the courier. 'I seen 'em come and I seen 'em go, but they's never been no white man could claw within a foot 'o the neck o' old Bill Kivingson!'

Kivingson! Bill Kivingson! *My Father!*

I approached the group. 'Gentlemen,' said I, 'you surely do not mean

Mr William Kivingson – a smallish man with a goatee and . . . ?'

'Still Bill! That's *him*!' came in full chorus.

'Why,' said I, 'it – it isn't possible that he should be performing actions such as you speak of! He is a harmless old man!'

'Harmless-*hell*!' snorted the fat old Pioneer. 'Harmless like a mess o' rattlesnakes!'

'But I'm his son!' I argued.

'I don't give a hoo-raw who you are! I'm his pal and I *know* Still Bill Kivingson – knowed him before you was born. It's good night, all, fer me!'

Now of course my natural thought was to go and get my father and make him retire for the night; but the hotel clerk laid a kind restraining hand upon my arm.

'Lay off o' him, son,' he said. 'When Still Bill gits a-goin', you jest got to give him a clean track and keep well under kivver. I ain't seen him speed none in twenty years, but I know what he *could* do. Jest you go to bed and lay off o' him.

'He won't hurt nobody,' he continued. 'All the old-timers'll keep out of his way, and he never did kill no bartenders, or such, in his life, because he needs 'em. Don't you worry about him. It's just them animile sperrits which has been plugged up fer a long time, coming out an' sniffin' around. O' course, if he should happen to think o' somebody he don't like, he might bother 'em some; but they ain't no one about Trinity he ain't made up with long ago.'

I debated the matter in my mind and came to the conclusion that I had better follow the clerk's advice. Who was I, that I should obstruct the course of a hero of the 'Dobe Walls, equipped with a cap and ball?

I lay awake for several hours, the tumult of the street pouring in at my window. Occasionally I heard above the hum of voices a pistol shot, which never failed to produce deep silence – after a great shuffling of feet. The pedestrians seemed to be seeking shelter. In the hush which followed these explosions there would come a voice, uplifted in warlike declamation. I could not make out the words, but there seemed to be a familiar ring to the belligerent chant.

When I went down the stairs the next morning, leaving Ellen at her toilet, a strange sight presented itself. It was nine o'clock. Outside, the sun was shining from a turquoise sky, and the air was soft as down, yet the lobby of the hotel was packed with men and women who stood gazing through the windows upon that scene of peace and quiet as if a terrible storm raged without.

Across the street, I could see, the stores were filled with similar crowds. The streets were deserted. An old man disengaged himself from the throng and sidled over to me. It was the hotel clerk.

'Son,' said he, 'I don't like fer to tell you-all, but yore old man, Still Bill, he's a-goin' good and strong this mornin'. He's plum' busted this celebration, which it can't go on with him a-streamin' up and down the streets like a pestilence. He's a-holdin' forth down yonder at the Moose, an' every now an' then he comes a-boilin' up this way to see if they's any defenceless folks he can devastate. Son, yore dad is a wolf – a curly wolf, that's all – and time don't change him none.'

'He certainly is a long-winded ole body,' declared another. 'I reckon it's his superflus energy o' twenty year a-bubbin' out all to onct. He allows he has decided to postpone the parade an' celebration until to-morrow and that he ain't goin' to permit no moosee dedication a-a-a-tall. He ain't decided yet whether he'll move this town plum' away or not.'

At that moment a high treble yell smote the air, and the crowd stayed back from the windows. I peered outside to see, far down the street, a small figure rocketing along at amazing speed. Clad in buckskins, feathered at the hems, a wide hat, it gave him the appearance of an animated mushroom, and waving a long-barrelled revolver, my father surged along in a billow of sound. While I watched, shamefaced, some of his expressions came to my ears.

'I'm a howlin' wolf from ole Mizzou, an' I'm a-huntin' gore!' he bawled. 'I picks my teeth with bowie-knives, an' the bark o' six-guns is music to my ears! Yee-owo-wow! I'm a snake in the grass, an' I hiss when you pass, an' I'm searchin' for folks to eat! Wow!'

He had a clear path, and he swirled along the street for a block or two, then doubled back and disappeared in a vocal storm.

'Ain't he a bear?' inquired the hotel clerk; and I could see that among these Pioneers my father's exhibitions, however much it shamed me, had aroused considerable admiration.

'Has he hurt anybody?' I inquired nervously.

'*Hurt* 'em, son?' said the hotel clerk. '*Hurt* 'em? Boy, they ain't anybody get near enough to old Hell-on-Wheels out there to let him *hurt* 'em. He never *hurts* no one if he gits 'em. He jest KILLS 'em. An' he ain't bin able for to ketch no one here.'

'Has he been going all night long?'

'All night,' replied the clerk. 'He ain't paused for drink for man or beast to date. An' bimeby we're goin' to set a bear trap out there in the street so business can proceed. Sim Leggins has gone after the trap now.

Sim is the authorities, an' a pussonal friend o' yer dad's, but he's decided Still Bill has got his twenty years' worth.'

Beyond the shadow of a doubt I should shortly have nerved myself to going after my father – there is no question in my mind but that I should have done it; but while I was steeling myself, my wife appeared – my wife, the immaculate Ellen, appeared in the crowded lobby, clad in a Japanese kimono, her hair in curl-papers.

'What is this I hear?' she demanded. 'The members of my committee tell me that our dedication is being postponed by some beast of a man – what does this mean?'

I had not the heart to tell her that it was my father. I could never have found the heart to do so. But at that moment he disclosed his identity by reappearing in the street – gun in hand and a yell in his throat.

Again he careened past the hotel, the crowd falling back dismayed – and as I stood there, the picture of embarrassment, if nothing more, my wife edged close to the window and stared.

'Come back, Ellen, dear,' I said. 'They say he's very dangerous to people he does not like.'

That was an unfortunate slip. I had never before suggested that my father did not like my wife – certainly he had never intimated such a thing.

'Yee-ow-wow!' yelled my father, as he swung back towards his Blue Moose retreat and disappeared.

My wife hurriedly left the hotel in a flutter of Japanese colouring, and with a toss of bedroom headgear. The crowd gasped. She was heading straight for the door of the Blue Moose. I followed – I have never permitted my wife to go where I do not go myself – and the crowd trailed along, nervously.

At the door of the Blue Moose saloon I paused, my heart beating with grave concern.

Imagine my feelings! My beloved wife, unappreciative of the danger attached to an eruption of twenty years of repressed pioneerial fervour, mindful only of the jeopardy of social standing, had flung herself headlong into the arms of Peril.

And my beloved father was Peril!

About me pressed the faces of the people, grey with apprehension, each head bent towards the door of the Blue Moose in a listening attitude.

Shortly I should have plunged through those doors regardless of consequences; shortly I should have rushed to my obvious duty.

From the interior of the Blue Moose arose a voice – a woman's voice – the voice of Ellen, my wife.

The door suddenly flew open with a bang, scattering the crowd like frightened sheep. My wife appeared. In one hand she held a long cap-and-ball revolver. In the other she clasped the left ear of a meek old gentleman, who was very white as to face, and who rubbed his hands together nervously.

'At your time of life, too!' my wife was saying. 'You ought to be ashamed of yourself, you silly old man!'

The crowd collected itself again, amazed, startled.

'Now, Elly –' quavered my father.

'Hush!' she ordered, in tones such as I never wish to hear again. 'Not another word, you ridiculous old man!'

And up the street, now teeming with an astounded multitude, she led the relentless howl wolf and snake in the grass, while I, who seemed destined always to be in the rear of the procession, followed, still harassed by emotion.

'I'm going to lock you up in a closet until the next train leaves,' my wife was saying. 'You – '

'Don't lose my gun, Elly,' my father exhorted humbly. 'It's the one with notches on it.'

A little boy, perhaps ten years of age, was running along beside them, whooping shrilly.

'Here, boy!' said Ellen, pushing the famous revolver into the youngster's hands. 'Here's a nice plaything for you!'

'And now, ladies and gentlemen,' said my wife, in closing her brief remarks at the dedication of the museum, 'it is with a feeling of deepest reverence towards the wonderful men of that early period, and to those equally wonderful men who came at a later day to develop and perpetuate the path of progress that we dedicate this small monument in the hope that it will ever keep green the memory of the Spanish explorers and the American Pioneer!'

I have a high regard for my father as a Pioneer, which is not shared by my wife, Ellen.

The Queen and I

☆★☆★☆★☆★☆★☆★☆★☆★☆★☆★☆★☆★☆★☆★☆★☆

SUE TOWNSEND

A Breath of Air

The Queen winced as Jack Barker ground his cigarette out on the silk rug. A faint smell of burning rose between them. Jack fought the urge to apologize. The Queen stared at Jack disdainfully. His stomach gurgled. Her picture had hung in his classroom when he was struggling to learn his nine times tables. In his boyhood he used to look to the Queen for inspiration. Prince Charles bent down and picked up the cigarette stub. He looked for somewhere to put it, but, finding nowhere suitable, he slipped it into his pocket.

Princess Margaret said, 'Lilibet I've *got* to have a fag. Please!'

'May we open the windows, Mr Barker?' asked the Queen. Her accent cut into Jack like a crystal. He half expected to bleed.

'No chance,' he replied.

'Am I to have a house of my own, Mr Barker, or must I share with my daughter and son-in-law?' The Queen Mother gave Jack her famous smile, but her hands were twisting the full skirt of her periwinkle dress into a knot.

'You'll get a pensioner's bungalow. It's your entitlement as an ordinary citizen of this country.'

'A bungalow, good. I couldn't manage stairs. Will my staff be living in or out?'

Jack laughed and looked at his fellow Republicans. Six men and six women, hand-picked to witness this historic occasion. They laughed along with Jack.

'You don't seem to understand. There'll be no staff, no dressers, no cooks, secretaries, cleaners, chauffeurs.'

Turning to the Queen he said, 'You'll have to nip in now and then, help your mum out. But she'll probably be entitled to Meals on Wheels.'

The Queen Mother looked quite pleased to hear this. 'So I shan't starve?'

'Under the People's Republican Party's rule, nobody in Britain will starve,' said Jack.

Prince Charles cleared his throat and said, 'Er, may one, er, enquire as to where. . . ? That is, the location . . . ?'

'If you're asking me where you're all going, I'm not telling you. All I can say at the moment is that you'll all be in the same street, but you'll have strangers as next-door neighbours, working-class people. Here's a list of what you can take with you.'

Jack held out photocopies of each of the lists his wife had compiled only two hours before. The lists were headed: *Essential Items; Furniture; Fittings, suitable for two-bedroomed council house and pensioner's bungalow.* The Queen Mother's list was much shorter, she noticed. Jack held the papers out, but nobody came forward to take them. Jack didn't move. He knew that one of them would crack. Eventually Diana got up, she hated scenes. She took the papers from Jack and gave each member of the Royal Family their list. There was quiet for a few moments while they read. Jack fiddled with the gun in his pocket. Only he knew that it wasn't loaded.

'Mr Barker, there is no mention of dogs here,' said the Queen.

'One per family,' said Jack.

'Horses?' asked Charles.

'Would you keep a horse in a council house garden?'

'No. Quite. One wasn't thinking.'

'Clothes aren't on the list,' said Diana, shyly.

'You won't be needing much. Just the bare essentials. You won't be making personal appearances, will you?'

Princess Anne rose and stood next to her father. 'Thank God for that! At least something good has come out of this bloody shambles. Are you all right, Pa?'

Prince Philip was in a state of shock and had been ever since the previous night when he had turned on the television for Election Night Special at 11.25 and seen the announcement of the election of Jack Barker, founder and leader of the People's Republican Party, as the member for Kensington West. Prince Philip had watched incredulously as Barker had addressed the joyous crowds in the Town Hall. Middle-aged poll tax payers had cheered alongside young people wearing ragged jeans and nose rings. He had lifted the telephone and advised his wife to watch the television set. Half an hour later, she rang him back. 'Philip, please come to my room.'

They had sat up until the early hours as one Republican candidate after another had been declared elected in front of cheering crowds of British citizenry. Gradually their children had joined them. At 7.30 am the servants brought them breakfast, but nobody ate. By 11 am the People's Republican Party had won 451 seats and John Major, the Conservative Prime Minister, had reluctantly conceded defeat. Shortly afterwards, Jack Barker announced that he was Prime Minister. His first job, he said, would be to go to Buckingham Palace and order the Queen to abdicate. . . .

Never So Humble

It was dusk when the furniture van drew up outside Number Nine Hellebore Close. The Queen looked stonily at her new home. The house looked grimly back through the gloom, as though it bore a grudge. Its windows were boarded. Somebody violent and strong had driven in six-inch nails and connected hardboard panels to the window frames. A small sycamore tree was growing from the upstairs guttering.

The Queen adjusted her headscarf and straightened her back. She looked at the mean front door: our furniture will never fit through, she thought, and we will have to share a wall – what was the technical term? Something celebratory. A *party* wall, that was it! The door of Number Eleven opened and a man in a tee shirt and overalls came out and stood on his concrete step. A woman joined him, blonde and fleshy, wearing clothes a size too small and red fluffy mules. The fluff waved about in the evening breeze, looking like creatures on the sea bed searching for plankton.

The man and the woman were husband and wife – Beverley and Tony Threadgold – the Queen's new neighbours. They gawped at the removal van, not bothering to disguise their curiosity. The house next door to them had been empty for over a year so the Threadgolds had enjoyed the luxury of comparative privacy. They'd shouted, banged doors and made love without vocal restraint, and now it was over. It was a sad day for them. They hoped their new neighbours would be reasonably, but not too, respectable.

The driver of the removal van went round and opened the door for the Queen. She climbed down, grateful for the volume of material in her tweed skirt.

'Come on, Philip,' she encouraged, but Philip sat on, in the front of the van, clutching his briefcase to him, as though it were a hot water bottle and he were a hypothermia victim.

'Philip, this gentleman has a family to go home to.'

The driver was pleased to be called a gentleman by the Queen.

'No 'urry,' he said, graciously.

But in truth he couldn't wait to get back to his own council house, to tell his wife about the journey up the M1. About how he and the Queen had talked of homeopathic medicine and dogs and the problems of adolescent children.

'I'll give you an 'and in with your stuff,' he offered.

'How kind, but the Republican Party suggested that my husband and I must get used to coping for ourselves.'

The driver confided, 'Nobody in our house voted for 'em. We always vote Conservative, always.'

The Queen confided, 'Somebody in *our* house supported them.'

The driver nodded towards Prince Philip. 'Not 'im?'

The Queen laughed at the thought.

A second removal van roared into the close. The doors opened immediately and the Queen's grandchildren climbed out. The Queen waved and the little boys ran towards her. Prince Charles helped his wife out of the van. Diana had dressed for adversity: denim and cowboy boots. She looked at Number Eight Hellebore Close and shuddered. But Prince Charles smiled. Here, at last, was the simple life. . . .

Eric Makes His Move

One morning the Queen received an envelope addressed to:

The Occupant
9 Hellebore Close
Flowers Estate
Middleton
MI2 9WL

Inside was a handwritten letter written on blue notepaper.

Erilob
39 Fox's Den Lane
Upper Hangton
nr Kettering
Northamptonshire

To Her Majesty
Elizabeth II, by the
Grace of God of the
United Kingdom of Great
Britain and Northern
Ireland, and of her other
Realms and Territories Queen,
Head of the Commonwealth,
Defender of the Faith.

Dear Your Majesty,

Please allow me to humbly introduce myself. I am Eric Tremainc,

> a mere loyal subject, who has been horrified by what has happened to this country and its once great peoples. I know that that coward and traitor Jack Barker has forbidden your subjects to approach you like this, but I have decided to throw my towel into the ring and defy him. If it means that one day I will face execution for my presumption, then so be it. (I have already lost two fingers in an industrial accident, so I have got less to lose than most people.)

The Queen broke off reading, snatched the grill pan and threw two burning slices of toast out of the window. Black smoke filled the kitchen. She used Tremaine's letter to disperse it. When the room was reasonably clear, she carried on reading.

> Your Majesty, I have put my head on the block and started a movement, it is called Bring Our Monarch Back, or B.O.M.B. for short. My wife Lobelia is quite good with words (see above for the amusing name of our house, evidence of Lobelia's handiwork!).
>
> You are not alone, your Majesty! Many in Upper Hangton are behind you!
>
> Lobelia and I are going into Kettering this afternoon to recruit members for B.O.M.B. Normally we keep away from the hurly-burly of big towns, but we have overcome our reluctance. The Cause is greater than our dislike of the metropolitan whirl that is Kettering in the nineties, I fear.
>
> Lobelia, my wife of thirty-two years, has never been one to push herself forward. She had preferred in the past to leave more confident types such as myself to bathe in the limelight. (I am the Chairman of several societies, Model Railways, Upper Hangton Residents Committee, Keep Dogs in the Parks Campaign – there are more, but enough!)
>
> But my retiring wife is prepared to approach total and absolute strangers and talk to them about B.O.M.B. in Kettering town centre, mark you! This is a mark of her disgust at what has happened to our beloved Royal Family. Jack Barker is pandering to the appetites of the people and trying to bring us all down to the level of the animals. He won't be content until we are all being sexually promiscuous in the fields and farmyards of our once green and pleasant land.
>
> Pigs like Barker will not accept that some of us are born to rule and others need to be ruled, and ordered about for their own good.

Well, I must stop now. I have to call in at number thirty-one and pick up the B.O.M.B. leaflets. Mr Bond, the owner of the aforesaid thirty-one has kindly desk-top published the above-mentioned leaflets!

B.O.M.B. is yet small, but it will grow! Soon there will be branches of B.O.M.B. in every hamlet, village, town, city and urban conurbation in the land! Fear not! You will once again sit on the Throne.

I remain, your Majesty,
your most humble subject,
Eric P. Tremaine

The Queen put Tremaine's letter on to Philip's tray. She thought it might amuse him but when she returned twenty minutes later she saw that the breakfast had not been eaten and that the letter appeared to be unread: it was still tucked at the same angle under the bowl of cold porridge.

'I've had this rather amusing letter this morning, darling, shall I read it out to you?' she said brightly. The doctor had said that Prince Philip must be stimulated. 'It's from a chap called Eric P. Tremaine. I wonder if the "P" stands for Philip? Quite a coincidence if it did, eh?'

The Queen knew that she was talking to her husband as though he were a simple-minded slug, but she couldn't stop herself. He wouldn't talk, wouldn't move, wouldn't *eat* now. It was absolutely *infuriating*. It was time to call the doctor again. She couldn't watch him starve to death. He was so thin now that he didn't resemble himself at all. He had white hair and a white beard and, without his tinted contact lenses, his eyes looked like the colour of the stone-washed denim that people in Hell Close seemed so fond of wearing.

He suddenly lifted his head from the pillow and shouted, 'I want Hélène!'

'Who's Hélène, dear?' asked the Queen.

But Philip's head sank back. His eyes closed and he appeared to go to sleep. The Queen went downstairs and picked up the telephone receiver. It was dead. She jiggled the black knob about, but there was no reassuring purr in her ear. British Telecom had carried out their threat to cut her off because she hadn't paid her deposit. . . .

Reading the News

One afternoon, Violet Toby knocked on the Queen's back door and walked straight into the kitchen. She was holding that day's edition of the *Middleton Mercury*. Harris poked his head out from under the kitchen table and growled at Violet, but she kicked out at him with the sharp point of a high-heeled shoe and he retreated. Violet found the Queen in the living room ironing a silk blouse. The Queen was having difficulty with the collar.

'Wretched thing keeps puckering,' she said.

Violet took the iron from the Queen, and checked the variable control switch. 'You got it on linen,' she said. 'Tha's why.'

The Queen switched the iron off and invited Violet to sit down.

Violet said, 'I wondered if you've seen this. It's about your mam.'

She handed the Queen the open newspaper. On page seven, under a report that a white tee-shirt had been stolen from a washing line in the early hours of Sunday morning in Pigston Magna, was another small news item:

> FORMER QUEEN MOTHER DIES
>
> The former Queen Mother, who in 1967 opened the Casualty Department at Middleton Royal Hospital, has died in Hellebore Close, the Flowers Estate. She was 92.

The Queen gave the newspaper back to Violet who said, 'Don't you want to cut it out?'

'No,' said the Queen. 'It's hardly worth keeping, is it?' Then she noticed that the front page headline screamed: 'LOAN CRISIS: JAPAN ISSUES ULTIMATUM.' She took the newspaper back from Violet and read that Jack Barker had been closeted in an eight-hour meeting with Treasury Officials, and the Japanese Finance Minister the previous day. No statement had been issued to the waiting media.

The *Middleton Mercury*'s financial correspondent, Marcus Moore, wrote that in his opinion, Britain faced its gravest crisis since the dark days of the War. He continued indignantly,

> 'No details about the precise collateral for the multi-billion yen loan have been made public. Mr Barker's commitment to open government must now be seen as a sham. Why oh why, are we being kept in the dark? What has Britain pledged to give Japan? The *Middleton Mercury* insists, "WE MUST BE TOLD".'

'Interesting, this Japanese loan thing,' said the Queen as she handed the paper back to Violet for the second time.

'Is it?' said Violet. 'I couldn't care less about politics myself. It don't affect my life, does it?'

'But I thought you supported Jack Barker, Violet,' said the Queen.

'Yeah, I do,' said Violet, 'But he'll be out on 'is arse soon, won't 'e?'

The Queen thought about the worsening financial crisis and agreed that Violet could be right. As she folded the ironing board away, and put it in the understairs cupboard, she wondered how she would feel about returning to Buckingham Palace. It would be awfully nice to have other, unseen hands to do her ironing for her of course, but the prospect of resuming her official duties made her shudder. She hoped that Jack would find a way out of his difficulties.

Bicycles

☆★☆★☆★☆★☆★☆★☆★☆★☆

JEROME K. JEROME

On Monday afternoon Harris came round; he had a cycling paper in his hand.

I said: 'If you take my advice, you will leave it alone.'

Harris said: 'Leave what alone?'

I said: 'That brand-new, patent, revolution in cycling, record-breaking, tomfoolishness, whatever it may be, the advertisement of which you have there in your hand.'

He said: 'Well, I don't know; there will be some steep hills for us to negotiate; I guess we shall want a good brake.'

I said: 'We shall want a brake, I agree; what we shall not want is a mechanical surprise that we don't understand, and that never acts when it is wanted.'

'This thing,' he said, 'acts automatically.'

'You needn't tell me,' I said. 'I know exactly what it will do, by instinct. Going uphill it will jam the wheel so effectively that we shall have to carry the machine bodily. The air at the top of the hill will do it good, and it will suddenly come right again. Going downhill it will start reflecting what a nuisance it has been. This will lead to remorse, and finally to despair. It will say to itself: "I'm not fit to be a brake. I don't help these fellows; I only hinder them. I'm a curse, that's what I am"; and, without a word of warning, it will "chuck" the whole business. That is what that brake will do. Leave it alone. You are a good fellow,' I continued, 'but you have one fault.'

'What?' he asked indignantly.

'You have too much faith,' I answered. 'If you read an advertisement, you go away and believe it. Every experiment that every fool has thought of in connection with cycling you have tried. Your guardian angel appears to be a capable and conscientious spirit, and hitherto she has seen you through; take my advice and don't try her too far. She must have had a busy time since you started cycling. Don't go on till you make her mad.'

He said: 'If every man talked like that there would be no advancement made in any department of life. If nobody ever tried a new thing the world would come to a standstill. It is by – '

'I know all that can be said on that side of the argument,' I interrupted. 'I agree in trying new experiments up to thirty-five; *after* thirty-five I consider a man is entitled to think of himself. You and I have done our duty in this direction, you especially. You have been blown up by a patent gas lamp – ' He said: 'I really think, you know, that was my fault; I think I must have screwed it up too tight.'

I said: 'I am quite willing to believe that if there was a wrong way of handling the thing that is the way you handle it. You should take that tendency of yours into consideration; it bears upon the argument. Myself, I did not notice what you did; I only know we were riding peacefully and pleasantly along the Whitby Road, discussing the Thirty Years War, when your lamp went off like a pistol shot. The start sent me into the ditch; and your wife's face, when I told her there was nothing the matter and that she was not to worry, because the two men would carry you upstairs, and the doctor would be round in a minute bringing the nurse with him, still lingers in my memory.'

He said: 'I wish you had thought to pick up the lamp. I should like to have found out what was the cause of its going off like that.'

I said: 'There was not time to pick up the lamp. I calculate it would have taken two hours to have collected it. As to its "going off", the mere fact of its being advertised as the safest lamp ever invented would of itself, to anyone but you, have suggested accident. Then there was that electric lamp,' I continued.

'Well, that really did give a fine light,' he replied; 'you said so yourself.'

I said: 'It gave a brilliant light in the King's Road, Brighton, and frightened a horse. The moment we got into the dark beyond Kemp Town it went out, and you were summoned for riding without a light. You may remember that on sunny afternoons you used to ride about with that lamp shining for all it was worth. When lighting-up time came it was naturally tired, and wanted a rest.'

'It was a bit irritating, that lamp,' he murmured; 'I remember it.'

I said: 'It irritated me; it must have been worse for you. Then, there are saddles,' I went on – I wished to get this lesson home to him. 'Can you think of any saddle ever advertised that you have *not* tried?'

He said: 'It has been an idea of mine that the right saddle is to be found.'

I said: 'You give up that idea; this is an imperfect world of joy and sorrow mingled. There may be a better land where bicycle saddles are made out of rainbow, stuffed with cloud; in this world the simplest thing is to get used to something hard. There was that saddle you bought in Birmingham; it was divided in the middle, and looked like a pair of kidneys.'

He said: 'You mean that one constructed on anatomical principles.'

'Very likely,' I replied. 'The box you bought it in had a picture on the cover, representing a sitting skeleton – or rather that part of a skeleton which does sit.'

He said: 'It was quite correct; it showed you the true position of the – '

I said: 'We will not go into details; the picture always seemed to me indelicate.'

He said: 'Medically speaking, it was right.'

'Possibly,' I said, 'for a man who rode in nothing but his bones. I only know that I tried it myself, and that to a man who wore flesh it was agony. Every time you went over a stone or a rut it nipped you; it was like riding on an irritable lobster. You rode that for a month.'

'I thought it only right to give it a fair trial,' he answered.

I said: 'You gave your whole family a fair trial also; if you will allow me the use of slang. Your wife told me that never in the whole course of your married life had she known you so bad tempered, so unchristian-like, as you were that month. Then you remember that other saddle, the one with the spring under it.'

He said: 'You mean "the Spiral".'

I said: 'I mean the one that jerked you up and down like a jack-in-the-box; sometimes you came down again in the right place, and sometimes you didn't. I am not referring to these matters merely to recall painful memories, but I want to impress you with the folly of trying experiments at your time of life.'

He said: 'I wish you wouldn't harp so much on my age. A man at thirty-four – '

'A man at what?'

He said: 'If you don't want the thing, don't have it. If your machine runs away with you down a mountain, and you and George get flung through a church roof, don't blame me.'

'I cannot promise for George,' I said; 'a little thing will sometimes irritate him, as you know. If such an accident as you suggest happens, he may be cross, but I will undertake to explain to him that it was not your fault.'

'Is the thing all right?' he asked.

'The tandem,' I replied, 'is well.'

He said: 'Have you overhauled it? '

I said: 'I have not, nor is anyone else going to overhaul it. The thing is now in working order, and it is going to remain in working order till we start.'

I have had experience of this 'overhauling'. There was a man at Folkestone; I used to meet him on the Lees. He proposed one evening we should go for a long bicycle ride together on the following day, and I agreed. I got up early, for me; I made an effort, and was pleased with myself. He came half an hour late: I was waiting for him in the garden. It was a lovely day. He said:

'That's a good-looking machine of yours. How does it run?'

'Oh, like most of them!' I answered; 'easily enough in the morning; goes a little stiffly after lunch.'

He caught hold of it by the front wheel and the fork, and shook it violently.

I said: 'Don't do that; you'll hurt it.'

I did not see why he should shake it; it had not done anything to him. Besides, if it wanted shaking, I was the proper person to shake it. I felt much as I should had he started whacking my dog.

He said: 'This front wheel wobbles.'

I said: 'It doesn't if you don't wobble it.' It didn't wobble, as a matter of fact – nothing worth calling a wobble.

He said: 'This is dangerous; have you got a screw-hammer?'

I ought to have been firm, but I thought that perhaps he really did know something about the business. I went to the tool shed to see what I could find. When I came back he was sitting on the ground with the front wheel between his legs. He was playing with it, twiddling it round between his fingers; the remnant of the machine was lying on the gravel path beside him.

He said: 'Something has happened to this front wheel of yours.'

'It looks like it, doesn't it?' I answered. But he was the sort of man that never understands satire.

He said: 'It looks to me as if the bearings were all wrong.'

I said: 'Don't you trouble about it any more; you will make yourself tired. Let us put it back and get off.'

He said: 'We may as well see what is the matter with it, now it is out.' He talked as though it had dropped out by accident.

Before I could stop him he had unscrewed something somewhere, and out rolled all over the path some dozen or so little balls.

'Catch 'em!' he shouted; 'catch 'em! We mustn't lose any of them.' He was quite excited about them.

We grovelled round for half an hour, and found sixteen. He said he hoped we had got them all, because, if not, it would make a serious difference to the machine. He said there was nothing you should be more careful about in taking a bicycle to pieces than seeing you did not lose any of the balls. He explained that you ought to count them as you took them out, and see that exactly the same number went back in each place. I promised, if ever I took a bicycle to pieces I would remember his advice.

I put the balls for safety in my hat, and I put my hat upon the doorstep. It was not a sensible thing to do, I admit. As a matter of fact, it was a silly thing to do. I am not as a rule addle-headed; his influence must have affected me.

He then said that while he was about it he would see to the chain for me, and at once began taking off the gear-case. I did try to persuade him from that. I told him what an experienced friend of mine once said to me solemnly:

'If anything goes wrong with your gear-case, sell the machine and buy a new one; it comes cheaper.'

He said: 'People talk like that who understand nothing about machines. Nothing is easier than taking off a gear-case.'

I had to confess he was right. In less than five minutes he had the gear-case in two pieces, lying on the path, and was grovelling for screws. He said it was always a mystery to him the way screws disappeared.

We were still looking for the screws when Ethelbertha came out. She seemed surprised to find us there; she said she thought we had started hours ago.

He said: 'We shan't be long now. I'm just helping your husband to overhaul this machine of his. It's a good machine; but they all want going over occasionally.'

Ethelbertha said: 'If you want to wash yourselves when you have done you might go into the back kitchen, if you don't mind; the girls have just finished the bedrooms.'

She told me that if she met Kate they would probably go for a sail; but that in any case she would be back to lunch. I would have given a sovereign to be going with her. I was getting heartily sick of standing about watching this fool breaking up my bicycle.

Common sense continued to whisper to me: 'Stop him, before he does any more mischief. You have a right to protect your own property from the ravages of a lunatic. Take him by the scruff of the neck, and kick him out of the gate!'

But I am weak when it comes to hurting other people's feelings, and I let him muddle on.

He gave up looking for the rest of the screws. He said screws had a knack of turning up when you least expected them, and that now he would see to the chain. He tightened it till it would not move; next he loosened it until it was twice as loose as it was before. Then he said we had better think about getting the front wheel back into its place again.

I held the fork open, and he worried with the wheel. At the end of ten minutes I suggested he should hold the forks, and that I should handle the wheel; and we changed places. At the end of his first minute he dropped the machine, and took a short walk round the croquet lawn, with his hands pressed together between his thighs. He explained as he walked that the thing to be careful about was to avoid getting your fingers pinched between the forks and the spokes of the wheel. I replied I was convinced, from my own experience, that there was much truth in what he said. He wrapped himself up in a couple of dusters, and we commenced again. At length we did get the thing into position; and the moment it was in position he burst out laughing.

I said: 'What's the joke?'

He said: 'Well, I am an ass!'

It was the first thing he had said that made me respect him. I asked him what had led him to the discovery.

He said: 'We've forgotten the balls!'

I looked for my hat; it was lying topsyturvy in the middle of the path, and Ethelbertha's favourite hound was swallowing the balls as fast as he could pick them up.

'He will kill himself,' said Ebbson – I have never met him since that day, thank the Lord; but I think his name was Ebbson – 'they are solid steel.'

I said: 'I am not troubling about the dog. He has had a bootlace and a packet of needles already this week. Nature's the best guide; puppies seem to require this kind of stimulant. What I am thinking about is my bicycle.'

He was of a cheerful disposition. He said: 'Well, we must put back all we can find, and trust to providence.'

We found eleven. We fixed six on one side and five on the other, and half an hour later the wheel was in its place again. It need hardly be added that it really did wobble now; a child might have noticed it. Ebbson said it would do for the present. He appeared to be getting a bit tired himself. If I had let him, he would, I believe, at this point have gone home. I was determined now, however, that he should stop and finish; I had abandoned all thoughts of a ride. My pride in the machine he had killed. My only interest lay now in seeing him scratch and bump and pinch himself. I revived his drooping spirits with a glass of beer and some judicious praise. I said:

'Watching you do this is of real use to me. It is not only your skill and dexterity that fascinates me, it is your cheery confidence in yourself, your inexplicable hopefulness, that does me good.'

Thus encouraged, he set to work to refix the gear-case. He stood the bicycle against the house, and worked from the off side. Then he stood it against a tree, and worked from the near side. Then I held it for him, while he lay on the ground with his head between the wheels, and worked at it from below, and dropped oil upon himself. Then he took it away from me, and doubled himself across it like a pack-saddle, till he lost his balance and slid over on to his head. Three times he said:

'Thank heaven, that's right at last !'

And twice he said:

'No, I'm damned if it is after all!'

What he said the third time I try to forget.

Then he lost his temper and tried bullying the thing. The bicycle, I was glad to see, showed spirit; and the subsequent proceedings degenerated into little else than a rough-and-tumble fight between him and the machine. One moment the bicycle would be on the gravel path, and he on top of it; the next, the position would be reversed – he on the gravel path, the bicycle on him. Now he would be standing flushed with victory, the bicycle firmly fixed between his legs. But his triumph would be short-lived. By a sudden, quick movement it would free itself, and, turning upon him, hit him sharply over the head with one of its handles.

At a quarter to one, dirty and dishevelled, cut and bleeding, he said: 'I think that will do'; and rose and wiped his brow.

The bicycle looked as if it also had had enough of it. Which had received most punishment it would have been difficult to say. I took him into the back kitchen, where, so far as was possible without soda and proper tools, he cleaned himself, and sent him home.

The bicycle I put into a cab and took round to the nearest repairing shop. The foreman of the works came up and looked at it.

'What do you want me to do with that?' said he.

'I want you,' I said, 'so far as is possible, to restore it.'

'It's a bit far gone,' said he; 'but I'll do my best.'

He did his best, which came to two pounds ten. But it was never the same machine again; and at the end of the season I left it in an agent's hands to sell. I wished to deceive nobody; I instructed the man to advertise it as a last year's machine. The agent advised me not to mention any date. He said: 'In this business it isn't a question of what is true and what isn't; it's a question of what you can get people to believe. Now, between you and me, it don't look like a last year's machine; so far as looks are concerned, it might be a ten-year-old. We'll say nothing about date; we'll just get what we can.'

I left the matter to him, and he got me five pounds, which he said was more than he had expected.

There are two ways you can get exercise out of a bicycle: you can 'overhaul' it, or you can ride it. On the whole, I am not sure that a man who takes his pleasure overhauling does not have the best of the bargain. He is independent of the weather and the wind; the state of the roads troubles him not. Give him a screw-hammer, a bundle of rags, an oil-can, and something to sit down upon, and he is happy for the day. He has to put up with certain disadvantages, of course; there is no joy without alloy. He himself always looks like a tinker, and his machine always suggests the idea that, having stolen it, he has tried to disguise it; but as he rarely gets beyond the first milestone with it, this, perhaps, does not much matter. The mistake some people make is in thinking they can get both forms of sport out of the same machine. This is impossible; no machine will stand the double strain. You must make up your mind whether you are going to be an 'overhauler' or a rider. Personally, I prefer to ride, therefore I take care to have near me nothing that can tempt me to overhaul. When anything happens to my machine I wheel it to the nearest repairing shop. If I am too far from the town or village to walk, I sit by the roadside and wait till a cart comes along. My chief danger, I always find, is from the wandering overhauler. The sight of a broken-down machine is to the overhauler as a wayside corpse to a crow; he swoops down upon it with a friendly yell of triumph. At first I used to try politeness. I would say:

'It is nothing; don't you trouble. You ride on, and enjoy yourself, I beg it of you as a favour; please go away.'

Experience has taught me, however, that courtesy is of no use in such an extremity. Now I say:

'You go away and leave the thing alone, or I will knock your silly head off.'

And if you look determined, and have a good stout cudgel in your hand, you can generally drive him off.

George came in later in the day. He said:

'Well, do you think everything will be ready?'

I said: 'Everything will be ready by Wednesday, except, perhaps, you and Harris.'

He said: 'Is the tandem all right?'

'The tandem, ' I said, 'is well.'

He said: 'You don't think it wants overhauling?'

I replied: 'Age and experience have taught me that there are few matters concerning which a man does well to be positive. Consequently, there remain to me now but a limited number of questions upon which I feel any degree of certainty. Among such still-unshaken beliefs, however, is the conviction that that tandem does not want overhauling. I also feel a presentiment that, provided my life is spared, no human being between now and Wednesday morning is going to overhaul it.'

George said: 'I should not show temper over the matter, if I were you. There will come a day, perhaps not far distant, when that bicycle, with a couple of mountains between it and the nearest repairing shop, will, in spite of your chronic desire for rest, *have* to be overhauled. Then you will clamour for people to tell you where you put the oil-can, and what you have done with the screw-hammer. Then, while you exert yourself holding the thing steady against a tree, you will suggest that somebody else should clean the chain and pump the back wheel.'

I felt there was justice in George's rebuke – also a certain amount of prophetic wisdom. I said:

'Forgive me if I seemed unresponsive. The truth is, Harris was round here this morning –'

George said: 'Say no more; I understand. Besides, what I came to talk to you about was another matter. Look at that.'

He handed me a small book bound in red cloth. It was a guide to English conversation for the use of German travellers. It commenced 'On a Steamboat', and terminated 'At the Doctor's'; its longest chapter being devoted to conversation in a railway carriage, among, apparently, a compartment load of quarrelsome and ill-mannered lunatics: 'Can you not get farther away from me, sir?' – 'It is impossible, madam; my neighbour, here, is very stout' – 'Shall we not endeavour to arrange our legs?' – 'Please have the goodness to keep your elbows down' – 'Pray do not inconvenience yourself, madam, if my shoulder is of any accommodation to you,' whether intended to be said sarcastically or not, there was nothing to indicate – 'I really must request you to move a little, madam, I can hardly breathe,' the author's idea being, presumably, that by this time the whole party was mixed up together on the floor. The chapter concluded with the phrase: 'Here we are at our destination, God be thanked! (*Gott sei dank!*)' a pious exclamation, which under the circumstances must have taken the form of a chorus.

At the end of the book was an appendix, giving the German traveller hints concerning the preservation of his health and comfort during his sojourn in English towns; chief among such hints being advice to him to always travel with a supply of disinfectant powder, to always lock his bedroom door at night, and to always carefully count his small change.

'It is not a brilliant publication,' I remarked, handing the book back to George; 'it is not a book that personally I would recommend to any German about to visit England; I think it would get him disliked. But I have read books published in London for the use of English travellers abroad every whit as foolish. Some educated idiot, misunderstanding seven languages, would appear to go about writing these books for the misinformation and false guidance of modern Europe.'

'You cannot deny,' said George, 'that these books are in large request. They are bought by the thousand, I know. In every town in Europe there must be people going about talking this sort of thing.'

'Maybe,' I replied; 'but fortunately, nobody understands them. I have noticed, myself, men standing on railway platforms and at street corners reading aloud from such books. Nobody knows what language they are speaking; nobody has the slightest knowledge of what they are saying. This is, perhaps, as well; were they understood they would probably be assaulted.'

George said: 'Maybe you are right; my idea is to see what would happen if they were understood. My proposal is to get to London early on Wednesday morning, and spend an hour or two going about and shopping with the aid of this book. There are one or two little things I want – a hat and a pair of bedroom slippers, among other articles. Our boat does not leave Tilbury till twelve, and that just gives us time. I want to try this sort of talk where I can properly judge of its effect. I want to see how the foreigner feels when he is talked to in this way.'

It struck me as a sporting idea. In my enthusiasm I offered to accompany him, and wait outside the shop. I said I thought that Harris would like to be in it, too – or rather outside.

George said that was not quite his scheme. His proposal was that Harris and I should accompany him into the shop. With Harris, who looks formidable, to support him, and myself at the door to call the police if necessary, he said he was willing to adventure the thing.

We walked round to Harris's, and put the proposal before him. He examined the book, especially the chapters dealing with the purchase of shoes and hats. He said:

'If George talks to any bootmaker or any hatter the things that are put down here, it is not support he will want; it is carrying to the hospital that he will need.'

That made George angry.

'You talk,' said George, 'as though I were a foolhardy boy without any sense. I shall select from the more polite and less irritating speeches; the grosser insults I shall avoid.'

This being clearly understood, Harris gave in his adhesion; and our start was fixed for early Wednesday morning.

The Dalkey Archive

☆★☆★☆★☆★☆★☆★☆★☆★☆★☆★☆★☆★☆★☆★☆

FLANN O'BRIEN

The old coloured houses of irregular size along the narrow quays of the Liffey seem to lean outward as if to study themselves in the water; but on his pleasant walk there this time, Mick's eye was not dwelling pleasurably on them. He was thinking, though not in gloom. There had come to him an idea that seemed bright, masterly, bold even. True, it would not dissipate the underwater ghost of Augustine nor extinguish the neuro-psychotic aberrations of De Selby but he became convinced it would enable him *to do something* to prevent, perhaps permanently but certainly for the present, the carrying out of any genuine plan to visit the human race with havoc. He was pleased. He resolved to go to a quiet place where alcoholic drinks were to be had and then, please God, not have one but try something healthy, refreshing, harmless. Plain thinking – planning – was called for.

And Father Cobble? Yes, Mick would keep that arrangement to bring him on a visit to De Selby. The visit might well be valuable and, also, he was glad that Hackett had reneged. He felt Hackett's presence might have been a complication, even an obstacle, and this was also true of the steps he would have to take later to give effect to his new idea.

His steps led him to the Metropole in Dublin's main street. It was not called a cinema, restaurant, dance hall or drinking den, though it contained all of these delights. Drinking was done in a quiet, softly-lighted lounge downstairs where tables were sequestered by tall fixed screens of dark wood. It was a favourite resort of parish priests from the country and, though service was by waitresses, lady customers were excluded.

He sat down and ordered a small Vichy water. When another order had been served in the division next to him he was sharply startled by the unseen customer's thanks, unmistakable in content if not in tone.

– In gratitude for that bottle, me dear colleen, I will make a novena for the implenishment of your soul irreciprocally to Saint Martin of Tours himself.

No help for it: Mick picked up his drink and moved in. Happily, Sergeant Fottrell was alone. In old-fashioned courtesy he stood up and put out a hand.

– Well, the Lord forbid but you must be following me detectively?

Mick laughed.

– No indeed. I wanted a quiet drink and thought nobody would know me down here.

– Ah, but the divil minds his own children.

Curiously, this unscheduled collision with the sergeant did not seem to erode Mick's half-formed desire to be by himself. In fact he was glad to see the sergeant. He apologized once more for having failed to retrieve his bicycle from the station in Dalkey. The sergeant took his long upper lip from his glass of barley wine with a wince of total absolution.

– Where the bicycle is, he said gravely, is a far safer place than the high highroad itself, intuitively.

– Oh, I just thought it might be in the way.

– It is under lock and key in cell number two and you are far better in your health to be divorced from it. Tell me this item: how did you find Policeman Pluck?

– I had met him before, of course. A very pleasant man.

– What was he doing perceptively?

– He was busy mending a puncture.

– Ah-ha!

The sergeant sniggered, took another sup from his drink and frowned slightly in thought.

– That will be the third puncture in seven days, he said, in what seemed to be a tone of satisfaction.

– That looks a pretty awful record, Mick replied. Is it sheer bad luck or is it the bad roads?

– 'Tis the Council must take the credit for the little back roads, the worst in Ireland. But Policeman Pluck got his punctures at half one on Monday, two o'clock on Wednesday, and half six on Sunday.

– How on earth do you know that? Does he keep a diary of them?

– He does not. I know the dates and times protruberantly because if was my good self who carried out the punctures with my penknife.

– Good heavens, why?

– For Policeman Pluck's good luck. But sitting here I have been considering meditatively those talking pictures upstairs. They are a quaint achievious science certainly.

– They are a great advance on silent films.

– You know how they are worked?

– Oh yes. The photo-electric cell.

– Yes then. Why if you can turn light into sound you cannot turn sound into light?

– You mean invent a *phono*-electric cell?

– Of a particular certainty, but for sure that invention would be a hard pancake. I do often contemplate what sort of a light the noble American Constitution would make, given out by President Roosevelt.

– A very interesting speculation.

– Or a speech by Arthur Griffith?

– Yes indeed.

– Charles Stewart Parnell held the dear belief that all Ireland's woes and tears were the true result of being so fond of green. Wrap the green flag round me, boys. If you put that grand man's speeches through the cell (and many a month he spent in a cell himself) wouldn't it be the hemochromic thing if the solution was a bright green light?

Mick laughed at this, and at the whole wonderful idea. There had been, he seemed to remember, an organ that 'played' light on a screen, enchanting patterns of mixes and colour. But that was not what the sergeant had conceived.

– Yes. And that would be the colour of Caruso's voice, or John McCormack singing *Down by the Sally Gardens*? But tell me, Sergeant. Why did you persistently puncture Policeman Pluck's tyres?

The sergeant beckoned the waitress, ordered a barley wine for himself and a small bottle of 'that' for his friend. Then he leaned forward confidentially.

– Did you ever discover or hear tell of mollycules? he asked.

– I did of course.

– Would it surprise or collapse you to know that the Mollycule Theory is at work in the parish of Dalkey?

– Well . . . yes and no.

– It is doing terrible destruction, he continued, the half of the people is suffering from it, it is worse than the smallpox.

– Could it not be taken in hand by the Dispensary Doctor or the National Teachers, or do you think it is a matter for the head of the family?

– The lock, stock and barrel of it all, he replied almost fiercely, is the County Council.

– It seems a complicated thing all right.

The sergeant drank delicately, deep in thought.

– Michael Gilhaney, a man I know, he said finally, is an example of a man that is nearly banjaxed from the operation of the Mollycule Theory. Would it astonish you ominously to hear that he is in danger of being a bicycle?

Mick shook his head in polite incomprehension.

– He is nearly sixty years of age by plain computation, the sergeant said, and if he is itself, he has spent no less than thirty-five years riding his bicycle over the rocky roadsteads and up and down the pertimious hills and into the deep ditches when the road goes astray in the strain of the winter. He is always going to a particular destination or other on his bicycle at every hour of the day or coming back from there at every other hour. If it wasn't that his bicycle was stolen every Monday he would be sure to be more than halfway now.

– Halfway to where?

– Halfway to being a bloody bicycle himself.

Had Sergeant Fottrell for once betrayed himself into drunken rambling? His fancies were usually amusing but not so good when they were meaningless. When Mick said something of the kind the sergeant stared at him impatiently.

– Did you ever study the Mollycule Theory when you were a lad? he asked. Mick said no, not in any detail.

– That is a very serious defalcation and an abstruse exacerbation, he said severely, but I'll tell you the size of it. Everything is composed of small mollycules of itself and they are flying around in concentric circles and arcs and segments and innumerable various other routes too numerous to mention collectively, never standing still or resting but spinning away and darting hither and thither and back again, all the time on the go. Do you follow me intelligently? Mollycules?

– I think I do.

– They are as lively as twenty punky leprechauns doing a jig on the top of a flat tombstone. Now take a sheep. What is a sheep only millions of little bits of sheepness whirling around doing intricate convulsions inside the baste. What else is it but that?

– That would be bound to make the sheep dizzy, Mick observed, especially if the whirling was going on inside the head as well.

The sergeant gave him a look which no doubt he himself would describe as one of non-possum and noli-me-tangere.

– That's a most foolhardy remark, he said sharply, because the nerve-strings and the sheep's head itself are whirling into the same bargain and you can cancel out one whirl against the other and there you are – like simplifying a division sum when you have fives above and below the bar.

– To say the truth I did not think of that.

– Mollycules is a very intricate theorem and can be worked out with algebra but you would want to take it by degrees with rulers and cosines and familiar other instruments and then at the wind-up not believe what you had proved at all. If that happened you would have to go back over it till you got a place where you could believe your own facts and figures as exactly delineated from Hall and Knight's Algebra and then go on again from that particular place till you had the whole pancake properly believed and not have bits of it half-believed or a doubt in your head hurting you like when you lose the stud of your shirt in the middle of the bed.

– Very true, Mick decided to say.

– If you hit a rock hard enough and often enough with an iron hammer, some mollycules of the rock will go into the hammer and contrariwise likewise.

– That is well known, he agreed.

– The gross and net result of it is that people who spend most of their natural lives riding iron bicycles over the rocky roadsteads of the parish get their personalities mixed up with the personalities of their bicycles as a result of the interchanging of the mollycules of each of them, and you would be surprised at the number of people in country parts who are nearly half people and half bicycles.

Mick made a little gasp of astonishment that made a sound like the air coming from a bad puncture.

– Good Lord, I suppose you're right.

– And you would be unutterably flibbergasted if you knew the number of stout bicycles that partake serenely of humanity.

Here the sergeant produced his pipe, a thing he did very rarely in public, and in silence commenced the laborious business of filling and ramming it from his battered tin of very dark tobacco. Mick began to muse and think of country places he had known in his younger days. He thought of one place he had been fond of.

Brown bogs and black bogs were neatly arranged on each side of the road with rectangular boxes carved out of them here and there, each with a filling of yellow-brown brown-yellow water. Far away near the sky tiny people were stooped at their turf-work, cutting out precisely-shaped sods with their patent spades and building them into a tall memorial the height of a horse and cart. Sounds came from them, delivered to his ears without charge by the west wind, sounds of laughing and whistling and bits of verses from the old bog-songs. Nearer, a house stood attended by three trees and surrounded by the happiness of a coterie of fowls, all of them picking and rooting and disputating loudly in the unrelenting manufacture of their eggs. The house was quiet in itself and silent but a canopy of lazy smoke had been erected over the chimney to indicate that people were within engaged on tasks. Ahead of him went the road, running swiftly across the flat land and pausing slightly to climb slowly up a hill that was waiting for it in a place where there was tall grass, grey boulders and rank stunted trees. The whole overhead was occupied by the sky, translucent, impenetrable, ineffable and incomparable, with a fine island of cloud anchored in the calm two yards to the right of Mr Jarvis's outhouse.

The scene was real and incontrovertible but at variance with the talk of the sergeant. Was it not monstrous to allege that the little people winning turf far away were partly bicycles? He took a sideways view of him. He had now compacted his turflike tobacco and produced a box of matches.

– Are you sure about the humanity of bicycles? Mick enquired of him. Does it not go against the doctrine of original sin? Or is the Molecule Theory as dangerous as you say?

The sergeant was drawing fiercely at the pipe as his match spluttered.

– It is between twice and three times as dangerous as it might be, he replied gloomily. Early in the morning I often think it is four times and, for goodness' sake, if you lived here for a few days and gave full and free rein to your observation and inspection, you would know how certain the sureness of the certainty is.

– Policeman Pluck did not look like a bicycle, Mick said. He had no back wheel on him and hadn't so much as a bell on his right thumb.

The sergeant looked at him with some commiseration.

– You cannot expect him to grow handlebars out of his neck but I have seen him attempt things more acutely indescribable than that. Did you ever notice the queer behaviour of bicycles in the country, or the more-man-bicycles?

– I did not.

– It's an indigenous catastrophe. When a man lets things go too far, you will not see much because he spends a lot of time leaning with one elbow on walls or standing propped up by one foot at the path. Such a man is a futile phenomenon of great charm and intensity and a very dangerous article.

– Dangerous to other people, you mean?

– Dangerous to himself and everybody. I once knew a man named Doyle. He was thirty-one per cent.

– Well, that's not too serious.

The sergeant was puffing industriously, his pipe now in fine order.

– Maybe. You can thank me. There were three Doyle brothers in the house and they were too contemptuously poor to have a bicycle apiece. Some people never know how fortunate they are when they are poorer than each other. But bedamn but one of the brothers won a prize of ten pounds in *John Bull*. When I got precise wind of this tiding I knew I would have to take quick steps unless there was to be two new bicycles in the family, because you will understand that I can steal only a limited number of bicycles in a month. Luckily I knew the postman well and I gave him a talking-to to divert the cheque to myself. The postman! Ah, great, sweet, brown stirabout!

Recollection of this public servant seemed to move the sergeant to sad sardonic chuckles, with intricate gesturings of his red hands.

– The postman? Mick asked.

– Seventy-two per cent, he said quietly.

– Great Lord!

– A round of twenty-nine miles on the bicycle every single day for forty years, hail, rain or snowballs. There was very little hope of getting his number down below fifty again. I got him to cash the cheque in a private sub-office and we split the money in the public interest paternalistically.

Funny thing, Mick did not feel that the sergeant had been dishonest; he had been sentimental, rather, and the state of the postman meant that no moral issue was involved.

He asked the sergeant how the bicycle, for its part, would behave from day to day in a situation like this.

– The behaviour of a bicycle with a very high content of *homo sapiens*, he explained, is very cunning and entirely remarkable. You never see them moving by themselves but you meet them in the least accountable places unexpectedly. Did you ever see a bicycle leaning against the dresser in a warm kitchen when it is pouring outside?

– I did.

– Not very far from the fire?

– Yes.

– Near enough to the family to hear the conversation?

– I suppose so.

– Not a thousand miles from where they keep the eatables?

– I did not notice that. Good Lord, you do not mean to say that these bicycles *eat food*?

– They were never seen doing it, nobody ever caught them with a mouthful of seedy cake. All I know is that food disappears.

– What!

– It is not the first time I have noticed crumbs at the front wheels of some of those gentlemen.

Rather feebly Mick gestured to the waitress and ordered another drink. The sergeant was in deadly earnest, no doubt about that. And this was the man Mick had decided to call in to help him in resolving the great St Augustine enigma. He felt strangely depressed.

– Nobody takes any notice, the sergeant said softly. Tom thinks that Pat is responsible for missing grubsteaks, and Pat thinks that Tom is instrumental. Very few of the people guess what is going on in such a fearsomely infractional house. There are other things, too . . . but it's better not to talk of them.

– Oh come now, Sergeant. What sort of other things?

– Well, a man riding a lady's bicycle. It's the height of sulphurous immorality, the PP would be within his rights in forbidding such a low character put as much as his nose inside the church.

– Yes . . . such conduct is unseemly.

– God help the nation that weakens on such matters. You would have bicycles demanding votes, and they would look for seats on the County Council to make the roads far worse than they are for their own ulterior motivation. But against that and on the other hand, a good bicycle is a great companion, a friend, there is great charm about it.

– All the same, I doubt if I'll ever again get up on that bicycle of mine you have in the station out in Dalkey.

The sergeant shook his head genially.

– Ah now, a little of it is a good thing, it makes you hardy and puts iron into you. But shure walking too far too often too quickly isn't safe at all either. The cracking of your feet on the road makes a certain amount of road come up into you. When a man dies they say he returns to clay funereally but too much walking fills you up with clay far sooner (or buries bits of you along the road) and brings your death halfway to meet you. It is not easy to know fastidiously what is the best way to move yourself from one place to another.

There was a little silence. Mick thought of mentioning how intact one could remain by restricting oneself to air travel but decided not to; the sergeant would surely object on the ground of cost. Mick noticed his face had become clouded and that he was staring into the bowl of his pipe.

– I will tell you a secret confidentially, he said in a low voice. My own grandfather was eighty-three when we buried him. For five years before his death he was a horse.

– *A horse?*

– A horse in everything but extraneous externalities, because he had spent years of his life – far too many for safety, be the pipers – in the saddle. Usually he was lazy and quiet but now and again he would go for a smart gallop, clearing the hedges in great style. Did you ever see a man on two legs galloping?

– I did not.

– Well, I am given to understand it is a great sight. He always said he won the Grand National when he was a lot younger and used to annoy the life out of his family with stories about the intricate jumps and the insoluble tallness of them.

– And the grandfather got himself into this condition by too much horse-riding?

– That was the size of it. His old horse Dan was in the contrary way of thinking and gave so much trouble, coming into the house at night, interfering with young girls during the day and committing indictable offences, that they had to shoot him. The polis of the time was not sympathetic exiguously. They said they would have to arrest the horse and have him up at the next Petty Sessions unless he was done away with. So the family shot him but if you ask me it was my grandfather they shot and it is the horse that is buried in Cloncoonla churchyard.

The sergeant fell to musing on his complicated ancestry but had the presence of mind to beckon the waitress with his pipe and order a repeat dose of the quiet medicine.

– In a way, Mick observed, your grandfather's case was not so bad. I mean, a horse is at least a creature, a living thing, man's companion on earth and indeed he is accounted everywhere a noble animal. Now, if it was a pig . . .

The sergeant turned and beamed on him, and gave a long contented puff at his pipe.

– You say that from a good heart, and it is subsidiary and solemn of you. The Irish people have great graw for the horse. When Tipperary Tim died, the cabhorse that won the Grand National and the only one of the whole field left standing, be the holy God you'd swear it was a beloved Archbishop that had gone to his eternal reward. Strong men was seen crying.

– Yes, and think of Orby, the great horse that won the National for Boss Croker. To this day he lies there at Sandyford.

– Ah yes. And then there was Master McGrath, the dog that was faster than the wind. A statue of him stands at a crossroads down in Tipp, where the mother comes from.

Both of them pleasurably savoured their kinship with the higher animals, though personally Mick drew the line at becoming one of them by a process of prolonged carnal intercussion.

– Well, Sergeant, I am delighted that we are quite agreed on one thing at least. Human metamorphosis vis-à-vis an iron bicycle is quite another matter. And there is more to it than the monstrous exchange of tissue for metal.

– And what would that be? the sergeant asked curiously.

– All decent Irishmen should have a proper national outlook. Practically any bike you have in Ireland was made in either Birmingham or Coventry.

– I see the point intimately. Yes. There is also an element of treason entailed. Quite right.

It seemed that this point had never occurred to him and a frown gathered about him as he inwardly considered it, puffing stolidly and compacting the tobacco in his bowl with a well-charred finger.

– Oh, now, he said at last, faith and the bicycle is no hilarity of itself as a gigantic social problem. In me younger days it led to a hanging.

– Is that so?

– It did bedad. I was stationed in Borrisokane at the time and there was a very famous man there be the name of McDadd. McDadd held the national record for the hundred miles on the solid tyre. I need not tell you with exactitude what the solid tyre did for him. We had to hang the bicycle.

– Hang the bicycle?

– McDadd had a first-class grudge against another man named MacDonaghy but he did not go near MacDonaghy. He knew how things stood there, and he gave MacDonaghy's bicycle a ferocious thrashing with a crowbar. After that McDadd and MacDonaghy had a fast fist fight and MacDonaghy – a dark man with glasses – did not live to know who the winner was.

– Well, wouldn't that be a case of manslaughter?

– Not with the sergeant we had in them days. He held it was murder most foul and a bad case of criminality into the same bargain. We couldn't find McDadd for a long time or make sure where the most of him was. We had to arrest his bicycle as well as himself and we minutely watched the two of them under secret observation for a week to see where the majority of McDadd was and whether the bicycle was mostly in McDadd's backside *pari passu* and vice versa if you understand my meaning.

– I think I do, but I can also see the possibility of a charge of conspiracy.

– Maybe so, maybe not. The sergeant gave his ruling at the end of the week. His position was painful in the extremity of pain because he was a close friend of McDadd after office hours. He condemned the bicycle and it was the bicycle that was hanged.

It seemed to Mick a very summary form of justice, and apparently the sentence had been imposed and carried out without the formality of court proceedings.

– I think that perhaps there was a miscarriage of the carriageway there, he commented.

– They were rough days, the sergeant replied, smoking thoughtfully. But there was a great wake afterwards, and the bicycle was buried in the same grave as MacDonaghy. Did you ever see a bicycle-shaped coffin?

– No.

– It is a very inconvoluted item of wood-working, you would want to be a master-class carpenter to make a good job of the handlebars, to say nothing of the pedals and the backstep.

– I don't doubt that.

– Ah yes. The days of racing on the solid tyre were sad days for Ireland.

The sergeant fell silent again. One could almost hear the gentle wash of the tide of memory in his head.

– There were tragedic cases, too, of another kind entirely. I remember an old man. He was harmless enough but he had the people driven loopy by the queer way he moved and walked. He'd go up a little gentle hill at a speed of maybe half a mile an hour but at other times he would run so fast that you'd swear he was doing up to fifteen emm pee aitch. And that's a fact by damn.

– Did anybody find out what was wrong with him?

– One very intelligent, perspicuous and infractious man did. It was meself. Do you know what was wrong with the poor bugger?

– No. What?

– He was suffering severely from Sturmey Archer. He was the first in the country to fit the three-speed gear at the turn of the century.

– Yes, I think I can see the various possible complications. For instance, I think racing bikes have forks with special springing in them. Yes. It's all very interesting. But now, I promised to be home early and I'm going to buy a final drink.

Mick beckoned the waitress.

– I want to ask you about something, he added.

As the drinks were coming he bethought himself, as they say in the old books. He had enjoyed the sergeant's peroration and his abstruse subject. It would be fitting, perhaps, to call him the poor man's De Selby. But the latter was still his preoccupation – perhaps he should say his night-and-day obsession. Yet he had a plan now, one that was at once ingenious and daring. He thought it would be only wise and judicious to have the sergeant participate unwittingly in it, for if he were to find certain things out afterwards of his own motion, his undoubted gift for the maladroit could in the end wreck the scheme. Mick had already in his mind assigned a part – again an unwitting one – to Hackett. The date and timing of the operation depended now on one thing only: finding out how De Selby proposed to circulate his deadly DMP substance simultaneously all over the world so as to obviate the condition of insulation, the sort of seal that had obtained in the case of the submarine cavern at Dalkey.

He was not clear how he could do this in a reasonably short time, and prolonged twisting and turning of his own brain yielded no guess about how this mighty task could be accomplished. Even a world Power with tens of thousands of aeroplanes would be daunted by such an undertaking and, supernatural as De Selby's contacts seemed to be, it was doubtful indeed if flights of angels could be invoked. In fact there was no proof that the Almighty approved of De Selby at all. God might be on Mick's side.

– Sergeant Fottrell, he said seriously, I suppose you know Mr De Selby of the Vico Road?

A gentle frown gathered on the face.

– An exemplary and august personality, he replied, but a whit contumacious.

That was promising: respect leavened with suspicion.

– Exactly. I know him rather well myself but he has me worried. In that house of his in the woods he has been carrying out experiments. He is a scientist, of course.

– Ah yes. Piercing insentiently the dim secrets of the holy world.

– Now I am not saying that he is breaking the law. But I do know that he is endangering the community. He does not know, and probably could not be persuaded, that his experiments might get out of control and visit us all with an epidemic of appalling disease, with goodness knows how many people dying like flies and passing on the pestilence to other people as they do so; not only here in Dublin and Dalkey but possibly in England and other parts of the world.

The sergeant had rekindled his pipe.

– That is a most unfavourable and incontinent tiding, he said. That is worse than the question of the bicycles.

– I'm glad you look at it in that way. You are a man, Sergeant, who is bigger than his job, otherwise you would not have stolen bicycles to curtail the deadly cycling of afflicted parties and indeed deliberately puncturing Policeman Pluck's machine.

This speech obviously pleased the sergeant, as Mick intended it would.

– There are times, he said, when I must take my superior officer to be the Man Above. It is my plain duty to guard members of the human race, sometimes from themselves. Not everybody understands the far from scrutable periculums of the intricate world.

– I quite agree. Now I happen to know that Mr De Selby has been artificially incubating the bacteria which cause typhoid fever in humans. Typhoid is a very serious and dangerous disease, even worse than typhus.

– An insatiable importunity.

– Yes.

– An indiscriminate exacerbation much to be inveighed against meticulously.

– Mr De Selby has tens of millions of those microbes in a metal container like a little keg. He has it in his house, locked in a safe.

– A safe, faith?

– Yes. In the interest of humanity I plan to carry off this container of dangerous bugs away from the scientist's house – steal it if you will – and put it in some safe place where it will do no harm.

– Ah! Well now! Steal it? Yes indeed. I would consider that not contumelious or derogatory.

– Then I can rely, Sergeant, on your co-operation?

He was now relaxed, apparently relieved that the project was no more than to take away something which was, while dangerous, of no monetary value.

– Not only my co-operation but my active condonement of the *res ipsa*. But locked in a safe? I do not know the skills of poking a safe's lock.

– Nor do I. And blowing it up or using force would be very dangerous. But that sort of hazard does not arise at all. The safe looks massive and strong but it is old-fashioned. Look at this!

From a small inside pocket of his jacket Mick extracted a key and held it up.

– I've told you, Sergeant, that our friend is careless, he said, and perhaps I should have said criminally careless and quite reckless. This is the key of the safe. I picked it up from the floor of his sitting-room on a recent visit.

– Well great cripes, the sergeant cried blankly.

– Our task is really simple enough, Mick continued. First we must see to it that on a given evening Mr De Selby is not at home. I think I can arrange that without much trouble. When he is out, there will be nobody else there. And our intrusion will be brief.

– Succinctly so, by dad.

– When we've got the container we will hide it in the shrubbery, near the little gate at the Vico Road. We will then go home. The following morning early I will collect it in a taxi. Then leave the rest to me. The only little snag is how to get into the house.

– That would not be a fastidious worry, the sergeant replied pleasantly, for if he is as careless as you say, I could deal deftly with a window, without wincing.

– But not break one, I hope. We don't want to alarm or alert him.

– No then. I have a good pen-knife.

– Ah, that is the business, Sergeant. We can take it that everything is agreed then?

– Except the date of the accomplishment.

– Yes. I'll let you know that in good time.

Mick rose, and in good conspirator's fashion, put out his hand. The sergeant grasped it.

– To the grand defence and preservation of the race of Adam, he intoned solemnly.

The Long Dark Tea-Time of the Soul

☆★☆

DOUGLAS ADAMS

The sun broke in through the upper windows of a house in North London and struck the peacefully sleeping figure of a man.

The room in which he slept was large and bedraggled and did not much benefit from the sudden intrusion of light. The sun crept slowly across the bedclothes, as if nervous of what it might find amongst them, slunk down the side of the bed, moved in a rather startled way across some objects it encountered on the floor, toyed nervously with a couple of motes of dust, lit briefly on a stuffed fruitbat hanging in the corner, and fled.

This was about as big an appearance as the sun ever put in here, and it lasted for about an hour or so, during which time the sleeping figure scarcely stirred.

At eleven o'clock the phone rang, and still the figure did not respond, any more than it had responded when the phone had rung at twenty-five to seven in the morning, again at twenty to seven, again at ten to seven, and again for ten minutes continuously starting at five to seven, after which it had settled into a long and significant silence, disturbed only by the braying of police sirens in a nearby street at around nine o'clock, the delivery of a large eighteenth-century dual manual harpsichord at around nine-fifteen, and the collection of same by bailiffs at a little after ten. This was a not uncommon sort of occurrence – the people concerned were accustomed to finding the key under the doormat, and the man in the bed was accustomed to sleeping through it. You would probably not say that he was sleeping the sleep of the just, unless you meant the just asleep, but it was certainly the sleep of someone who was not fooling about when he climbed into bed of a night and turned off the light.

The room was not a room to elevate the soul. Louis XIV, to pick a name at random, would not have liked it, would have found it not sunny enough, and insufficiently full of mirrors. He would have desired someone to pick up the socks, put the records away, and maybe burn the place down. Michelangelo would have been distressed by its proportions, which were neither lofty nor shaped by any noticeable inner harmony or symmetry, other than that all parts of the room were pretty much equally full of old coffee mugs, shoes and brimming ashtrays, most of which were now sharing their tasks with each other. The walls were painted in almost precisely that shade of green which Raffaello Sanzio would have bitten off his own right hand at the wrist rather than use, and Hercules, on seeing the room, would probably have returned half an hour later armed with a navigable river. It was, in short, a dump, and was likely to remain so for as long as it remained in the custody of Mr Svlad, or 'Dirk', Gently, né Cjelli.

At last Gently stirred.

The sheets and blankets were pulled up tightly around his head, but from somewhere halfway down the length of the bed a hand slowly emerged from under the bedclothes and its fingers felt their way in little tapping movements along the floor. Working from experience, they neatly circumvented a bowl of something very nasty that had been sitting there since Michaelmas, and eventually happened upon a half-empty pack of untipped Gauloises and a box of matches. The fingers shook a crumpled white tube free of the pack, seized it and the box of matches, and then started to poke a way through the sheets tangled together at the top of the bed, like a magician prodding at a handkerchief from which he intends to release a flock of doves.

The cigarette was at last inserted into the hole. The cigarette was lit. For a while the bed itself appeared to be smoking the cigarette in great heaving drags. It coughed long, loud and shudderingly and then began at last to breathe in a more measured rhythm. In this way, Dirk Gently achieved consciousness.

He lay there for a while feeling a terrible sense of worry and guilt about something weighing on his shoulders. He wished he could forget about it, and promptly did. He levered himself out of bed and a few minutes later padded downstairs.

The mail on the doormat consisted of the usual things: a rude letter threatening to take away his American Express card, an invitation to apply for an American Express card, and a few bills of the more hysterical and unrealistic type. He couldn't understand why they kept sending them. The cost of the postage seemed merely to be good money thrown after bad. He shook his head in wonderment at the malevolent incompetence of the world, threw the mail away, entered the kitchen and approached the fridge with caution.

It stood in the corner.

The kitchen was large and shrouded in a deep gloom that was not relieved, only turned yellow, by the action of switching on the light. Dirk squatted down in front of the fridge and carefully examined the edge of the door. He found what he was looking for. In fact he found more than he was looking for.

Near the bottom of the door, across the narrow gap which separated the door from the main body of the fridge, which held the strip of grey insulating rubber, lay a single human hair. It was stuck there with dried saliva. That he had expected. He had stuck it there himself three days earlier and had checked it on several occasions since then. What he had not expected to find was a second hair.

He frowned at it in alarm. A *second* hair?

It was stuck across the gap in the same way as the first one, only this hair was near the top of the fridge door, and he had not put it there. He peered at it closely, and even went so far as to go and open the old shutters in the kitchen windows to let some extra light in upon the scene.

The daylight shouldered its way in like a squad of policemen, and did a lot of *what's-all-this*ing around the room which, like the bedroom, would have presented anyone of an aesthetic disposition with difficulties. Like most of the rooms in Dirk's house it was large, looming and utterly dishevelled. It simply sneered at anyone's attempts to tidy it, sneered at them and brushed them aside like one of the small pile of dead and disheartened flies that lay beneath the window, on top of a pile of old pizza boxes.

The light revealed the second hair for what it was – a grey hair at root, dyed a vivid metallic orange. Dirk pursed his lips and thought very deeply. He didn't need to think hard in order to realize who the hair belonged to – there was only one person who regularly entered the kitchen looking as if her head had been used for extracting metal oxides from industrial waste – but he did have seriously to consider the implications of the discovery that she had been plastering her hair across the door of his fridge.

It meant that the silently waged conflict between himself and his cleaning lady had escalated to a new and more frightening level. It was now, Dirk reckoned, fully three months since this fridge door had been opened, and each of them was grimly determined not to be the one to open it first. The fridge no longer merely stood there in the corner of the kitchen, it actually lurked. Dirk could quite clearly remember the day on which the thing had started lurking. It was about a week ago, when Dirk had tried a simple subterfuge to trick Elena – the old bat's name was Elena, pronounced to rhyme with cleaner, which was an irony that Dirk now no longer relished – into opening the fridge door. The subterfuge had been deftly deflected and had nearly rebounded horribly on Dirk.

He had resorted to the strategy of going to the local mini-market to buy a few simple groceries. Nothing contentious – a little milk, some eggs, some bacon, a carton or two of chocolate custard and a simple half-pound of butter. He had left them, innocently, on top of the fridge as if to say, 'Oh, when you have a moment, perhaps you could pop these inside . . .'

When he had returned that evening his heart bounded to see that they were no longer on top of the fridge. They were gone! They had not been merely moved aside or put on a shelf, they were nowhere to be seen. She must finally have capitulated and put them away. In the fridge. And she would surely have cleaned it out once it was actually open. For the first and only time his heart swelled with warmth and gratitude towards her, and he was about to fling open the door of the thing in relief and triumph when an eighth sense (at the last count, Dirk reckoned he had eleven) warned him to be very, very careful, and to consider first where Elena might have put the cleared out contents of the fridge.

A nameless doubt gnawed at his mind as he moved noiselessly towards the garbage bin beneath the sink. Holding his breath, he opened the lid and looked.

There, nestling in the folds of the fresh black bin liner, were his eggs, his bacon, his chocolate custard and his simple half-pound of butter. Two milk bottles stood rinsed and neatly lined up by the sink into which their contents had presumably been poured.

She had thrown it away.

Rather than open the fridge door, she had thrown his food away. He looked round slowly at the grimy, squat, white monolith, and that was the exact moment at which he realized without a shadow of a doubt that his fridge had now begun seriously to lurk.

He made himself a stiff black coffee and sat, slightly trembling. He had not even looked directly at the sink, but he knew that he must unconsciously have noticed the two clean milk bottles there, and some busy part of his mind had been alarmed by them.

The next day he had explained all this away to himself. He was becoming needlessly paranoiac. It had surely been an innocent or careless mistake on Elena's part. She had probably been brooding distractedly on her son's attack of bronchitis, peevishness or homosexuality or whatever it was that regularly prevented her from either turning up, or from having noticeable effect when she did. She was Italian and probably had absent-mindedly mistaken his food for garbage.

But the business with the hair changed all that. It established beyond all possible doubt that she knew exactly what she was doing. She was under no circumstances going to open the fridge door until he had opened it first, and he was under no circumstances going to open the fridge until she had.

Obviously she had not noticed his hair, otherwise it would have been her most effective course simply to pull it off, thus tricking him into thinking she had opened the fridge. He should presumably now remove her hair in the hope of pulling that same trick on her, but even as he sat there he knew that somehow that wouldn't work, and that they were locked into a tightening spiral of non-fridge-opening that would lead them both to madness or perdition.

He wondered if he could hire someone to come and open the fridge.

No. He was not in a position to hire anybody to do anything. He was not even in a position to pay Elena for the last three weeks. The only reason he didn't ask her to leave was that sacking somebody inevitably involved paying them off, and this he was in no position to do. His secretary had finally left him on her own initiative and gone off to do something reprehensible in the travel business. Dirk had attempted to cast scorn on her preferring monotony of pay over –

'*Regularity* of pay,' she had calmly corrected him.

– over job satisfaction.

She had nearly said, 'Over *what*?', but at that moment she realized that if she said that she would have to listen to his reply, which would be bound to infuriate her into arguing back. It occurred to her for the first time that the only way of escaping was just not to get drawn into these arguments. If she simply did not respond this time, then she was free to leave. She tried it. She felt a sudden freedom. She left. A week later, in much the same mood, she married an airline cabin steward called Smith.

Dirk had kicked her desk over, and then had to pick it up himself later when she didn't come back.

The detective business was currently as brisk as the tomb. Nobody, it seemed, wished to have anything detected. He had recently, to make ends meet, taken up doing palmistry in drag on Thursday evenings, but he wasn't comfortable with it. He could have withstood it – the hateful, abject humiliation of it all was something to which he had, in different ways, now become accustomed, and he was quite anonymous in his little tent in the back garden of the pub – he could have withstood it all if he hadn't been so horribly, excruciatingly good at it. It made him break out in a sweat of self-loathing. He tried by every means to cheat, to fake, to be deliberately and cynically bad, but whatever fakery he tried to introduce always failed and he invariably ended up being right.

His worst moment had come about as a result of the poor woman from Oxfordshire who had come in to see him one evening. Being in something of a waggish mood, he had suggested that she should keep an eye on her husband, who, judging by her marriage line, looked to be a bit of a flighty type. It transpired that her husband was in fact a fighter pilot, and that his plane had been lost in an exercise over the North Sea only a fortnight earlier.

Dirk had been flustered by this and had soothed meaninglessly at her. He was certain, he said, that her husband would be restored to her in the fullness of time, that all would be well, and that all manner of things would be well and so on. The woman said that she thought this was not very likely seeing as the world record for staying alive in the North Sea was rather less than an hour, and since no trace of her husband had been found in two weeks it seemed fanciful to imagine that he was anything other than stone dead, and she was trying to get used to the idea, thank you very much. She said it rather tartly.

Dirk had lost all control at this point and started to babble.

He said that it was very clear from reading her hands that the great sum of money she had coming to her would be no consolation to her for the loss of her dear, dear husband, but that at least it might comfort her to know that he had gone on to that great something or other in the sky, that he was floating on the fleeciest of white clouds, looking very handsome in his new set of wings, and that he was terribly sorry to be talking such appalling drivel but she had caught him rather by surprise. Would she care for some tea, or some vodka, or some soup?

The woman demurred. She said she had only wandered into the tent by accident, she had been looking for the lavatories, and what was that about the money?

'Complete gibberish,' Dirk had explained. He was in great difficulties, what with having the falsetto to keep up. 'I was making it up as I went along,' he said. 'Please allow me to tender my most profound apologies for intruding so clumsily on your private grief, and to escort you to, er, or rather, direct you to the, well, what I can only in the circumstances call the lavatory, which is out of the tent and on the left.'

Dirk had been cast down by this encounter, but was then utterly horrified a few days later when he discovered that the very following morning the unfortunate woman had learnt that she had won £250,000 on the Premium Bonds. He spent several hours that night standing on the roof of his house, shaking his fist at the dark sky and shouting, 'Stop it!' until a neighbour complained to the police that he couldn't sleep. The police had come round in a screaming squad car and woken up the rest of the neighbourhood as well.

Today, this morning, Dirk sat in his kitchen and stared dejectedly at his fridge. The bloody-minded ebullience which he usually relied on to carry him through the day had been knocked out of him in its very opening moments by the business with the fridge. His will sat imprisoned in it, locked up by a single hair.

What he needed, he thought, was a client. Please, God, he thought, if there is a god, any god, bring me a client. Just a simple client, the simpler the better. Credulous and rich. Someone like that chap yesterday. He tapped his fingers on the table.

The problem was that the more credulous the client, the more Dirk fell foul at the end of his own better nature, which was constantly rearing up and embarrassing him at the most inopportune moments. Dirk frequently threatened to hurl his better nature to the ground and kneel on its windpipe, but it usually managed to get the better of him by dressing itself up as guilt and self-loathing, in which guise it could throw him right out of the ring.

Credulous and rich. Just so that he could pay off some, perhaps even just one, of the more prominent and sensational bills. He lit a cigarette. The smoke curled upwards in the morning light and attached itself to the ceiling.

Like that chap yesterday . . .

He paused.

The chap yesterday . . .

The world held its breath.

Quietly and gently there settled on him the knowledge that something, somewhere, was ghastly. Something was terribly wrong.

There was a disaster hanging silently in the air around him waiting for him to notice it. His knees tingled.

What he needed, he had been thinking, was a client. He had been thinking that as a matter of habit. It was what he always thought at this time of the morning. What he had forgotten was that he had one.

He stared wildly at his watch. Nearly eleven-thirty. He shook his head to try and clear the silent ringing between his ears, then made a hysterical lunge for his hat and his great leather coat that hung behind the door.

Fifteen seconds later he left the house, five hours late but moving fast.

A Sunday Kind of Love

☆★☆★☆★☆★☆★☆★☆★☆★☆★☆★☆★☆★☆★☆★☆★☆

TOM WOLFE

Love! Attar of libido in the air! It is 8:45 A.M. Thursday morning in the IRT subway station at 50th Street and Broadway and already two kids are hung up in a kind of herringbone weave of arms and legs, which proves, one has to admit, that love is not *confined* to Sunday in New York. Still, the odds! All the faces come popping in clots out of the Seventh Avenue local, past the King Size Ice Cream machine, and the turnstiles start whacking away as if the world were breaking up on the reefs. Four steps past the turnstiles everybody is already backed up haunch to paunch for the climb up the ramp and the stairs to the surface, a great funnel of flesh, wool, felt, leather, rubber and steaming alumicron, with the blood squeezing through everybody's old sclerotic arteries in hopped-up spurts from too much coffee and the effort of surfacing from the subway at the rush hour. Yet there on the landing are a boy and a girl, both about eighteen, in one of those utter, My Sin, backbreaking embraces.

He envelops her not only with his arms but with his chest, which has the American teenager concave shape to it. She has her head cocked at a 90-degree angle and they both have their eyes pressed shut for all they are worth and some incredibly feverish action going with each other's mouths. All round them, ten, scores, it seems like hundreds, of faces and bodies are perspiring, trooping and bellying up the stairs with arteriosclerotic grimaces past a showcase full of such novel items as Joy Buzzers, Squirting Nickels, Finger Rats, Scary Tarantulas and spoons with realistic dead flies on them, past Fred's barbershop, which is just off the landing and has glossy photographs of young men with the kind of baroque haircuts one can get in there, and up onto 50th Street into a madhouse of traffic and shops with weird lingerie and gray hair-dyeing displays in the windows, signs for free teacup readings and a pool-playing match between the Playboy Bunnies and Downey's Showgirls, and then everybody pounds on toward the Time-Life Building, the Brill Building or NBC.

The boy and the girl just keep on writhing in their embroilment. Her hand is sliding up the back of his neck, which he turns when her fingers wander into the intricate formal gardens of his Chicago Boxcar hairdo at the base of the skull. The turn causes his face to start to mash in the ciliated hull of her beehive hairdo, and so she rolls her head 180 degrees to the other side, using their mouths for the pivot. But aside from good hair grooming, they are oblivious to everything but each other. Everybody gives them a once-over. Disgusting! Amusing! How touching! A few kids pass by and say things like 'Swing it, baby.' But the great majority in that heaving funnel up the stairs seem to be as much astounded as anything else. The vision of love at rush hour cannot strike anyone exactly as romance. It is a feat, like a fat man crossing the English Channel in a barrel. It is an earnest accomplishment against the tide. It is a piece of slightly gross heroics, after the manner of those knobby, varicose old men who come out from some place in baggy shorts every year and run through the streets of Boston in the Marathon race. And somehow that is the gaffe against love all week long in New York, for everybody, not just two kids writhing under their coiffures in the 50th Street subway station; too hurried, too crowded, too hard, and no time for dalliance. Which explains why the real thing in New York is, as it says in the song, a Sunday kind of love.

There is Saturday, but Saturday is not much better than Monday through Friday. Saturday is the day for errands in New York. More millions of shoppers are pouring in to keep the place jammed up. Everybody is bobbing around, running up to Yorkville to pick up these arty cheeses for this evening, or down to Fourth Avenue to try to find this Van Vechten book, *Parties*, to complete the set for somebody, or off to the cleaner's, the dentist's, the hairdresser's, or some guy's who is going to loan you his station wagon to pick up two flush doors to make tables out of, or over to some place somebody mentioned that is supposed to have fabulous cuts of meat and the butcher wears a straw hat and arm garters and is colorfully rude.

True, there is Saturday night, and Friday night. They are fine for dates and good times in New York. But for the dalliance of love, they are just as stupefying and wound up as the rest of the week. On Friday and Saturday nights everybody is making some kind of scene. It may be a cellar cabaret in the Village where five guys from some place talk 'Jamaican' and pound steel drums and the Connecticut teenagers wear plaid ponchos and knee-high boots and drink such things as Passion Climax cocktails, which are made of apple cider with water-melon balls thrown in. Or it may be some cellar in the East 50's, a discotheque, where the alabaster kids come on in sleeveless minksides jackets, tweed evening dresses and cool-it Modernismus hairdos. But either way, it's a scene, a production, and soon the evening begins to whirl, like the whole world with the bed-spins, in a montage of taxis, slithery legs slithering in, slithery legs slithering out, worsted, piqué, grins, eye teeth, glissandos, buffoondos, tips, par lamps, doormen, lines, magenta ropes, white dickies, mirrors and bar bottles, pink men and shawl-collared coats, hatcheck girls and neon peach fingernails, taxis, keys, broken lamps and no coat hangers. . . .

And, then, an unbelievable dawning; Sunday, in New York.

George G., who writes 'Z' ads for a department store, keeps saying that all it takes for him is to smell coffee being made at a certain point in the percolation. It doesn't matter where. It could be the worst death-ball hamburger dive. All he has to do is smell it, and suddenly he finds himself swimming, drowning dissolving in his own reverie of New York's Sunday kind of love.

Anne A.'s apartment was nothing, he keeps saying, and that was the funny thing. She lived in Chelsea. It was this one room with a cameo-style carving of a bored Medusa on the facing of the mantelpiece, this one room plus a kitchen, in a brownstone sunk down behind a lot of loft buildings and truck terminals and so forth. Beautiful Chelsea. But on Sunday morning by 10:30 the sun would be hitting cleanly between two rearview buildings and making it through the old no man's land of gas effluvia ducts, restaurant vents, aerials, fire escapes, stairwell doors, clotheslines, chimneys, skylights, vestigial lightning rods, Mansard slopes, and those peculiarly bleak, filthy and misshapen backsides of New York buildings, into Anne's kitchen.

George would be sitting at this rickety little table with an oilcloth over it. How he goes on about it! The place was grimy. You couldn't keep the soot out. The place was beautiful. Anne is at the stove making coffee. The smell of the coffee being made, just the smell . . . already he is turned on. She had on a great terrycloth bathrobe with a sash belt. The way she moved around inside that bathrobe with the sun shining in the window always got him. It was the *at*mosphere of the thing. There she was, moving around in that great fluffy bathrobe with the sun hitting her hair, and they had all the time in the world. There wasn't even one flatulent truck horn out on Eighth Avenue. Nobody was clobbering their way down the stairs in high heels out in the hall at 10 minutes to 9.

Anne would make scrambled eggs, plain scrambled eggs, but it was a feast. It was incredible. She would bring out a couple of these little smoked fish with golden skin and some smoked oysters that always came in a little can with ornate lettering and royal colors and flourishes and some Kissebrot bread and black cherry preserves, and then the coffee. They had about a million cups of coffee apiece, until the warmth seemed to seep through your whole viscera. And then cigarettes. The cigarettes were like some soothing incense. The radiator was always making a hissing sound and then a clunk. The sun was shining in and the fire escapes and effluvia ducts were just silhouettes out there someplace. George would tear off another slice of Kissebrot and pile on some black cherry preserves and drink some more coffee and have another cigarette, and Anne crossed her legs under her terrycloth bathrobe and crossed her arms and drew on her cigarette, and that was the way it went.

'It was the *torpor*, boy,' he says. 'It was beautiful. Torpor is a beautiful, underrated thing. Torpor is a luxury. Especially in this stupid town. There in that kitchen it was like being in a perfect cocoon of love. Everything was beautiful, a perfect cocoon.'

By and by they would get dressed, always in as shiftless a getup as possible. She would put on a big heavy sweater, a raincoat and a pair of faded slacks that gripped her like neopreme rubber. He would put on a pair of corduroy pants, a crew sweater with moth holes and a raincoat. Then they would go out and walk down to 14th Street for the Sunday paper.

All of a sudden it was great out there on the street in New York. All those damnable millions who come careening into Manhattan all week weren't there. The town was empty. To a man and woman shuffling along there, torpid, in the cocoon of love, it was as if all of rotten Gotham had improved overnight. Even the people looked better. There would be one of those old dolls with little flabby arms all hunched up in a coat of pastel oatmeal texture, the kind whose lumpy old legs you keep seeing as she heaves her way up the subway stairs ahead of you and holds everybody up because she is so flabby and decrepit . . . and today, Sunday, on good, clean, empty 14th Street, she just looked like a nice old lady. There was no one around to make her look slow, stupid, unfit, unhip, expendable. That was the thing about Sunday. The weasel millions were absent. And Anne walking along beside him with a thready old pair of slacks gripping her like neopreme rubber looked like possibly the most marvelous vision the world had ever come up with, and the cocoon of love was perfect. It was like having your cake and eating it, too. On the one hand, here it was, boy, the prize: New York. All the buildings, the Gotham spires, were sitting up all over the landscape in silhouette like ikons representing all that was great, glorious and triumphant in New York. And, on the other hand, there were no weasel millions bellying past you and eating crullers on the run with the crumbs flaking off the corners of their mouths as a reminder of how much *Angst* and *Welthustle* you had to put into the town to get any of that out of it for yourself. All there was was the cocoon of love, which was complete. It was like being inside a scenic Easter Egg where you look in and the Gotham spires are just standing there like a little gemlike backdrop.

By and by the two of them would be back in the apartment sprawled out on the floor rustling through the Sunday paper, all that even black ink appliquéd on big fat fronds of paper. Anne would put an E. Power Biggs organ record on the hi-fi, and pretty soon the old trammeler's bass chords would be vibrating through you as if he had clamped a diathermy machine on your solar plexus. So there they would be, sprawled out on the floor, rustling through the Sunday paper, getting bathed and massaged by E. Power Biggs' sonic waves. It was like taking peyote or something. This marvelously high feeling would come over them, as though they were psychedelic, and the most commonplace objects took on this great radiance and significance. It was like old Aldous Huxley in his drug experiments, sitting there hooking down peyote buttons and staring at a clay geranium pot on a table, which gradually became the most fabulous geranium pot in God's world. The way it curved . . . why, it curved 360 d-e-g-r-e-e-s! And the clay . . . why, it was the color of the earth itself! And the top . . . It had a r-i-m on it! George had the same feeling. Anne's apartment . . . it was hung all over the place with the usual New York working girl's modern prints, the Picasso scrawls, the Mondrians curling at the corners . . . somehow nobody ever gets even a mat for a Mondrian print . . . the Toulouse-Lautrecs with that guy with the chin kicking his silhouette leg, the Klees, that Paul Klee is cute . . . why, all of a sudden these were the most beautiful things in the whole hagiology of art . . . the way that guy with the chin k-i-c-k-s t-h-a-t l-e-g, the way that Paul Klee h-i-t-s t-h-a-t b-a-l-l . . . the way that apartment just wrapped around them like a cocoon, with lint under the couch like angel's hair, and the plum cover on the bed lying halfway on the floor in folds like the folds in a Tiepolo cherub's silks, and the bored Medusa on the mantelpiece looking like the most splendidly, gloriously b-o-r-e-d Medusa in the face of time!

'Now, that was love,' says George, 'and there has never been anything like it. I don't know what happens to it. Unless it's Monday. Monday sort of happens to it in New York.'

Cleaning

☆★☆★☆★☆★☆★☆★☆★☆★☆★☆

VICTORIA WOOD

A large, messy, stripped-pine kitchen. Ursula, a large messy lady novelist in a smock sits drinking tea with Kent, a disdainful Northern man.

URSULA You know, it's amazing: you're the only person who's answered the advert. I just cannot get a cleaner. I'm afraid it's all rather neglected in here.

KENT Well, yes, I was just admiring that blue mink hat, but I see now it's a mouldy pizza.

URSULA I'm a novelist, and it's so hard to do everything. Is the tea all right?

KENT Not really.

URSULA Oh sorry, is it too strong?

KENT I'm just a bit perturbed by the way it's taken the tarnish off this teaspoon.

URSULA Biscuit?

KENT Have they got chemicals in?

URSULA Preservatives?

KENT I was hoping for disinfectant.

URSULA No, I baked them myself.

KENT I bet Mr Kipling's worried.

URSULA Aren't you going to finish it?

KENT I'll keep it by me – you never know, I may need to force a lock.

Pause.

Anyone ever told you you've got a look of Molly Weir?

URSULA No.

KENT I'm not surprised.

URSULA Have you been a cleaner for long?

KENT Well, I was abroad for some years.

URSULA Really?

KENT Lived with Picasso, actually.

URSULA The painter?

KENT Yes. I had a put-u-up in the back bedroom. I had to come away. It was nice, but, you know, everything tasted of turps. Henry Moore was the same – a stranger to Harpic.

URSULA You obviously know a lot about cleaning.

KENT I was approached by 'Mastermind' to set the questions for the specialized subject 'The history of the J-cloth from 1963 to the present time'.

URSULA Goodness, so you're a sort of academic are you?

KENT Oh yes. I was all set to be an Oxford don a few months back – it was just a question of me scraping up the bus-fare – but I couldn't see eye to eye with them over the gown. I said Joan Crawford had it right – a padded shoulder demands a platform shoe.

URSULA I don't really notice clothes – I've had this for years.

KENT My mother had something similar.

URSULA Really?

KENT She used to throw it over her bubble car in the cold weather.

URSULA This is a lovely old farm table, isn't it? Do you like stripped pine?

KENT No, I don't. I was brought up in a dresser drawer, so all this brings back the stench of unbearable poverty.

URSULA Oh goodness! Will you be able to clean it, then, do you think?

KENT Oh yes. In fact I shall probably get a better finish if I'm shuddering.

URSULA You see, being a novelist, I get rather engrossed, rather tend to let the housework go . . .

KENT Mm, it's the first time I've seen windows so dirty they were soundproof.

URSULA I've been working so hard, I must sort myself out, change this drcss . . .

KENT You know that soup down your front?

URSULA Whoops.

KENT Well, they don't make it any more. And I wouldn't go swimming till you've washed your hair; it could be another Torrey Canyon.

URSULA It's just my deadline – my novel . . .

KENT There's only one woman novelist struck home with me: Shirley Conran, *Superwoman* – I could not put it down.

URSULA The new one, *Lace*, have you read that?

KENT How they could call it explicit! I read right through and I was still no wiser over getting felt-tip off formica.

URSULA Do you think you'll be able to take this little job?

KENT Not really, no. I couldn't clean for a woman, I find them a very unnecessary sex.

URSULA But my name was on the card, it was a woman's name.

KENT That's no real indication of gender; it could have been an auxiliary fireman dropping a heavy hint.

URSULA So I can't twist your arm?

KENT I'd rather you didn't touch anything of mine. I'm very squeamish, skin-wise. In fact my social life took a real up-turn when I found they did Marigold gloves in large sizes.

URSULA You're a novelist's dream, I could listen to you all afternoon – do stay.

KENT No, I can't settle. I keep fretting about dysentery.

URSULA Oh, just a few secs. I mean, where are you from, for instance?

KENT Well, I was born under a pile of anthracite on the East Lancs Road. My father was a steeple-jack; he got drunk one day and never came down. I left home at fifteen when my mother caught me in bed with a Bleachmatic. I toured the working-men's clubs with a magic act; I used to close with a song. When I got better at it I used to saw myself in half and finish with a duet. Then I went to Monte, modelling . . .

URSULA I'd forgotten all about him.

KENT Who?

URSULA Monty Modlyn.

KENT Monte Carlo, as a model. Got into drugs, marijuana, then cocaine, then Shake 'n' Vac. Then I became a monk, but we had words over my safari jacket.

URSULA Do you have a close relationship with anyone?

KENT Well, I've hung round a few lavatories, but I usually only stay long enough to buff up the taps. I'm a loner. There'll never be more than one slice in my toaster.

URSULA Do you still see your mother?

KENT Oh yes, I go round once a week, take her some Duraglit or a packet of firelighters. I do have four brothers.

URSULA What do they do?

KENT They're a string quartet.

URSULA So is cleaning your main source of income?

KENT Well, I won quite a bit of Northumberland in a raffle, so I don't go short.

URSULA So, you don't really need this job?

KENT No.

URSULA What a pity! You know, I'd love to put you in a novel.

KENT Oh, you can put me in a novel.

URSULA Really?

KENT Piece of pastry – two pounds an hour, four hours a week, I can squeeze you in between Beryl Bainbridge's seventh, and Melvyn Bragg's twenty-fourth. Just change my name and call me broad-shouldered, all right?

David Copperfield

☆★☆★☆★☆★☆★☆★☆★☆★☆★☆★☆★☆★☆★☆★☆

CHARLES DICKENS

I inquired about my aunt among the boatmen first, and received various answers. One said she lived in the South Foreland Light, and had singed her whiskers by doing so; another, that she was made fast to the great buoy outside the harbour, and could only be visited at half-tide; a third, that she was locked up in Maidstone Jail for child-stealing; a fourth, that she was seen to mount a broom, in the last high wind, and make direct for Calais. The fly-drivers, among whom I inquired next, were equally jocose and equally disrespectful; and the shopkeepers, not liking my appearance, generally replied, without hearing what I had to say, that they had got nothing for me. I felt more miserable and destitute than I had done at any period of my running away. My money was all gone, I had nothing left to dispose of: I was hungry, thirsty, and worn out; and seemed as distant from my end as if I had remained in London.

The morning had worn away in these inquiries, and I was sitting on the step of an empty shop at a street corner, near the market-place, deliberating upon wandering towards those other places which had been mentioned, when a fly-driver, coming by with his carriage, dropped a horsecloth. Something good-natured in the man's face, as I handed it up, encouraged me to ask him if he could tell me where Miss Trotwood lived; though I had asked the question so often, that it almost died upon my lips.

'Trotwood,' said he. 'Let me see. I know the name, too. Old lady?'

'Yes,' I said, 'rather.'

'Pretty stiff in the back?' said he, making himself upright.

'Yes,' I said. 'I should think it very likely.'

'Carries a bag?' said he: 'bag with a good deal of room in it: is gruffish, and comes down upon you, sharp?'

My heart sank within me as I acknowledged the undoubted accuracy of this description.

'Why then, I tell you what,' said he. 'If you go up there,' pointing with his whip towards the heights, 'and keep right on till you come to some houses facing the sea, I think you'll hear of her. My opinion is, she won't stand anything, so here's a penny for you.'

I accepted the gift thankfully, and bought a loaf with it. Dispatching this refreshment by the way, I went in the direction my friend had indicated, and walked on a good distance without coming to the houses he had mentioned. At length I saw some before me; and approaching them, went into a little shop (it was what we used to call a general shop, at home), and inquired if they could have the goodness to tell me where Miss Trotwood lived. I addressed myself to a man behind the counter, who was weighing some rice for a young woman; but the latter, taking the inquiry to herself, turned round quickly.

'My mistress?' she said. 'What do you want with her, boy?'

'I want,' I replied, 'to speak to her, if you please.'

'To beg of her, you mean,' retorted the damsel.

'No,' I said, 'indeed.' But suddenly remembering that in truth I came for no other purpose, I held my peace in confusion, and felt my face burn.

My aunt's handmaid, as I supposed she was from what she had said, put her rice in a little basket and walked out of the shop; telling me that I could follow her, if I wanted to know where Miss Trotwood lived. I needed no second permission; though I was by this time in such a state of consternation and agitation, that my legs shook under me. I followed the young woman, and we soon came to a very neat little cottage with cheerful bow-windows: in front of it, a small square gravelled court or garden full of flowers, carefully tended, and smelling deliciously.

'This is Miss Trotwood's,' said the young woman. 'Now you know; and that's all I have got to say.' With which words she hurried into the house, as if to shake off the responsibility of my appearance; and left me standing at the garden-gate, looking disconsolately over the top of it towards the parlour-window, where a muslin curtain partly undrawn in the middle, a large round green screen or fan fastened on to the window-sill, a small table, and a great chair, suggested to me that my aunt might be at that moment seated in awful state.

My shoes were by this time in a woeful condition. The soles had shed themselves bit by bit, and the upper leathers had broken and burst until the very shape and form of shoes had departed from them. My hat (which had served me for a night-cap, too) was so crushed and bent, that no old battered handleless saucepan on a dunghill need have been ashamed to vie with it. My shirt and trousers, stained with heat, dew, grass, and the Kentish soil on which I had slept – and torn besides – might have frightened the birds from my aunt's garden, as I stood at the gate. My hair had known no comb or brush since I left London. My face, neck and hands, from unaccustomed exposure to the air and sun, were burnt to a berry-brown. From head to foot I was powdered almost as white with chalk and dust, as if I had come out of a lime-kiln. In this plight, and with a strong consciousness of it, I waited to introduce myself to, and make my first impression on, my formidable aunt.

The unbroken stillness of the parlour-window leading me to infer, after a while, that she was not there, I lifted up my eyes to the window above it, where I saw a florid, pleasant-looking gentleman, with a grey head, who shut up one eye in a grotesque manner, nodded his head at me several times, shook it at me as often, laughed, and went away.

I had been discomposed enough before; but I was so much the more discomposed by this unexpected behaviour, that I was on the point of slinking off, to think how I had best proceed, when there came out of the house a lady with her handkerchief tied over her cap, and a pair of gardening gloves on her hands, wearing a gardening pocket like a toll-man's apron, and carrying a great knife. I knew her immediately to be Miss Betsey, for she came stalking out of the house exactly as my poor mother had so often described her stalking up our garden at Blunderstone Rookery.

'Go away!' said Miss Betsey, shaking her head, and making a distant chop in the air with her knife. 'Go along! No boys here!'

I watched her, with my heart at my lips, as she marched to a corner of her garden, and stooped to dig up some little root there. Then, without a scrap of courage, but with a great deal of desperation, I went softly in and stood beside her, touching her with my finger.

'If you please, ma'am,' I began.

She started and looked up.

'If you please, aunt.'

'EH?' exclaimed Miss Betsey, in a tone of amazement I have never heard approached.

'If you please, aunt, I am your nephew.'

'Oh, Lord!' said my aunt. And sat flat down in the garden-path.

'I am David Copperfield, of Blunderstone, in Suffolk – where you came, on the night when I was born, and saw my dear mama. I have been very unhappy since she died. I have been slighted, and taught nothing, and thrown upon myself, and put to work not fit for me. It made me run away to you. I was robbed at first setting out, and have walked all the way, and have never slept in a bed since I began the journey.' Here my self-support gave way all at once; and with a movement of my hands, intended to show her my ragged state, and call it to witness that I had suffered something, I broke into a passion of crying, which I suppose had been pent up within me all the week.

My aunt, with every sort of expression but wonder discharged from her countenance, sat on the gravel, staring at me, until I began to cry; when she got up in a great hurry, collared me, and took me into the parlour. Her first proceeding there was to unlock a tall press, bring out several bottles, and pour some of the contents of each into my mouth. I think they must have been taken out at random, for I am sure I tasted aniseed water, anchovy sauce, and salad dressing. When she had administered these restoratives, as I was still quite hysterical, and unable to control my sobs, she put me on the sofa, with a shawl under my head, and the handkerchief from her own head under my feet, lest I should sully the cover; and then, sitting herself down behind the green fan or screen I have already mentioned, so that I could not see her face, ejaculated at intervals, 'Mercy on us!' letting those exclamations off like minute guns.

After a time she rang the bell. 'Janet,' said my aunt, when her servant came in. 'Go upstairs, give my compliments to Mr Dick, and say I wish to speak to him.'

Janet looked a little surprised to see me lying stiffly on the sofa (I was afraid to move lest it should be displeasing to my aunt), but went on her errand. My aunt, with her hands behind her, walked up and down the room, until the gentleman who had squinted at me from the upper window came in laughing.

'Mr Dick,' said my aunt, 'don't be a fool, because nobody can be more discreet than you can, when you choose. We all know that. So don't be a fool, whatever you are.'

The gentleman was serious immediately, and looked at me, I thought, as if he would entreat me to say nothing about the window.

'Mr Dick,' said my aunt, 'you have heard me mention David Copperfield? Now don't pretend not to have a memory, because you and I know better.'

'David Copperfield?' said Mr Dick, who did not appear to me to remember much about it. '*David* Copperfield? Oh yes, to be sure. David, certainly.'

'Well,' said my aunt, 'this is his boy, his son. He would be as like his father as it's possible to be, if he was not so like his mother, too.'

'His son?' said Mr Dick. 'David's son? Indeed!'

'Yes,' pursued my aunt, 'and he has done a pretty piece of business. He has run away. Ah! His sister, Betsey Trotwood, never would have run away.' My aunt shook her head firmly, confident in the character and behaviour of the girl who never was born.

'Oh! you think she wouldn't run away?' said Mr Dick.

'Bless and save the man,' exclaimed my aunt, sharply, 'how he talks! Don't I know she wouldn't? She would have lived with her god-mother, and we should have been devoted to one another. Where, in the name of wonder, should his sister, Betsey Trotwood, have run from or to?'

'Nowhere,' said Mr Dick.

'Well then,' returned my aunt, softened by the reply, 'how can you pretend to be wool-gathering, Dick, when you are as sharp as a surgeon's lancet? Now, here you see young David Copperfield, and the question I put to you is, what shall I do with him?'

'What shall you do with him?' said Mr Dick, feebly, scratching his head. 'Oh! do with him?'

'Yes,' said my aunt, with a grave look, and her forefinger held up. 'Come! I want some very sound advice.'

'Why, if I was you,' said Mr Dick, considering, and looking vacantly at me, 'I should – ' The contemplation of me seemed to inspire him with a sudden idea, and he added, briskly, 'I should wash him!'

'Janet,' said my aunt, turning round with a quiet triumph, which I did not then understand, 'Mr Dick sets us all right. Heat the bath!'

Although I was deeply interested in this dialogue, I could not help observing my aunt, Mr Dick, and Janet, while it was in progress, and completing a survey I had already been engaged in making of the room.

My aunt was a tall, hard-featured lady, but by no means ill-looking. There was an inflexibility in her face, in her voice, in her gait and carriage, amply sufficient to account for the effect she had made upon a gentle creature like my mother; but her features were rather handsome than otherwise, though unbending and austere. I particularly noticed that she had a very quick, bright eye. Her hair, which was grey, was arranged in two plain divisions, under what I believe would be called a mob-cap; I mean a cap, much more common then than now, with side-pieces fastened under the chin. Her dress was of a lavender colour, and perfectly neat; but scantily made, as if she desired to be as little encumbered as possible. I remember that I thought it, in form, more like a riding-habit with the superfluous skirt cut off, than anything else. She wore at her side a gentleman's gold watch, if I might judge from its size and make, with an appropriate chain and seals; she had some linen at her throat not unlike a shirt-collar, and things at her wrists like little shirt-wristbands.

Mr Dick, as I have already said, was grey-headed and florid: I should have said all about him, in saying so, had not his head been curiously bowed – not by age; it reminded me of one of Mr Creakle's boys' heads after a beating – and his grey eyes prominent and large, with a strange kind of watery brightness in them that made me, in combination with his vacant manner, his submission to my aunt, and his childish delight when she praised him, suspect him of being a little mad; though, if he were mad, how he came to be there, puzzled me extremely. He was dressed like any other ordinary gentleman, in a loose grey morning coat and waistcoat, and white trousers; and had his watch in his fob, and his money in his pockets: which he rattled as if he were very proud of it.

Janet was a pretty blooming girl, of about nineteen or twenty, and a perfect picture of neatness. Though I made no further observation of her at the moment, I may mention here what I did not discover until afterwards, namely, that she was one of a series of protégées whom my aunt had taken into her service expressly to educate in a renouncement of mankind, and who had generally completed their abjuration by marrying the baker.

The room was as neat as Janet or my aunt. As I laid down my pen, a moment since, to think of it, the air from the sea came blowing in again, mixed with the perfume of the flowers; and I saw the old-fashioned furniture brightly rubbed and polished, my aunt's inviolable chair and table by the round green fan in the bow-window, the drugget-covered carpet, the cat, the kettle-holder, the two canaries, the old china, the punch-bowl full of dried rose-leaves, the tall press guarding all sorts of bottles and pots, and, wonderfully out of keeping with the rest, my dusty self upon the sofa, taking note of everything.

Janet had gone away to get the bath ready, when my aunt to my great alarm, became in one moment rigid with indignation, and had hardly voice to cry out, 'Janet! Donkeys!'

Upon which, Janet came running up the stairs as if the house were in flames, darted out on a little piece of green in front, and warned off two saddle-donkeys, lady-ridden, that had presumed to set hoof upon it; while my aunt, rushing out of the house, seized the bridle of a third animal laden with a bestriding child, turned him, led him forth from those sacred precincts, and boxed the ears of the unlucky urchin in attendance who had dared to profane that hallowed ground.

To this hour I don't know whether my aunt had any lawful right of way over that patch of green; but she had settled it in her own mind that she had, and it was all the same to her. The one great outrage of her life, demanding to be constantly avenged, was the passage of a donkey over that immaculate spot. In whatever occupation she was engaged, however interesting to her the conversation in which she was taking part, a donkey turned the current of her ideas in a moment, and she was upon him straight. Jugs of water, and watering-pots, were kept in secret places ready to be discharged on the offending boys; sticks were laid in ambush behind the doors; sallies were made at all hours; and incessant war prevailed. Perhaps this was an agreeable excitement to the donkey-boys; or perhaps the more sagacious of the donkeys, understanding how the case stood, delighted with constitutional obstinacy in coming that way. I only know that there were three alarms before the bath was ready; and that on the occasion of the last and most desperate of all, I saw my aunt engage, single-handed, with a sandy-headed lad of fifteen, and bump his sandy head against her own gate, before he seemed to comprehend what was the matter. These interruptions were the more ridiculous to me, because she was giving me broth out of a table-spoon at the time (having firmly persuaded herself that I was actually starving, and must receive nourishment at first in very small quantities), and, while my mouth was yet open to receive the spoon, she would put it back into the basin, cry 'Janet! Donkeys!' and go out to the assault.

The bath was a great comfort. For I began to be sensible of acute pains in my limbs from lying out in the fields, and was now so tired and low that I could hardly keep myself awake for five minutes together. When I had bathed they (I mean my aunt and Janet) enrobed me in a shirt and a pair of trousers belonging to Mr Dick, and tied me up in two or three great shawls. What sort of bundle I looked like, I don't know, but I felt a very hot one. Feeling also very faint and drowsy, I soon lay down on the sofa again and fell asleep.

It might have been a dream, originating in the fancy which had occupied my mind so long, but I awoke with the impression that my aunt had come and bent over me, and had put my hair away from my face, and laid my head more comfortably, and had then stood looking at me. The words, 'Pretty fellow,' or 'Poor fellow,' seemed to be in my ears, too; but certainly there was nothing else, when I awoke, to lead me to believe that they had been uttered by my aunt, who sat in the bow-window gazing at the sea from behind the green fan, which was mounted on a kind of swivel, and turned any way.

We dined soon after I awoke, of a roast fowl and a pudding; I sitting at table, not unlike a trussed bird myself, and moving my arms with considerable difficulty. But as my aunt had swathed me up, I made no complaint of being inconvenienced. All this time, I was deeply anxious to know what she was going to do with me; but she took her dinner in profound silence, except when she occasionally fixed her eyes on me sitting opposite, and said, 'Mercy upon us!' which did not by any means relieve my anxiety.

The cloth being drawn, and some sherry put upon the table (of which I had a glass), my aunt sent up for Mr Dick again, who joined us, and looked as wise as he could when she requested him to attend to my story, which she elicited from me, gradually, by a course of questions. During my recital, she kept her eyes on Mr Dick, who I thought would have gone to sleep but for that, and who, whensoever he lapsed into a smile, was checked by a frown from my aunt.

'Whatever possessed that poor unfortunate Baby, that she must go and be married again,' said my aunt, when I had finished. '*I* can't conceive.'

'Perhaps she fell in love with her second husband,' Mr Dick suggested.

'Fell in love!' repeated my aunt. 'What do you mean? What business had she to do it?'

'Perhaps,' Mr Dick simpered, after thinking a little, 'she did it for pleasure.'

'Pleasure, indeed!' replied my aunt. 'A mighty pleasure for the poor Baby to fix her simple faith upon any dog of a fellow, certain to ill-use her in some way or other. What did she propose to herself, I should like to know! She had had one husband. She had seen David Copperfield out of the world, who was always running after wax dolls from his cradle. She had got a baby – oh, there were a pair of babies when she gave birth to this child sitting here, that Friday night! – and what more did she want?'

Mr Dick secretly shook his head at me, as if he thought there was no getting over this.

'She couldn't even have a baby like anybody else,' said my aunt. 'Where was this child's sister, Betsey Trotwood? Not forthcoming. Don't tell me!'

Mr Dick seemed quite frightened.

'That little man of a doctor, with his head on one side,' said my aunt, 'Jellips, or whatever his name was, what was *he* about? All he could do was to say to me, like a robin redbreast – as he *is* – "it's a boy." A boy! Yah, the imbecility of the whole set of 'em!'

The heartiness of the ejaculation startled Mr Dick exceedingly; and me, too, if I am to tell the truth.

'And then, as if this was not enough, and she had not stood sufficiently in the light of this child's sister, Betsey Trotwood,' said my aunt, 'she marries a second time – goes and marries a Murderer – or a man with a name like it – and stands in *this* child's light! And the natural consequence is, as anybody but a baby might have foreseen, that he prowls and wanders. He's as like Cain before he was grown up, as he can be.'

Mr Dick looked hard at me, as if to identify me in this character.

'And then there's that woman with the Pagan name,' said my aunt, 'that Peggotty, *she* goes and gets married next. Because she has not seen enough of the evil attending such things, *she* goes and gets married next, as the child relates. I only hope,' said my aunt, shaking her head, 'that her husband is one of those Poker husbands who abound in the newspapers, and will beat her well with one.'

I could not bear to hear my old nurse so decried, and made the subject of such a wish. I told my aunt that indeed she was mistaken. That Peggotty was the best, the truest, the most faithful, most devoted, and most self-denying friend and servant in the world; who had ever loved me dearly, who had ever loved my mother dearly; who had held my mother's dying head upon her arm, on whose face my mother had imprinted her last grateful kiss. And my remembrance of them both, choking me, I broke down as I was trying to say that her home was my home, and that all she had was mine, and that I would have gone to her for shelter, but for her humble station, which made me fear that I might bring some trouble on her – I broke down, I say, as I was trying to say so, and laid my face in my hands upon the table.

'Well, well!' said my aunt, 'the child is right to stand by those who have stood by him. – Janet! Donkeys!'

I thoroughly believe that but for those unfortunate donkeys, we should have come to a good understanding; for my aunt had laid her hand on my shoulder, and the impulse was upon me, thus emboldened, to embrace her and beseech her protection. But the interruption, and the disorder she was thrown into by the struggle outside, put an end to all softer ideas for the present, and kept my aunt indignantly declaiming to Mr Dick about her determination to appeal for redress to the laws of her country, and to bring actions for trespass against the whole donkey proprietorship of Dover, until tea-time.

After tea, we sat at the window – on the look-out, as I imagined, from my aunt's sharp expression of face, for more invaders – until dusk, when Janet set candles, and a backgammon-board, on the table, and pulled down the blinds.

'Now, Mr Dick,' said my aunt, with her grave look, and her forefinger up as before, 'I am going to ask you another question. Look at this child.'

'David's son?' said Mr Dick, with an attentive, puzzled face.

'Exactly so,' returned my aunt. 'What would you do with him, now?'

'Do with David's son?' said Mr Dick.

'Ay,' replied my aunt, 'with David's son.'

'Oh!' said Mr Dick. 'Yes. Do with – I should put him to bed.'

'Janet!' cried my aunt, with the same complacent triumph that I had remarked before. 'Mr Dick sets us all right. If the bed is ready, we'll take him up to it.'

Janet reporting it to be quite ready, I was taken up to it; kindly, but in some sort like a prisoner; my aunt going in front, and Janet bringing up the rear. The only circumstance which gave me any new hope, was my aunt's stopping on the stairs to inquire about a smell of fire that was prevalent there; and Janet's replying that she had been making tinder down in the kitchen, of my old shirt. But there were no other clothes in my room than the odd heap of things I wore; and when I was left there, with a little taper which my aunt forewarned me would burn exactly five minutes, I heard them lock my door on the outside. Turning these things over in my mind, I deemed it possible that my aunt who could know nothing of me, might suspect I had a habit of running away, and took precautions, on that account, to have me in safe keeping.

The room was a pleasant one, at the top of the house, overlooking the sea, on which the moon was shining brilliantly. After I had said my prayers, and the candle had burnt out, I remember how I still sat looking at the moonlight on the water, as if I could hope to read my fortune in it, as in a bright book; or to see my mother with her child, coming from Heaven, along that shining path, to look upon me as she had looked when I last saw her sweet face. I remember how the solemn feeling with which at length I turned my eyes away, yielded to the sensation of gratitude and rest which the sight of the white-curtained bed – and how much more the lying softly down upon it, nestling in the snow-white sheets! – inspired. I remember how I thought of all the solitary places under the night sky where I had slept, and how I prayed that I never might be houseless any more, and never might forget the houseless. I remember how I seemed to float, then, down the melancholy glory of that track upon the sea, away into the world of dreams.

Stop Me If You've Heard It

☆★☆

NOËL COWARD

'Please God,' she whispered to herself. 'Don't let it be the one about the Englishman and the Scotsman and the American in the railway carriage, nor the one about the old lady and the parrot, nor the one about the couple arriving at the seaside hotel on their honeymoon night! I'll settle for any of the others, but please, please merciful God, not one of those three – I can't bear it. If it's one of those three, particularly the Englishman and the Scotsman and the American in the railway carriage, I shall go mad – I shall do something awful – I'll shriek – I'll make a hideous scene – I'll bash his head in with a bottle – '

Her husband, sitting opposite to her at the table, cleared his throat. Her whole body became rigid at the sound. With a great effort she took a cigarette out of a little blue enamel pot in front of her and lit it. Some of the general conversation at the table died away into polite attentiveness. She was aware, wretchedly aware, of the quick, resigned glance that Louis Bennet exchanged with Susan Lake. She looked at her host, Carroll Davis, leaning forward politely, his good-looking face blank. Carroll was kind; Carroll understood; his manners were dictated by his heart – he wouldn't hurt Budge's feelings for the world; he would listen appreciatively and laugh at the right moments, saving his loudest, most convincing laugh for the point at the end, and Budge would never know, never remotely suspect for an instant, that he hadn't been amused.

The others would laugh too, of course, but there would be an undertone of malice – their alert, cruel minds would be silently communicating with one another. 'Poor Budge,' they would be saying, 'the kiss of death on every party – he never knows when to stop. In the old days he used to be funny on the stage, but now he's even lost that. Why does Carroll ask him? Obviously, for Marty's sake – she *must* know how awful he is. She *must* realize, deep down, that she's married to the most monumental cracking bore. Why doesn't she leave him? Why doesn't she at least come to parties without him? She knows we're all old friends – she knows we love her. Why the hell doesn't she leave that aggressive, overeager little megalomaniac at home?'

Marty drew deeply at her cigarette. Jane and Shirley and Bobby Peek were still talking and laughing at the other end of the table. They had not noticed – yet. They were still unaware of doom. Budge shot them a quick, resentful look and cleared his throat again. They glanced up, and the light went out of their faces. Shirley stabbed out her cigarette, put her head back and closed her eyes. Marty felt an insane desire to lean forward and slap her face violently. 'Listen, you languid, supercilious bitch, Budge Ripley's going to tell a story. Sit up and listen, and mind your manners! He was telling stories – amusing people – millions of people – making them laugh until they cried, making them forget their troubles – making them happy – before you were born. All right, all right – he may be a bore now – he may have lost his touch, but mind your manners – lean forward, look interested, whatever you feel – bitch – spoiled, supercilious bitch.'

'Stop me if you've heard it.' Budge's voice grated in the silence. He caught her eye, and, painting an encouraging smile on her face, she leaned forward. No more than a split second could have passed before he began, but in that split second the years of her life with him rolled out before her – jerkily and confused in memory, like a panorama she had been taken to see at Earl's Court when she was a child.

She had been getting on quite well twenty years ago when she had first met him – chorus and understudy and small parts here and there. She had never been pretty, but there was something about her that people liked, a comic quality of personality. Carroll had always asked her to his grandest parties regardless of the fact that she was really small fry in the theatre compared with his other guests. She had had wit always, a realistic, unaffected cockney humour, quick as a whip but without malice. It was at one of Carroll's parties, in this same house, that Budge had first noticed her. It was in this same house three years later, after she had slept with him hundreds of times, that he had told her that his divorce was through and that they could get married. Seventeen years ago that was. They had moved into Number 18 – she had been so proud, so grateful, and he had been so sweet. No more stage work for her, no more prancing on and off for finales and opening choruses. She ran the house fairly well, went to all Budge's first nights in a box or stalls; stood with him afterward in the dressing room while people came rushing in to say how marvellous he was. 'Funnier than ever.' 'I laughed till I was sick.' 'Nobody like you, Budge, the comic genius of the age – your inventiveness – your pathos too – only really great comedians have that particular quality, that subtle balance between grave and gay – '

They gave parties at Number 18 – gay and amusing, lasting sometimes until dawn. Several years of happiness passed – several years of excitement and success and occasional holidays in the South of France. Then, insidiously, the rot began to set in – very gradually at first, so gradually, indeed, that it was a long time before she even suspected it. A strange rot, composed of circumstances, small, psychological maladjustments, mutual irritations, sudden outbursts of temper; the subtle cause of it all still obscure, still buried deep.

It was about then that he began to be unfaithful to her – nothing serious – just an occasional roll in the hay with someone who took his fancy. Marty found out about this almost immediately, and it hurt her immeasurably. She reasoned with herself, of course; she exerted every ounce of common sense and self-control, and succeeded bleakly insofar that she said nothing and did nothing, but from then on everything was different. There was no security anymore, and no peace of mind. It was not that she cared so desperately about him popping into bed every now and then with someone else – only a fool, married happily for years to a famous star, would make a fuss about that. It was something deeper, something that bewildered and gnawed at her, something more important that she knew to exist but somehow could not identify.

It was later – quite a long while later – that the truth suddenly became clear to her, that the answer to this riddle, which had tortured her for so long, suddenly flashed into her consciousness with all the blatant clarity of a neon light – a neon light sign flashing on and off with hideous monotony one vulgar, piteous word, jealousy. Budge was jealous of her. He was jealous of her wit, her gaiety, her friends. She could have slept with other men as much as she liked, and he would have forgiven her; she could have drunk herself into a coma every night, and he would have been loving and concerned and understanding; but because she was herself, because people of all kinds found her good company, because she could, without effort, embroider an ordinary anecdote with genuine humour and infectious gaiety and be loved and welcomed for it – this he could never forgive; for this, she realized in that blinding flash of revelation, he would hate her until the day he died.

'Stop me if you've heard it!' That idiotic, insincere phrase – that false, unconvincing opening gambit – as though people ever had the courage to stop anyone however many times they'd heard it! Human beings could be brave – incredibly brave about many things. They could fly in jet-propelled planes; fling themselves from the sky in parachutes; hurl themselves fully clothed into turbulent seas to rescue drowning children; crawl on their mortal stomachs through bullet-spattered mud and take pins out of unexploded bombs or shells or whatever they were, but no one, no one in the whole twisting, agonized world was brave enough to say loudly and clearly, 'Yes, I have heard it. It is dull and unfunny; it bores the liver and lights out of me. I have heard it over and over again, and if I have to hear it once more in any of the years that lie between me and the grave, I'll plunge a fork into your silly throat – I'll pull out your clacking tongue with my nails.'

Marty suddenly caught sight of her hands. One was resting on the table; the other was holding her cigarette; both were trembling. She looked miserably round the table. They were all listening with exaggerated courtesy. Shirley was looking down, her long scarlet-tipped fingers scratching about among the bread crumbs by her plate, making them into little patterns, a circle with one larger one in the middle, then a triangle. Budge's voice grated on. The Englishman, the Scotsman and the American, 'I say you know,' 'Och aye,' 'Gee.' Marty stared across the years at his face. There it was, aged a little, but not much changed since she had loved it so; the same kindly, rather protuberant blue eyes, the fleshy nose, the straw-colored hair, the wide comedian's mouth. His head was bent forward eagerly. He was talking a trifle too quickly because somewhere writhing deep within him was a suspicion that his audience was not wholly with him, he hadn't quite got them. He finished the Scotsman's bit. Bobby Peek laughed, and Marty could have flung her arms round his neck and hugged him for it.

Budge's eyes shone with pleasure – 'Gee, Buddy!' There was quite a loud laugh at the end of the story.

Carroll's kindness triumphed over his wisdom. 'That was wonderful, Budge,' he said. 'Nobody can tell a story like you!'

Marty's heart died in her. She made a swift, instinctive movement to get up from the table. Budge looked at her, and his eyes hardened. She sat still as death, chained to her chair. He cleared his throat again.

'Marty half getting up like that reminded me of a good one,' he said. 'Do you know the one about the shy lady at the dinner party who wanted to go to the telephone?'

There was a polite murmur round the table. Shirley took her compact out of her bag and scrutinized her face in the little mirror. Louis Bennet coughed and exchanged another meaning glance with Susan. Budge pushed back his chair, recrossed his legs and started. . . .

Marty stared down into her lap. There was some gold embroidery on her dress and it seemed to be expanding and changing into curious shapes because her eyes were filled with tears.

A hundred years later they were driving home. It was very late and the streets were almost empty. Budge was bunched up in his corner, sulky and silent. Marty stared at the back of Gordon's neck. Gordon drove well, but he was inclined to take risks. As a rule she was nervous and made him go slowly, but tonight she didn't care; she wouldn't have minded if he had driven at sixty miles an hour, careering along Oxford Street, crashing all the lights.

They arrived at Number 18 still in silence. Budge said good night to Gordon, and they went into the house. Rose had left the drink tray on the dining-room table and a plate of curly-looking sandwiches.

Budge poured himself out a whisky and soda. 'I'm going on up,' he said. 'I'm tired.'

Suddenly something seemed to crack inside Marty's head and she started to laugh. There was an ugly note in the laugh which she recognized, but she had neither the strength nor the will to do anything about it.

'You must be,' she said. 'Oh, my God, you certainly must be!'

Budge stopped at the door and turned and looked at her.

'And what exactly do you mean by that?' he asked.

'Don't you know?' she said, and her voice sounded shrill and hysterical. 'Don't you really know? Haven't you got the faintest idea?'

Budge's already red face flushed and he advanced two steps toward her. 'What's the matter with you?'

Marty backed away from him, still laughing miserably.

'This is a good one,' she said. 'Stop me if you've heard it. Stop me if you've heard it or not, because if you don't you'll never forgive me and I shall never forgive myself.'

Budge frowned. 'Are you drunk?'

Marty shook her head dumbly. She felt the tears starting and tried to wipe them away with the back of her hand. Budge came closer to her and looked carefully into her face. There was no more anger in his eyes, only bewilderment. She tried to look away, to escape from that puzzled, anxious face. She backed farther and, feeling the edge of a chair under her knees, sank down into it.

'What's the matter?' Budge persisted. 'You're not ill or anything, are you? Is it anything to do with me? What have I done?'

He put his hand on her arm. She felt the warmth of it through her sleeve. Suddenly her hysteria evaporated. She felt utterly exhausted, but no longer wild, no longer shrill and nerve-strained and cruel. She put her hand up, and pressed his more firmly onto her arm. Then she gave a little giggle, not a very convincing one really, but good enough.

'You may well ask what you've done,' she said. 'You may well ask if it's anything to do with you –'

Her voice broke, and, bringing her face against his stomach, she started crying thoroughly and satisfyingly.

Budge remained silent, but his other hand smoothed her hair away from her forehead. After a moment or two she controlled herself a bit and pushed him gently away.

'You've given me a miserable evening,' she said huskily. 'You never took your eyes off Shirley Dale from the beginning of supper to the end. You then behave like a sulky little boy all the way home in the car, and, to round the whole thing off, you help yourself to a drink without even asking if I want one and tell me you're tired! You're an inconsiderate, lecherous little pig and I can't imagine why I ever let you lead me to the Registry Office.'

She rose to her feet and put her arms round him tightly. She felt his body relax.

He gave a complacent chuckle. 'Of all the bloody fools,' he said. The warmth was back in his voice, the crisis had passed and the truth was stamped down again deep into the ground.

He led her over to the table and mixed her a drink. 'Shirley Dale, indeed – you must be out of your mind!'

She stood there with one arm still around him, sipping her drink. Nothing more was said until he had switched off the lights and they had gone upstairs. They talked ordinarily while they undressed; the familiarity of the bedroom seemed overeager to put their hearts at ease.

Later on, after he had attacked his teeth in the bathroom with his customary violence, sprinkled himself with Floris 127 and put on his pyjamas, he came over and sat on the edge of her bed.

She smiled and reached out and patted his hand. Then gently, almost timidly, as though she were not quite sure of her ground, she pulled him toward her. 'I've got something to tell you,' she said. 'Stop me if you've heard it.'

A Country Christmas

☆★☆★☆★☆★☆★☆★☆★☆★☆★☆★☆★☆★☆★☆★☆★☆

DIRK BOGARDE

I was just lying there: it was very warm and safe-feeling. I knew it was still dark because there was no ragged line of light round the curtains and I could hear Flora snoring, or moaning, in her bed. My sister was probably curled up with her head under the quilt. She always slept like that, only this time I couldn't see her because it was dark. But if I turned my head and looked through Flora's room I could see the orange glimmer round Lally's bedroom door, and that was her getting up. So, worse luck, as soon as she'd got on her pinafore, tidied up her hair and shaken her alarm clock (she always did this to see if it was still working even though she could hear it ticking, but it was just something she did anyway, to be quite certain), I knew the door would creak open and she'd come through the rooms and tell us to start waking up, quick sharp, and that another day was starting and there was this or that to do if we wanted any breakfast. I knew it by heart, I suppose.

'Time to wake up! Lots to do before breakfast!' she said. (You see?) And then she saw I was awake. 'There's a surprise for you all outside . . . better get your skates on before it goes.' She was holding her candle high so that shadows danced across the bumpy plaster walls and made the beams black and wavery. She had her indoor shoes in her other hand, so as not to wake us up, except that she had already woken us.

'What is it?' I said and sat up, and felt the cold slither right down my back.

'Been a fall of snow overnight. Still as still . . . but it won't lie. Best put on your woolly stockings from the top drawer. It's a very cold morning.' And then she opened the door to the stairs and went rustling down while I reached for the box of Swan Vestas by the candlestick.

When we all got down to the kitchen, and after I'd looked to see if all was well with the Weekend (which it was), the light was goldeny brown from the paraffin lamp and the candle, and the range was crackling and Lally was pumping up the Primus . . . the other one had a singing kettle on it – well, not exactly singing, but sighing really. It was still dark outside, but if you pressed hard against the cold glass, and shaded your face against the lamplight with your hands, you could see, as clear as clear, that everything outside was white.

'It'll be light in a few minutes, near eight o'clock, and as soon as it is, and as soon as you've had a good hot drink, taken your Virol, got on your Wellingtons, then it's off with you all to do a bit of wooding for the kindling pile while I get the toast and porridge ready. And I want no arguments!' She looked very serious, one hand on hip, bread knife in the other. I mean, it was sticking up! You couldn't argue with her.

'What's for breakfast?' I said, pouring milk from the milk-can into a jug.

'Tea, toast and six eggs! And out of my way, I've a busy day today.' She wagged the knife at me, 'Toot de sweet, now!'

My sister came clumping down the stairs doing up her snake-belt. It was her most favourite thing, and she'd pinched it from me, but I had a second, so it didn't worry me really. But she wore it even with her good flannel skirt from school. Not just her shorts, like she did in summer. 'You said it was snowing!' she grumbled. 'That's what you said, ' and she began to pull up her school socks which were woollen and awful-looking things. Wrinkled grey worms.

'It *was* snowing! I said there had been a light fall, if I'm right – and no one try to correct me. It's stopped now, and you'll come to no harm and I reckon you won't see a polar bear, no more a penguin, where you are going. And please set the sugar on the table. Flora! Flora! Come along now, do. Breakfast is about to begin. Flora! Do I have to bang a gong?'

'She wouldn't know what a gong was,' I said. 'And the wood will be all snowy, all the kindling and everything.'

'So what's the use?' said my sister huffing about looking for the Tate and Lyle on the dresser.

'The use is that I need the kindling, so shake the snow off – don't dare bring it into the house and make all the rest sodden!'

'But there is masses of kindling, we got piles yesterday!'

'And you'll get piles today! Or else my name is not Ellen Jane . . . '

My sister looked at me across the table and made a twisty face, and we both began to snort a bit, and Lally suddenly got a bit red in the face, the way she did when she thought we were being rotten behind her back but she didn't know. Like the Bindie Bucket business.

'What's all the sniggering in aid of, pray? That range uses the kindling like straw, and there's the sitting-room fire to be lit to air the room for your parents, and I want the copper lit this afternoon . . .' She started to slice up the big cottage loaf for toast. You could see she was being a bit huffy about the sniggering part because she suddenly said, quite crossly, 'Your grammar! Upon my word! What would your father say? "Good Grammar Teached Here Gooder Up The Stairs." That's what. "Is" and "are", remember. And now out of my way.'

But you could see she was fretting, and then Flora came down the stairs looking pretty silly in a raggedy woollen red and yellow tartan hat which she said was her Tam o'Shanter. And it had a stupid pom-pom on the top which wobbled about. She looked really jolly funny, wandering about the kitchen pulling the hat this way and that.

Lally took the kettle off the Primus and poured it into the big brown teapot. 'I want no more private laughter from you two,' she said, 'and no *quibbling*! No quibbling at all. Wooding after your tea and Virol, breakfast *after*. Then you all get washed and do teeth.' And looking at Flora she said, in her Polite-to-Guest voice, 'Flora dear, what are you about? Not in the house dear, not in the house.' And then she set the jar of Virol on a saucer and put three spoons round it, like the spokes in a wheel.

Flora pulled out her chair and sat down. She wasn't a bit afraid of Lally, mostly because Lally was always so terribly sweet to her. When she spoke to her, anyway.

'It's against the cold,' she said firmly. I thought she was very brave. 'My father says that our heads are like yon chimney. All the heat in your body just rises up and goes out of the top of your head. And he was a soldier in the war and he should know.'

'Well . . . quite right. But your head will be nice and warm in my kitchen, now I've got it all cosy and comfy for you, so I'll be obliged if you'd remove your hat at my table, please. You'll lose nothing through the top of your head except your brains. Off with it, please, Madam Caledonia!'

So Lally won. Well, she nearly always did. So the silly Tam o'Shanter came off and we drank our tea, had the Virol and licked the spoons.

Lally poured herself another cup of tea. 'I'm not washing all that money down the drains! You lick it clean. Cost your parents a lot of money to keep you healthy. Lick now! Quick sharp! It's just like caramel!'

She was being really quite bullying, but it was now light outside, and she was in a hurry. 'I'll need milk today. So when you've done the wooding and washed, and if the snow isn't too thick, I'll thank you to hop skip it down to the dairy and ask Miss Aleford, if she's there, or Len Diplock if he's in the yard, for two pints of fresh –' and then she stopped and said we'd never remember, and so when we came back from the wooding she'd have a list. And to hurry up about it.

The snow wasn't really thick. We left footprints, but it wasn't right up to our knees or anything wonderful like that, or even up to our ankles. It was just white. But everything was very still and early morning. Down at the Court, where we had to go for the milk, there was a waver of thin smoke meandering up in the air, and my sister said that at least *someone* else was up at dawn, and not just us.

Flora stood looking at the whiteness. The sky was grey with little orange specks in it like the back of a plaice. The Downs were smooth and soft, and you couldn't even see the white horse on High-And-Over because he was covered, and so was the gorse. Everything was smooth and clean like big fat pillows. I almost really liked Flora when she said that the cottage looked like a 'wee ship' in a white sea. But I *knew* it looked like a ship, I just found the 'wee' part boring: it was the way she spoke. And the cottage did look strange up on the very top of Great Meadow with nothing, except the elms round the church, for miles and miles. We started wooding away, but secretly I was a bit worried that perhaps our parents wouldn't be able to get up the road. The O.M. was the best car in the world, but the lane to the cottage was deep in snow. Only I didn't say anything, except to tell Flora not to pick up any old bits of elderberry bush. She was stuffing the wooding-sack full with it, and I had to take it all out and explain to her why not.

'Well! *Why* not? It's as dry as dry. It just snaps – '

'And it smells terrible on the fire. All the house smells if you burn it.'

'Smells of what? What does it smell of?'

My sister looked at me with a squinty smiling face. 'You tell her,' she said.

'No, you. You're the girl.'

'Whatever has *that* got to do with it?'

'Well. You are both girls. It's easier to tell a girl if you are a girl.'

'My feet are cold, thank you kindly,' said Flora. 'So, what *do* I gather if I don't gather the easy stuff. Elderberry. And why not? You haven't said.'

'Because,' I said, with my breath drifting out round me like fog, 'because it smells of bindie. That's why. So don't pick it up.'

Flora looked pinched, but she just shrugged. 'I don't know what you mean. I think you are being horrid and making me feel daft because I'm

Scots! Well I am and I don't. Feel silly, I mean. I don't know what your old bindie means so I'll just go on picking it up. So there.'

'It smells like *dog's* bindie,' hissed my sister.

Flora went quite white. She dropped some sticks and looked worried. 'What's bindie for goodness' sake? What's that?'

My sister started to drag the wooding-sack through the snow across the little churchyard where we were looking for the kindling among the ash and the elms. 'It's what dogs do in the street. Not at lamp-posts, that's just widdle. Bindie is much worse. *Much* worse. And that's what elderberry wood smells of.'

Flora screamed suddenly, her Tam o'Shanter went tilty, and she beat her hands against her coat.

'It's everywhere! I can smell it! It's terrible! My coat is ruined. Oh dearie me –'

'No need to deary-you. It only smells like it in the fire. That's all. I mean, there isn't any bindie actually *on* the twigs . . .'

But she covered her ears up and started to scramble down the path to the gate. 'You *are* awful! Awful! I feel sick. I'll go and tell on you two . . .'

I watched her sliding and stumbling down the hill. But we had work to do.

'Let her go. Good riddance,' said my sister. 'So silly about a little bit of bindie. Goodness. Anyway, she gets in the way. We can do it quicker together because we know what is and what isn't. After we've got the milk, will you come to Baker's with me? There is a dear little matchbox there with a whole fishing-kit inside. It's only a penny. How much have you got?'

'Two pennies,' I said, stuffing some sticks into the sack, having shaken off all the snow and frost.

'Oh good!' said my sister. 'So you can buy one too. There's a little round thing with a funny mouse in it, and you have to get the glass balls into its eyes. It's a penny too. You'll love that.'

The next day was pretty good because there was a thaw in the night, so that made it all right for our father and mother to be on time. I mean the O.M. would be able to get up the lane. So we all went out, well wrapped up with scarves and Wellingtons and gloves and everything, and stamped about at the end of the muddy lane between 2 o'clock and 3 o'clock, as our father had promised to be there, and Mrs Daukes kept running down her path and said we'd all perish from the cold but she never asked us to come into her parlour and that was because Mr Daukes was probably still unconscious with his bad head and bandages everywhere. So Lally said. And then, just as it was beginning to get dusk, because we had got past the shortest day, we saw the headlights, the little ones, of the O.M. as it turned left at Piggy Corner and started to climb up the hill. It was exactly ten past three, and we all started cheering and waving, except silly Flora. She had just about got over her sulking on account of the bindie-wood business, but didn't know about cheering her father and mother because she only had a father and he wasn't worth cheering for anyway.

And then the huffle and bustle, the kissing and laughing, and our mother looking so pretty all wrapped up in the big moleskin travelling-rug, with her leather helmet and huge great goggles. Our father always drove with the hood folded away. It was a 'sports car', he said, so it was suitable. But our mother didn't very much like getting her hair all blown everywhere, so that's why she had to wear the helmet, like my father. Hers was brown and his black, and they had gauntlet gloves and all the luggage was in the big box strapped at the back. Minnehaha was in his basket with the wire front, under the tonneau cover at the back, and I was told to carry him up first and let him have a sniff round the sitting-room, locked in, while we all unloaded the car and got our mother safely up to the house. She was a bit wobbly from the drive, and from not being very strong after her fall down the stairs.

But Lally steadied her up the path and we all helped carry the parcels and cases. Just as it got really dark and my father started to cover the car for the night by putting up the hood and slotting in the isinglass windows (I had to help, and it was a jolly cold and fiddly job, I can tell you), I said, very politely, 'Where is the tree, Papa?'

He straightened up and put his hands to his mouth and said, 'Oh! My god!', which was pretty awful, but he looked so worried that I pretended I hadn't heard what he said and just went on talking and screwing the things that held the windows down.

'I know the goose is there – Lally said it was a "giant of a bird" – and there was the box of crackers, because I saw the name in wriggly writing, but there isn't a tree.'

And there wasn't, and our mother was quite amused when we told her and said it really didn't matter, we'd do without a tree this year because there had been so many problems for our father to worry about. He just forgot it, and it wouldn't have fitted into the car anyway. We had Minnehaha, crackers, the goose, even the pudding from October, and we had *them*, safe and sound. So that seemed reasonable, and Lally brought in the tea and a big dish of buttery crumpets with a lid on, and so I just forgot the tree. Well, sort of.

Minnehaha had almost settled down by this time, of course. He was pretty old, and he knew the cottage, and so he just went poking about here and there, sniffing, and in the end he jumped up on my father's lap and sat looking about him, his ears rather flat to his head. Flora said, 'I think he's scenting your wee mice in the cage. Cats have a wonderful sense of smell, that's how they find their prey.'

I really did want to give her a bonk on the nose, but Lally gave me one of her looks, and I just shrugged, and Lally said the mice were miles away in the lean-to, on a high shelf, and that Minnehaha was too old to 'caper about mousing'. It was kind of her, but I wasn't altogether certain. I didn't like the flat ears bit. But, of course, he *could* just have been listening for strange sounds after our house in Hampstead. His tail was twitching slowly, and I felt a bit worried. But I *did* want to bonk Flora for putting the idea into his head.

The lean-to was a bit cold. It had a tin roof and wooden walls, and no curtains or anything at the windows to keep out the draughts. But the Weekend seemed all right up on its shelf, and I'd given them a good chunk of fresh apple, some corn and a big fistful of hay for their bedding. There was a good smell everywhere of not only onions and paraffin, but creosote and turpentine. There were sacks of potatoes, a big row of marrows, jars of gooseberries and greengages, rows of our father's painting things and canvases stacked in a corner, and a line of stone jars full of ginger beer and parsnip wine which our mother 'put up' at the end of every summer. I liked the lean-to very much. It was sort of outside the house but inside the house at the same time, because if you opened one door you were in the garden, and the other one opened right into the kitchen with the glowing range and the copper and all the dishes and pots and pans. It was really very decent.

We didn't have Christmas stockings now that we were more grown up. So even though I woke up early, even before Lally, because you could see there was no light round her door, there wasn't much point in being awake because of no Christmas stocking, which was a bit sad. I remembered feeling it in the dark, the nuts in the toe, the tangerine a bit squashy if you weren't careful, the interesting rustling of paper and the liquorice-strap (that was easy to tell by being flat *and* round), and the cracker wagging about at the top. It was pretty exciting, but now there was no stocking and no tree. I just hoped there were presents of some sort. I had asked for a theatre from Mr Pollock's shop in Hoxton, but I didn't suppose our father had had the time to go there, not if he forgot the tree.

So I went to sleep again, and only woke up when Lally gave me a push and said, 'Happy Christmas, and you, Miss Fernackerpan! Wake up! It's Christmas morning and your parents' tea to get. Bonnie Caledonia! Wake up! Happy Christmas!' And carrying her candlestick and her indoor shoes, she went off down the stairs. She was so bossy and busy that you just *had* to get up, and this morning there was no wooding to do, so we had to wash our faces and hands first off. We each had a bowl and jug of freezing water, and a big slop pail, and shared the soap. So it was all a bit of a muddle, except the girls got dressed while I washed, and then I gave Flora the Lifebuoy, and then my sister took it. We poured the bowls into the slop bucket and I had to carry it down and empty it in the drain outside the lean-to.

In the kitchen, kettles were boiling, the goose was on the table looking very white and dead beside a carrier bag from MacFisheries. Lally said, don't touch, because it was full of innards and she needed them and we'd have to manage best we could about breakfast and clear ourselves places because she was up to her eyes. Anyway, we had boiled eggs, no porridge today, and toast and rhubarb and ginger jam.

Then we all had to go down to the Court to get the milk and some cream. Our mother came down to see how we all were, and get another cup of tea and make the stuffing for the MacFisheries goose. She looked pretty in her kimono with a huge gold dragon on the back, and when I asked where our father was she just shook her head and said she really didn't know. I was pretty sure she really did but wasn't saying. So we went down to the Court, not down Great Meadow, because it was all muddy and boggy and my sister said there were some cows down in the corner and Flora said she was scared witless of cows. But I didn't take much notice of that because she was witless anyway, so how could she be scared out of something she hadn't got? We walked, sploshed really, down the lane, and the chalky water was gurgling and spilling down the ruts because of the thaw, and there was no sound except for our sloshing and the water burbling.

'You'd think the world had stopped just because it's Christmas Day. It feels so funny,' said Flora, who was pretty funny herself.

The dairy at the Court was very interesting because it was half underground and half not, so that it would never get warm even in the very hottest summer. And it never did. There were little ferns growing along under the big slate shelves where the bowls of buttermilk and whey, skimmed, and 'Today's' and 'Yesterday's' stood. Everything was usually covered in muslin because of the flies from the yard, only, not today, because it was so cold even the ferns had gone all limp. But Miss Barbara Aleford was fussing about the very moment we pushed open the door. Inside it smelled lovely and damp, earthy and then sweet from the milk, and she was pouring a big crock of new milk into the bowls with 'Today's' on them.

'Heigh ho! Heigh ho!' she cried loudly and set the big crock down with a crack on the slate shelf. 'Happy Christmas! Wonderful day! See you've got your cans with you and that doesn't leave me to guess you need some delicious new milk from my animals. Got it right?'

I said that was right and gave her the cans.

'Today's or Yesterday's? All the same to me. In this cold Yesterday's will do you just as well and you can come down tomorrow and get some Today's. Capital!'

She was quite tall, with earphone things curled round the side of her head, and men's corduroy breeches and canvas gaiters, and Lally once said that she was a poor soul who was grieving for her fiancé who had gone missing in the war. But she was still waiting for him because, at any old time, she told Lally, he'd just turn up. He knew the way like the back of his hand, and his pipe and baccy pouch were still in the front parlour where he'd left them.

It was a bit difficult to think of Miss Barbara with a fiancé, and waiting so long in those awful breeches, and her big red hands and earphones and all, when perhaps the fiancé had just gone away somewhere. Like our grandfather who, our mother said, suddenly hop-skipped it off to South America without so much as a by-your-leave or even a kiss to his wife, and just never came back. Wrote some letters but never came back. Just went off. Perhaps our grandmother had got into a bit of a huff. People did do that and it could make you very disagreeable. My sister did sometimes, and sometimes Lally.

Miss Barbara was ladling the Yesterday's into the milk cans and humming under her breath. 'Bring your white mice again? Remember last summer and the harvest mice? Terrible that was! You got so upset . . .'

I remembered the harvest mice all right. I'd brought them back to the farm from the gleaning and they'd jumped out of my pocket and Miss Barbara had trodden on one in her huge old boots and killed it dead. So of course, I got upset, anyone would. Silly woman. So that's why I bought Sat and Sun in a pet shop in Lewes, to make up for it. Being dead, I mean.

I said yes, they were in the lean-to and very well, thank you, and she ladled the milk and said that Mrs Daukes, up the top, had told her that my mother was not so well, on account of she had a nasty fall down the stairs not long ago . . . and how sorry she was if she'd lost it . . . and then she went quite red in the face and told me not to mind. Which I didn't. Grown-ups are very peculiar sometimes. Really . . .

When we put the lids on the milk cans and thanked her, she wrote down what we owed on a slate on the wall and said, 'Take your mama some nice brown eggs, a present from me, help to build her up.' As if she was a castle or something. Still, it was very kind, and she put them in a brown paper bag with *Eat more fruit* on it, and gave it to Flora to carry, on account of we had the cans. Then we all called, 'Happy Christmas', and shuffled about on the wet stone floor and went out into the slushy yard. All the way to the lane we could hear her singing – well, that's what she would have called it – 'If I Had a Talking Picture of Youhoooo'. She was really a bit batty.

Our father was in the lean-to when we got back. He was looking very nice, wearing his painting smock which Mr Dick, the shepherd, had given him, and he smelled of turpentine. He had a saw in one hand and a clump of mistletoe which he'd cut from the old apple tree in the orchard. He held it over Flora's head and said we had to have a bit of mistletoe in the house so that he could kiss all the girls, and Flora made a soppy face and gave him the eggs instead.

Inside, the kitchen smelled of roasting goose and gravy, and the range was red hot and the copper boiling with steam tumbling about, and our mother, in a cotton frock, was getting the chestnuts ready for the sprouts. Everyone was very happy, busy and cheerful. You'd never know we had forgotten the tree. Our father hung the mistletoe in the door between the kitchen and the hallway and Lally said it would be a terrible nuisance there and couldn't we have it in the dining-room, over the table, and he said well, how could he kiss them all if it was over the table unless they all got on it? Anyway, Lally won, as usual. So he nailed it to a big beam above the table in the Big Dining-Room, which we never really used except for parties or Christmas. The door to *their* sitting-room was shut, and locked, and we had to go and take off our Wellingtons and coats and things and then he called to our mother, 'Margaret! I think it's high time for the presents, don't you?' and Lally and our mother came into the hall, and our father took off his smock and opened the sitting-room door.

And there it was.

The most beautiful tree you've ever seen. All gold and silver. Shining in the firelight. And we all cried out in surprise, and our father said the only thing was not to touch it really, because it was all made of holly branches and he'd had to paint all the leaves gold and silver by hand and it had taken him half the night. Our mother said that was his punishment for forgetting the tree in the first place, and Lally said it was a good thing she wasn't about to do any washing because her clothes' prop was now covered in holly and thick as a hedgehog with nails, and our father said there was quite a gap in the fence down at the Daukeses' cottage. Then they had sherry. Even Lally had a sip, but not too much on account of she'd be tipsy taking the goose out of the oven. All round the gold and silver tree were the presents, including Flora's haggis – you could tell them easily because they were round and wrapped in tartan paper, and there was a huge box for me and I knew what it was by shaking it. It was the Pollock's Theatre. So they hadn't forgotten after all. And they had made the tree.

After we'd opened all the presents our parents went down to the village to telephone *The Times*. You always had to telephone *The Times* to check that everything was all right and that nothing terrible had happened in some place like the Sahara or Berlin. You never could be certain, our father said, that some 'idiot' hadn't got himself assassinated or pushed off a cliff, and that really meant just 'killed' in simple English. But he had to 'check in'. So they did, on Christmas morning even, from the Star at the Market Cross because it had a telephone. Lally said *nothing* stopped for *The Times*, it was all go.

I hoped, with my fingers crossed, that nothing awful *had* happened when they telephoned, because if it had, that meant our father would rush back to London no matter what. So no Christmas dinner. I just prayed there wouldn't be another airship crash, like the R.101, or another Emperor crowned in Abyssinia. Things like that got in the way. But it was all right, and they came back safe and sound. When I asked them, my mother laughed, looking so pretty with sparky eyes and said no, nothing to make our father go to *The Times*, just a bit of trouble in the Punjab but then there always was, so we'd have a decent time and dinner was at three o'clock on the dot.

The Metropolitan Touch

☆★☆

P. G. WODEHOUSE

Nobody is more alive than I am to the fact that young Bingo Little is in many respects a sound old egg. In one way and another he has made life pretty interesting for me at intervals ever since we were at school. As a companion for a cheery hour I think I would choose him before anybody. On the other hand, I'm bound to say that there are things about him that could be improved. His habit of falling in love with every second girl he sees is one of them; and another is his way of letting the world in on the secrets of his heart. If you want shrinking reticence, don't go to Bingo, because he's got about as much of it as a soap advertisement.

I mean to say – well, here's the telegram I got from him one evening in November, about a month after I'd got back to town from my visit to Twing Hall:

> I say Bertie old man I am in love at last. She is the most wonderful girl Bertie old man. This is the real thing at last Bertie. Come here at once and bring Jeeves. Oh I say you know that tobacco shop in Bond Street on the left side as you go up. Will you get me a hundred of their special cigarettes and send them to me here. I have run out. I know when you see her you will think she is the most wonderful girl. Mind you bring Jeeves. Don't forget the cigarettes.
>
> *Bingo.*

It had been handed in at Twing Post Office. In other words, he had submitted that frightful rot to the goggling eye of a village post-mistress who was probably the mainspring of local gossip and would have the place ringing with the news before nightfall. He couldn't have given himself away more completely if he had hired the town crier. When I was a kid, I used to read stories about knights and vikings and that species of chappie who would get up without a blush in the middle of a crowded banquet and loose off a song about how perfectly priceless they thought their best girl. I've often felt that those days would have suited young Bingo down to the ground.

Jeeves had brought the thing in with the evening drink, and I slung it over to him.

'It's about due, of course,' I said. 'Young Bingo hasn't been in love for at least a couple of months. I wonder who it is this time?'

'Miss Mary Burgess, sir,' said Jeeves, 'the niece of the Reverend Mr Heppenstall. She is staying at Twing Vicarage.'

'Great Scott!' I knew that Jeeves knew practically everything in the world, but this sounded like second-sight. 'How do you know that?'

'When we were visiting Twing Hall in the summer, sir, I formed a somewhat close friendship with Mr Heppenstall's butler. He is good enough to keep me abreast of the local news from time to time. From his account, sir, the young lady appears to be a very estimable young lady. Of a somewhat serious nature, I understand. Mr Little is very *épris*, sir. Brookfield, my correspondent, writes that last week he observed him in the moonlight at an advanced hour gazing up at his window.'

'Whose window! Brookfield's?'

'Yes, sir. Presumably under the impression that it was the young lady's.'

'But what the deuce is he doing at Twing at all?'

'Mr Little was compelled to resume his old position as tutor to Lord Wickhammersley's son at Twing Hall, sir. Owing to having been unsuccessful in some speculations at Hurst Park at the end of October.'

'Good Lord, Jeeves! Is there anything you don't know?'

'I couldn't say, sir.'

I picked up the telegram.

'I suppose he wants us to go down and help him out a bit?'

'That would appear to be his motive in dispatching the message, sir.'

'Well, what shall we do? Go?'

'I would advocate it, sir. If I may say so, I think that Mr Little should be encouraged in this particular matter.'

'You think he's picked a winner this time?'

'I hear nothing but excellent reports of the young lady, sir. I think it is beyond question that she would be an admirable influence for Mr Little, should the affair come to a happy conclusion. Such a union would also, I fancy, go far to restore Mr Little to the good graces of his uncle, the young lady being well connected and possessing private means. In short, sir, I think that if there is anything that we can do we should do it.'

'Well, with you behind him,' I said, 'I don't see how he can fail to click.'

'You are very good, sir,' said Jeeves. 'The tribute is much appreciated.'

Bingo met us at Twing station next day, and insisted on my sending Jeeves on in the car with the bags while he and I walked. He started in about the female the moment we had begun to hoof it.

'She is very wonderful, Bertie. She is not one of these flippant, shallow-minded modern girls. She is sweetly grave and beautifully earnest. She reminds me of – what is the name I want?'

'Marie Lloyd?'

'Saint Cecilia,' said young Bingo, eyeing me with a good deal of loathing. 'She reminds me of Saint Cecilia. She makes me yearn to be a better, nobler, deeper, broader man.'

'What beats me,' I said, following up a train of thought, 'is what principle you pick them on. The girls you fall in love with, I mean. I mean to say, what's your system? As far as I can see, no two of them are alike. First it was Mabel the waitress, then Honoria Glossop, then that fearful blister Charlotte Corday Rowbotham –'

I own that Bingo had the decency to shudder. Thinking of Charlotte always made me shudder, too.

'You don't seriously mean, Bertie, that you are intending to compare the feeling I have for Mary Burgess, the holy devotion, the spiritual –'

'Oh, all right, let it go,' I said. 'I say, old lad, aren't we going rather a long way round?'

Considering that we were supposed to be heading for Twing Hall, it seemed to me that we were making a longish job of it. The Hall is about two miles from the station by the main road, and we had cut off down a lane, gone across country for a bit, climbed a stile or two, and were now working our way across a field that ended in another lane.

'She sometimes takes her little brother for a walk round this way,' explained Bingo. 'I thought we would meet her and bow, and you could see her, you know, and then we would walk on.'

'Of course,' I said, 'that's enough excitement for anyone, and undoubtedly a corking reward for tramping three miles out of one's way over ploughed fields with tight boots, but don't we do anything else? Don't we tack on to the girl and buzz along with her?'

'Good Lord!' said Bingo, honestly amazed. 'You don't suppose I've got nerve enough for that, do you? I just look at her from afar off and all that sort of thing. Quick! Here she comes! No I'm wrong!'

It was like that song of Harry Lauder's where he's waiting for the girl and says 'This is her-r-r. No, it's a rabbut.' Young Bingo made me stand there in the teeth of a nor'-east half-gale for ten minutes, keeping me on my toes with a series of false alarms, and I was just thinking of suggesting that we should lay off and give the rest of the proceedings a miss, when round the corner there came a fox-terrier, and Bingo quivered like an aspen. Then there hove in sight a small boy and he shook like jelly. Finally, like a star whose entrance has been worked up by the *personnel* of the *ensemble*, a girl appeared, and his emotion was painful to witness. His face got so red that, what with his white collar and the fact that the wind had turned his nose blue, he looked more like a French flag than anything else. He sagged from the waist upwards, as if he had been filleted.

He was just raising his fingers limply to his cap when he suddenly saw that the girl wasn't alone. A chappie in clerical costume was also among those present, and the sight of him didn't seem to do Bingo a bit of good. His face got redder and his nose bluer, and it wasn't till they had nearly passed that he managed to get hold of his cap.

The girl bowed, the curate said, 'Ah, Little. Rough weather,' the dog barked, and then they toddled on and the entertainment was over.

The curate was a new factor in the situation to me. I reported his movements to Jeeves when I got to the Hall. Of course, Jeeves knew all about it already.

'That is the Reverend Mr Wingham, Mr Heppenstall's new curate, sir. I gathered from Brookfield that he is Mr Little's rival, and at the moment the young lady appears to favour him. Mr Wingham has the advantage of being on the premises. He and the young lady play duets after dinner, which acts as a bond. Mr Little on these occasions, I understand, prowls about in the road, chafing visibly.'

'That seems to be all the poor fish is able to do, dash it. He can chafe all right, but there he stops. He's lost his pep. He's got no dash. Why, when we met her just now, he hadn't even the common manly courage to say "Good evening"!'

'I gather that Mr Little's affection is not unmingled with awe, sir.'

'Well, how are we to help a man when he's such a rabbit as that? Have you anything to suggest? I shall be seeing him after dinner, and he's sure to ask first thing what you advise.'

'In my opinion, sir, the most judicious course for Mr Little to pursue would be to concentrate on the young gentleman.'

'The small brother? How do you mean?'

'Make a friend of him, sir – take him for walks and so forth.'

'It doesn't sound one of your red-hottest ideas. I must say I expected something fruitier than that.'

'It would be a beginning, sir, and might lead to better things.'

'Well, I'll tell him. I liked the look of her, Jeeves.'

'A thoroughly estimable young lady, sir.'

I slipped Bingo the tip from the stable that night, and was glad to observe that it seemed to cheer him up.

'Jeeves is always right,' he said. 'I ought to have thought of it myself. I'll start in tomorrow.'

It was amazing how the chappie bucked up. Long before I left for town it had become a mere commonplace for him to speak to the girl. I mean he didn't simply look stuffed when they met. The brother was forming a bond that was a dashed sight stronger than the curate's duets. She and Bingo used to take him for walks together. I asked Bingo what they talked about on these occasions, and he said Wilfred's future. The girl hoped that Wilfred would one day become a curate, but Bingo said no, there was something about curates he didn't quite like.

The day we left, Bingo came to see us off with Wilfred frisking about him like an old college chum. The last I saw of them, Bingo was standing him chocolates out of the slot-machine. A scene of peace and cheery goodwill. Dashed promising, I thought.

Which made it all the more of a jar, about a fortnight later, when his telegram arrived. As follows:

> Bertie old man I say Bertie could you possibly come down here at once. Everything gone wrong hang it all. Dash it Bertie you simply must come. I am in a state of absolute despair and heart-broken. Would you mind sending another hundred of those cigarettes. Bring Jeeves when you come Bertie. You simply must come Bertie. I rely on you. Don't forget to bring Jeeves.
>
> *Bingo.*

For a chap who's perpetually hard-up, I must say that young Bingo is the most wasteful telegraphist I ever struck. He's got no notion of condensing. The silly ass simply pours out his wounded soul at twopence a word, or whatever it is, without a thought.

'How about it, Jeeves?' I said. 'I'm getting a bit fed up. I can't go chucking all my engagements every second week in order to biff down to

Twing and rally round young Bingo. Send him a wire telling him to end it all in the village pond.'

'If you could spare me for the night, sir, I should be glad to run down and investigate.'

'Oh, dash it! Well, I suppose there's nothing else to be done. After all, you're the fellow he wants. All right, carry on.'

Jeeves got back late the next day.

'Well?' I said.

Jeeves appeared perturbed. He allowed his left eyebrow to flicker upwards in a concerned sort of manner.

'I have done what I could, sir,' he said, 'but I fear Mr Little's chances do not appear bright. Since our last visit, sir, there has been a decidedly sinister and disquieting development.'

'Oh, what's that?'

'You may remember Mr Steggles, sir – the young gentleman who was studying for an examination with Mr Heppenstall at the Vicarage?'

'What's Steggles got to do with it?' I asked.

'I gather from Brookfield, sir, who chanced to overhear a conversation, that Mr Steggles is interesting himself in the affair.'

'Good Lord! What, making a book on it?'

'I understand that he is accepting wagers from those in his immediate circle, sir. Against Mr Little, whose chances he does not seem to fancy.'

'I don't like that, Jeeves.'

'No, sir. It is sinister.'

'From what I know of Steggles there will be dirty work.'

'It has already occurred, sir.'

'Already?'

'Yes, sir. It seems that, in pursuance of the policy which he has been good enough to allow me to suggest to him, Mr Little escorted Master Burgess to the church bazaar, and there met Mr Steggles, who was in the company of young Master Heppenstall, the Reverend Mr Heppenstall's second son, who is home from Rugby just now, having recently recovered from an attack of mumps. The encounter took place in the refreshment-room, where Mr Steggles was at that moment entertaining Master Heppenstall. To cut a long story short, sir, the two gentlemen became extremely interested in the hearty manner in which the lads were fortifying themselves; and Mr Steggles offered to back his nominee in a weight-for-age eating contest against Master Burgess for a pound a side. Mr Little admitted to me that he was conscious of a certain hesitation as to what the upshot might be, should Miss Burgess get to hear of the matter, but his sporting blood was too much for him and he agreed to the contest. This was duly carried out, both lads exhibiting the utmost willingness and enthusiasm, and eventually Master Burgess justified Mr Little's confidence by winning, but only after a bitter struggle. Next day both contestants were in considerable pain; inquiries were made and confessions extorted, and Mr Little – I learn from Brookfield, who happened to be near the door of the drawing-room at the moment – had an extremely unpleasant interview with the young lady, which ended in her desiring him never to speak to her again.'

There's no getting away from the fact that, if ever a man required watching, it's Steggles. Machiavelli could have taken his correspondence course.

'It was a put-up job, Jeeves!' I said. 'I mean, Steggles worked the whole thing on purpose. It's his old nobbling game.'

'There would seem to be no doubt about that, sir.'

'Well, he seems to have dished poor old Bingo all right.'

'That is the prevalent opinion, sir. Brookfield tells me that down in the village at the Cow and Horses seven to one is being freely offered on Mr Wingham and finding no takers.'

'Good Lord! Are they betting about it down in the village, too?'

'Yes, sir. And in adjoining hamlets also. The affair has caused widespread interest. I am told that there is a certain sporting reaction in even so distant a spot as Lower Bingley.'

'Well, I don't see what there is to do. If Bingo is such a chump – '

'One is fighting a losing battle, I fear, sir, but I did venture to indicate to Mr Little a course of action which might prove of advantage. I recommended him to busy himself with good works.'

'Good works?'

'About the village, sir. Reading to the bedridden – chatting with the sick – that sort of thing, sir. We can but trust that good results will ensue.'

'Yes, I suppose so,' I said doubtfully. 'But, by gosh, if I was a sick man I'd hate to have a loony like young Bingo coming and gibbering at my bedside.'

'There *is* that aspect of the matter, sir,' said Jeeves.

I didn't hear a word from Bingo for a couple of weeks, and I took it after a while that he had found the going too hard and had chucked in the towel. And then, one night not long before Christmas, I came back to the flat pretty latish, having been out dancing at the Embassy. I was fairly tired, having swung a practically non-stop shoe from shortly after dinner till two AM, and bed seemed to be indicated. Judge of my chagrin and all that sort of thing, therefore, when, tottering to my room and switching on the light, I observed the foul features of young Bingo all over the pillow. The blighter had appeared from nowhere and was in my bed, sleeping like an infant with a sort of happy, dreamy smile on his map.

A bit thick I mean to say! We Woosters are all for the good old medieval hosp. and all that, but when it comes to finding chappies collaring your bed, the thing becomes a trifle too mouldy. I hove a shoe, and Bingo sat up, gurgling.

''s matter? 's matter?' said young Bingo.

'What the deuce are you doing in my bed?' I said.

'Oh, hallo, Bertie! So there you are!'

'Yes, here I am. What are you doing in my bed?'

'I came up to town for the night on business.'

'Yes, but what are you doing in my bed?'

'Dash it all, Bertie,' said young Bingo querulously, 'don't keep harping on your beastly bed. There's another made up in the spare room. I saw Jeeves make it with my own eyes. I believe he meant it for me, but I knew what a perfect host you were, so I just turned in here. I say, Bertie, old man,' said Bingo, apparently fed up with the discussion about sleeping-quarters, 'I see daylight.'

'Well, it's getting on for three in the morning.'

'I was speaking figuratively, you ass. I meant that hope has begun to dawn. About Mary Burgess, you know. Sit down and I'll tell you all about it.'

'I won't. I'm going to sleep.'

'To begin with,' said young Bingo, settling himself comfortably against the pillows and helping himself to a cigarette from my private box, 'I must once again pay a marked tribute to good old Jeeves. A modern Solomon. I was badly up against it when I came to him for advice, but he rolled up with a tip which has put me – I use the term advisedly and in a conservative spirit – on velvet. He may have told you that he recommended me to win back the lost ground by busying myself with good works? Bertie, old man,' said young Bingo earnestly, 'for the last two weeks I've been comforting the sick to such an extent that, if I had a brother and you brought him to me on a sick-bed at this moment, by Jove, old man, I'd heave a brick at him. However, though it took it out of me like the deuce, the scheme worked splendidly. She softened visibly before I'd been at it a week. Started to bow again when we met in the street, and so forth. About a couple of days ago she distinctly smiled – in a sort of faint, saint-like kind of way, you know – when I ran into her outside the Vicarage. And yesterday – I say, you remember that curate chap, Wingham? Fellow with a long nose.'

'Of course I remember him. Your rival.'

'Rival?' Bingo raised his eyebrows. 'Oh, well, I suppose you could have called him that at one time. Though it sounds a little far-fetched.'

'Does it?' I said, stung by the sickening complacency of the chump's manner. 'Well, let me tell you that the last I heard was that at the Cow and Horses in Twing village and all over the place as far as Lower Bingley they were offering seven to one on the curate and finding no takers.'

Bingo started violently and sprayed cigarette-ash all over my bed.

'Betting!' he gargled. 'Betting! You don't mean that they're betting on this holy, sacred . . . Oh, I say, dash it all! Haven't people any sense of decency and reverence? Is nothing safe from their beastly, sordid graspingness? I wonder,' said young Bingo thoughtfully, 'if there's a chance of my getting any of that seven-to-one money? Seven to one! What a price! Who's offering it, do you know? Oh, well, I suppose it wouldn't do. No, I suppose it wouldn't be quite the thing.'

'You seem dashed confident,' I said. 'I'd always thought that Wingham – '

'Oh, I'm not worried about him,' said Bingo. 'I was just going to tell you. Wingham's got the mumps, and won't be out and about for weeks. And, jolly as that is in itself, it's not all. You see, he was producing the Village School Christmas Entertainment, and now I've taken over the job. I went to old Heppenstall last night and clinched the contract. Well, you see what that means. It means that I shall be absolutely the centre of the village life and thought for three solid weeks, with a terrific triumph to wind up with. Everybody looking up to me and fawning on me, don't you see, and all that. It's bound to have a powerful effect on Mary's mind. It will show her that I am capable of serious effort; that there is a solid foundation of worth in me; that, mere butterfly as she may once have thought me, I am in reality – '

'Oh, all right, let it go!'

'It's a big thing, you know, this Christmas Entertainment. Old Heppenstall is very much wrapped up in it. Nibs from all over the countryside rolling up. The Squire present, with family. A big chance for me, Bertie, my boy, and I mean to make the most of it. Of course, I'm handicapped a bit by not having been in on the thing from the start. Will you credit it that that uninspired doughnut of a curate wanted to give the public some rotten little fairy play out of a book for children published about fifty years ago without one good laugh or the semblance of a gag in it? It's too late to alter the thing entirely, but at least I can jazz it up. I'm going to write them in something zippy to brighten the thing up a bit.'

'You can't write.'

'Well, when I say write, I mean pinch. That's why I've popped up to town. I've been to see that revue, *Cuddle Up!* at the Palladium, tonight. Full of good stuff. Of course, it's rather hard to get anything in the nature of a big spectacular effect in the Twing Village Hall, with no scenery to speak of and a chorus of practically imbecile kids of ages ranging from nine to fourteen, but I think I see my way. Have you seen *Cuddle Up!*?'

'Yes. Twice.'

'Well, there's some good stuff in the first act, and I can lift practically all the numbers. Then there's that show at the Palace. I can see the *matinée* of that tomorrow before I leave. There's sure to be some decent bits in that. Don't you worry about my not being able to write a hit. Leave it to me, laddie, leave it to me. And now, my dear old chap,' said young Bingo, snuggling down cosily, 'you mustn't keep me up talking all night. It's all right for you fellows who have nothing to do, but I'm a busy man. Good night, old thing. Close the door quietly after you and switch out the light. Breakfast, about ten tomorrow, I suppose, what? Right-o. Good night.'

For the next three weeks I didn't see Bingo. He became a sort of Voice Heard Off, developing a habit of ringing me up on long-distance and consulting me on various points arising at rehearsal, until the day when he got me out of bed at eight in the morning to ask whether I thought *Merry Christmas!* was a good title. I told him then that this nuisance must now cease, and after that he cheesed it, and practically passed out of my life, till one afternoon when I got back to the flat to dress for dinner and found Jeeves inspecting a whacking big poster sort of thing which he had draped over the back of an armchair.

'Good Lord, Jeeves!' I said. I was feeling rather weak that day, and the thing shook me. 'What on earth's that?'

'Mr Little sent it to me, sir, and desired me to bring it to your notice.'

'Well, you've certainly done it!'

I took another look at the object. There was no doubt about it, it caught the eye. It was about seven feet long, and most of the lettering in about as bright red ink as I ever struck.

This was how it ran:

Twing Village Hall,
Friday, December 23rd,
Richard Little
presents
A New and Original Revue Entitled

WHAT HO, TWING!!

Book by
Richard Little
Lyrics by
Richard Little
Music by
Richard Little
With the Full Twing Juvenile
Company and Chorus.
Scenic Effects by
Richard Little
Produced by
Richard Little

'What do you make of it, Jeeves?' I said.

'I confess I am a little doubtful, sir. I think Mr Little would have done better to follow my advice and confine himself to good works about the village.'

'You think the thing will be a frost?'

'I could not hazard a conjecture, sir. But my experience has been that what pleases the London public is not always so acceptable to the rural mind. The metropolitan touch sometimes proves a trifle too exotic for the provinces.'

'I suppose I ought to go down and see the dashed thing?'

'I think Mr Little would be wounded were you not present, sir.'

The Village Hall at Twing is a smallish building, smelling of apples. It was full when I turned up on the evening of the twenty-third, for I had purposely timed myself to arrive not long before the kick-off. I had had experience of one or two of these binges, and didn't want to run any risk of coming early and finding myself shoved into a seat in one of the front rows where I wouldn't be able to execute a quiet sneak into the open air halfway through the proceedings, if the occasion seemed to demand it. I secured a nice strategic position near the door at the back of the hall.

From where I stood I had a good view of the audience. As always on these occasions, the first few rows were occupied by the Nibs – consisting of the Squire, a fairly mauve old sportsman with white whiskers, his family, a platoon of local parsons and perhaps a couple of dozen of prominent pew-holders. Then came a dense squash of what you might call the lower middle classes. And at the back, where I was, we came down with a jerk in the social scale, this end of the hall being given up almost entirely to a collection of frankly Tough Eggs, who had rolled up not so much for any love of the drama as because there was a free tea after the show. Take it for all in all, a representative gathering of Twing life and thought. The Nibs were whispering in a pleased manner to each other, the Lower Middles were sitting up very straight, as if they'd been bleached, and the Tough Eggs whiled away the time by cracking nuts and exchanging low rustic wheezes. The girl, Mary Burgess, was at the piano playing a waltz. Beside her stood the curate, Wingham, apparently recovered. The temperature, I should think, was about a hundred and twenty-seven.

Somebody jabbed me heartily in the lower ribs, and I perceived the man Steggles.

'Hallo!' he said. 'I didn't know you were coming down.'

I didn't like the chap, but we Woosters can wear the mask. I beamed a bit.

'Oh, yes,' I said. 'Bingo wanted me to roll up and see his show.'

'I hear he's giving us something pretty ambitious,' said the man Steggles. 'Big effects and all that sort of thing.'

'I believe so.'

'Of course, it means a lot to him, doesn't it? He's told you about the girl, of course?'

'Yes. And I hear you're laying seven to one against him,' I said, eyeing the blighter a trifle austerely.

He didn't even quiver.

'Just a little flutter to relieve the monotony of country life,' he said. 'But you've got the facts a bit wrong. It's down in the village that they're laying seven to one. I can do you better than that, if you feel in a speculative mood. How about a tenner at a hundred to eight?'

'Good Lord! Are you giving that?'

'Yes. Somehow,' said Steggles meditatively, 'I have a sort of feeling, a kind of premonition that something's going to go wrong tonight. You know what Little is. A bungler, if ever there was one. Something tells me that this show of his is going to be a frost. And if it is, of course, I should think it would prejudice the girl against him pretty badly. His standing always was rather shaky.'

'Are you going to try and smash up the show?' I said sternly.

'Me!' said Steggles. 'Why, what could I do? Half a minute, I want to go and speak to a man.'

He buzzed off, leaving me distinctly disturbed. I could see from the fellow's eye that he was meditating some of his customary rough stuff, and I thought Bingo ought to be warned. But there wasn't time and I couldn't get at him. Almost immediately after Steggles had left me the curtain went up.

Except as a prompter, Bingo wasn't much in evidence in the early part of the performance. The thing at the outset was merely one of those weird dramas which you dig out of books published around Christmas time and entitled *Twelve Little Plays for the Tots*, or something like that. The kids drooled on in the usual manner, the booming voice of Bingo ringing out from time to time behind the scenes when the fatheads forgot their lines; and the audience was settling down into the sort of torpor usual on these occasions, when the first of Bingo's interpolated bits occurred. It was that number which What's-her-name sings in that revue at the Palace – you would recognize the tune if I hummed it, but I can never get hold of the dashed thing. It always got three encores at the Palace, and it went well now, even with a squeaky-voiced child jumping on and off the key like a chamois of the Alps leaping from crag to crag. Even the Tough Eggs liked it. At the end of the second refrain the entire house was shouting for an encore, and the kid with the voice like a slate-pencil took a deep breath and started to let it go once more.

At this point all the lights went out.

I don't know when I've had anything so sudden and devastating happen to me before. They didn't flicker. They just went out. The hall was in complete darkness.

Well, of course, that sort of broke the spell, as you might put it. People started to shout directions, and the Tough Eggs stamped their feet and settled down for a pleasant time. And, of course, young Bingo had to make an ass of himself. His voice suddenly shot at us out of the darkness.

'Ladies and gentlemen, something has gone wrong with the lights – '

The Tough Eggs were tickled by this bit of information straight from the stable. They took it up as a sort of battle-cry. Then, after about five minutes, the lights went up again, and the show was resumed.

It took ten minutes after that to get the audience back into its state of coma, but eventually they began to settle down, and everything was going nicely when a small boy with a face like a turbot edged out in front of the curtain, which had been lowered after a pretty painful scene about a wishing-ring or a fairy's curse or something of that sort, and started to sing that song of George Thingummy's out of *Cuddle Up!* You know the one I mean. 'Always Listen to Mother, Girls!' it's called, and he gets the audience to join in and sing the refrain. Quite a ripeish ballad, and one which I myself have frequently sung in my bath with not a little vim; but by no means – as anyone but a perfect sapheaded prune like young Bingo would have known – by no means the sort of thing for a children's Christmas entertainment in the old village hall. Right from the start of the first refrain the bulk of the audience had begun to stiffen in their seats and fan themselves, and the Burgess girl at the piano was accompanying in a stunned, mechanical sort of way, while the curate at her side averted his gaze in a pained manner. The Tough Eggs, however, were all for it.

At the end of the second refrain the kid stopped and began to sidle towards the wings. Upon which the following brief duologue took place:

YOUNG BINGO (*Voice heard, off, ringing against the rafters*): 'Go on!'

THE KID (*coyly*): 'I don't like to.'

YOUNG BINGO (*still louder*): 'Go on, you little blighter, or I'll slay you!'

I suppose the kid thought it over swiftly and realized that Bingo, being in a position to get at him, had better be conciliated, whatever the harvest might be; for he shuffled down to the front and, having shut his eyes and giggled hysterically, said: 'Ladies and gentlemen, I will now call upon Squire Tressidder to oblige by singing the refrain!'

You know, with the most charitable feelings towards him, there are moments when you can't help thinking that young Bingo ought to be in some sort of a home. I suppose, poor fish, he had pictured this as the big punch of the evening. He had imagined, I take it, that the Squire would spring jovially to his feet, rip the song off his chest, and all would be gaiety and mirth. Well, what happened was simply that old Tressidder – and, mark you, I'm not blaming him – just sat where he was, swelling and turning a brighter purple every second. The lower middle classes remained in frozen silence, waiting for the roof to fall. The only section of the audience that really seemed to enjoy the idea was the Tough Eggs, who yelled with enthusiasm. It was jam for the Tough Eggs.

And then the lights went out again.

When they went up, some minutes later, they disclosed the Squire marching stiffly out at the head of his family, fed up to the eyebrows; the

Burgess girl at the piano with a pale, set look; and the curate gazing at her with something in his expression that seemed to suggest that, although all this was no doubt deplorable, he had spotted the silver lining.

The show went on once more. There were great chunks of Plays-for-the-Tots dialogue, and then the girl at the piano struck up the prelude to that Orange-Girl number that's the big hit of the Palace revue. I took it that this was to be Bingo's smashing act one finale. The entire company was on the stage, and a clutching hand had appeared round the edge of the curtain, ready to pull at the right moment. It looked like the finale all right. It wasn't long before I realized that it was something more. It was the finish.

I take it you know that Orange number at the Palace? It goes:

Oh, won't you something something oranges,
  My something oranges,
  My something oranges;
Oh, won't you something something something I forget,
Something something something tumty tumty yet:
Oh –

or words to that effect. It's a dashed clever lyric, and the tune's good, too; but the thing that made the number was the business where the girls take oranges out of their baskets, you know, and toss them lightly to the audience. I don't know if you've ever noticed it, but it always seems to tickle an audience to bits when they get things thrown at them from the stage. Every time I've been to the Palace the customers have simply gone wild over this number.

But at the Palace, of course, the oranges are made of yellow wool, and the girls don't so much chuck them as drop them limply into the first and second rows. I began to gather that the business was going to be treated rather differently tonight when a dashed great chunk of pips and mildew sailed past my ear and burst on the wall behind me. Another landed with a squelch on the neck of one of the Nibs in the third row. And then a third took me right on the tip of the nose, and I kind of lost interest in the proceedings for a while.

When I had scrubbed my face and got my eye to stop watering for a moment, I saw that the evening's entertainment had begun to resemble one of Belfast's livelier nights. The air was thick with shrieks and fruit. The kids on the stage, with Bingo buzzing distractedly to and fro in their midst, were having the time of their lives. I suppose they realized that this couldn't go on for ever, and were making the most of their chances. The Tough Eggs had begun to pick up all the oranges that hadn't burst and were shooting them back, so that the audience got it both coming and going. In fact, take it all round, there was a certain amount of confusion; and, just as things had begun really to hot up, out went the lights again.

It seemed to me about my time for leaving, so I slid for the door. I was hardly outside when the audience began to stream out. They surged about me in twos and threes, and I've never seen a public body so dashed unanimous on any point. To a man – and to a woman – they were cursing poor old Bingo; and there was a large and rapidly growing school of thought which held that the best thing to do would be to waylay him as he emerged and splash him about in the village pond a bit.

There were such a dickens of a lot of these enthusiasts and they looked so jolly determined that it seemed to me that the only matey thing to do was to go behind and warn young Bingo to turn his coatcollar up and breeze off snakily by some side exit. I went behind, and found him sitting on a box in the wings, perspiring pretty freely and looking more or less like the spot marked with a cross where the accident happened. His hair was standing up and his ears were hanging down, and one harsh word would undoubtedly have made him burst into tears.

'Bertie,' he said hollowly, as he saw me, 'it was that blighter Steggles! I caught one of the kids before he could get away and got it all out of him. Steggles substituted real oranges for the balls of wool which with infinite sweat and at a cost of nearly a quid I had specially prepared. Well, I will now proceed to tear him limb from limb. It'll be something to do.'

I hated to spoil his day-dreams, but it had to be.

'Good heavens, man,' I said, 'you haven't time for frivolous amusements now. You've got to get out. And quick!'

'Bertie,' said Bingo in a dull voice, 'she was here just now. She said it was all my fault and that she would never speak to me again. She said she had always suspected me of being a heartless practical joker, and now she knew. She said – Oh, well, she ticked me off properly.'

'That's the least of your troubles,' I said. It seemed impossible to rouse the poor zib to a sense of his position. 'Do you realize that about two hundred of Twing's heftiest are waiting for you outside to chuck you into the pond?'

'No!'

'Absolutely!'

For a moment the poor chap seemed crushed. But only for a moment. There has always been something of the good old English bulldog breed about Bingo. A strange, sweet smile flickered for an instant over his face.

'It's all right,' he said. 'I can sneak out through the cellar and climb over the wall at the back. They can't intimidate *me*!'

It couldn't have been more than a week later when Jeeves, after he had brought me my tea, gently steered me away from the sporting page of the *Morning Post* and directed my attention to an announcement in the engagements and marriages column.

It was a brief statement that a marriage had been arranged and would shortly take place between the Hon. and Rev. Hubert Wingham, third son of the Right Hon. the Earl of Sturridge, and Mary, only daughter of the late Matthew Burgess, of Weatherly Court, Hants.

'Of course,' I said, after I had given it the east-to-west, 'I expected this, Jeeves.'

'Yes, sir.'

'She would never forgive him what happened that night.'

'No, sir.'

'Well,' I said, as I took a sip of the fragrant and steaming, 'I don't suppose it will take old Bingo long to get over it. It's about the hundred and eleventh time this sort of thing has happened to him. You're the man I'm sorry for.'

'Me, sir?'

'Well, dash it all, you can't have forgotten what a deuce of a lot of trouble you took to bring the thing off for Bingo. It's too bad that all your work should have been wasted.'

'Not entirely wasted, sir.'

'Eh?'

'It is true that my efforts to bring about the match between Mr Little and the young lady were not successful, but I still look back upon the matter with a certain satisfaction.'

'Because you did your best, you mean?'

'Not entirely, sir, though of course that thought also gives me pleasure. I was alluding more particularly to the fact that I found the affair financially remunerative.'

'Financially remunerative? What do you mean?'

'When I learned that Mr Steggles had interested himself in the contest, sir, I went shares with my friend Brookfield and bought the book which had been made on the issue by the landlord of the Cow and Horses. It has proved a highly profitable investment. Your breakfast will be ready almost immediately, sir. Kidneys on toast and mushrooms. I will bring it when you ring.'

The Moon's a Balloon

☆★☆★☆★☆★☆★☆★☆★☆★☆★☆★☆★☆★☆★☆★☆★☆★☆★☆

DAVID NIVEN

Apart from the Chinese, the only people in the world who pack their sons off to the tender care of unknown and often homosexual schoolmasters at the exact moment when they are most in need of parental love and influence, are the British so-called upper and middle classes.

I had not been long at boarding school before I discovered that life could be hell. There was a great deal of bullying and for a six-year-old, the spectacle of a gang of twelve-year-olds bearing down, cracking wet towels like whips, can be terrifying.

For the most part, the masters were even more frightening. It would be charitable to think that they were shell-shocked heroes returned from the hell of Mons and Vimy, but it seems more probable that they were sadistic perverts who had been dredged up from the bottom of the educational barrel at a time of acute manpower shortage.

One, a Mr Croome, when he tired of pulling ears halfway out of our heads (I still have one that sticks out almost at right angles thanks to this son of a bitch), and delivering, for the smallest mistake in declension, back-handed slaps that knocked one off one's bench, delighted in saying, 'Show me the hand that wrote this', and then bringing down the sharp edge of a heavy ruler across the offending wrist.

He took the last class on Friday evening and I remember praying every week that he would die before then so that I could somehow reach the haven of Saturday and Sunday and the comparative safety of the weekend.

I don't think I have ever been so frightened of a human being in my life. Once he made me lean out of a fourth floor window – a stupefying height for a little boy – then he shut the window across the small of my back, ordered two other equally terrified boys to hold my feet and laid into me mightily with a cane. All this for some mistake in – 'common are sacerdos dux vates parens et conjux . . .'

Years later, when I was at Sandhurst and playing in the Rugby football fifteen, big enough and ugly enough to take care of myself, I had an overpowering urge to see the bastard again, face to face.

I went down to the school, filled with vindictiveness. I don't know what I intended to do really, but when I got there I found the school deserted; its prison-like exercise yard full of rubbish and old newspapers. The fourth floor window, out of which I had dangled, was broken and open to the rain – it didn't even look very high.

My mother, at the time, however, would not believe my tales of woe or rather Uncle Tommy persuaded her that they were nonsense, telling her that all boys exaggerated and that anyway she could not be expected to know anything about English schools.

After two years of this purgatory, I got a large and painful boil as a result of the bad food. 'Oh!' said the matron, 'that's nothing, don't make such a fuss!', and lopped off the top of it with a pair of scissors. The ensuing infection was pretty horrible and put me in hospital.

The next term, I was removed and sent to Heatherdown at Ascot.

At this point, I don't believe my mother was actually taking in washing, but, as sure as hell, she was sending very little out, and it must have been a fearful drain on her resources. Heatherdown was far more expensive than Worthing; certainly only a token subscription to the family coffers was being made by Uncle Tommy and she still had her thumb in the dyke of my father's debts, but I was blissfully unconscious of all this and wallowed in my good fortune.

Heatherdown was a very different cup of tea, very carriage-trade, very protected and, compared to Worthing, very soft, very snobbish. Everybody went from there to Eton. Gone were the sadistic masters and the school bullies tying small boys to hot radiators; no more scissor-wielding matrons; no more ex-naval cooks with finger nails like toe nails doling out their nauseous confections; and, receding like a bad dream, were the flinty playground and the evil-smelling doorless lavatories, open to the elements and to the helpful advice of schoolmates.

Instead, I found a world of cleanliness and kindly masters; motherly matrons; green playing fields; a lake; delicious food and a swimming pool. In short . . . schoolboy heaven.

The only grown-ups who hit me were the headmaster who, under great provocation, occasionally uncorked a dose of the cane; and a dear old gentleman who taught divinity, called Mr Hodgson, who sometimes brandished a clothes brush known as 'Dixon and Parker' because if, as rarely happened, he hit someone with it, the name of the maker was left imprinted on the bum.

After the appalling apprenticeship of Worthing, I could not believe that life could be so perfect. Released from fear and oppression, the whole thing went to my head.

Almost nine, I became something of a clown. This was hastened on when, for some strange reason, my balls dropped three years earlier than they should have done.

I was in the choir at the time, the possessor of a voice of guileless purity. Sometimes I was entrusted with solo passages and it was on such an occasion, and in front of a full house, that disaster struck.

Ascot Sunday – parents staying for the race meeting in smart country houses nearby had filled the chapel to capacity. Alone, I was piping my way through 'There is a green hill far away, without a city wall' . . . Suddenly, on the word 'wall' a fearful braying sound issued from the angelic face of the soloist. I tried for the note again: this time it sounded like a Rolls-Royce klaxon of the period. The paper-thin discipline of the choir quickly disintegrated . . . repressed laughter became contagious and finally, general.

Immediately after chapel, I was caned by the headmaster – Sammy Day. He had once played cricket for England and still had one of the best late cuts in the business. It hurt a lot and, considering the medical evidence that was from then on permanently with me, was rather unfair.

Boys are terrible snobs and I was annually unnerved when the school list came out, to see some of my contemporaries sniggering because in between the young marquesses and dukes with their splendid addresses, was –

Niven, D. Rose Cottage, Bembridge, I.W.

It had become necessary for the house in London to be sold and our permanent address was now as advertised – a converted fisherman's cottage which had a reputation for unreliability. When the East wind blew, the front door got stuck and when the West wind blew, the back door could not be opened – only the combined weight of the family seemed to keep it anchored to the ground. I adored it and was happier there than I had ever been, especially because, with a rare flash of genius, my mother decided that during the holidays she would be alone with her children.

Uncle Tommy was barred – I don't know where he went – to the Carlton Club, I suppose.

After the sudden descent of my testicles, I was removed from the choir as a bad risk and became the 'bellows man' and the musical success of each service (we suffered through two a day) depended entirely on my prowess behind the organ. This was a position of great trust, but the newly found clown in me could not resist the opportunities it offered. For a small price – two chocolate whirls, one Cadbury's Milk Flake or a brace of Turkish delights – I could be bribed to let the air out of the bellows on important occasions. The whole school, on the selected day, would be in the know and would sit through an endless sermon hugging itself with delicious anticipation.

It took careful preparation but I could generally arrange matters so that a rude noise could be subtly injected into the proceedings, usually just after an Amen. I could redress the situation rapidly by quick pumping and only the connoisseurs could detect that it was not a mistake . . . the boys were all connoisseurs.

Once I tried it when the Bishop of Ripon was in the middle of a special address. This was my masterpiece and also my downfall but the bribes were mountainous.

It was a highly technical job and involved surreptitiously and noiselessly keeping the bellows half-filled for several minutes after the end of the preceding hymn. I had intended to let this air out in a series of well-spaced small squeaks and trills thus keeping the boys happy during what promised to be a long, trying period, but something went wrong and it all came out at once and on a most unfortunate cue . . . a quotation from Proverbs 7, 'I have perfumed my bed with myrrh, aloes and cinnamon . . .'

It was as if the bellows could not contain themselves any longer – a tremendous fart rent the air. All was confusion.

The school was infiltrated with informers and I was soon dealt with once more by the long-suffering Sammy Day.

I loved Heatherdown and tried hard to uphold the agricultural standards of the landed gentry with whom I was rubbing shoulders.

Every summer on the First Sunday After the Derby (it is not thus described in the Book of Common Prayer but so many boys of noble birth had racehorse owner fathers that at Heatherdown, it far outranked Rogation Sunday, the Sunday after Advent, and the Twenty-first Sunday after Trinity) a prize was given to the boy with the most beautiful garden. Each boy had one about the size of a lavatory mat in a small commercial hotel, but immense ingenuity and forethought were displayed by the owners. Actually, these allotments were status symbols of the worst kind, and boys whose family estates employed an army of gardeners proudly displayed the most exotic flowers and shrubs, delivered for planting hot from the family greenhouses while the more modest smallholders nurtured colourful annuals and arranged them in intricate patterns.

I could only manage a bi-annual crop of mustard and cress.

The year that Humorist won the Derby saw that rare phenomenon, a drought in England, and my crop, carefully timed for the Flower Show, failed, burned to a crisp.

By now the self-appointed jester to the upper classes, I decided to fill the gap, and creeping out of the dormitory after dark, I made my way downstairs and flitting from tree to tree in the moonlight, arrived at a well-known gap in the wall which separated Heatherdown from Heathfield – the girls' school next door.

From preliminary reconnaissance, I knew that this gap opened on to the kitchen garden. I selected a huge vegetable marrow plant, pulled it up by the roots and once safely back on the male side of the wall, hid it behind a piece of corrugated iron.

It took some while and several near heart attacks but I finally made it back to bed. The next morning I retrieved the marrow and in the hubbub caused by the arrival of other boys' parents in Daimlers and Rolls-Royces, managed to plant my prize on my poor piece of desert.

It didn't go down very well. The Countess of Jersey – one of the parents – presented the prizes.

She didn't give one to me and later, I was caned again by a no longer affable Sammy Day: not for making a nonsense of the Flower Show which could have been justified – but for *stealing* which put a totally different connotation on the thing.

After this, I went rapidly downhill from popular school clown to unpopular school nuisance. Striving to maintain my waning reputation, I fell in the lake and nearly drowned, purposely split the seat of my trousers on the school walk through Ascot and was caught trying to get into the Racecourse – a hideous crime. Poor Brian Franks, a Bembridge friend, near death's door with pneumonia at Wixenford, a school nearby, received from me on the day of his 'crisis', a large chocolate box inside which was a smaller box, then a smaller box and so on down the scale to a match box with a piece of dog's mess in it.

Not a funny joke, especially for the Matron who opened it, but then I didn't know Brian was ill.

Brian overcame his illness and my gift and has remained a life-long friend but the Matron took a dim view, the smoke signals went up between Wixenford and Heatherdown and Sammy Day decided that his school could get along without me.

I was ten and a half when I was expelled.

The Provincial Lady In Wartime

E. M. DELAFIELD

September 1st, 1939. – Enquire of Robert whether he does not think that, in view of times in which we live, diary of daily events might be of ultimate historical value to posterity. He replies that It Depends.

Explain that I do not mean events of national importance, which may safely be left to the Press, but only chronicle of ordinary English citizen's reactions to war which now appears inevitable.

Robert's only reply – if reply it can be called – is to enquire whether I am really quite certain that Cook takes a medium size in gas-masks. Personally, he should have thought a large, if not out-size, was indicated. Am forced to realize that Cook's gas-mask is intrinsically of greater importance than problematical contribution to literature by myself, but am all the same slightly aggrieved. Better nature fortunately prevails, and I suggest that Cook had better be asked to clear up the point once and for all. Inclination on the part of Robert to ring the bell has to be checked, and I go instead to kitchen passage door and ask if Cook will please come here for a moment.

She does come, and Robert selects frightful-looking appliances, each with a snout projecting below a little talc window, from pile which has stood in corner of the study for some days.

Cook shows a slight inclination towards coyness when Robert adjusts one on her head with stout crosspiece, and replies from within, when questioned, that It'll do nicely, sir, thank you. (Voice sounds very hollow and sepulchral.)

Robert still dissatisfied and tells me that Cook's nose is in quite the wrong place, and he always thought it would be, and that what she needs is a large size. Cook is accordingly extracted from the medium-size, and emerges looking heated, and much inclined to say that she'd rather make do with this one if it's all the same to us, and get back to her fish-cakes before they're spoilt. This total misapprehension as to the importance of the situation is rather sharply dealt with by Robert, as ARP Organizer for the district, and he again inducts Cook into a gas-mask and this time declares the results to be much more satisfactory.

Cook (evidently thinks Robert most unreasonable) asserts that she's sure it'll do beautifully – this surely very curious adverb to select? – and departs with a look implying that she has been caused to waste a good deal of valuable time.

Cook's gas-mask is put into cardboard box and marked with her name, and a similar provision made for everybody in the house, after which Robert remarks, rather strangely, that *that's* a good job done.

Telephone bell rings, Vicky can be heard rushing to answer it, and shortly afterwards appears, looking delighted, to say that that was Mr Humphrey Holloway, the billeting officer, to say that we may expect three evacuated children and one teacher from East Poplar at eleven o'clock tonight.

Have been expecting this, in a way, for days and days, and am fully prepared to take it with absolute calm, and am therefore not pleased when Vicky adopts an *air capable* and says: It'll be all right, I'm not to throw a fit, she can easily get everything ready. (Dear Vicky in many ways a great comfort, and her position as House prefect at school much to her credit, but cannot agree to be treated as though already in advanced stage of senile decay.)

I answer repressively that she can help me to get the beds made up, and we proceed to top-floor attics, hitherto occupied by Robin, who has now, says Vicky, himself been evacuated to erstwhile spare bedroom.

Make up four beds, already erected by Robin and the gardener in corners, as though about to play Puss-in-the-Corner, and collect as many mats from different parts of the house as can be spared, and at least two that can't. Vicky undertakes to put flowers in each room before nightfall, and informs me that picture of Infant Samuel on the wall is *definitely* old-fashioned and must go. Feel sentimental about this and inclined to be slightly hurt, until she suddenly rather touchingly adds that, as a matter of fact, she thinks she would like to have it in her own room – to which wc accordingly rcmovc it.

Robin returns from mysterious errand to the village, for which he has borrowed the car, looks all round the rooms rather vaguely and says: Everything seems splendid – which I think is overestimating the amenities provided, which consist mainly of very old nursery screen with pictures pasted on it, green rush-bottomed chairs, patchwork quilts and painted white furniture. He removes his trouser-press with an air of deep concern and announces, as he goes, that the evacuated children can read all his books if they want to. Look round at volumes of Aldous Huxley, André Maurois, Neo-Georgian Poets, the *New Yorker* and a number of Greek textbooks, and remove them all.

Inspection of the schoolroom – also to be devoted to evacuated children – follows, and I am informed by Vicky that they may use the rocking-horse, the doll's house and all the toys, but that she has locked the bookcases. Am quite unable to decide whether I should, or should not, attempt interference here.

(Remembrance awakens, quite involuntarily, of outmoded educational methods adopted by Mr Fairchild. But results, on the whole, not what one would wish to see, and dismiss the recollection at once.)

Vicky asks whether she hadn't better tell Cook, Winnie and May about the arrival of what she calls 'The little evacuments', and I say Certainly, and am extremely relieved at not having to do it myself. Call after her that she is to say they will want a hot meal on arrival but that if Cook will leave the things out, I will get it ready myself and nobody is to sit up.

Reply reaches me later to the effect that Cook will be sitting up in *any* case, to listen-in to any announcements that may be on the wireless.

Announcement, actually, is made at six o'clock of general mobilization in England and France.

I say, Well, it's a relief it's come at last, Robin delivers a short speech about the Balkan States and their political significance, which is not, he thinks, sufficiently appreciated by the Government – and Vicky declares that if there's a war, she ought to become a VAD and not go back to school.

Robert says nothing.

Very shortly afterwards he becomes extremely active over the necessity of conforming to the black-out regulations, and tells me that from henceforward no chink of light must be allowed to show from any window whatever.

He then instructs us all to turn on every light in the house and draw all the blinds and curtains while he makes a tour of inspection outside. We all obey in frenzied haste, as though a fleet of enemy aircraft had already been sighted making straight for this house and no other, and then have to wait some fifteen minutes before Robert comes in again and says that practically every curtain in the place will have to be lined with black and that sheets of brown paper must be nailed up over several of the windows. Undertake to do all before nightfall tomorrow, and make a note to get in supply of candles, matches, and at least two electric torches.

Telephone rings again after dinner, and conviction overwhelms me that I am to receive information of world-shaking importance, probably under oath of secrecy. Call turns out to be, once more, from Mr Holloway, to say that evacuees are not expected before midnight. Return to paper-games with Robin and Vicky.

Telephone immediately rings again.

Aunt Blanche, speaking from London, wishes to know if we should care to take her as paying guest for the duration of the war. It isn't, she says frenziedly, that she would *mind* being bombed, or is in the least afraid of anything that Hitler – who is, she feels perfectly certain, simply the Devil in disguise – may do to her, but the friend with whom she shares a flat has joined up as an Ambulance driver and says that she will be doing twenty-four-hour shifts, and sleeping on a camp bed in the Adelphi, and that as the lease of their flat will be up on September 25th, they had better give it up. The friend, to Aunt Blanche's certain knowledge, will never see sixty-five again, and Aunt Blanche has protested strongly against the whole scheme – but to no avail. Pussy – Mrs Winter-Gammon – has bought a pair of slacks and been given an armlet, and may be called up at any moment.

I express whole-hearted condemnation of Mrs Winter-Gammon – whom I have never liked – and put my hand over the mouthpiece of the telephone to hiss at Robert that it's Aunt Blanche, and she wants to come as PG, and Robert looks rather gloomy but finally nods – like Jove – and I tell Aunt Blanche how delighted we shall all be to have her here as long as she likes.

Aunt Blanche thanks us all – sounding tearful – and repeats again that it isn't *air-raids* she minds – not for one minute – and enquires if Robin is nineteen yet – which he won't be for nearly a year. She then gives me quantities of information about relations and acquaintances.

William is an ARP Warden and Angela is acting as his skeleton staff – which Aunt Blanche thinks has a very odd sound. Emma Hay is said to be looking for a job as Organiser, but what she wants to organise is not known. Old Uncle A. has refused to leave London and has offered his services to the War Office, but in view of his age – eighty-two – is afraid that he may not be sent on active service.

She asks what is happening to Caroline Concannon, that nice Rose and poor Cissie Crabbe.

Rose is still in London, I tell her, and will no doubt instantly find Hospital work – Caroline married years ago and went to Kenya and is tiresome about never answering letters – and Cissie Crabbe I haven't seen or heard of for ages.

Very likely not, replies Aunt Blanche in a lugubrious voice, but at a time like this one is bound to recollect old ties. Can only return a respectful assent to this, but do not really see the force of it.

Aunt Blanche then tells me about old Mrs Winter-Gammon all over again, and I make much the same comments as before, and she further reverts to her attitude about air-raids. Perceive that this conversation is likely to go on all night unless steps are taken to check Aunt Blanche decisively, and I therefore tell her that we are expecting a party of evacuees at any moment – (can distinctly hear Vicky exclaiming loudly: Not till midnight – exclamation no doubt equally audible to Aunt Blanche) – and that I *must* ring off.

Of course, of course, cries Aunt Blanche, but she just felt she *had* to have news of all of us, because at a time like this –

Can see nothing for it but to replace receiver sharply, hoping she may think we have been cut off by exchange.

Return to paper-games and am in the midst of searching my mind for famous Admiral whose name begins with D – nothing but Nelson occurs to me – when I perceive that Robin is smoking a pipe.

Am most anxious to let dear Robin develop along his own lines without undue interference, but am inwardly shattered by this unexpected sight, and by rather green tinge all over his face. Do not say anything, but all hope of discovering Admiral whose name begins with D has now left me, as mind definitely – though temporarily, I hope – refuses to function.

Shortly afterwards pipe goes out, but Robin – greener than ever – re-lights it firmly. Vicky says Isn't it marvellous, he got it in the village this afternoon – at which Robin looks at me with rather apologetic smile, and I feel the least I can do is to smile back again. Am rather better after this.

Vicky embarks on prolonged discussion as to desirability or otherwise of her sitting up till twelve to receive little evacuments, when front-door bell peals violently, and everyone except Robert says: Here they are!

Winnie can be heard flying along kitchen passage at quite unprecedented speed, never before noticeable when answering any bell whatever, and almost instantly appears to say that Robert is Wanted, please – which sounds like a warrant for his arrest, or something equally dramatic.

Vicky at once says that it's quite impossible for her to go to bed till she knows what it is.

Robin relights pipe, which has gone out for the seventh time.

Suspense is shortly afterwards relieved when Robert reappears in drawing-room and says that a crack of light is distinctly visible through the pantry window and a special constable has called to say that it must immediately be extinguished.

Vicky asks in awed tones how he knew about it and is told briefly that he was making his rounds, and we are all a good deal impressed by so much promptitude and efficiency. Later on, Robert tells me privately that special constable was only young Leslie Oakford from the Home Farm, and that he has been told not to make so much noise another time. Can see that Robert is in slight state of conflict between patriotic desire to obey all regulations, and private inner conviction that young Leslie is making a nuisance of himself. Am glad to note that patriotism prevails, and pantry light is replaced by sinister-looking blue bulb and heavily draped shade.

Telephone rings once more – Humphrey Holloway thinks, apologetically, that we may like to know that evacuated children now not expected at all, but may be replaced next Monday by three young babies and one mother. Can only say Very well, and ask what has happened. Humphrey Holloway doesn't know. He adds that all is very difficult, and one hundred and forty children evacuated to Bude are said to have arrived at very small, remote moorland village instead. On the other hand, Miss Pankerton – who asked for six boys – has got them, and is reported to be very happy. (Can only hope the six boys are, too.) Lady B. – whose house could very well take in three dozen – has announced that she is turning it into a Convalescent Home for Officers, and can therefore receive no evacuees at all. Am indignant at this, and say so, but H. H. evidently too weary for anything but complete resignation, and simply replies that many of the teachers are more difficult than the children, and that the mothers are the worst of all.

(Mental note here, to the effect that no more unpopular section of the community exists, anywhere, than mothers as a whole.)

Robert, when told that evacuees are *not* coming tonight, says Thank God and we prepare to go upstairs when Vicky makes dramatic appearance in vest and pants and announces that there is No Blind in the WC. Robert points out, shortly and sharply, that no necessity exists for turning on the light at all; Vicky disagrees and is disposed to argue the point, and I beg her to retire to bed instantly.

Impression prevails as of having lived through at least two European wars since morning, but this view certainly exaggerated and will doubtless disperse after sleep.

September 3rd, 1939. – England at war with Germany. Announcement is made by Prime Minister over the radio at eleven-fifteen and is heard by us in village church, where wireless has been placed on the pulpit.

Everyone takes it very quietly and general feeling summed up by old Mrs S. at the Post Office who says to me, after mentioning that her two sons have both been called up: Well, we've got to *show* 'Itler, haven't we? Agree, emphatically, that we have.

September 7th. – Discuss entire situation as it affects ourselves with Robert, the children and Cook.

Robert says: Better shut up the house as we shan't be able to afford to live anywhere, after the war – but is brought round to less drastic views and agrees to shutting up drawing-room and two bedrooms only. He also advocates letting one maid go – which is as well since both have instantly informed me that they feel it their duty to leave and look for war work.

Cook displays unexpectedly sporting spirit, pats me on the shoulder with quite unprecedented familiarity, and assures me that I'm not to worry – she'll see me through, whatever happens. Am extremely touched and inclined to shed tears. Will Cook agree to let Aunt Blanche take over the housekeeping, if Robert is away all day, the children at school, and I am doing war work in London and coming down here one week out of four? (This course indicated by absolute necessity of earning some money if possible, and inability to remain out of touch with current happenings in London.)

Yes, Cook declares stoutly, she will agree to anything and she quite understands how I'm situated. (Hope that some time or other she may make this equally clear to me.) We evolve hurried scheme for establishment of Aunt Blanche, from whom nothing as to date of arrival has as yet been heard, and for weekly Help for the Rough from the village.

Cook also asserts that May can do as she likes, but Winnie is a silly girl who doesn't know what's good for her, and she thinks she can talk her round all right. She *does* talk her round, and Winnie announces a change of mind and says she'll be glad to stay on, please. Should much like to know how Cook accomplished this, but can probably never hope to do so.

Spend most of the day listening to News from the wireless and shutting up the drawing-room and two bedrooms, which involves moving most of the smaller furniture into the middle of the room and draping everything with dust-sheets.

Robin – still dealing with pipe, which goes out oftener than ever – has much to say about enlisting, and Vicky equally urgent – with less foundation – on undesirability of her returning to school. School, however, telegraphs to say that reopening will take place as usual, on appointed date.

September 8th. – Am awakened at 1.10 A.M. by telephone. Imagination, as usual, runs riot and while springing out of bed, into dressing-gown and downstairs, has had ample time to present air-raid, assembly of household in the cellar, incendiary bombs, house in flames and all buried beneath the ruins. Collide with Robert on the landing – he says briefly that It's probably an ARP call and dashes down, and I hear him snatch up receiver.

Reach the telephone myself in time to hear him say Yes, he'll come at once. He'll get out the car. He'll be at the station in twenty minutes' time.

What station?

Robert hangs up the receiver and informs me that that was the station-master. An old lady has arrived from London, the train having taken twelve hours to do the journey – usually accomplished in five – and says that we are expecting her, she sent a telegram. She is, the station-master thinks, a bit upset.

I ask in a dazed way if it's an evacuee, and Robert says No, it's Aunt Blanche, and the telegram must, like the train, have been delayed.

Am torn between compassion for Aunt Blanche – station-master's description almost certainly an understatement – and undoubted dismay at unpropitious hour of her arrival. Can see nothing for it but to assure Robert – untruthfully – that I can Easily Manage, and will have everything ready by the time he's back from station. This is accomplished without awakening household, and make mental note to the effect that air-raid warning itself will probably leave Cook and Winnie quite impervious and serenely wrapped in slumber.

Proceed to make up bed in North Room, recently swathed by my own hands in dust-sheets and now rapidly disinterred, put in hot-water bottle, and make tea and cut bread-and-butter. (*N.B.*: State of kitchen, as to cleanliness and tidiness, gratifying. Larder less good, and why four half-loaves of stale bread standing uncovered on shelf? Also note that cat, Thompson, evidently goes to bed nightly on scullery shelf. Hope that Robert, who to my certain knowledge puts Thompson out every night, will never discover this.)

Have agreeable sense of having dealt promptly and efficiently with war emergency – this leads to speculation as to which Ministerial Department will put me in charge of its workings, and idle vision of taking office as Cabinet Minister and Robert's astonishment at appointment. Memory, for no known reason, at this point recalls the fact that Aunt Blanche will want hot water to wash in and that I have forgotten to provide any. Hasten to repair omission – boiler fire, as I expected, practically extinct and I stoke it up and put on another kettle and fetch can from bathroom. (Brass cans all in need of polish, and enamel ones all chipped. Am discouraged.)

Long wait ensues, and drink tea prepared for Aunt Blanche myself, and put on yet another kettle. Decide that I shall have time to dress, go upstairs, and immediately hear car approaching and dash down again. Car fails to materialize and make second excursion, which results in unpleasant discovery in front of the mirror that my hair is on end and my face pale blue with cold. Do the best I can to repair ravages of the night, though not to much avail, and put on clothes.

On reaching dining-room, find that electric kettle has boiled over and has flooded the carpet. Abandon all idea of Ministerial appointment and devote myself to swabbing up hot water, in the midst of which car returns. Opening of front door reveals that both headlights have turned blue and emit minute ray of pallid light only. This effect achieved by Robert unknown to me, and am much impressed.

Aunt Blanche is in tears, and has brought three suit-cases, one bundle of rugs, a small wooden box, a portable typewriter, a hat-box and a trunk. She is in deep distress and says that she would have spent the night in the station willingly, but the station-master wouldn't let her. Station-master equally adamant at her suggestion of walking to the Hotel – other end of the town – and assured her it was full of the Militia. Further offer from Aunt Blanche of walking about the streets till breakfast-time also repudiated and telephone call accomplished by strong-minded station-master without further attention to her protests.

I tell Aunt Blanche five separate times how glad I am to have her, and that we are not in the least disturbed by nocturnal arrival, and finally lead her into the dining-room where she is restored by tea and bread-and-butter. Journey, she asserts, was terrible – train crowded, but everyone good-tempered – no food, but what can you expect in wartime? – and she hopes I won't think she has brought too much luggage. No, not at all – because she *has* two *large* trunks, but they are waiting at the station.

Take Aunt Blanche to the North Room, on entering which she again cries a good deal but says it is only because I am so kind and I mustn't think her in any way unnerved because that's the last thing she ever is – and get to bed at 3.15.

Hot-water bottle cold as a stone and cannot imagine why I didn't refill it, but not worth going down again. Later on decide that it *is* worth going down again, but don't do so. Remainder of the night passed in similar vacillations.

September 12th. – Aunt Blanche settling down, and national calamity evidently bringing out best in many of us, Cook included, but exception must be made in regard to Lady Boxe, who keeps large ambulance permanently stationed in drive and says that house is to be a Hospital (Officers only) and is therefore not available for evacuees. No officers materialize, but Lady B. reported to have been seen in full Red Cross uniform with snow-white veil floating in the breeze behind her. (Undoubtedly very trying colour next to any but a youthful face; but am not proud of this reflection and keep it to myself.)

Everybody else in neighbourhood has received evacuees, most of whom arrive without a word of warning and prove to be of age and sex diametrically opposite to those expected.

Rectory turns its dining-room into a dormitory and Our Vicar's Wife struggles gallantly with two mothers and three children under five, one of whom is thought to be suffering from fits. Both her maids have declared that they must find war work and immediately departed in search of it. I send Vicky up to see what she can do, and she is proved to be helpful, practical, and able to keep a firm hand over the under-fives.

Am full of admiration for Our Vicar's Wife and very sorry for her, but feel she is at least better off than Lady Frobisher, who rings up to ask me if I know how one gets rid of *lice*? Refer her to the chemist, who tells me later that if he has been asked that question once in the last week, he's been asked it twenty times.

Elderly neighbours, Major and Mrs Bergery, recent arrivals at small house in the village, are given two evacuated teachers and appear in consequence to be deeply depressed. The teachers sit about and drink cups of tea and assert that the organization at the *London* end was wonderful, but at *this* end there isn't any organization at all. Moreover, they are here to teach – which they do for about four hours in the day – but not for anything else. Mrs Bergery suggests that they should collect all the evacuated children in the village and play with them, but this not well received.

Our Vicar, appealed to by the Major, calls on the teachers and effects a slight improvement. They offer, although without much enthusiasm, to organize an hour of Recreative Education five days a week. He supposes, says Our Vicar, that this means play, and closes with the suggestion at once.

Light relief is afforded by Miss Pankerton, who is, we all agree, having the time of her life. Miss P. – who has, for no known reason, sprung into long blue trousers and leather jerkin – strides about the village marshalling six pallid and wizened little boys from Bethnal Green in front of her. Extraordinary legend is current that she has taught them to sing 'Under a spreading chestnut-tree, the village smithy stands', and that they roar it in chorus with great docility in her presence, but have a version of their own which she has accidentally overheard from the bathroom and that this runs:

Under a spreading chestnut-tree
Stands the bloody ARP
So says the – ing BBC

Aunt Blanche, in telling me this, adds that: 'It's really wonderful, considering the eldest is only seven years old.' Surely a comment of rather singular leniency?

Our own evacuees make extraordinarily brief appearance, coming – as usual – on day and at hour when least expected, and consisting of menacing-looking woman with twins of three and baby said to be eighteen months old but looking more like ten weeks. Mother comes into the open from the very beginning, saying that she doesn't fancy the country, and it will upset the children, and none of it is what she's accustomed to. Do my best for them with cups of tea, cakes, toys for the children and flowers in bedroom. Only the cups of tea afford even moderate satisfaction, and mother leaves the house at dawn next day to find Humphrey Holloway and inform him that he is to telegraph to Dad to come and fetch them away immediately – which he does twenty-four hours later. Feel much cast-down, and apologize to H. H., who informs me in reply that evacuees from all parts of the country are hastening back to danger zone as rapidly as possible, as being infinitely preferable to rural hospitality. Where this *isn't* happening, adds Humphrey in tones of deepest gloom, it is the country hostesses who are proving inadequate and clamouring for the removal of their guests.

Cannot believe this to be an accurate summary of the situation, and feel that Humphrey is unduly pessimistic owing to overwork as Billeting Officer. He admits this may be so, and further says that, now he comes to think of it, some of the families in village are quite pleased with the London children. Adds – as usual – that the *real* difficulty is the mothers.

Are we, I ask, to have other evacuees in place of departed failures? Try to sound as though I hope we are – but am only too well aware that effort is poor and could convince nobody. H. H. says that he will see what he can do, which I think equal, as a reply, to anything ever perpetrated by Roman oracle.

September 13th. – Question of evacuees solved by Aunt Blanche, who proposes that we should receive two children of Coventry clergyman and his wife, personally known to her, and their nurse. Children are charming, says Aunt Blanche – girls aged six and four – and nurse young Irishwoman about whom she knows nothing but that she is *not* a Romanist and is called Doreen Fitzgerald. Send cordial invitation to all three.

September 17th. – Installation of Doreen Fitzgerald, Marigold and Margery. Children pretty and apparently good. D. Fitzgerald has bright red hair but plain face and to all suggestions simply replies: Certainly I shall.

House and bedrooms once more reorganized, schoolroom temporarily reverts to being a nursery again – am inwardly delighted by this but refrain from saying so – and D. Fitzgerald, asked if she will look after rooms herself, again repeats: Certainly I shall. Effect of this is one of slight patronage, combined with willing spirit.

Weather continues lovely, garden all Michaelmas daisies, dahlias and nasturtiums – autumn roses a failure, but cannot expect everything – and Aunt Blanche and I walk about under the apple-trees and round the tennis-court and ask one another who could ever believe that England is at war? Answer is, alas, only too evident – but neither of us makes it aloud.

Petrol rationing, which was to have started yesterday, postponed for a week. (*Query*: Is this an ingenious device for giving the whole country agreeable surprise, thereby improving public morale?) Robin and Vicky immediately point out that it is Vicky's last day at home, and ask if they couldn't go to a film and have tea at the café? Agree to this at once and am much moved by their delighted expressions of gratitude.

Long talk with Aunt Blanche occupies most of the afternoon. She has much to say about Pussy – old Mrs Winter-Gammon. Pussy, declares Aunt Blanche, has behaved neither wisely, considerately nor even with common decency. She may look many years younger than her age, but sixty-six is sixty-six and is *not* the proper time of life for driving a heavy ambulance. Pussy might easily be a grandmother. She *isn't* a grandmother, as it happens, because Providence has – wisely, thinks Aunt Blanche – withheld from her the blessing of children, but so far as age goes, she could very well be a grandmother ten times over.

Where, I enquire, are Mrs Winter-Gammon and the ambulance in action?

Nowhere, cries Aunt Blanche. Mrs W.-G. has pranced off in this irresponsible way to an ARP Station in the Adelphi – extraordinary place, all underground, somewhere underneath the Savoy – and so far has done nothing whatever except Stand By with crowds and crowds of others. She is on a twenty-four-hour shift and supposed to sleep on a camp-bed in a Women's Restroom without any ventilation whatever in a pandemonium of noise. Suggest that if this goes on long enough old Mrs W.-G. will almost certainly become a nervous wreck before very long and be sent home incapacitated.

Aunt Blanche answers, rather curtly, that I don't know Pussy and that in any case the flat has now been given up and she herself has no intention of resuming life with Pussy. She has had more to put up with than people realize and it has now come to the parting of the ways. Opening here afforded leads me to discussion of plans with Aunt Blanche. Can she, and will she, remain on here in charge of household if I go to London and take up a job, preferably in the nature of speaking or writing, so that I can return home for, say, one week in every four? Cook – really pivot on whom the whole thing turns – has already expressed approval of the scheme.

Aunt Blanche – usually perhaps inclined to err on the side of indecisiveness – rises to the occasion magnificently and declares firmly that Of Course she will. She adds, in apt imitation of D. Fitzgerald, Certainly I shall – and we both laugh. Am startled beyond measure when she adds that it doesn't seem *right* that my abilities should be wasted down here, when they might be made use of in wider spheres by the Government. Can only hope that Government will take view similar to Aunt Blanche's.

Practical discussion follows, and I explain that dear Rose has asked me on a postcard, days ago, if I know anyone who might take over tiny two-roomed furnished flat in Buckingham Street, Strand, belonging to unknown cousin of her own, gone with RNVR to East Africa. Have informed her, by telephone, that I might consider doing so myself, and will make definite pronouncement shortly.

Go! says Aunt Blanche dramatically. This is no time for making two bites at a cherry, and she herself will remain at the helm here and regard the welfare of Robert and the evacuated children as her form of national service. It seems to her more suited to the elderly, she adds rather caustically, than jumping into a pair of trousers and muddling about in an ambulance.

Think better to ignore this reference and content myself with thanking Aunt Blanche warmly. Suggest writing to Rose at once, securing flat, but Aunt Blanche boldly advocates a trunk call and says that this is a case of Vital Importance and in no way contrary to the spirit of national economy or Government's request to refrain from unnecessary telephoning.

Hours later, Aunt Blanche startles Marigold, Margery and myself – engaged in peacefully playing game of Happy Families – by emitting a scream and asking: Did I say *Buckingham* Street?

Yes, I did.

Then, I shall be positively next door to Adelphi, underworld, ARP Station, ambulance and Pussy. Within one minute's walk. But, what is far more important, I shall be able to see there delightful young friend, also standing by, to whom Aunt Blanche is devoted and of whom I must have heard her speak. Serena Thingamy.

Acknowledge Serena Thingamy – have never been told surname – but attention distracted by infant Margery who has remained glued to Happy Families throughout and now asks with brassy determination for Master Bones the Butcher's Son. Produce Master Potts by mistake, am rebuked gravely by Margery and screamed at by Marigold, and at the same time informed by Aunt Blanche that she can never remember the girl's name but I *must* know whom she means – dear little Serena Fiddlededee. Agree that I do, promise to go down into the underworld in search of her, and give full attention to collecting remaining unit of Mr Bun the Baker's family.

Robin and Vicky come back after dark – I have several times visualized fearful car smash, and even gone so far as to compose inscription on tombstone – and declare that driving without any lights is absolutely *marvellous* and that film – *Beau Geste* – was super.

September 18th. – Departure of Vicky in the company of athletic-looking science mistress who meets her at Exeter station. Robin and I see them off, with customary sense of desolation, and console ourselves with cocoa and buns in the town. Robin then says he will meet me later, as he wishes to make enquiries about being placed on the Reserve of the Devon Regiment.

Am torn between pride, tenderness, incredulity and horror, but can only acquiesce.

September 20th. – Robin informed by military authorities that he is to return to school for the present.

September 21st. – Am struck, not for the first time, by extraordinary way in which final arrangements never *are* final, but continue to lead on to still further activities until parallel with eternity suggests itself, and brain in danger of reeling.

Spend much time in consulting lists with which writing-desk is littered and trying to decipher mysterious abbreviations such as Sp. W. about T-cloths and Wind cl. in s. room, and give Aunt Blanche many directions as to care of evacuees and Robert's taste in breakfast dishes. No cereal on any account, and eggs not to be poached more than twice a week. Evacuees, on the other hand, require cereals every day and are said by Doreen Fitzgerald not to like bacon. Just as well, replies Aunt Blanche, as this is shortly to be rationed. This takes me into conversational byway concerning food shortage in Berlin, and our pity for the German people with whom, Aunt Blanche and I declare, we have no quarrel whatever, and who must on no account be identified with Nazi Party, let alone with Nazi Government. The whole thing, says Aunt Blanche, will be brought to an end by German revolution. I entirely agree, but ask when, to which she replies with a long story about Hitler's astrologer. Hitler's astrologer – a woman – has predicted every event in his career with astounding accuracy, and the Führer has consulted her regularly. Recently, however, she has – with some lack of discretion – informed him that his downfall, if not his assassination, is now a matter of months, and as a result, astrology has been forbidden in Germany. The astrologer is said to have disappeared.

Express suitable sentiments in return, and turn on wireless for the Four O'clock News. Am, I hope, duly appreciative of BBC Home Service, but struck by something a little unnatural in almost total omission of any reference in their bulletins to any reverses presumably suffered by the Allies. Ministry of Information probably responsible for this, and cannot help wondering what its functions *really* are. Shall perhaps discover this if proffered services, recently placed at Ministry's disposal by myself, should be accepted.

Say as much to Aunt Blanche, who replies – a little extravagantly – that she only wishes they would put me in charge of the whole thing. Am quite unable to echo this aspiration and in any case am aware that it will not be realized.

Pay parting call on Our Vicar's Wife, and find her very pale but full of determination and not to be daunted by the fact that she has no maids at all. Members of the Women's Institute have, she says, come to the rescue and several of them taking it in turns to come up and Give a Hand in the Mornings, which is, we agree, what is really needed everywhere. They have also formed a Mending Pool – which is, Our Vicar's Wife says, wartime expression denoting ordinary old-fashioned working-party.

Doubt has been cast on the possibility of continuing WI Monthly Meetings but this dispersed by announcement, said to have come from the Lord Privy Seal, no less, that they are to be continued. Mrs F. from the mill – our secretary – has undertaken to inform all members that the Lord Privy Seal says that we are to go on with our meetings just the same and so it will be all right.

Enquire after Rectory evacuees – can see two of them chasing the cat in garden – and Our Vicar's Wife says Oh, well, there they are, poor little things, and one mother has written to her husband to come and fetch her and the child away but he hasn't done so, for which Our Vicar's Wife doesn't blame him – and the other mother seems to be settling down and has offered to do the washing-up. The child who had fits is very well-behaved and the other two will, suggests Our Vicar's Wife optimistically, come into line presently. She then tells me how they went out and picked up fir-cones and were unfortunately inspired to throw them down lavatory pan to see if they floated, with subsequent jamming of the drain.

Still, everything is all right and both she and Our Vicar quite feel that nothing at all matters except total destruction of Hitlerism. Applaud her heartily and offer to try to find maid in London and send her down. Meanwhile, has she tried Labour Exchange? She has, but results not good. Only one candidate available for interview, who said that she had hitherto looked after dogs. Particularly sick dogs, with mange. Further enquiries as to her ability to cook only elicited information that she used to cook for the dogs – and Our Vicar's Wife compelled to dismiss application as unsuitable.

Conversation is interrupted by fearful outburst of screams from infant evacuees in garden between whom mysterious feud has suddenly leapt into being, impelling them to fly at one another's throats. Our Vicar's Wife taps on window-pane sharply – to no effect whatever – but assures me that It's Always Happening, and they'll settle down presently, and the mothers will be sure to come out and separate them in a minute.

One of them does so, slaps both combatants heartily, and then leads them, bellowing, indoors.

Can see that Our Vicar's Wife – usually so ready with enlightened theories on upbringing of children, of whom she has none of her own – is so worn-out as to let anybody do anything, and am heartily sorry for her.

Tell her so – she smiles wanly, but repeats that she will put up with anything so long as Hitler *goes* – and we part affectionately.

Meet several people in the village, and exchange comments on such topics as food-rationing, possible shortage of sugar, and inability ever to go anywhere on proposed petrol allowance. Extraordinary and characteristically English tendency on the part of everybody to go into fits of laughter and say Well, we're all in the same boat, aren't we, and we've got to *show* 'Itler he can't go on like that, haven't we?

Agree that we have, and that we will.

On reaching home Winnie informs me that Mr Humphrey Holloway is in the drawing-room and wishes to speak to me. Tell her to bring in an extra cup for tea and ask Cook for some chocolate biscuits.

Find H. H. – middle-aged bachelor who has recently bought small bungalow on the Common – exchanging views about Stalin with Aunt Blanche. Neither thinks well of him. Ask Aunt Blanche if she has heard the Four O'clock News – Yes, she has, and there was nothing. Nothing turns out to be that Hitler, speaking yesterday in Danzig, has declared that Great Britain is responsible for the war, and that Mr Chamberlain, speaking today in Parliament, has reaffirmed British determination to redeem Europe from perpetual fear of Nazi aggression. Thank Heaven for that, says Aunt Blanche piously, we've got to fight it out to a finish now, and would Mr Holloway very kindly pass her the brown bread-and-butter.

It turns out that H. H. has heard I am going up to London tomorrow and would I care to go up with him in his car, as he wishes to offer his services to the Government, but has been three times rejected for the Army owing to myopia and hayfever. The roads, he asserts, will very likely be blocked with military transport, especially in Salisbury neighbourhood, but he proposes – if I agree – to start at seven o'clock in the morning.

Accept gratefully, and enquire in general terms how local evacuees are getting on? Better, returns H. H. guardedly, than in some parts of the country, from all he hears. Recent warning broadcast from BBC regarding probability of London children gathering and eating deadly nightshade from the hedges, though doubtless well-intended, has had disastrous effect on numerous London parents, who have hurriedly reclaimed their offspring from this perilous possibility.

Point out that real deadly nightshade is exceedingly rare in any hedge, but Aunt Blanche says compassionately that probably the BBC doesn't know this, error on the subject being extremely common. Am rather taken aback at this attitude towards the BBC and can see that H. H. is too, but Aunt Blanche quite unmoved and merely asks whether the blackberry jelly is homemade. Adds that she will willingly help to make more if Marigold, Margery and Doreen Fitzgerald will pick the blackberries.

Accept this gratefully and hope it is not unpatriotic to couple it with a plea that Aunt Blanche will neither make, nor allow Cook to make, any marrow jam – as can perfectly remember its extreme and universal unpopularity in 1916, '17 and '18.

Robin, due to return to school tomorrow, comes in late and embarks on discussion with H. H. concerning probability or otherwise of repeal of the arms embargo in the USA. This becomes so absorbing that when H. H. takes his leave, Robin offers to accompany him in order to continue it, and does so.

Aunt Blanche says that Robin is a very dear boy and it seems only yesterday that he was running about in his little yellow smock and look at him now! My own thoughts have been following very similar lines, but quite realize that morale – so important to us all at present juncture – will be impaired if I dwell upon them for even two minutes. Suggest instead that Children's Hour now considerably overdue, and we might play Ludo with little evacuees, to which Aunt Blanche at once assents, but adds that she can play just as well while going on with her knitting.

Towards seven o'clock Robert returns from ARP office – large, ice-cold room kindly lent by Guild of Congregational Ladies – is informed of suggestion that H. H. should motor me to London, to which he replies with a reminder that I must take my gas-mask, and, after a long silence, tells me that he has a new helper in the office who is driving him mad. She is, he tells me in reply to urgent questioning, a Mrs Wimbush, and she has a swivel eye.

As Robert adds nothing to this, feel constrained to ask What Else?

Elicit by degrees that Mrs Wimbush is giving her services voluntarily, that she types quickly and accurately, is thoroughly efficient, never makes a mistake, arrives with the utmost punctuality, and always knows where to find everything.

Nevertheless, Robert finds her intolerable.

Am very sorry for him and say that I can quite understand it – which I can – and refer to Dr Fell. Evening spent in remembering quantities of things that I meant to tell Cook, Winnie, Aunt Blanche and the gardener about proper conduct of the house in my absence.

Also write long letter to mother of Marigold and Margery, begging her to come down and see them when she can, and assuring her of the well-being of both. (Just as I finish this, Robin informs me that Marigold was sick in the bathroom after her supper, but decide not to reopen letter on that account.) Make all farewells overnight and assert that I shall leave the house noiselessly without disturbing anyone at dawn.

September 22nd. – Ideal of noiseless departure not wholly realized (never really thought it would be); as Robert appears in dressing-gown and pyjamas to carry my suit-case downstairs for me, Cook, from behind partially closed kitchen-passage door, thrusts a cup of tea into my hand, and dog Benjy, evidently under impression that I am about to take him for an early walk, capers joyfully round and round, barking.

Moreover, Humphrey Holloway, on stroke of seven precisely, drives up to hall door by no means inaudibly.

Say goodbye to Robert – promise to let him hear the minute I know about my job – snatch up gas-mask in horrible little cardboard container, and go. Have extraordinarily strong premonition that I shall never see home again. (Have often had this before.) Humphrey H. and I exchange good-mornings, he asks, in reference to my luggage, if that is All, and we drive away.

Incredibly lovely September morning, with white mists curling above the meadows and cobwebs glittering in the hedges, and am reminded of Pip's departure from the village early in the morning in *Great Expectations*. Ask H. H. if he knows it and he says Yes, quite well – but adds that he doesn't remember a word of it. Subject is allowed to drop. Roads are empty, car flies along and we reach Mere at hour which admits of breakfast and purchase of newspapers. Am, as usual, unable to resist remarkable little column entitled *Inside Information* in *Daily Sketch*, which has hitherto proved uncannily correct in every forecast made. Should much like to know how this is achieved.

Likewise buy and read *The Times*, excellent in its own way but, as H. H. and I agree, quite a different cup of tea. Resume car again and drive off with equal speed. H. H. makes no idle conversation, which is all to the good, and am forced to the conclusion that men, in this respect, far better than women. When he eventually breaks silence, it is to suggest that we should drive round by Stonehenge and have a look at it. The sight of Stonehenge, thinks H. H., will help us to realize the insignificance of our own troubles.

Am delighted to look at Stonehenge and theoretically believe H. H. to be right, but am practically certain, from past experience, that neither Stonehenge nor any other monument, however large and ancient, will really cause actual present difficulties to vanish into instant nothingness. (*Note*: Theory one thing, real life quite another. Do not say anything of this aloud.)

Overtake the military, soon afterwards, sitting in heaps on large Army lorries and all looking very youthful. They wave, and laugh, and sing 'We'll Hang Out the Washing on the Siegfried Line' and 'South of the Border'.

Wave back again, and am dreadfully reminded of 1914. In order to dispel this, owing to importance of keeping morale in good repair, talk to Humphrey H. about – as usual – evacuees, and we exchange anecdotes.

H. H. tells me of rich woman who is reported to have said that the secret of the whole thing is to Keep the Classes Separate and that High School children must never, on any account, be asked to sit down to meals with Secondary School children. Am appalled and agree heartily with his assertion that if we get a Bolshevik régime over here, it will be no more than some of us deserve.

I then tell H. H. about builder in South Wales who received three London school children and complained that two cried every night and the third was a young tough who knocked everything about, and all must be removed or his wife would have immediate nervous breakdown. Weeping infants accordingly handed over to elderly widow, and tough sent off in deep disgrace to share billet of teacher. Two days later – it may have been more, but two days sounds well – widow appears before billeting officer, with all three evacuees, and declares her intention of keeping the lot. The tough, in tears, is behind her pushing juniors in a little go-cart. No further complaints heard from either side.

H. H. seems touched, and says with great emphasis that that's exactly what he means. (This passes muster at the time, but on thinking it over, can see no real justification for the assertion.)

Interchange of stories interrupted by roarings overhead, and I look up with some horror at wingless machine, flying low and presenting appearance as of giant species of unwholesome-looking insect. H. H. – association of ideas quite unmistakable – abruptly observes that he hopes I have remembered to bring my gas-mask. Everyone up here, he asserts, will be wearing them.

Does he mean *wearing* them, I ask, or only just wearing them?

He means just wearing them, slung over one shoulder. Sure enough shortly afterwards pass group of school children picking blackberries in the hedges, each one with little square box – looking exactly like picnic lunch – hanging down behind.

After this, gas-masks absolutely universal and perceive that my own cardboard container, slung on string, is quite *démodé* and must be supplied with more decorative case. Great variety of colour and material evidently obtainable, from white waterproof to gay red and blue checks.

Traffic still very scarce, even when proceeding up Putney Hill, and H. H. says he's never seen anything like it and won't mind driving into London at all, although he usually stops just outside, but this is all as simple as possible.

Very soon afterwards he dashes briskly down one-way street and is turned back by the police into Trafalgar Square, round which we drive three times before H. H. gets into right line of traffic for the Strand. He also makes abortive effort to shoot direct down Buckingham Street – likewise one-way – but am able to head him off in time.

Strand has very little traffic, but men along edges of pavement are energetically hawking gas-mask cases, and also small and inferior-looking document, evidently of facetious nature, purporting to be Last Will and Testament of Adolf Hitler.

Am reminded of cheap and vulgar conundrum, brought home by Robin, as to What Hitler said when he fell through the bed. Reply is: At last I'm in Poland. Dismiss immediately passing fancy of repeating this to Humphrey Holloway, and instead make him civil speech of gratitude for having brought me to my door. In return he extracts my suit-case and gas-mask, from car, declares that it has been a pleasure, and drives off.

September 23rd. – Installed in Buckingham Street top-floor flat, very nicely furnished and Rose's cousin's taste in pictures – reproductions of Frith's Derby Day, Ramsgate Sands and Paddington Station – delight me and provide ideal escape from present-day surroundings. Foresee that much time will be spent sitting at writing-table looking at them, instead of writing. (*Query*: Should this be viewed as sheer waste of time, or reasonable relaxation? *Answer*: Reminiscent of Robert – can only be that It Depends.)

This thought takes me straight to telephone, so as to put through trunk call home. Operator tells me austerely that full fee of half a crown will be charged for three minutes, and I cancel call. Ring up Rose instead, at cost of twopence only, and arrange to meet her for lunch on Wednesday.

Is she, I enquire, very busy?

No, not at present. But she is Standing By.

Gather from tone in which she says this that it will be useless to ask if she can think of anything for me to do, so ring off.

Ministry of Information will no doubt be in better position to suggest employment.

Meanwhile, am under oath to Aunt Blanche to go down to Adelphi underworld and look up Serena Fiddlededee, and also – has said Aunt Blanche – let her know if Pussy Winter-Gammon has come to her senses yet. Just as I am departing on this errand, occupier of ground-floor offices emerges and informs me that he is owner of the house, and has never really approved of the subletting of top flat. Still, there it is, it's done now. But he thinks it right that I should be in possession of following facts:

This house is three hundred years old and will burn like tinder if – am not sure he didn't say *when* – incendiary bomb falls on the roof.

It is well within official danger zone.

The basement is quite as unsafe as the rest of the house.

The stairs are extremely steep, narrow and winding, and anyone running down them in a hurry in the night would have to do so in pitch darkness and would almost certainly end up with a broken neck at the bottom.

If I choose to sleep in the house, I shall be quite alone there. (Can well understand this, after all he has been saying about its disadvantages.)

Rather more hopeful note is struck when he continues to the effect that there *is* an air-raid shelter within two minutes' walk, and it will accommodate a hundred and fifty people.

I undertake to make myself instantly familiar with its whereabouts, and to go there without fail in the event of an air-raid alarm.

Conversation concludes with the owner's assurance that whatever I do is done on my own responsibility, in which I acquiesce, and my departure into Buckingham Street.

Spirits rather dashed until I glance up and see entire sky peppered with huge silver balloons, which look lovely. Cannot imagine why they have never been thought of before and used for purely decorative purposes.

Find entrance to Adelphi underground organization strongly guarded by two pallid-looking ARP officials to whom I show pass, furnished by Aunt Blanche, *via* – presumably – Miss Serena Fiddledede. Perceive that I am getting into the habit of thinking of her by this name and must take firm hold of myself if I am not to make use of it when we meet face to face.

Descend lower and lower down concrete-paved slope – classical parallel here with Proserpina's excursion into Kingdom of Pluto – and emerge under huge vaults full of ambulances ranged in rows, with large cars sandwiched between.

Trousered women are standing and walking about in every direction, and great number of men with armlets. Irrelevant reflection here to the effect that this preponderance of masculine society, so invaluable at any social gathering, is never to be seen on ordinary occasions.

Rather disquieting notice written in red chalk on matchboard partitions, indicates directions to be taken by Decontaminated Women, Walking Cases, Stretcher-bearers and others – but am presently relieved by perceiving arrow with inscription: To No. 1 Canteen – where I accordingly proceed. Canteen is large room, insufficiently lit, with several long tables, a counter with urns and plates, kitchen behind, and at least one hundred and fifty people standing and sitting about, all looking exactly like the people already seen outside.

Wireless is blaring out rather inferior witticisms, gramophone emitting raucous rendering of 'We'll Hang Out the Washing on the Siegfried Line' and very vocal game of darts proceeding merrily. Am temporarily stunned, but understand that everybody is only Standing By. Now I come to think of it, am doing so myself.

Atmosphere thick with cigarette smoke and no apparent ventilation anywhere. Noise indescribable. Remember with some horror that Aunt Blanche said everybody was doing twenty-four-hour shifts and sleeping on camp-beds on the premises. Am deeply impressed by this devotion to duty and ask myself if I could possibly do as much. Answer probably No.

Very pretty girl with dark curls – in slacks, like everybody else – screams into my ear, in order to make herself heard: Am I looking for anyone? Should like to ask for Serena, whom I have always thought charming, but impossible to shriek back: Have you anybody here called

Serena Fiddlededee? – name still a complete blank. Am consequently obliged to enquire for my only other acquaintance in the underworld, old Mrs Winter-Gammon – not charming at all.

Very pretty girl giggles and says Oh, do I mean Granny Bo-Peep? which immediately strikes me as most brilliant nickname ever invented and entirely suited to Mrs Winter-Gammon. She is at once pointed out, buying Gold Flake cigarettes at Canteen counter, and I look at her with considerable disfavour. Cannot possibly be less than sixty-six, but has put herself into diminutive pair of blue trousers, short-sleeved wool jumper, and wears her hair, which is snow-white, in roguish mop of curls bolt upright all over her head. Old Mrs W.-G. stands about five foot high, and is very slim and active, and now chatting away merrily to about a dozen ambulance men.

Pretty girl informs me very gloomily that Granny Bo-Peep is the Sunbeam of the Adelphi.

Am filled with horror and say that I made a mistake, I don't really want to see her after all. Mrs W.-G. has, however, seen me and withdrawal becomes impossible. She positively dances up to me, and carols out her astonishment and delight at my presence. Am disgusted at hearing myself replying with cordiality amounting to enthusiasm.

She enquires affectionately after Aunt Blanche, and I say that she sent her love – cannot be *absolutely* certain that she didn't really say something of the kind – and Mrs W.-G. smiles indulgently and says Poor dear old Blanche, she'll be better and happier out of it all in the country, and offers to show me round.

We proceed to inspect ambulances – ready day and night – motor cars, all numbered and marked Stretcher Parties – Red Cross Station – fully equipped and seems thoroughly well organized, which is more than can be said for Women's Rest-room, packed with uncomfortable-looking little camp-beds of varying designs, tin helmets slung on hooks round matchboarded walls, two upright wooden chairs and large printed sheet giving Instructions in the event of an Air-raid Warning. Several women – still in trousers and jumpers – huddle exhaustedly on the camp-beds, and atmosphere blue with cigarette smoke.

Noise is, if possible, greater in Rest-room than anywhere else in the building as it is situated between Canteen and ambulance station, where every now and then all engines are started up and run for five minutes. Canteen wireless and gramophone both clearly audible, also rather amateurish rendering of 'South of the Border' on unlocated, but not distant, piano.

Screech out enquiry as to whether anyone can ever manage to sleep in here, and Mrs W.-G. replies Yes, indeed, it is a comfort to have Winston in the Cabinet. This takes me outside the door, and am able to repeat enquiry which is, this time, audible.

Mrs. W.-G. – very sunny – assures me that the young ones sleep through everything. As for old campaigners like herself, what does it matter? She went through the last war practically side by side with Our Boys behind the lines, as near to the trenches as she could get. Lord Kitchener on more than one occasion said to her: Mrs Winter-Gammon, if only the regulations allowed me to do so, *you* are the person whom I should recommend for the Victoria Cross. That, of course, says Mrs W.-G. modestly, was nonsense – (should think so indeed) – but Lord K. had ridiculous weakness for her. Personally, she never could understand what people meant by calling him a woman-hater. Still, there it was. She supposes that she *was* rather a privileged person in the war.

Have strong inclination to ask if she means the Crimean War, but enquire instead what work she is engaged on here and now. Well, at the moment, she is Standing By, affirms Mrs W.-G. lighting cigarette and sticking it into one corner of her mouth at rakish angle. She will, when the emergency arises, drive a car. She had originally volunteered to drive an ambulance but proved – hee-hee-hee – to be too tiny. Her feet wouldn't reach the pedals and her hands wouldn't turn the wheel.

Am obliged, on Mrs W.-G.'s displayal of what look to me like four particularly frail claws, to admit the justice of this.

She adds that, in the meantime, she doesn't mind what she does. She just gives a hand here, there and everywhere, and tries to jolly everybody along. People sometimes say to her that she will destroy herself, she gives out so much all the time – but to this her only reply is: What does it matter if she does? Why, just nothing at all!

Am wholly in agreement, and much inclined to say so. Ruffianly-looking man in red singlet, khaki shorts and armlet goes by and Mrs W.-G. calls out merrily: Hoo-hoo! to which he makes no reply whatever, and she tells me that he is one of the demolition squad and a dear boy, a very special friend of hers, and she loves pulling his leg.

Am unsympathetically silent, but old Mrs W.-G. at once heaps coals of fire on my head by offering me coffee and a cigarette from the Canteen, and we sit down at comparatively empty table to strains of 'The Siegfried Line' from gramophone and 'In the Shadows' from the wireless. Coffee is unexpectedly good and serves to support me through merry chatter of Granny Bo-Peep, who has more to say of her own war service, past and present.

Coma comes on, partly due to airless and smoke-laden atmosphere, partly to mental exhaustion, and am by no means clear whether Mrs W.-G.'s reminiscences are not now taking us back to Peninsular War or possibly even Wars of the Roses.

Am sharply roused by series of shrill blasts from powerful whistle: Mrs W.-G. leaps up like a (small) chamois and says, It's a mock Air-raid alarm, only for practice – I'm not to be frightened – which I wasn't, and shouldn't dream of being, and anyhow shouldn't show it if I was – and she must be off to her post. She then scampers away, tossing her curls as she goes, darts out at one door and darts in again at another – curls now extinguished under tin-hat – pulling on leather jacket as she runs. Quantities of other people all do the same, though with less celerity.

Can hear engines, presumably of ambulances, being started and temporarily displacing gramophone and wireless.

Spirited game of darts going on in one corner amongst group already pointed out to me by old Mrs W.-G. as those dear, jolly boys of the Demolition Squad, comes to an abrupt end, and only Canteen workers remain, conversing earnestly behind plates of buns, bananas and chocolate biscuits. Can plainly hear one of them telling another that practically every organization in London is turning voluntary workers away by the hundred, as there is nothing for them to do. *At present*, she adds darkly. Friend returns that it is the same story all over the country. Land Army alone has had to choke off several thousand applicants – and as for civil aviation –

Before I can learn what is happening about civil aviation – but am prepared to bet that it's being told to Stand By – I am accosted by Aunt Blanche's friend, Serena Fiddlededee. She is young and rather pretty, with enormous round eyes, and looks as if she might – at outside estimate – weigh seven and a half stone. Trousers brown, which is a relief after so much navy blue, jumper scarlet and leather jacket orange. General effect gay and decorative. Quite idle fancy flits through my mind of adopting similar attire and achieving similar result whilst at the selfsame moment the voice of common sense informs me that a considerable number of years separates me from Serena and the wearing of bright colours alike. (Opening here for interesting speculation: Do not all women think of themselves as still looking exactly as they did at twenty-five, whilst perfectly aware that as many years again have passed over their heads?)

Serena astonishes me by expressing delight at seeing me, and asks eagerly if I have come to join up. Can only say that I have and I haven't. Am more than anxious to take up work for King and Country but admit that, so far, every attempt to do so has been met with discouragement.

Serena says Yes, yes – she knows it's like that – and she herself wouldn't be here now if she hadn't dashed round to the Commandant two days before war was declared at all and offered to scrub all the floors with disinfectant. After that, they said she might drive one of the cars.

And has she?

Serena sighs, and rolls her enormous eyes, and admits that she was once sent to fetch the Commandant's laundry from Streatham. All the other drivers were most fearfully jealous, because none of *them* have done anything at all except Stand By.

I enquire why Serena isn't taking part in the mock air-raid, and she says negligently that she's off duty just now but hasn't yet summoned up energy to go all the way to Belsize Park where she inconveniently lives. She adds that she is rather sorry, in a way, to miss the test, because the last one they had was quite exciting. A girl called Moffat or Muffet was the first driver in the line and had, Serena thinks, only just passed her 'L' test and God alone knows how she'd done that. And instead of driving up the ramp, round the corner and out into the Adelphi, she'd shot straight forward, missed the Commandant by millimetres, knocked down part of the structure of Gentlemen and reversed onto the bumpers of the car behind. You could, avers Serena, absolutely *see* the battle-bowlers rising from the heads of the four stretcher-bearers inside the car. Moffat or Muffet, shortly after this dramatic performance, was sacked.

Serena then offers me coffee and a cigarette. I reply, though gratefully, that I have already had both and she assures me that this war is really being won on coffee and cigarettes, by women in trousers. Speaking of trousers, have I seen Granny Bo-Peep. Yes, I have. Serena goes off into fits of laughter, and says Really, this war is terribly funny *in its own way*, isn't it? Reply that I see what she means – which I do – and that, so far, it's quite unlike any other war. One keeps on wondering when something is going to happen. Yes, agrees Serena mournfully, and when one says that, everybody looks horrified and asks if one *wants* to be bombed by the Germans and see the Nelson Column go crashing into Trafalgar Square. They never, says Serena in a rather resentful tone, suggest the Albert Hall crashing into Kensington, which for her part she could view with equanimity.

We then refer to Aunt Blanche – how she stood Granny Bo-Peep as long as she did is a mystery to Serena – the evacuees at home – how lucky I am to have really nice ones. No lice? interpolates Serena, sounding astonished. Certainly no lice. They're not in the *least* like that. Charming children, very well brought-up – sometimes I am inclined to think, better brought-up than Robin and Vicky – to which Serena civilly ejaculates Impossible!

Canteen comes under discussion – very well run and no skin on the cocoa, which Serena thinks is *the* test. Open day and night because workers are on twenty-four-hour shift. Enquire of Serena whether she ever gets any sleep in the Rest-room, and she replies rather doubtfully that she thinks she does, sometimes. On the whole most of her sleeping is done at home. She has four Jewish Refugees in her flat – very, very nice ones, but too many of them – and they cook her the most excellent Viennese dishes. Originally she had only one refugee, but gradually a mother, a cousin, and a little boy have joined the party, Serena doesn't know how. They all fit into one bedroom and the kitchen and she herself has remaining bedroom and sitting-room, only she's never there.

Suggest that she should make use of Buckingham Street flat whenever convenient, and she accepts and says may she go there immediately and have a bath?

Certainly.

We proceed at once to Rest-room for Serena to collect her things, and she shows me horrible-looking little canvas affair about three inches off the floor, swung on poles like inferior sort of hammock. Is that her bed?

Yes, says Serena, and she has shown it to a doctor friend who has condemned it at sight, with rather strangely-worded observation that any bed of that shape is always more or less fatal in the long run, as it throws the kidneys on the bum.

Conduct Serena to top-storey flat, present her with spare latch-key and beg her to come in when she likes and rest on properly constructed divan, which presumably is not open to similar objection.

Am touched when she assures me that I am an angel and have probably saved her life.

Wish I could remember whether I have ever heard her surname, and if so, what it is.

September 23rd. – Postcard from Our Vicar who writes because he feels he ought, in view of recent conversation, to let me know that he has had a letter from a friend in Northumberland on whom two evacuated teachers are billeted, both of whom are *very nice indeed*. Make beds, and play with children, and have offered to dig potatoes. It is a satisfaction, adds

Our Vicar across one corner, to know that we were mistaken in saying that everyone complained of the teachers. There are evidently exceptions.

Think well of Our Vicar for this, and wonder if anyone will ever say that mothers, in some cases, are also satisfactory inmates.

Should doubt it.

Spend large part of the day asking practically everybody I can think of, by telephone or letter, if they can suggest a war job for me.

Most of them reply that they are engaged in similar quest on their own account.

Go out into Trafalgar Square and see gigantic poster on Nelson's plinth asking me what form MY service is taking.

Other hoardings of London give equally prominent display to such announcements as that 300,000 Nurses are wanted, 41,000 Ambulance Drivers, and 500,000 Air-raid Wardens. Get into touch with Organizations requiring these numerous volunteers, and am told that queue five and a half miles long is already besieging their doors.

Ring up influential man at BBC – name given me by Sir W. Frobisher as being dear old friend of his – and influential man tells me in tones of horror that they have a list of really *first-class* writers and speakers whom they can call upon at any moment – which, I gather, they have no intention of doing – and really couldn't possibly make any use of me whatever. At the same time, of course, I can always feel I'm Standing By.

I say Yes, indeed, and ring off.

Solitary ray of light comes from Serena Fiddledeedee whom I hear in bathroom – on door of which she has pinned paper marked ENGAGED – at unnatural hour of 2 p.m. and who emerges in order to say that *until* I start work at the Ministry of Information, she thinks the Adelphi Canteen might be glad of occasional help, if voluntary, and given on night-shift.

Pass over reference to Ministry of Information and at once agree to go and offer assistance at Canteen. Serena declares herself delighted, and offers to introduce me there tonight.

Meanwhile, why not go and see Brigadier Pinflitton, said to be important person in ARP circles? Serena knows him well, and will ring up and say that I am coming and that he will do well to make sure of my assistance before I am snapped up elsewhere.

I beg Serena to modify this last improbable adjuration, but admit that I should be glad of introduction to Brigadier P. if there is the slightest chance of his being able to tell me of something I can do. What does Serena think?

Serena thinks there's almost certain to be a fire-engine or something that I could drive, or perhaps I might decontaminate someone – which leads her on to an enquiry about my gas-mask. How, she wishes to know, do I get on inside it? Serena herself always feels as if she must faint after wearing it for two seconds. She thinks one ought to practise sitting in it in the evenings sometimes.

Rather unalluring picture is conjured up by this, but admit that Serena may be right, and I suggest supper together one evening, followed by sessions in our respective gas-masks.

We can, I say, listen to Sir Walford Davies.

Serena says That would be lovely, and offers to obtain black paper for windows of flat, and put it up for me with drawing-pins.

Meanwhile she will do what she can about Brigadier Pinflitton, but wiser to write than to ring up as he is deaf as a post.

September 25th. – No summons from Brigadier Pinflitton, the Ministry of Information, the BBC or anybody else.

Letter from Felicity Fairmead enquiring if she could come and help me, as she is willing to do anything and is certain that I must be fearfully busy.

Reply-paid telegram from Rose asking if I know any influential person on the British Medical Council to whom she could apply for post.

Letter from dear Robin, expressing concern lest I should be overworking, and anxiety to know exactly what form my exertions on behalf of the nation are taking.

Tremendous scene of reunion – not of my seeking – takes place in underworld between myself and Granny Bo-Peep, cantering up at midnight for cup of coffee and cigarettes. What, she cries, am I here again? Now, that's what she calls setting a *real* example.

Everyone within hearing looks at me with loathing and I explain that I am doing nothing whatever.

Old Mrs W.-G., unmoved, goes on to say that seeing me here reminds her of coffee-stall run by herself at the Front in nineteen-fourteen. The boys loved it, she herself loved it, Lord Roberts loved it. Ah, well, Mrs W.-G. is an old woman now and has to content herself with trotting about in the background doing what she can to cheer up the rest of the world.

Am sorry to say that Demolition Squad, Stretcher-bearers and Ambulance men evince greatest partiality for Mrs W.-G. and gather round her in groups.

They are, says Serena, a low lot – the other night two of them had a fight and an ambulance man who went to separate them emerged bitten to the bone.

Should be delighted to hear further revelations, but supper rush begins and feel that I had better withdraw.

September 27th. – Day pursues usual routine, so unthinkable a month ago, now so familiar, and continually recalling early Novels of the Future by H. G. Wells – now definitely established as minor prophet. Have very often wondered why all prophecies so invariably of a disturbing nature, predicting unpleasant state of affairs all round. Prophets apparently quite insensible to any brighter aspects of the future.

Ring up five more influential friends between nine and twelve to ask if they know of any national work I can undertake. One proves to be on duty as LCC ambulance driver – at which I am very angry and wonder how on earth she managed to get the job – two more reply that I am the tenth person at least to ask this and that they don't know of anything whatever for me, and the remaining two assure me that I must just *wait*, and in time I shall be told what to do.

Ask myself rhetorically whether it was for this that I left home?

Conscience officiously replies that I left home partly because I had no wish to spend the whole of the war in doing domestic work, partly because I felt too cut-off owing to distance between Devonshire and London, and partly from dim idea that London will be more central if I wish to reach Robin or Vicky in any emergency.

Meet Rose for luncheon. She says that she has offered her services to every hospital in London without success. The Hospitals, says Rose gloomily, are all fully staffed, and the beds are all empty, and nobody is allowed to go in however ill they are, and the medical staff goes to bed at ten o'clock every night and isn't called till eleven next morning because they haven't anything to do. The nurses, owing to similar inactivity, are all quarrelling amongst themselves and throwing the splints at one another's heads.

I express concern but no surprise, having heard much the same thing repeatedly in the course of the last three weeks. Tell Rose in return that I am fully expecting to be offered employment of great national importance by the Government at any moment. Can see by Rose's expression that she is not in the least taken in by this. She enquires rather sceptically if I have yet applied for work as voluntary helper on night-shift at Serena's canteen, and I reply with quiet dignity that I shall do so directly I can get anybody to attend to me.

Rose, at this, laughs heartily, and I feel strongly impelled to ask whether the war has made her hysterical – but restrain myself. We drink quantities of coffee, and Rose tells me what she thinks about the Balkans, Stalin's attitude, the chances of an air-raid over London within the week, and the probable duration of the war. In reply I give her my considered opinion regarding the impregnability or otherwise of the Siegfried Line, the neutrality of America, Hitler's intentions with regard to Rumania, and the effect of the petrol rationing on this country as a whole.

We then separate with mutual assurances of letting one another know if we Hear of Anything. In the meanwhile, says Rose rather doubtfully, do I remember the Blowfields? Sir Archibald Blowfield is something in the Ministry of Information, and it might be worth while ringing them up.

I do ring them up in the course of the afternoon, and Lady Blowfield – voice sounds melancholy over the telephone – replies that of course she remembers me well, we met at Valescure in the dear old days. Have never set foot in Valescure in my life, but allow this to pass, and explain that my services as lecturer, writer, or even shorthand typist, are entirely at the disposal of my country if only somebody will be good enough to utilize them.

Lady Blowfield emits a laugh – saddest sound I think I have ever heard – and replies that thousands and thousands of highly-qualified applicants are waiting in a queue outside her husband's office. In *time*, no doubt, they will be needed, but at present there is Nothing, Nothing, Nothing! Unspeakably hollow effect of these last words sends my morale practically down to zero, but I rally and thank her very much. (What for?)

Have I tried the Land Army? enquires Lady Blowfield.

No, I haven't. If the plough, boots, smock and breeches are indicated, something tells me that I should be of very little use to the Land Army.

Well, says Lady Blowfield with a heavy sigh, she's terribly, terribly sorry. There seems nothing for anybody to do, really, except wait for the bombs to rain down upon their heads.

Decline absolutely to subscribe to this view, and enquire after Sir Archibald.

Oh, Archibald is killing himself. Slowly but surely. He works eighteen hours a day, Sundays and all, and neither eats nor sleeps.

Then why, I urge, not let me come and help him, and set him free for an occasional meal at least? But to this Lady Blowfield replies that I don't understand at all. There will be work for us all eventually – provided we are not Wiped Out instantly – but for the moment we must *wait*. I enquire rather peevishly how long, and she returns that the war, whatever some people may say, is quite likely to go on for years and years. Archibald, personally, has estimated the probable duration at exactly twenty-two years and six months. Feel that if I listen to Lady Blowfield for another moment I shall probably shoot myself, and ring off.

Just as I am preparing to listen to the Budget announcement on the Six O'clock News, telephone rings and I feel convinced that I am to be sent for by someone at a moment's notice, to do something, somewhere, and dash to the receiver.

Call turns out to be from old friend Cissie Crabbe, asking if I can find her a war job. Am horrified at hearing myself replying that in time, no doubt, we shall all be needed, but for the moment there is nothing to do but *wait*.

Budget announcement follows and is all that one could have foreseen, and more. Evolve hasty scheme for learning to cook and turning home into a boarding-house after the war, as the only possible hope of remaining there at all.

September 28th. – Go through now habitual performance of pinning up brown paper over the windows and drawing curtains before departing to underworld. Night is as light as possible, and in any case only two minutes' walk.

Just as I arrive, Serena emerges in trousers, little suède jacket and tin hat, beneath which her eyes look positively gigantic. She tells me she is off duty for an hour, and suggests that we should go and drink coffee somewhere.

We creep along the street, feeling for edges of the pavement with our feet, and eventually reach a Lyons Corner House, entrance to which is superbly buttressed by mountainous stacks of sandbags with tiny little aperture dramatically marked 'In' and 'Out' on piece of unpainted wood. Serena points out that this makes it all look much more war-like than if 'In' and 'Out' had been printed in the ordinary way on cardboard.

She then takes off her tin hat, shows me her new gas-mask container – very elegant little vermilion affair with white spots, in waterproof – and utters to the effect that, for her part, she has worked it all out whilst Standing By and finds that her income tax will *definitely* be in excess of her income, which simplifies the whole thing. Ask if she minds, and Serena says No, not in the least, and orders coffee.

She tells me that ever since I last saw her she has been, as usual, sitting about in the underworld, but that this afternoon everybody was told to attend a lecture on the treatment of Shock. The first shock that Serena herself anticipates is the one we shall all experience when we get something to do. Tell her of my conversation over the telephone with Lady Blowfield and Serena says Pah! to the idea of a twenty-two-years war and informs me that she was taken out two days ago to have a drink by a very nice man in the Air Force, and he said Six months at the very outside – and he ought to know.

We talk about the Canteen – am definitely of opinion that I shall never willingly eat sausage-and-mashed again as long as I live – the income tax once more – the pronouncement of the cleaner of the Canteen that the chief trouble with Hitler is that he's such a *fidget* – and the balloon barrage, which, Serena assures me in the tone of one giving inside information, is all to come down in November. (When I indignantly ask why, she is unable to substantiate the statement in any way.)

We smoke cigarettes, order more coffee, and I admit to Serena that I don't think I've ever really understood about the balloons. Serena offers to explain – which I think patronizing but submit to – and I own to rather fantastic idea as to each balloon containing an observer, more or less resembling the look-out in crow's-nest of old-fashioned sailing vessel. This subsequently discarded on being told, probably by Serena herself, that invisible network of wires connect the balloons to one another, all wires being electrified and dealing instant death to approaching enemy aircraft.

Serena now throws over electrified-wire theory completely, and says Oh, no, it isn't like that at all. Each balloon is attached to a huge lorry below, in which sits a Man, perpetually on guard. She has actually seen one of the lorries, in front of the Admiralty, with the Man inside sitting reading a newspaper, and another man close by to keep him company, cooking something on a little oil-stove.

Shortly afterwards Serena declares that she *must* go – positively *must*.

She then remains where she is for twenty minutes more, and when she does go, leaves her gas-mask behind her and we have to go back for it. The waiter who produces it congratulates Serena on having her name inside the case. Not a day, he says in an offhand manner, passes without half-a-dozen gas-masks being left behind by their owners and half of them have no name, and the other half just have 'Bert' or 'Mum' or 'Our Stanley', which, he says, doesn't take you anywhere at all.

He is thanked by Serena, whom I then escort to entrance of underworld, where she trails away swinging her tin helmet and assuring me that she will probably get the sack for being late if anybody sees her.

September 30th. – Am invited by Serena to have tea at her flat, Jewish refugees said to be spending day with relations at Bromley. Not, says Serena, that she wants to get rid of them – she likes them – but their absence does make more room in the flat.

On arrival it turns out that oldest of the refugees has changed his mind about Bromley and remained behind. He says he has a letter to write.

Serena introduces me – refugee speaks no English and I no German and we content ourselves with handshakes, bows, smiles and more handshakes. He looks patriarchal and dignified, sitting over electric fire in large great-coat.

Serena says he feels the cold. They all feel the cold. She can't bear to contemplate what it will be like for them when the cold really begins – which it hasn't done at all so far – and she has already piled upon their beds all the blankets she possesses. On going to buy others at large Store, she is told that all blankets have been, are being, and will be, bought by the Government and that if by any extraordinary chance one or two *do* get through, they will cost five times more than ever before.

Beg her not to be taken in by this for one moment and quote case of Robert's aunt, elderly maiden lady living in Chester, who has, since outbreak of war, purchased set of silver dessert-knives, large chiming clock, bolt of white muslin, new rabbit-skin neck-tie and twenty-four lead pencils – none of which she required – solely because she has been told in shops that these will in future be unobtainable. Serena looks impressed and refugee and I shake hands once more.

Serena takes me to her sitting-room, squeezes past two colossal trunks in very small hall, which Serena explains as being luggage of her refugees. The rest of it is in the kitchen and under the beds, except largest trunk of all which couldn't be got beyond ground floor and has had to be left with hall-porter.

Four O'clock News on wireless follows. Listeners once more informed of perfect unanimity on all points between French and English Governments. Make idle suggestion to Serena that it would be much more interesting if we were suddenly to be told that there had been several sharp divergences of opinion. And probably much truer too, says Serena cynically, and anyway, if they always agree so perfectly, why meet at all? She calls it waste of time and money.

Am rather scandalized at this, and say so, and Serena immediately declares that she didn't mean a word of it, and produces tea and admirable cakes made by Austrian refugee. Conversation takes the form –

extraordinarily prevalent in all circles nowadays – of exchanging rather singular pieces of information, never obtained by direct means but always heard of through friends of friends.

Roughly tabulated, Serena's news is to following effect:

The whole of the BBC is really functioning from a place in the Cotswolds, and Broadcasting House is full of nothing but sandbags.

A Home for Prostitutes has been evacuated from a danger zone outside London to Aldershot.

(At this I protest, and Serena admits that it was related by young naval officer who has reputation as a wit.)

A large number of war casualties have already reached London, having come up the Thames in barges, and are installed in blocks of empty flats by the river – but nobody knows they're there.

Hitler and Ribbentrop are no longer on speaking terms.

Hitler and Ribbentrop have made it up again.

The Russians are going to turn dog on the Nazis at any moment.

In return for all this, I am in a position to inform Serena:

That the War Office is going to Carnarvon Castle.

A letter has been received in London from a German living in Berlin, with a private message under the stamp saying that a revolution is expected to break out at any minute.

President Roosevelt has been flown over the Siegfried Line and flown back to Washington again, in the strictest secrecy.

The deb. at the canteen, on being offered a marshmallow out of a paper bag, has said: What *is* a marshmallow? (Probably related to a High Court Judge.)

The Russians are determined to assassinate Stalin at the first opportunity.

A woman fainted in the middle of Regent Street yesterday and two stretcher-bearers came to the rescue and put her on the stretcher, then dropped it and fractured both her arms. Serena assures me that in the event of her being injured in any air-raid she has quite decided to emulate Sir Philip Sidney and give everybody else precedence.

Talking of that, would it be a good idea to practise wearing our gas-masks?

Agree, though rather reluctantly, and we accordingly put them on and sit opposite one another in respective armchairs, exchanging sepulchral-sounding remarks from behind talc-and-rubber snouts.

Serena says she wishes to time herself, as she doesn't think she will be able to breathe for more than four minutes at the very most.

Explain that this is all nerves. Gas-masks may be rather warm – (am streaming from every pore) – and perhaps rather uncomfortable, and certainly unbecoming – but any sensible person can breathe inside them for hours.

Serena says I shall be sorry when she goes off into a dead faint.

The door opens suddenly and remaining Austrian refugees, returned early from Bromley, walk in and, at sight presented by Serena and myself, are startled nearly out of their senses and enquire in great agitation What is happening.

Remove gas-mask quickly – Serena hasn't fainted at all but is crimson in the face, and hair very untidy – and we all bow and shake hands.

Letter-writing refugee joins us – shakes hands again – and we talk agreeably round tea-table till the letter-motif recurs – they all say they have letters to write, and – presumably final – handshaking closes séance.

Just as I prepare to leave, Serena's bell rings and she says It's J. L. and I'm to wait, because she wants me to meet him.

J. L. turns out to be rather distinguished-looking man, face perfectly familiar to me from *Radio Times* and other periodicals as he is well-known writer and broadcaster. (Wish I hadn't been so obliging about gas-mask, as hair certainly more untidy than Serena's and have not had the sense to powder my nose.)

J. L. is civility itself and pretends to have heard of me often – am perfectly certain he hasn't – and even makes rather indefinite reference to my Work, which he qualifies as well known, but wisely gives conversation another turn immediately without committing himself further.

Serena produces sherry and enquires what J. L. is doing.

Well, J. L. is writing a book.

He is, as a matter of fact, going on with identical book – merely a novel – that he was writing before war began. It isn't that he *wants* to do it, or that he thinks anybody else wants him to do it. But he is over military age, and the fourteen different organizations to whom he has offered his services have replied, without exception, that they have far more people already than they know what to do with.

He adds pathetically that authors, no doubt, are very useless people.

Not more so than anybody else, Serena replies. Why can't they be used for propaganda?

J. L. and I – with one voice – assure her that every author in the United Kingdom has had exactly this idea, and has laid it before the Ministry of Information, and has been told in return to Stand By for the present.

In the case of Sir Hugh Walpole, to J. L.'s certain knowledge, a Form was returned on which he was required to state all particulars of his qualifications, where educated, and to which periodicals he has contributed, also names of any books he may ever have had published.

Serena enquires witheringly if they didn't want to know whether the books had been published at Sir H. W.'s own expense, and we all agree that if this is official reaction to Sir H.'s offer, the rest of us need not trouble to make any.

Try to console J. L. with assurance that there is to be a boom in books, as nobody will be able to do anything amusing in the evenings, what with black-out, petrol restrictions, and limitations of theatre and cinema openings, so they will have to fall back on reading.

Realize too late that this not very happily expressed.

J. L. says Yes indeed, and tells me that he finds poetry more helpful than anything else. The Elizabethans for choice. Don't I agree?

Reply at once that I am less familiar with the Elizabethan poets than I should like to be, and hope he may think this means that I know plenty of others. (Am quite unable to recall any poetry at all at the moment, except 'How they Brought the Good News from Ghent' and cannot imagine why in the world I should have thought of that.)

Ah, says J. L. very thoughtfully, there is a lot to be said for prose. He personally finds that the Greeks provide him with escapist literature. Plato.

Should not at all wish him to know that *The Fairchild Family* performs the same service for me – but remember with shame that E. M. Forster, in admirable wireless talk, has told us *not* to be ashamed of our taste in reading.

Should like to know if he would apply this to *The Fairchild Family* and can only hope that he would.

Refer to Dickens – compromise here between truth and desire to sound reasonably cultured – but J. L. looks distressed, says Ah yes – really? and changes conversation at once.

Can see that I have dished myself with him for good.

Talk about black-out – Serena alleges that anonymous friend of hers goes out in the dark with extra layer of chalk-white powder on her nose, so as to be seen, and resembles Dong with the Luminous Nose.

J. L. not in the least amused and merely replies that there are little disks on sale, covered with luminous paint, or that pedestrians are now allowed electric torch if pointed downwards, and shrouded in tissue-paper. Serena makes fresh start, and enquires whether he doesn't know Sir Archibald and Lady Blowfield – acquaintances of mine.

He does know them – had hoped that Sir A. could offer him war work – but that neither here nor there. Lady Blowfield is a charming woman.

I say Yes, isn't she – which is quite contrary to my real opinion. Moreover, am only distressed at this lapse from truth because aware that Serena will recognize it as such. Spiritual and moral degradation well within sight, but cannot dwell on this now. (*Query*: Is it in any way true that war very often brings out the best in civil population? *Answer*: So far as I am concerned, Not at all.)

Suggestion from Serena that Sir Archibald and Lady Blowfield both take rather pessimistic view of international situation causes J. L. to state it as his considered opinion that no one, be he whom he may, *no one*, is in a position at this moment to predict with certainty what the Future may hold.

Do not like to point out to him that no one ever has been, and shortly afterwards J. L. departs, telling Serena that he will ring her up when he knows any more. (Any more what?)

October 1st. – Am at last introduced by Serena Fiddlededee to underworld Commandant. She is dark, rather good-looking young woman wearing out-size slacks and leather jacket, using immensely long black cigarette-holder, and writing at wooden trestle-table piled with papers.

Serena – voice sunk to quite unnaturally timid murmur – explains that I am very anxious to make myself of use in any way whatever, while waiting to be summoned by Ministry of Information.

The Commandant – who has evidently heard this kind of thing before – utters short incredulous ejaculation, in which I very nearly join, knowing even better than she does herself how thoroughly well justified it is.

Serena – voice meeker than ever – whispers that I can drive a car if necessary, and have passed my First Aid examination – (hope she isn't going to mention date of this achievement which would take us a long way back indeed) – and am also well used to Home Nursing. Moreover, I can write shorthand and use a typewriter.

Commandant goes on writing rapidly and utters without looking up for a moment – which I think highly offensive. Utterance is to the effect that there are no paid jobs going.

Oh, says Serena, sounding shocked, we never thought of anything like *that*. This is to be voluntary work, and anything in the world, and at any hour.

Commandant – still writing – strikes a bell sharply.

It has been said that the Canteen wants an extra hand, suggests Serena, now almost inaudible. She knows that I should be perfectly willing to work all through the night, or perhaps all day on Sundays, so as to relieve others. And, naturally, voluntary work. To this Commandant – gaze glued to her rapidly-moving pen – mutters something to the effect that voluntary work is all very well –

Have seldom met more un-endearing personality.

Bell is answered by charming-looking elderly lady wearing overall, and armlet badge inscribed *Messenger*, which seems to me unsuitable.

Commandant – tones very peremptory indeed – orders her to Bring the Canteen Time-Sheet. Grey-haired messenger flies away like the wind. Cannot possibly have gone more than five yards from the door before the bell is again struck, and on her reappearance Commandant says sharply that she has just asked for Canteen Time-Sheet. Why hasn't it come?

Obvious reply is that it hasn't come because only a pair of wings could have brought it in the time – but no one says this, and Messenger again departs and can be heard covering the ground at race-track speed.

Commandant continues to write – says Damn once, under her breath, as though attacked by sudden doubt whether war will stop exactly as and when she has ordained – and drops cigarette-ash all over the table.

Serena looks at me and profanely winks enormous eye.

Bell is once more banged – am prepared to wager it will be broken before week is out at this rate. It is this time answered by smart-looking person in blue trousers and singlet and admirable make-up. Looks about twenty-five, but has prematurely grey hair, and am conscious that this gives me distinct satisfaction.

(Not very commendable reaction.)

Am overcome with astonishment when she enquires of Commandant in brusque, official tones: Isn't it time you had some lunch, darling?

Commandant for the first time raises her eyes and answers No, darling, she can't possibly bother with lunch, but she wants a staff car instantly, to go out to Wimbledon for her. It's urgent.

Serena looks hopeful but remains modestly silent while Commandant and Darling rustle through quantities of lists and swear vigorously, saying that it's a most extraordinary thing, the Time-Sheets ought to be always available at a second's notice, and they never *are*.

Darling eventually turns to Serena, just as previous – and infinitely preferable – Messenger returns breathless, and asks curtly, Who is on the Staff Car? Serena indicates that she is herself scheduled for it, is asked why she didn't say so, and commanded to get car out instantly and dash to Wimbledon.

Am deeply impressed by this call to action, but disappointed when Commandant instructs her to go *straight* to No. 478 Mottisfont Road, Wimbledon, and ask for clean handkerchief, which Commandant forgot to bring this morning.

She is to come *straight* back, as quickly as possible, *with* the handkerchief. Has she, adds Commandant suspiciously, quite understood?

Serena replies that she has. Tell myself that in her place I should reply No, it's all too complicated for me to grasp – but judging from lifelong experience, this is a complete fallacy and should in reality say nothing of the kind but merely wish, long afterwards, that I had.

Departure of Serena, in search, no doubt, of tin helmet and gas-mask, and am left, together with elderly Messenger, to be ignored by Commandant whilst she and Darling embark on earnest argument concerning Commandant's next meal, which turns out to be lunch, although time now five o'clock in the afternoon.

She must, says Darling, absolutely *must* have something. She has been here since nine o'clock and during that time what has she had? One cup of coffee and a tomato. It isn't enough on which to do a heavy day's work.

Commandant – writing again resumed and eyes again on paper – asserts that it's all she wants. She hasn't time for more. Does Darling realize that there's a *war* on, and not a minute to spare?

Yes, argues Darling, but she could eat something without leaving her desk for a second. Will she try some soup?

No.

Then a cup of tea and some buns?

No, no, no. *Nothing*.

She *must* take some black coffee. Absolutely and definitely must. Oh, very well, cries Commandant – at the same time striking table quite violently with her hand, which produces confusion among the papers. (Can foresee fresh trouble with mislaid Time-Sheets in immediate future.) Very well – black coffee, and she'll have it here. Instantly.

Darling dashes from the room throwing murderous look at elderly Messenger who has temporarily obstructed the dash.

Commandant writes more frenziedly than ever and snaps out single word *What*, which sounds like a bark, and is evidently addressed to Messenger, who respectfully lays Canteen Time-Sheet on table. This not a success, as Commandant snatches it up again and cries *Not* on the table, my God, *not* on the table! and scans it at red-hot speed.

She then writes again, as though nothing had happened.

Decide that if I am to be here indefinitely I may as well sit down, and do so.

Elderly Messenger gives me terrified, but I think admiring, look. Evidently this display of initiative quite unusual, and am, in fact, rather struck by it myself.

Darling reappears with a tray. Black coffee has materialized and is flanked by large plate of scrambled eggs on toast, two rock-buns and a banana.

All are placed at Commandant's elbow and she wields a fork with one hand and continues to write with the other.

Have sudden impulse to quote to her historical anecdote of British Sovereign remarking to celebrated historian: Scribble, scribble, scribble, Mr Gibbon.

Do not, naturally, give way to it.

Darling asks me coldly If I want anything, and on my replying that I have offered my services to Canteen tells me to go *at once* to Mrs Peacock. Decide to assume that this means I am to be permitted to serve my country, if only with coffee and eggs, so depart, and Elderly Messenger creeps out with me.

I ask if she will be kind enough to take me to Mrs Peacock and she says Of course, and we proceed quietly – no rushing or dashing. (*Query*: Will not this dilatory spirit lose us the war? *Answer*: Undoubtedly, Nonsense!) Make note not to let myself be affected by aura of agitation surrounding Commandant and friend.

Messenger takes me past cars, ambulances, Rest-room, from which unholy din of feminine voices proceeds, and gives me information.

A Society Deb. is working in the Canteen. She is the only one in the whole place. A reporter came to interview her once and she was photographed kneeling on one knee beside an ambulance wheel, holding tools and things. Photograph published in several papers and underneath it was printed: Débutante Jennifer Jamfather Stands By on Home Front.

Reach Mrs Peacock, who is behind Canteen counter, sitting on a box, and looks kind but harassed.

She has a bad leg. Not a permanent bad leg but it gets in the way, and she will be glad of extra help.

Feel much encouraged by this. Nobody else has made faintest suggestion of being glad of extra help – on the contrary.

Raise my voice so as to be audible above gramophone ('Little Sir Echo') and wireless (. . . And so, bairns, we bid Goodbye to Bonnie

Scotland) – roarings and bellowings of Darts Finals being played in a corner, and clatter of dishes from the kitchen – and announce that I am Come to Help – which I think sounds as if I were one of the Ministering Children Forty Years After.

Mrs. Peacock, evidently too dejected even to summon up customary formula that there is nothing for me to do except Stand By as she is turning helpers away by the hundred every hour, smiles rather wanly and says I am very kind.

What, I enquire, can I do?

At the moment nothing. (Can this be a recrudescence of Stand By theme?)

The five o'clock rush is over, and the seven o'clock rush hasn't begun. Mrs Peacock is taking the opportunity of sitting for a moment. She heroically makes rather half-hearted attempt at offering me half packing-case, which I at once decline, and ask about her leg.

Mrs P. displays it, swathed in bandages beneath her stocking, and tells me how her husband had two boxes of sand, shovel and bucket prepared for emergency use – (this evidently euphemism for incendiary bombs) – and gave full instructions to household as to use of them, demonstrating in back garden. Mrs P. herself took part in this, she adds impressively. I say Yes, yes, to encourage her, and she goes on. Telephone call then obliged her to leave the scene – interpolation here about nature of the call involving explanation as to young married niece – husband a sailor, dear little baby with beautiful big blue eyes – from whom call emanated.

Ninth pip-pip-pip compelled Mrs P. to ring off and, in retracing her steps, she crossed first-floor landing on which husband, without a word of warning, had meanwhile caused boxes of sand, shovel and bucket to be ranged, with a view to permanent instalment there. Mrs P. – not expecting any of them – unfortunately caught her foot in the shovel, crashed into the sand-boxes, and was cut to the bone by edge of the bucket.

She concludes by telling me that it really was a lesson. Am not clear of what nature, or to whom, but sympathize very much and say I shall hope to save her as much as possible.

Hope this proceeds from unmixed benevolence, but am inclined to think it is largely actuated by desire to establish myself definitely as canteen worker – in which it meets with success.

Return to Buckingham Street flat again coincides with exit of owner, who at once enquires whether I have ascertained whereabouts of nearest air-raid shelter.

Well, yes, I have in a way. That is to say, the ARP establishment in Adelphi is within three minutes' walk, and I could go there. Owner returns severely that that is Not Good Enough. He must beg of me to take this question seriously, and pace the distance between bedroom and shelter and find out how long it would take to get there in the event of an emergency. Moreover, he declares there is a shelter nearer than the Adelphi, and proceeds to indicate it.

Undertake, reluctantly, to conduct a brief rehearsal of my own exodus under stimulus of air-raid alarm, and subsequently do so.

This takes the form of rather interesting little experiment in which I lay out warm clothes, heavy coat, *Our Mutual Friend* – Shakespeare much more impressive but cannot rise to it – small bottle of boiled sweets – sugar said to increase energy and restore impaired morale – and electric torch. Undress and get into bed, then sound imaginary tocsin, look at my watch, and leap up.

Dressing is accomplished without mishap and proceed downstairs and into street with *Our Mutual Friend*, boiled sweets and electric torch. Am shocked to find myself strongly inclined to run like a lamplighter, in spite of repeated instructions issued to the contrary. If this is the case when no raid at all is taking place, ask myself what it would be like with bombers overhead – and do not care to contemplate reply.

Street seems very dark, and am twice in collision with other pedestrians. Reaction to this is merry laughter on both sides. (Effect of black-out on national hilarity quite excellent.)

Turn briskly down side street and up to entrance of air-raid shelter, which turns out to be locked. Masculine voice enquires where I think I am going, and I say, Is it the police? No, it is the Air-raid Warden. Explain entire situation; he commends my forethought and says that on the first sound of siren alarm He Will be There. Assure him in return that in that case we shall meet, as I shall also Be There, with equal celerity, and we part – cannot say whether temporarily or for ever.

Wrist-watch, in pocket of coat, reveals that entire performance has occupied four and a half minutes only.

Am much impressed, and walk back reflecting on my own efficiency and wondering how best to ensure that it shall be appreciated by Robert, to whom I propose to write spirited account.

Return to flat reveals that I have left all the electric lights burning – though behind blue shades – and forgotten gas-mask, still lying in readiness on table.

Decide to put off writing account to Robert.

Undress and get into bed again, leaving clothes and other properties ready as before – gas-mask in prominent position on shoes – but realize that if I have to go through whole performance all over again tonight, shall be very angry indeed.

October 2nd. – No alarm takes place. Wake at two o'clock and hear something which I think may be a warbling note from a siren – which we have been told to expect – but if so, warbler very poor and indeterminate performer, and come to the conclusion that it is not worth my attention and go to sleep again.

Post – now very late every day – does not arrive until after breakfast.

Short note from Robert informs me that all is well, he does not care about the way the Russians are behaving – (he never has) – his ARP office has more volunteers than he knows what to do with – and young Cramp from the garage, who offered to learn method of dealing with unexploded bombs, has withdrawn after ten minutes' instruction on the grounds that he thinks it seems rather dangerous.

Robert hopes I am enjoying the black-out – which I think is satirical – and has not forwarded joint letter received from Robin as there is nothing much in it. (Could willingly strangle him for this.)

Vicky's letter, addressed to me, makes some amends, as she writes ecstatically about heavenly new dormitory, divine concert and utterly twee air-raid shelter newly constructed (towards which parents will no doubt be asked to contribute). Vicky's only complaint is to the effect that no air-raid has yet occurred, which is very dull.

Also receive immensely long and chatty letter from Aunt Blanche. Marigold and Margery are well, Doreen Fitzgerald and Cook have failed to reach identity of views regarding question of the children's supper but this has now been adjusted by Aunt Blanche and I am not to worry, and Robert seems quite all right, though not saying much.

Our Vicar's Wife has been to tea – worn to a thread and looking like death – but has declared that she is getting on splendidly and the evacuees are settling down, and a nephew of a friend of hers, in the Militia, has told his mother, who has written it to his aunt, who has passed it on to Our Vicar's Wife, that all Berlin is seething with discontent, and a revolution in Germany is scheduled for the first Monday in November.

Is this, asks Aunt Blanche rhetorically, what the Press calls Wishful Thinking?

She concludes with affectionate enquiries as to my well-being, begs me to go and see old Uncle A. when I have time, and is longing to hear what post I have been offered by the Ministry of Information. *P.S.*: What about the Sweep? Cook has been asking.

Have never yet either left home, or got back to it, without being told that Cook is asking about the Sweep.

Large proportion of mail consists of letters, full of eloquence, from tradespeople who say that they are now faced with a difficult situation which will, however, be improved on receipt of my esteemed cheque.

Irresistible conviction comes over me that my situation is even more difficult than theirs, and, moreover, no cheques are in the least likely to come and improve it.

Turn, in hopes of consolation, to remainder of mail and am confronted with Felicity Fairmead's writing – very spidery – on envelope, and typewritten letter within, which she has forgotten to sign. Tells me that she is using typewriter with a view to training for war work, and adds candidly that she can't help hoping war may be over before she finds it. This, says Felicity, is awful, she knows very well, but she can't help it. She is deeply ashamed of her utter uselessness, as she is doing nothing whatever except staying as Paying Guest in the country with delicate friend whose husband is in France, and who has three small children, also delicate, and one maid who isn't any use, so that Felicity and friend make the beds, look after the children, do most of the cooking and keep the garden in order. Both feel how wrong it is not to be doing real work for the country, and this has driven Felicity to the typewriter and friend to the knitting of socks and Balaclava helmets.

Felicity concludes with wistful supposition that *I* am doing something splendid.

Should be very sorry to enlighten her on this point, and shall feel constrained to leave letter unanswered until reality of my position corresponds rather more to Felicity's ideas.

Meanwhile, have serious thoughts of sending copies of her letter to numerous domestic helpers of my acquaintance who have seen fit to leave their posts at a moment's notice in order to seek more spectacular jobs elsewhere.

Remaining item in the post is a letter-card – which I have customary difficulty in tearing open and only succeed at the expense of one corner – and proves to be from Barbara Carruthers *née* Blenkinsop, now living in Midlands. She informs me that this war is upsetting her very much: it really is dreadful for *her*, she says, because she has children, and situation may get very difficult later on and they may have to do without things and she has always taken so much trouble to see that they have *everything*. They are at present in Westmorland, but this is a considerable expense and moreover petrol regulations make it impossible to go and see them, and train-service – about which Barbara is indignant and says it is *very* hard on her – most unsatisfactory. How long do I think war is going on? She had arranged for her elder boys to go to excellent Preparatory School near London this autumn, but school has moved to Wales, which isn't at all the same thing, and Barbara does feel it's rather too bad. And what do I think about food shortage? It is *most* unfair if her children are to be rationed, and she would even be prepared to pay extra for them to have additional supplies. She concludes by sending me her love and enquiring casually whether Robin has been sent to France yet, or is he just too young?

Am so disgusted at Barbara's whole attitude that I dramatically tear up letter into fragments and cast it from me, but realize later that it should have been kept in order that I might send suitable reply.

Draft this in my own mind several times in course of the day, until positively vitriolic indictment is evolved which will undoubtedly never see the light of day, and would probably land me in the Old Bailey on a charge of defamatory libel if it did.

Purchase overall for use in Canteen, debate the question of trousers and decide that I must be strong-minded enough to remain in customary clothing which is perfectly adequate to work behind the counter. Find myself almost immediately afterwards trying on very nice pair of navy-blue slacks, thinking that I look well in them and buying them.

Am prepared to take any bet that I shall wear them every time I go on duty.

As this is not to happen till nine o'clock tonight, determine to look up the Weatherbys, who might possibly be able to suggest whole-time National Service job – and old Uncle A. about whom Aunt Blanche evidently feels anxious.

Ring up Uncle A. – his housekeeper says he will be delighted to see me at tea-time – and also Mrs Weatherby, living in Chelsea, who invites me to lunch and says her husband, distinguished Civil Servant, will be in and would much like to meet me. Imagination instantly suggests that he has heard of me (in what connection cannot possibly conceive), and, on learning that he is to be privileged to see me at his table, will at once realize that Civil Service would be the better for my assistance in some highly authoritative capacity.

Spend hours wondering what clothes would make me look most efficient, but am quite clear *not* slacks for the Civil Service. Finally decide on black coat and skirt, white blouse with frill of austere, *not* frilly, type, and cone-shaped black hat. Find that I look like inferior witch in third-rate pantomime in the latter, and take it off again. Only alternative is powder-blue with rainbow-like swathings, quite out of the question. Feel myself obliged to go out and buy small black hat, with brim like a jockey-cap and red edging. Have no idea whether this is in accordance with Civil Service tastes or not, but feel that I look nice in it.

Walk to Chelsea, and on looking into small mirror in handbag realize that I don't after all. Can do nothing about it, and simply ask hall-porter for Mrs Weatherby, and am taken up in lift to sixth-floor flat, very modern and austere, colouring entirely neutral and statuette – to me wholly revolting – of misshapen green cat occupying top of bookcase, dominating whole of the room.

Hostess comes in – cannot remember if we are on Christian-name terms or not, but inclined to think not and do not risk it – greets me very kindly and again repeats that her husband wishes to meet me.

(Civil Service appointment definitely in sight, and decide to offer Serena job as my private secretary.)

Discuss view of the river from window – Mrs Weatherby says block of flats would be an excellent target from the air, at which we both laugh agreeably – extraordinary behaviour of the Ministry of Information, and delightful autumnal colouring in neighbourhood of Bovey Tracy, which Mrs Weatherby says she knows well.

Entrance of Mr Weatherby puts an end to this interchange, and we are introduced. Mr W. very tall and cadaverous, and has a beard, which makes me think of Agrippa.

He says that he has been wishing to meet me, but does not add why. Produces sherry and we talk about black-out, President Roosevelt – I say that his behaviour throughout entire crisis has been magnificent and moves me beyond measure – Mrs Weatherby agrees, but Agrippa seems surprised and I feel would like to contradict me but politeness forbids – and we pass on to cocker spaniels, do not know how or why.

Admirable parlourmaid – uniform, demeanour and manner all equally superior to those of Winnie, or even departed May – announces that Luncheon is served, madam, and just as I prepare to swallow remainder of sherry rapidly, pallid elderly gentleman crawls in, leaning on stick and awakening in me instant conviction that he is not long for this world.

Impression turns out to be not without foundation as it transpires that he is Agrippa's uncle, and has recently undergone major operation at London Nursing Home but was desired to leave it at five minutes' notice in order that bed should be available if and when required. Uncle asserts that he met this – as well he might – with protests but was unfortunately too feeble to enforce them and accordingly found himself, so he declares, on the pavement while still unable to stand. From this fearful plight he has been retrieved by Agrippa, and given hospitality of which he cannot speak gratefully enough.

Story concludes with examples of other, similar cases, of which we all seem to know several, and Mrs Weatherby's solemn assurance that all the beds of all the Hospitals and Nursing Homes in England are standing empty, and that no civilian person is to be allowed to be ill until the war is over.

Agrippa's uncle shakes his head, and looks worse than ever, and soon after he has pecked at chicken soufflé, waved away sweet omelette and turned his head from the sight of Camembert cheese, he is compelled by united efforts of the Weatherbys to drink a glass of excellent port and retire from the room.

They tell me how very ill he has been – can well believe it – and that there was another patient even more ill, in room next to his at Nursing Home, who was likewise desired to leave. She, however, defeated the authorities by dying before they had time to get her packing done.

Find myself exclaiming 'Well done!' in enthusiastic tone before I have time to stop myself, and am shocked. So, I think, are the Weatherbys – rightly.

Agrippa changes the conversation and asks my opinion about the value of the natural resources of Moravia. Fortunately answers his own question, at considerable length.

Cannot see that any of this, however interesting, is leading in the direction of war work for me.

On returning to drawing-room and superb coffee which recalls Cook's efforts at home rather sadly to my mind – I myself turn conversation forcibly into desired channel.

What an extraordinary thing it is, I say, that so many intelligent and experienced people are not, so far as one can tell, being utilized by the Government in any way!

Mrs Weatherby replies that she thinks most people who are *really* trained for anything worth while have found no difficulty whatever in getting jobs, and Agrippa declares that it is largely a question of Standing By, and will continue to be so for many months to come.

Does he, then, think that this will be a long war?

Agrippa, assuming expression of preternatural discretion, replies that he must not, naturally, commit himself. Government officials, nowadays, have to be exceedingly careful in what they say as I shall, he has no doubt, readily understand.

Mrs Weatherby strikes in to the effect that it is difficult to see how the war can be a very *short* one, and yet it seems unlikely to be a very *long* one.

I enquire whether she thinks it is going to be a middling one, and then feel I have spoken flippantly and that both disapprove of me.

Should like to leave at once, but custom and decency alike forbid as have only this moment finished coffee.

Ask whether anything has been heard of Pamela Pringle, known to all three of us, at which Agrippa's face lights up in the most extraordinary way and he exclaims that she is, poor dear, quite an invalid but as charming as ever.

Mrs Weatherby – face not lighting up at all but, on the contrary, resembling a thunder-cloud – explains that Pamela, since war started, has developed unspecified form of Heart and retired to large house near the New Forest where she lies on the sofa, in *eau-de-nil* velvet wrapper, and has all her friends down to stay in turns.

Her husband has a job with the Army and is said to be in Morocco, and she has despatched the children to relations in America, saying that this is a terrible sacrifice, but done for their own sakes.

Can only reply, although I hope indulgently, that it all sounds to me exactly like dear Pamela. This comment more of a success with Mrs W. than with Agrippa, who stands up – looks as if he might touch the ceiling – and says that he must get back to work.

Have abandoned all serious hope of his offering me a post of national importance, or even of no importance at all, but put out timid feeler to the effect that he must be very busy just now.

Yes, yes, he is. He won't get back before eight o'clock tonight, if then. At one time it was eleven o'clock, but things are for the moment a little easier, though no doubt this is only temporary. (*Query*: Why is it that all those occupied in serving the country are completely overwhelmed by pressure of work but do not apparently dream of utilizing assistance pressed upon them by hundreds of willing helpers? *Answer* comes there none.)

Agrippa and I exchange unenthusiastic farewells, but he sticks to his guns to the last and says that he has always wanted to meet me. Does not, naturally, add whether the achievement of this ambition has proved disappointing or the reverse.

Linger on for a few moments in frail and unworthy hope that Mrs Weatherby may say something more, preferably scandalous, about Pamela Pringle, but she only refers, rather bleakly, to Agrippa's uncle and his low state of health and asserts that she does not know what the British Medical Association can be thinking about.

Agree that I don't either – which is true not only now but at all times – and take my leave. Tell her how much I have liked seeing them both, and am conscious of departing from spirit of truth in saying so, but cannot, obviously, inform her that the only parts of the entertainment I have really enjoyed are her excellent lunch and hearing about Pamela.

Go out in search of bus – all very few and far between now – and contemplate visit to hairdresser's, but conscience officiously points out that visits to hairdresser constitute an unnecessary expense and could very well be replaced by ordinary shampoo in bedroom basin at flat. Inner prompting – probably the Devil – urges that Trade must be Kept Going and that it is my duty to help on the commercial life of the nation.

Debate this earnestly, find that bus has passed the spot at which I intended to get out, make undecided effort to stop it, then change my mind and sit down again and am urged by conductor to Make up My Mind. I shall have to move a lot faster than that, he jocosely remarks, when them aeroplanes are overhead. Much amusement is occasioned to passengers in general, and we all part in high spirits.

Loser Wins

☆★☆★☆★☆★☆★☆★☆★☆★☆★☆★☆★☆★☆

PAUL THEROUX

The insects warbled at the windows, and on the wall a pale gecko chattered and flicked its tail. It was one of those intimate late-night pauses – we had been drinking for two hours and had passed the point of drunken chit-chat. Then, to break the silence, I said, 'I've lost my spare pair of glasses.'

'I hadn't noticed,' said Strang. A surveyor, he had the abrupt manner of one who works alone. He was mapping this part of the state and he had made Ayer Hitam his base. His wife, Milly, was devoted to him, people said; it seemed an unusual piece of praise. Strang picked up his drink. 'You won't find them.'

'It's an excuse to go down to Singapore for a new pair.'

Strang looked thoughtful. I expected him to say something about Singapore. We were alone. Stanley Chee had slammed the door for the last time and had left a tray of drinks on the bar that we could sign for on the chit-pad.

Still Strang didn't reply. The ensuing silence made my sentence about Singapore a frivolous echo. He walked over and poured himself a large gin, emptied a bottle of tonic into the tall glass and pinched a new slice of lemon into it.

'I ever tell you about the Parrishes?'

A rhetorical question: he was still talking.

'Married couple I met up in Kota Bahru. Jungle bashers. Milly and I lived there our first year – looked like paradise to us, if you could stand the sand-flies. Didn't see much of the Parrishes. They quarrelled an awful lot, so we stayed as far away as possible from their arguments. Seemed unlucky. We'd only been married a few months.' He smiled. 'Old Parrish took quite a shine to Milly.'

'What did the Parrishes argue about?' Was this what he wanted me to ask? I hoped he was not expecting me to drag the story out of him. I wanted him to keep talking and let it flow over me. But even at the best of times Strang was no spellbinder; tonight he seemed agitated.

'See, that shows you've never been spliced,' he said. 'Married people argue about everything – anything. A tone of voice, saying please, the colour of the wallpaper, something you forgot, the speed of the fan, food, friends, the weather. That tie of yours – if you had a wife she'd hate you for it. A bone of contention,' said Strang slowly, 'is just a bone.'

'Perhaps I have that in store for me.' I filled my own drink and signed for that and Strang's.

'Take my advice,' he said. 'No – it was something you said a minute ago. Oh, you lost your specs. That's what I was going to say. The Parrishes argued about everything, but most of all they argued about things they lost. I mean, things *she* lost. She was incredible. At first he barely noticed it. She lost small things, lipstick, her cigarettes, her comb. She didn't bother to look for them. She was very county – her parents had money, and she had a kind of contempt for it. Usually she didn't even try to replace the things she lost. The funny thing is, she seemed to do it on purpose – to lose things she hated.

'He was the local magistrate. An Outward Bound type. After a week in court he was dead keen to go camping. Old Parrish – he looked like a goat, little pointed beard and those sort of hairy ears. They went on these camping trips and invariably she lost something en route – the house keys, her watch, the matches, you name it. But she was a terrific map-reader and he was appalling, so he really depended on her. I think he had some love for her. He was a lot older than she was – he'd married her on a Long Leave.

'Once, he showed how much he loved her. She lost fifty dollars. Not a hard thing to do – it was a fifty-dollar note, the one with the mosque on it. I would have cried, myself, but she just shrugged, and knowing how she was continually losing things he was sympathetic. "Poor thing," he says, "you must feel a right charlie." But not a bit of it. She had always had money. She didn't take a blind bit of notice, and she was annoyed that he pitied her for losing the fifty sheets. Hated him for noticing it.

'They went off on their camping trips – expeditions was more like it – and always to the same general area. Old Parrish had told me one or two things about it. There was one of these up-country lakes, with a strange island in the middle of it. They couldn't find it on the map, but they knew roughly where it was supposed to be – there's never been a detailed survey done of the Malaysian interior. But that's where the Parrishes were headed every weekend during that dry season. The attraction was the monkeys. Apparently, the local *sakais* – they might have been Laruts – had deported some wild monkeys there. The monkeys got too stroppy around the village, so being peace-loving buggers the *sakais* just caught them and tied them up and brought them to the island where they wouldn't bother anyone. There were about a dozen of these beasts, surrounded by water. An island of wild monkeys – imagine landing there on a dark night!

'In the meantime, we saw the Parrishes occasionally in the compound during the week and that's where I kept up to date with the story. As I say, his first reaction when she lost things was to be sympathetic. But afterwards, it irritated him. She lost her handbag and he shouted at her. She lost her watch – it was one he had given her – and he wouldn't speak to her for days. She mislaid the bathplug, lost some jewellery, his passport disappeared. And that's the way it went – bloody annoying. I don't know what effect this had on her. I suppose she thought she deserved his anger. People who lose things get all knotted up about it, and the fear of losing things makes them do it all the more. That's what I thought then.

'And the things she lost were never found. It was uncanny, as if she just wished them away. He said she didn't miss them.

'Then, on one of these expeditions she lost the paraffin. Doesn't seem like much, but the place was full of leeches and a splash of paraffin was the only thing that'd shake them loose from your arms or legs. They both suffered that weekend and didn't find the island either. Then, the next weekend, she lost the compass, and that's when the real trouble started. Instead of pitying her, or getting angry, or ignoring it, old Parrish laughed. He saw how losing the compass inconvenienced her in her map-reading, and she was so shaken by that horrible laugh of his she was all the more determined to do without it. She succeeded, too. She used a topographical map and somehow found the right landmarks and led them back the way they'd come.

'But Parrish still laughed. I remember the day she lost the car-keys – *his* car-keys, mind you, because she'd lost practically everything she owned and now it was his stuff up the spout. You could hear old Parrish halfway to Malacca. Then it was the malaria tablets. Parrish laughed even harder – he said he'd been in the Federation so long he was immune to it, but being young and new to the place she'd get a fever, and he found that screamingly funny. This was too much for her, and when his wedding ring just went missing – God only knows how *that* happened – and Parrish just laughed, that was the last straw. I suppose it didn't help matters when Parrish set off for the court-house in the morning saying, "What are you going to lose today, my darling?"

'Oh, there was much more. He talked about it at parties, laughing his head off, while she sulked in a corner, and we expected to find him dead the next morning with a knitting-needle jammed through his wig.

'But, to make a long story short, they went off on one of their usual expeditions. No compass, no paludrine, no torch – she'd lost practically everything. By this time, they knew their way, and they spent all that Saturday bush-whacking through the *ulu*. They were still headed in that deliberate way of theirs for the monkey island, and now I remember that a lot of people called him "Monkey" Parrish. She claimed it was mythical, didn't exist, except in the crazy fantasies of a lot of *sakais*; but Monkey said, "I know what you've done with it, my darling – you've lost that island!" And naturally he laughed.

'They were making camp that night in a grove of bamboos when it happened. It was dusk, and looking up they saw one of those enormous clouds of flying foxes in the sky. Ever see them? They're really fruit-bats, four feet from tip to tip, and they beat the air slowly. You get them in the *ulu* near the coast. Eerie, they are – scare the wits out of you the way they fly, and they're ugly as old boots. You can tell the old ones by the way they move, sort of dropping behind and losing altitude while the younger ones push their noses on ahead. It's one of the weirdest sights in this country, those flying foxes setting off in the twilight, looking so fat and fearsome in the sky. Like a bad dream, a kind of monster film – they come out of nowhere.

'She said, "Look they're heading for the island."

'He said, "Don't be silly – they're flying east, to the coast."

' "There's the light," she said, "that's west." She claimed the bats preferred islands and would be homing in on one where there was fruit – monkey food. The wild monkeys slept at night, so they wouldn't bother the bats. She said, "I'm going to have a look."

' "There's no torch," he says, and he laughs like hell.

' "There's a moon," she says. And without another word she's crashing through the bamboos in the direction the foxes are flying. Parrish – Monkey Parrish – just laughed and sat down by the fire to have a pipe before bed. Can you see him there, chuckling to himself about this wife of his who loses everything, how he suddenly realizes that she's lost herself and he has a fit of laughter? Great hoots echoing through the jungle as old Parrish sees he's rid of her at last!

'Maybe. But look at it another way. The next morning he wakes up and sees she's not there. She never came back. At first he slaps his thigh and laughs and shouts, "She's lost!" Then he looks around. No map, no compass, no torch – only that low dense jungle that stretches for hundreds of miles across the top of the country, dropping leeches on anyone who's silly enough to walk through it. And the more he thinks about it the more it becomes plain to him that *he's* the one who's lost – she's wished him away, like the wedding ring and the torch and the fifty-dollar bill. Suddenly, he's not laughing any more.

'I'm only guessing. I don't really know what he was thinking. I had the story from her, just before she left the country. She said there were only two monkeys on the island, a male and a female, bickering the whole time, like her and her late husband. Yes, *late* husband. No one ever found him – certainly not her, but she wouldn't would she?'

William and Photography

☆★☆

RICHMAL CROMPTON

Mrs Adolphus Crane was William's mother's second cousin and William's godmother. Among the many senseless institutions of grown-up life the institutions of godmothers and godfathers seemed to William the most senseless of all. Moreover, Mrs Adolphus Crane was rich and immensely respectable – the last person whom Fate should have selected as his godmother. Fortunately, she lived at a distance, and so was spared the horrible spectacle of William's daily crimes. His meetings with her had not been fortunate, so far, in spite of his family's earnest desire that he should impress her favourably.

There had been that terrible meeting two months ago. William was running a race with one of his friends. It was quite a novel race invented by William. The competitors each had their mouths full of water and the one who could run the farthest without either swallowing his load or discharging it, won. William in the course of the race encountered Mrs Adolphus Crane, who was on her way to William's house to pay him a surprise visit. She recognized him and addressed to him a kindly, affectionate remark. Of course, if he had had time to think over the matter from all points of view, he might have conceived the idea of swallowing the water before he answered. But, as he afterwards explained, he had no time to think. The worst of it was that the painful incident was witnessed by almost all William's family from the drawing-room window. Mrs Adolphus Crane's visit on that occasion was a very short one. She seemed slightly distant. It was felt strongly that something must be done to win back her favour. William disclaimed all responsibility.

'Well, I can't help it. I *can't* help it. I don't mind. Honestly I don't mind if she doesn't like me. Well, I don't mind if she doesn't come again, either.'

'But, William, she's your godmother.'

'Well,' said the goaded William. 'I can't help *that*. I didn't do *that*.'

When Mrs Adolphus Crane's birthday came, William's mother attacked him again.

'You ought to give her something William, you know, especially after the way you treated her the last time she came over.'

'I've nothin' to give her,' said William simply. 'She can have that book Uncle George gave me, if she likes. Yes, she can have that.' He warmed to the subject. 'You know. The one about Ancient Hist'ry. I don't mind her having it a bit.'

'But you haven't read it.'

'I don't mind not readin' it,' said William generously. 'I – I'd like her to have it,' he went on.

But it was Mrs Brown who had the great inspiration.

'We'll have William's photograph taken for her.'

It was quite simple to say that, and it was quite simple to make an appointment at the photographer's, but it was another matter to provide an escort for him. Mrs Brown happened to have a bad cold; Mr Brown was at the office; Robert, William's grown-up brother, flatly refused to go with him. So, after a conversation that lasted almost an hour, William's elder sister Ethel was induced, mainly by bribery and corruption, to go with William to the photographer's. But she took a friend with her to act as a buffer state.

William, at the appointed hour, was in a state of suppressed fury. To William the lowest depth of humiliation was having his photograph taken. Mrs Brown had expended much honest toil upon him. He had been washed and brushed and combed and manicured till his spirits had sunk below zero. To William, complete cleanliness was quite incompatible with happiness. He had been encased in his 'best suit' – a thing of hard, unbending cloth; with that horror of horrors, a stiff collar.

'Won't a jersey do?' he had asked plaintively. 'It'll probably make me ill – give me a sore throat or somethin' – this tight thing at my neck, an' I wouldn't like to be ill – 'cause of giving you trouble,' he ended piously.

Mrs Brown was touched – she was the one being in the world who never lost faith in William.

'But you wear it every Sunday, dear,' she protested.

'Sundays is different,' he said. 'Everyone wears silly things on Sundays – but, but s'pose I met someone on my way there.' His horror was pathetic.

'Well, you look very nice, dear. Where are your gloves?'

'*Gloves!*' he said indignantly.

'Yes – to keep your hands clean till you get there.'

'Is anyone goin' to *give* me anythin' for doin' all this?'

She sighed.

'No, dear. It's to give pleasure to your godmother. I know you like to give people pleasure.' William was silent, cogitating over this entirely new aspect of his character.

He set off down the road with Ethel and her friend Blanche. Bosom friends of his, with jerseys, with normal dirty hands and faces, passed him and stared at him in amazement.

He acknowledged their presence only by a cold stare. On ordinary days he was a familiar figure on that road himself, also comfortably jerseyed and gloriously dirty. He would then have greeted them with a war-whoop and a friendly punch. But now he was an outcast, a pariah, a thing apart – a boy in his best clothes and kid gloves on an ordinary morning.

The photographer was awaiting them. William returned his smile of welcome with a scowl.

'So this is our little friend?' said the photographer. 'And what is his name?'

William grew purple.

Ethel began to enjoy it.

'Willie,' she said.

Now, there were many insults that William had learned to endure with outward equanimity, but this was not one. Ethel knew perfectly well his feeling with regard to the name 'Willie'. It was a deliberate revenge because she had to waste a whole morning on him. Moreover, Ethel had various scores to wipe off against William, and it was not often that she had him entirely at her mercy.

William growled. That is the only word that describes the sound emitted.

'Pretty name for a pretty boy,' commented the photographer in sprightly vein.

Ethel and Blanche gurgled. William, dark and scowling, looked unspeakable things at them.

'Come forward,' said the photographer invitingly. 'Any preparations? Fancy dress?'

'I think not,' gurgled Ethel.

'I have some nice costumes,' he persisted. 'A little page? Bubbles? But perhaps the hair is hardly suitable. Cupid? I have some pretty wings and drapery. But perhaps the little boy's expression is hardly – No, I think not,' hastily, as he encountered the fixed intensity of William's scowling gaze. 'Remove the cap and gloves, my little chap.'

He looked up and down William's shining, immaculate person. 'Ah, very nice.'

He waved Ethel and Blanche to a seat.

'Now, my boy –'

He waved the infuriated William to a rustic woodland scene at the other end.

'Now, stand just here. That's right. No, not quite so stiff – and – no, not quite so hunched up, my little chap . . . the hands resting carelessly . . . one on the hip, I think . . . just easy and natural . . . *that's* right . . . but no, hardly. Relax the brow a little. And – ah, no . . . not a grimace . . . it would spoil a pretty picture . . . the feet *so* . . . and the head *so* . . . the hair is slightly deranged . . . that's better.'

Let it stand to William's eternal credit that he resisted the temptation to bite the photographer's hand as it strayed among his short locks. At last he was posed and the photographer returned to the camera, but during his return William moved feet, hands, and head to an easier position. The photographer sighed.

'Ah, he's moved. William's moved. What a pity! We'll have to begin all over again.'

He returned to William, and very patiently he rearranged William's feet and hands and head.

'The toes turned out – not in, you see, Willie, and the hands *so*, and the head slightly on one side . . . *so*, no, not right down on to the shoulder . . . ah, that's right . . . that's sweet, a very pretty picture.'

Ethel had retired hysterically behind a screen.

The photographer returned to his camera. William promptly composed his limbs more comfortably.

'Ah, what a pity! Willie's moved again. We shall have to commence afresh.'

He returned to William and again put his unwilling head on one side, his hand upon his hip, and turned William's stout boots at a graceful angle.

He returned. William was clinging doggedly to his pose. Anything to put an end to this torture.

'Ah, right,' commented the photographer. 'Splendid! Ve-ery pretty. The head just a lee-eetle more on one side. The expression a lee-eetle less – melancholy. A smile, please – just a lee-eetle smile. Ah, no,' hastily, as William savagely bared his teeth, 'perhaps it is better without the smile.'

Suppressed gurgles came from behind the screen where Ethel clung helplessly to Blanche. 'One more, please. *Sitting*, I think, this time. The legs crossed – easily and naturally – *so*. The elbow resting on the arm of the chair and the cheek upon the hand – *so*.' He retired to a distance and examined the effect, with his head on one side. 'A little spoilt by the expression, perhaps – but very pretty. The expression a lee-eetle less – er – fierce, if you will pardon the word.' William here deigned to speak.

'I can't look any different to this,' he remarked coldly.

'Now, think of the things I say,' went on the photographer, brightly. 'Sweeties? Ah!' looking merrily at William's unchanging ferocious expression. 'Do I see a saucy little smile?' As a matter of fact, he didn't, because at that moment Ethel, her eyes streaming, peeped round the screen for another look at the priceless sight of William in his best suit, in the familiar attitude of the Bard of Avon. Encountering the concentrated fury of William's gaze, she retired hastily.

'Seaside with spade and bucket?' went on the photographer, watching William's unchanging expression. 'Pantomimes? That nice, soft, furry pussy cat you've got at home?' But seeing William's expression change from one of scornful fury to one of Nebuchadnezzan rage and fury, he hastily pressed the little ball lest worse should follow.

Ethel's description of the morning considerably enlivened the lunch table. Only Mrs Brown did not join in the roars of laughter.

'But I think it sounds very nice, dear,' she said, 'very nice. I'm very much looking forward to the proofs coming.'

'Well, it was priceless,' said Ethel. 'It was ever so much funnier than the pantomime. I wouldn't have missed it for anything. For years to come, if I feel depressed, I shall just think of William this morning. His face . . . oh, his face!'

William defended himself.

'My face is jus' like anyone else's face,' he said indignantly. 'I don't know why you're all laughing. There's nothin' funny about my face. I've never *done* anythin' to it. It's no different to other people's. It doesn't make *me* laugh.'

'No, dear,' said Mrs Brown soothingly, 'it's very nice – very nice, indeed. And I'm sure it will be a beautiful photograph.'

The proofs arrived the next week. They were highly appreciated by William's family. There were two positions. In one, William in an attitude of intellectual contemplation, glowered at them from an artistic background; in the other, he stood stiffly with one hand on his hip, his toes (in spite of all) turned resolutely in, and glared ferociously and defiantly upon the world in general. Mrs Brown was delighted. 'I think it's awfully nice,' she said, 'and he looks so smart and clean.'

William, mystified by Robert's and Ethel's reception of them, carried them up to his room and studied them long and earnestly.

'Well, I can't see wot's *funny* about them,' he said at last, half indignantly and half mystified. 'It doesn't seem funny to *me*.'

'You'll have to write a letter to your godmother, dear,' said Mrs Brown, as Mrs Adolphus Crane's birthday drew near.

'*Me*?' said William bitterly. 'I should think I've done *enough* for her.'

'No,' said Mrs Brown firmly, 'you *must* write a letter.'

'I dunno what to say to her.'

'Say whatever comes into your head.'

'I dunno how to *spell* all the words that come in my head.'

'I'll help you, dear.'

Seeing no escape, William sat gloomily down at the table and was supplied with pen, ink, and paper. He looked round disapprovingly.

'S'pose I wear out the nib?' he said sadly. Mrs Brown obligingly placed a box of nibs at his elbow. He sighed wearily. Life sometimes is hardly worth living.

After much patient thought he got as far as 'Dear Godmother.' He occupied the next ten minutes in seeing how far you could bend apart the two halves of a nib without breaking them. After breaking six, he wearied of the occupation and returned to his letter. With deeply-furrowed brow and protruding tongue he continued his efforts. 'Many happy returns of your birthday. I hopp you are verry well. I am very well and so is mother and father and Ethel and Robbert.' He gazed out of the window and chewed the end of his penholder into splinters. Some he swallowed, then choked, and had to retire for a drink of water. Then he demanded a fresh pen. After about fifteen minutes he returned to his epistolary efforts.

'It is not raning today,' he wrote, after much thought. Then, 'It did not rane yesterday and we are hoppin' it will not rane tomorrow.'

Having exhausted that topic, he scratched his head in despair, wrinkled up his brows, and chewed his penholder again.

'I have a hole in my stocking,' was his next effort. Then, 'I have had my phottograf took and send it for a birthday present. Some people think it funny but to me it seems alrite. I hopp you will like it. Your loving godsun, William.'

Mrs Adolphus Crane was touched, both by letter and photograph.

'I must have been wrong,' she said with penitence. 'He looks so *good*. And there's something rather *sad* about his face.'

She asked William to her birthday tea-party. To William this was the climax of a long chain of insults.

'But I don't *want* to go to tea with her,' he said in dismay.

'But she wants you, darling,' said Mrs Brown. 'I expect she liked your photograph.'

'I'm not going,' said William testily, 'if they're all going to be laughing at my photograph all the time. I'm jus' sick of people laughing at my photograph.'

'Of course they won't, dear,' said Mrs Brown. 'It's a very nice photograph. You look a bit – depressed in it, that's all.'

'Well, that's not *funny*,' he said indignantly.

'Of course not, dear. You'll behave nicely, won't you?'

'I'll behave ordinary,' he said coldly, 'but I don't want to go. I don't want to go 'cause – 'cause – 'cause –' he sought silently for a reason that might appeal to a grown-up mind, then, with a brilliant inspiration, ''cause I don't want my best clothes to get all wore out.'

'I don't think they will, dear,' she said; 'don't worry about that.'

William dejectedly promised not to.

The afternoon of Mrs Adolphus Crane's birthday dawned bright and clear, and William, resigned and martyred, set off. He arrived early and was shown into Mrs Adolphus Crane's magnificent drawing-room. An air of magisterial magnificence shed gloom over Mrs Adolphus Crane's whole house. Mrs Adolphus Crane, as magisterial, and magnificent and depressing and enormous as her house, entered.

'Good afternoon, William. Now I've a pleasant little surprise for you.' William's gloomy countenance brightened. 'I've put your photograph into my album. There! What an honour for a little boy!' William's countenance relapsed into gloom.

'You can look at the album while I'm getting ready, and then when the guests come you can show it to them. Won't that be nice?' She departed.

William was trapped – trapped in a huge and horrible drawing-room by a huge and horrible woman, and he would have to stay there at least two hours. And Ginger and Henry were bird-nesting! Oh, the horror of it. Why was he chosen by Fate for this penance? He felt a sudden fury against the art of photography in general. William's sudden furies against anything demanded some immediate outlet.

So William, with the aid of a pencil, looked at Mrs Adolphus Crane's family album till Mrs Adolphus Crane was ready. Then she arrived, and soon after her the guests, or rather such of them as had not had the presence of mind to invent excuses for their absence. For, funeral affairs were Mrs Adolphus Crane's parties. Liveliness and hilarity dropped slain on the doorstep. The guests came sadly into the drawing-room, and Mrs Adolphus Crane dispensed gloom from the hearthrug. Her voice was low and deep.

'How do you do . . . thank you so much . . . I doubt whether I shall live to see another . . . yes, my nerves! By the way – my little godson –' They turned to look at William who was sitting in silent misery in a corner, his hands on his knees. He returned their interested stares with his best company frown. On the chair by him was the album. 'Have you seen the family album?' went on Mrs Adolphus Crane. 'It's most interesting. Do look at it.' A group of visitors sadly gathered round it and one of them opened it. Mrs Adolphus Crane did not join them. She knew her album by heart. She took her knitting, sat down by the fire, and poured forth her knowledge.

'The first one is great uncle Joshua,' she said, 'a splendid old man. Never touched tobacco or alcoholic drinks in his life.'

They looked at great uncle Joshua. He sat, grim and earnest and respectable, with his hand on the table. But a lately-added pipe, in pencil, adorned his mouth, and his hand seemed to encircle a tankard. Quite suddenly animation returned to the group by the album. They began to believe that they were going to enjoy it, after all.

'Then comes my poor, dear mother.' Poor, dear mother wore a large eye-glass with a black ribbon and a wild Indian head-dress. The group by the album grew large. There seemed to be some magnetic attraction about it.

'Then comes my paternal uncle James, a very handsome man.'

Paternal uncle James might have been a very handsome man before his nose had been elongated for several inches, and his lips curved into an enormous smile, showing gigantic teeth. He smoked a large, vulgar-looking pipe.

'A beautiful character, too,' said Mrs Adolphus Crane. She continued the family catalogue, and the visitors followed the photographs in the album. They were all embellished. Some had pipes, some had blue noses, some had black eyes, some giant spectacles, some comic head-dresses. Some had received more attention than others. Aunt Julia, 'a most saintly woman,' positively leered from her 'cabinet,' with a huge nose, and a black eye, and a cigar in her mouth. The album was handed from one to another. An unwonted hilarity and vivacity reigned supreme – and always there were crowds round the album.

Mrs Adolphus Crane was surprised, but vaguely flattered. Her party seemed more successful than usual. People seemed to be taking quite a lot of notice of William, too. One young curate, who had wept tears over the album, pressed half a crown into William's hand. By some unerring instinct they guessed the author of the outrage. As a matter of fact, Mrs Adolphus Crane did not happen to look at her album till several months later, and then it did not occur to her to connect it with William. But this afternoon she somehow connected the strange spirit of cheerfulness that pervaded her drawing-room with him, and was most gracious to him.

'He's been *so* good,' she said to Mrs Brown when she arrived to take William home; 'quite helped to make my little party a success.'

Mrs Brown concealed her amazement as best she could.

'But what did you *do*, William?' she said on the way home as William plodded along beside her, his hands in his pockets lovingly fingering his half-crown.

'Me?' said William innocently. 'Nothin'.'

The White Wedding

☆★☆★☆★☆★☆★☆★☆★☆★☆★☆★☆★☆★☆★☆★☆★☆★☆

DAVID NOBBS

The doors at the back of the abbey church creaked open, and the radiant bride appeared on the arm of her noticeably less radiant father.

Jenny Rodenhurst looked stunning in her wedding dress, which had achieved that elegance of simplicity which only money can buy. It was entirely white, and successfully combined traditionalism with modernity. Her accessories were extremely spare, in view of all the suffering in the Third World. Her lengthy train was held by two bridesmaids. One of them was very young, and the other one was very fat.

Her father, Laurence Rodenhurst, was as perfectly dressed as it is possible for a man to be without ceasing to look like a dentist.

Leslie Horton, water bailiff and organist, who hated to be called Les, launched himself into a hefty rendition of 'Here Comes The Bride'; and a brief burst of sunlight poured through the memorial stained-glass window dedicated to the King's Own Yorkshire Light Infantry, on whose side God had been in two world wars, though this hadn't prevented them suffering heavy casualties.

The sizeable congregation craned their necks with varying degrees of shameless curiosity to watch the bridal procession, as it moved slowly past the stall of devotional literature, past the red arrow that indicated the distressingly slow progress of the Tower Appeal Fund, past the empty back pews and massive columns of the austere Norman nave, towards the less fearsome, more decorated beauty of the Early English chancel. Now the bride and her father were level with the least important of the guests, the third cousins twice removed, the employees who just couldn't not be invited, and the funny little man with the big ears who turned up unbidden at all the weddings.

Rita Simcock, mother of the groom and wife of the town's premier maker of toasting forks, was painfully aware that there were more people on the bride's side than on theirs, that the people on the bride's side were better dressed and more stylish. She was painfully aware that her younger son, Paul, the groom, was unemployed, and hadn't had the haircut that he had promised, and looked a mess. She was painfully aware that her elder son, the cynical Elvis, although he had a philosophy degree from the University of Keele, was also unemployed, there being no vacancies for philosophers at the Job Centre just then, and looked almost as great a mess as Paul.

Liz Rodenhurst, mother of the lovely bride, a year older than Rita but looking ten years younger, was aware of all these things too, but her main emotion as she watched the slow procession was one of irritation with her daughter for having had her beautiful hair cropped short before this day of all days. It emphasized the slight heaviness of her jaw. How perverse the young were. But then it was perverse of Jenny to marry Paul at all. 'If only I'd had the sense not to advise against it,' she thought.

The procession had reached the more important guests, first cousins twice removed, second cousins once removed, friends, uncles, aunts with unsuitable hats, Rita's slightly glazed parents, brothers, mothers, one wishing her son's hair was shorter, the other wishing her daughter's hair was longer – was nobody happy on this happy day? Certainly not the Reverend J. D. Thoroughgood. Hardly a genuine churchgoer among the whole caboosh.

As Laurence came level with Liz, he gave her a brief glance. 'What kind of a dash am I cutting?' it asked.

In reply Liz smiled, a brief demonstration of a smile, indicating to her husband that he was to remember to look happy.

Laurence nodded imperceptibly, then smiled bravely, though not entirely successfully. He was a tall, slim man with cool eyes, handsome in a rather theoretical way, like a drawing of a good-looking man. His hair was receding quietly, sensibly, with impeccable manners. Men considered him a fine figure of a man. Women didn't.

Ted Simcock nudged Paul, who stepped forward, almost tripping. At the sight of Paul, Laurence's smile flickered, then fluttered bravely, like an upside-down Union Jack in a stiff, biting, easterly wind. And the sunlight disappeared brutally, as if it had been switched off.

Paul Simcock, the badly groomed groom, was twenty-one, and very nervous. His face seemed to be trying to hide beneath all that hair. His tie was very loosely tied – a compromise which pleased nobody. His inexpensive suit had almost been fashionable teenage wear when he had bought it. Five years later it was a museum piece. He had filled out in those five years, and it barely met around his groin, buttocks, chest and shoulders. He felt as if *it* had put *him* on in a great hurry. Buttons would burst and the zip fly open if he so much as gazed at a hard-boiled egg and Danish caviare canapé, and a pint of Theakston's Best would be out of the question. How he wished now that he hadn't been so stubborn in refusing his father's offer of a new suit.

How he wished he hadn't chosen the uncouth Neil Hodgson as best man.

The organ music ceased. 'Dearly beloved,' said the Reverend J. D. Thoroughgood rather severely, as if hinting that they would be more dearly beloved if more regularly seen at church. 'We are gathered here together in the sight of God . . .'

'I don't believe in Him,' thought Jenny. 'I wish we'd done it in a registry office.'

'. . . woman in Holy Matrimony, which is an honourable estate,' continued the vicar, whose own daughter had run off to London seventeen years ago and had never been seen again. Some said he retained the old words in all his services because for him time had stopped at that moment. '. . . instituted of God in the time of man's innocency . . .'

Liz Rodenhurst looked round at exactly the same time as Ted Simcock. Her eyes glinted, and Ted, father of the groom, spurned offerer of new suits, turned away hastily and hung on the vicar's words with exaggerated attention.

Liz smiled.

'. . . and therefore is not by any to be enterprized, nor taken in hand, unadvisedly, lightly, or wantonly, to satisfy men's carnal lusts and appetites.'

'No mention of women's carnal lusts and appetites, I notice,' thought Liz.

'. . . but reverently, discreetly, advisedly, soberly . . .'

'Oh I hope so,' thought Rodney Sillitoe, managing director of Cock-A-Doodle Chickens and close friend of the groom's parents. 'I'll be watching her.'

'I'll be watching him,' thought his wife Betty, who was overdressed as usual. 'If he lets the side down today . . .'

'. . . for which Matrimony was ordained,' continued the vicar in his strong, steady, undramatic Yorkshire voice, so unlike those comedy vicars on television which his wife always switched off, though they amused him as evidence of the media's tiny minds – not that either of them watched comedy or indeed television much, especially since time had stopped. 'First it was ordained for the procreation of children . . .'

'Yes, well,' said Paul Simcock silently, but half expecting to be heard by God, because under the powerful influence of the devotional atmosphere it seemed possible that He might exist after all. 'I'm afraid we jumped the gun a bit there.'

'. . . the Lord, and to the praise of his Holy Name.' The Reverend J. D. Thoroughgood's voice brought a touch of the hard limestone country into this town of the softer plains. 'Secondly, it was ordained for a remedy against sin, and to avoid fornication.'

'Sorry,' said Ted Simcock to his maker, and to his horror it almost came out aloud. His face, always slightly red, as if he overdid things, went even redder. He was a broad, bulky man, with slightly coarse features and fierce shaggy brows. His thick black hair was turning grey. Men didn't consider him much of a figure of a man. Women did.

'. . . that such persons as have not the gift of continency . . .'

'All right?' whispered Rita's mother, the seventy-six-year-old Clarrie Spragg.

'Oh aye.' Percy Spragg's answering whisper was much too loud, and Rita turned to give her father a frantic, warning glare.

'. . . themselves undefiled members of Christ's body. Thirdly . . .'

This time it was Ted's eyes that were drawn to Liz's fractionally before she gave him an unmistakeably meaningful glance. Laurence turned and saw Ted looking in his wife's direction, and Ted developed a sudden interest in the magnificent hammer-beam roof. Another burst of sunlight was streaming into the huge old church. The day was improving.

'Therefore, if any man can shew any just cause why they may not lawfully be joined together, let him now speak, or else hereafter for ever hold his peace.'

The Reverend J. D. Thoroughgood paused dramatically, and swept a severe gaze over the congregation. The sunshine seemed very far away, in another world.

'Make somebody say something, please, oh Lord,' prayed Laurence with a fervour that surprised him. 'Save my daughter from this unsuitable marriage.'

'I require and charge you both,' said the vicar, damping Laurence's brief hope, and the church darkened again as the summer's day played grim meteorological jests with their emotions, 'as ye will answer at the dreadful day of judgement . . .'

'I don't dread it,' thought Rita. 'That's the day I come into my own.'

'. . . know any impediment, why ye may not be lawfully joined together in Matrimony, ye do now confess it. For be ye well assured, that so many as are coupled together otherwise than God's Word doth allow are not joined together by God; neither is their Matrimony lawful.'

Paul and Jenny smiled at each other a little uneasily, long-haired cheap-suited groom beside close-cropped, beautifully gowned bride, but united in their youth, their vulnerability and their love. They joined hands, and gave each other a little squeeze, and held their peace. Afterwards, both admitted that they had felt shivers and goose pimples at that moment.

'Wilt thou have this woman to thy wedded wife, to live together . . . ?'

'He promised me he'd have a haircut,' said Rita to herself. 'He promised.' She had achieved, with her bottle-green two-piece suit and pink hat, the difficult feat of looking puritanical and over-dressed at the same time. Her austere hair style and natural air of worry made her look older than her forty-seven years. She had a hunched appearance, as if she were trying not to take up too much space.

'. . . and in health, and forsaking all other, keep thee only unto her, so long as ye both shall live?'

'Oh Jane!' called out the immaculate Neville Badger silently from the bride's side of the church, and this dapper doyen of the town's lawyers also had a moment of horror when he thought that everyone must have heard, so loud did his agonized private cry seem to him: 'Oh, Jane! Do you remember our wedding in this church?'

'I will,' whispered Paul, after a moment when it seemed that he would never speak.

The Reverend J. D. Thoroughgood turned to Jenny. Was it possible that he didn't think of his own daughter at this moment?

'Wilt thou have this man to thy wedded . . .?'

'Look happy, Laurence,' Laurence told himself. 'If you look happy long enough, you may even start to feel happy.'

'. . . keep thee only unto him, so long as ye both shall live?'

'Oh Lord,' prayed the immaculate Neville Badger. 'Why did you take her from me?'

'I will,' said Jenny clearly, with an outward confidence that contrasted sharply with Paul's delivery and made her parents feel that the money they had spent on her education had not been entirely wasted.

There was a slight commotion towards the back of the congregation. A second cousin twice removed had been overcome by emotion, and had to be removed. Rita was painfully conscious that it was on their side of the church.

Outside, in the bustling summer streets, people were peering at details of skiing holidays which they couldn't afford, gawping at dresses which they would never wear, and slowly reading the meagre lists of unappetizing catering vacancies in the Job Centre. To the town's seventy thousand inhabitants, the abbey church was so familiar as to be almost invisible.

The ancient market town had expanded rapidly with a mixture of light industry and heavy engineering, which were both now declining. A combination of ignorant councillors, apathetic citizens and ruthless property developers had removed almost all traces of its ancient heritage, except for the abbey church and the street names. Few tourists stopped off on their way to York, Durham and Edinburgh.

It wasn't surprising, therefore, that at the moment when the great West Door creaked open, nobody was looking at the abbey, except for a visiting Greek-Cypriot builder who was staring open-mouthed at the scaffolding which encased the massive tower.

Then suddenly the assertive strains of Leslie Horton, water bailiff and organist, who hated to be called Les, were mingling with the hum of the Saturday afternoon traffic. Now people stopped and stared, eager to see the lovely bride, the lucky groom, the proud parents, the hats and dresses of the aunts and cousins.

Six bachelor philatelists, on their way to an exhibition in the annexe of the Alderman Cartwright Memorial Museum (entrance by the side door, in West Riding Passage), watched from the top deck of a bright yellow corporation bus as the wedding guests filtered slowly under the four beautifully carved recessed arches of the Norman doorway. The philatelists were in a good mood, being as yet unaware that the exhibition of wildlife stamps had closed at one, due to local government cutbacks. One of them said, 'They haven't got too bad a day for it,' and the other five were not disposed to argue. For the paths were almost dry now after the last brief shower, and there was almost as much blue in the sky as cloud.

The wedding guests stood around in uneasy knots, not quite knowing what to do with themselves, while the funny little man with big ears who turned up unbidden at all the weddings hurried off to the Baptist Chapel, where a promising event was scheduled for three o'clock.

'Did you see Paul's hair?' said Rita Simcock in a low voice.

'I could hardly miss it,' said Ted rather less softly. 'It was on the top of his head, as usual.'

'S'ssh!' she hissed. 'He promised he'd have it cut, Ted. He promised. I mean . . . what *will* they think? They already think we're not good enough for them.'

'He's a dentist, Rita, not First Lord of the Admiralty,' said Ted.

'S'ssh! Here they come,' whispered Rita urgently. 'Look happy!' She turned to face the Rodenhurst parents, who were approaching with the immaculate Neville Badger. 'Didn't it go off well?' she said, giving a radiant smile that had no radiance in it.

'Very well,' said Liz.

'You must be very happy,' said Neville Badger. He was in his early fifties, but his recent grief seemed to set him apart as a member of the previous generation. 'Jenny looked a picture,' he said, turning to Liz and Laurence. 'A picture. I think she's putting on a bit of weight. It suits her.'

'Do you all know each other?' said Laurence. 'No? Ah! Neville Badger, a very old friend. Paul's parents, Ted and Rita Simcock.'

Neville Badger shook hands with Ted and Rita. Ted said, 'I own the Jupiter Foundry. I expect you've heard of us.' Rita frowned at him. Neville Badger didn't hear him, because of a passing motorcyclist with a faulty silencer and a hang-up about his virility; and when Ted repeated his statement, Neville Badger said, 'Actually, no.'

'Oh,' said Ted. 'Well, we . . . er . . . we make fire irons, companion sets, door knockers, toasting forks . . .'

'Are you a dentist, Mr Badger?' said Rita, breaking in hastily before Ted gave the whole of his firm's sales list, and smiling excessively.

'Oh no! No!' said Neville Badger too vehemently. He gave Laurence an uneasy, apologetic glance. 'No. I'm with Badger, Badger, Fox and Badger.'

'Taxidermists?' asked Ted.

'Solicitors!' said Rita frantically. She flashed him an angry glare, then switched on another nervously ingratiating smile for Neville. The sky was dotted with small white clouds, and in another remarkable meteorological coincidence . . . or celestial joke . . . the sun was popping in and out in ironical counterpoint to Rita's expressions. The sun shone when she frowned. The skies darkened when she smiled.

'I love a good wedding, don't you, Mr Badger?' she said.

'Yes, I . . . I do . . . I . . . excuse me.'

Neville Badger moved off abruptly. Rita stared after him in horrified astonishment, and the sun came out.

'His wife died six weeks ago,' explained Liz.

Two bright pink spots appeared on Rita's cheeks, and Ted gave her a look which said, 'You've done it again.'

Rodney and Betty Sillitoe were approaching. Rodney was forty-eight, Betty fifty-one, but she looked the younger. Rodney Sillitoe was wearing a very good suit, but it looked as if he had fallen asleep in a chicken coop while wearing it. Betty Sillitoe was so enthusiastically overdressed that she almost carried it off. Her dyed blonde hair peeped cheerfully out at the world round the edges of a yellow hat which wouldn't have been out of place in the Royal Enclosure at Ascot. Betty was always the first to draw attention to her dark roots. She dyed her hair to sparkle, not deceive.

'Well, that all went off splendidly,' she said.

Ted made the introductions. Rita wished he'd tried to hide the pride in his voice when he added, 'Rodney's the big wheel behind Cock-A-Doodle Chickens,' as if he were a prize salmon Ted had caught, and she knew that Liz had picked this up. Why else should she have exclaimed, as she shook hands with Rodney and gazed into his grizzled, lined face, 'Ah! A man of power!'

'Your girl looks a picture,' the big wheel behind Cock-A-Doodle Chickens told her. 'A picture.'

Rita tried to hide her irritation at all this praise of Jenny, and then found that she had a far greater irritation to hide. Her parents were hobbling painfully towards them.

Percy Spragg was a bow-legged, barrel-chested old man who appeared to be wearing a demob suit. Clarrie Spragg was a bow-legged, barrel-chested old woman whose face had set over the years into a fearsome and entirely misleading hardness in repose. She looked as if she had bought her clothes at a 1940s jumble sale at which she had arrived late. They looked to Rita as they bore down upon her like two pill boxes left over from our wartime coastal defences.

'Well, that were grand,' said Clarrie Spragg.

'Grand,' echoed Percy Spragg.

Ted effected the introductions reluctantly.

'By 'eck, your daughter's a belter,' Percy Spragg told the Rodenhursts, who flinched and smiled at the same time. Rita glared at her father, and Clarrie Spragg wasn't too pleased either.

Clarrie managed to force herself in between Percy and the group. She whispered grimly, 'Just you mind your Ps and Qs, Percy Spragg.' Her expression softened. 'All right?' she whispered.

'Oh aye,' said Percy Spragg much too loudly, and a playful gust sent his words streaming out over the gravestones which surrounded the abbey church. 'I've only been once since breakfast.'

Rita glared, and Ted hurried over to remove a Co-op carrier bag which was being drummed against one of the gravestones by the wind. As he bent to pick it up, another gust lifted Liz's dress and revealed an achingly tempting knee. He looked away hastily.

'Right, everybody,' said Nigel Thick, the carefully classless young photographer from Marwoods of Moor Street. 'We're all set. Let's have the happy couple.'

There was a murmur of conversation and excitement, a communal release from tension like an echo of a distant mass orgasm, as the guests found that they had a definite role to play once more. They were watchers, admirers, murmurers of 'aaaah!' at appropriate moments. The uneasy knots broke up and re-formed in a homogeneous mass. Except for Elvis Simcock, who prowled on the edges looking cynical, as befitted a young man who had studied the great philosophers and knew how weak-minded mass sentimentality is.

Paul and Jenny stood framed against the magnificent West Doorway of the old abbey church. A low-flying military aircraft struck a discordant note.

'I feel awful,' whispered Jenny, smiling rather desperately.

'Why?' whispered her husband of ten minutes.

'Right! Big smiles! Radiance pouring from every pore!' commanded the classless Nigel Thick. He thought that the taking of wedding photos was beneath him, but he was clever enough not to show this. He came out with all the right words, delivered with automated enthusiasm.

Radiance poured somewhat stickily from every pore, and froze on the cool breeze.

'Great! Terrific!' lied Nigel Thick.

'Wearing white,' whispered Jenny, free to answer Paul's question at last. 'Hypocrisy's the national disease, and we've started to build our marriage on hypocritical foundations.'

'Jenny!' whispered Paul.

'OK,' said the young photographer classlessly. 'Now a nice dreamy one. Two lovebirds gazing into each other's eyes.'

Two extremely embarrassed and shy lovebirds gazed into each other's eyes.

'Aaaaah!' went the uncles and aunts and cousins.

'Great!' said Nigel Thick, who intended to change his name to Barry Precious and become famous. 'Tremendous. Fabulous.'

'The cost of my dress could feed an African family for twenty years,' whispered Jenny.

'Jenny! Forget all that just for today,' whispered Paul.

'OK,' said Nigel Thick. 'Now a real sexy one.'

The happy couple made a brave stab at a real sexy one, and Jenny blushed prettily.

'Nice!' said Nigel Thick. 'Very nice.' Nice was the least complimentary of all his adjectives. He only used it when he meant 'Really awful!' but the massed ranks of the guests didn't seem to feel that it was awful. Another satisfied communal 'Aaaah!' drifted away across the town's jumbled-up skyline towards the foetid River Gadd.

'If our child grows up selfish and deceitful, it'll be our fault,' said Jenny. She didn't need to whisper, as a police siren was blaring.

'Jenny!' said Paul.

'OK,' shouted Nigel Thick, in competition with the siren. 'Let's go for something a bit more informal. Right? OK.'

'Is that all the man I've committed myself to for life can say – "Jenny!"?' said Jenny.

'Jenny!'

Jenny laughed and gave Paul a quick, spontaneous kiss. She had almost forgotten the watching throng.

'Good,' said Nigel Thick. 'Great. Terrific. Fantabulous.'

' "Committed for life!" ' whispered Paul, as the siren faded into the western suburbs. 'It sounds like a prison sentence.'

'Oh Paul, you don't think that, do you?'

'No! Love! 'Course I don't.'

They kissed.

'Aaaah!' went the crowd.

'Ugh!' went the cynical Elvis Simcock.

'Very good!' went the classless Nigel Thick. 'Terrific! Nice one! Tremendous!'

Jenny and Paul disengaged in some confusion, as self-consciousness returned.

'OK,' said Nigel Thick. 'Happy couple out. Four proud parents in.' One day these people would have coffee-table books of his photographs. His mother still called them his 'snaps'. He was sure she did it deliberately.

The four proud parents took up their positions, Simcocks together, Rodenhursts together.

'Anything you ever want in the ironmongery line, Laurence,' said Ted. 'Custom-built door knockers, personalized coal scuttles, you name it, I'll give it at cost price.'

'Well well!' said Laurence. 'It seems that this union can be of great benefit to our family, Liz!'

Liz and Ted both gave Laurence sharp looks. Rita gave Ted a furious look. Laurence's smooth face remained innocent of expression.

'OK,' said Nigel Thick. '*Big* smiles. Happiest day of your life.'

They all smiled, with varying degrees of artificiality and success.

'Terrific,' lied Nigel Thick.

'In fact, Ted,' said Liz, 'we already have one of your companion sets in our drawing room.'

'Oh! In your "drawing room"! Well well!' said Ted. He added, somewhat archly: 'I trust it's giving satisfactory service.'

'Actually the tongs have buckled,' said Laurence.

'OK,' said Nigel Thick. 'Nice dignified one. Nice and solemn. Four pillars of local society, linked by wedlock.'

They found being dignified and solemn easier than smiling.

'Great! Tremendous! Magnificent!'

'I'll bring you a replacement,' said Ted. 'Gratis. Have no fear.'

'Ted!' hissed Rita. 'Don't talk business at functions. Mr Rodenhurst doesn't talk about dental appointments at functions.'

'OK,' said the future Barry Precious classlessly. 'Now change partners. Symbolize that you're all one big happy family.'

The two couples changed places.

'Actually, I think you're both due for a check-up,' said Laurence smoothly, his face a mask. 'I'll get my girl to send you one of our cards.'

'OK,' said Nigel Thick. 'Arms round each other. Nice and friendly. No inhibitions.'

Liz's arm went round Ted, and he felt his bottom being stroked. Had he imagined it? No! There it was again, and a quick playful nip. He was terrified. Of course his bottom, by its very nature, was round the back, out of sight of people he was facing, but still . . . ! Liz's arm was round his waist now. One finger stroked him very gently. It was too small a gesture to be seen by the assembled guests. But still . . . ! He could feel the sweat running down his back.

Laurence put his arm round Rita with fastidious distaste. He looked like the leader of a nation embracing the wife of a hated rival at the end of a conference at which only a meaningless, bland communiqué had been issued.

'Relax!' said Nigel Thick. 'Let it all hang out.'

Laurence regarded this phrase with extreme distaste. He found it impossible to comply but, for the sake of Jenny and social decorum, he did manage to make a bit of it almost hang out. Rita smiled like the Queen being offered sheeps' eyes at a Bedouin banquet. Ted and Liz were more successful.

'Great! Terrific! Fantabulous! Marvellous! OK. Happy couple back in, with the two brothers.'

A robin watched beadily from its vantage point on a nearby gravestone as the four proud parents moved away. Ted gave Liz a warning look. Laurence noticed it, but Rita didn't. She was too busy indicating to Elvis that he was to smile. He made a wry face at her.

Elvis Simcock was twenty-four. He was taller, more self-possessed and wilder than his brother, and he was the only man at the wedding not wearing a suit, though he could have looked quite smart in his red cord jacket and tight brown trousers if he'd wanted to.

Simon Rodenhurst, Jenny's older brother, who was twenty-three, was well dressed in a rather anonymous way, a provincial professional young man who had never felt any urge to rebel. He worked for the estate agents, Trellis, Trellis, Openshaw and Finch. His face had an immature, unformed look, as if it were waiting for his personality to be delivered.

'Elvis?' said Jenny. 'Have you met my brother Simon?'

'No. That's one of the many pleasures I've missed out on so far,' said Elvis Simcock, and his 'hello' to Simon Rodenhurst was barely more than a grunt.

'OK. Big smiles. Bags of brotherly love,' said Nigel Thick.

Paul's and Jenny's smiles were a bit strained. Simon's was perfectly judged. The cynical Elvis's was grotesque, way over the top, a grinning fiend.

'Amazing!' said Nigel Thick, with more than his customary accuracy. He took pictures of the four proud parents with the happy couple, of the happy couple with the two bridesmaids, of the two bridesmaids together, of the very young bridesmaid on her own and therefore also inevitably of the very fat bridesmaid on her own, of the bride on her own and therefore also inevitably of the groom on his own, of the proud parents and the happy couple with Rita's parents. Ted's parents and Laurence's parents were dead, and Liz's widowed mother had remarried, lived in South Africa, and had been advised by her doctor not to travel.

Finally, Nigel Thick took pictures of all the guests, clustered round the great doorway in an amorphous throng. This picture offended his artistic sensibilities, but pleased his commercial instincts. It was ghastly, but everyone in it would buy a copy.

'Right,' he said. 'Say cheese.'

'Cheese,' said everybody except Laurence and Ted. Laurence said nothing. Ted said 'fromage'. There was a little laughter, but not enough.

'Great!' said the carefully classless Nigel Thick. 'Tremendous. Terrific. Marvellous. Fantastic. Fantabulous.' . . .

Sotto voce, as they walked away between the graves, the Simcock parents sparred.

'Why did you have to say "fromage"?'

'People laughed.'

'Out of pity and embarrassment. Why do you have to ruin the greatest day of my life?'

'I thought our wedding was supposed to be the greatest day of your life.'

'It was supposed to be.'

The Sexes

☆★☆★☆★☆★☆★☆★☆★☆★☆★☆

DOROTHY PARKER

The young man with the scenic cravat glanced nervously down the sofa at the girl in the fringed dress. She was examining her handkerchief; it might have been the first one of its kind she had seen, so deep was her interest in its material, form, and possibilities. The young man cleared his throat, without necessity or success, producing a small, syncopated noise.

'Want a cigarette?' he said.

'No, thank you,' she said. 'Thank you ever so much just the same.'

'Sorry I've only got these kind,' he said. 'You got any of your own?'

'I really don't know,' she said. 'I probably have, thank you.'

'Because if you haven't,' he said, 'it wouldn't take me a minute to go up to the corner and get you some.'

'Oh, thank you, but I wouldn't have you go to all that trouble for anything,' she said. 'It's awfully sweet of you to think of it. Thank you ever so much.'

'Will you for God's sakes stop thanking me?' he said.

'Really,' she said, 'I didn't know I was saying anything out of the way. I'm awfully sorry if I hurt your feelings. I know what it feels like to get your feelings hurt. I'm sure I didn't realize it was an insult to say 'thank you' to a person. I'm not exactly in the habit of having people swear at me because I say "thank you" to them.'

'I did not swear at you!' he said.

'Oh, you didn't?' she said. 'I see.'

'My God,' he said, 'all I said, I simply asked you if I couldn't go out and get you some cigarettes. Is there anything in that to get up in the air about? '

'Who's up in the air?' she said. 'I'm sure I didn't know it was a criminal offence to say I wouldn't dream of giving you all that trouble. I'm afraid I must be awfully stupid, or something.'

'Do you want me to go out and get you some cigarettes; or don't you?' he said.

'Goodness,' she said, 'if you want to go so much, please don't feel you have to stay here. I wouldn't have you feel you had to stay for anything.'

'Ah, don't be that way, will you?' he said.

'Be what way?' she said. 'I'm not being any way.'

'What's the matter?' he said.

'Why, nothing,' she said. 'Why?'

'You've been funny all evening,' he said. 'Hardly said a word to me, ever since I came in.'

'I'm terribly sorry you haven't been having a good time,' she said. 'For goodness' sakes, don't feel you have to stay here and be bored. I'm sure there are millions of places you could be having a lot more fun. The only thing, I'm a little bit sorry I didn't know before, that's all. When you said you were coming over tonight, I broke a lot of dates to go to the theatre and everything. But it doesn't make a bit of difference. I'd much rather have you go and have a good time. It isn't very pleasant to sit here and feel you're boring a person to death.'

'I'm not bored!' he said. 'I don't want to go any place! Ah, honey, won't you tell me what's the matter? Ah, please.'

'I haven't the faintest idea what you're talking about,' she said. 'There isn't a thing on earth the matter. I don't know what you mean.'

'Yes, you do,' he said. 'There's something the trouble. Is it anything I've done, or anything?'

'Goodness,' she said, 'I'm sure it isn't any of my business, anything you do. I certainly wouldn't feel I had any right to criticize.'

'Will you stop talking like that?' he said. 'Will you, please?'

'Talking like what?' she said.

'You know,' he said. 'That's the way you were talking over the telephone today, too. You were so snotty when I called you up, I was afraid to talk to you.'

'I beg your pardon,' she said. 'What did you say I was?'

'Well, I'm sorry,' he said. 'I didn't mean to say that. You get me so balled up.'

'You see,' she said, 'I'm really not in the habit of hearing language like that. I've never had a thing like that said to me in my life.'

'I told you I was sorry, didn't I?' he said. 'Honest, honey, I didn't mean it. I don't know how I came to say a thing like that. Will you excuse me? Please?'

'Oh, certainly,' she said. 'Goodness, don't feel you have to apologize to me. It doesn't make any difference at all. It just seems a little bit funny to have somebody you were in the habit of thinking was a gentleman come to your home and use language like that to you, that's all. But it doesn't make the slightest bit of difference.'

'I guess nothing I say makes any difference to you,' he said. 'You seem to be sore at me.'

'I'm sore at you?' she said. 'I can't understand what put that idea in your head. Why should I be sore at you?'

'That's what I'm asking you,' he said. 'Won't you tell me what I've done? Have I done something to hurt your feelings, honey? The way you were, over the phone, you had me worried all day. I couldn't do a lick of work.'

'I certainly wouldn't like to feel,' she said, 'that I was interfering with your work. I know there are lots of girls that don't think anything of doing things like that, but I think it's terrible. It certainly isn't very nice to sit here and have someone tell you you interfere with his business.'

'I didn't say that!' he said. 'I didn't say it!'

'Oh, didn't you?' she said. 'Well, that was the impression I got. It must be my stupidity.'

'I guess maybe I better go,' he said. 'I can't get right. Everything I say seems to make you sorer and sorer. Would you rather I'd go?'

'Please do just exactly whatever you like,' she said. 'I'm sure that last thing I want to do is have you stay here when you'd rather be some place else. Why don't you go some place where you won't be bored? Why don't you go up to Florence Leaming's? I know she'd love to have you.'

'I don't want to go up to Florence Leaming's!' he said. 'What would I want to go up to Florence Leaming's for? She gives me a pain.'

'Oh, really?' she said. 'She didn't seem to be giving you so much of a pain at Elsie's party last night, I notice. I notice you couldn't even talk to anybody else, that's how much of a pain she gave you.'

'Yeah, and you know why I was talking to her?' he said.

'Why, I suppose you think she's attractive,' she said. 'I suppose some people do. It's perfectly natural. Some people think she's quite pretty.'

'I don't know whether she's pretty or not,' he said. 'I wouldn't know her if I saw her again. Why I was talking to her was you wouldn't even give me a tumble, last night. I came up and tried to talk to you, and you just said, "Oh, how do you do" – just like that, "Oh, how do you do" – and you turned right away and wouldn't look at me.'

'I wouldn't look at you?' she said. 'Oh, that's awfully funny. Oh, that's marvellous. You don't mind if I laugh, do you?'

'Go ahead and laugh your head off,' he said. 'But you wouldn't.'

'Well, the minute you came in the room,' she said, 'you started making such a fuss over Florence Leaming, I thought you never wanted to see anybody else. You two seemed to be having such a wonderful time together, goodness knows I wouldn't have butted in for anything.'

'My God,' he said, 'this what's-her-name girl came up and began talking to me before I even saw anybody else, and what could I do? I couldn't sock her in the nose, could I?'

'I certainly didn't see you try,' she said.

'You saw me try to talk to you, didn't you?' he said. 'And what did you do? "Oh, how do you do." Then this what's-her-name came up again, and there I was, stuck. Florence Leaming! I think she's terrible. Know what I think of her? I think she's a damn little fool. That's what I think of her.'

'Well, of course,' she said, 'that's the impression she always gave me, but I don't know. I've heard people say she's pretty. Honestly I have.'

'Why, she can't be pretty in the same room with you,' he said.

'She has got an awfully funny nose,' she said. 'I really feel sorry for a girl with a nose like that.'

'She's got a terrible nose,' he said. 'You've got a beautiful nose. Gee, you've got a pretty nose.'

'Oh, I have not,' she said. 'You're crazy.'

'And beautiful eyes,' he said, 'and beautiful hair and a beautiful mouth. And beautiful hands. Let me have one of the little hands. Ah, look atta little hand! Who's got the prettiest hands in the world? Who's the sweetest girl in the world?'

'I don't know,' she said. 'Who?'

'You don't know!' he said. 'You do so, too, know.'

'I do not,' she said. 'Who? Florence Leaming?'

'Oh, Florence Leaming, my eye!' he said. 'Getting sore about Florence Leaming! And me not sleeping all last night and not doing a stroke of work all day because you wouldn't speak to me! A girl like you getting sore about a girl like Florence Leaming!'

'I think you're just perfectly crazy,' she said. 'I was not sore! What on earth ever made you think I was? You're simply crazy. Ow, my new pearl beads! Wait a second till I take them off. There!'

The Murder of the Mandarin

ARNOLD BENNETT

I

'What's that you're saying about murder?' asked Mrs Cheswardine as she came into the large drawing-room, carrying the supper-tray.

'Put it down here,' said her husband, referring to the supper-tray, and pointing to a little table which stood two legs off and two legs on the hearth-rug.

'That apron suits you immensely,' murmured Woodruff, the friend of the family, as he stretched his long limbs into the fender towards the fire, farther even than the long limbs of Cheswardine. Each man occupied an easy-chair on either side of the hearth; each was very tall, and each was forty.

Mrs Cheswardine, with a whisk infinitely graceful, set the tray on the table, took a seat behind it on a chair that looked like a toddling grand-nephew of the arm-chairs, and nervously smoothed out the apron.

As a matter of fact, the apron did suit her immensely. It is astounding, delicious, adorable, the effect of a natty little domestic apron suddenly put on over an elaborate and costly frock, especially when you can hear the rustle of a silk petticoat beneath, and more especially when the apron is smoothed out by jewelled fingers. Every man knows this. Every woman knows it. Mrs Cheswardine knew it. In such matters Mrs Cheswardine knew exactly what she was about. She delighted, when her husband brought Woodruff in late of a night, as he frequently did after a turn at the club, to prepare with her own hands – the servants being in bed – a little snack of supper for them. Tomato sandwiches, for instance, miraculously thin, together with champagne or Bass. The men preferred Bass, naturally, but if Mrs Cheswardine had a fancy for a sip of champagne out of her husband's tumbler, Bass was not forthcoming.

Tonight it was champagne.

Woodruff opened it, as he always did, and involuntarily poured out a libation on the hearth, as he almost always did. Good-natured, ungainly, long-suffering men seldom achieve the art of opening champagne.

Mrs Cheswardine tapped her pink-slippered foot impatiently.

'You're all nerves tonight,' Woodruff laughed, 'and you've made me nervous.' And at length he got some of the champagne into a tumbler.

'No, I'm not,' Mrs Cheswardine contradicted him.

'Yes, you are, Vera,' Woodruff insisted calmly.

She smiled. The use of that elegant Christian name, with its faint suggestion of Russian archduchesses, had a strange effect on her, particularly from the lips of Woodruff. She was proud of it, and of her surname too – one of the oldest surnames in the Five Towns. The syllables of 'Vera' invariably soothed her, like a charm. Woodruff, and Cheswardine also, had called her Vera during the whole of her life; and she was thirty. They had all three lived in different houses at the top end of Trafalgar Road, Bursley. Woodruff fell in love with her first, when she was eighteen, but with no practical result. He was a brown-haired man, personable despite his ungainliness, but he failed to perceive that to worship from afar off is not the best way to capture a young woman with large eyes and an emotional disposition. Cheswardine, who had a black beard, simply came along and married the little thing. She fluttered down on to his shoulders like a pigeon. She adored him, feared him, cooed to him, worried him, and knew that there were depths of his mind which she would never plumb. Woodruff, after being best man, went on loving, meekly and yet philosophically, and found his chief joy in just these suppers. The arrangement suited Vera; and as for the husband and the hopeless admirer, they had always been fast friends.

'I asked you what you were saying about murder,' said Vera sharply, 'but it seems – '

'Oh! Did you?' Woodruff apologized. 'I was saying that murder isn't such an impossible thing as it appears. Anyone might commit a murder.'

'Then you want to defend Harrisford? Do you hear what he says, Stephen?'

The notorious and terrible Harrisford murders were agitating the Five Towns that November. People read, talked, and dreamt murder; for several weeks they took murder to all their meals.

'He doesn't want to defend Harrisford at all,' said Cheswardine, with a superior masculine air, 'and of course anyone might commit a murder. I might.'

'Stephen! How horrid you are!'

'You might, even!' said Woodruff, gazing at Vera.

'Charlie! Why, the blood alone – '

'There isn't always blood,' said the oracular husband.

'Listen here,' proceeded Woodruff, who read variously and enjoyed philosophical speculation. 'Supposing that by just taking thought, by just wishing it, an Englishman could kill a mandarin in China and make himself rich for life, without anybody knowing anything about it! How many mandarins do you suppose there would be left in China at the end of a week!'

'At the end of twenty-four hours, rather,' said Cheswardine grimly.

'Not one,' said Woodruff.

'But that's absurd,' Vera objected, disturbed. When these two men began their philosophical discussions they always succeeded in disturbing her. She hated to see life in a queer light. She hated to think.

'It isn't absurd,' Woodruff replied. 'It simply shows that what prevents wholesale murder is not the wickedness of it, but the fear of being found out, and the general mess, and seeing the corpse, and so on.'

Vera shuddered.

'And I'm not sure,' Woodruff proceeded, 'that murder is so very much more wicked than lots of other things.'

'Usury, for instance,' Cheswardine put in.

'Or bigamy,' said Woodruff.

'But an Englishman *couldn't* kill a mandarin in China by just wishing it,' said Vera, looking up.

'How do we know?' said Woodruff, in his patient voice. 'How do we know? You remember what I was telling you about thought-transference last week. It was in *Borderland*.'

Vera felt as if there was no more solid ground to stand on, and it angered her to be plunging about in a bog.

'I think it's simply silly,' she remarked. 'No, thanks.'

She said 'No, thanks' to her husband, when he tendered his glass.

He moved the glass still closer to her lips.

'I said "No, thanks," ' she repeated dryly.

'Just a mouthful,' he urged.

'I'm not thirsty.'

'Then you'd better go to bed,' said he.

He had a habit of sending her to bed abruptly. She did not dislike it. But she had various ways of going. Tonight it was the way of an archduchess.

II

Woodruff, in stating that Vera was all nerves that evening, was quite right. She was. And neither her husband nor Woodruff knew the reason.

The reason had to do most intimately with frocks.

Vera had been married ten years. But no one would have guessed it, to watch her girlish figure and her birdlike ways. You see, she was the only child in the house. She often bitterly regretted the absence of offspring to the name and honour of Cheswardine. She envied other wives their babies. She doted on babies. She said continually that in her deliberate opinion the proper mission of women was babies. She was the sort of woman that regards a cathedral as a place built especially to sit in and dream soft domestic dreams; the sort of woman that adores music simply because it makes her dream. And Vera's brown studies, which were frequent, consisted chiefly of babies. But as babies amused themselves by coming down the chimneys of all the other houses in Bursley, and avoiding her house, she sought comfort in frocks. She made the best of herself. And it was a good best. Her figure was as near perfect as a woman's can be, and then there were those fine emotional eyes, and that flutteringness of the pigeon, and an ever-changing charm of gesture. Vera had become the best-dressed woman in Bursley. And that is saying something. Her husband was wealthy, with an increasing income, though, of course, as an earthenware manufacturer, and the son and grandson of an earthenware manufacturer, he joined heartily in the general Five Towns lamentation that there was no longer any money to be made out of 'pots'. He liked to have a well-dressed woman about the house, and he allowed her an incredible allowance, the amount of which was breathed with awe among Vera's friends; a hundred a year, in fact. He paid it to her quarterly, by cheque. Such was his method.

Now a ball was to be given by the members of the Ladies' Hockey Club (or such of them as had not been maimed for life in the pursuit of this noble pastime) on the very night after the conversation about murder. Vera belonged to the Hockey Club (in a purely ornamental sense), and she had procured a frock for the ball which was calculated to crown her reputation as a mirror of elegance. The skirt had – but no (see the columns of the *Staffordshire Signal* for the 9th November, 1901). The mischief was that the gown lacked, for its final perfection, one particular thing, and that particular thing was separated from Vera by the glass front of Brunt's celebrated shop at Hanbridge. Vera could have managed without it. The gown would still have been brilliant without it. But Vera had seen it, and she *wanted* it.

Its cost was a guinea.

Well, you will say, what is a guinea to a dainty creature with a hundred a year? Let her go and buy the article. The point is that she couldn't, because she had only six and sevenpence left in the wide world. (And six weeks to Christmas!) She had squandered – oh, soul above money! – twenty-five pounds, and more than twenty-five pounds, since the 29th of September. Well, you will say, credit, in other words, tick? No, no, no! The giant Stephen absolutely and utterly forbade her to procure anything whatever on credit. She was afraid of him. She knew just how far she could go with Stephen. He was great and terrible. Well, you will say, why couldn't she blandish and cajole Stephen for a sovereign or so? Impossible! She had a hundred a year on the clear understanding that it was never exceeded nor anticipated. Well, you will discreetly hint, there are certain devices known to housewives. . . . Hush! Vera had already employed them. Six and sevenpence was not merely all that remained to her of her dress allowance; it was all that remained to her of her household allowance till the next Monday.

Hence her nerves.

There that poor unfortunate woman lay, with her unconscious tyrant of a husband snoring beside her, desolately wakeful under the night-light in the large, luxurious bedroom – three servants sleeping overhead, champagne in the cellar, furs in the wardrobe, valuable lace round her neck at that very instant, grand piano in the drawing-room, horses in the stable, stuffed bear in the hall – and her life was made a blank for want of fourteen and fivepence! And she had nobody to confide in. How true it is that the human soul is solitary, that content is the only true riches, and that to be happy we must be good!

It was at that juncture of despair that she thought of mandarins. Or rather – I may as well be frank – she had been thinking of mandarins all the time since retiring to rest. There *might* be something in Charlie's mandarin theory. . . . According to Charlie, so many queer, inexplicable things happened in the world. Occult – subliminal – astral – thoughtwaves. These expressions and many more occurred to her as she recollected Charlie's disconcerting conversations. There *might*. . . . One never knew.

Suddenly she thought of her husband's pockets, bulging with silver, with gold, and with bank-notes. Tantalizing vision! No! She could not steal. Besides, he might wake up.

And she returned to mandarins. She got herself into a very morbid and two-o'clock-in-the-morning state of mind. Suppose it was a dodge that *did* work. (Of course, she was extremely superstitious; we all are.) She began to reflect seriously upon China. She remembered having heard that Chinese mandarins were very corrupt; that they ground the faces of the poor, and put innocent victims to the torture; in short, that they were sinful and horrid persons, scoundrels unfit for mercy. Then she pondered upon the remotest parts of China, regions where Europeans never could penetrate. No doubt there was some unimportant mandarin, somewhere in these regions, to whose district his death would be a decided blessing, to kill whom would indeed be an act of humanity. Probably a mandarin without wife or family; a bachelor mandarin whom no relative would regret; or, in the alternative, a mandarin with many wives, whose disgusting polygamy merited severe punishment! An old mandarin already pretty nearly dead; or, in the alternative, a young one just commencing a career of infamy!

'I'm awfully silly,' she whispered to herself. 'But still, if there *should* be anything in it. And I must, I must, I must have that thing for my dress!'

She looked again at the dim forms of her husband's clothes, pitched anyhow on an ottoman. No! She could not stoop to theft!

So she murdered a mandarin; lying in bed there; not any particular mandarin, a vague mandarin, the mandarin most convenient and suitable under all the circumstances. She deliberately wished him dead, on the off-chance of acquiring riches, or, more accurately, because she was short of fourteen and fivepence in order to look perfectly splendid at a ball.

In the morning when she woke up – her husband had already departed to the works – she thought how foolish she had been in the night. She did not feel sorry for having desired the death of a fellow-creature. Not at all. She felt sorry because she was convinced, in the cold light of day, that the charm would not work. Charlie's notions were really too ridiculous, too preposterous. No! She must reconcile herself to wearing a ball dress which was less than perfection, and all for the want of fourteen and fivepence. And she had more nerves than ever!

She had nerves to such an extent that when she went to unlock the drawer of her own private toilet-table, in which her prudent and fussy husband forced her to lock up her rings and brooches every night, she attacked the wrong drawer – an empty unfastened drawer that she never used. And lo! The empty drawer was not empty. There was a sovereign lying in it!

This gave her a start, connecting the discovery, as naturally at the first blush she did, with the mandarin.

Surely it couldn't be, after all.

Then she came to her senses. What absurdity! A coincidence, of course, nothing else? Besides, a mere sovereign! It wasn't enough. Charlie had said 'rich for life'. The sovereign must have lain there for months and months, forgotten.

However, it was none the less a sovereign. She picked it up, thanked Providence, ordered the dog-cart, and drove straight to Brunt's. The particular thing that she acquired was an exceedingly thin, slim, and fetching silver belt – a marvel for the money, and the ideal waist decoration for her wonderful white muslin gown. She bought it, and left the shop.

And as she came out of the shop, she saw a street urchin holding out the poster of the early edition of the *Signal*. And she read on the poster, in large letters: 'DEATH OF LI HUNG CHANG.' It is no exaggeration to say that she nearly fainted. Only by the exercise of that hard self-control, of which women alone are capable, did she refrain from tumbling against the blue-clad breast of Adams, the Cheswardine coachman.

She purchased the *Signal* with well-feigned calm, opened it and read: '*Stop-press news. Pekin. Li Hung Chang, the celebrated Chinese statesman, died at two o'clock this morning.* – Reuter.'

III

Vera reclined on the sofa that afternoon, and the sofa was drawn round in front of the drawing-room fire. And she wore her fluffiest and languidest *peignoir*. And there was a perfume of eau de Cologne in the apartment. Vera was having a headache; she was having it in her grand, her official manner. Stephen had had to lunch alone. He had been told that in all probability his suffering wife would not be well enough to go to the ball. Whereupon he had grunted. As a fact, Vera's headache was extremely real, and she was very upset indeed.

The death of Li Hung Chang was heavy on her soul. Occultism was justified of itself. The affair lay beyond coincidence. She had always *known* that there was something in occultism, supernaturalism, so-called superstitions, what not. But she had never expected to prove the faith that was in her by such a homicidal act on her own part. It was detestable of Charlie to have mentioned the thing at all. He had no right to play with fire. And as for her husband, words could give but the merest rough outline of her resentment against Stephen. A pretty state of things that a woman with a position such as she had to keep up should be reduced to six and sevenpence! Stephen, no doubt, expected her to visit the pawnshop. It would serve him right if she did so – and he met her coming out under the three brass balls! Did she not dress solely and wholly to please him? Not in the least to please herself! Personally she had a mind set on higher things, impossible aspirations. But he liked fine clothes. And it was her duty to satisfy him. She strove to satisfy him in all matters. She lived for him. She sacrificed herself to him completely. And what did she get in return? Nothing! Nothing! Nothing! All men were selfish. And women were their victims. . . . Stephen, with his silly bullying rules against credit and so forth. . . . The worst of men was that they had no sense.

She put a new dose of eau de Cologne on her forehead, and leaned on one elbow. On the mantelpiece lay the tissue parcel containing the slim silver belt, the price of Li's death. She wanted to stick it in the fire. And only the fact that it would not burn prevented her savagely doing so. There was something wrong, too, with the occultism. To receive a paltry sovereign for murdering the greatest statesman of the Eastern hemisphere was simply grotesque. Moreover, she had most distinctly not wanted to deprive China of a distinguished man. She had expressly stipulated for an inferior and insignificant mandarin, one that could be spared and that was unknown to Reuter. She supposed she ought to have looked up China at the Wedgwood Institution and selected a definite mandarin with a definite place of residence. But could she be expected to go about a murder deliberately like that?

With regard to the gross inadequacy of the fiscal return for her deed, perhaps that was her own fault. She had not wished for more. Her brain had been so occupied by the belt that she had wished only for the belt. But, perhaps, on the other hand, vast wealth was to come. Perhaps something might occur that very night. That would be better. Yet would it be better? However rich she might become, Stephen would coolly take charge of her riches, and dole them out to her, and make rules for her concerning them. And besides, Charlie would suspect her guilt. Charlie understood her, and perused her thoughts far better than Stephen did. She would never be able to conceal the truth from Charlie. The conversation, the death of Li within two hours, and then a sudden fortune accruing to her – Charlie would inevitably put two and two together and divine her shameful secret.

The outlook was thoroughly black anyway.

She then fell asleep.

When she awoke, some considerable time afterwards, Stephen was calling to her. It was his voice, indeed, that had aroused her. The room was dark.

'I say, Vera,' he demanded, in a low, slightly inimical tone, 'have you taken a sovereign out of the empty drawer in your toilet-table?'

'No,' she said quickly, without thinking.

'Ah!' he observed reflectively, 'I knew I was right.' He paused, and added, coldly, 'If you aren't better you ought to go to bed.'

Then he left her, shutting the door with a noise that showed a certain lack of sympathy with her headache.

She sprang up. Her first feeling was one of thankfulness that that brief interview had occurred in darkness. So Stephen was aware of the existence of the sovereign! The sovereign was not occult. Possibly he had put it there. And what did he know he was 'right' about?

She lighted the gas, and gazed at herself in the glass, realizing that she no longer had a headache, and endeavouring to arrange her ideas.

'What's this?' said another voice at the door. She glanced round hastily, guiltily. It was Charlie.

'Steve telephoned me you were too ill to go to the dance,' explained Charlie, 'so I thought I'd come and make inquiries. I quite expected to find you in bed with a nurse and a doctor or two at least. What is it?' He smiled.

'Nothing,' she replied. 'Only a headache. It's gone now.'

She stood against the mantelpiece, so that he should not see the white parcel.

'That's good,' said Charlie.

There was a pause.

'Strange, Li Hung Chang dying last night, just after we had been talking about killing mandarins,' she said. She could not keep off the subject. It attracted her like a snake, and she approached it in spite of the fact that she fervently wished not to approach it.

'Yes,' said Charlie. 'But Li wasn't a mandarin, you know. And he didn't die after we had been talking about mandarins. He died before.'

'Oh! I thought it said in the paper he died at two o'clock this morning.'

'Two a.m. in Pekin,' Charlie answered. 'You must remember that Pekin time is many hours earlier than our time. It lies so far eastward.'

'Oh!' she said again.

Stephen hurried in, with a worried air.

'Ah! It's you, Charlie!'

'She isn't absolutely dying, I find,' said Charlie, turning to Vera: 'You are going to the dance after all – aren't you?'

'I say, Vera,' Stephen interrupted, 'either you or I must have a scene with Martha. I've always suspected that confounded housemaid. So I put a marked sovereign in a drawer this morning, and it was gone at lunch-time. She'd better hook it instantly. Of course I shan't prosecute.'

'Martha!' cried Vera. 'Stephen, what on earth are you thinking of? I wish you would leave the servants to me. If you think you can manage this house in your spare time from the works, you are welcome to try. But don't blame me for the consequences.' Glances of triumph flashed in her eyes.

'But I tell you – '

'Nonsense,' said Vera. 'I took the sovereign. I saw it there and I took it, and just to punish you, I've spent it. It's not at all nice to lay traps for servants like that.'

'Then why did you tell me just now you hadn't taken it?' Stephen demanded crossly.

'I didn't feel well enough to argue with you then,' Vera replied.

'You've recovered precious quick,' retorted Stephen with grimness.

'Of course, if you want to make a scene before strangers,' Vera whimpered (poor Charlie a stranger!), 'I'll go to bed.'

Stephen knew when he was beaten.

She went to the Hockey dance, though. She and Stephen and Charlie and his young sister, aged seventeen, all descended together to the Town Hall in a brougham. The young girl admired Vera's belt excessively, and looked forward to the moment when she too should be a bewitching and captivating wife like Vera, in short, a woman of the world, worshipped by grave, bearded men. And both the men were under the spell of Vera's incurable charm, capricious, surprising, exasperating, indefinable, indispensable to their lives.

'Stupid superstitions!' reflected Vera. 'But of course I never believed it really.'

And she cast down her eyes to gloat over the belt.

1066 and All That

☆★☆★☆★☆★☆★☆★☆★☆★☆★☆★☆★☆★☆★☆★☆★☆★☆★☆

W. C. SELLAR and R. J. YEATMAN

Charles I and the Civil War

With the ascension of Charles I to the throne we come at last to the Central Period of English History (not to be confused with the Middle Ages, of course), consisting in the *utterly memorable Struggle between the Cavaliers* (*Wrong but Wromantic*) *and the Roundheads* (*Right and Repulsive*).

Charles I was a Cavalier King and therefore had a small pointed beard, long flowing curls, a large, flat, flowing hat, and *gay attire*. The Roundheads, on the other hand, were clean-shaven and wore tall, conical hats, white ties, and *sombre garments*. Under these circumstances a Civil War was inevitable.

The Roundheads, of course, were so called because Cromwell had all their heads made perfectly round, in order that they should present a uniform appearance when drawn up in line.

Besides this, if any man lost his head in action, it could be used as a cannon-ball by the artillery (which was done at the Siege of Worcester).

For a long time before the Civil War, however, Charles had been quarrelling with the Roundheads about what was right. Charles explained that there was a doctrine called the Divine Right of Kings, which said that:

(a) He was King, and that was right.
(b) Kings were divine, and that was right.
(c) Kings were right, and that was right.
(d) Everything was all right.

But so determined were the Roundheads that all this was all wrong that they drew up a Petition called the Petition of Right to show in more detail which things were wrong. This Petition said:

(a) That it was wrong for anyone to be put to death more than once for the same offence.
(b) *Habeas Corpus*, which meant that it was wrong if people were put in prison except for some reason, and that people who had been mutilated by the King, such as Prynne, who had often had his ears cut off, should always be allowed to keep their bodies.
(c) That Charles's memorable methods of getting money, such as Rummage and Scroungeage, were wrong.

But the most important cause of the Civil War was

Ship Money

Charles I said that any money which was Ship Money belonged to him; but while the Roundheads declared that Ship Money could be found only in the Cinq Ports, Charles maintained that no one but the King could guess right which was Ship Money and which wasn't. This was, of course, part of his Divine Right. The climax came when a villager called Hampden (memorable for his dauntless breast) advised the King to divine again.

This so upset Charles that he went back to Westminster, and after cinquing several ports burst into the House of Commons and asked in a very royal way for some birds which he said were in there. The Parliament, who were mostly Puritans, were so shocked that they began making solemn Leagues and Countenances. Charles therefore became very angry and complaining that the birds had flown raised his standard at Nottingham and declared war against Hampden and the Roundheads.

The War

At first the King was successful owing to Prince Rupert of Hentzau, his famous cavalry leader, who was very dashing in all directions. After this, many indecisive battles were fought at such places as Newbury, Edgehill, Newbury, Chalgrove Field, Newbury, etc., in all of which the Cavaliers were rather victorious.

The Roundheads therefore made a new plan in order to win the war after all. This was called the Self-Denying Ordnance and said that everyone had to deny everything he had done up to that date, and that nobody was allowed to admit who he was: thus the war could be started again from the beginning. When the Roundheads had done this they were called the New Moral Army and were dressed up as Ironclads and put under the command of Oliver Cromwell, whose Christian name was Oliver and who was therefore affectionately known as 'Old Nick'.

Cromwell was not only moral and completely round in the head but had a large (round) wart on the nose. He was consequently victorious in all the remaining battles such as Newbury, Marston Moor, Edgehill (change for Chalgrove), Naseby, Newbury, etc.

Blood and Ironclads

When Charles I had been defeated he was brought to trial by the Rump Parliament – so-called because it had been sitting for such a long time – and was found guilty of being defeated in a war against himself, which was, of course, a form of High Treason. He was therefore ordered by Cromwell to go and have his head cut off (it was, the Roundheads pointed out, the wrong shape, anyway). So romantic was Charles, however, that this made little difference to him and it is very memorable that he walked and talked Half an hour after his Head was cut off.

On seeing this, Cromwell was so angry that he picked up the mace (the new and terrible Instrument of Government which he had invented) and, pointing it at the Head, shouted: 'Take away that Marble,' and announced that his policy in future would be just Blood and Ironclads. In order to carry out this policy he divided the country into twelve districts and set a Serjeant-Major over each of them.

Rule of the Serjeant-Majors

Nothing sickened the people of the rule of the Serjeant-Majors so much as their cruel habit of examining little boys *viva-voce*. For this purpose the unfortunate children were dressed in their most uncomfortable satins and placed on a stool. The Serjeant-Major would then ask such difficult questions as 'How's your Father?' or 'Animal, Vegetable, or Mineral?' and those who could not answer were given a cruel medicine called Pride's Purge. All this was called the Crommonwealth and was right but repulsive.

The Crowning Mercy

The Roundheads at length decided to offer Cromwell the Crown. Cromwell, however, was unwilling and declared it was a Crowning Mercy when he found that it would not fit, having been designed for a Cavalier King.

Soon after, Cromwell died of a surfeit of Pride, Purges, Warts, and other Baubles.

Shy Rights: Why Not Pretty Soon?

☆★☆★☆★☆★☆★☆★☆★☆★☆★☆★☆★☆★☆★☆★☆★☆★☆

GARRISON KEILLOR

Recently I read about a group of fat people who had organized to fight discrimination against themselves. They said that society oppresses the overweight by being thinner than them and that the term 'overweight' itself is oppressive because it implies a 'right' weight that the fatso has failed to make. Only weightists use such terms, they said; they demanded to be called 'total' people and to be thought of in terms of wholeness; and they referred to thin people as being 'not all there.'

Don't get me wrong. This is fine with me. If, to quote the article if I may, 'Fat Leaders Demand Expanded Rights Act, Claim Broad Base of Support,' I have no objections to it whatsoever. I feel that it is their right to speak up and I admire them for doing so, though of course this is only my own opinion. I could be wrong.

Nevertheless, after reading the article, I wrote a letter to President Jimmy Carter demanding that his administration take action to end discrimination against shy persons sometime in the very near future. I pointed out three target areas – laws, schools, and attitudes – where shy rights maybe could be safeguarded. I tried not to be pushy but I laid it on the line. 'Mr President,' I concluded, 'you'll probably kill me for saying this but compared to what you've done for other groups, we shys have settled for "peanuts." As you may know, we are not ones to make threats, but it is clear to me that if we don't get some action on this, it could be a darned quiet summer. It is up to you, Mr President. Whatever you decide will be okay by me. Yours very cordially.'

I never got around to mailing the letter, but evidently word got around in the shy community that I had written it, and I've noticed that most shy persons are not speaking to me these days. I guess they think the letter went too far. Probably they feel that making demands is a betrayal of the shy movement (or 'gesture,' as many shys call it) and an insult to shy pride and that it risks the loss of some of the gains we have already made, such as social security and library cards.

Perhaps they are right. I don't claim to have all the answers. I just feel that we ought to begin, at least, to think about some demands that we *might* make if, for example, we *had* to someday. That's all. I'm not saying we should make fools of ourselves, for heaven's sake!

Shut up (A Slogan)

Sometimes I feel that maybe we shy persons have borne our terrible burden for far too long now. Labeled by society as 'wimps,' 'dorks,' 'creeps,' and 'sissies,' stereotyped as Milquetoasts and Walter Mittys, and tagged as potential psychopaths ('He kept pretty much to himself,' every psychopath's landlady is quoted as saying after the arrest, and for weeks thereafter every shy person is treated like a leper), we shys are desperately misunderstood on every hand. Because we don't 'talk out' our feelings, it is assumed that we haven't any. It is assumed that we never exclaim, retort, or cry out, though naturally we do on occasions when it seems called for.

Would anyone dare to say to a woman or a Third World person, 'Oh, don't be a woman! Oh, don't be so Third!'? And yet people make bold with us whenever they please and put an arm around us and tell us not to be shy.

Hundreds of thousands of our shy brothers and sisters (and 'cousins twice-removed,' as militant shys refer to each other) are victimized every year by self-help programs that promise to 'cure' shyness through hand-buzzer treatments, shout training, spicy diets, silence-aversion therapy, and every other gimmick in the book. Many of them claim to have 'overcome' their shyness, but the sad fact is that they are afraid to say otherwise.

To us in the shy movement, however, shyness is not a disability or disease to be 'overcome.' It is simply the way we are. And in our own quiet way, we are secretly proud of it. It isn't something we shout about at public rallies and marches. It is Shy Pride. And while we don't have a Shy Pride Week, we do have many private moments when we keep our thoughts to ourselves, such as 'Shy is nice,' 'Walk short,' 'Be proud – shut up,' and 'Shy is beautiful, for the most part.' These are some that I thought up myself. Perhaps other shy persons have some of their own, I don't know.

A 'Number One' Disgrace

Discrimination against the shy is our country's number one disgrace in my own personal opinion. Millions of men and women are denied equal employment, educational and recreational opportunities, and rewarding personal relationships simply because of their shyness. These injustices are nearly impossible to identify, not only because the shy person will not speak up when discriminated against, but also because the shy person almost always *anticipates* being denied these rights and doesn't ask for them in the first place. (In fact, most shys will politely decline a right when it is offered to them.)

Most shy lawyers agree that shys can never obtain justice under our current adversary system of law. The Sixth Amendment, for example, which gives the accused the right to confront his accusers, is anti-shy on the face of it. It effectively denies shy persons the right to accuse anyone of anything.

One solution might be to shift the burden of proof to the defendant in case the plaintiff chooses to remain silent. Or we could create a special second-class citizenship that would take away some rights, such as free speech, bearing arms, and running for public office, in exchange for some other rights that we need more. In any case, we need some sort of fairly totally new concept of law if we shys are ever going to enjoy equality, if indeed that is the sort of thing we could ever enjoy.

A Million-Dollar Ripoff

Every year, shy persons lose millions of dollars in the form of overcharges that aren't questioned, shoddy products never returned to stores, refunds never asked for, and bad food in restaurants that we eat anyway, not to mention all the money we lose and are too shy to claim when somebody else finds it.

A few months ago, a shy friend of mine whom I will call Duke Hand (not his real name) stood at a supermarket checkout counter and watched the cashier ring up thirty fifteen-cent Peanut Dream candy bars and a $3.75 copy of *Playhouse* for $18.25. He gave her a twenty-dollar bill and thanked her for his change, but as he reached for his purchases, she said, 'Hold on. There's something wrong here.'

'No, really, it's OK,' he said.

'Let me see that cash register slip,' she said.

'No, really, thanks anyway,' he whispered. Out of the corner of his eye, he could see that he had attracted attention. Other shoppers in the vicinity had sensed that something was up, perhaps an attempted price-tag switch or insufficient identification, and were looking his way. 'It's not for me,' he pleaded. 'I'm only buying this for a friend.'

Nevertheless, he had to stand there in mute agony while she counted all of the Peanut Dreams and refigured the total and the correct change. (In fairness to her, it should be pointed out that Duke, while eventually passing on each copy of *Playhouse* to a friend, first reads it himself.)

Perhaps one solution might be for clerks and other business personnel to try to be a little bit more careful about this sort of thing in the first place. OK?

How About Shy History?

To many of us shys, myself included, the worst tragedy is the oppression of shy children in the schools, and while we don't presume to tell educators how to do their work, work that they have been specially trained to do, we do feel that schools must begin immediately to develop programs of shy history, or at the very least to give it a little consideration.

History books are blatantly prejudiced against shyness and shy personhood. They devote chapter after chapter to the accomplishments of famous persons and quote them at great length, and say nothing at all, or very little, about countless others who had very little to say, who never sought fame, and whose names are lost to history.

Where in the history books do we find mention of The Lady in Black, Kilroy, The Unknown Soldier, The Forgotten Man, The Little Guy, not to mention America's many noted recluses?

Where, for example, can we find a single paragraph on America's hundreds of scale models, those brave men of average height whose job it was to pose beside immense objects such as pyramids and dynamos so as to indicate scale in drawings and photographs? The only credit that scale models ever received was a line in the caption – 'For an idea of its size, note man (arrow, at left).' And yet, without them, such inventions as the dirigible, the steam shovel, and the swing-span bridge would have looked like mere toys, and natural wonders such as Old Faithful, the Grand Canyon, and the giant sequoia would have been dismissed as hoaxes. It was truly a thankless job.

Shys On 'Strike'

The scale models themselves never wanted any thanks. All they wanted was a rope or device of some type to keep them from falling off tall structures, plus a tent to rest in between drawings, and in 1906, after one model was carried away by a tidal wave that he had been hired to pose in front of, they formed a union and went on strike.

Briefly, the scale models were joined by a contingent of shy artists' models who had posed for what they thought was to be a small monument showing the Battle of Bull Run only to discover that it was actually a large bas-relief entitled 'The Bathers' and who sat down on the job, bringing the work to a halt. While the artists' models quickly won a new contract and went back to work (on a non-representational basis), the scale models' strike was never settled.

True to their nature, the scale models did not picket the work sites or negotiate with their employers. They simply stood quietly a short distance away and, when asked about their demands, pointed to the next man. A year later, when the union attempted to take a vote on the old contract, it found that most of the scale models had moved away and left no forwarding addresses.

It was the last attempt by shy persons to organize themselves anywhere in the country.

Now Is the Time, We Think

Now is probably as good a time as any for this country to face up to its shameful treatment of the shy and to do something, almost anything, about it. On the other hand, maybe it would be better to wait for a while and see what happens. All I know is that it isn't easy trying to write a manifesto for a bunch of people who dare not speak their names. And that the shy movement is being inverted by a tiny handful of shy militants who do not speak for the majority of shy persons, nor even very often for themselves. This secret cadre, whose members are not known even to each other, advocate doing 'less than nothing.' They believe in tokenism, and the smaller the token the better. They seek only to promote more self-consciousness: that ultimate shyness that shy mystics call 'the fear of fear itself.' What is even more terrifying is the ultimate goal of this radical wing: They believe that they shall inherit the earth, and they will not stop until they do. Believe me, we moderates have our faces to the wall.

Perhaps you are saying, 'What can *I* do? I share your concern at the plight of the shy and wholeheartedly endorse your two-(or three-) point program for shy equality. I pledge myself to work vigorously for its adoption. My check for ($10 $25 $50 $100 $–) is enclosed. In addition, I agree to (circulate petitions, hold fund-raising party in my home, write to congressman and senator, serve on local committee, write letters to newspapers, hand out literature door-to-door during National Friends of the Shy Drive).'

Just remember: You said it, not me.

Philippa's Fox-hunt

EDITH SOMERVILLE AND MARTIN ROSS

No one can accuse Philippa and me of having married in haste. As a matter of fact, it was but little under five years from that autumn evening on the river when I had said what is called in Ireland 'the hard word,' to the day in August when I was led to the altar by my best man, and was subsequently led away from it by Mrs Sinclair Yeates. About two years out of the five had been spent by me at Shreelane in ceaseless warfare with drains, eaveshoots, chimneys, pumps; all those fundamentals, in short, that the ingenuous and improving tenant expects to find established as a basis from which to rise to higher things. As far as rising to higher things went, frequent ascents to the roof to search for leaks summed up my achievements; in fact, I suffered so general a shrinkage of my ideals that the triumph of making the hall-door bell ring blinded me to the fact that the rat-holes in the hall floor were nailed up with pieces of tin biscuit boxes, and that the casual visitor could, instead of leaving a card, have easily written his name in the damp on the walls.

Philippa, however, proved adorably callous to these and similar shortcomings. She regarded Shreelane and its floundering, foundering *ménage* of incapables in the light of a gigantic picnic in a foreign land; she held long conversations daily with Mrs Cadogan, in order, as she informed me, to acquire the language; without any ulterior domestic intention she engaged kitchenmaids because of the beauty of their eyes, and housemaids because they had such delightfully picturesque old mothers, and she declined to correct the phraseology of the parlourmaid, whose painful habit it was to whisper 'Do ye choose cherry or clarry?' when proffering the wine. Fast-days, perhaps, afforded my wife her first insight into the sterner realities of Irish housekeeping. Philippa had what are known as High Church proclivities, and took the matter seriously.

'I don't know how we are to manage for the servants' dinner tomorrow,

Sinclair,' she said, coming to my office one Thursday morning; 'Julia says she "promised God this long time that she wouldn't eat an egg on a fast-day," and the kitchen maid says she won't eat herrings "without they're fried with onions," and Mrs Cadogan says she will "not go to them extremes for servants." '

'I should let Mrs Cadogan settle the menu herself,' I suggested.

'I asked her to do that,' replied Philippa, 'and she only said she "thanked God *she* had no appetite!" '

The lady of the house here fell away into unseasonable laughter.

I made the demoralizing suggestion that, as we were going away for a couple of nights, we might safely leave them to fight it out, and the problem was abandoned.

Philippa had been much called on by the neighbourhood in all its shades and grades, and daily she and her trousseau frocks presented themselves at hall doors of varying dimensions in due acknowledgment of civilities. In Ireland, it may be noted, the process known in England as 'summering and wintering' a newcomer does not obtain; sociability and curiosity alike forbid delay. The visit to which we owed our escape from the intricacies of the fast-day was to the Knoxes of Castle Knox, relations in some remote and tribal way of my landlord, Mr Flurry of that ilk. It involved a short journey by train, and my wife's longest basket-trunk; it also, which was more serious, involved my being lent a horse to go out cubbing the following morning.

At Castle Knox we sank into an almost forgotten environment of draught-proof windows and doors, of deep carpets, of silent servants instead of clattering belligerents. Philippa told me afterwards that it had only been by an effort that she had restrained herself from snatching up the train of her wedding-gown as she paced across the wide hall on little Sir Valentine's arm. After three weeks at Shreelane she found it difficult to remember that the floor was neither damp nor dusty.

I had the good fortune to be of the limited number of those who got on with Lady Knox, chiefly, I imagine, because I was as a worm before her, and thankfully permitted her to do all the talking.

'Your wife is extremely pretty,' she pronounced autocratically, surveying Philippa between the candle-shades; 'does she ride?'

Lady Knox was a short square lady, with a weather-beaten face, and an eye decisive from long habit of taking her own line across country and elsewhere. She would have made a very imposing little coachman, and would have caused her stable helpers to rue the day they had the presumption to be born; it struck me that Sir Valentine sometimes did so.

'I'm glad you like her looks,' I replied, 'as I fear you will find her thoroughly despicable otherwise; for one thing, she not only can't ride, but she believes that I can!'

'Oh, come, you're not as bad as all that!' my hostess was good enough to say; 'I'm going to put you up on Sorcerer tomorrow, and we'll see you at the top of the hunt – if there is one. That young Knox hasn't a notion how to draw these woods.'

'Well, the best run we had last year out of this place was with Flurry's hounds,' struck in Miss Sally, sole daughter of Sir Valentine's house and home, from her place halfway down the table. It was not difficult to see that she and her mother held different views on the subject of Mr Flurry Knox.

'I call it a criminal thing in any one's great-great-grandfather to rear up a preposterous troop of sons and plant them all out in his own country,' Lady Knox said to me with apparent irrelevance. 'I detest collaterals. Blood may be thicker than water, but it is also a great deal nastier. In this country I find that fifteenth cousins consider themselves near relations if they live within twenty miles of one!'

Having before now taken in the position with regard to Flurry Knox, I took care to accept these remarks as generalities, and turned the conversation to other themes.

'I see Mrs Yeates is doing wonders with Mr Hamilton,' said Lady Knox presently, following the direction of my eyes, which had strayed away to where Philippa was beaming upon her left-hand neighbour, a mildewed-looking old clergyman, who was delivering a long dissertation, the purport of which we were happily unable to catch.

'She has always had a gift for the Church,' I said.

'Not curates?' said Lady Knox, in her deep voice.

I made haste to reply that it was the elders of the Church who were venerated by my wife.

'Well, she has her fancy in old Eustace Hamilton; he's elderly enough!' said Lady Knox. 'I wonder if she'd venerate him as much if she knew that he had fought with his sister-in-law, and they haven't spoken for thirty years! Though for the matter of that,' she added, 'I think it shows his good sense!'

'Mrs Knox is rather a friend of mine,' I ventured.

'Is she? H'm! Well, she's not one of mine!' replied my hostess, with her usual definiteness. 'I'll say one thing for her, I believe, she's always been a sportswoman. She's very rich, you know, and they say she only married old Badger Knox to save his hounds from being sold to pay his debts, and then she took the horn from him and hunted them herself. Has she been rude to your wife yet? No? Oh, well, she will. It's a mere question of time. She hates all English people. You know the story they tell of her? She was coming from London, and when she was getting her ticket the man asked if she had said a ticket for York. "No, thank God, Cork!" says Mrs Knox.'

'Well, I rather agree with her!' said I; 'but why did she fight with Mr Hamilton?'

'Oh, nobody knows. I don't believe they know themselves! Whatever it was, the old lady drives five miles to Fortwilliam every Sunday, rather than go to his church, just outside her own back gates,' Lady Knox said with a laugh like a terrier's bark. 'I wish I'd fought with him myself,' she said; 'he gives us forty minutes every Sunday.'

As I struggled into my boots the following morning, I felt that Sir Valentine's acid confidences on cub-hunting, bestowed on me at midnight, did credit to his judgment. 'A very moderate amusement, my dear Major,' he had said, in his dry little voice; 'you should stick to shooting. No one expects you to shoot before daybreak.'

It was six o'clock as I crept downstairs, and found Lady Knox and Miss Sally at breakfast, with two lamps on the table, and a foggy daylight oozing in from under the half-raised blinds. Philippa was already in the hall, pumping up her bicycle, in a state of excitement at the prospect of her first experience of hunting that would have been more comprehensible to me had she been going to ride a strange horse, as I was. As I bolted my food I saw the horses being led past the windows, and a faint twang of a horn told that Flurry Knox and his hounds were not far off.

Miss Sally jumped up.

'If I'm not on the Cockatoo before the hounds come up, I shall never get there!' she said, hobbling out of the room in the toils of her safety habit. Her small, alert face looked very childish under her riding-hat; the lamp-light struck sparks out of her thick coil of golden-red hair: I wondered how I had ever thought her like her prim little father.

She was already on her white cob when I got to the hall door, and Flurry Knox was riding over the glistening wet grass with his hounds, while his whip, Dr Jerome Hickey, was having a stirring time with the young entry and the rabbit-holes. They moved on without stopping, up a back avenue, under tall and dripping trees, to a thick laurel covert, at some little distance from the house. Into this the hounds were thrown, and the usual period of fidgety inaction set in for the riders, of whom all told, there were about half a dozen. Lady Knox, square and solid, on her big, confidential iron-grey, was near me, and her eyes were on me and my mount; with her rubicund face and white collar she was more than ever like a coachman.

'Sorcerer looks as if he suited you well,' she said, after a few minutes of silence, during which the hounds rustled and crackled steadily through the laurels; 'he's a little high on the leg, and so are you, you know, so you show each other off.'

Sorcerer was standing like a rock, with his good-looking head in the air and his eyes fastened on the covert. His manners, so far, had been those of a perfect gentleman, and were in marked contrast to those of Miss Sally's cob, who was sidling, hopping, and snatching unappeasably at his bit. Philippa had disappeared from view down the avenue ahead. The fog was melting, and the sun threw long blades of light through the trees; everything was quiet, and in the distance the curtained windows of the house marked the warm repose of Sir Valentine, and those of the party who shared his opinion of cubbing.

'Hark! Hark to cry there!'

It was Flurry's voice, away at the other side of the covert. The rustling and brushing through the laurels became more vehement, then passed out of hearing.

'He never will leave his hounds alone,' said Lady Knox disapprovingly.

Miss Sally and the Cockatoo moved away in a series of heraldic capers towards the end of the laurel plantation, and at the same moment I saw Philippa on her bicycle shoot into view on the drive ahead of us.

'I've seen a fox!' she screamed, white with what I believe to have been personal terror, though she says it was excitement; 'it passed quite close to me!'

'What way did he go?' bellowed a voice which I recognized as Dr Hickey's, somewhere in the deep of the laurels.

'Down the drive!' returned Philippa, with a pea-hen quality in her tones with which I was quite unacquainted.

An electrifying screech of 'Gone away!' was projected from the laurels by Dr Hickey.

'Gone away!' chanted Flurry's horn at the top of the covert.

'This is what he calls cubbing!' said Lady Knox, 'a mere farce!' but none the less she loosed her sedate monster into a canter.

Sorcerer got his hind legs under him, and hardened his crest against the bit, as we all hustled along the drive after the flying figure of my wife. I knew very little about horses, but I realized that even with the hounds tumbling hysterically out of the covert, Sorcerer comported himself with the manners of the best society. Up a side road I saw Flurry Knox opening half of a gate and cramming through it; in a moment we also had crammed through, and the turf of a pasture field was under our feet. Dr Hickey leaned forward and took hold of his horse; I did likewise, with the trifling difference that my horse took hold of me, and I steered for Flurry Knox with single-hearted purpose, the hounds, already a field ahead, being merely an exciting and noisy accompaniment of this endeavour. A heavy stone wall was the first occurrence of note. Flurry chose a place where the top was loose, and his clumsy-looking brown mare changed feet on the rattling stones like a fairy. Sorcerer came at it, tense and collected as a bow at full stretch, and sailed steeply into the air; I saw the wall far beneath me, with an unsuspected ditch on the far side, and I felt my hat following me at the full stretch of its guard as we swept over it, then, with a long slant, we descended to earth some sixteen feet from where we had left it, and I was possessor of the gratifying fact that I had achieved a good-sized 'fly,' and had not perceptibly moved in my saddle. Subsequent disillusioning experience has taught me that but few horses jump like Sorcerer, so gallantly, so sympathetically, and with such supreme mastery of the subject; but none the less the enthusiasm that he imparted to me has never been extinguished, and that October morning ride revealed to me the unsuspected intoxication of fox-hunting.

Behind me I heard the scrabbling of the Cockatoo's little hoofs among the loose stone, and Lady Knox, galloping on my left, jerked a maternal chin over her shoulder to mark her daughter's progress. For my part, had there been an entire circus behind me, I was far too much occupied with ramming on my hat and trying to hold Sorcerer, to have looked round, and all my spare faculties were devoted to steering for Flurry, who had taken a right-handed turn, and was at that moment surmounting a bank of uncertain and briary aspect. I surmounted it also, with the swiftness and simplicity for which the Quaker's methods of bank jumping had not prepared me, and two or three fields, traversed at the same steeplechase pace, brought us to a road and to an abrupt check. There, suddenly, were the hounds, scrambling in baffled silence down into the road from the opposite bank, to look for the line they had overrun, and there, amazingly, was Philippa, engaged in excited converse with several men with spades over their shoulders.

'Did ye see the fox, boys?' shouted Flurry, addressing the group.

'We did! We did!' cried my wife and her friends in chorus; 'he ran up the road!'

'We'd be badly off without Mrs Yeates!' said Flurry, as he whirled his mare round and clattered up the road with a hustle of hounds after him.

It occurred to me as forcibly as any mere earthly thing can occur to those who are wrapped in the sublimities of a run, that, for a young woman who had never before seen a fox out of a cage at the Zoo, Philippa was taking to hunting very kindly. Her cheeks were a most brilliant pink, her blue eyes shone.

'Oh, Sinclair!' she exclaimed, 'they say he's going for Aussolas, and there's a road I can ride all the way!'

'Ye can, miss! Sure we'll show you!' chorused her cortège.

Her foot was on the pedal ready to mount. Decidedly my wife was in no need of assistance from me.

Up the road a hound gave a yelp of discovery, and flung himself over a stile into the fields; the rest of the pack went squealing and jostling after him, and I followed Flurry over one of those infinitely varied erections, pleasantly termed 'gaps' in Ireland. On this occasion the gap was made of three razor-edged slabs of slate leaning against an iron bar, and Sorcerer conveyed to me his thorough knowledge of the matter by a lift of his hind quarters that made me feel as if I were being skilfully kicked downstairs. To what extent I looked it, I cannot say, nor providentially can Philippa, as she had already started. I only know that undeserved good luck restored to me my stirrup before Sorcerer got away with me in the next field.

What followed was, I am told, a very fast fifteen minutes; for me time was not; the empty fields rushed past uncounted, fences came and went in a flash, while the wind sang in my ears, and the dazzle of the early sun was in my eyes. I saw the hounds occasionally, sometimes pouring over a green bank, as the charging breaker lifts and flings itself, sometimes driving across a field, as the white tongues of foam slide racing over the sand; and always ahead of me was Flurry Knox, going as a man goes who knows his country, who knows his horse, and whose heart is wholly and absolutely in the right place.

Do what I would, Sorcerer's implacable stride carried me closer and closer to the brown mare, till, as I thundered down the slope of a long field, I was not twenty yards behind Flurry. Sorcerer had stiffened his neck to iron, and to slow him down was beyond me; but I fought his head away to the right, and found myself coming hard and steady at a stone-faced bank with broken ground in front of it. Flurry bore away to the left, shouting something that I did not understand. That Sorcerer shortened his stride at the right moment was entirely due to his own judgment; standing well away from the jump, he rose like a stag out of the tussocky ground, and as he swung my twelve stone six into the air the obstacle revealed itself to him and me as consisting not of one bank but of two, and between the two lay a deep grassy lane, half choked with furze. I have often been asked to state the width of the *bohireen*, and can only reply that in my opinion it was at least eighteen feet; Flurry Knox and Dr Hickey, who did not jump it, say that it is not more than five. What Sorcerer did with it I cannot say; the sensation was of a towering flight with a kick back in it, a biggish drop, and a landing on cee-springs, still on the downhill grade. That was how one of the best horses in Ireland took one of Ireland's most ignorant riders over a very nasty place.

A sombre line of fir-wood lay ahead, rimmed with a grey wall, and in another couple of minutes we had pulled up on the Aussolas road, and were watching the hounds struggling over the wall into Aussolas demesne.

'No hurry now,' said Flurry, turning in his saddle to watch the Cockatoo jump into the road, 'he's to ground in the big earth inside. Well, Major, it's well for you that's a big-jumped horse. I thought you were a dead man a while ago when you faced him at the *bohireen*!'

I was disclaiming intention in the matter when Lady Knox and the others joined us.

'I thought you told me your wife was no sportswoman,' she said to me, critically scanning Sorcerer's legs for cuts the while, 'but when I saw her a minute ago she had abandoned her bicycle and was running across country like –'

'Look at her now!' interrupted Miss Sally. 'Oh! – oh!' In the interval between these exclamations my incredulous eyes beheld my wife in mid air, hand in hand with a couple of stalwart country boys, with whom she was leaping in unison from the top of a bank on to the road.

Every one, even the saturnine Dr Hickey, began to laugh; I rode back to Philippa, who was exchanging compliments and congratulations with her escort.

'Oh, Sinclair!' she cried, 'wasn't it splendid? I saw you jumping, and everything! Where are they going now?'

'My dear girl,' I said, with marital disapproval, 'you're killing yourself. Where's your bicycle?'

'Oh, it's punctured in a sort of lane, back there. It's all right' and then they' – she breathlessly waved her hand at her attendants – 'they showed me the way.'

'Begor! You proved very good, miss!' said a grinning cavalier.

'Faith she did!' said another, polishing his shining brow with his white flannel coat-sleeve, 'she lepped like a haarse!'

'And may I ask how you propose to go home?' said I.

'I don't know and I don't care! I'm not going home!' She cast an entirely disobedient eye at me. 'And your eye-glass is hanging down your back and your tie is bulging out over your waistcoat!'

The little group of riders had begun to move away.

'We're going on into Aussolas,' called out Flurry; 'come on, and make my grandmother give you some breakfast, Mrs Yeates; she always has it at eight o'clock.'

The front gates were close at hand, and we turned in under the tall beech-trees, with the unswept leaves rustling round the horses' feet, and the lovely blue of the October morning sky filling the spaces between smooth grey branches and golden leaves. The woods rang with the voices of the hounds, enjoying an untrammelled rabbit hunt, while the Master and the Whip, both on foot, strolled along unconcernedly with their bridles over their arms, making themselves agreeable to my wife, an occasional touch of Flurry's horn, or a crack of Dr Hickey's whip, just indicating to the pack that the authorities still took a friendly interest in their doings.

Down a grassy glade in the wood a party of old Mrs Knox's young horses suddenly swept into view, headed by an old mare, who, with her tail over her back, stampeded ponderously past our cavalcade, shaking and swinging her handsome old head, while her youthful friends bucked and kicked and snapped at each other round her with the ferocious humour of their kind.

'Here, Jerome, take the horn,' said Flurry to Dr Hickey; 'I'm going to see Mrs Yeates up to the house, the way these tomfools won't gallop on top of her.'

From this point it seems to me that Philippa's adventures are more worthy of record than mine, and as she has favoured me with a full account of them, I venture to think my version may be relied on.

Mrs Knox was already at breakfast when Philippa was led, quaking, into her formidable presence. My wife's acquaintance with Mrs Knox was, so far, limited to a state visit on either side, and she found but little comfort in Flurry's assurances that his grandmother wouldn't mind if he brought all the hounds in to breakfast, coupled with the statement that she would put her eyes on sticks for the Major.

Whatever the truth of this may have been, Mrs Knox received her guest with an equanimity quite unshaken by the fact that her boots were in the fender instead of on her feet, and that a couple of shawls of varying dimensions and degrees of age did not conceal the inner presence of a magenta flannel dressing-jacket. She installed Philippa at the table and plied her with food, oblivious as to whether the needful implements with which to eat it were forthcoming or no. She told Flurry where a vixen had reared her family, and she watched him ride away, with some biting comment on his mare's hocks screamed after him from the window.

The dining-room at Aussolas Castle is one of the many rooms in Ireland in which Cromwell is said to have stabled his horse (and probably no one would have objected less than Mrs Knox had she been consulted in the matter). Philippa questions if the room had ever been tidied up since, and she endorses Flurry's observation that 'there wasn't a day in the year you wouldn't get feeding for a hen and chickens on the floor'. Opposite to Philippa, on a Louis Quinze chair, sat Mrs Knox's woolly dog, its suspicious little eyes peering at her out of their setting of pink lids and dirty white wool. A couple of young horses outside the windows tore at the matted creepers on the walls, or thrust faces that were half-shy, half-impudent, into the room. Portly pigeons waddled to and fro on the broad window-sill, sometimes flying in to perch on the picture-frames, while they kept up incessantly a hoarse and pompous cooing.

Animals and children are, as a rule, alike destructive to conversation; but Mrs Knox, when she chose, *bien entendu*, could have made herself agreeable in a Noah's ark, and Philippa has a gift of sympathetic attention that personal experience has taught me to regard with distrust as well as respect, while it has often made me realize the worldly wisdom of Kingsley's injunction:

Be good, sweet maid, and let who will be clever.

Family prayers, declaimed by Mrs Knox with alarming austerity, followed close on breakfast, Philippa and a vinegar-faced henchwoman forming the family. The prayers were long, and through the open window as they progressed came distantly a whoop or two; the declamatory tones staggered a little, and then continued at a distinctly higher rate of speed.

'Ma'am! Ma'am!' whispered a small voice at the window.

Mrs Knox made a repressive gesture and held on her way. A sudden outcry of hounds followed, and the owner of the whisper, a small boy with a face freckled like a turkey's egg, darted from the window and dragged a donkey and bath-chair into view. Philippa admits to having lost the thread of the discourse, but she thinks that the 'Amen' that immediately ensued can hardly have come in its usual place. Mrs Knox shut the book abruptly, scrambled up from her knees, and said, 'They've found!'

In a surprisingly short space of time she had added to her attire her boots, a fur cape, and a garden hat, and was in the bath-chair, the small boy stimulating the donkey with the success peculiar to his class, while Philippa hung on behind.

The woods of Aussolas are hilly and extensive, and on that particular morning it seemed that they held as many foxes as hounds. In vain was the horn blown and the whips cracked, small rejoicing parties of hounds, each with a fox of its own, scoured to and fro: every labourer in the vicinity had left his work, and was sedulously heading every fox with yells that would have befitted a tiger hunt, and sticks and stones when occasion served.

'Will I pull out as far as the big rosydandhrum, ma'am?' inquired the small boy; 'I seen three of the dogs go in it, and they yowling.'

'You will,' said Mrs Knox, thumping the donkey on the back with her umbrella; 'here! Jeremiah Regan! Come down out of that with that pitchfork! Do you want to kill the fox, you fool?'

'I do not, your honour, ma'am,' responded Jeremiah Regan, a tall young countryman, emerging from a bramble brake.

'Did you see him?' said Mrs Knox eagerly.

'I seen himself and his ten pups drinking below at the lake ere yestherday, your honour, ma'am, and he as big as a chestnut horse!' said Jeremiah.

'Faugh! Yesterday!' snorted Mrs Knox; 'go on to the rhododendrons, Johnny!'

The party, reinforced by Jeremiah and the pitchfork, progressed at a high rate of speed along the shrubbery path, encountering *en route* Lady Knox, stooping on to her horse's neck under the sweeping branches of the laurels.

'Your horse is too high for my coverts, Lady Knox,' said the lady of the manor, with a malicious eye at Lady Knox's flushed face and dinged hat; 'I'm afraid you will be left behind like Absalom when the hounds go away!'

'As they never do anything here but hunt rabbits,' retorted her ladyship, 'I don't think that's likely.'

Mrs Knox gave her donkey another whack, and passed on.

'Rabbits, my dear!' she said scornfully to Philippa. 'That's all she knows about it. I declare it disgusts me to see a woman of that age making such a Judy of herself! Rabbits indeed!'

Down in the thicket of rhododendron everything was very quiet for a time. Philippa strained her eyes in vain to see any of the riders; the horn-blowing and the whip-cracking passed on almost out of hearing. Once or twice a hound worked through the rhododendrons, glanced at the party, and hurried on, immersed in business. All at once, Johnny, the donkey-boy, whispered excitedly:

'Look at he! Look at he!' and pointed to a boulder of grey rock that stood out among the dark evergreens. A big yellow cub was crouching on it; he instantly slid into the shelter of the bushes, and the irrepressible Jeremiah, uttering a rending shriek, plunged into the thicket after him. Two or three hounds came rushing at the sound, and after this Philippa says she finds some difficulty in recalling the proper order of events; chiefly, she confesses, because of the wholly ridiculous tears of excitement that blurred her eyes.

'We ran,' she said, 'we simply tore, and the donkey galloped, and as for that old Mrs Knox, she was giving cracked screams to the hounds all the time, and they were screaming too; and then somehow we were all out on the road!'

What seems to have occurred was that three couple of hounds, Jeremiah Regan, and Mrs Knox's equipage, amongst them somehow hustled the cub out of Aussolas demesne and up on to a hill on the farther side of the road. Jeremiah was sent back by his mistress to fetch Flurry, and the rest of the party pursued a thrilling course along the road, parallel with that of the hounds, who were hunting slowly through the gorse on the hill-side.

'Upon my honour and word, Mrs Yeates, my dear, we have the hunt to ourselves!' said Mrs Knox to the panting Philippa, as they pounded along the road. 'Johnny, d'ye see the fox?'

'I do, ma'am!' shrieked Johnny, who possessed the usual field-glass vision bestowed upon his kind. 'Look at him over-right us on the hill above! Hi! The spotty dog have him! No, he's gone from him! *Gwan out o' that!*' This to the donkey, with blows that sounded like the beating of carpets, and produced rather more dust.

They had left Aussolas some half a mile behind, when, from a strip of wood on their right, the fox suddenly slipped over the bank on to the road just ahead of them, ran up it for a few yards, and whisked in at a small entrance gate, with the three couple of hounds yelling on a red-hot scent, not thirty yards behind. The bath-chair party whirled in at their heels, Philippa and the donkey considerably blown, Johnny scarlet through his freckles, but as fresh as paint, the old lady blind and deaf to all things save the chase. The hounds went raging through the shrubs beside the drive, and away down a grassy slope towards a shallow glen, in the bottom of which ran a little stream, and after them over the grass bumped the bath-chair. At the stream they turned sharply and ran up the glen towards the avenue, which crossed it by means of a rough stone viaduct.

' 'Pon me conscience, he's into the old culvert!' exclaimed Mrs Knox; 'there was one of my hounds choked there once, long ago! Beat on the donkey, Johnny!'

At this juncture Philippa's narrative again becomes incoherent, not to say breathless. She is, however, positive that it was somewhere about here that the upset of the bath-chair occurred, but she cannot be clear as to whether she picked up the donkey or Mrs Knox, or whether she herself was picked up by Johnny while Mrs Knox picked up the donkey. From my knowledge of Mrs Knox I should say she picked up herself and no one else. At all events, the next salient point is the palpitating moment when Mrs Knox, Johnny, and Philippa successively applying an eye to the opening of the culvert by which the stream trickled under the viaduct, while five dripping hounds bayed and leaped around them, discovered by more senses than that of sight that the fox was in it, and furthermore that one of the hounds was in it too.

'There's a sthrong grating before him at the far end,' said Johnny, his head in at the mouth of the hole, his voice sounding as if he were talking into a jug, 'the two of them's fighting in it; they'll be choked surely!'

'Then don't stand gabbling there, you little fool, but get in and pull the hound out!' exclaimed Mrs Knox, who was balancing herself on a stone in the stream.

'I'd be in dread, ma'am,' whined Johnny.

'Balderdash!' said the implacable Mrs Knox. 'In with you!'

I understand that Philippa assisted Johnny into the culvert, and presume that it was in so doing that she acquired the two Robinson Crusoe bare footprints which decorated her jacket when I next met her.

'Have you got hold of him yet, Johnny?' cried Mrs Knox up the culvert.

'I have, ma'am, by the tail,' responded Johnny's voice, sepulchral in the depths.

'Can you stir him, Johnny?'

'I cannot, ma'am, and the wather is rising in it.'

'Well, please God, they'll not open the mill dam!' remarked Mrs Knox philosophically to Philippa, as she caught hold of Johnny's dirty ankles. 'Hold on to the tail, Johnny!'

She hauled, with, as might be expected, no appreciable result. 'Run, my dear, and look for somebody, and we'll have that fox yet!'

Philippa ran, whither she knew not, pursued by fearful visions of bursting mill-dams, and maddened foxes at bay. As she sped up the avenue she heard voices, robust male voices, in a shrubbery, and made for them. Advancing along an embowered walk towards her was what she took for one wild instant to be a funeral; a second glance showed her that it was a party of clergymen of all ages, walking by twos and threes in the dappled shade of the over-arching trees. Obviously she had intruded her sacrilegious presence into a Clerical Meeting. She acknowledges that at this awe-inspiring spectacle she faltered, but the thought of Johnny, the hound, and the fox, suffocating, possibly drowning together in the culvert, nerved her. She does not remember what she said or how she said it, but I fancy she must have conveyed to them the impression that old Mrs Knox was being drowned, as she immediately found herself heading a charge of the Irish Church towards the scene of disaster.

Fate has not always used me well, but on this occasion it was mercifully decreed that I and the other members of the hunt should be privileged to arrive in time to see my wife and her rescue party precipitating themselves down the glen.

'Holy Biddy!' ejaculated Flurry, 'is she running a paper-chase with all the parsons? But look! For pity's sake will you look at my grandmother and my Uncle Eustace?'

Mrs Knox and her sworn enemy the old clergyman, whom I had met at dinner the night before, were standing, apparently in the stream, tugging at two bare legs that projected from a hole in the viaduct, and arguing at the top of their voices. The bath-chair lay on its side with the donkey grazing beside it, on the bank a stout archdeacon was tendering advice, and the hounds danced and howled round the entire group.

'I tell you, Eliza, you had better let the archdeacon try,' thundered Mr Hamilton.

'Then I tell you I will not!' vociferated Mrs Knox, with a tug at the end of the sentence that elicited a subterranean lament from Johnny. 'Now who was right about the second grating? I told you so twenty years ago!'

Exactly as Philippa and her rescue party arrived, the efforts of Mrs Knox and her brother-in-law triumphed. The struggling, sopping form of Johnny was slowly drawn from the hole, drenched, speechless, but clinging to the stern of a hound, who, in its turn, had its jaws fast in the hind quarters of a limp, yellow cub.

'Oh, it's dead!' wailed Philippa, 'I *did* think I should have been in time to save it!'

'Well, if that doesn't beat all!' said Dr Hickey.

The Love-Philtre of Ikey Schoenstein

☆★☆

O. HENRY

The Blue Light drug store is downtown, between the Bowery and First Avenue, where the distance between the two streets is the shortest. The Blue Light does not consider that pharmacy is a thing of bric-à-brac, scent and ice-cream soda. If you ask it for pain-killer it will not give you a bonbon.

The Blue Light scorns the labor-saving arts of modern pharmacy. It macerates its opium and percolates its own laudanum and paregoric. To this day pills are made behind its tall prescription desk – pills rolled out on its own pill-tile, divided with a spatula, rolled with the finger and thumb, dusted with calcined magnesia and delivered in little round pasteboard pill-boxes. The store is on a corner about which coveys of ragged-plumed, hilarious children play and become candidates for the cough drops and soothing syrups that wait for them inside.

Ikey Schoenstein was the night clerk of the Blue Light and the friend of his customers. Thus it is on the East Side, where the heart of pharmacy is not glacé. There, as it should be, the druggist is a counsellor, a confessor, an adviser, an able and willing missionary and mentor whose learning is respected, whose occult wisdom is venerated and whose medicine is often poured, untasted, into the gutter. Therefore Ikey's corniform, bespectacled nose and narrow, knowledge-bowed figure was well known in the vicinity of the Blue Light, and his advice and notice were much desired.

Ikey roomed and breakfasted at Mrs Riddle's two squares away. Mrs Riddle had a daughter named Rosy. The circumlocution has been in vain – you must have guessed it – Ikey adored Rosy. She tinctured all his thoughts; she was the compound extract of all that was chemically pure and officinal – the dispensatory contained nothing equal to her. But Ikey was timid, and his hopes remained insoluble in the menstruum of his backwardness and fears. Behind his counter he was a superior being, calmly conscious of special knowledge and worth; outside he was a weak-kneed, purblind, motorman-cursed rambler, with ill-fitting clothes stained with chemicals and smelling of socotrine aloes and valerianate of ammonia.

The fly in Ikey's ointment (thrice welcome, pat trope!) was Chunk McGowan.

Mr McGowan was also striving to catch the bright smiles tossed about by Rosy. But he was no out-fielder as Ikey was; he picked them off the bat. At the same time he was Ikey's friend and customer, and often dropped in at the Blue Light Drug Store to have a bruise painted with iodine or get a cut rubber-plastered after a pleasant evening spent along the Bowery.

One afternoon McGowan drifted in in his silent, easy way, and sat, comely, smooth-faced, hard, indomitable, good-natured, upon a stool.

'Ikey,' said he, when his friend had fetched his mortar and sat opposite, grinding gum benzoin to a powder, 'get busy with your ear. It's drugs for me if you've got the line I need.'

Ikey scanned the countenance of Mr McGowan for the usual evidence of conflict, but found none.

'Take your coat off,' he ordered. 'I guess already that you have been stuck in the ribs with a knife. I have many times told you those Dagoes would do you up.'

Mr McGowan smiled. 'Not them,' he said. 'Not any Dagoes. But you've located the diagnosis all right enough – it's under my coat, near the ribs. Say! Ikey – Rosy and me are goin' to run away and get married tonight.'

Ikey's left forefinger was doubled over the edge of the mortar, holding it steady. He gave it a wild rap with the pestle, but felt it not. Meanwhile Mr McGowan's smile faded to a look of perplexed gloom.

'That is,' he continued, 'if she keeps in the notion until the time comes. We've been layin' pipes for the getaway for two weeks. One day she says she will; the same evenin' she says nixy. We've agreed on tonight, and Rosy's stuck to the affirmative this time for two whole days. But it's five hours yet till the time, and I'm afraid she'll stand me up when it comes to the scratch.'

'You said you wanted drugs,' remarked Ikey.

Mr McGowan looked ill at ease and harassed – a condition opposed to his usual line of demeanor. He made a patent-medicine almanac into a roll and fitted it with unprofitable carefulness about his finger.

'I wouldn't have this double handicap make a false start tonight for a million,' he said. 'I've got a little flat up in Harlem all ready, with chrysanthemums on the table and a kettle ready to boil. And I've engaged a pulpit pounder to be ready at his house for us at 9.30. It's got to come off. And if Rosy don't change her mind again!' – Mr McGowan ceased, a prey to his doubts.

'I don't see then yet,' said Ikey, shortly, 'what makes it that you talk of drugs, or what I can be doing about it.'

'Old man Riddle don't like me a little bit,' went on the uneasy suitor, bent upon marshalling his arguments. 'For a week he hasn't let Rosy step outside the door with me. If it wasn't for losin' a boarder they'd have bounced me long ago. I'm makin' $20 a week and she'll never regret flyin' the coop with Chunk McGowan.'

'You will excuse me, Chunk,' said Ikey. 'I must make a prescription that is to be called for soon.'

'Say,' said McGowan, looking up suddenly, 'say, Ikey, ain't there a drug of some kind – some kind of powders that'll make a girl like you better if you give 'em to her?'

Ikey's lip beneath his nose curled with the scorn of superior enlightenment; but before he could answer, McGowan continued:

'Tim Lacy told me he got some once from a croaker uptown and fed 'em to his girl in soda water. From the very first dose he was ace-high and everybody else looked like thirty cents to her. They was married in less than two weeks.'

Strong and simple was Chunk McGowan. A better reader of men than Ikey was could have seen that his tough frame was strung upon fine wires. Like a good general who was about to invade the enemy's territory he was seeking to guard every point against possible failure.

'I thought,' went on Chunk, hopefully, 'that if I had one of them powders to give Rosy when I see her at supper tonight it might brace her up and keep her from reneging on the proposition to skip. I guess she don't need a mule team to drag her away, but women are better at coaching than they are at running bases. If the stuff'll work just for a couple of hours it'll do the trick.'

'When is this foolishness of running away to be happening?' asked Ikey.

'Nine o'clock,' said Mr McGowan. 'Supper's at seven. At eight Rosy goes to bed with a headache, at nine old Parvenzano lets me through to his backyard, where there's a board off Riddle's fence, next door. I go under her window and help her down the fire-escape. We've got to make it early on the preacher's account. It's all dead easy if Rosy don't balk when the flag drops. Can you fix me one of them powders, Ikey?'

Ikey Schoenstein rubbed his nose slowly.

'Chunk,' said he, 'it is of drugs of that nature that pharmaceutists must have much carefulness. To you alone of my acquaintance would I intrust a powder like that. But for you I shall make it, and you shall see how it makes Rosy to think of you.'

Ikey went behind the prescription desk. There he crushed to a powder two soluble tablets, each containing a quarter of a grain of morphia. To them he added a little sugar of milk to increase the bulk, and folded the mixture neatly in a white paper. Taken by an adult this powder would insure several hours of heavy slumber without danger to the sleeper. This he handed to Chunk McGowan, telling him to administer it in a liquid if possible, and received the hearty thanks of the backyard Lochinvar.

The subtlety of Ikey's action becomes apparent upon recital of his subsequent move. He sent a messenger for Mr Riddle and disclosed the plans of Mr McGowan for eloping with Rosy. Mr Riddle was a stout man, brick-dusty of complexion and sudden in action.

'Much obliged,' he said, briefly, to Ikey. 'The lazy Irish loafer! My own room's just above Rosy's. I'll just go up there myself after supper and load the shot-gun and wait. If he comes in my backyard he'll go away in a ambulance instead of a bridal chaise.'

With Rosy held in the clutches of Morpheus for a many-hours deep slumber, and the blood-thirsty parent waiting, armed and forewarned, Ikey felt that his rival was close, indeed, upon discomfiture.

All night in the Blue Light Drug Store he waited at his duties for chance news of the tragedy, but none came.

At eight o'clock in the morning the day clerk arrived and Ikey started hurriedly for Mrs Riddle's to learn the outcome. And, lo! As he stepped out of the store who but Chunk McGowan sprang from a passing street car and grasped his hand – Chunk McGowan with a victor's smile and flushed with joy.

'Pulled it off,' said Chunk with Elysium in his grin. 'Rosy hit the fire-escape on time to a second, and we was under the wire at the Reverend's at 9.30¼. She's up at the flat – she cooked eggs this mornin' in a blue kimono – Lord! How lucky I am! You must pace up some day, Ikey, and feed with us. I've got a job down near the bridge, and that's where I'm heading for now.'

'The – the – powder?' stammered Ikey.

'Oh, that stuff you gave me!' said Chunk, broadening his grin; 'well, it was this way. I sat down at the supper table last night at Riddle's, and I looked at Rosy, and I says to myself, "Chunk, if you get the girl get her on the square – don't try any hocus-pocus with a thoroughbred like her." And I keeps the paper you give me in my pocket. And then my lamps fall on another party present, who, I says to myself, is failin' in a proper affection toward his comin' son-in-law, so I watches my chance and dumps that powder in old man Riddle's coffee – see?'

The Man They Tried To Kill

☆★☆★☆★☆★☆★☆★☆★☆★☆★☆★☆★☆★☆★☆★☆★☆★☆★☆★☆★☆

BEN ELTON

Lovelorn Egghead

Geoffrey sat alone in the big open-plan office of the Institute of Industrial Research where he worked. He was surrounded by computers and they all winked and flashed at him, but, despite being intimately acquainted with every one of them, Geoffrey neither winked nor flashed back. He wasn't thinking of computers. He was thinking of a beautiful girl, and how one day in the not too distant future, he, Geoffrey, would set that girl free and by doing so would win her love. He would achieve this end with his fantastic research development. A research development so colossal and stupendous it made Penicillin look positively mouldy.

There was a bottle in front of Geoffrey and he was allowing himself a small toast, a little celebration, to mark the imminent realization of all his wildest dreams. Not all of them obviously, not the one set in a nunnery where all the novices turned out to be Dolly Parton for instance, nor the one about the recurring ostrich, but all the ones fit to print. The dreams about success, peer group respect, enormous mountains of serious cash and setting free the most beautiful girl in the world, hence winning her love. If that wasn't worth a sloosh of pop whilst alone in the old research lab, then Geoffrey wasn't the man he thought he was. And Geoffrey certainly was the man he thought he was, because Geoffrey's was a thorough and precise mind and it wasn't the sort of thing he would make a mistake about.

So there he was, warm glow of satisfaction in his gut, love for a good woman in his heart, a little drinkie on the table, and bent over the arm of his chair staring at the carpet and dribbling.

Unwelcome Visitors

There was a buzz from the intercom. Obviously somebody was at the door. Geoffrey was a bit annoyed. He had no wish to be disturbed by anyone, unless of course it was by the girl of his dreams, or possibly Dolly Parton in a wimple, but since these were both rather unlikely, any visitors were unwelcome. Actually Geoffrey had no idea just how unwelcome these visitors would turn out to be. For they were professional killers – which is nearly as bad as having the Jehovah's Witnesses knock on your door.

With difficulty Geoffrey got up, or at least partly up. He managed to get to his feet but it wasn't what you would call a particularly perpendicular performance. None the less, it was the best Geoffrey could manage under the circumstances. He fixed his eye upon the intercom some thirty yards across the room. A room crowded with obstacles. Getting across it was going to take some concentration. There were computers, printers, swivel chairs, kettles, stuffed Snoopy and amusing stickers proclaiming that you didn't have to be mad to work there but it helped.

These stickers were originally developed by psychologists as a test to enable office managers to determine an employee's utter dullness. If, for instance, the manager is seeking to find a person to whom may safely be entrusted the organization of the coffee-making rota. If he needs a reliable sort who will ensure that a good tin is provided for the sugar so that the office does not end up with a soggy paper bag containing forty-seven congealed brown sugar globules. All the manager has to do is spy out the employees with the sticker on their computer amusingly proclaiming that 'You don't have to be mad to work here but it helps'. That person will be guaranteed dull, dependable and sane as a pair of corduroy trousers.

Geoffrey lurched forward towards the vast expanse of potential croppers that lay between him and the buzzer. His work place was one of those modern open-plan areas where everything is rendered much more frank and relaxed by virtue of there being no nasty walls to divide people or doors to intimidate them. The actual result of course being that everyone develops nervous ticks due to never knowing who's eavesdropping on them and never feeling safe to have a really good bitch.

An added disadvantage of these spaces, especially if you happen to be in the condition that Geoffrey was in, is that plug and telephone sockets stick up out of the floor in the most unexpected places and there are wires everywhere. It was whilst attempting to negotiate a particularly tangled bit of technology that Geoffrey skidded on the bit of pizza that was left over from a leaving bash which had taken place on the previous Friday evening.

The Leaving Bash From Hell

Geoffrey lay on the carpet tiles, with his head in a waste-paper bin, quietly cursing. The leaving bash from hell had returned to haunt him.

All leaving bashes are awful. Perhaps not as awful as birthday bashes where one is forced to annoy an entire restaurant by singing *Happy Birthday* whilst a waiter proudly brings forth a mound of whipped cream with a sparkler in it, but pretty bad, none the less – and this leaving bash was worse. The nightmare had started with the card. Geoffrey had barely known Suzy, the lucky recipient of all that office warmth, symbolized, as it was, by a large picture of Snoopy holding a horseshoe. However, he had felt obliged to rack his brains for twenty minutes trying to think of something witty to write. Eventually he had decided on 'I don't know who you are, but very best wishes'. The biro had scarcely come to a standstill when he deeply regretted his decision. Paranoia consumed him, the phrase was too hard, too dismissive. The scrawled sentence Geoffrey had written seemed to dissolve before his eyes and reform into the words, 'Bugger off, nobody'. After all, that was what his message implied wasn't it? In that instant Geoffrey convinced himself that the girl would be very hurt and that the rest of the lab would despise him for messing up their nice card. Already he could feel the icy hand of social ostracism fingering his collar.

In desperation he opened a bracket. Impulsively he wrote,' Just joking, really, it's been great working with you.' Geoffrey closed the bracket and descended fully and completely into the paranoid zone. Talk about making a bad thing worse! Maybe he should just go have a shit in the poor woman's pending tray! The first joke had been merely tasteless, now he had turned it into pure hate mail. Everything he had written seemed to just deliberately and maliciously draw attention to the fact that he had scarcely ever spoken to the girl and did not care whether she lived or died. Frantically Geoffrey considered a second bracket, a square one, just a simple and affectionate message to repair the damage of the previous two efforts. Perhaps something along the lines of, 'Actually I want you to be the mother of my children! . . .' or, 'Listen Suzy, name your price to forget about the whole thing.' Fortunately for Geoffrey reason returned to its throne. He realized that there would not be sufficient brackets in a book of algebra to extricate him from the tact swamp into which he had dived. He would simply have to let it go.

Geoffrey firmly closed the card and, with a weak smile, handed it back to Denise, unofficial social secretary for the whole building and the girl with the 'mad' sticker on her desk.

Denise, who had about as much tact as the Wehrmacht, reopened the card and read Geoffrey's message. 'Oh that's *lovely*,' she said, in a voice that you could have beaten down and forged into drill bits. 'I'm *sure* Suzy will see the joke.'

Attending the 'do' itself had been worse than writing the card. There is a type of white wine which is produced in continental Europe specifically for leaving 'do's in Britain. It is described as 'an elegant, delicate, fruity dry' which is Euro-plonkspeak for abrasive and it is made by putting sandpaper and lemon juice into a blender. Within two sips from his or her plastic cup the unhappy imbiber's throat becomes coated in a thick layer of bitter tasting phlegm which can only be removed with a pan scrubber. Unless of course you happen to be talking to the boss, in which case the phlegm will instantly leap out of the back of your neck and cling desperately to his tie.

This wine also contains a special kind of alcohol that cannot get you happy-drunk but can only get you bored-drunk, which was the state that everybody was in when the 'do' finally wound down at about eight-thirty.

This is an appalling time for an after-work social to end. Up until eight-twenty everyone has spent the entire time making desperate conversation and wishing they were somewhere else. Then suddenly, with no warning, people are sufficiently bored-pissed on plastic cups of warm French expectorant to agree to going on for a curry.

It is a strange factor of this kind of euphorically dull drunkenness ('Oh go on then, sod it, why not? The evening's buggered anyway.') that it lasts for only twenty-five minutes. This is exactly long enough to get trapped in a curry house between two people you have absolutely no desire to talk to, who are on a different table from the person you have vaguely begun to fancy, while you watch one person order three – no better make if four – popadums each, and someone else order a large brandy. All of which you know you are going to have to pay for a fifteenth of, even though you're not particularly hungry and you can't drink any more yourself because you're driving.

All of this had taken place on Friday night, and now it was late Sunday afternoon and the leaving bash from hell was back. Like some evil curse from a darker age it refused to let Geoffrey be. Having caused him untold worry, bored him stupid and cost him over twenty quid, it had now dumped him down with a thud on the carpet tiles and left him with his head in a waste-paper basket, wherein, a polystyrene cup was in the process of pouring half an inch of cold coffee with a fag end in it, up his nose. How much more could one leaving bash do to a man?

English Comprehension

The buzzer was still buzzing, Geoffrey wanted to shout 'All right, hang on, where's the fire, dickheads,' but he was a realist and in his condition he didn't reckon he would be up to making himself understood. If you're going to start being brusque with people, the last thing you want is them looking puzzled and replying, 'You what?' It detracts from your impact.

With some difficulty, Geoffrey extricated his head from the waste-paper bin that the pizza had dumped it in, and continued his uncertain stagger across the room, finally arriving at the intercom buzzer.

On the second attempt Geoffrey managed to press the button . . . 'Yurgh,' he grunted into the microphone. Which translated meant 'Yes, who is it?' However, since no interpreter was available at the other end, the two killers waiting on the pavement had to make do with 'Yurgh'.

'Uhm yeah,' shouted one of the killers, for the traffic was loud in the street, 'we're looking for Dr Geoffrey Peason. He around?'

'Yes, that's me, come on up,' said Dr Geoffrey Peason – or rather he didn't because he was having a bit of trouble getting his tongue and larynx to cooperate with each other. The sentence had departed from his brain in perfect condition, but by the time it struggled out of the inter-com into the street it had become 'Urg-ats-mm-uhmonup'.

The two men in the street did not know what to make of this cryptic message. They couldn't see the condition Geoffrey was in so they just presumed that they were dealing with a foreigner, or perhaps a mental defective.

The more talkative killer began again, employing the accepted method of communication employed by the British whenever they encounter someone who does not appear to understand English. He raised his voice.

All over Europe, each summer, can be seen the sad picture of frus-trated, purple-faced Britons screaming in the faces of non-comprehending natives, 'WHERE . . . IS . . . THE . . . PUBLIC . . . CON-VE-NIENCE'. The curious theory that a strange language can be rendered understandable by increasing the volume at which it is spoken is one of the great mysteries of the British abroad.

In Paris the cause of the commotion is slightly different. Most Pari-sians do in fact speak some English, but out of pure bloody-minded snobbishness they refuse to do so in the company of the British. When accosted by a desperate, sweaty, confused Brit asking, 'Excuse me, but do you speak English?' the immaculately dressed Parisian will raise a lang-uid eyebrow and enquire, 'Yes, do you speak French?' It is a little known historical fact that it was this irritating habit which was the principle cause of the Hundred Years' War.

Anyway, in an effort to make himself understood, the man in the street raised his voice. Since he had already been shouting to get above the traffic noise the effort caused veins to stand out on his forehead. He accompanied this tonsil tingling rant with an elaborate pantomime, this being another aspect of the standard British method of getting your message across to foreigners – scream at the top of your voice and wave your arms about in massive but vague physical gesticulations.

This sad display provides mainland Europeans (again, particularly, the French) with endless entertainment. Outside the Georges Pompidou Centre in Paris, there can always be found a cluster of extremely dull mime artists in tights and bowler hats with flowers sticking out of them, miming walking into a high wind. These irritating performances are invariably accompanied by a clutch of Americans, Brits and Japanese delightedly assuring each other that the bowler hatted one indeed looks *exactly* like he's walking into a high wind, or quite anyway. The locals of course, know that far more fun can be had watching a British tourist attempt to mime 'Can you direct me to the Museum of Contemporary Sculpture please?' and what's more he won't shove his bowler hat under your nose at the end of it.

Judging A Book By Its Cover

So there they were, the two men on the pavement, one of them roaring at the intercom and miming wildly. Geoffrey, deciding that actions speak louder than words, even words as loud as the ones making the intercom shudder, pressed the lock transmission button, thus providing the first clear message of the whole communication.

After the obligatory electronic lock dance, in which a person and door push against each other to the tune of a buzzer going on and off, the door swung open and the men stumbled in.

They took the lift to the floor marked 'Transport, Fuel and Engine Research' and emerged from it to find Dr Geoffrey Peason waiting for them. Geoffrey held out a shaking hand and tried to greet them cordially but he wasn't really up to it and the two men clearly weren't very impressed with him. However, at first they made at least a pretence at the easy good manners which killers are wont to adopt before unmasking themselves as the angel of death.

They enquired again after Dr Geoffrey Peason stating that they had business with him regarding his recent application for a patent. Dr Peason, also attempting easy good manners but blowing it by dribbling a bit, again replied that he was the said Peason, Doctor of Physics and patent applicant, and what could he do for them? Unfortunately Geoffrey still was not making himself very clearly understood and the visitors' tone became impatient.

'Now listen Sonny, we haven't got a lot of time to waste, so you pull yourself together, all right? And tell us where Peason is.'

Geoffrey was suddenly very tired. He hated being patronized and he hated being dismissed as of no importance. It was always happening to him. He turned his back on the men and staggered back to his chair. Plonking himself down rather heavily he knocked his bottle onto the floor.

'Bollocks,' he said, or rather 'Burgles', an exclamation which he accompanied with an impulsive looking gesture of despair.

Faced with this incoherent hurdle to their enquiries the two men's tone became markedly more intimidating.

'Where's Peason?' the talkative one barked. 'This is where he works isn't it? Our information is that he's always here Sundays.'

Again Dr Peason tried to explain that he was the man they sought, but the men just did not have the patience to listen to him. They had been briefed to pay a visit on a brilliant scientist and inventor. A man who had invented something quite brilliant and scientific. Confronted by this slurring, unpleasant, uncoordinated young man in a leather jacket and torn jeans, they assumed that the doctor was out. However, since the dribbling rocker was clearly their only available source of information they had no choice but to continue their clumsy enquiries.

Advancing towards Geoffrey one of the men slipped on the pizza.

'I just did that,' said Geoffrey trying once more to be friendly, but still failing completely to make himself understood.

'Don't laugh at me you disgusting little git,' barked the man. He grabbed Geoffrey's cap from Geoffrey's head. Geoffrey was wearing a cap he particularly liked, it was a comedy cap. It had a stuffed arm holding a hammer emerging out of it which appeared to be beating the wearer on his own head. The man wiped the pizza from his shoe with Geoffrey's hat.

Geoffrey may have been having more trouble than usual making himself understood that day but this last gesture confirmed an understanding that had been dawning on him for some time: that he was in the presence of a couple of potentially very dangerous people.

Pizza-shoe roughly crammed the hat back on Geoffrey's head.

'Where's the Doc zit face?' he demanded.

Geoffrey gulped.

'He can't tell you nothing, can he,' said the other, speaking for the first time.

'Look at the state he's in. Let's search the building.'

And with that Geoffrey's interrogators stalked from the room, leaving Geoffrey rather shaken by his unpleasant encounter. Not as shaken as he would have been if he had realized that, had he not been a spastic, he would have been murdered. But none the less, pretty shaken.

Being a spastic had not done Geoffrey a lot of favours in his life. In fact it could be said to have been a total and utter drag from start to finish. However, in that brief moment, being a spastic had actually made up for quite a number of its shortcomings as a physical condition. It had unquestionably saved Geoffrey's life, because if Geoffrey had not been a spastic, or CP sufferer as some people call it, the two thugs would certainly have killed him

This is not to say that they refrained from such a course of action out of any sense of sympathy; they did not say to themselves, 'Oh look, hell, the poor bugger's been knocking glasses off tables all his life and probably never been able to masturbate properly. Let's give him a break eh?' No, the two thugs in question were far too hard of heart for that. It was simply that it never occurred to them that the strange, guttural sounding, twitchy chap sat before them could be the brilliant scientist and inventor whom they had been ordered to murder. But he was.

People with disabilities are very used to being looked through, over, and around. Judged by their covers so to speak. They no longer find it surprising when it is presumed that they have little or no potential and nothing to add to a conversation (other than a conversation on the subject of disability). This is not to say that it gets any easier to put up with, spending one's entire life being underestimated never ceases to be anything other than an horrendous strain, but people with disabilities certainly recognize the attitude. Geoffrey did, he was always being either ignored or patronized and on this occasion he was extremely fortunate that it was the case.

The Declaration

☆★☆★☆★☆★☆★☆★☆★☆★☆★☆★☆★☆★☆

JANE AUSTEN

The next day opened a new scene at Longbourn. Mr Collins made his declaration in form. Having resolved to do it without loss of time, as his leave of absence extended only to the following Saturday, and having no feelings of diffidence to make it distressing to himself even at the moment, he set about it in a very orderly manner, with all the observances which he supposed a regular part of the business. On finding Mrs Bennet, Elizabeth, and one of the younger girls together, soon after breakfast, he addressed the mother in these words.

'May I hope, Madam, for your interest with your fair daughter Elizabeth, when I solicit for the honour of a private audience with her in the course of this morning?'

Before Elizabeth had time for any thing but a blush of surprise, Mrs Bennet instantly answered,

'Oh dear! – Yes – certainly. – I am sure Lizzy will be very happy – I am sure she can have no objection. – Come, Kitty, I want you up stairs.' And gathering her work together, she was hastening away, when Elizabeth called out,

'Dear Ma'am, do not go. – I beg you will not go. – Mr Collins must excuse me. – He can have nothing to say to me that any body need not hear. I am going away myself.'

'No, no, nonsense, Lizzy. – I desire you will stay where you are.' – And upon Elizabeth's seeming really, with vexed and embarrassed looks, about to escape, she added, 'Lizzy, I *insist* upon your staying and hearing Mr Collins.'

Elizabeth would not oppose such an injunction – and a moment's consideration making her also sensible that it would be wisest to get it over as soon and as quietly as possible, she sat down again, and tried to conceal by incessant employment the feelings which were divided between distress and diversion. Mrs Bennet and Kitty walked off, and as soon as they were gone Mr Collins began.

'Believe me, my dear Miss Elizabeth, that your modesty, so far from doing you any disservice, rather adds to your other perfections. You would have been less amiable in my eyes had there *not* been this little unwillingness; but allow me to assure you that I have your respected mother's permission for this address. You can hardly doubt the purport of my discourse, however your natural delicacy may lead you to dissemble; my attentions have been too marked to be mistaken. Almost as soon as I entered the house I singled you out as the companion of my future life. But before I am run away with by my feelings on this subject, perhaps it will be advisable for me to state my reasons for marrying – and moreover for coming into Hertfordshire with the design of selecting a wife, as I certainly did.'

The idea of Mr Collins, with all his solemn composure, being run away with by his feelings, made Elizabeth so near laughing that she could not use the short pause he allowed in any attempt to stop him farther, and he continued:

'My reasons for marrying are, first, that I think it a right thing for every clergyman in easy circumstances (like myself) to set the example of matrimony in his parish. Secondly, that I am convinced it will add very greatly to my happiness; and thirdly – which perhaps I ought to have mentioned earlier, that it is the particular advice and recommendation of the very noble lady whom I have the honour of calling patroness. Twice has she condescended to give me her opinion (unasked too!) on this subject; and it was but the very Saturday night before I left Hunsford – between our pools at quadrille, while Mrs Jenkinson was arranging Miss de Bourgh's footstool, that she said, "Mr Collins, you must marry. A clergyman like you must marry. – Chuse properly, chuse a gentlewoman for *my* sake; and for your *own*, let her be an active, useful sort of person, not brought up high, but able to make a small income go a good way. This is my advice. Find such a woman as soon as you can, bring her to Hunsford, and I will visit her." Allow me, by the way to observe, my fair cousin, that I do not reckon the notice and kindness of Lady Catherine de Bourgh as among the least of the advantages in my power to offer. You will find her manners beyond any thing I can describe; and your wit and vivacity I think must be acceptable to her, especially when tempered with the silence and respect which her rank will inevitably excite. Thus much for my general intention in favour of matrimony; it remains to be told why my views were directed to Longbourn instead of my own neighbourhood, where I assure you there are many amiable young women. But the fact is, that being, as I am, to inherit this estate after the death of your honoured father, (who, however, may live many years longer), I could not satisfy myself without resolving to chuse a wife from among his daughters, that the loss to them might be as little as possible, when the melancholy event takes place – which, however, as I have already said, may not be for several years. This has been my motive, my fair cousin, and I flatter myself it will not sink me in your esteem. And now nothing remains for me but to assure you in the most animated language of the violence of my affection. To fortune I am perfectly indifferent, and shall make no demand of that nature on your father, since I am well aware that it could not be complied with; and that one thousand pounds in the 4 per cents. which will not be yours till after your mother's decease, is all that you may ever be entitled to. On that head, therefore, I shall be uniformly silent; and you may assure yourself that no ungenerous reproach shall ever pass my lips when we are married.'

It was absolutely necessary to interrupt him now.

'You are too hasty, Sir,' she cried. 'You forget that I have made no answer. Let me do it without farther loss of time. Accept my thanks for the compliment you are paying me. I am very sensible of the honour of your proposals, but it is impossible for me to do otherwise than decline them.'

'I am not now to learn,' replied Mr Collins, with a formal wave of the hand, 'that it is usual with young ladies to reject the addresses of the man whom they secretly mean to accept, when he first applies for their favour; and that sometimes the refusal is repeated a second or even a third time. I am therefore by no means discouraged by what you have just said, and shall hope to lead you to the altar ere long.'

'Upon my word, Sir,' cried Elizabeth, 'your hope is rather an extraordinary one after my declaration. I do assure you that I am not one of those young ladies (if such young ladies there are) who are so daring as to risk their happiness on the chance of being asked a second time. I am perfectly serious in my refusal. – You could not make *me* happy, and I am convinced that I am the last woman in the world who would make *you* so. – Nay, were your friend Lady Catherine to know me, I am persuaded she would find me in every respect ill qualified for the situation.'

'Were it certain that Lady Catherine would think so,' said Mr Collins very gravely – 'but I cannot imagine that her ladyship would at all disapprove of you. And you may be certain that when I have the honour of seeing her again I shall speak in the highest terms of your modesty, economy, and other amiable qualifications.'

'Indeed, Mr Collins, all praise of me will be unnecessary. You must give me leave to judge for myself, and pay me the compliment of believing what I say. I wish you very happy and very rich, and by refusing your hand, do all in my power to prevent your being otherwise. In making me the offer, you must have satisfied the delicacy of your feelings with regard to my family, and may take possession of Longbourn estate whenever it falls, without any self-reproach. This matter may be considered, therefore, as finally settled.' And rising as she thus spoke, she would have quitted the room, had not Mr Collins thus addressed her.

'When I do myself the honour of speaking to you next in this subject I shall hope to receive a more favourable answer than you have now given me; though I am far from accusing you of cruelty at present, because I know it to be the established custom of your sex to reject a man on the first application, and perhaps you have even now said as much to encourage my suit as would be consistent with the true delicacy of the female character.'

'Really, Mr Collins,' cried Elizabeth with some warmth, 'you puzzle me exceedingly. If what I have hitherto said can appear to you in the form of encouragement, I know not how to express my refusal in such a way as may convince you of its being one.'

'You must give me leave to flatter myself, my dear cousin, that your refusal of my addresses is merely words of course. My reasons for believing it are briefly these: – It does not appear to me that my hand is unworthy your acceptance, or that the establishment I can offer would be any other than highly desirable. My situation in life, my connections with the family of de Bourgh, and my relationship to your own, are circumstances highly in my favour; and you should take it into farther consideration that in spite of your manifold attractions, it is by no means certain that another offer of marriage may ever be made you. Your portion is unhappily so small that it will in all likelihood undo the effects of your loveliness and amiable qualifications. As I must therefore conclude that you are not serious in your rejection of me, I shall chuse to attribute it to your wish of increasing my love by suspense, according to the usual practice of elegant females.'

'I do assure you, Sir, that I have no pretension whatever to that kind of elegance which consists in tormenting a respectable man. I would rather be paid the compliment of being believed. I thank you again and again for the honour you have done me in your proposals, but to accept them is absolutely impossible. My feelings in every respect forbid it. Can I speak plainer? Do not consider me now as an elegant female intending to plague you, but as a rational creature speaking the truth from her heart.'

'You are uniformly charming!' cried he, with an air of awkward gallantry; 'and I am persuaded that when sanctioned by the express authority of both your excellent parents, my proposals will not fail of being acceptable.'

To such perseverance in wilful self-deception Elizabeth would make no reply, and immediately and in silence withdrew; determined, if he persisted in considering her repeated refusals as flattering encouragement, to apply to her father, whose negative might be uttered in such a manner as must be decisive, and whose behaviour at least could not be mistaken for the affectation and coquetry of an elegant female.

Mr Collins was not left long to the silent contemplation of his successful love; for Mrs Bennet, having dawdled about in the vestibule to watch for the end of the conference, no sooner saw Elizabeth open the door and with quick step pass her towards the staircase, than she entered the breakfast-room, and congratulated both him and herself in warm terms on the happy prospect of their nearer connection. Mr Collins received and returned these felicitations with equal pleasure, and then proceeded to relate the particulars of their interview, with the result of which he trusted he had every reason to be satisfied, since the refusal which his cousin had steadfastly given him would naturally flow from her bashful modesty and the genuine delicacy of her character.

This information, however, startled Mrs Bennet; – she would have been glad to be equally satisfied that her daughter had meant to encourage him by protesting against his proposals, but she dared not to believe it, and could not help saying so.

'But depend upon it, Mr Collins,' she added, 'that Lizzy shall be brought to reason. I will speak to her about it myself directly. She is a very headstrong foolish girl, and does not know her own interest; but I will *make* her know it.'

'Pardon me for interrupting you, Madam,' cried Mr Collins; 'but if she is really headstrong and foolish, I know not whether she would altogether be a very desirable wife to a man in my situation, who naturally looks for happiness in the marriage state. If therefore she actually persists in rejecting my suit, perhaps it were better not to force her into accepting me, because if liable to such defects of temper, she could not contribute much to my felicity.'

'Sir, you quite misunderstand me,' said Mrs Bennet, alarmed. 'Lizzy is only headstrong in such matters as these. In every thing else she is as good natured a girl as ever lived. I will go directly to Mr Bennet, and we shall very soon settle it with her, I am sure.'

She would not give him time to reply, but hurrying instantly to her husband, called out as she entered the library,

'Oh! Mr Bennet, you are wanted immediately; we are all in an uproar. You must come and make Lizzy marry Mr Collins, for she vows she will not have him, and if you do not make haste he will change his mind and not have *her*.'

Mr Bennet raised his eyes from his book as she entered, and fixed them on her face with a calm unconcern which was not in the least altered by her communication.

'I have not the pleasure of understanding you,' said he, when she had finished her speech. 'Of what are you talking?'

'Of Mr Collins and Lizzy. Lizzy declares she will not have Mr Collins, and Mr Collins begins to say that he will not have Lizzy.'

'And what am I to do on the occasion? – It seems an hopeless business.'

'Speak to Lizzy about it yourself. Tell her that you insist upon her marrying him.'

'Let her be called down. She shall hear my opinion.'

Mrs Bennet rang the bell, and Miss Elizabeth was summoned to the library.

'Come here, child,' cried her father as she appeared. 'I have sent for you on an affair of importance. I understand that Mr Collins has made you an offer of marriage. Is it true?' Elizabeth replied that it was. 'Very well – and this offer of marriage you have refused?'

'I have, Sir.'

'Very well. We now come to the point. Your mother insists upon your accepting it. Is not it so, Mrs Bennet?'

'Yes, or I will never see her again.'

'An unhappy alternative is before you, Elizabeth. From this day you must be a stranger to one of your parents. – Your mother will never see you again if you do *not* marry Mr Collins, and I will never see you again if you *do*.'

The Wash-Tub

☆★☆★☆★☆★☆★☆★☆★☆★☆★☆★☆★☆

W. SOMERSET MAUGHAN

Positano stands on the side of a steep hill, a disarray of huddled white houses, their tiled roofs washed pale by the suns of a hundred years; but unlike many of these Italian towns perched out of harm's way on a rocky eminence it does not offer you at one delightful glance all it has to give. It has quaint streets that zig-zag up the hill, and battered, painted houses in the baroque style, but very late, in which Neapolitan noblemen led for a season lives of penurious grandeur. It is indeed almost excessively picturesque and in winter its two or three modest hotels are crowded with painters, male and female, who in their different ways acknowledge by their daily labours the emotion it has excited in them. Some take infinite pains to place on canvas every window and every tile their peering eyes can discover and doubtless achieve the satisfaction that rewards honest industry. 'At all events it's sincere,' they say modestly when they show you their work. Some, rugged and dashing, in a fine frenzy attack their canvas with a pallet knife charged with a wad of paint, and they say: 'You see, what I was trying to bring out was my personality.' They slightly close their eyes and tentatively murmur: 'I think it's rather me, don't you?' And there are some who give you highly entertaining arrangements of spheres and cubes and utter sombrely: 'That's how I see it!' These for the most part are strong silent men who waste no words.

But Positano looks full south and the chances are that in summer you will have it to yourself. The hotel is clean and cool and there is a terrace, overhung with vines, where you can sit at night and look at the sea bespangled with dim stars. Down at the Marine, on the quay, is a little tavern where you can dine under an archway off anchovies and ham, macaroni and fresh-caught mullet, and drink cold wine. Once a day the steamer from Naples comes in, bringing the mail, and for a quarter of an hour gives the beach (there is no port and the passengers are landed in small boats) an air of animation.

One August, tiring of Capri where I had been staying, I made up my mind to spend a few days at Positano, so I hired a fishing-boat and rowed over. I stopped on the way in a shady cove to bathe and lunch and sleep, and did not arrive till evening. I strolled up the hill, my two bags following me on the heads of two sturdy women, to the hotel, and was surprised to learn that I was not its only guest. The waiter, whose name was Giuseppe, was an old friend of mine, and at that season he was boots, porter, chambermaid, and cook as well. He told me that an American signore had been staying there for three months.

'Is he a painter or writer or something?' I asked.

'No, *Signore*, he's a gentleman.'

Odd, I thought. No foreigners came to Positano at that time of year but German *Wandervogel*, looking hot and dusty, with satchels on their backs, and they only stayed overnight. I could not imagine anyone wishing to spend three months there; unless of course he were hiding. And since all London had been excited by the flight earlier in the year of an eminent, but dishonest, financier, the amusing thought occurred to me that this mysterious stranger was perhaps he. I knew him slightly and trusted that my sudden arrival would not disconcert him.

'You'll see the *Signore* at the Marina,' said Giuseppe, as I was setting out to go down again. 'He always dines there.'

He was certainly not there when I arrived. I asked what there was for dinner and drank an americano, which is by no means a bad substitute for a cocktail. In a few minutes, however, a man walked in who could be no other than my fellow-guest at the hotel and I had a moment's disappointment when I saw that it was not the absconding financier. A tall, elderly man, bronzed after his summer on the Mediterranean, with a handsome, thin face. He wore a very neat, even smart, suit of cream-coloured silk and no hat. His grey hair was cut very short, but was still thick. There was ease in his bearing, and elegance. He looked round the half-dozen tables under the archway at which the natives of the place were playing cards or dominoes and his eyes rested on me. They smiled pleasantly. He came up.

'I hear you have just arrived at the hotel. Giuseppe suggested that as he couldn't come down here to effect an introduction you wouldn't mind if I introduced myself. Would it bore you to dine with a total stranger?'

'Of course not. Sit down.'

He turned to the maid who was laying a cover for me and in beautiful Italian told her that I would eat with him. He looked at my americano.

'I have got them to stock a little gin and French vermouth for me. Would you allow me to mix you a very dry Martini?'

'Without hesitation.'

'It gives an exotic note to the surroundings which brings out the local colour.'

He certainly made a very good cocktail and with added appetite we ate the ham and anchovies with which our dinner began. My host had a pleasant humour and his fluent conversation was agreeable.

'You must forgive me if I talk too much,' he said presently. 'This is the first chance I've had to speak English for three months. I don't suppose you will stay here long and I mean to make the most of it.'

'Three months is a long time to stay at Positano.'

'I've hired a boat and I bathe and fish. I read a great deal. I have a good many books here and if there's anything I can lend you I shall be very glad.'

'I think I have enough reading matter. But I should love to look at what you have. It's always fun looking at other people's books.'

He gave me a sharp look and his eyes twinkled.

'It also tells you a good deal about them,' he murmured.

When we finished dinner we went on talking. The stranger was well-read and interested in a diversity of topics. He spoke with so much knowledge of painting that I wondered if he was an art critic or a dealer. But then it appeared that he had been reading Suetonius and I came to the conclusion that he was a college professor. I asked him his name.

'Barnaby,' he answered.

'That's a name that has recently acquired an amazing celebrity.'

'Oh, how so?'

'Have you never heard of the celebrated Mrs Barnaby? She's a compatriot of yours.'

'I admit that I've seen her name in the papers rather frequently of late. Do you know her?'

'Yes, quite well. She gave the grandest parties all last season and I went to them whenever she asked me. Everyone did. She's an astounding woman. She came to London to do the season, and, by George, she did it. She just swept everything before her.'

'I understand she's very rich?'

'Fabulously, I believe, but it's not that that has made her success. Plenty of American women have money. Mrs Barnaby has got where she has by sheer force of character. She never pretends to be anything but what she is. She's natural. She's priceless. You know her history, of course?'

My friend smiled.

'Mrs Barnaby may be a great celebrity in London, but to the best of my belief in America she is almost inconceivably unknown.'

I smiled also, but within me; I could well imagine how shocked this distinguished and cultured man would be by the rollicking humour, the frankness, with its tang of the soil, and the rich and vital experience of the amazing Mrs Barnaby.

'Well, I'll tell you about her. Her husband appears to be a very rough diamond; he's a great hulking fellow, she says, who could fell a steer with his fist. He's known in Arizona as One-Bullet Mike.'

'Good gracious! Why?'

'Well, years ago in the old days he killed two men with a single shot. She says he's handier with his gun even now than any man West of the Rockies. He's a miner, but he's been a cowpuncher, a gun-runner, and God knows what in his day.'

'A thoroughly Western type,' said my professor a trifle acidly, I thought.

'Something of a desperado, I imagine. Mrs Barnaby's stories about him are a real treat. Of course everyone's been begging her to let him come over, but she says he'd never leave the wide open spaces. He struck oil a year or two ago and now he's got all the money in the world. He must be a great character. I've heard her keep the whole dinner-table spellbound when she's talked of the old days when they roughed it together. It gives you quite a thrill when you see this grey-haired woman, not at all pretty, but exquisitely dressed, with the most wonderful pearls, and hear her tell how she washed the miners' clothes and cooked for the camp. Your American women have an adaptability that's really stupendous. When you see Mrs Barnaby sitting at the head of her table, perfectly at home with princes of the blood, ambassadors, cabinet ministers, and the duke of this and the duke of that, it seems almost incredible that only a few years ago she was cooking the food of seventy miners.'

'Can she read or write?'

'I suppose her invitations are written by her secretary, but she's by no means an ignorant woman. She told me she used to make a point of reading for an hour every night after the fellows in camp had gone to bed.'

'Remarkable!'

'On the other hand One-Bullet Mike only learnt to write his name when he suddenly found himself under the necessity of signing cheques.'

We walked up the hill to our hotel and before separating for the night arranged to take our luncheon with us next day and row over to a cove that my friend had discovered. We spent a charming day bathing, reading, eating, sleeping, and talking, and we dined together in the evening. The following morning, after breakfast on the terrace, I reminded Barnaby of his promise to show me his books.

'Come right along.'

I accompanied him to his bedroom, where Giuseppe, the waiter, was making his bed. The first thing I caught sight of was a photograph in a gorgeous frame of the celebrated Mrs Barnaby. My friend caught sight of it too and suddenly turned pale with anger.

'You fool, Giuseppe. Why have you taken that photograph out of my wardrobe? Why the devil did you think I put it away?'

'I didn't know, Signore. That's why I put it back on the Signore's table. I thought he liked to see the portrait of his *signora*.'

I was staggered.

'Is my Mrs Barnaby your wife?' I cried.

'She is.'

'Good Lord, are you One-Bullet Mike?'

'Do I look it?'

I began to laugh.

'I'm bound to say you don't.'

I glanced at his hands. He smiled grimly and held them out.

'No, sir. I have never felled a steer with my naked fist.'

For a moment we stared at one another in silence.

'She'll never forgive me,' he moaned. 'She wanted me to take a false name, and when I wouldn't she was quite vexed with me. She said it wasn't safe. I said it was bad enough to hide myself in Positano for three months, but I'd be damned if I'd use any other name than my own.' He hesitated. 'I throw myself on your mercy. I can do nothing but trust to your generosity not to disclose a secret that you have discovered by the most unlikely chance.'

'I will be as silent as the grave, but honestly I don't understand. What does it all mean?'

'I am a doctor by profession and for the last thirty years my wife and I have lived in Pennsylvania. I don't know if I have struck you as a roughneck, but I venture to say that Mrs Barnaby is one of the most cultivated women I have ever known. Then a cousin of hers died and left her a very large fortune. There's no mistake about that. My wife is a very, very rich woman. She has always read a great deal of English fiction and her one desire was to have a London season and entertain and do all the grand things she had read about in books. It was her money and although the prospect did not particularly tempt me, I was very glad that she should gratify her wish. We sailed last April. The young Duke and Duchess of Hereford happened to be on board.'

'I know. It was they who first launched Mrs Barnaby. They were crazy about her. They've boomed her like an army of press-agents.'

'I was ill when we sailed, I had a carbuncle which confined me to my stateroom, and Mrs Barnaby was left to look after herself. Her deck-chair happened to be next the duchess's, and from a remark she overheard it occurred to her that the English aristocracy were not so wrapped up in our social leaders as one might have expected. My wife is a quick little woman and she remarked to me that if you had an ancestor who signed Magna Carta perhaps you were not excessively impressed because the grandfather of one of your acquaintances sold skunks and the grandfather of another ran ferryboats. My wife has a very keen sense of humour. Getting into conversation with the duchess, she told her a little Western anecdote, and to make it more interesting told it as having happened to herself. Its success was immediate. The duchess begged for another and my wife ventured a little further. Twenty-four hours later she had the duke and duchess eating out of her hand. She used to come down to my stateroom at intervals and tell me of her progress. In the innocence of my heart, I was tickled to death and since I had nothing else to do, I sent to the library for the works of Bret Harte and primed her with effective touches.'

I slapped my forehead.

'We said she was as good as Bret Harte,' I cried.

'I had a grand time thinking of the consternation of my wife's friends when at the end of the voyage I appeared and we told them the truth. But I reckoned without my wife. The day before we reached Southampton Mrs Barnaby told me that the Herefords were arranging parties for her. The duchess was crazy to introduce her to all sorts of wonderful people. It was a chance in a thousand; but of course I should spoil everything, she admitted that she had been forced by the course of events to represent me as very different from what I was. I did not know that she had already transformed me into One-Bullet Mike, but I had a shrewd suspicion that she had forgotten to mention that I was on board. Well, to make a long story short, she asked me to go to Paris for a week or two till she had consolidated her position. I didn't mind that. I was much more inclined to do a little work at the Sorbonne than to go to parties in Mayfair, and so leaving her to go on to Southampton, I got off at

Cherbourg. But when I had been in Paris ten days she flew over to see me. She told me that her success had exceeded her wildest dreams: it was ten times more wonderful than any of the novels; but my appearance would ruin it all. Very well, I said, I would stay in Paris. She didn't like the idea of that; she said she'd never have a moment's peace so long as I was so near and I might run across someone who knew me. I suggested Vienna or Rome. They wouldn't do either, and at last I came here and here have I been hiding like a criminal for three interminable months.'

'Do you mean to say you never killed the two gamblers, shooting one with your right hand and the other with your left?'

'Sir, I have never fired a pistol in my life.'

'And what about the attack on your log-cabin by the Mexican bandits when your wife loaded your guns for you and you stood the siege for three days till the Federal troops rescued you?'

Mr Barnaby smiled grimly.

'I never heard that one. Isn't it a trifle crude?'

'Crude! It was as good as any Wild West picture.'

'If I may venture a guess, that is where my wife in all probability got the idea.'

'But the wash-tub. Washing the miners' clothes and all that. You don't know how she made us roar with that story. Why, she swam into London Society in her wash-tub.'

I began to laugh.

'She's made the most gorgeous fools of us all,' I said.

'She's made a pretty considerable fool of me, I would have you observe,' remarked Mr Barnaby.

'She's a marvellous woman and you're right to be proud of her. I always said she was priceless. She realized the passion for romance that beats in every British heart and she's given us exactly what we wanted. I wouldn't betray her for worlds.'

'It's all very fine for you, sir. London may have gained a wonderful hostess, but I'm beginning to think that I have lost a perfectly good wife.'

'The only place for One-Bullet Mike is the great open West. My dear Mr Barnaby, there is only one course open to you now. You must continue to disappear.'

'I'm very much obliged to you.'

I thought he replied with a good deal of acidity.

The Lost Continent

☆★☆★☆★☆★☆★☆★☆★☆★☆★☆★☆★☆★☆★☆★☆★☆★☆★☆★☆★☆

BILL BRYSON

I had always thought that New England was nothing but maple trees and white churches and old guys in checked shirts sitting around iron stoves in country general stores swapping tall tales and spitting in the cracker barrel. But if lower New Hampshire was anything to go by, clearly I had been misinformed. There was just modern commercial squalor – shopping centres, gas stations, motels. Every once in a while there would be a white church or clapboard inn standing incongruously in the midst of Burger Kings and Texacos. But far from mollifying the ugliness, it only intensified it, reminding you what had been thrown away for the sake of drive-thru burgers and cheap gasoline.

At Salisbury, I joined old Route 1, intending to follow it up the coast through Maine. Route 1, as the name suggests, is the patriarch of American roads, the first federal highway. It stretches for 2,500 miles from the Canadian border to the Florida Keys. For forty years it was the main highway along the eastern seaboard, connecting all the big cities of the North – Boston, New York, Philadelphia, Baltimore, Washington – with the beaches and citrus groves of the South. It must have been wonderful in the 1930s and 1940s to drive from Maine to Florida on vacation, going through all those big marvellous cities and then passing on to the hills of Virginia and the green mountains of the Carolinas, getting warmer with the passing miles. But by the 1960s Route 1 had become too congested to be practical – a third of all Americans live within twenty miles of it – and Interstate 95 was built to zip traffic up and down the coast with only the most fleeting sense of a changing landscape. Today Route 1 is still there, but you would need weeks to drive its entire length. Now it is just a local road, an endless city street, an epic stretch of shopping malls.

I had hoped that here in rural New England it would retain something of its former charm, but it seemed not to. I drove through a chill morning drizzle and wondered if ever I would find the real New England. At Portsmouth, an instantly forgettable little town, I crossed over into Maine on an iron bridge over the grey Piscataqua River. Seen through the rhythmic swish of windscreen wipers, Maine too looked ominously unpromising, a further sprawl of shopping centres and muddy new housing developments.

Beyond Kennebunkport the suburbs at last gave way to forest. Here and there massive brown boulders emerged eerily from the earth, like subterranean creatures coming up for air, and occasionally I caught glimpses of the sea – a grey plain, cold and bleak. I drove and drove, thinking that any moment now I would encounter the fabled Maine of lobster-pots and surf-battered shores and lonely lighthouses standing on rocks of granite, but the towns I passed through were just messy and drear, and the countryside was wooded and unmemorable. Once, outside Falmouth, the road ran for a mile or so along a silvery bay with a long, low bridge leading over it to a landscape of snug farms nestled in a fold of hills, and I got briefly excited. But it was a false alarm and the landscape quickly grew dull again. The rest of the time the real Maine eluded me. It was always just over there, like the amusement parks my dad used to miss.

At Wiscasset, a third of the way up the coast to New Brunswick, I lost heart altogether. Wiscasset bills itself on the signboard at the edge of town as the prettiest village in Maine, which doesn't say a whole lot for the rest of the state. I don't mean to suggest that Wiscasset was awful, because it wasn't. It had a steep main street lined with craft shops and other yuppie emporia sloping down to a placid inlet of the Atlantic. Two old wooden ships sat rotting on the bank. It was OK. It just wasn't worth driving four hours to get there.

Abruptly I decided to abandon Route 1 and plunge northward, into the dense pine forests of central Maine, heading in an irregular line for the White Mountains, on a road that went up and down, up and down, like a rucked carpet. After a few miles I began to sense a change of atmosphere. The clouds were low and shapeless, the daylight meagre. Winter clearly was closing in. I was only seventy miles or so from Canada and it was evident that winters here were long and severe. It was written in the crumbling roads and in the huge stacks of firewood that stood outside each lonely cabin. Many chimneys were already sprouting a wintry wisp of smoke. It was barely October, but already the land had the cold and lifeless feel of winter. It was the kind of atmosphere that makes you want to turn up your collar and head for home.

Just beyond Gilead I passed into New Hampshire and the landscape became more interesting. The White Mountains rose up before me, big and round, the colour of wood-ash. Presumably they take their name from the birch trees that cover them. I drove on an empty highway through a forest of trembling leaves. The skies were still flat and low, the weather cold, but at least I was out of the monotony of the Maine woods. The road rose and fell and swept along the edge of a boulder-strewn creek. The scenery was infinitely better – but still there was no colour, none of the brilliant golds and reds of autumn that I had been led to expect. Everything from the ground to the sky was a dull, cadaverous grey.

I drove past Mt Washington, the highest peak in the north-eastern US (6,288 feet, for those of you who are keeping notes). But its real claim to fame is as the windiest place in America. It's something to do with . . . well, with the way the wind blows, of course. Anyway, the highest wind speed ever recorded anywhere on earth was logged on the top of Mt Washington in April 1934 when a gust of – pencils ready? – 231 miles an hour whistled through. That must have been an experience and a half for the meteorologists who worked up there. Can you imagine trying to describe a wind like that to somebody? 'Well, it was, you know, real . . . *windy*. I mean, *really* windy. Do you know what I'm saying?' It must be very frustrating to have a truly unique experience.

Just beyond it, I came to Bretton Woods, which I had always pictured as a quaint little town. But in fact there was no town at all, just a hotel and a ski lift. The hotel was huge and looked like a medieval fortress, but with a bright red roof. It looked like a cross between Monte Cassino and a Pizza Hut. It was here in 1944 that economists and politicians from twenty-eight nations got together and agreed to set up the International Monetary Fund and the World Bank. It certainly looked a nice place to make economic history. As John Maynard Keynes remarked at the time in a letter to his brother, Milton: 'It has been a most satisfactory week. The negotiations have been cordial, the food here is superb and the waiters are ever so pretty.'

I stopped for the night at Littleton, which, as the name suggests, was a little town near the Vermont border. I pulled into the Littleton Motel on the main street. On the office door was a sign that said 'If you want ice or advice, come before 6.30. I'm taking the wife to dinner. ("And about time too!" – wife).' Inside was an old guy on crutches who told me I was very lucky because he had just one room left. It would be $42 plus tax. When he saw me start to froth and back off, he hastily added, 'It's a real nice room. Got a brand new TV. Nice carpets. Beautiful little shower. We've got the cleanest rooms in town. We're famous for that.' He swept an arm over a selection of testimonials from satisfied customers which he displayed under glass on the counter-top. 'Our room must have been the cleanest room in town!' – A. K., Aardvark Falls, Ky. 'Boy, was our room ever clean! And such nice carpets!' – Mr and Mrs J. F., Spotweld, Ohio. That sort of thing.

Somehow I doubted the veracity of these claims, but I was too weary to return to the road, so with a sigh I said all right and signed in. I took my key and a bucket of ice (at $42 plus tax I intended to have everything that was going) and went with them to my room. And by golly it *was* the cleanest room in town. The TV was brand new and the carpet was plush. The bed was comfortable and the shower really was a beauty. I felt instantly ashamed of myself and retracted all my bad thoughts about the proprietor. ('I was a pompous little shit to have doubted you.' – Mr B. B., Des Moines, Iowa.)

I ate fourteen ice-cubes and watched the early evening news. This was followed by an old episode of *Gilligan's Island*, which the TV station had thoughtfully put on as an inducement to its non-brain-damaged viewers to get up immediately and go do something more useful. This I did. I went out and had a look around the town. The reason I had chosen to stop for the night at Littleton was that a book I had with me referred to it as picturesque. In point of fact, if Littleton was characterized by anything it was a singular lack of picturesqueness. The town consisted principally of one long street of mostly undistinguished buildings, with a supermarket parking lot in the middle and the shell of a disused gas station a couple of doors away. This, I think we can agree, does not constitute picturesqueness. Happily, the town had other virtues. For one thing, it was the friendliest little place I had ever seen. I went into the Topic of the Town restaurant. The other customers smiled at me, the lady at the cash register showed me where to put my jacket, and the waitress, a plump and dimpled little lady, couldn't do enough for me. It was as if they had all been given some kind of marvellous tranquillizer.

The waitress brought me a menu and I made the mistake of saying thank you. 'You're welcome,' she said. Once you start this there's no stopping. She came and wiped the table with a damp cloth. 'Thank you,' I said. 'You're welcome,' she said. She brought me some cutlery wrapped in a paper napkin. I hesitated, but I couldn't stop myself. 'Thank you,' I said. 'You're welcome,' she said. Then came a place mat with Topic of the Town written on it, and then a glass of water and then a clean ashtray, and then a little basket of Saltine crackers wrapped in cellophane, and at each we had our polite exchange. I ordered the fried chicken special. As I waited I became uncomfortably aware that the people at the next table were watching me and smiling at me in a deranged fashion. The waitress was watching me too, from a position by the kitchen doorway. It was all rather unnerving. Every few moments she would come over and top up my iced water and tell me that my food would only be a minute.

'Thank you,' I'd say.

'You're welcome,' she'd say.

Eventually the waitress came out of the kitchen with a tray the size of a table-top and started setting down plates of food in front of me – soup, salad, a platter of chicken, a basket of steaming rolls. It all looked delicious. Suddenly I realized that I was starving.

'Can I get you anything else?' she said.

'No, this is just fine, thank you,' I answered, knife and fork plugged in my fists, ready to lunge at the food.

'Would you like some ketchup?'

'No thank you.'

'Would you like a little more dressing for your salad?'

'No thank you.'

'Have you got enough gravy?'

There was enough gravy to drown a horse. 'Yes, plenty of gravy, thank you.'

'How about a cup of coffee?'

'Really, I'm fine.'

'You sure there's nothing I can do for you?'

'Well, you might just piss off and let me eat my dinner,' I wanted to say, but I didn't, of course. I just smiled sweetly and said no thank you and after a while she withdrew. But she stood with a pitcher of iced water and watched me closely the whole meal. Every time I took a sip of water, she would come forward and top up my glass. Once when I reached for the pepper, she misread my intentions and started forward with the water pitcher, but then had to retreat. After that, whenever my hands left the cutlery for any reason, I would semi-mime an explanation to her of what I was about to do – 'I'm just going to butter my roll now' – so that she wouldn't rush over to give me more water. And all the while the people at the next table watched me eat and smiled encouragingly. I couldn't wait to get out of there.

When at last I finished the waitress came over and offered me dessert. 'How about a piece of pie? We've got blueberry, blackberry, raspberry, boysenberry, huckleberry, whortleberry, cherry berry, hairy berry, chuckberry and berry-berry.'

'Gosh, no thanks, I'm too full,' I said placing my hands on my stomach. I looked as if I had stuffed a pillow under my shirt.

'Well, how about some ice-cream? We've got chocolate chip, chocolate fudge, chocolate ripple, chocolate-vanilla fudge, chocolate nut fudge, chocolate marshmallow swirl, chocolate mint with fudge chips, and fudge nut with or without chocolate chips.'

'Have you got just plain chocolate?'

'No, I'm afraid there's not much call for that.'

'I don't think I'll have anything then.'

'Well, how about a piece of cake. We've got –'

'Really, no thank you.'

'A cup of coffee?'

'No thank you.'

'You sure now?'

'Yes, thank you.'

'Well, I'll just get you a little more water then,' and she was off for the water jug before I could get her to give me my bill. The people at the next table watched this with interest and smiled a smile that said 'We are completely off our heads. How are you?'

Afterwards, I had a walk around the town – that is to say, I walked up one side of the street and down the other. For the size of place it was a nice town. It had two bookstores, a picture gallery, a gift shop, a movie-house. People on the sidewalk smiled at me as I passed. This was beginning to worry me. Nobody, even in America, is *that* friendly. What did they want from me? Up at the far end of the street there was a BP service station, the first one I had seen in America. Feeling vaguely homesick for Blighty, I walked up to have a look at it and was disappointed to see that there wasn't anything particularly British about it. The guy behind the counter wasn't even wearing a turban. When he saw me looking in the window he smiled at me with the same strange, unsettling smile. Suddenly I realized what it was – it was the look of someone from outer space, that odd, curiously malevolent B-movie smile of a race of interplanetary creatures who have taken over a small town in the middle of nowhere as their first step towards becoming . . . *Earth Masters*. I know this sounds improbable, but crazier things have happened – look who was in the White House, for Christ's sake. As I strolled back to the motel, I gave everyone I passed that same eerie smile, thinking I ought to keep on their good side, just in case. 'And you never know,' I remarked to myself in a low voice, 'if they do take over the planet, there might be some openings for a guy of your talents.'

Deflowered but not For-Lawn

☆★☆

MAUREEN LIPMAN

Are you sitting comfortably? Then get up. This is no time for sloth. Against all possible odds, my lobelias are up. Red where I planted blue, blue where I planted red and puce where they've been strangled by the busy lizzies, but to a first-time gardener they represent Wisley, Kew Gardens and Capability Lipman rolled into one. London pride isn't in it!

It all started with the purchase of two halves of a wooden ale keg and four antique Salford chimney pots. You know, the sort of things that once you couldn't get the Salford rag and bone man to take away for less than ten bob and a pair of nylons, and which now sell upwards of £60 a pot with extra for original soot.

They looked very cute on the patio, but lacked the necessary sprouting foliage to give them that rustic look so beloved by your average Salford roof. I bought a trowel from Woolies and put in some soil. It fell straight through to the patio. I kept adding until the pot was full and the garden was virtually empty. I then added my fuchsias and lobelias and a spiky looking creature, name of Potentilla, and waited with breath that can only be described as bated.

Each morning, I've taken my Morning-Starter tea on to the patio and, in dressing-gown and cucumbers, surveyed my domain. Gentle reader, the little buggers have grown! Albeit not above the tops of the pots, but on a clear day were one to be standing on a medium-sized stool or step-ladder one would have seen a display which would have had Bill Sowerbutts at his most underwhelmed. 'Now for the big stuff,' I told my husband Jack. 'I'm off to the Ally Pally Garden Centre for to buy a watering can and some slug pellets.' And it's highly unnecessary to point out that slugs can't climb chimney pots because it was the front lawn I now had in mind – total transformation of same. Sixty-three pounds later I returned home in a car which resembled the camouflaged truck driven by Radar in *M.A.S.H.* Lilac, wisteria, begonias by the boxful, honeysuckle, pansies and enough lobelias to border the Borders of Scotland. I had to leave Simone, my Mother's Help, there. Not as a deposit, but it was her or a bay tree, and I reckoned she'd be lousy in a lamb casserole (even though she was a wonderful girl who came from Hull, two qualifications which are totally synonymous).

Before I left, I asked the cashier for some soil. 'Soil?' she gawped, 'Oh, we don't sell *soil* here.' Her amazement was such that it was like asking for a Spam sandwich in Bloom's. 'But . . . but . . . it's a garden centre,' I spluttered. 'I mean, what am I to do with all these plants and no soil?' Patiently, and with more than a little of the air of a midwife, she gave me some leaflets on home deliveries. I thanked her and, while writing out two cheques and considering a home loam, I asked her in what other substance people planted plants.

'Potting compost and peat.'

My ears went up like elevators. Hadn't I been growing my own compost for three years from Pushkin Rosenthal's cat litter? A short discussion followed about the acid nature of cat poo as opposed to dog poo and within minutes a third cheque was written out and the boot of my car written off with the weight of three bags full of non-feline compost.

I won't go into the business of the actual planting – fascinating though it is to us of the 'Gang Green-Fingers'. I will say, however, that had I realized that each lobelia strip contained twelve plants and that there were eight rows of strips, I might very well have jacked in the whole procedure and got a little man in. I will also say that when Stan, our weekly, arrived to plant the tiny bay tree, he took great pleasure in pointing out to me that the nine-foot-high tree growing profusely by my front gate for the last ten years was none other than *Laura nobilis*. Yes, you've guessed it, a bay tree.

But are we downhearted? Does it bother me that every plant entering our portals appears to see a sign reading, 'Abandon Hope All Ye Who Enter Here'? Do I care that the two £20 rhododendron bushes both suffer from premature ejaculation and spring into glorious flower on April 28th – and drop clean dead by the 29th? Leap Year or not? Do I give a damn that the apricot tree was struck by forked lightning and now bears beige prunes? Or that one side of the lawn is so completely waterlogged in all seasons that the only suggestion the lawn expert offered was that we might keep ducks?

Am I for-lawn? Fingers off the buzzer and no conferring. Quite frankly, I don't give a sod. When that first passion flower opens its glorious face for one glorious day, I shall bloom. When the first little bunch of tiny black grapes starts dropping all over the car, tasting of stoat pee, I shall feel divine, and as for the miracle of my seven yuccas – let him who is without yuccas cast the first yuck! My dears, they have flowered – all seven of them. First came the pokers, looming, Cleese-like, out of the leaves, then suddenly, one day last week, they burst into bells – the palest, greenest, whitest bells – hanging in majestic clusters all over the show. I mean, I've got the message, man. As old Rambling Syd Rumpo used to say, 'The answer lies in the soil.' If you can get it, of course.

My mother wouldn't agree. 'She cares more about those plants than she does about anything,' she audibly whispered as I Baby Bio'd my spiders. For this, read 'The kids' drawers look like they've been burgled, there are stains in the toilet and she's busy with her mist spray.' Mother's idea of a perfect lawn is all-over concrete with two squares of soil full of everlastings and a sheet of Astroturf for the deckchairs.

My late mother-in-law, however, was a genius, and I think it's her genes I'm feeling the vibes from. 'Lakey' sang opera to her plants, and they never let her down. Her idea of a really good aria was 'Collect the labels the gifts are free/With Black and Greens, the family tea'. Verdi it wasn't, but verdant was her patch and her cucumbers were legendary. She used to mate them, serenading the while. An early form of sex therapy, I guess.

However, there is one snake in my grass: the hose. *Hoses*! They make me so permanently angry that I'd like nothing better than to line 'em up and circumcise 'em en masse. Without a blessing.

All right, my garden is fairly large – what? – 150ft-ish? – but there ought to be a way of watering it without emerging at the end of an hour wringing wet, covered in compost and with your inner-soles stuck to your feet in damp corrugated waves. Here's the scenario: woman gingerly turns on outside tap in hope that water emission will indicate location of nozzle amidst several yards of hosepipe. Nothing happens. Woman goes to investigate, finds nozzle, but no water coming through it. She picks up and examines nozzle. Nothing apparently wrong. She shakes part of hosepipe, releasing kink, and water gushes frantically through nozzle and up woman's nose, sending glasses aquaplaning on to concrete surface. Woman curses nozzles throughout the land and moves down towards bottom of garden, pulling hoseline behind her as she sprays.

Halfway down garden hoseline yanks her back, having wound its way round bike abandoned on patio. Woman drops nozzle on to flower-bed and runs back to release pipe from under wheel-guard. Races back to find antirrhinums flattened by force of jet from nozzle. Proceeding down towards rose-bed (i.e. shady patch covered by apple tree, soil like tarmac, won't grow anything except self-seeded mint), woman sprays roses for couple of minutes before spattering starts and water slows down to dribble. Woman walks back, in search of kinks. No kinks, but second connection point has unconnected and water is gushing on to lawn. Woman can't be bothered to turn off water at tap before attempting to reconnect junction. As she pushes plastic hose into joining device, water pressure causes fan-shaped waterfall to hit woman's crutch and inside leg of trousers, causing her to dance backwards like circus horse. Defeated, woman walks back to turn off tap, then returns to junction, unscrews cap, replaces hose in threaded bit, realizes cap now on upside down, removes hose, realigns cap and reseals join. Wet and weary she trudges back, turns on tap, walks back to nozzle, which spits into life and weakly sprays two and a half miniature rose bushes before junction connecting hosepipe to tap falls off wall.

Woman slowly and menacingly walks back in new, light pink sandals she forgot to change out of before assault course began, and, cursing and swearing like a merchant seaman denied leave, jams hose back on to tap. Half an hour has passed and three quarters of one garden bed has been watered. Woman falls to knees and prays for rain.

Then there's the garden furniture schism. During the four days of brilliant sunshine we had in May I became obsessed with the need to buy lounging chairs. Considering that I never sit down for long enough to know the meaning of the word 'lounge' and that if I do I'm covered in prickly heat within minutes, this was, you'll agree, an unnecessary necessity.

Anyway, my mother was staying at the time and it gave us something to do other than rearranging each other's rearrangements. So, off we went to Fenwick's, John Lewis, several garden centres and a huge Sainsbury's Homebase off the North Circular. I should point out that my idea of buying anything means going to one shop and ordering it, while my mother's idea is to ring every shop in the 'G' for garden section of the Yellow Pages to compare prices, make a list, ring them all back to check they've understood her original enquiry, then visit each one to look at the goods, and finally decide to leave the purchase until next year's January sales. Several boiling hours later we'd lounged in every adjustable lounger this side of Hatch End and encountered a whole new set of dilemmas. For example, some plastic chairs can be left out all summer so long as you remove the covers. These look *exactly* like the ones which can't be left out in so much as a light drizzle except they have a little label secreted under the seating. Then there are the wrought iron ones, some of which are £16 and others £65 per chair for no discernible reason, except to make the buyer over-wrought. Then there's the incredibly posh-looking German ones which only sell with matching table, parasol, table napkins, coasters, candle holders and probably Bratwurst slicer, and for which you need a second mortgage. Not to mention the rustic wooden ones which look golden the first year, then, after being left out all year as recommended, turn a curious sort of elephant grey and take chunks out of your Gotex'd bum.

Finally, at Sainsbury's, I found them. Four green-and-white cushioned, all-weather plastic adjustable loungers plus one on wheels for chasing sunshine, plus matching table-cloth for existing table. Reasonable and rugged. Thank the Lord, we'd done it! The assistant placed two huge flat packs (with instructions – hah!) in my trolley, then went to the storeroom to bring down the other four boxes. During the wait my mother said, 'You know what you *do* need?' (thereby implying that what I've just ordered is a frivolous extra, which I'm sort of suspecting anyway). I indicated I didn't know what I did need, so she told me, 'Tiles.' 'Tiles?' 'Yes, tiles. Around that little wash basin in the guest-room toilet. There's absolutely no splash-back. At all!' This latter she made sound as unthinkable a deficiency as having no door on your oven. 'You should get a double row of nice matching tiles on each side. It would *make* that toilet.'

I was fortunately stopped from making the cynical response which would have sprung from my lips in spite of the resolution I'd made three times that day not to make any such cynical remarks, by the arrival of the four extra flat packs, and we duly loaded the trolley and got in line at the check-out. Whilst I waited, Mother disappeared. Not a good sign. She would undoubtedly be asking somebody something. She was.

Red-faced with anxiety she rushed up to me. 'Don't buy them, Maureen. I've just spoken to the man. You won't believe it! What a good job I thought to mention it. What do you think – the covers won't come off!!'

'So, I'll wash the whole thing in the machine.'

'Are you mad? They're all foam-lined. They'll bunch up! It's nothing to me, I mean, it's no skin off my nose, but if you do buy them you'll be sorry! You'll have to buy new again next year. It'll be a complete dead loss. They have to have removable covers. You ask anybody – excuse me asking' (this to the woman ahead of us in the queue) 'but are you buying chairs with removable covers or are they all in one? There, you see. My daughter says it doesn't matter but they get filthy, don't they, when you can't take them off? There you are, Maureen, this lady agrees with me. Yes, she is on television. I'm her mother – where are you going, Maureen – ?'

I pushed the trolley back to the shelves, unloaded five huge boxes back into place, hurled the matching tablecloth across two aisles, and was heading back through the superstore in search of the super sodding exit. Mother followed.

'Well, don't say it's my fault – I don't mind what you do. It's not my money, but I'm right. You'll see.'

I branched off at the tile section, intending to buy a pack of twelve tiles for over the wretched sink, as a way of diverting my mind. After a couple of minutes' contemplation of colours I felt a tap on my shoulder.

'What are you *doing*?' asked Mother incredulously.

'I'm choosing the tiles for the toilet,' I said in measured tones.

She gawped at me, aghast. 'What? NOW?'

'Well, as I'm in the tile section I thought I'd choose them here.'

'But – but – you haven't measured the space! What if you haven't got enough? What if you've got too many? What if – No, you've got to get it measured properly by a man . . . '

I replaced the tiles, abandoned my trolley and all thoughts of either chairs or an amicable journey home. It's July as I write this and outside the rain pours down on four ancient canvas director's chairs, two torn deck chairs and a parasol that used to be green and white, but is now white and grey, courtesy of every pigeon in town.

The fact is that my garden is full of earthly delights, mostly bought at vast expense from every beckoning garden centre. Mother stands purse-lipped as I lash out another thirty or forty quid on plants and says, 'Do you know, I've never had to buy a single thing for my garden. Ever. They just come up every year. Doesn't that happen in London?' I've got a monkey puzzle tree, an ancient gazebo, gooseberries, purple clematis, and I'm training a wisteria to throw itself up the side of the house. Meanwhile, my passion flower *is* in flower, three or four fantastic flowers a day. They make the most beautiful buttonholes.

My garden gives me grubby nails, backache and total pleasure. The three taciturn, shirtless men who spend an hour crimping the lawn each week and grunt monosyllabically every time I speak to them, have no idea that they are bringing up my baby. I don't expect them to love it as I do, but I do expect them to be equally interested in its development. It may be a bit short of floribunda, but it's full of the green stuff in more ways than one. Or, as Andrew Marvell used to say, 'Annihilating all that's made/To a green thought in a green shade.' 'E was a marvel, that Andrew. Also a Hull lad. Need I say more?

The Canterville Ghost

☆★☆★☆★☆★☆★☆★☆★☆★☆★☆★☆★☆★☆★☆★☆★☆★☆★☆

OSCAR WILDE

One

When Mr Hiram B. Otis, the American Minister, bought Canterville Chase, everyone told him he was doing a very foolish thing, as there was no doubt at all that the place was haunted. Indeed, Lord Canterville himself, who was a man of the most punctilious honour, had felt it his duty to mention the fact to Mr Otis, when they came to discuss terms.

'We have not cared to live in the place ourselves,' said Lord Canterville, 'since my grand-aunt, the Dowager Duchess of Bolton, was frightened into a fit, from which she never really recovered, by two skeleton hands being placed on her shoulders as she was dressing for dinner, and I feel bound to tell you, Mr Otis, that the ghost has been seen by several living members of my family, as well as by the rector of the parish, the Rev Augustus Dampier, who is a fellow of King's College, Cambridge. After the unfortunate accident to the Duchess, none of our younger servants would stay with us, and Lady Canterville often got very little sleep at night, in consequence of the mysterious noises that came from the corridor and the library.'

'My Lord,' answered the Minister, 'I will take the furniture and the ghost at a valuation. I come from a modern country, where we have everything that money can buy; and with all our spry young fellows painting the Old World red, and carrying off your best actresses and prima-donnas, I reckon that if there were such a thing as a ghost in Europe, we'd have it at home in a very short time in one of our public museums, or on the road as a show.'

'I fear that the ghost exists,' said Lord Canterville, smiling, 'though it may have resisted the overtures of your enterprising impresarios. It has been well known for three centuries, since 1584 in fact, and always makes its appearance before the death of any member of our family.'

'Well, so does the family doctor for that matter, Lord Canterville. But there is no such thing, sir, as a ghost, and I guess the laws of nature are not going to be suspended for the British aristocracy.'

'You are certainly very natural in America,' answered Lord Canterville, who did not quite understand Mr Otis's last observation, 'and if you don't mind a ghost in the house, it is all right. Only you must remember I warned you.'

A few weeks after this, the purchase was completed, and at the close of the season the Minister and his family went down to Canterville Chase. Mrs Otis, who, as Miss Lucretia R. Tappan, of West 53rd Street, had been a celebrated New York belle, was now a very handsome middle-aged woman, with fine eyes, and a superb profile. Many American ladies on leaving their native land adopt an appearance of chronic ill-health, under the impression that it is a form of European refinement, but Mrs Otis had never fallen into this error. She had a magnificent constitution, and a really wonderful amount of animal spirits. Indeed, in many respects, she was quite English, and was an excellent example of the fact that we have really everything in common with America nowadays, except, of course, language. Her eldest son, christened Washington by his parents in a moment of patriotism, which he never ceased to regret, was a fair-haired, rather good-looking young man, who had qualified himself for American diplomacy by leading the German at the Newport Casino for three successive seasons, and even in London was well known as an excellent dancer. Gardenias and the peerage were his only weaknesses. Otherwise he was extremely sensible. Miss Virginia E. Otis was a little girl of fifteen, lithe and lovely as a fawn, and with a fine freedom in her large blue eyes. She was a wonderful amazon, and had once raced old Lord Bilton on her pony twice round the park, winning by a length and a half, just in front of Achilles' statue, to the huge delight of the young Duke of Cheshire, who proposed to her on the spot, and was sent back to Eton that very night by his guardians, in floods of tears. After Virginia came the twins, who were usually called 'The Stars and Stripes' as they were always getting swished. They were delightful boys, and with the exception of the worthy Minister the only true republicans of the family.

As Canterville Chase is seven miles from Ascot, the nearest railway station, Mr Otis had telegraphed for a waggonette to meet them, and they started on their drive in high spirits. It was a lovely July evening, and the air was delicate with the scent of the pinewoods. Now and then they heard a wood pigeon brooding over its own sweet voice, or saw, deep in the rustling fern, the burnished breast of the pheasant. Little squirrels peered at them from the beech-trees as they went by, and the rabbits scudded away through the brushwood and over the mossy knolls, with their white tails in the air. As they entered the avenue of Canterville Chase, however, the sky became suddenly overcast with clouds, a curious stillness seemed to hold the atmosphere, a great flight of rooks passed silently over their heads, and, before they reached the house, some big drops of rain had fallen.

Standing on the steps to receive them was an old woman, neatly dressed in black silk, with a white cap and apron. This was Mrs Umney, the housekeeper, whom Mrs Otis, at Lady Canterville's earnest request, had consented to keep on in her former position. She made them each a low curtsey as they alighted, and said in a quaint, old-fashioned manner, 'I bid you welcome to Canterville Chase.' Following her, they passed through the fine Tudor hall into the library, a long, low room, panelled in black oak, at the end of which was a large stained-glass window. Here they found tea laid out for them, and, after taking off their wraps, they sat down and began to look round, while Mrs Umney waited on them.

Suddenly Mrs Otis caught sight of a dull red stain on the floor just by the fireplace and, quite unconscious of what it really signified, said to Mrs Umney, 'I am afraid something has been spilt there.'

'Yes, madam,' replied the old housekeeper in a low voice, 'blood has been spilt on that spot.'

'How horrid,' cried Mrs Otis; 'I don't at all care for blood-stains in a sitting-room. It must be removed at once.'

The old woman smiled, and answered in the same low, mysterious voice, 'It is the blood of Lady Eleanore de Canterville, who was murdered on that very spot by her own husband, Sir Simon de Canterville, in 1575. Sir Simon survived her nine years, and disappeared suddenly under very mysterious circumstances. His body has never been discovered, but his guilty spirit still haunts the Chase. The blood-stain has been much admired by tourists and others, and cannot be removed.'

'That is all nonsense,' cried Washington Otis; 'Pinkerton's Champion Stain Remover and Paragon Detergent will clean it up in no time,' and before the terrified housekeeper could interfere he had fallen upon his knees, and was rapidly scouring the floor with a small stick of what looked like a black cosmetic. In a few moments no trace of the blood-stain could be seen.

'I knew Pinkerton would do it,' he exclaimed triumphantly, as he looked round at his admiring family; but no sooner had he said these words than a terrible flash of lightning lit up the sombre room, a fearful peal of thunder made them all start to their feet, and Mrs Umney fainted.

'What a monstrous climate!' said the American Minister calmly, as he lit a long cheroot. 'I guess the old country is so overpopulated that they have not enough decent weather for everybody. I have always been of opinion that emigration is the only thing for England.'

'My dear Hiram,' cried Mrs Otis, 'what can we do with a woman who faints?'

'Charge it to her like breakages,' answered the Minister; 'she won't faint after that'; and in a few moments Mrs Umney certainly came to. There was no doubt, however, that she was extremely upset, and she sternly warned Mr Otis to beware of some trouble coming to the house.

'I have seen things with my own eyes, sir,' she said, 'that would make any Christian's hair stand on end, and many and many a night I have not closed my eyes in sleep for the awful things that are done here.' Mr Otis, however, and his wife warmly assured the honest soul that they were not afraid of ghosts, and, after invoking the blessings of Providence on her new master and mistress, and making arrangements for an increase of salary, the old housekeeper tottered off to her own room.

Two

The storm raged fiercely all that night, but nothing of particular note occurred. The next morning, however, when they came down to breakfast, they found the terrible stain of blood once again on the floor. 'I don't think it can be the fault of the Paragon Detergent,' said Washington, 'for I have tried it with everything. It must be the ghost.' He accordingly rubbed out the stain a second time, but the second morning it appeared again. The third morning also it was there, though the library had been locked up at night by Mr Otis himself, and the key carried upstairs. The whole family were now quite interested; Mr Otis began to suspect that he had been too dogmatic in his denial of the existence of ghosts, Mrs Otis expressed her intention of joining the Psychical Society, and Washington prepared a long letter to Messrs Myers and Podmore on the subject of the Permanence of Sanguineous Stains when connected with crime. That night all doubts about the objective existence of phantasmata were removed for ever.

The day had been warm and sunny; and, in the cool of the evening, the whole family went out for a drive. They did not return home till nine o'clock, when they had a light supper. The conversation in no way turned upon ghosts, so there were not even those primary conditions of receptive expectation which so often precede the presentation of psychical phenomena. The subjects discussed, as I have since learned from Mr Otis, were merely such as form the ordinary conversation of cultured Americans of the better class, such as the immense superiority of Miss Fanny Davenport over Sarah Bernhardt as an actress; the difficulty of obtaining green corn, buckwheat cakes, and hominy, even in the best English houses; the importance of Boston in the development of the world-soul; the advantages of the baggage check system in railway travelling; and the sweetness of the New York accent as compared to the London drawl. No mention at all was made of the supernatural, nor was Sir Simon de Canterville alluded to in any way. At eleven o'clock the family retired, and by half past all the lights were out. Some time after, Mr Otis was awakened by a curious noise in the corridor, outside his room. It sounded like the clank of metal, and seemed to be coming nearer every moment. He got up at once, struck a match, and looked at the time. It was exactly one o'clock. He was quite calm, and felt his pulse, which was not at all feverish. The strange noise still continued, and with it he heard distinctly the sound of footsteps. He put on his slippers, took a small oblong phial out of his dressing-case, and opened the door. Right in front of him he saw, in the wan moonlight, an old man of terrible aspect. His eyes were as red as burning coals; long grey hair fell over his shoulders in matted coils; his garments, which were of antique cut, were soiled and ragged, and from his wrists and ankles hung heavy manacles and rusty gyves.

'My dear sir,' said Mr Otis, 'I really must insist on your oiling those chains, and have brought you for that purpose a small bottle of the Tammany Rising Sun Lubricator. It is said to be completely efficacious upon one application, and there are several testimonials to that effect on the wrapper from some of our most eminent native divines. I shall leave it here for you by the bedroom candles, and will be happy to supply you with more should you require it.' With these words the United States Minister laid the bottle down on a marble table, and, closing his door, retired to rest.

For a moment the Canterville ghost stood quite motionless in natural indignation; then, dashing the bottle violently upon the polished floor, he fled down the corridor, uttering hollow groans, and emitting a ghastly green light. Just, however, as he reached the top of the great oak staircase, a door was flung open, two little white-robed figures appeared, and a large pillow whizzed past his head! There was evidently no time to be lost, so, hastily adopting the Fourth Dimension of Space as a means of escape, he vanished through the wainscoting, and the house became quite quiet.

On reaching a small secret chamber in the left wing, he leaned up against a moonbeam to recover his breath, and began to try and realize his position. Never, in a brilliant and uninterrupted career of three hundred years, had he been so grossly insulted. He thought of the Dowager Duchess, whom he had frightened into a fit as she stood before the glass in her lace and diamonds; of the four housemaids, who had gone off into hysterics when he merely grinned at them through the curtains of one of the spare bedrooms; of the rector of the parish, whose candle he had blown out as he was coming late one night from the library, and who had been under the care of Sir William Gull ever since, a perfect martyr to nervous disorders; and of old Madame de Tremouillac, who, having wakened up one morning early and seen a skeleton seated in an arm-chair by the fire reading her diary, had been confined to her bed for six weeks with an attack of brain fever, and, on her recovery, had become reconciled to the Church, and had broken off her connection with that notorious sceptic Monsieur de Voltaire. He remembered the terrible night when the wicked Lord Canterville was found choking in his dressing-room, with the knave of diamonds halfway down his throat, and confessed, just before he died, that he had cheated Charles James Fox out of £50,000 at Crockford's by means of that very card, and swore that the ghost had made him swallow it. All his great achievements came back to him again, from the butler who had shot himself in the pantry because he had seen a green hand tapping at the window pane, to the beautiful Lady Stutfield, who was always obliged to wear a black velvet band round her throat to hide the mark of five fingers burnt upon her white skin, and who drowned herself at last in the carp-pond at the end of the King's Walk. With the enthusiastic egotism of the true artist he went over his most celebrated performances, and smiled bitterly to himself as he recalled to mind his last appearance as 'Red Ruben, or the Strangled Babe', his début as 'Gaunt Gibeon, the Blood-sucker of Bexley Moor', and the furore he had excited one lovely June evening by merely playing ninepins with his own bones upon the lawn-tennis ground. And after all this, some wretched modern Americans were to come and offer him the Rising Sun Lubricator, and throw pillows at his head! It was quite unbearable. Besides, no ghosts in history had ever been treated in this manner. Accordingly, he determined to have vengeance, and remained till daylight in an attitude of deep thought.

Three

The next morning when the Otis family met at breakfast, they discussed the ghost at some length. The United States Minister was naturally a little annoyed to find that his present had not been accepted. 'I have no wish,' he said, 'to do the ghost any personal injury, and I must say that, considering the length of time he has been in the house, I don't think it is at all polite to throw pillows at him' – a very just remark, at which, I am sorry to say, the twins burst into shouts of laughter. 'Upon the other hand,' he continued, 'if he really declines to use the Rising Sun Lubricator, we shall have to take his chains from him. It would be quite impossible to sleep, with such a noise going on outside the bedrooms.'

For the rest of the week, however, they were undisturbed, the only thing that excited any attention being the continual renewal of the blood-stain on the library floor. This certainly was very strange, as the door was always locked at night by Mr Otis, and the windows kept closely barred. The chameleon-like colour, also, of the stain excited a good deal of comment. Some mornings, it was a dull (almost Indian) red, then it would be vermilion, then a rich purple, and once when they came down for family prayers, according to the simple rites of the Free American Reformed Episcopalian Church, they found it a bright emerald-green. These kaleidoscopic changes naturally amused the party very much, and bets on the subject were freely made every evening. The only person who did not enter into the joke was little Virginia, who, for some unexplained reason, was always a good deal distressed at the sight of the blood-stain, and very nearly cried the morning it was emerald-green.

The second appearance of the ghost was on Sunday night. Shortly after they had gone to bed they were suddenly alarmed by a fearful crash in the hall. Rushing downstairs, they found that a large suit of old armour had become detached from its stand, and had fallen on the stone floor, while, seated in a high-backed chair, was the Canterville ghost, rubbing his knees with an expression of acute agony on his face. The twins, having brought their peashooters with them, at once discharged two pellets on him, with that accuracy of aim which can only be attained by long and careful practice on a writing-master, while the United States Minister covered him with his revolver, and called upon him, in accordance with Californian etiquette, to hold up his hands! The ghost started up with a wild shriek of rage, and swept through them like a mist, extinguishing Washington Otis's candle as he passed, and so leaving them all in total darkness. On reaching the top of the staircase he recovered himself, and determined to give his celebrated peal of demoniac laughter. This he had on more than one occasion found extremely useful. It was said to have turned Lord Raker's wig grey in a single night, and had certainly made three of Lady Canterville's French governesses give warning before their month was up. He accordingly laughed his most horrible laugh, till the old vaulted roof rang and rang again, but hardly had the fearful echo died away when a door opened, and Mrs Otis came out in a light blue dressing-gown. 'I am afraid you are far from well,' she said, 'and have brought you a bottle of Dr Dobell's tincture. If it is indigestion, you will find it a most excellent remedy.' The ghost glared at her in fury, and began at once to make preparations for turning himself into a large black dog, an accomplishment for which he was justly renowned, and to which the family doctor always attributed the permanent idiocy of Lord Canterville's uncle, the Hon Thomas Horton. The sound of approaching footsteps, however, made him hesitate in his fell purpose, so he contented himself with becoming faintly phosphorescent, and vanished with a deep churchyard groan, just as the twins had come up to him.

On reaching his room he entirely broke down, and became a prey to the most violent agitation. The vulgarity of the twins, and the gross materialism of Mrs Otis, were naturally extremely annoying, but what really distressed him most was, that he had been unable to wear the suit of mail. He had hoped that even modern Americans would be thrilled by the sight of a Spectre In Armour, if for no more sensible reason, at least out of respect for their national poet Longfellow, over whose graceful and attractive poetry he himself had whiled away many a weary hour when the Cantervilles were up in town. Besides, it was his own suit. He had worn it with success at the Kenilworth tournament, and had been highly complimented on it by no less a person than the Virgin Queen herself. Yet when he had put it on, he had been completely overpowered by the weight of the huge breastplate and steel casque, and had fallen heavily on the stone pavement, barking both his knees severely, and bruising the knuckles of his right hand.

For some days after this he was extremely ill, and hardly stirred out of his room at all, except to keep the blood-stain in proper repair. However, by taking great care of himself, he recovered, and resolved to make a third attempt to frighten the United States Minister and his family. He selected Friday, the 17th of August, for his appearance, and spent most of that day in looking over his wardrobe, ultimately deciding in favour of a large slouched hat with a red feather, a winding-sheet frilled at the wrists and neck, and a rusty dagger. Towards evening a violent storm of rain came on, and the wind was so high that all the windows and doors in the old house shook and rattled. In fact, it was just such weather as he loved. His plan of action was this. He was to make his way quietly to Washington Otis's room, gibber at him from the foot of the bed, and stab himself three times in the throat to the sound of slow music. He bore Washington a special grudge, being quite aware that it was he who was in the habit of removing the famous Canterville blood-stain, by means of Pinkerton's Paragon Detergent. Having reduced the reckless and foolhardy youth to a condition of abject terror, he was then to proceed to the room occupied by the United States Minister and his wife, and there to place a clammy hand on Mrs Otis's forehead, while he hissed into her trembling husband's ear the awful secrets of the charnel-house. With regard to little Virginia, he had not quite made up his mind. She had never insulted him in any way, and was pretty and gentle. A few hollow groans from the wardrobe, he thought, would be more than sufficient, or, if that failed to wake her, he might grabble at the counterpane with palsy-twitching fingers. As for the twins, he was quite determined to teach them a lesson. The first thing to be done was, of course, to sit upon their chests, so as to produce the stifling sensation of nightmare. Then, as their beds were quite close to each other, to stand between them in the form of a green icy-cold corpse, till they became paralysed with fear, and finally, to throw off the winding-sheet, and crawl round the room, with white bleached bones and one rolling eyeball, in the character of 'Dumb Daniel, or the Suicide's Skeleton', a rôle in which he had on more than one occasion produced a great effect, and which he considered quite equal to his famous part of 'Martin the Maniac, or the Masked Mystery'.

At half past ten he heard the family going to bed. For some time he was disturbed by wild shrieks of laughter from the twins, who, with the light-hearted gaiety of schoolboys, were evidently amusing themselves before they retired to rest, but at a quarter past eleven all was still, and, as midnight sounded, he sallied forth. The owl beat against the window panes, the raven croaked from the old yew-tree, and the wind wandered moaning round the house like a lost soul; but the Otis family slept unconscious of their doom, and high above the rain and storm he could hear the steady snoring of the Minister for the United States. He stepped stealthily out of the wainscoting, with an evil smile on his cruel, wrinkled mouth, and the moon hid her face in a cloud as he stole past the great oriel window, where his own arms and those of his murdered wife were blazoned in azure and gold. On and on he glided, like an evil shadow, the very darkness seeming to loathe him as he passed. Once he thought he heard something call, and stopped; but it was only the baying of a dog from the Red Farm, and he went on, muttering strange sixteenth-century curses, and ever and anon brandishing the rusty dagger in the midnight air. Finally he reached the corner of the passage that led to luckless Washington's room. For a moment he paused there, the wind blowing his long grey locks about his head, and twisting into grotesque and fantastic folds the nameless horror of the dead man's shroud. Then the clock struck the quarter, and he felt the time was come. He chuckled to himself, and turned the corner; but no sooner had he done so, than, with a piteous wail of terror, he fell back, and hid his blanched face in his long, bony hands. Right in front of him was standing a horrible spectre, motionless as a carven image, and monstrous as a madman's dream! Its head was bald and burnished; its face round, and fat, and white; and hideous laughter seemed to have writhed its features into an eternal grin. From the eyes streamed rays of scarlet light, the mouth was a wide well of fire, and a hideous garment, like to his own, swathed with its silent snows the Titan form. On its breast was a placard with strange writing in antique characters, some scroll of shame it seemed, some record of wild sins, some awful calendar of crime, and, with its right hand, it bore aloft a falchion of gleaming steel.

Never having seen a ghost before, he naturally was terribly frightened, and, after a second hasty glance at the awful phantom, he fled back to his room, tripping up in his long winding-sheet as he sped down the corridor, and finally dropping the rusty dagger into the Minister's jack-boots, where it was found in the morning by the butler. Once in the privacy of his own apartment, he flung himself down on a small pallet-bed, and hid his face under the clothes. After a time, however, the brave old Canterville spirit asserted itself, and he determined to go and speak to the other ghost as soon as it was daylight. Accordingly, just as the dawn was touching the hills with silver, he returned towards the spot where he had first laid eyes on the grisly phantom, feeling that, after all, two ghosts were better than one, and that, by the aid of his new friend, he might safely grapple with the twins. On reaching the spot, however, a terrible sight met his gaze. Something had evidently happened to the spectre, for the light had entirely faded from its hollow eyes, the gleaming falchion had fallen from its hand, and it was leaning up against the wall in a strained and uncomfortable attitude. He rushed forward and seized it in his arms, when, to his horror, the head slipped off and rolled on the floor, the body assumed a recumbent posture, and he found himself clasping a white dimity bed-curtain, with a sweeping-brush, a kitchen cleaver, and a hollow turnip lying at his feet! Unable to understand this curious transformation, he clutched the placard with feverish haste, and there, in the grey morning light, he read these fearful words:

YE OTIS GHOSTE.
Ye Onlie True and
Originale Spook.
Beware of Ye
Imitations.
All others are
Counterfeite.

The whole thing flashed across him. He had been tricked, foiled, and outwitted! The old Canterville look came into his eyes; he ground his toothless gums together; and, raising his withered hands high above his head, swore, according to the picturesque phraseology of the antique school, that when Chanticleer had sounded twice his merry horn, deeds of blood would be wrought, and Murder walk abroad with silent feet.

Hardly had he finished this awful oath when, from the red-tiled roof of a distant homestead, a cock crew. He laughed a long, low, bitter laugh, and waited. Hour after hour he waited, but the cock, for some strange reason, did not crow again. Finally, at half past seven, the arrival of the housemaids made him give up his fearful vigil, and he stalked back to his room, thinking of his vain hope and baffled purpose. There he consulted several books of ancient chivalry, of which he was exceedingly fond, and found that, on every occasion on which his oath had been used, Chanticleer had always crowed a second time. 'Perdition seize the naughty fowl,' he muttered, 'I have seen the day when, with my stout spear, I would have run him through the gorge, and made him crow for me an 'twere in death!' He then retired to a comfortable lead coffin, and stayed there till evening.

Four

The next day the ghost was very weak and tired. The terrible excitement of the last four weeks was beginning to have its effect. His nerves were completely shattered, and he started at the slightest noise. For five days he kept his room, and at last made up his mind to give up the point of the blood-stain on the library floor. If the Otis family did not want it, they clearly did not deserve it. They were evidently people on a low, material plane of existence, and quite incapable of appreciating the symbolic value of sensuous phenomena. The question of phantasmic apparitions, and the development of astral bodies, was of course quite a different matter, and really not under his control. It was his solemn duty to appear in the corridor once a week, and to gibber from the large oriel window on the first and third Wednesday in every month, and he did not see how he could honourably escape from his obligations. It is quite true that his life had been very evil, but, upon the other hand, he was most conscientious in all things connected with the supernatural. For the next three Saturdays, accordingly, he traversed the corridor as usual between midnight and three o'clock, taking every possible precaution against being either heard or seen. He removed his boots, trod as lightly as possible on the old worm-eaten boards, wore a large black velvet cloak, and was careful to use the Rising Sun Lubricator for oiling his chains. I am bound to acknowledge that it was with a good deal of difficulty that he brought himself to adopt this last mode of protection. However, one night, while the family were at dinner, he slipped into Mr Otis's bedroom and carried off the bottle. He felt a little humiliated at first, but afterwards was sensible enough to see that there was a great deal to be said for the invention, and, to a certain degree, it served his purpose. Still, in spite of everything, he was not left unmolested. Strings were continually being stretched across the corridor, over which he tripped in the dark, and on one occasion, while dressed for the part of 'Black Isaac, or the Huntsman of Hogley Woods', he met with a severe fall, through treading on a butter-slide, which the twins had constructed from the entrance of the Tapestry Chamber to the top of the oak staircase. This last insult so enraged him, that he resolved to assert his dignity, and determined to visit the insolent young Etonians the next night in his celebrated character of 'Reckless Rupert, or the Headless Earl'.

He had not appeared in this disguise for more than seventy years; in fact, not since he had so frightened pretty Lady Barbara Modish by means of it, that she suddenly broke off her engagement with the present Lord Canterville's grandfather, and ran away to Gretna Green with handsome Jack Castleton, declaring that nothing in the world would induce her to marry into a family that allowed such a horrible phantom to walk up and down the terrace at twilight. Poor Jack was afterwards shot in a duel by Lord Canterville on Wandsworth Common, and Lady Barbara died of a broken heart at Tunbridge Wells before the year was out, so, in every way, it had been a great success. It was, however, an extremely difficult 'make-up', if I may use such a theatrical expression in connection with one of the greatest mysteries of the supernatural, or, to employ a more scientific term, the higher-natural world and it took him fully three hours to make his preparations. At last everything was ready, and he was very pleased with his appearance. The big leather riding-boots that went with the dress were just a little too large for him, and he could only find one of the two horse-pistols, but, on the whole, he was quite satisfied, and at a quarter past one he glided out of the wainscoting and crept down the corridor. On reaching the room occupied by the twins, which I should mention was called the Blue Bed Chamber, on account of the colour of its hangings, he found the door just ajar. Wishing to make an effective entrance, he flung it wide open, when a heavy jug of water fell right down on him, wetting him to the skin, and just missing his left shoulder by a couple of inches. At the same moment he heard stifled shrieks of laughter proceeding from the four-post bed. The shock to his nervous system was so great that he fled back to his room as hard as he could go, and the next day he was laid up with a severe cold. The only thing that at all consoled him in the whole affair was the fact that he had not brought his head with him, for, had he done so, the consequences might have been very serious.

He now gave up all hope of ever frightening this rude American family, and contented himself, as a rule, with creeping about the passages in list slippers, with a thick red muffler round his throat for fear of draughts, and a small arquebuse, in case he should be attacked by the twins. The final blow he received occurred on the 19th of September. He had gone downstairs to the great entrance-hall, feeling sure that there, at any rate, he would be quite unmolested, and was amusing himself by making satirical remarks on the large Saroni photographs of the United States Minister and his wife, which had now taken the place of the Canterville family pictures. He was simply but neatly clad in a long shroud, spotted with churchyard mould, had tied up his jaw with a strip of yellow linen, and carried a small lantern and a sexton's spade. In fact, he was dressed for the character of 'Jonas the Graveless, or the Corpse-Snatcher of Chertsey Barn', one of his most remarkable impersonations, and one which the Cantervilles had every reason to remember, as it was the real origin of their quarrel with their neighbour, Lord Rufford. It was about a quarter past two o'clock in the morning, and, as far as he could ascertain, no one was stirring. As he was strolling towards the library, however, to see if there were any traces left of the bloodstain, suddenly there leaped out on him from a dark corner two figures, who waved their arms wildly above their heads, and shrieked out 'BOO!' in his ear.

Seized with a panic, which, under the circumstances, was only natural, he rushed for the staircase, but found Washington Otis waiting for him there with the big garden-syringe; and being thus hemmed in by his enemies on every side, and driven almost to bay, he vanished into the great iron stove, which, fortunately for him, was not lit, and had to make his way home through the flues and chimneys, arriving at his own room in a terrible state of dirt, disorder, and despair.

After this he was not seen again on any nocturnal expedition. The twins lay in wait for him on several occasions, and strewed the passages with nutshells every night to the great annoyance of their parents and the servants, but it was of no avail. It was quite evident that his feelings were so wounded that he would not appear. Mr Otis consequently resumed his great work on the history of the Democratic Party, on which he had been engaged for some years; Mrs Otis organized a wonderful clambake, which amazed the whole county; the boys took to lacrosse, euchre, poker, and other American national games; and Virginia rode about the lanes on her pony, accompanied by the young Duke of Cheshire, who had come to spend the last week of his holidays at Canterville Chase. It was generally assumed that the ghost had gone away, and, in fact, Mr Otis wrote a letter to that effect to Lord Canterville, who, in reply, expressed his great pleasure at the news, and sent his best congratulations to the Minister's worthy wife.

The Otises, however, were deceived, for the ghost was still in the house, and though now almost an invalid, was by no means ready to let matters rest, particularly as he heard that among the guests was the young Duke of Cheshire, whose grand-uncle, Lord Francis Stilton, had once bet a hundred guineas with Colonel Carbury that he would play dice with the Canterville ghost, and was found the next morning lying on the floor of the card-room in such a helpless paralytic state, that though he lived on to a great age, he was never able to say anything again but 'Double Sixes'. The story was well known at the time, though, of course, out of respect to the feelings of the two noble families, every attempt was made to hush it up; and a full account of all the circumstances connected with it will be found in the third volume of Lord Tattle's *Recollections of the Prince Regent and his Friends*. The ghost, then, was naturally very anxious to show that he had not lost his influence over the Stiltons, with whom, indeed, he was distantly connected, his own first cousin having been married *en secondes noces* to the Sieur de Bulkeley, from whom, as everyone knows, the Dukes of Cheshire are lineally descended. Accordingly, he made arrangements for appearing to Virginia's little lover in his celebrated impersonation of 'The Vampire Monk, or, the Bloodless Benedictine', a performance so horrible that when old Lady Startup saw it, which she did on one fatal New Year's Eve, in the year 1764, she went off into the most piercing shrieks, which culminated in violent apoplexy, and died in three days, after disinheriting the Cantervilles, who were her nearest relations, and leaving all her money to her London apothecary. At the last moment, however, his terror of the twins prevented his leaving his room, and the little Duke slept in peace under the great feathered canopy in the Royal Bedchamber, and dreamed of Virginia.

Five

A few days after this, Virginia and her curly-haired cavalier went out riding on Brockley meadows, where she tore her habit so badly in getting through a hedge, that, on her return home, she made up her mind to go up by the back staircase so as not to be seen. As she was running past the Tapestry Chamber, the door of which happened to be open, she fancied she saw some one inside, and thinking it was her mother's maid, who sometimes used to bring her work there, looked in to ask her to mend her habit. To her immense surprise, however, it was the Canterville Ghost himself! He was sitting by the window, watching the ruined gold of the yellow trees fly through the air, and the red leaves dancing madly down the long avenue. His head was leaning on his hand, and his whole attitude was one of extreme depression. Indeed, so forlorn, and so much out of repair did he look, that little Virginia, whose first idea had been to run away and lock herself in her room, was filled with pity, and determined to try and comfort him. So light was her footfall, and so deep his melancholy, that he was not aware of her presence till she spoke to him.

'I am so sorry for you,' she said, 'but my brothers are going back to Eton tomorrow, and then, if you behave yourself, no one will annoy you.'

'It is absurd asking me to behave myself,' he answered, looking round in astonishment at the pretty little girl who had ventured to address him, 'quite absurd. I must rattle my chains, and groan through keyholes, and walk about at night, if that is what you mean. It is my only reason for existing.'

'It is no reason at all for existing, and you know you have been very wicked. Mrs Umney told us, the first day we arrived here, that you had killed your wife.'

'Well, I quite admit it,' said the Ghost petulantly, 'but it was a purely family matter, and concerned no one else.'

'It is very wrong to kill any one,' said Virginia, who at times had a sweet Puritan gravity, caught from some old New England ancestor.

'Oh, I hate the cheap severity of abstract ethics! My wife was very plain, never had my ruffs properly starched, and knew nothing about cookery. Why, there was a buck I had shot in Hogley Woods, a magnificent pricket, and do you know how she had it sent up to table? However, it is no matter now, for it is all over, and I don't think it was very nice of her brothers to starve me to death, though I did kill her.'

'Starve you to death? Oh, Mr Ghost, I mean Sir Simon, are you hungry? I have a sandwich in my case. Would you like it?'

'No, thank you, I never eat anything now; but it is very kind of you, all the same, and you are much nicer than the rest of your horrid, rude, vulgar, dishonest family.'

'Stop!' cried Virginia, stamping her foot, 'it is you who are rude, and horrid, and vulgar; and as for dishonesty, you know you stole the paints out of my box to try and furbish up that ridiculous blood-stain in the library. First you took all my reds, including the vermilion, and I couldn't do any more sunsets, then you took the emerald-green and the chrome-yellow, and finally I had nothing left but indigo and Chinese white, and could only do moonlight scenes, which are always depressing to look at, and not at all easy to paint. I never told on you, though I was very much annoyed, and it was most ridiculous, the whole thing, for who ever heard of emerald-green blood?'

'Well, really,' said the Ghost, rather meekly, 'what was I to do? It is a very difficult thing to get real blood nowadays, and, as your brother began it all with his Paragon Detergent, I certainly saw no reason why I should not have your paints. As for colour, that is always a matter of taste: the Cantervilles have blue blood, for instance, the very bluest in England; but I know you Americans don't care for things of this kind.'

'You know nothing about it, and the best thing you can do is to emigrate and improve your mind. My father will be only too happy to give you a free passage, and though there is a heavy duty on spirits of every kind, there will be no difficulty about the Custom House, as the officers are all Democrats. Once in New York, you are sure to be a great success. I know lots of people there who would give a hundred thousand dollars to have a grandfather, and much more than that to have a family Ghost.'

'I don't think I should like America.'

'I suppose because we have no ruins and no curiosities,' said Virginia satirically.

'No ruins! No curiosities!' answered the Ghost; 'you have your navy and your manners.'

'Good evening; I will go and ask papa to get the twins an extra week's holiday.'

'Please don't go, Miss Virginia,' he cried; 'I am so lonely and so unhappy, and I really don't know what to do. I want to go to sleep and I cannot.'

'That's quite absurd. You have merely to go to bed and blow out the candle. It is very difficult sometimes to keep awake, especially at church, but there is no difficulty at all about sleeping. Why, even babies know how to do that, and they are not very clever.'

'I have not slept for three hundred years,' he said sadly, and Virginia's beautiful blue eyes opened in wonder; 'for three hundred years I have not slept, and I am so tired.'

Virginia grew quite grave, and her little lips trembled like rose-leaves. She came towards him, and kneeling down at his side, looked up into his old withered face.

'Poor, poor Ghost,' she murmured; 'have you no place where you can sleep?'

'Far away beyond the pine-woods,' he answered, in a low dreamy voice, 'there is a little garden. There the grass grows long and deep, there are the great white stars of the hemlock flower, there the nightingale sings all night long. All night long he sings, and the cold, crystal moon looks down, and the yew-tree spreads out its giant arms over the sleepers.'

Virginia's eyes grew dim with tears, and she hid her face in her hands.

'You mean the Garden of Death,' she whispered.

'Yes, Death. Death must be so beautiful. To lie in the soft brown earth, with the grasses waving above one's head, and listen to silence. To have no yesterday, and no tomorrow. To forget time, to forgive life, to be at peace. You can help me. You can open for me the portals of Death's house, for Love is always with you, and Love is stronger than Death is.'

Virginia trembled, a cold shudder ran through her, and for a few moments there was silence. She felt as if she was in a terrible dream.

Then the Ghost spoke again, and his voice sounded like the sighing of the wind.

'Have you ever read the old prophecy on the library window?'

'Oh, often,' cried the little girl, looking up; 'I know it quite well. It is painted in curious black letters, and it is difficult to read. There are only six lines:

When a golden girl can win
Prayer from out the lips of sin,
When the barren almond bears,
And a little child gives away its tears,
Then shall all the house be still
And peace come to Canterville.

But I don't know what they mean.'

'They mean,' he said sadly, 'that you must weep for me for my sins, because I have no tears, and pray with me for my soul, because I have no faith, and then, if you have always been sweet, and good, and gentle, the Angel of Death will have mercy on me. You will see fearful shapes in darkness, and wicked voices will whisper in your ear, but they will not harm you, for against the purity of a little child the powers of Hell cannot prevail.'

Virginia made no answer, and the Ghost wrung his hands in wild despair as he looked down at her bowed golden head. Suddenly she stood up, very pale, and with a strange light in her eyes. 'I am not afraid,' she said firmly, 'and I will ask the Angel to have mercy on you.'

He rose from his seat with a faint cry of joy, and taking her hand bent over it with old-fashioned grace and kissed it. His fingers were as cold as ice, and his lips burned like fire, but Virginia did not falter, as he led her across the dusky room. On the faded green tapestry were broidered little huntsmen. They blew their tasselled horns and with their tiny hands waved to her to go back. 'Go back! Little Virginia,' they cried, 'go back!' but the Ghost clutched her hand more tightly, and she shut her eyes against them. Horrible animals with lizard tails, and goggle eyes, blinked at her from the carven chimney-piece, and murmured, 'Beware! little Virginia, beware! We may never see you again,' but the Ghost glided on more swiftly, and Virginia did not listen. When they reached the end of the room he stopped, and muttered some words she could not understand. She opened her eyes, and saw the wall slowly fading away like a mist, and a great black cavern in front of her. A bitter cold wind swept round them, and she felt something pulling at her dress. 'Quick, quick,' cried the Ghost, 'or it will be too late,' and, in a moment, the wainscoting had closed behind them, and the Tapestry Chamber was empty.

Six

About ten minutes later, the bell rang for tea, and, as Virginia did not come down, Mrs Otis sent up one of the footmen to tell her. After a little time he returned and said that he could not find Miss Virginia anywhere. As she was in the habit of going out to the garden every evening to get flowers for the dinner-table, Mrs Otis was not at all alarmed at first, but when six o'clock struck, and Virginia did not appear, she became really agitated, and sent the boys out to look for her, while she herself and Mr Otis searched every room in the house. At half-past six the boys came back and said that they could find no trace of their sister anywhere. They were all now in the greatest state of excitement, and did not know what to do, when Mr Otis suddenly remembered that, some few days before, he had given a band of gypsies permission to camp in the park. He accordingly at once set off for Blackfell Hollow, where he knew they were, accompanied by his eldest son and two of the farm-servants. The little Duke of Cheshire, who was perfectly frantic with anxiety, begged hard to be allowed to go too, but Mr Otis would not allow him, as he was afraid there might be a scuffle. On arriving at the spot, however, he found that the gypsies had gone, and it was evident that their departure had been rather sudden, as the fire was still burning, and some plates were lying on the grass. Having sent off Washington and the two men to scour the district, he ran home, and despatched telegrams to all the police inspectors in the county, telling them to look out for a little girl who had been kidnapped by tramps or gypsies. He then ordered his horse to be brought round, and, after insisting on his wife and the three boys sitting down to dinner, rode off down the Ascot Road with a groom. He had hardly, however, gone a couple of miles when he heard somebody galloping after him, and, looking round, saw the little Duke coming up on his pony, with his face very flushed and no hat. 'I'm awfully sorry, Mr Otis,' gasped out the boy, 'but I can't eat any dinner as long as Virginia is lost. Please, don't be angry with me; if you had let us be engaged last year, there would never have been all this trouble. You won't send me back, will you? I can't go! I won't go!'

The Minister could not help smiling at the handsome young scape-grace, and was a good deal touched at his devotion to Virginia, so leaning down from his horse, he patted him kindly on the shoulders, and said, 'Well, Cecil, if you won't go back I suppose you must come with me, but I must get you a hat at Ascot.'

'Oh, bother my hat! I want Virginia!' cried the little Duke, laughing, and they galloped on to the railway station. There Mr Otis inquired of the station-master if any one answering the description of Virginia had been seen on the platform, but could get no news of her. The station-master, however, wired up and down the line, and assured him that a strict watch would be kept for her, and, after having bought a hat for the little Duke from a linen-draper, who was just putting up his shutters, Mr Otis rode off to Bexley, a village about four miles away, which he was told was a well-known haunt of the gypsies, as there was a large common next to it. Here they roused up the rural policeman, but could get no information from him, and, after riding all over the common, they turned their horses' heads homewards, and reached the Chase about eleven o'clock, dead-tired and almost heart-broken. They found Washington and the twins waiting for them at the gate-house with lanterns, as the avenue was very dark. Not the slightest trace of Virginia had been discovered. The gypsies had been caught on Broxley meadows, but she was not with them, and they had explained their sudden departure by saying that they had mistaken the date of Chorton Fair, and had gone off in a hurry for fear they might be late. Indeed, they had been quite distressed at hearing of Virginia's disappearance, as they were very grateful to Mr Otis for having allowed them to camp in his park, and four of their number had stayed behind to help in the search. The carp-pond had been dragged, and the whole Chase thoroughly gone over, but without any result. It was evident that, for that night at any rate, Virginia was lost to them; and it was in a state of the deepest depression that Mr Otis and the boys walked up to the house, the groom following behind with the two horses and the pony. In the hall they found a group of frightened servants, and lying on a sofa in the library was poor Mrs Otis, almost out of her mind with terror and anxiety, and having her forehead bathed with eau-de-cologne by the old housekeeper. Mr Otis at once insisted on her having something to eat, and ordered up supper for the whole party. It was a melancholy meal, as hardly any one spoke, and even the twins were awestruck and subdued, as they were very fond of their sister. When they had finished, Mr Otis, in spite of the entreaties of the little Duke, ordered them all to bed, saying that nothing more could be done that night, and that he would telegraph in the morning to Scotland Yard for some detectives to be sent down immediately. Just as they were passing out of the dining-room, midnight began to boom from the clock tower, and when the last stroke sounded they heard a crash and a sudden shrill cry; a dreadful peal of thunder shook the house, a strain of unearthly music floated through the air, a panel at the top of the staircase flew back with a loud noise, and out on the landing, looking very pale and white, with a little casket in her hand, stepped Virginia. In a moment they had all rushed up to her. Mrs Otis clasped her passionately in her arms, the Duke smothered her with violent kisses, and the twins executed a wild war-dance round the group.

'Good heavens! Child, where have you been?' said Mr Otis, rather angrily, thinking that she had been playing some foolish trick on them. 'Cecil and I have been riding all over the country looking for you, and your mother has been frightened to death. You must never play these practical jokes any more.'

'Except on the Ghost! Except on the Ghost!' shrieked the twins, as they capered about.

'My own darling, thank God you are found; you must never leave my side again,' murmured Mrs Otis, as she kissed the trembling child, and smoothed the tangled gold of her hair.

'Papa,' said Virginia quietly, 'I have been with the Ghost. He is dead, and you must come and see him. He had been very wicked, but he was really sorry for all that he had done, and he gave me this box of beautiful jewels before he died.'

The whole family gazed at her in mute astonishment, but she was quite grave and serious; and turning round, she led them through the opening in the wainscoting down a narrow secret corridor, Washington following with a lighted candle, which he had caught up from the table. Finally, they came to a great oak door, studded with rusty nails. When Virginia touched it, it swung back on its heavy hinges, and they found themselves in a little low room, with a vaulted ceiling, and one tiny grated window. Imbedded in the wall was a huge iron ring, and chained to it was a gaunt skeleton, that was stretched out at full length on the stone floor, and seemed to be trying to grasp with its long fleshless fingers an old-fashioned trencher and ewer, that were placed just out of its reach. The jug had evidently been once filled with water, as it was covered inside with green mould. There was nothing on the trencher but a pile of dust. Virginia knelt down beside the skeleton, and, folding her little hands together, began to pray silently, while the rest of the party looked on in wonder at the terrible tragedy whose secret was now disclosed to them.

'Hallo!' suddenly exclaimed one of the twins, who had been looking out of the window to try and discover in what wing of the house the room was situated. 'Hallo! The old withered almond-tree has blossomed. I can see the flowers quite plainly in the moonlight.'

'God has forgiven him,' said Virginia gravely, as she rose to her feet, and a beautiful light seemed to illumine her face.

'What an angel you are!' cried the young Duke, and he put his arm round her neck and kissed her.

Seven

Four days after these curious incidents a funeral started from Canterville Chase at about eleven o'clock at night. The hearse was drawn by eight black horses, each of which carried on its head a great tuft of nodding ostrich-plumes, and the leaden coffin was covered by a rich purple pall, on which was embroidered in gold the Canterville coat-of-arms. By the side of the hearse and the coaches walked the servants with lighted torches, and the whole procession was wonderfully impressive. Lord Canterville was the chief mourner, having come up specially from Wales to attend the funeral, and sat in the first carriage along with little Virginia. Then came the United States Minister and his wife, then Washington and the three boys, and in the last carriage was Mrs Umney. It was generally felt that, as she had been frightened by the ghost for more than fifty years of her life, she had a right to see the last of him. A deep grave had been dug in the corner of the churchyard, just under the old yew-tree, and the service was read in the most impressive manner by the Rev Augustus Dampier. When the ceremony was over, the servants, according to an old custom observed in the Canterville family, extinguished their torches, and, as the coffin was being lowered into the grave, Virginia stepped forward and laid on it a large cross made of white and pink almond-blossoms. As she did so, the moon came out from behind a cloud, and flooded with its silent silver the little churchyard, and from a distant copse a nightingale began to sing. She thought of the ghost's description of the Garden of Death, her eyes became dim with tears, and she hardly spoke a word during the drive home.

The next morning, before Lord Canterville went up to town, Mr Otis had an interview with him on the subject of the jewels the ghost had given to Virginia. They were perfectly magnificent, especially a certain ruby necklace with old Venetian setting, which was really a superb specimen of sixteenth-century work, and their value was so great that Mr Otis felt considerable scruples about allowing his daughter to accept them.

'My Lord,' he said, 'I know that in this country mortmain is held to apply to trinkets as well as to land, and it is quite clear to me that these jewels are, or should be, heirlooms in your family. I must beg you, accordingly, to take them to London with you, and to regard them simply as a portion of your property which has been restored to you under certain strange conditions. As for my daughter, she is merely a child, and has as yet, I am glad to say, but little interest in such appurtenances of idle luxury. I am also informed by Mrs Otis, who, I may say, is no mean authority upon Art – having had the privilege of spending several winters in Boston when she was a girl – that these gems are of great monetary worth, and if offered for sale would fetch a tall price. Under these circumstances, Lord Canterville, I feel sure that you will recognize how impossible it would be for me to allow them to remain in the possession of any member of my family; and, indeed, all such vain gauds and toys, however suitable or necessary to the dignity of the British aristocracy, would be completely out of place among those who have been brought up on the severe, and I believe immortal, principles of republican simplicity. Perhaps I should mention that Virginia is very anxious that you should allow her to retain the box as a memento of your unfortunate but misguided ancestor. As it is extremely old, and consequently a good deal out of repair, you may perhaps think fit to comply with her request. For my own part, I confess I am a good deal surprised to find a child of mine expressing sympathy with medievalism in any form, and can only account for it by the fact that Virginia was born in one of your London suburbs shortly after Mrs Otis had returned from a trip to Athens.'

Lord Canterville listened very gravely to the worthy Minister's speech, pulling his grey moustache now and then to hide an involuntary smile, and when Mr Otis had ended, he shook him cordially by the hand, and said, 'My dear sir, your charming little daughter rendered my unlucky ancestor, Sir Simon, a very important service, and I and my family are much indebted to her for her marvellous courage and pluck. The jewels are clearly hers, and, egad, I believe that if I were heartless enough to take them from her, the wicked old fellow would be out of his grave in a fortnight, leading me the devil of a life. As for their being heirlooms, nothing is an heirloom that is not so mentioned in a will or legal document, and the existence of these jewels has been quite unknown. I assure you I have no more claim on them than your butler, and when Miss Virginia grows up I daresay she will be pleased to have pretty things to wear. Besides, you forget, Mr Otis, that you took the furniture and the ghost at a valuation, and anything that belonged to the ghost passed at once into your possession, as, whatever activity Sir Simon may have shown in the corridor at night, in point of law he was really dead, and you acquired his property by purchase.'

Mr Otis was a good deal distressed at Lord Canterville's refusal, and begged him to reconsider his decision, but the good-natured peer was quite firm, and finally induced the Minister to allow his daughter to retain the present the ghost had given her, and when, in the spring of 1890, the young Duchess of Cheshire was presented at the Queen's first drawing-room on the occasion of her marriage, her jewels were the universal theme of admiration. For Virginia received the coronet, which is the reward of all good little American girls, and was married to her boy-lover as soon as he came of age. They were both so charming, and they loved each other so much, that everyone was delighted at the match, except the old Marchioness of Dumbleton, who had tried to catch the Duke for one of her seven unmarried daughters, and had given no less than three expensive dinner-parties for that purpose, and, strange to say, Mr Otis himself. Mr Otis was extremely fond of the young Duke personally, but, theoretically, he objected to titles, and, to use his own words, 'was not without apprehension lest, amid the enervating influences of a pleasure-loving aristocracy, the true principles of republican simplicity should be forgotten.' His objections, however, were completely overruled, and I believe that when he walked up the aisle of St George's, Hanover Square, with his daughter leaning on his arm, there was not a prouder man in the whole length and breadth of England.

The Duke and Duchess, after the honeymoon was over, went down to Canterville Chase, and on the day after their arrival they walked over in the afternoon to the lonely churchyard by the pine-woods. There had been a great deal of difficulty at first about the inscription on Sir Simon's tombstone, but finally it had been decided to engrave on it simply the initials of the old gentleman's name, and the verse from the library window. The Duchess had brought with her some lovely roses, which she strewed upon the grave, and after they had stood by it for some time they strolled into the ruined chancel of the old abbey. There the Duchess sat down on a fallen pillar, while her husband lay at her feet smoking a cigarette and looking up at her beautiful eyes. Suddenly he threw his cigarette away, took hold of her hand, and said to her, 'Virginia, a wife should have no secrets from her husband.'

'Dear Cecil! I have no secrets from you.'

'Yes, you have,' he answered, smiling, 'you have never told me what happened to you when you were locked up with the ghost.'

'I have never told any one, Cecil,' said Virginia gravely.

'I know that, but you might tell me.'

'Please don't ask me, Cecil. I cannot tell you. Poor Sir Simon! I owe him a great deal. Yes, don't laugh, Cecil, I really do. He made me see what Life is, and what Death signifies, and why Love is stronger than both.'

The Duke rose and kissed his wife lovingly.

'You can have your secret as long as I have your heart,' he murmured.

'You have always had that, Cecil.'

'And you will tell our children some day, won't you?'

Virginia blushed.

Smiling Through

☆★☆★☆★☆★☆★☆★☆★☆★☆★☆★☆★☆★☆★☆★☆★☆

ALAN COREN

Computer scientists in California believe they have evidence that the Mona Lisa was originally wearing a necklace.

Dr John Asmus, who headed a team which investigated the picture using computer image analysis techniques, told yesterday's annual meeting of the American Association for the Advancement of Science that Leonardo da Vinci probably changed his mind about the portrait and painted over the necklace.

the Independent

'Hallo!' shouted Leonardo da Vinci, into the cocoa tin. 'Is that Florence 2?'

He put the tin to his ear.

From somewhere deep inside came a sound not unlike a cockroach running through iron filings. He took his ear out of the tin again.

'Speak up!' he shouted.

The tin squawked, unintelligibly.

He pulled on the string. Beyond his attic dormer, it tautened above the umber roofscape, scattering sparrows. He was about to put the tin to his ear again, when the string went suddenly slack.

'Sod it,' said Leonardo.

He put the cocoa tin back on his desk, and ran out of his studio, slamming the door. Caught in the slipstream of his flying cloak, a preliminary cartoon for *The Battle of Anghiari* trembled on his easel, floated to the floor, and came to rest face up. The moted sunlight fell across two battered Medici grenadiers crouching in a muddy crater. *'If you knows of a better 'ole . . .'* the caption began; but, like so much else these days, it was unfinished, and would in all likelihood remain so.

On the landing, Leonardo sprang into the lift, plummeted, screamed, and was hurled off his feet as it stopped without warning between floors. He rang the emergency handbell, and was winched slowly down by a bloomered pupil.

'Up the spout,' muttered Leonardo.

'*Up the spout,* Master?' murmured the pupil.

'It is a technical phrase I have invented,' replied Leonardo da Vinci, straightening his plume, 'to describe lifts.'

'Is it like *on the blink*, Master?' enquired the pupil.

'No,' said Leonardo. '*On the blink* describes telephones.'

'Is Florence 1 on the blink again, then?'

'Yes. There is a fault on the line. It is my opinion the knot has come out of Florence 2.'

'It is nevertheless,' said the pupil, simpering warmly, 'a wonderful invention, and a boon to man!'

'Inventing the cocoa tin was the hard part,' said Leonardo. He sniffed, bitterly. 'You would think that once you'd come up with the cocoa tin, it would all be downhill after that. You would think the string would be a doddle. It's a bugger, science. Half the time, it makes no bloody sense at all.' He pushed into the new revolving door which led to his workshop, and the pupil pushed in behind him. After about ten minutes of banging and shrieking, the pupil came out in front.

'Up the blink, Master?' murmured the pupil, gloomily watching Leonardo's shredded cloak smouldering in the door's boiler. 'On the spout?'

'Down the tubes,' muttered Leonardo. He dusted himself off, and peered into the bustling workshop, on the far side of which a tiny buskinned man was throwing vegetables into a large glass cylinder. 'Hallo, what's that little twerp Giovanni up to now?'

The pupil examined his clipboard.

'Where are we?' he said. 'Tuesday, Tuesday, yes, Tuesday he is supposed to be on rotary-wing research. He is down here as developing the Leonardo Gnat.'

Cursing, Leonardo ran across and snatched an imminent cucumber from Giovanni's little hands; in the confusion, a chicken scrambled out of the glass cylinder and fled, clucking.

'That's never a helicopter!' cried Leonardo.

'Insofar as you would have a job getting to Pisa in it,' replied the pupil, 'that is true. However, Master, it works on the same principle. It is what we call a spin-off. If I may be permitted?'

Leonardo prodded the cylinder with his patent umbrella. The ferrule dropped off.

'Two minutes,' he said. 'But God help you if it turns out to be another bloody toaster. They'll never send the fire brigade out four days in a row.'

Giovanni, who had meanwhile been turning a large key protruding from the base of the cylinder, now took a deep breath, and flicked a switch. Inside the cylinder, blades whirled, howling; a white lumpy mass spread across the ceiling. Leonardo looked slowly up, as the substance coalesced into soft stalactites; a blob fell into his beard, and he licked it off.

'Vichyssoise, is it?' he enquired, levelly.

'Leek and turnip, actually,' said Giovanni. He spooned a quantity from Leonardo's hat, and tasted it. 'Could do with a bit more garlic?'

Leonardo swung his umbrella. It turned, naturally enough, inside out, but the residual sturdiness was still enough to fell Giovanni where he stood. Slowly, his ear swelled, glowing.

'I want this one,' said Leonardo to the pupil-foreman, 'on the next train to Santa Maria della Grazie.'

'*The Last Supper*, Master?' cried the pupil-foreman, aghast. 'Are you sure he's up to it?'

'I'm a dab hand with apostles,' retorted Giovanni, struggling to his feet, 'also glassware. You could drink out of my goblets.'

'He will not be painting the wall,' said Leonardo, 'he will be plastering it prior to undercoat, as per ours of the 14th ultimo, plus removing all rubbish from site and making good.'

'Bloody hell!' cried Giovanni. 'All I forgot was the lid! I have not even mentioned the fact that the amazing new Vincimix comes with a range of attachments which chop, shred, slice, and whip the pips out of a quince before you can say Jack Robinson.'

At which point, all the windows blew in.

Slowly, Leonardo da Vinci walked through the settling dust, and looked out. A blackened face looked back at him. Neither spoke. Leonardo turned and walked back through the room.

'You'll have to go by horse,' he said to Giovanni.

'Do not be downcast, Master,' said the pupil-foreman. 'Nobody said trains were easy.'

Leonardo stared at the floor.

'Funny,' he said, 'the lid hops up and down all right on the kettle.'

The clock struck ten. Absently, Leonardo picked up the fallen cuckoo, walked out of the workshop, into the sunlit street, climbed on his bicycle, and began pedalling slowly towards Fiesole, scattering nuts and spokes. By the time he reached the house of Zanoki del Giocondo, he was carrying a wheel and a saddlebag, and sweating.

He tugged the bell-rope.

'I phoned,' he gasped, when she answered the door.

'The knot came out,' she replied.

'I thought so,' he said. He cleared his throat. 'Is he in?'

'He's out in his tank.'

'I thought he'd like that,' said Leonardo. 'I thought it might get him out of the house.' He walked into the hall. 'I hope he doesn't suspect anything, mind.'

'No. He thinks you're a faggot. Nobody else gives him presents.' A neighbour passed, and peered, and smiled. La Gioconda nodded, and closed the front door. 'How long is he likely to stay out?' she said. 'I don't know anything about tanks.'

'Days, possibly,' said Leonardo. 'We haven't cracked this business of the tracks. It tends to go round in circles until the engine seizes up. Even if he manages to get the lid open again, he won't have the faintest idea where he is.'

'But we ought to do a bit more of the painting, first?'

'You can't be too careful,' said Leonardo da Vinci. He propped his wheel against the dado, and opened his saddlebag, and took out his palette and his easel; but as he was following her through the house and out into the garden – not simply for the light but for the assuaging of neighbourly curiosity – he could not help noticing the way a sunbeam fell across her plump shoulder, and the way her hips rolled.

So they decided to do a bit more of the painting afterwards, instead.

And when they were in the garden, finally, he put the necklace around her neck, and fastened the clasp, and she cried aloud:

'Diamonds!'

'What else?' he said.

So she sat in her chair, with her hands folded and a broad smile on her tawny face, and Leonardo da Vinci's brushes flicked back and forth, and the neighbours peered from between the mullions, and were satisfied.

And then it began to rain.

Not seriously enough to drive them in; just a warm summer blob or two. But one such, unfortunately, fell on her necklace, and, after a few moments, she looked down, and stared; and then she said, carefully:

'The diamonds appear to be going grey.'

'Ah,' said Leonardo.

'Is that usual?'

Leonardo came out from behind his easel, and looked at them.

'It could be,' he said, 'With this new process.'

'I'm sorry?'

'It's a bit technical,' said Leonardo.

'Try me.'

'You start off with coal,' said Leonardo.

'I see.'

She stared at him for a long while after that, until Leonardo went back behind his easel. He picked up his brush.

He looked at her.

Her lip curled.

He put the brush down again.

'It isn't much of a smile,' said Leonardo da Vinci.

'It isn't much of a necklace,' said Mona Lisa.

The Darling Buds of May

☆★☆

H. E. BATES

After distributing the eight ice-creams – they were the largest vanilla, chocolate, and raspberry super-bumpers, each in yellow, brown, and almost purple stripes – Pop Larkin climbed up into the cab of the gentian blue, home-painted thirty-hundredweight truck, laughing happily.

'Perfick wevver! You kids all right at the back there? Ma, hitch up a bit!'

Ma, in her salmon jumper, was almost two yards wide.

'I said you kids all right there?'

'How do you think they can hear,' Ma said, 'with you revving up all the time?'

Pop laughed again and let the engine idle. The strong May sunlight, the first hot sun of the year, made the bonnet of the truck gleam like brilliant blue enamel. All down the road, winding through the valley, miles of pink apple orchards were in late bloom, showing petals like light confetti.

'Zinnia and Petunia, Primrose, Victoria, Montgomery, Mariette!' – Pop unrolled the handsome ribbon of six names but heard only five separate answers, each voice choked and clotted with ice-cream.

'Where's Mariette? Ain't Mariette there?'

'I'm here, Pop.'

'That's all right, then. Thought you'd fell overboard.'

'No, I'm here, Pop, I'm here.'

'Perfick!' Pop said. 'You think I ought to get more ice-creams? It's so hot Ma's is nearly melted.'

Ma shook all over, laughing like a jelly. Little rivers of yellow, brown, and pinkish-purple cream were running down over her huge lardy hands. In her handsome big black eyes the cloudless blue May sky was reflected, making them dance as she threw out the splendid bank of her bosom, quivering under its salmon jumper. At thirty-five she still had a head of hair like black silk cotton, curly and thick as it fell to her fat olive shoulders. Her stomach and thighs bulged like a hopsack under the tight brown skirt and in her remarkably small delicate cream ears her round pearl drop earrings trembled like young white cherries.

'Hitch up a bit I said, Ma! Give father a bit o' room.' Pop Larkin, who was thin, sharp, quick-eyed, jocular, and already going shining bald on top, with narrow brown side-linings to make up for it, nudged against the mass of flesh like a piglet against a sow. 'Can't get the clutch in.'

Ma hitched up a centimetre or two, still laughing.

'Perfick!' Pop said. 'No, it ain't though. Where'd I put that money?'

Ice-cream in his right hand, he began to feel in the pockets of his leather jacket with the other.

'I had it when I bought the ice-creams. Don't say I dropped it. Here, Ma, hold my ice-cream.'

Ma held the ice-cream, taking a neat lick at a melting edge of it with a red sparkling tongue.

'All right, all right. Panic over. Put it in with the crisps.'

Packets of potato crisps crackled out of his pocket, together with a bundle of pound notes, rolled up, perhaps a hundred of them, and clasped with a thick elastic band.

'Anybody want some crisps? Don't all speak at once! – anybody –'

'Please!'

Pop leaned out of the driving cab and with two deft backhand movements threw packets of potato crisps into the back of the truck.

'Crisps, Ma?'

'Please,' Ma said. 'Lovely. Just what I wanted.'

Pop took from his pocket a third packet of potato crisps and handed it over to Ma, taking his ice-cream back and licking the dripping underside of it at the same time.

'All right. All set now.' He let in the clutch at last, holding his ice-cream against the wheel. 'Perfick! Ma, take a look at that sky!'

Soon, in perfect sunlight, between orchards that lifted gentle pink branches in the lightest breath of wind, the truck was passing strawberry fields.

'Got the straw on,' Pop said. 'Won't be above anuvver few days now.'

In June it would be strawberries for picking, followed by cherries before the month ended, and then more cherries through all the month of July. Sometimes, in good summers, apples began before August did, and with them early plums and pears. In August and again in September it was apples. In September also it was hops and in October potatoes. At strawberries alone, with a big family, you could earn fifteen pounds a day.

'See that, kids?' Pop slowed down the truck, idling past the long rows of fresh yellow straw. 'Anybody don't want to go strawberry-picking?'

In the answering burst of voices Pop thought, for the second time, that he couldn't hear the voice of Mariette.

'What's up with Mariette, Ma?'

'Mariette? Why?'

'Ain't heard her laughing much today.'

'I expect she's thinking,' Ma said.

Lost in silent astonishment at this possibility, Pop licked the last melting pink and chocolate-yellow cream from its paper and let the paper fly out of the window.

'Thinking? What's she got to think about?'

'She's going to have a baby.'

'Oh?' Pop said. 'Well, that don't matter. Perfick. Jolly good.'

Ma did not seem unduly worried either.

'Who is it?' Pop said.

'She can't make up her mind.'

Ma sat happily munching crisps, staring at cherry orchards as they sailed past the truck, every bough hung with swelling fruit, palest pink on the sunnier edges of the trees.

'Have to make up her mind some time, won't she?' Pop said.

'Why?'

'Oh! I just thought,' Pop said.

Ma, who had almost finished the crisps, poured the last remaining golden crumbs into the palm of her left hand. Over the years, as she had grown fatter, the three big turquoise and pearl rings she wore had grown tighter and tighter on her fingers, so that every now and then she had to have them cut off, enlarged, and put back again.

'She thinks it's either that Charles boy who worked at the farm,' Ma said, 'Or else that chap who works on the railway line. Harry somebody.'

'I know him,' Pop said. 'He's married.'

'The other one's overseas now,' Ma said. 'Tripoli or somewhere.'

'Well, he'll get leave.'

'Not for a year he won't,' Ma said. 'And perhaps not then if he hears.'

'Ah! well, we'll think of something,' Pop said. 'Like some more crisps? How about some chocolate? Let's stop and have a beer. Got a crate in the back.'

'Not now,' Ma said. 'Wait till we get home now. We'll have a Guinness then and I'll warm the fish-and-chips up.'

Pop drove happily, both hands free now, staring with pleasure at the cherries, the apples, and the strawberry fields, all so lovely under the May sunlight, and thinking with pleasure too of his six children and the splendid, handsome names he and Ma had given them. Jolly good names, perfick, every one of them, he thought. There was a reason for them all.

Montgomery, the only boy, had been named after the general. Primrose had come in the Spring. Zinnia and Petunia were twins and they were the flowers Ma liked most. Victoria, the youngest girl, had been born in plum-time.

Suddenly he couldn't remember why they had called the eldest Mariette.

'Ma,' he said, 'trying to think why we called her Mariette. Why did we?'

'I wanted to call her after that Queen,' Ma said. 'I always felt sorry for that Queen.'

'What Queen?'

'The French one, Marie Antoinette. But you said it was too long. You'd never say it, you said.'

'Oh! I remember,' Pop said. 'I remember now. We put the two together.'

Ten minutes later they were home. With pride and satisfaction Pop gazed on home as it suddenly appeared beyond its scrubby fringe of woodland, half filled with bluebells, half with scratching red-brown hens.

'Home looks nice,' he said. 'Allus does though, don't it? Perfick.'

'Lovely,' Ma said.

'We're all right,' Pop said. 'Got nothing to worry about, Ma, have we?'

'Not that I can think of,' Ma said.

Pop drew the truck to a standstill in a dusty yard of nettles, old oil drums, corrugated pig-sties, and piles of rusty iron in which a line of white ducks, three grey goats, and a second batch of red-brown hens set up a concerted, trembling fuss of heads and wings, as if delighted.

'Just in time for dinner!' Pop said. It was almost four o'clock. 'Anybody not hungry?'

He leapt down from the cab. Like him, everybody was laughing. He knew they were all hungry; they always were.

'Down you come, you kids. Down.'

Letting down the back-board and holding up both arms, he took the youngest children one by one, jumping them down to the yard, laughing and kissing them as they came.

Presently only Mariette remained on the truck, wearing jodhpurs and a pale lemon shirt, standing erect, black-haired, soft-eyed, olive-skinned, and so well-made in a slender and delicate way that he could not believe that Ma, at seventeen too, had once looked exactly like her.

'It's all right. I can get down myself, Pop.'

Pop held up his arms, looking at her tenderly.

'Ah! come on. Ma's told me.'

'Let me get down myself, Pop.'

He stood watching her. Her eyes roamed past him, flashing and dark as her mother's, searching the yard.

It suddenly crossed his mind that she was afraid of something, not happy, and he half-opened his mouth to comment on this unlikely, disturbing, unheard-of fact when she suddenly shook her black head and startled him by saying:

'Pop, there's a man in the yard. There's a man over there by the horse-box. Watching us.'

Pop walked across the yard towards the horse-box. He owned two horses, one a young black mare for Mariette, the other a piebald pony for the other kids. Mariette, who was crazy about horses, rode to point-to-points, sometimes went hunting, and even jumped at shows. She was wonderful about horses. She looked amazing on a horse. Perfick, he thought.

'Hullo, hullo, hullo,' he said. 'Good morning, afternoon rather. Looking for me?'

The man, young, spectacled, pale-faced, trilby-hatted, with a small brown tooth-brush moustache, carried a black brief-case under his arm.

'Mr Sidney Larkin?'

'Larkin, that's me,' Pop said. He laughed in ringing fashion. 'Larkin by name, Larkin by nature. What can I do for you? Nice wevver.'

'I'm from the office of the Inspector of Taxes.'

Pop stood blank and innocent, staggered by the very existence of such a person.

'Inspector of *what*?'

'Taxes. Inland Revenue.'

'You must have come to the wrong house,' Pop said.

'You are Mr Sidney Larkin?' The young man snapped open the brief-case, took out a paper, and glanced at it quickly, nervously touching his spectacles with the back of his hand. 'Sidney Charles Larkin.'

'That's me. That's me all right,' Pop said.

'According to our records,' the young man said, 'you have made no return of income for the past year.'

'Return?' Pop said. 'What return? Why? Nobody asked me.'

'You should have had a form,' the young man said. He took a yellow-buff sheet of paper from the brief-case and held it up. 'One like this.'

'Form?' Pop said. 'Form?'

Ma was crossing the yard with a box of groceries under one arm and a bag of fruit in the other. Three big ripe pineapples stuck cactus-like heads from the top of the huge paper bag. The twins loved pineapple. Especially fresh. Much better than tinned, they thought.

'Ma, did we have a form like this?' Pop called. 'Never had no form, did we?'

'Never seen one. Sure we never.'

'Come over here, Ma, a minute. This gentleman's from the Inspector of Summat or other.'

'I got dinner to get,' Ma said and strode blandly on with groceries and pineapples, huge as a buffalo. 'You want your dinner, don't you?'

Pop turned with an air of balmy indifference to the young man, who was staring incredulously at the receding figure of Ma as if she were part of the menagerie of hens, goats, ducks, and horses.

'No, never had no form. Ma says so.'

'You should have done. Two at least were sent. If not three.'

'Well, Ma says so. Ma ought to know. Ma's the one who does the paper work.'

The young man opened his mouth to speak and for a moment it was as if a strangled, startled gurgle came out. His voice choked itself back, however, and in reality the sound came from a drove of fifteen young turkeys winding down from the strip of woodland.

'Won't hurt you,' Pop said. 'How about a nice hen-bird for Christmas? Put your name on it now.'

'This form has to be returned to the Inspector,' the young man said. 'There is a statutory obligation –'

'Can't return it if I ain't got it,' Pop said. 'Now can I?'

'Here's another.'

As he recoiled from the buff-yellow sheet of paper Pop saw Mariette walking across the yard, slender, long-striding, on her way to the wooden, brush-roofed stable where both pony and horse were kept.

'I got no time for forms,' Pop said. 'Gawd Awmighty, I got pigs to feed.

Turkeys to feed. Hens to feed. Kids to feed. I ain't had no dinner. Nobody ain't had no dinner.'

Suddenly the young man was not listening. With amazement he was following the progress of Mariette's dark, yellow-shirted figure across the yard.

'My eldest daughter,' Pop said. 'Crazy on horses. Mad on riding. You do any riding, Mister – Mister – I never caught your name.'

'Charlton.'

'Like to meet her, Mister Charlton?' Pop said. The young man was still staring, mouth partly open. Between his fingers the tax form fluttered in the breezy sunlit air.

'Mariette, come over here a jiff. Young man here's crazy on horses, like you. Wants to meet you. Comes from the Ministry of Revenue or summat.'

In astonished silence the young man stared at the new celestial body, in its yellow shirt, as it floated across the background of rusty iron, pig-sties, abandoned oil-drums, goat-chewn hawthorn bushes, and dusty earth.

'Mister Charlton, this is my eldest, Mariette. The one who's mad on horses. Rides everywhere. You've very like seen her picture in the papers.'

'Hullo,' Mariette said. 'I spotted you first.'

'That's right, she saw you,' Pop said. 'Who's that nice young feller in the yard, she said.'

'So you', Mariette said, 'like riding too?'

The eyes of the young man groped at the sunlight as if still unable correctly to focus the celestial body smiling at him from three feet away.

'I say every kid should have a horse,' Pop said. 'Nothing like a horse. I'm going to get every one of my kids a horse.'

Suddenly the young man woke from mesmerism, making a startling statement.

'I saw you riding over at Barfield,' he said. 'In the third race. At Easter. You came second.'

'I hope you won a bob or two on her,' Pop said.

Again he laughed in ringing fashion, bringing from beyond the stable an echo of goose voices as three swaggering grey-white birds emerged from a barricade of nettles, to be followed presently by the half-sleepy, dainty figures of a dozen guinea-fowl.

'Pity we didn't know you were coming,' Pop said. 'We're killing a goose tomorrow. Always kill a goose or a turkey or a few chickens at the weekend. Or else guinea-fowl. Like guinea-fowl?'

If the young man had any kind of answer ready it was snatched from him by the voice of Ma, calling suddenly from the house:

'Dinner's nearly ready. Anybody coming in or am I slaving for nothing?'

'We're coming, Ma!' Pop turned with eager, tempting relish to the young man, still speechless, still struggling with his efforts to focus correctly the dark-haired girl. 'Well, we got to go, Mister Charlton. Sorry. Ma won't have no waiting.'

'Now, Mr Larkin, about this form –'

'Did you see me at Newchurch?' Mariette said. 'I rode there too.'

'As a matter of fact, I did – I did, yes – But, Mr Larkin, about this form –'

'What form?' Mariette said.

'Oh! some form, some form,' Pop said. 'I tell you what, Mister Charlton, you come in and have a bite o' dinner with us. No, no trouble. Tons o' grub – '

'I've eaten, thank you. I've eaten.'

'Well, cuppa tea then. Cuppa coffee. Bottle o' beer. Bottle o' Guinness. Drop o' cider.'

The entire body of the young man seemed to swirl helplessly, as if half-intoxicated, out of balance, on its axis. 'Oh! yes, do,' Mariette said and by the time he had recovered he found himself being led by Pop Larkin towards the house, from which Ma was already calling a second time:

'If nobody don't come in three minutes I'll give it to the cats.'

'Know anybody who wants a pure white kitten?' Pop said. 'Don't want a pure white kitten, do you?'

'So you were at Newchurch too,' Mariette said. 'I wish I'd known.'

A moment later Pop threw up his hands in a gesture of near ecstasy at the overpowering beauty, which suddenly seemed to strike him all afresh, of the May afternoon.

'Beautiful, ain't it?' he said. 'Perfick. I got a beautiful place here. Don't you think I got a beautiful place here, Mister Charlton?'

In the kitchen a radio was loudly playing jazz. In the living-room next door, where the curtains were half-drawn, a television set was on, giving to the nine faces crowded about the table a grey-purple, flickering glow.

'Have just what you fancy, Mister Charlton,' Pop said. 'If you don't see it here, ask for it. Bottle o' beer? Glass o' sherry? Pass the vinegar, Ma.'

Soon the young man, arms crooked at the crowded table, was nursing a cup of tea. In the centre of the table stood the three pineapples, flanked on all sides by plates of fish-and-chips, more coloured blocks of ice-cream, pots of raspberry and strawberry jam, bottles of tomato-ketchup and Guinness, bottles of Worcester sauce and cups of tea, chocolate biscuits and piles of icy buns.

'Perhaps Mister Charlton would like a couple o' sardines with his tea?' Pop said. 'Montgomery, fetch the sardines.'

Mr Charlton, bemused by the name of Montgomery, protested faintly that he did not like sardines.

'Mister Charlton saw Mariette riding at Barfield,' Pop said.

'And at Newchurch,' Mariette said.

'Funny we didn't see you there,' Ma said, 'we was all there.'

'Mister Charlton', Pop said, 'loves horses.'

'Turn up the contrast,' Ma said, 'it's getting dark.'

In the television's flickering purplish light the young man watched the faces about the table, as they munched on fish-and-chips, ice-cream, tomato-ketchup, and jam, becoming more and more like pallid, eyeless ghouls. Pop had placed him between Ma and Mariette and presently he detected under the great breathing bank of Ma's bosom, now mauve-salmon in the flickering light, the shape of two white kittens somehow nestling on the bulging precipice of her lap. Occasionally the kittens miaowed prettily and Ma fed them with scraps of fish and batter.

Above the noise of jazz, television voices, kittens, geese hawking at the kitchen door, and the chattering voices of the family he found it hard to make himself heard.

'Mr Larkin, about this form. If you've got any difficulties I could help you fill it in.'

'All right,' Pop said, 'you fill it in.'

'It's still too dark,' Ma said. 'Turn it up a bit. It never stays where you put it nowadays.'

'I'll give the damn thing one more week to behave itself,' Pop said. 'And if it don't then I'll turn it in for another.'

Mr Charlton spread the yellow-buff form on the table in front of him and then took out his fountain pen and unscrewed the cap.

'Ma, is there any more ice-cream?' Primrose said.

'In the fridge,' Ma said. 'Big block o' strawberry *mousse*. Get that.'

'Full name: Sidney Charles Larkin,' Mr Charlton said and wrote it down. 'Occupation? Dealer?'

'Don't you call him dealer,' Ma said. 'I'll give you dealer. He owns land.'

'Well, landowner – '

'Farmer,' Pop said.

'Well, farmer,' Mr Charlton said. 'I'm very sorry. Farmer.'

'Mariette, cut the pineapple,' Ma said. 'Montgomery, go into the kitchen and fetch that pint jug of cream.'

While Mr Charlton filled in the form Mariette stood up, reached for the bread knife, and started to cut the pineapples, putting thick juicy slices on plates over which Ma poured heavy yellow cream.

'Real Jersey,' Ma said. 'From our cow.'

Every time Mariette reached over for another plate she brushed the sleeve of Mr Charlton, who either made sketchy blobs on the tax form or could not write at all.

'How many children?' Mr Charlton said. 'Six? Is that right? No more?'

'Well, not yet, old man. Plenty o' time though. Give us a chance,' Pop said and again laughed in ringing fashion.

'Gone again,' Ma said. 'You can't see a blessed thing. Montgomery, Primrose – switch it off and change it for the set in our bedroom.'

In the half-darkness that now smothered the room Mr Charlton felt something smooth, sinuous, and slender brush against his right calf. For one shimmering, unnerving moment he sat convinced that it was Mariette's leg entwining itself about his own. As it curled towards his thigh he felt his throat begin choking but suddenly he looked down to realize that already the geese were under the table, where Ma was feeding them with scraps of fish, half-cold chips, and crumbled icy buns.

Unnerved, he found it difficult to frame his next important question.

'Of course this is confidential in every way,' he said, 'but at what would you estimate your income?'

'Estimate, estimate?' Pop said. 'Income? What income?'

Montgomery and Primrose, who had carried one television set away, now brought in another, larger than the first.

'Steady there, steady!' Ma said. 'Watch where you're looking. Mind the cocktail cabinet.'

'Hear that, Ma?' Pop said. 'Income!'

Ma, as she had done in the truck, started laughing like a jelly.

'Outcome more likely,' she said. 'Outcome I should say.'

'Six kids to feed and clothe,' Pop said. 'This place to run. Fodder to buy. Wheat as dear as gold dust. Pig-food enough to frighten you to death. Living all the time going up and up. Vet's fees. Fowl pest. Foot-and-mouth. Swine fever. Birds all the time dying. Income, old man? *Income?* I should like some, old man.'

Before Mr Charlton could answer this the second television set threw across the room its pallid, unreal glow, now in a curious nightmare green. At the same moment the twins, Zinnia and Petunia, demanded more pineapple. The geese made shovelling noises under the table and Mariette, rising to cut fresh slices, suddenly turned to Mr Charlton with modest, almost whispered apology.

'I'm awfully sorry, Mr Charlton. I didn't offer you any pineapple. Would you like some?'

'No thanks. I'm not allowed it. I find it too acid.'

'What a shame. Won't you change your mind? They're nice ripe ones.'

'Ought to be,' Ma said. 'Cost enough.'

'I'm afraid I'm simply not allowed it,' Mr Charlton said. 'I have to go very carefully. I have to manage mostly on eggs and that sort of thing.'

'Eggs?' Pop said. 'Eggs? Why didn't you say so? Got plenty of eggs, Ma, haven't we? Give Mister Charlton a boiled egg or two wiv his tea.'

'How would you like that?' Ma said. 'A couple o' boiled eggs, Mister Charlton? What do you say?'

To the delight of Ma, Mr Charlton confessed that that was what he really wanted.

'I'll do them,' Mariette said. 'Three minutes? Four? How long?'

'Very light,' Mr Charlton said. 'Three.'

'Nice big 'uns! – brown!' Pop called to Mariette as she went into the kitchen, where the geese presently followed her, brushing past Mr Charlton's legs again as they passed, once more to give him that shimmering, shocking moment of unnerving ecstasy.

'About this income,' Mr Charlton said. 'Can you give me an estimate? Just an estimate.'

'Estimate it'll be an' all, old man,' Pop said. 'Lucky if we clear a fiver a week, ain't we, Ma?'

'Fiver? I'd like to see one,' Ma said.

'We want boiled eggs, too!' the twins said, as in one voice. 'Can we have boiled eggs?'

'Give over. Can't you see I'm cutting the pineapple?' Ma said.

Everybody except Mr Charlton had large second helpings of pineapple, with more cream. When Ma had finished ladling out the cream she poured the remainder of it into a tablespoon and then licked the spoon with her big red tongue. After two or three spoonsful she cleaned the spoon with her finger and fed one of the white kittens with cream. On the television screen a posse of cowboys fired thirty revolvers into a mountainside and Mr Charlton said:

'I'm afraid we have to know what your income is, Mr Larkin. Supposing –'

'All right,' Pop said, 'that's a fair question, old man. Fair for me, fair for another. How much do *you* get?'

'Oh! well, me, not all that much. Civil servant, you know –'

'Nice safe job, though.'

'Nice safe job, yes. I suppose so.'

'Nothing like a nice safe job,' Pop said. 'As long as you're happy. Do you reckon you're happy?'

Mr Charlton, who did not look at all happy, said quickly:

'Supposing I put down a provisional five hundred?'

'Hundred weeks in a year now, Ma,' Pop said, laughing again. 'Well, put it down, old man, put it down. No harm in putting it down.'

'Now the names of children,' Mr Charlton said.

While Pop was reciting, with customary pride, the full names of the children, beginning with the youngest, Zinnia Florence and Petunia Mary, the twins, Mariette came back with two large brown boiled eggs in violet plastic egg-cups to hear Pop say:

'Nightingales in them woods up there behind the house, Mr Charlton. Singing all day.'

'Do nightingales sing all day?' Mr Charlton said. 'I wasn't aware –'

'All day, all night,' Pop said. 'Like everything else in the mating season they go hell for leather.'

The plate holding the two eggs was embroidered with slices of the thinnest white bread-and-butter. Mariette had cut them herself. And now Mr Charlton looked at them, as he looked at the eggs, with reluctance and trepidation, as if not wanting to tamper with their fresh, neat virginity.

'I've been looking at you,' Ma said. 'I don't think you get enough to eat by half.'

'I live in lodgings,' Mr Charlton said. 'It's not always –'

'We want to have some of your egg!' the twins said. 'Give us some of your egg!'

'Now you've started summat,' Pop said.

A moment later Mr Charlton announced the startling discovery that the twins were just alike; he simply couldn't tell one from the other.

'You're quick,' Pop said. 'You're quick.'

'It's gone dark again,' Ma said. 'Turn up the contrast. And Montgomery, fetch me my Guinness. There's a good boy.'

Soon, while Ma drank Guinness and Pop spoke passionately again of nightingales, bluebells that clothed the copses, 'fick as carpets, ficker in fact,' and how soon it would be the great time of the year, the time he loved most, the time of strawberry-fields and cherries everywhere, Mr Charlton found himself with a twin on each knee, dipping white fingers of bread and butter into delicious craters of warm golden egg-yolk.

'I hope the eggs are done right?' Mariette said.

'Perfect.'

'Perfick they will be an' all if she does 'em, you can bet you,' Pop said. 'Perfick!'

Mr Charlton had given up, for the time being, all thought of the buff-yellow form. A goose brushed his legs again. Outside, somewhere in the yard, a dog barked and the drove of turkeys seemed to respond in bubbling chorus. Far beyond them, in broken, throaty tones, a cuckoo called, almost in its June voice, and when it was silent the entire afternoon simmered in a single marvellous moment of quietness, breathlessly.

'If you don't mind me saying so,' Ma said, 'a few days in the country'd do you a world of good.'

'What are we having Sunday, Ma?' Pop said. 'Turkey?'

'What you like. Just what you fancy.'

'Roast pork,' Montgomery said. 'I like roast pork. With them brown onions.'

'Or goose,' Pop said. 'How about goose? We ain't had goose since Easter.'

In enthusiastic tones Pop went on to ask Mr Charlton whether he preferred goose, turkey, or roast pork but Mr Charlton, bewildered, trying to clean his misty spectacles and at the same time cut into thin fingers the last of his bread-and-butter, confessed he hardly knew.

'Well, I tell you what,' Ma said, 'we'll have goose *and* roast pork. Then I can do apple sauce for the two.'

'Perfick,' Pop said. 'Perfick. Primrose, pass me the tomato-ketchup. I've got a bit of iced bun to finish up.'

'Dinner on Sunday then,' Ma said. 'About two o'clock.'

Mr Charlton, who was unable to decide from this whether he had been invited to dinner or not, felt fate softly brush his legs again in the shape of a goose-neck. At the same time he saw Mariette smile at him with intensely dark, glowing eyes, almost as if she had in fact brushed his leg with her own, and he felt his limbs again begin melting.

Across the fields a cuckoo called again and Pop echoed it with a belch that seemed to surprise him not only by its length and richness but by the fact that it was a belch at all.

'Manners,' he said. 'Pardon,' and beat his chest in stern, suppressive apology. 'Wind all of a sudden.'

'What's on now?' Ma said. On the television screen all shooting had died and two men on horses, one a piebald, were riding up the valley, waving farewell hands.

'Nobody's birthday, Sunday, is it?' Pop said.

'Nobody's birthday before August,' Ma said.

'Then it's mine,' Mariette said. 'I'll be eighteen.'

'Pity it ain't nobody's birthday,' Pop said. 'We might have had a few fireworks.'

Suddenly all the geese were gone from the kitchen and Ma, marvelling at this fact, started laughing like a jelly again and said:

'They did that once before. They heard us talking!'

'Tell you what,' Pop said, 'if you've had enough, Mister Charlton, why don't you get Mariette to take you as far as the wood and hear them nightingales? I don't think you believe they sing all day, do you?'

'Oh! yes, I –'

'Shall we ride or walk?' Mariette said. 'I don't mind the pony if you want to ride.'

'I think I'd rather walk.'

'In that case I'll run and change into a dress,' she said. 'It's getting a bit warm for jodhpurs.'

While Mariette had gone upstairs the twins abandoned Mr Charlton's egg-less plate and fetched jam-jars from the kitchen.

'Going to the stall,' they said. 'Think we'll put honeysuckle on today instead of bluebells.'

As they ran off Pop said:

'That's the flower-stall they keep at the corner of the road down there. Wild flowers. Tuppence a bunch for motorists. Everybody works here, y'know.'

'I think I passed it,' Mr Charlton said, 'as I walked up from the bus.'

'That's the one,' Pop said. 'Everybody's got to work here so's we can scratch a living. Montgomery, you'd better get off to your goats and start milking 'em.'

Presently Ma, concerned at Mr Charlton's air of retreat, uncertainty, and fatigue, spread hands like lardy legs of pork across her salmon jumper and said with earnest kindness:

'Taking your holiday soon, Mr Charlton? Where do you usually go?'

'I hadn't –'

'You should come strawberry-picking with us,' Ma said. 'Do you the world of good. Else cherry-picking. Best holiday in the world if the weather's nice. Make yourself a lot o' money too.'

'Perfick,' Pop said. 'Don't cost nothing either. Here's Mariette. Perfick, I tell you.'

Mr Charlton rose from the table to find himself stunned by a new astral body, now in a lime green dress with broad black belt, a flouncing skirt, loose neck, and short scalloped sleeves. Her beautiful dark eyes were smiling at him splendidly.

'Is that your shantung?' Ma said. 'You'll be warm enough in that, dear, will you?'

'Oh! it's hot,' Mariette said. 'It's nice to feel the breeze blowing round my legs again. You ready, Mr Charlton?'

Mr Charlton, the buff-yellow form forgotten, turned and followed Mariette, who actually stretched out a friendly hand. As they crossed a yard noisy with hawking geese, mumbling turkeys, and braying goats being led to milking by Montgomery Pop called:

'Remember about Sunday, Mr Charlton, won't you? Don't forget about Sunday.'

'You really mean it?' Mr Charlton halted and turned back, amazed. 'Are you quite sure?'

'Sure?' Pop said. 'Blimey, old man, I'm going to kill the geese any minute now.'

'Thank you. Thank you very much.'

'One goose or two, Ma?' Pop called. 'Two geese be enough? or shall we have three?'

Mr Charlton, still stunned and amazed, turned to face the waiting figure of Mariette and saw it miraculously framed against piles of junk, rampant nettles and, in the near distance, deep strips of bluebells fenced away, in the strip of woodland, from flocks of brown marauding hens. Her legs, in pale beige silk stockings, were surprisingly shapely and slender. Her breasts protruded with grace from the soft lime shantung.

He could not believe in this figure. Nor, five minutes later, could he believe that the yard of nettles and junk, Pop's beautiful, incredible paradise, lay only a hundred yards away, screened by thickets of hornbeam and hazel, oaks in olive flower and may-trees carrying blossom as rich and thick as Ma's lavish Jersey cream.

'You didn't really believe about the nightingales, did you?'

'No.'

'Listen,' she said. 'You will.'

Walking along the woodland path, Mr Charlton could hear only a single untangled chorus of evening bird-song, unseparated into species, confusing as the tuning of orchestra strings.

'Let's stand here by the gate and listen,' Mariette said. 'Let's stand and listen here.'

Mr Charlton, transfixed, utterly bemused, stood by the gate and listened. Patches of evening sunlight, broken gold, sprinkled down through oak-branches, like delicate quivering translations in light of the bird-notes themselves.

'No, not that one,' Mariette said. 'That's a blackbird. Not the one over there, either. That's a wren. Now – that one. The one in the chestnut up there. The one with the long notes and then the long pause. Can you hear it now? That's a nightingale.'

Mr Charlton listened, hardly breathing, and heard for the first time in his life, in a conscious moment, the voice of a nightingale singing against a May evening sky.

Enthralled, still hardly believing it, he turned to see the deep black eyes holding him in utter captivation and heard her say again:

'You really didn't believe it, did you?'

'I must say I didn't.'

'I tell you something else you didn't believe either.'

'What was that?'

'You didn't believe about me, did you?' she said. 'You didn't believe I was the same girl you saw riding at Easter, did you?'

'No,' he said. 'How did you know?'

'I guessed,' she said. 'I could see it in your eyes. I was watching you.'

She lifted her hands and held them suddenly against his cheeks without either boldness or hesitation but with a lightness of touch that woke in Mr Charlton's legs exactly the same melting, unnerving sensation as when the geese had brushed against him under the table. A moment later he saw her lips upraised.

'Who did you think I was?'

Mr Charlton made a startling, embarrassed confession.

'I thought – well, I was actually told you were someone else in point of fact – that you were a niece of Lady Planson-Forbes – you know, at Carrington Hall –'

Mariette began laughing, in ringing tones, very much like her father.

'Now you've just found I wasn't.'

'Well, yes –'

'You feel it makes any difference?'

'Well, in point of fact –'

'I'm just the same, aren't I?' She smiled and he found his eyes level with her bare, olive shoulder. 'I'm just me. The same girl, just me. Just the same.'

Again she touched his face with her hands and Mr Charlton took hurried refuge in a sudden recollection of the buff-yellow form.

'By the way I mustn't forget to get your father to sign that form before I go –'

'You'll have to sign it for him,' she said, 'or Ma will. He can't write his name.'

She laughed again and Mr Charlton, his limbs melting once more as she lifted his hand to her bare warm shoulder, heard consciously but dizzily, for the second time in his life, a passionate burst of song from the nightingales.

At the same moment, back in the house, Pop returned to the kitchen after wringing the necks of three fat geese and poured himself a much-needed glass of beer.

'A few days like this, Ma,' he said, ''ll put a bit o' paint on the strawberries.'

Ma was raking the kitchen fire, putting on to it empty ice-cream cartons, scraps of fish-and-chips, egg-shells, pineapple tops, and Mr Charlton's buff-yellow paper.

'I don't know as I shan't get a few bottles o' port wine in for Sunday,' Pop said, 'so we can celebrate.'

'Celebrate what?'

'Well,' Pop said, 'what about Mariette?'

Ma laughed again, jumper shaking like a salmon jelly.

'The only thing is,' Pop said, 'I hope he won't want to take her away from here.' He carried his beer to the kitchen door and from there contemplated, almost with reverence, the paradisiacal scene beyond. 'Gawd A'mighty, Ma, you know we got a beautiful place here. Paradise. I don't know what we'd do if she were took away from here.'

Standing in the evening sunlight, gazing across the pile of junk, the nettles, the rusting hovels, and the scratching, dusty hens, Pop sighed loudly and with such content that the sound seemed to travel with perfect definition across the surrounding fields of buttercups and may, gathering its echo at last from the mingled sounds of the remaining geese, the voices of cuckoos calling as they flew across the meadows and the small, passionate, invisible nightingales.

'Perfick,' Pop said. 'You couldn't wish for nothing more perfick nowhere.'

On Thrift

☆★☆★☆★☆★☆★☆★☆★☆★☆★☆★☆

GROUCHO MARX

The people who talk about the dear departed days are usually over fifty. They nostalgically remember the horse and buggy, the bicycle built for two, penny candy, and that structure in the back yard that looked like a telephone booth but wasn't. Many other cherished things have disappeared, but why go on? If you're over fifty you probably remember them as clearly as I do.

The word 'thrifty,' for example, has no meaning today except as a name for a chain of drug stores. The *Wall Street Journal* says that the entire country is living on a precarious precipice of debt; the government is deeply in hock and so are most of its citizens. It's a joy ride, they add, but nobody in Washington seems to give a damn.

In the old days, when people were poor they lived poor. Today they live rich. I've discussed this with many wage earners in the eight-to-ten-thousand-dollar-a-year class and, in most cases, they admit that almost everything they own, they don't – their automobiles, their television sets, their houses, and the furniture. Their philosophy seems to be, 'What the hell – we may be dead tomorrow!' However, if their prediction is a few decades off, many of them will spend their old age living off the state.

Cleanliness may be next to godliness, but to my mind thriftiness would be closer. I consider myself one of the last survivors of a dying era. I'm the type that turns out the lights when I leave a room. I turn the water taps securely to make sure they don't drip. Although I have a cook, I go to the supermarket myself and pick out the food that she will eventually ruin. People are astonished when they see me at the vegetable bin, carefully weighing the merits of two heads of cabbage, pinching tomatoes, and an occasional tootsie. Since my face is fairly well known, this is frequently a source of embarrassment, but I can't help myself. I'm convinced that thrift, in my case, is an innate trait that springs from a debt-ridden childhood and can no more be overcome than old age (which I passed some years ago).

I am not alone in this. I have many prosperous friends who are also frugal in peculiar ways. I have a friend who uses a fresh handkerchief each day, but on retiring, before throwing the used one in the laundry hamper, he gives it one last stentorian blow. I questioned him about this one day and he said, 'I try to get as much mileage as I can out of each day's handkerchief, and I don't feel too bad when I catch a cold. That's when I really get my money's worth!'

I have another friend (you didn't imagine I had two, did you?), who earns about two hundred thousand dollars a year. He will take you to Romanoff's in a Rolls Royce and then park it two or three blocks away so that he won't have to tip the parking attendant. It isn't that he's stingy. He explains, 'If I go to an expensive restaurant and spend fifty or sixty dollars for dinner, I want the management to park my car gratis.'

I know another chap who is completely bald, and yet whenever he goes to a restaurant, even in the winter, he leaves his hat in the car. As a result, he frequently has a heavy cold, and about twice a year he comes down with pneumonia. But he says he doesn't care. 'I refuse to tip some hat check girl fifty cents just to hang my hat on a hook. I wouldn't mind so much if she kept the money, but she doesn't get a penny of it. Part of the swag is kept by the restaurant and the rest goes to some sinister combine in Chicago that controls these concessions.'

I give my wife a liberal allowance, but when we dine out I groan in despair when she suddenly discovers that she has no cigarettes. I then have to plank down a buck to some short-skirted babe for a pack of cigarettes that I can buy almost anywhere for two bits. Seventy-five cents shot! Almost the price of a Martini, which I desperately need after paying a dollar for a pack of cigarettes.

Jack Benny, in real life, is an extremely generous fellow, but his theatrical image is that of a parsimonious skinflint who would risk his life for a buck. People roar with laughter at his miserliness. They think it's terribly funny that he regards money as something that shouldn't be squandered. We'll see who laughs last!

Fred Allen, a great man (and, boy, could we use him today!), one summer rented a cottage in Maine for three hundred dollars for the season. Being an actor, and the landlord being from Maine, he was obliged to pay the rent in advance. Early in June Fred was offered two thousand dollars a week to write a short column every other day for one of the syndicates. This was long ago when two thousand dollars was still a lot of money, but Fred turned down the offer. I asked him why. 'I paid three hundred dollars for that cottage up in Maine,' he said, 'and if I accept this job I'll have to stay in New York. I'd be out the three hundred dollars.'

The syndicate then raised its offer to three thousand dollars a week. Again Fred turned it down. They then offered four thousand dollars and once more he refused.

'Why don't you forget about the three hundred dollars?' I asked. 'You could take one week's salary from the syndicate and own that cottage outright.'

But Allen, too, had curious notions about money. He was extremely generous but he couldn't stand waste. He was also extremely stubborn. 'I paid three hundred dollars to live in that cottage this summer,' he said, 'and that landlord is not going to get my money for nothing!'

I once played a season on the Orpheum Circuit with a very funny comedian named Doc Rockwell. He had his own way of saving money. The first week in Chicago, Doc bought six blue serge double-breasted suits for one hundred and fifty dollars, and if you're any good at mathematics you know this comes to twenty-five dollars apiece. He would wear each suit for about a month and then, when it was partially covered with spots and a few rips, he would throw it away. He had it all figured out. 'This way,' he explained, 'I don't have to pay for any cleaning and pressing and, besides, I'm always wearing a brand-new suit.'

Years ago, when playing the small time, most actors used to dine at the Automat. The food was wonderful and I'm sure it still is but, unfortunately, I can't eat there any more because of the autograph hunters. For years I've been telling my daughter, Melinda, what wonderful restaurants they are. I told her that all you had to do was get a lot of nickels from the cashier, drop them in various slots and, presto, you had a meal fit for a king (assuming there are any still around).

The last time I went to New York I took Melinda along. We were on our way to a very expensive restaurant when she asked me if we couldn't have lunch at the Automat. I said, 'No, you wouldn't like it. It's terribly crowded and the food isn't any good.'

'But Daddy,' she said, 'you told me just a few weeks ago that the food is as good as at any restaurant in New York.'

Well, she had me there. The pressure a child can put on a parent is beyond belief – unless you are a parent. So before I knew it I was standing in front of the cashier's cage at Horn and Hardart's Automat, changing enough nickels for two meals.

Melinda, far more excited than she would have been at '21' or the Pavillon, ran around dropping nickels into slots as though this was to be her last meal. I decided on a roast beef sandwich and carefully inserted ten nickels in the proper slot, but for some reason the little glass door didn't open. I then tapped gently on the window with a coin, but the door still didn't budge. I tried hammering on the door with my fist. Suddenly a stout woman came rushing out from behind the façade of glass windows and said, 'Are you the gent who's been thumpin' on my window?'

'I certainly am,' I answered.

'Well, don't y'know ya have to put in ten nickels t'get a fifty cent roast beef san'wich? Whatsamatter? You stupid 'r somethin'? Didn't ya go to school?'

By this time some of the other diners, overhearing the argument, began gathering around us and, to my dismay, recognized me. I tried to ignore them and again asked for my sandwich.

The female bruiser said, 'Let me tell ya a thing 'r two. We get guys like you every day. Ya think, just because this is a automatic rest'rant, y'can get away with somethin'!'

By this time a goodly crowd surrounded us. A bus boy broke through and spotted me. 'Hey,' he said, 'ain't you a big star on TV? What're ya arguin' with the poor dame for over a lousy nickel? Inna first place, what're ya eatin' in a dump like this for? If I had yer dough ya wouldn't catch me eatin' in no joint like this!'

I said, with considerable dignity, 'I came here because my daughter wanted to eat at the Automat.'

'Oh yeah?' he sneered. 'So where's yer daughter?'

'Over there some place,' I said. What I didn't know was that Melinda, not wishing to be embarrassed, had quietly sneaked out when the ruckus started and was waiting for me outside. I imagine she expected me to come out soon, on my head.

The argument with the bus boy and the female wrestler continued. And now, to make everything still sillier, people began asking for my autograph. A heavy-set woman behind me, determined to attract my attention, was jerking my coat-tails. Lucky for me she wasn't tugging at my trousers; otherwise I would soon have been standing there in my jockey shorts.

The floorwalker (or whoever he was, manager perhaps) came over and said, 'Mr Marx, I've always enjoyed your work, but why are you making such a scene over a nickel? You should be ashamed of yourself.'

'Why?' I asked indignantly. 'Just because I want my roast beef sandwich?'

'You know our machines don't lie,' he said. 'If you dropped ten nickels into the roast beef sandwich slot you would now be enjoying as fine a sandwich as you can get any place in New York.'

The woman from behind the glass windows chimed in, 'He only put in nine nickels and he knows y'need ten for a roast beef san'wich! Why don't he stick in another nickel an' get his lousy san'wich?'

The manager turned on her accusingly, 'Did I hear you call our sandwich a *lousy* sandwich?!'

'Oh no, sir, I didn't mean our san'wich was lousy,' she explained hurriedly. 'I only meant he was a lousy cheap-skate for not puttin' in the extra lousy nickel.'

Between the back-and-forth dialogue and the scribbling of autographs and worrying whether, by this time, Melinda had been picked up by white slavers and was now on a ship bound for Brazil, I was ready to beat a retreat.

'It's not the nickel, it's the principle of the thing,' I said. 'Just give me back my ten nickels and I'll dine in some bistro where I'm treated with the respect that a star is entitled to!'

The woman poured nine nickels into my chubby fist. I threw them up in the air and said, 'There! That'll show you that money means nothing to me!'

I then stalked out, picked up Melinda and went to the Colony, where we had a lovely lunch for $27.60. And I want to announce to the whole world that I will never set foot in the Automat again until they have the decency to send me the nickel they still owe me.

The Royal Me

☆★☆★☆★☆★☆★☆★☆★☆★☆★☆★☆★☆★☆★☆

DAME EDNA EVERAGE

'Push Darling, *push*! Push harder, *harder*!'

Princess Diana was expecting her first baby and I was talking to her.

'Push as hard as you can!' I exhorted her at the top of my voice. But it was no use. She was calling me from a public phone and her coin had stuck in the slot. To an ordinary member of the public she just looked like a heavily pregnant Princess Diana lookalike, hammering furiously at a defective British Telecom instrument on the fifth floor of Harrods from which she regularly gave me an incognito tinkle. I knew she'd phone again, probably from Buckingham Palace next time, since her confinement was drawing very near and I had promised to give her my famous stretch mark recipe (patent applied for).

Royalty aren't the only people calling me for advice, marriage counselling or just a friendly gossip. Winnie Mandela, Joan Collins, Mother Teresa, Fergie, Imelda Marcos, Raisa Gorbachev, Princess Michael of Kent, Pia Zadora, Margaret Thatcher, Madonna, Princess Susan of Albania, Fawn Hall, Dame Janet Baker and Barry Manilow are just a few of my regular callers who expect me to drop everything while they pour their hearts out. A couple on this list even call me long distance *collect*: no prizes for guessing who! But let's face it, Possums, it is a big compliment to me that these folk feel there is someone on the planet they can 'let it all hang out' with who won't go rushing into print. They know that whatever they say to me, however intimate, will never go any further; well, no further than the pages of this book which is only going to be read by a few million extremely discreet people.

Princess Diana had been shopping for her new bubba that day and had just wanted a little help with her shopping list and, I suspect, a little motherly advice as well. It only seems yesterday when my own waters broke but in the days and weeks leading up to that historic event I suffered the usual fears and anxieties especially in crowded places like department stores where I would have given *anything* for the phone number of a kind, caring and supportive Megastar. That was a few years ago and my adorable royal caller now has two lovely kiddies but at little private dinners at Kensington Palace whenever the subject of stretch marks comes up – as it does quite often – she always says proudly, 'I don't have any, *thanks* to Dame Edna.'

I wish I could persuade all the members of the Royal Family to drop my honorific when they are talking to me and just call me Edna. To one of them I once said, 'For heaven's sake, Liz, *please* try! I come from Australia where informality is the keynote.'

'I'll try, I promise I will!' exclaimed my gorgeous friend. 'But you have such an aura about you, it would seem disrespectful. To me you will always be a Dame.'

Compliments like that don't grow on trees, do they, Readers? And the little lady whose anonymity I am protecting certainly knows how to dish out the compliments. In fact she does so in a big way every New Year's Day.

For some years I had been unofficial Australian royalty – a bit of a paradox really considering I am as left-wing as they come. I know for a fact, however, that everyone has to have someone to look up to; it is a human need and folk get rather pinched, peaky and run-down without a glittering role model to put on a pedestal. The same goes for my fellow Australians, for no matter how emancipated, Americanized or republican they may pretend to be, statistics have proved that they still buy twice as many newspapers or magazines if there's a snap of me or the Queen on the cover. I'm sorry but they do.

I first met my British opposite number at one of those star-studded back-stage line-ups after a big glittering charity Gala. We stood in line as the Royal party headed by the Queen moved slowly down, chatting to each star, whilst a carefully vetted group of paparazzi took flash photos of the encounters. No prizes for guessing whose pickie made page one world-wide the next day. A lot of the stars seemed nervous. Little Leo Sayer on my right was almost shaking until I leant down and patted him gently on the head. Even suave David Frost was discreetly puffing a minty aerosol between his famous lips and probably blowing another hole in the ozone layer if he'd only known it.

The glittering party at last drew level with me and the theatre manager performed the introduction. Our eyes met, then our fingers as I prepared to curtsy. Did I imagine it or had *her* legs given a little bob? I wasn't the only one to notice since a slight gasp ran down the line of superstars and only then did I make my own graceful obeisance to my Sovereign. Dr Sidney Shardenfreude (whom I see for my children) has told me that people who are really going to hit it off in a big way with each other know from the first instant of eye contact, and we knew it then. Eye contact wasn't coming easy by the way, since the royal orbs were pretty well fixed on my tiara which is studded with a few *serious* stones. I keep it in a Swiss bank most of the time incidentally, and the one I sometimes wear in the street is fake (muggers, please note!).

Her little gloved hand was still in mine and I suddenly became aware that she was trying to push something into my palm. It felt like a small piece of paper. At that instant our eyes met once more and hers wore a look of pained entreaty that I will never forget. 'Please, Edna,' they seemed to conjure me. '*Please* keep my secret. Act normally.' Luckily I am a highly sensitive, acutely tuned organism used to acting normally, and my fingers closed around that secret scrap. Meanwhile cameras flashed and TV lenses winked around us but no one could have noticed that covert exchange between two intensely private people caught in the full glare of publicity. We chatted of course about how marvellous my performance had been but they were empty words compared to the urgent messages our hearts were sending forth.

As soon as the ceremony was over and the Royal party had left the theatre I rushed to my dressing room and locked the door, standing for a moment with my back to it, breathing deeply. Only then did I open my right hand and, sure enough, nestling in my silver lurex palm was a scrunched-up piece of paper. I opened it quickly and spread it on my dressing table. What I read caused my heart to stop for a moment. I read the single word 'Help' in a trembling urgent handwriting and beneath it was a London telephone number which for obvious reasons I will not divulge. I have an uncanny memory as readers of this autobiography will be aware, so I stared at that phone number, zapped it into my brain, popped the paper into my mouth and tried to swallow it. No easy task either as spies reading this book will have found out long ago. I was still chewing as Madge let me into my luxury penthouse high above Mayfair half an hour later. I packed her off to bed, flung myself on a sofa and picked up the phone.

It did not ring for long. 'Hello?' a small famous voice challenged the transmitter.

'It's – it's Dame Edna here. You asked . . . ?'

'Yes, oh yes. Thank heaven you've called. I knew you wouldn't give me away and I knew somehow you'd understand. It's just . . .'

She broke off and I wondered if I could hear tears. What terrible trouble had this poor lass found herself in that she should turn to me in her agony?

'Please, dear,' I said, the way I can, warmly, caringly: 'Tell Edna what's the matter? I am here for you. I always will be.'

'You won't think I'm silly?' she said with the artlessness of a girl, tears still glistening in her voice. But on her lips, I like to think, a flickering smile of trust.

'*Silly*?' I almost shrieked. 'Why *all* of us are silly sometimes,' I declared. 'Even I have been silly sometimes in my life and if I ever write my autobiography I will send you a copy, silly bits and all.'*

'Well,' she began a little shyly, 'have you got a good pavlova recipe?'

'*What*?' I ejaculated, almost forgetting who I was talking to.

'You know, a recipe for an Australian pavlova cake,' she continued, oblivious to my exclamation of surprise. 'The Australian Prime Minister and party are coming to supper next Saturday night and I want to give them one of your national specialities but our chefs have drawn a blank. I knew only you could help save the day.'

'Who's that, Edna?' came a voice from our bedroom door and I saw my old bridesmaid standing there in her faded Oxfam winceyette, a glass of NightNurse *frappé* in her right hand and the bedroom extension in the other.

'Put that *down*, you stupid woman!' I yelled. 'Aren't I entitled to a minute's privacy? And change your nightie. It makes you look like Orphan Annie.'

The small voice on the phone said, 'I'm sorry? My nightie? What's wrong with it?'

'Not you!' I bellowed back after Madge had reluctantly replaced her receiver, or so I thought. 'I was talking to my lady-in-waiting, Your Majesty,' I added in a much nicer tone as I tried to pull myself together. 'I'll copy it out of my recipe book in the morning,' I promised in a practical voice, 'and drop it by at your place on my way to Harrods on Saturday morning. Will there be anyone home?'

'Better still,' said my midnight supplicant, 'pop over in the afternoon. Run up a pavlova for me and join us for dinner! That's if you're free?'

I pretended to look in a diary.

'We are!' came a New Zealand voice from the next room and funnily enough, Readers, that was the only time in my life, before or since, when I have felt that I could commit murder.

*I have.

The Queen said, 'Naturally bring any staff you may require.'

'That won't be necessary, Ma'am,' I said very audibly. 'I hope I can run up a passion-fruit pav on my ownsome.'

After a few other pleasantries, expressions of gratitude and mutual esteem we rang off. After that I had a nice bath, rubbed a little precious 'under-the-counter' Wombat Spleen Jelly into my crow's feet ('the dried-up beds of old smiles', to use my mother's marvellous expression), slipped into my favourite Janet Reger and gave Madge Allsop the rough edge of my tongue.

I can't say I slept too well either after that, in fact I felt distinctly queasy and I think it was probably something I'd eaten, more than likely the Queen's telephone number.

The pav was a triumph but the dinner was awful. My countrymen all seemed well topped up and the womenfolk looked as though they might have overdone the pre-Palace Valium. I blushed for my homeland quite frankly. Considering how many refined and acceptable Australian menfolk there are, it has always puzzled me why they never find their way into Parliament. The Australian Governor General was there as well, a man who is supposed to be the Queen's representative and as rough a diamond as you could ever meet. He looked a bit like a tram conductor in a hired suit. Spookily psychic that I am, I found out later that he had once had a job with the Tramways Union!

I had arrived earlier that afternoon with a motorcycle escort provided by the Palace and I was shown straight up to the Royal kitchen where the chief chef was at my beck and call, stiffening egg whites, squeezing passion-fruit, whipping cream and sifting castor sugar. It wasn't long before my new friend popped her pretty little head through the kitchen door to shyly thank me and ask me if there was anything I needed. Because I was wearing the stunning frock (designed by my son Kenny) that I intended to wear for dinner I asked her if I might borrow one of her aprons to protect me from 'pavlova splashback'. Did I imagine it or did she go just a tiny bit blank when I made this simple request? She repeated the word 'apron?' a few times rather vaguely and my heart went out to her as I suddenly realized that she, who enjoyed all these wonderful amenities, had probably never rejoiced in the proud uniform of a normal housewife. On her next birthday I sent her a gorgeous 'Venomous Insects of Australia' Irish linen apron with matching tea-towels, handcrafted in North Korea, and a lovely pair of yellow Marigolds.

The meal was, of course, scrumptious but the Australian party couldn't have tasted it since they were too far gone and smoking throughout, even offering ciggies to the Queen who declined with the sweetness of a Saint. I suppose you have to allow for the 'awestruck factor'. After all, this poor little band of overdressed waifs had been plucked out of nowhere and plonked down in a red and gold room with a forty-foot ceiling, Old Masters on the wall, a Royal couple and *me*! Only when my pavlova was wheeled in did they seem to come to life and when the port was passed around it looked as though they might easily outstay their welcome and settle down for the night, droning on and on about the shows they had been to see and the shopping they had done in London at the Australian tax-payer's expense.

I was amazed how my regal hostess managed to listen with seeming interest to the slurred shorthand her guests were talking, particularly when our Prime Minister rambled on about how they had all been to see the Trooping of the Guard and had Her Majesty, by any chance, managed to catch it?

How would she get rid of them? I wondered. As if by magic the answer came. Rising from a beautiful gold chair, the Queen said rather firmly: 'Would any of you care for a cup of coffee *before you go*?' It worked like a charm. Soon the bedraggled little party, their chins still flecked with meringue and passion-fruit, were being poured into their coats by winking footmen, the charming Prince had retired and I was alone with my hostess.

'How can I thank you?' she said, squeezing my hand, her gaze lingering for a moment on the Everage Diamond which blazed on my finger.

'No thanks needed, Possum,' I said daringly, but with sincerity. 'You coped magnificently tonight,' I added. 'How do you do it?'

'All in a day's work, Dame Edna,' she said with a weary smile. 'But it would be nice if Australia had a female Prime Minister one day. A woman of intelligence, dignity, refinement and beauty who could do justice to that wonderful sub-continent.'

'Perhaps,' I said wistfully. 'But where could such a woman be found, Your Majesty?'

The Queen gave me an old-fashioned look and another of her radiant smiles. 'She may be closer than you think, Dame Edna. Tell me, where do you stay in London?'

'I used to live in suites in some of the big hotels,' I confessed, ' but now I have my own gorgeous penthouse in Mayfair as well as my homes in Montreux, Mustique, Malibu and Melbourne. Why do you ask?'

'I hope,' hesitated the Queen, 'you won't think me forward, but my husband and I would like you always to feel at home in Buckingham Palace.'

I gasped, but the Queen went on, 'It must be a nightmare being always in the public eye as you are, living in a goldfish bowl. My life is private compared with yours. We would just like you to feel free to come and go here at any time of the day or night when the press are driving you bananas. Here is a key.'

Speechless with gratitude I accepted the small gold object and clenched it in my hand, feeling the bevel with my fingers.

'Regard this as your bolthole,' she said, as I slipped into my humanely culled acrylic. 'You can have your own shelf in the fridge.'

We gave each other a little squash and I was off in my limo down the Mall, where the lights of London seemed to shine more brightly than ever before.

Would I tell Madge? I wondered. No way! It would be as good as sending a press release to the *Sunday People*. The golden key in my clutch bag was my secret – *our* secret, I thought, glancing over my shoulder through the rear window of the limo at the receding Palace.

So when people ask me, as they often do, if I have met Royalty I smile a certain smile: Have I met them? Do I know them? Leave it out, do me a favour, you've got to be joking!!

The Diary of a Nobody

☆★☆★☆★☆★☆★☆★☆★☆★☆★☆★☆★☆★☆★☆★☆★☆★☆

GEORGE AND WEEDON GROSSMITH

April 27. Kept a little later than usual at the office, and as I was hurrying along a man stopped me, saying: 'Hulloh! That's a face I know.' I replied politely: 'Very likely; lots of people know *me*, although I may not know them.' He replied: 'But you know *me* – Teddy Finsworth.' So it was. He was at the same school with me. I had not seen him for years and years. No wonder I did not know him! At school he was at least a head taller than I was; now I am at least a head taller than he is, and he has a thick beard, almost grey. He insisted on my having a glass of wine (a thing I never do), and told me he lived at Middlesboro', where he was Deputy Town Clerk, a position which was as high as the Town Clerk of London – in fact, higher. He added that he was staying for a few days in London, with his uncle, Mr Edgar Paul Finsworth (of Finsworth and Pultwell). He said he was sure his uncle would be only too pleased to see me, and he had a nice house, Watney Lodge, only a few minutes' walk from Muswell Hill Station. I gave him our address, and we parted.

In the evening, to my surprise, he called with a very nice letter from Mr Finsworth, saying if we (including Carrie) would dine with them tomorrow (Sunday), at two o'clock, he would be delighted. Carrie did not like to go; but Teddy Finsworth pressed us so much we consented. Carrie sent Sarah round to the butcher's and countermanded our half-leg of mutton, which we had ordered for tomorrow.

April 28, Sunday. We found Watney Lodge farther off than we anticipated, and only arrived as the clock struck two, both feeling hot and uncomfortable. To make matters worse, a large collie dog pounced forward to receive us. He barked loudly and jumped up at Carrie, covering her light skirt, which she was wearing for the first time, with mud. Teddy Finsworth came out and drove the dog off and apologized. We were shown into the drawing-room, which was beautifully decorated. It was full of knick-knacks, and some plates hung up on the wall. There were several little wooden milk-stools with paintings on them; also a white wooden banjo, painted by one of Mr Paul Finsworth's nieces – a cousin of Teddy's.

Mr Paul Finsworth seemed quite a distinguished-looking elderly gentleman, and was most gallant to Carrie. There were a great many water-colours hanging on the walls, mostly different views of India, which were very bright. Mr Finsworth said they were painted by 'Simpz', and added that he was no judge of pictures himself but had been informed on good authority that they were worth some hundreds of pounds, although he had only paid a few shillings apiece for them, frames included, at a sale in the neighbourhood.

There was also a large picture in a very handsome frame, done in coloured crayons. It looked like a religious subject. I was very much struck with the lace collar, it looked so real, but I unfortunately made the remark that there was something about the expression of the face that was not quite pleasing. It looked pinched. Mr Finsworth sorrowfully replied: 'Yes, the face was done after death – my wife's sister.'

I felt terribly awkward and bowed apologetically, and in a whisper said I hoped I had not hurt his feelings. We both stood looking at the picture for a few minutes in silence, when Mr Finsworth took out a handkerchief and said: 'She was sitting in our garden last summer,' and blew his nose violently. He seemed quite affected, so I turned to look at something else and stood in front of a portrait of a jolly-looking middle-aged gentleman, with a red face and straw hat. I said to Mr Finsworth: 'Who is this jovial-looking gentleman? Life doesn't seem to trouble him much.' Mr Finsworth said: 'No, it doesn't. *He is dead too* – my brother.'

I was absolutely horrified at my own awkwardness. Fortunately at this moment Carrie entered with Mrs Finsworth, who had taken her upstairs to take off her bonnet and brush her skirt. Teddy said: 'Short is late,' but at that moment the gentleman referred to arrived, and I was introduced to him by Teddy, who said: 'Do you know Mr Short?' I replied, smiling, that I had not that pleasure, but I hoped it would not be *long* before I knew Mr *Short*. He evidently did not see my little joke, although I repeated it twice with a little laugh. I suddenly remembered it was Sunday, and Mr Short was perhaps *very particular*.

In this I was mistaken, for he was not at all particular in several of his remarks after dinner. In fact I was so ashamed of one of his observations that I took the opportunity to say to Mrs Finsworth that I feared she found Mr Short occasionally a little embarrassing. To my surprise she said: 'Oh! he is privileged you know.' I did *not* know as a matter of fact, and so I bowed apologetically. I fail to see why Mr Short should be privileged.

Another thing that annoyed me at dinner was that the collie dog, which jumped up at Carrie, was allowed to remain under the dining-room table. It kept growling and snapping at my boots every time I moved my foot. Feeling nervous rather, I spoke to Mrs Finsworth about the animal, and she remarked: 'It is only his play.' She jumped up and let in a frightfully ugly-looking spaniel called Bibbs, which had been scratching at the door. This dog also seemed to take a fancy to my boots, and I discovered afterwards that it had licked off every bit of blacking from them. I was positively ashamed of being seen in them. Mrs Finsworth, who, I must say, is not much of a Job's comforter, said: 'Oh! we are used to Bibbs doing that to our visitors.'

Mr Finsworth had up some fine port, although I question whether it is a good thing to take on the top of beer. It made me feel a little sleepy, while it had the effect of inducing Mr Short to become 'privileged' to rather an alarming extent. It being cold even for April, there was a fire in the drawing-room; we sat around in easy chairs, and Teddy and I waxed rather eloquent over the old school days, which had the effect of sending all the others to sleep. I was delighted, as far as Mr Short was concerned, that it *did* have that effect on him.

We stayed till four, and the walk home was remarkable only for the fact that several fools giggled at the unpolished state of my boots. Polished them myself when I got home. Went to church in the evening, and could scarcely keep awake. I will not take port on top of beer again.

April 29. I am getting quite accustomed to being snubbed by Lupin, and I do not mind being sat upon by Carrie, because I think she has a certain amount of right to do so; but I do think it hard to be at once snubbed by wife, son, and both my guests.

Gowing and Cummings had dropped in during the evening, and I suddenly remembered an extraordinary dream I had a few nights ago, and I thought I would tell them about it. I dreamt I saw some huge blocks of ice in a shop with a bright glare behind them. I walked into the shop and the heat was overpowering. I found that the blocks of ice were on fire. The whole thing was so real and yet so supernatural I woke up in a cold perspiration. Lupin, in a most contemptuous manner, said: 'What utter rot!'

Before I could reply, Gowing said there was nothing so completely uninteresting as other people's dreams.

I appealed to Cummings, but he said he was bound to agree with the others, and my dream was especially nonsensical. I said: 'It seemed so real to me.' Gowing replied: 'Yes, to *you*, perhaps, but not to *us*.' Whereupon they all roared.

Carrie, who had hitherto been quiet, said: 'He tells me his stupid dreams every morning nearly.' I replied: 'Very well, dear, I promise you I will never tell you or anyone else another dream of mine the longest day I live.' Lupin said: 'Hear! hear!' and helped himself to another glass of beer. The subject was fortunately changed, and Cummings read a most interesting article on the superiority of the bicycle to the horse.

May 10. Received a letter from Mr Franching, of Peckham, asking us to dine with him tonight, at seven o'clock, to meet Mr Hardfur Huttle, a very clever writer for the American papers. Franching apologized for the short notice; but said he had at the last moment been disappointed of two of his guests and regarded us as old friends who would not mind filling up the gap. Carrie rather demurred at the invitation; but I explained to her that Franching was very well off and influential, and we could not afford to offend him. 'And we are sure to get a good dinner and a good glass of champagne.' 'Which never agrees with you!' Carrie replied sharply. I regarded Carrie's observation as unsaid. Mr Franching asked us to wire a reply. As he had said nothing about dress in the letter, I wired back: 'With pleasure. Is it full dress?' and by leaving out our name, just got the message within the sixpence.

Got back early to give time to dress, which we received a telegram instructing us to do. I wanted Carrie to meet me at Franching's house; but she would not do so, so I had to go home to fetch her. What a long journey it is from Holloway to Peckham! Why do people live such a long way off? Having to change 'buses, I allowed plenty of time – in fact, too much; for we arrived at twenty minutes to seven, and Franching, so the servant said, had only just gone up to dress. However, he was down as the clock struck seven; he must have dressed very quickly.

I must say it was quite a distinguished party, and although we did not know anybody personally, they all seemed to be quite swells. Franching had got a professional waiter, and evidently spared no expense. There were flowers on the table round some fairy-lamps, and the effect, I must say, was exquisite. The wine was good and there was plenty of champagne, concerning which Franching said he, himself, never wished to taste better. We were ten in number, and a *menu* card to each. One lady said she always preserved the *menu* and got the guests to write their names on the back.

We all of us followed her example, except Mr Huttle, who was of course the important guest.

The dinner-party consisted of Mr Franching, Mr Hardfur Huttle, Mr and Mrs Samuel Hillbutter, Mrs Field, Mr and Mrs Purdick, Mr Pratt, Mr R. Kent, and, last, but not least, Mr and Mrs Charles Pooter. Franching said he was sorry he had no lady for me to take in to dinner. I replied that I preferred it, which I afterwards thought was a very uncomplimentary observation to make.

I sat next to Mrs Field at dinner. She seemed a well-informed lady, but was very deaf. It did not much matter, for Mr Hardfur Huttle did all the talking. He is a marvellously intellectual man and says things which from other people would seem quite alarming. How I wish I could remember even a quarter of his brilliant conversation. I made a few little reminding notes on the *menu* card.

One observation struck me as being absolutely powerful – though not to my way of thinking of course. Mrs Purdick happened to say: 'You are certainly unorthodox, Mr Huttle.' Mr Huttle, with a peculiar expression (I can see it now) said in a slow, rich voice: 'Mrs Purdick, "orthodox" is a grandiloquent word implying sticking-in-the-mud. If Columbus and Stephenson had been orthodox there would neither have been the discovery of America nor the steam-engine.' There was quite a silence. It appeared to me that such teaching was absolutely dangerous, and yet I felt – in fact we must all have felt – there was no answer to the argument. A little later on Mrs Purdick, who is Franching's sister and also acted as hostess, rose from the table, and Mr Huttle said: 'Why, ladies, do you deprive us of your company so soon? Why not wait while we have our cigars?'

The effect was electrical. The ladies (including Carrie) were in no way inclined to be deprived of Mr Huttle's fascinating society, and immediately resumed their seats, amid much laughter and a little chaff. Mr Huttle said: 'Well, that's a real good sign; you shall not be insulted by being called orthodox any longer.' Mrs Purdick, who seemed to be a bright and rather sharp woman, said: 'Mr Huttle, we will meet you halfway – that is, till you get halfway through your cigar. That, at all events, will be the happy medium.'

I shall never forget the effect the words, 'happy medium', had upon him. He was brilliant and most daring in his interpretation of the words.

He positively alarmed me. He said something like the following: 'Happy medium, indeed. Do you know "happy medium" are two words which mean "miserable mediocrity"? I say, go first class or third; marry a duchess or her kitchen-maid. The happy medium means respectability, and respectability means insipidness. Does it not, Mr Pooter?'

I was so taken aback by being personally appealed to, that I could only bow apologetically, and say I feared I was not competent to offer an opinion. Carrie was about to say something; but she was interrupted, for which I was rather pleased, for she is not clever at argument, and one has to be extra clever to discuss a subject with a man like Mr Huttle.

He continued, with an amazing eloquence that made his unwelcome opinions positively convincing: 'The happy medium is nothing more or less than a vulgar half-measure. A man who loves champagne and, finding a pint too little, fears to face a whole bottle and has recourse to an imperial pint, will never build a Brooklyn Bridge or an Eiffel Tower. No, he is half-hearted, he is a half-measure – respectable – in fact, a happy medium, and will spend the rest of his days in a suburban villa with a stucco-column portico, resembling a four-post bedstead.'

We all laughed.

'That sort of thing,' continued Mr Huttle, 'belongs to a soft man, with a soft beard, with a soft head, with a made tie that hooks on.'

This seemed rather personal, and twice I caught myself looking in the glass of the chiffonier; for *I* had on a tie that hooked on – and why not? If these remarks were not personal they were rather careless, and so were some of his subsequent observations, which must have made both Mr Franching and his guests rather uncomfortable. I don't think Mr Huttle meant to be personal, for he added: 'We don't know that class here in this country; but we do in America, and I've no use for them.'

Franching several times suggested that the wine should be passed round the table, which Mr Huttle did not heed; but continued as if he were giving a lecture:

'What we want in America is your homes. We live on wheels. Your simple, quiet life and home, Mr Franching, are charming. No display, no pretension! You make no difference in your dinner, I dare say, when you sit down by yourself and when you invite us. You have your own personal attendant – no hired waiter to breathe on the back of your head.'

I saw Franching palpably wince at this.

Mr Huttle continued: 'Just a small dinner with a few good things, such as you have this evening. You don't insult your guests by sending to the grocer for champagne at six shillings a bottle.'

I could not help thinking of 'Jackson Frères' at three-and-six!

'In fact,' said Mr Huttle, 'a man is little less than a murderer who does. That is the province of the milksop, who wastes his evening at home playing dominoes with his wife. I've heard of these people. We don't want them at this table. Our party is well selected. We've no use for deaf old women, who cannot follow intellectual conversation.'

All our eyes were turned to Mrs Field, who fortunately, being deaf, did not hear his remarks; but continued smiling approval.

'We have no representative at Mr Franching's table,' said Mr Huttle, 'of the unenlightened frivolous matron, who goes to a second-class dance at Bayswater and fancies she is in Society. Society does not know her; it has no use for her.'

Mr Huttle paused for a moment, and the opportunity was afforded for the ladies to rise. I asked Mr Franching quietly to excuse me, as I did not wish to miss the last train, which we very nearly did, by-the-by, through Carrie having mislaid the little cloth cricket-cap which she wears when we go out.

It was very late when Carrie and I got home; but on entering the sitting-room I said: 'Carrie, what do you think of Mr Hardfur Huttle?' She simply answered: 'How like Lupin!' The same idea occurred to me in the train. The comparison kept me awake half the night. Mr Huttle was, of course, an older and more influential man; but he *was* like Lupin, and it made me think how dangerous Lupin would be if he were older and more influential. I feel proud to think Lupin *does* resemble Mr Huttle in some ways. Lupin, like Mr Huttle, has original and sometimes wonderful ideas; but it is those ideas that are so dangerous. They make men extremely rich or extremely poor. They make or break men. I always feel people are happier who live a simple unsophisticated life. I believe *I* am happy because I am not ambitious. Somehow I feel that Lupin, since he has been with Mr Perkupp, has become content to settle down and follow the footsteps of his father. This is a comfort.

Trefusis and Rosina

☆★☆★☆★☆★☆★☆★☆★☆★☆★☆★☆★☆★☆★☆★☆★☆

STEPHEN FRY

In which Donald Trefusis and Rosina, Lady Madding, recall a night of love that never was.

Donald Trefusis first:

If I were asked to remember one evening above any others it would be that evening in June when, just down from Cambridge, I attended one of Jaquinda Marriott's extraordinary *salons* in Kerdiston Square.

Jaquinda, who had the most fascinating ears in Europe, was something of a mystery. Married to Archie Marriott, the sportsman and Shadow Chancellor of Oxford University, she was said to come originally from the Hungarian royal family, although all of us suspected her of more humble origins. It is certainly true that the birth records of one Mabel Blifford were destroyed in a fire in 1924 just six months before Jaquinda appeared on the scene. But whatever her provenance there was no doubting the perfection of those ears and the splendour of those *salons*. She collected people of talent rather as some people collect children from school – every day. Pianists, painters, poets, statesmen, novelists, princesses, even oboists were gathered together under those lovely, pendulous lobes and bidden to attend her *levées* and talk and play and smoke.

The *soirée* to which I refer was her second of the Season and I arrived late owing to an argument with a cabbie. He had advanced the claims of Baron Corvo as a novelist over those of Capt W. E. Johns and this I could not allow. When at last I extricated myself the party was in full swing. Ivor Novello and Cecil Beaton were wrapped in deep yellow *crêpe de chine* in the hallway, reciting passages from *The Old Curiosity Shop* in Danish, a fashionable pastime amongst the younger dandy set at the time. Minty Havercuck, the Duke of Montreech's young bride, in a devastating flounce of Berlin silk, talked animatedly to Malcolm Lowry and T. C. Worsley, whose dancing seemed in its heat and frenzy to stand as a kinetic symbol of our mad decade, as it rushed headlong towards destruction in perfect 5:8 time.

But all these sights receded into background mist for me as I beheld a young girl whom I had not seen for four years. Rosina Bantwigg, the younger and by far the second most lovely of the celebrated Bantwigg twins. She stood, her hands behind her back, her head cocked like an inquisitive librarian, listening to John Gielgud teach Sacheverell Sitwell how to time a joke. Oblivious to everything else, the ragtime music, the Prime Minister's feeble impression of Vesta Victoria, Unity Mitford's moustache, Cardinal Halloran's swimming trunks, I gazed on this enchanting creature hungrily. She turned for a moment and saw me. A bright smile lit up her face as she approached. 'Why Donald,' she said, 'how perfectly delightful.' The voice, the image, the smile are fixed now in my mind like stars in the sky. They pilot me through life, they are my one fixed point, the paradigm to which all else in my universe must strive. At that point, I rather injudiciously jerked my head back, shut my eyes and vomited all over her. The heat, the tallow, the hemp, I don't know what it was. Without stopping to look back I hurried from that room and out of that life for ever. She married Tom Madding of course. Never saw her again.

Rosina, Lady Madding, remembers the same evening:

Because of my connection with the Kirkmichael family – my grandmother, the Marchioness Gloweravon, was born the Lady Vyella Kirkmichael – I was afforded from an early age a glimpse of English drawing-room and country house society, before the Second War drew a thick black-out blind across that world and extinguished its brilliance for ever. It was that privileged *entrée* that so positively endorsed my already strong feelings of adolescent crypto-syndicalist anarcho-Marxist neo-Buddhist Presbyterianism. A mordantly cynical young hound I might have been in the 1930s, but even I, in my gauche rejection of all that my family stood for, could not fail but be captivated by the beauty, the charm and the effulgence of those relics of the century's golden Edwardian summer, whose brightness and warmth shone all the more strongly through the sombre gloom of a depressed decade.

Of course, my favourite parties were those given by Jaquinda Marriott in her London residence in, I think, Kerdiston Square. She called them *salons*, they weren't of course. No hair-dryers.

I remember one such evening in the May or June of 1932. Everyone had to come dressed as a paradox. Bertie Russell came as the group of groups which is not contained within that group: I came as Achilles, with my sister Castella as the tortoise. I felt most sorry for G. K. Chesterton who came as the answer to the question 'Is this a question?' and was ignored for the whole evening. It was a lovely summer's night, I was nineteen, the world was at my feet.

But every Eden contains a viper and the canker in the apple of this evening took the shape of the foul Brandelia Cawston who dedicated herself to spoiling my evening. She mocked me, trod deliberately on the train of my thought, dropped ash in my glass and yawned whenever I spoke. She had never liked me and she was doing her best to provoke me into vulgarity. And then, while I was listening to Osbert Sitwell teach Laurence Olivier how to do a German accent, I spotted young Donald Trefusis across the room. My heart missed a beat; here was the now tall and comely youth whom I had hero-worshipped to abstraction when I was still in pig-tails and sheep's ears. Brandelia Cawston spitefully pinched my arm. A glance at Donald told me that he had seen this and taken in the whole situation. I excused myself from Olivier and Sitwell and, followed by the odious Cawston girl, approached Donald. He jerked his head back and, reading his intentions perfectly, I stepped smartly to one side to allow him to puke all over the wretched Brandelia. Never was I more delighted. I had not seen anyone look to such disadvantage in society since Edgar Wallace's toupée caught fire in Cap Ferrat in 1924. I turned to thank my bold rescuer, but he had vanished, leaving not a wrack behind. I never saw him again. I think of the dear man always, wonder what became of him. Life can be so cruel. Let me wrestle now.

Green Forms

☆★☆★☆★☆★☆★☆★☆★☆★☆★☆★☆★☆★☆

ALAN BENNETT

An office. Plants on the window ledge and postcards on the wall imply that though this is a place of work that is not the be-all and end-all. So the office is cosy if a little run-down: in one of the interior windows a pane of glass is broken; one lamp wants a shade, another a bulb; the Venetian blind lacks several slats and the rubber plant is plainly on its last legs. These dilapidations are precise and will turn out to be important.

In this office are three desks, one occupied by DOREEN, *a married lady in her thirties, another by* DORIS, *an unmarried lady in her forties; the third is empty and plainly unused.*

There are two doors, one to the corridor and the other to a passage at the far end of which is an unseen toilet and washbasin. The desks are furnished with the usual office clutter and there is an In/Out tray by the corridor door for incoming/outgoing mail. Shelves are lined with buff folders containing papers, some so fat they are tied up with string. Other folders are piled on chairs, in dusty brown paper parcels on the tops of tin office cupboards and some have accumulated on the floor round the desks. There is a mass of miscellaneous information here which a computer would put paid to in five minutes. However there is no computer, just DORIS, *who is reading the newspaper and* DOREEN, *who is contemplating her desk.*

DOREEN Are green forms still going through Mrs Henstridge?
(*Pause*)
DORIS Newcastle.
DOREEN Newcastle?
DORIS Newcastle.
DOREEN You don't mean Manchester, Fordyce Road?

DORIS No. I mean Newcastle, Triad House.

DOREEN Then where's Mrs Henstridge? (*Pause*) She was green forms for as long as I can remember. And now you say it's Newcastle. (*Pause*) *Newcastle*?

DORIS Staff appointments and changes in personnel: Newcastle.

(*The green form is inside an inter-office envelope. One look inside the envelope tells* DOREEN *the form is green and therefore not their pigeon. If she does take the form out of the envelope she should not read it.*)

DOREEN Newcastle. Not Mrs Henstridge. Thin-faced woman. Blondeish. She had a son that wasn't right. Lived in Whingate.

DORIS I don't know where people live.

DOREEN Well where's she gone and got to if she's not doing green forms?

DORIS Search me.

DOREEN I can remember when it used to be Southport.

DORIS It isn't Southport.

DOREEN I'm not saying it is Southport. Southport is being wound down.

DORIS Up.

DOREEN Up what?

DORIS Wound up.

DOREEN Wound down. Wound up. Phrased out anyway. I hope she hasn't been made . . . you know . . .

DORIS What?

DOREEN Well . . . redundant. I wouldn't like to think she's been made redundant; she was very nicely spoken.

DORIS I haven't had the pleasure.

DOREEN Mrs Henstridge? Oh yes. You'll have gone up in the lift with her many a time. Smartish, oldish woman. Check costume. Brown swagger coat.

(*Pause*)

Fancy them phrasing out Southport. I never thought they'd phrase Southport out.

(*Pause*)

DORIS Phasing, not phrasing.

DOREEN Come again?

DORIS Phasing. The phrase is phase. Not phrase.

DOREEN What did I say?

DORIS Phrasing.

DOREEN Oh. Well. If you'd come up to me ten years ago and said 'They're going to phase out Southport' I'd have laughed in your face.

DORIS You wouldn't.

DOREEN I would.

DORIS You wouldn't. If someone had come up to you ten years ago and said 'They're phasing out Southport', you wouldn't have known what they were talking about: you didn't work here then.

(*Pause*)

DOREEN How's Mother?

DORIS Naught clever.

DOREEN No. I didn't think so, somehow.

DORIS Anyway, why single out Southport? I ran into Mr Butterfield in Planning and he says a question-mark definitely hangs over Ipswich.

DOREEN Ipswich! That's only been going five years.

DORIS Four. She was on the commode half the night again.

DOREEN Poor lamb.

DORIS I think she must have eaten something. You can't turn your back. Last time it was the vicar. I just caught him doling her out the Milk Tray, else that would have been another three o'clock in the morning do. She's on a knife edge. People don't realize. One coffee cream and it's three months devoted nursing down the drain. I'm trying to build her up.

DOREEN What I'm wondering is . . . Where will the axe fall next?

DORIS Axe? What axe? This isn't an axe. These are scheduled cutbacks. Selective redeployment as set out in the '78 report. Axe! I know one thing. It won't fall on yours truly.

DOREEN Why not?

DORIS Because I'm Grade 3, that's why.

DOREEN Well I'm substantively Grade 3. Technically I'm Grade 4 but I'm holding down a Grade 3 job. If Central hadn't gone and frozen gradings I'd have been made up months since. Wouldn't I?

DORIS They won't unfreeze gradings while differentials are depressed. Even in this cock-eyed group.

DOREEN No. I know.

DORIS I don't think people *are* out of work anyway. I was reading in the paper yesterday a firm in Warrington is sending £50,000 of seersucker slipovers to Finland. Does that sound like out of work?

DOREEN I can't see myself in seersucker somehow. Even in Finland. Anyway I'm not going to worry: I've got Clifford.

DORIS Oh, Clifford.

DOREEN That's the thing about marriage, there's always the two of you.

DORIS There's two of Mother and me.

DOREEN We've talked it over and Cliff says that in the event of a real downturn in the economic climate he could fall back on the smallholding and me do my home hairdressing. People are always going to want their hair done, inflation or no inflation, and there's always a demand for rhubarb.

DORIS Yes. Well. I hope it keeps fine for you.

DOREEN 'Which twin has the Toni?'. Remember? It's stood me in good stead has that. You don't catch me in a salon. Only you think it's Newcastle? This green form.

DORIS Newcastle.

DOREEN (*As she addresses it and to herself*) Not . . . Mrs . . . Henstridge. Off you go to Newcastle. (*She takes it to the Out tray by the door.*) We are getting on this morning. Proper little beavers. Oh, the *Bulletin's* come. (*It is in the tray.*) You didn't tell me the *Bulletin* had come. (*Reading from the* Bulletin.) 'It's goodbye to Leeds, Cardigan Road. Smiles and sadness at simple ceremony.' Fancy shutting down Cardigan Road. That would have been unthinkable five years ago. It has its own canteen.

DORIS What am I talking about? (*She goes over to the Out tray and takes out the envelope with the green form.*) Doris Rutter, you want your head examining. Newcastle?

DOREEN Oh, little Brenda Horsfall's dead. 'Death will leave gap at Goole.' You remember Brenda?

DORIS Doreen.

DOREEN You called.

DORIS Smack me.

(DOREEN *smacks her outstretched hand without looking up from the* Bulletin)

This isn't Newcastle.

DOREEN I never thought it was. I said all along it was Mrs Henstridge.

DORIS It's not, though. That's what confused me, you introducing her. Mrs Henstridge has got nothing to do with it.

DOREEN Better smack me then.

(DOREEN *gets smacked too.*)

DORIS Under the new procedure this belongs on the second floor. It has to go through Staff and Appointments.

DOREEN Oh, nice Mr Titmuss.

DORIS After that it goes to Newcastle. Hearken to the book of words. (DORIS *reads from a procedural manual.*) 'Selection and Appointments, North Western Area. Newcastle, Triad House. PO Box 230. Local and District Documentation:' (i.e. us) 'all communications on a district level to be routed through Area Staff and Selection with contingency copies to Records and relevant departments concerned.' We're not a relevant department concerned. Somebody on the second floor is living in the past. Docket it 'misrouted' and bung it straight back to Staff Selection.

DOREEN Mr Titmuss.

DORIS The very same. No, let me. I want to append a note.

DOREEN (*Still glued to the* Bulletin) 'Thirty-five years at Bristol, Hotwells Road: veteran Reg. punches his last clock.'

DORIS (*Typing*) 'Dear Stanley, don't I have troubles enough? What goes on down there on the second floor, or has your triumph in the badminton semi-finals gone to your head? Definitely your baby. Hard cheddar, Doris.' (*She staples it to the green form and puts it in the Out tray by the door.*) When were these pink forms due back in Personnel?

DOREEN Last Monday.

DORIS I suppose I ought to look through them. Though I don't see why we should break our backs for Mr Cunliffe. What have Personnel ever done for us? Except make our lives a misery.

DOREEN (*Reading from the* Bulletin) 'Say Jack and Nanette. Any kindred spirit passing through Rugeley, Staffs., and wanting a natter about the old prehistoric days at Bebington Road, remember, folks, coffee time is from 9 a.m. to 11 p.m.' People are nice.

DORIS Oh, Blood and Sand!

DOREEN Language.

DORIS That puts paid to Mr Cunliffe. No pink forms today. (*She holds up some forms.*) One PS104. Two PS104s. Three PS104s.

DOREEN I don't believe it. What do they think we are?

DORIS That's three hours' solid work. Three PS104s. I think a cigarette is called for.

(*The telephone rings.* DOREEN *answers it.*)

DOREEN 3507 Precepts and Invoices, Mrs Bidmead speaking. One moment, Mr Cunliffe. I'll see if she's in.

(DORIS *shakes her head.*)

She appears to have slipped out. Can I be of any assistance? Well if we have any pink forms, and at this moment in time I'm not sure that we have, one thing I do know: we are not sitting on them. At a guess I should say they're somewhere in the pipeline.

(*Putting her hand over the receiver.*) He's talking about shortfall.

DORIS He wasn't talking about shortfall when Mr Parry had shingles.

DOREEN You weren't talking about shortfall when Mr Parry had shingles. I seem to remember some of us working round the clock. (*Hand over the receiver.*) What does he tell the computer?

DORIS That's his problem. He's been to Newport Pagnell.

DOREEN Didn't they teach you that at Newport Pagnell? (*Hand over receiver.*) He says there's going to be an alteration. We'll be laughing on the other side of our faces. We won't know what's hit us. (*Shaken*) He's put the phone down. Doris.

DORIS What?

DOREEN What does he mean?

DORIS It means he wants these pink forms. I was going to do them but I'm not now. People will just have to learn to be polite. Personnel. Let them wait. I can find something else to do. These 104s. No. I can't face them. If only we didn't have to bother with these silly, faffing forms we could get on with some real work.

(*She picks up the* Bulletin *which* DOREEN *has discarded.*)

DOREEN Has it gone cold? It feels to me to have gone right cold.

DORIS Something about Newport Pagnell here. 'Newport Pagnell comes of age. Smiling graduates of the twenty-first computer course at Roker Park gather round C.I.S.S.I.E. (Computer Instructor for Senior Staffs In Electronics).' Cissie! (*She reads the item scornfully.*) 'Cissie is now a rather battered old lady and is soon to be replaced by a more sophisticated model. By the time you read this the old girl will have done her last print-out. Sorry, Cis, but it happens to us all. Ed.'

DOREEN I don't know why you don't go on a course or two.

DORIS And where am I supposed to put Mother in the meantime?

DOREEN Send her to that place at Bispham.

DORIS I don't want to go on a course. You just want me out of the way.

DOREEN It would improve your prospects.

DORIS I don't want prospects. Prospects is what I don't want. Prospects means you get woken up in the middle of the night and asked to fly with Mr Swithinbank to Saudi Arabia. Why? Because you've got prospects and you've been on the Far East course. Though when you come in on a morning and find three PS104s on your desk maybe it's preferable.

DOREEN What?

DORIS Saudi Arabia. PS104, 104, 104. Office stinking precept forms. Who bothers with precept forms these days?

DOREEN I hope she's not dead.

DORIS Who?

DOREEN Mrs Henstridge. I don't think she is. I seem to remember something about the Wirral.

DORIS She's probably been sacked. What grade was she? Wasn't she your grade?

DOREEN I don't know. Remind me to get Clifford some chops. He loves chops.

DORIS When we say redundancy we mean you, Mrs Henstridge.

DOREEN Tina's not on heat again, is she?

DORIS No. Why?

DOREEN You just seem a bit bitter today somehow.

DORIS You'd be bitter if you'd got a shovelful of 104s on your desk. One for a lampshade. One, would you believe it, for an electric light bulb. And the other. (*She looks for it.*) Where is it? . . . Why don't they get stuff direct from Stores like everybody else. Precepting for individual items. A gross of light bulbs, yes. That's worth a 104. But *one.* It's procedurally correct, but it's insanity. If everybody started putting in a 104 whenever they wanted a light bulb we should be swamped. One of them is for a washbasin plug. When I can find it. *A washbasin* plug! Then people say you're looking older!

DOREEN Listen. Tell me again. Mother. Which of her hips is the plastic one?

DORIS It depends which way you look at her. Left if you're looking at her. Right if she's looking at you. Why?

DOREEN It's just that Clifford's sister-in-law's had one fitted and I thought they might have a bit of something in common.

DORIS Why? Which side is hers?

DOREEN I don't know. I shall have to ask. Anyway, who says you're looking older?

DORIS I do. Where is it?

DOREEN What?

DORIS This other 104.

DOREEN What do you want it for?

DORIS I don't want it. I just want to know where it is for when I do want it.

DOREEN I wish I had your system.

DORIS All this rigmarole. They cost 5p to buy. And just think what our time's costing.

DOREEN We could apply for a washbasin plug if we wanted. We've lost ours.

DORIS We haven't lost it. It was pinched.

DOREEN It disappeared.

DORIS Nicked. By Personnel.

DOREEN Are you sure?

DORIS Positive. What sort of a mentality is it pinches a plug from a washbasin? Several of them have degrees.

DOREEN How do you know it was Personnel?

DORIS I saw it.

DOREEN Saw what?

DORIS I saw our plug.

DOREEN Where?

DORIS In the toilet in Personnel.

DOREEN On the fourth floor? What were you doing there?

DORIS Looking for our plug.

DOREEN How do you know it was ours?

DORIS Because I recognized it.

DOREEN They're standard issue.

DORIS Listen. When it disappeared last time it was the third time in six months, so I thought 'Right, Doris. We'll settle these buggers.' So I got a new one and cut a little nick in it. Then a fortnight later it went again. Nicked.

DOREEN You mean the one you'd nicked?

DORIS I didn't nick it. I put a nick in it. The one I'd put a nick in was nicked. Right?

DOREEN I see.

DORIS Well, when they had everybody down in the canteen for the efficiency drive, I took the opportunity to do a little fact-finding survey of the departmental toilets.

DOREEN Doris!

DORIS And guess where Doris found it? Personnel.

DOREEN Never.

DORIS Positive. Little nick in it. It must have been. Nobody else in their right mind is going to put a nick in their washbasin plug, are they?

DOREEN So why didn't you confront them with it? Lay it before Mr Skidmore.

DORIS Do you remember Miss Batty of Costing?

DOREEN Shy woman, a bit on the grey side. Wore a little blue coatee.

DORIS Well she'd keep missing their toilet seat: she'd go down to Stores to put in for a replacement, it'd last about a fortnight then it would get pinched. She'd put in for another. Same thing. It got so that she daren't go into Stores.

DOREEN I can imagine. She was a very refined woman.

DORIS Eventually when she got to her sixth replacement Miss Batty got a red hot poker and burnt her name on the underside. Unfortunately they had somebody down from the sixth floor to do with industrial psychology. He was in Costing talking about incentives and said could he use the toilet? Well, I suppose, being from the sixth floor he lifted the seat and the upshot was Miss Batty got sent on three months' unpaid leave and lost her grading. Hypertension. She now looks after her brother in Rhyl.

DOREEN Tragic.

DORIS So don't ask me why I didn't take it up with Mr Skidmore. Only I know. And Personnel know I know.

DOREEN Yes. We still haven't got a washbasin plug, though, have we?

DORIS No problem. When I want to fill the basin, like when I do my foot, I use one of the issue paperweights. What do you want a plug for?

DOREEN Same reason you want a rubber plant.

DORIS What rubber plant?

DOREEN I've got one now. A PS104. For a rubber plant.

DORIS A PS104 for a rubber plant. Who puts in a PS104 for a rubber plant?) *Pause, as* DORIS *compares documents.*) The same person who puts in a PS104 for a washbasin plug. What's the personnel number on yours?

DOREEN RB/57/212/X.

DORIS (*Reading out another document*) RB/57/212/X.

DOREEN (*Reading out another document*) RB/57/212/X.

DORIS (*Reading out another document*) RB/57/212/X.

DOREEN Doris.

DORIS Doreen?

DOREEN They're all from the same person. (*Pause*) Don't you feel chilly?

DORIS (*Slowly*) Somebody's going mad. . . .

Hunting with the Hoorays

☆★☆

JILLY COOPER

In my youth, hunt balls were held in vast country houses and were very, very wild. By midnight, the barrage of bread rolls was only exceeded by the squadrons of moths thundering out of the brocade as ancient four-posters heaved with occupants.

It was with excitement but some trepidation therefore that we accepted an invitation to the Cotswold Hunt Ball. Needing a dress, I borrowed my daughter's black strapless. A mild fit of sulks, because my husband said I looked like a badly wrapped Christmas cracker, gave me the excuse to sit in the back. The dress would never have got under a seat belt anyway; when my brother took his wife and daughters to a hunt ball in Shropshire, he had to borrow a horse box to accommodate the crinolines.

We kicked off with champagne at the house of the Joint Master, Tim Unwin. Those making feeble attempts to pace themselves drank Buck's Fizz. A hunting blade with a red Pentel was marking the list of forty people in the Unwin's party: 'Putting asterisks beside all the worst gropers,' he said. He had to guard his wife, he explained, pointing to an exquisite blonde. 'She's Polish, I'm Welsh. It makes for a wonderfully volatile marriage. We throw telephones at one another.'

Another beautiful blonde, Princess Michael's lady-in-waiting, floated across the room.

'I'm official lech-in-waiting tonight,' said my husband, pursuing her briskly.

The men looked even more glamorous than the women, gaudy peacocks in their different tailcoats, red with green collars for the Cotswold, red with maroon for the VWH (Vale of the White Horse), dark blue with buff for the Beaufort. Permission to wear the hunt coat – or one's button, as it is called – is given by the Master, like getting one's colours.

Soon they were capping each other's tales of earlier hunt balls: erotic scufflings in the dungeons at Berkeley Castle, Masters riding their horses round the ballroom followed by hounds. Our host remembered dancing most of one evening with a lampstand. 'Suddenly I noticed the then Master was solemnly chewing up a glass. My immediate unaltruistic thought was "Oh hell, he won't be able to take hounds out tomorrow." But he didn't come to any harm. If the glass is good, one doesn't.'

It was a bitterly cold night as we set out in convoys to the ball. Cars with silver foxes on the bonnets skidded over the roads, rattling cattle grids and lighting up the grey curls of traveller's joy and the last red beech leaves. Flakes of snow drifted down as we arrived at Cheltenham Town Hall. 'It's already fetlock deep in Stow-on-the-Wold,' bellowed a woman who had just arrived with a white windscreen.

In the Ladies, pale-shouldered women with weathered complexions fought for the mirror.

'I got bucked off into a cow-pat today,' wailed a pretty girl. 'I'll never get my breeches clean.'

'Soak them in Nappisan,' advised a large lady.

Soon four hundred people were tucking into a splendid dinner at £18.50 a head. On my left a late arrival seemed very familiar. Tall, raffish, handsome, like an unfrocked cherub making a guest appearance in *Minder*, he said he'd just left a crucial meeting in Maidenhead. He hunted with the Cotswold when business and racing allowed.

Suddenly I twigged: he was Michael Arnold, the Receiver who'd so audaciously hijacked the miners' five million pounds from a foreign bank last week.

'For what we are about to receiver,' I said, attacking my smoked mackerel.

What was extraordinary, he went on, was that he had suddenly bumped into one of the foreign bankers he'd been writing to for weeks trying to recoup the cash, out hunting. Neither of them had had any idea that they were members of the same hunt.

'Gosh,' I said, having visions of wads of tenners being handed over as they whizzed over hedges.

Mr Arnold, forty-nine, started hunting only three seasons ago, but has, he said, no difficulty keeping up. 'I'm as competitive about hunting as I am about business. Nanny hunts with the Cotswold too – she picks me up if I fall off,' he added.

'My cleaner used to hunt with the Beaufort,' I said, to keep my end up.

On my right, the Master, Tim Unwin, said that one of the keenest hunts in the country was the South Wales Banwen Miners: 'We keep drafting hounds to them. They always want a hound who's a pack leader.'

Perhaps they should call it Arthur.

Discussing obsessions with hunting, Tim cited a former Master who'd left a clause in his will saying he wanted his body fed to hounds so he could enjoy one last run.

'We got round it by scattering his ashes on the hounds' porridge.'

A diversion was caused by the late arrival of three young men from the Cambridge Harriers, all with ironed hair and smooth faces, who'd gone to Gloucester Town Hall by mistake. 'Fast man across country,' said Tim approvingly as one of them sat down opposite us. He was certainly the fastest eater, and raced through three courses in as many minutes.

The band was playing 'Red Red Wine'. The brilliantly lit ballroom beckoned. Tim swept me off to dance. A wonderful dancer, his only problem was that, being Master, he knew everyone . . . and every time he raised his hand, which was firmly clasping mine, to hail some chum, I shot right out of my dress – a chintzless wonder.

As the vast floor filled with couples, red coats with flying tails clashing gloriously with the stinging fuchsia pinks and electric blues of the girls' dresses, the ballroom looked like a shaken kaleidoscope. I couldn't help feeling that as well as class hatred, an element of sexual jealousy must motivate the hunt saboteurs: people in hunting kit look so good.

'If we went out in rags on rough ponies we wouldn't get half the flak,' said Tim Unwin. 'People get completely the wrong idea. Hunting isn't a rich elitist sport – people of all ages and classes come out with us. We've got millers, doctors and farmers as well as knights. I always think of Chaucer's *Canterbury Tales*.'

To prove the point, at that moment our fishmonger bopped past with his comely wife, and I was able to order some cod for the weekend.

It was also nice to see the huge number of young people who'd paid £11.50 for an after-dinner ticket. Sartorially there is a complete divide between the young girls, who all wear mid-calf dresses and look as though they are going to a drinks party, and the wrinklies, whose dresses go down to the ground.

'Ever since a short-sighted brigadier mistook my varicose veins for patterned stockings I've stuck to long,' sighed one woman.

With the richness of royalty in the area, each hunt is proud of its royal patrons. Princess Anne and Captain Phillips hunt with the Beaufort, Princess Michael also. But Prince Michael remains loyal to the Cotswold. Maybe it is the secret of a happy marriage for each to hunt with different packs.

Prince Charles goes out with the VWH. 'HRH has got a triffic sense of humour,' said a VWH stalwart. 'The other day a bobbed-tail fox went past, and he turned to me and said, "Looks more like a bloody corgi." Bloody funny, what?' he brayed with laughter.

Everyone was having a great time. The Receiver turned out to be a wonderful dancer, too, what with twinkling black suede feet and long muscular arms (presumably as a result of humping all that money around).

No one poured champagne over anyone else – at £15 a bottle they couldn't afford to. And with so many starving birds outside, people were far too conservation-conscious to hurl bread rolls.

12.30 a.m.: There was a rumpus in the hall. 'No, you can't come in,' a bossy official was saying to a group of people with snow in their hair. 'The doors shut at midnight.'

The next minute a pint-sized individual in a red coat, furious as a hunt terrier, was yelling into the official's navel.

'You don't understand, you must let us in. They're hunting over me le-and tomorrow.'

Three thousand acres near Winchcombe tipped the scales, and the doors were opened.

Hungry as hunters, we fell on breakfast. Back on the floor, the fastest eater, obviously still hungry, was nibbling his partner's bare shoulder. One local Casanova, with patent leather hair and an overdeveloped little finger from winding women round it, had the unenviable problem of having both his wife and current mistress as well as his discarded mistress present. The former two smirked slightly as the ex-mistress flounced up to him, breathing fire.

To shut her up, he bore her off to dance, and all round the floor one could see them rowing in that rigid-jawed upper class way, as though they'd had too many injections at the dentist.

Why do hunting people have such a reputation for adultery? Perhaps it is because they're so fit – at three o'clock in the morning no one was flagging – or because if you like chasing foxes, you enjoy chasing other things, or because, as one man explained to me, 'Only time one can really sleep with one's wife is two weeks in November. Then she can have the baby in August, and be back in time for cubbing.'

3.45 a.m.: Sadly mindful of icy roads, we called it a day. Outside there were already three inches of snow. As the long dresses trailed over the white pavements, flurrying flakes blurred the Regency houses, and young blades engaged in a snowball fight, we seemed to have gone back a hundred years.

Not unamiably, the attendant manning the Gents sleepily imitated them: 'Going to Georgie's drinks party? Ya. Is Rose going? Ya. Hunting tomorrow? Ya. Think they'll cancel? Ya.'

Suddenly the horn called and they all swarmed back, view-hallooing, to join the stampede of the 'Posthorn Gallop'. A passionately embracing couple, nearly knocked sideways in the rush, reluctantly disengaged themselves and joined in.

The anti-fox hunting brigade don't seem to realize that by trying to abolish hunting, they are taking a pair of scissors to the whole social tapestry of country life, which has lasted for generations. For, as R S Surtees commented, over a hundred years ago, the real business of a hunt ball 'is either to look out for a wife or look after a wife, or to look after somebody's else's wife'.

It has very little to do with foxes.

THE RECESSIONAL

☆★☆★☆★☆★☆★☆★☆★☆★☆★☆★☆★☆★☆★☆★☆★☆★☆

SAKI

Clovis sat in the hottest zone but two of a Turkish bath, alternately inert in statuesque contemplation and rapidly manœuvring a fountain-pen over the pages of a note-book.

'Don't interrupt me with your childish prattle,' he observed to Bertie van Tahn, who had slung himself languidly into a neighbouring chair and looked conversationally inclined; 'I'm writing deathless verse.'

Bertie looked interested.

'I say, what a boon you would be to portrait painters if you really got to be notorious as a poetry writer. If they couldn't get your likeness hung in the Academy as "Clovis Sangrail, Esq., at work on his latest poem," they could slip you in as a Study of the Nude or Orpheus descending into Jermyn Street. They always complain that modern dress handicaps them, whereas a towel and a fountain-pen – '

'It was Mrs Packletide's suggestion that I should write this thing,' said Clovis, ignoring the bypaths to fame that Bertie van Tahn was pointing out to him. 'You see, Loona Bimberton had a Coronation Ode accepted by the *New Infancy*, a paper that has been started with the idea of making the *New Age* seem elder and hidebound. "So clever of you, dear Loona," the Packletide remarked when she had read it; "of course, any one could write a Coronation Ode, but no one else would have thought of doing it." Loona protested that these things were extremely difficult to do, and gave us to understand that they were more or less the province of a gifted few. Now the Packletide has been rather decent to me in many ways, a sort of financial ambulance, you know, that carries you off the field when you're hard hit, which is a frequent occurrence with me, and I've no use whatever for Loona Bimberton, so I chipped in and said I could turn out that sort of stuff by the square yard if I gave my mind to it. Loona said I couldn't, and we got bets on, and between you and me I think the money's fairly safe. Of course, one of the conditions of the wager is that the thing has to be published in something or other, local newspapers barred; but Mrs. Packletide has endeared herself by many little acts of thoughtfulness to the editor of the *Smoky Chimney*, so if I can hammer out anything at all approaching the level of the usual Ode output we ought to be all right. So far I'm getting along so comfortably that I begin to be afraid that I must be one of the gifted few.'

'It's rather late in the day for a Coronation Ode, isn't it?' said Bertie.

'Of course,' said Clovis; 'this is going to be a Durbar Recessional, the sort of thing that you can keep by you for all time if you want to.'

'Now I understand your choice of a place to write it in,' said Bertie van Tahn, with the air of one who has suddenly unravelled a hitherto obscure problem; 'you want to get the local temperature.'

'I came here to get freedom from the inane interruptions of the mentally deficient,' said Clovis, 'but it seems I asked too much of fate.'

Bertie van Tahn prepared to use his towel as a weapon of precision, but reflecting that he had a good deal of unprotected coast-line himself, and that Clovis was equipped with a fountain-pen as well as a towel, he relapsed pacifically into the depths of his chair.

'May one hear extracts from the immortal work?' he asked. 'I promise that nothing that I hear now shall prejudice me against borrowing a copy of the *Smoky Chimney* at the right moment.'

'It's rather like casting pearls into a trough,' remarked Clovis pleasantly, 'but I don't mind reading you bits of it. It begins with a general dispersal of the Durbar participants:

' "Back to their homes in Himalayan heights
The stale pale elephants of Cutch Behar
Roll like great galleons on a tideless sea – " '

'I don't believe Cutch Behar is anywhere near the Himalayan region,' interrupted Bertie. 'You ought to have an atlas on hand when you do this sort of thing; and why stale and pale?'

'After the late hours and the excitement, of course,' said Clovis; 'and I said their *homes* were in the Himalayas. You can have Himalayan elephants in Cutch Behar, I suppose, just as you have Irish-bred horses running at Ascot.'

'You said they were going back to the Himalayas,' objected Bertie.

'Well, they would naturally be sent home to recuperate. It's the usual thing out there to turn elephants loose in the hills, just as we put horses out to grass in this country.'

Clovis could at least flatter himself that he had infused some of the reckless splendour of the East into his mendacity.

'Is it all going to be in blank verse?' asked the critic.

'Of course not; "Durbar" comes at the end of the fourth line.'

'That seems so cowardly; however, it explains why you pitched on Cutch Behar.'

'There is more connection between geographical place-names and poetical inspiration than is generally recognized; one of the chief reasons why there are so few really great poems about Russia in our language is that you can't possibly get a rhyme to names like Smolensk and Tobolsk and Minsk.'

Clovis spoke with the authority of one who has tried.

'Of course, you could rhyme Omsk with Tomsk,' he continued; 'in fact, they seem to be there for that purpose, but the public wouldn't stand that sort of thing indefinitely.'

'The public will stand a good deal,' said Bertie malevolently, 'and so small a proportion of it knows Russian that you could always have an explanatory footnote asserting that the last three letters in Smolensk are not pronounced. It's quite as believable as your statement about putting elephants out to grass in the Himalayan range.'

'I've got rather a nice bit,' resumed Clovis with unruffled serenity, 'giving an evening scene on the outskirts of a jungle village:

' "Where the coiled cobra in the gloaming gloats,
And prowling panthers stalk the wary goats." '

'There is practically no gloaming in tropical countries,' said Bertie indulgently; 'but I do like the masterly reticence with which you treat the cobra's motive for gloating. The unknown is proverbially the uncanny. I can picture nervous readers of the *Smoky Chimney* keeping the light turned on in their bedrooms all night out of sheer sickening uncertainty as to *what* the cobra might have been gloating about.'

'Cobras gloat naturally,' said Clovis, 'just as wolves are always ravening from mere force of habit, even after they've hopelessly overeaten themselves. I've got a fine bit of colour painting later on,' he added, 'where I describe the dawn coming up over the Brahmaputra river:

' "The amber dawn-drenched East with sun-shafts kissed,
Stained sanguine apricot and amethyst,
O'er the washed emerald of the mango groves
Hangs in a mist of opalescent mauves,
While painted parrot-flights impinge the haze
With scarlet, chalcedon and chrysoprase." '

'I've never seen the dawn come up over the Brahmaputra river,' said Bertie, 'so I can't say if it's a good description of the event, but it sounds more like an account of an extensive jewel robbery. Anyhow, the parrots give a good useful touch of local colour. I suppose you've introduced some tigers into the scenery? An Indian landscape would have rather a bare, unfinished look without a tiger or two in the middle distance.'

'I've got a hen-tiger somewhere in the poem,' said Clovis, hunting through his notes. 'Here she is:

' "The tawny tigress 'mid the tangled teak
Drags to her purring cubs' enraptured ears
The harsh death-rattle in the pea-fowl's beak,
A jungle lullaby of blood and tears." '

Bertie van Tahn rose hurriedly from his recumbent position and made for the glass door leading into the next compartment.

'I think your idea of home life in the jungle is perfectly horrid,' he said. 'The cobra was sinister enough, but the improvised rattle in the tiger-nursery is the limit. If you're going to make me turn hot and cold all over I may as well go into the steam room at once.'

'Just listen to this line,' said Clovis; 'it would make the reputation of any ordinary poet:

' "and overhead
The pendulum-patient Punkah, parent of stillborn breeze." '

'Most of your readers will think "punkah" is a kind of iced drink or half-time at polo,' said Bertie, and disappeared into the steam.

The *Smoky Chimney* duly published the 'Recessional,' but it proved to be its swan song, for the paper never attained to another issue.

Loona Bimberton gave up her intention of attending the Durbar and went into a nursing-home on the Sussex Downs. Nervous breakdown after a particularly strenuous season was the usually accepted explanation, but there are three or four people who know that she never really recovered from the dawn breaking over the Brahmaputra river.

Goodbye to All Cats

☆★☆★☆★☆★☆★☆★☆★☆★☆★☆★☆★☆★☆★☆★☆★☆★☆★☆★☆

P. G. WODEHOUSE

As the club kitten sauntered into the smoking room of the Drones Club and greeted those present with a friendly meow, Freddie Widgeon, who had been sitting in a corner with his head between his hands, rose stiffly.

'I had supposed,' he said, in a cold, level voice, 'that this was a quiet retreat for gentlemen. As I perceive that it is a blasted zoo, I will withdraw.'

And he left the room in a marked manner.

There was a good deal of surprise, not unmixed with consternation.

'What's the trouble?' asked an Egg, concerned. Such exhibitions of the naked emotions are rare at the Drones. 'Have they had a row?'

A Crumpet, always well-informed, shook his head.

'Freddie has had no personal breach with this particular kitten,' he said. 'It is simply that since that weekend at Matcham Scratchings he can't stand the sight of a cat.'

'Matcham what?'

'Scratchings. The ancestral home of Dahlia Prenderby in Oxfordshire.'

'I met Dahlia Prenderby once,' said the Egg. 'I thought she seemed a nice girl.'

'Freddie thought so, too. He loved her madly.'

'And lost her, of course?'

'Absolutely.'

'Do you know,' said a thoughtful Bean, 'I'll bet that if all the girls Freddie Widgeon has loved and lost were placed end to end – not that I suppose one could do it – they would reach halfway down Piccadilly.'

'Further than that,' said the Egg. 'Some of them were pretty tall. What beats me is why he ever bothers to love them. They always turn him down in the end. He might just as well never begin. Better, in fact, because in the time saved he could be reading some good book.'

'I think the trouble with Freddie,' said the Crumpet, 'is that he always gets off to a flying start. He's a goodlooking sort of chap who dances well and can wiggle his ears, and the girl is dazzled for the moment, and this encourages him. From what he tells me, he appears to have gone very big with this Prenderby girl at the outset. So much so, indeed, that when she invited him down to Matcham Scratchings he had already bought his copy of *What Every Young Bridegroom Ought To Know*.'

'Rummy, these old country house names,' mused the Bean. 'Why Scratchings, I wonder?'

'Freddie wondered, too, till he got to the place. Then he tells me he felt it was absolutely the *mot juste*. This girl Dahlia's family, you see, was one of those animal-loving families, and the house, he tells me, was just a frothing maelstrom of dumb chums. As far as the eye could reach, there were dogs scratching themselves and cats scratching the furniture. I believe, though he never met it socially, there was even a tame chimpanzee somewhere on the premises, no doubt scratching away as assiduously as the rest of them. You get these conditions here and there in the depths of the country, and this Matcham place was well away from the centre of things being about six miles from the nearest station.'

It was at this station that Dahlia Prenderby met Freddie in her two-seater, and on the way to the house there occurred a conversation which I consider significant – showing, as it does, the cordial relations existing between the young couple at that point in the proceedings. I mean, it was only later that the bitter awakening and all that sort of thing popped up.

'I do want you to be a success, Freddie,' said the girl, after talking a while of this and that. 'Some of the men I've asked down here have been such awful flops. The great thing is to make a good impression on Father.'

'I will,' said Freddie.

'He can be a little difficult at times.'

'Lead me to him,' said Freddie. 'That's all I ask. Lead me to him.'

'The trouble is, he doesn't much like young men.'

'He'll like me.'

'He will, will he?'

'Rather!'

'What makes you think that?'

'I'm a dashed fascinating chap.'

'Oh, you are?'

'Yes, I am.'

'You are, are you?'

'Rather!'

Upon which, she gave him a sort of push and he gave her a sort of push, and she giggled and he laughed like a paper bag bursting, and she gave him a kind of shove and he gave her a kind of shove, and she said 'You *are* a silly ass!' and he said 'What-ho!' All of which shows you, I mean to say, the stage they had got to by this time. Nothing definitely settled, of course, but Love obviously beginning to burgeon in the girl's heart.

Well, naturally, Freddie gave a good deal of thought during the drive to this father of whom the girl had spoken so feelingly, and he resolved that he would not fail her. The way he would suck up to the old dad would be nobody's business. He proposed to exert upon him the full force of his magnetic personality, and looked forward to registering a very substantial hit.

Which being so, I need scarcely tell you, knowing Freddie as you do, that his first act on entering Sir Mortimer Prenderby's orbit was to make the scaliest kind of floater, hitting him on the back of the neck with a tortoiseshell cat not ten minutes after his arrival.

His train having been a bit late, there was no time on reaching the house for any stately receptions or any of that 'Welcome to Meadowsweet Hall' stuff. The girl simply shot him up to his room and told him to dress like a streak, because dinner was in a quarter of an hour, and then buzzed off to don the soup and fish herself. And Freddie was just going well when, looking round for his shirt, which he had left on the bed, he saw a large tortoiseshell cat standing on it, kneading it with its paws.

Well, you know how a fellow feels about his shirt-front. For an instant, Freddie stood spellbound. Then with a hoarse cry he bounded forward, scooped up the animal, and, carrying it out on to the balcony, flung it into the void. And an elderly gentleman, coming round the corner at this moment, received a direct hit on the back of his neck.

'Hell!' cried the elderly gentleman.

A head popped out of a window.

'Whatever is the matter, Mortimer?'

'It's raining cats.'

'Nonsense. It's a lovely evening,' said the head, and disappeared.

Freddie thought an apology would be in order.

'I say,' he said.

The old gentleman looked in every direction of the compass, and finally located Freddie on his balcony.

'I say,' said Freddie, 'I'm awfully sorry you got that nasty buffet. It was me.'

'It was not you. It was a cat.'

'I know. I threw the cat.'

'Why?'

'Well . . .'

'Dam' fool.'

'I'm sorry,' said Freddie.

'Go to blazes,' said the old gentleman.

Freddie backed into the room, and the incident closed.

Freddie is a pretty slippy dresser, as a rule, but this episode had shaken him, and he not only lost a collar-stud but made a mess of the first two ties. The result was that the gong went while he was still in his shirtsleeves: and on emerging from his boudoir he was informed by a footman that the gang were already nuzzling their *bouillon* in the dining room. He pushed straight on there, accordingly, and sank into a chair beside his hostess just in time to dead-heat with the final spoonful.

Awkward, of course, but he was feeling in pretty good form owing to the pleasantness of the thought that he was shoving his knees under the same board as the girl Dahlia: so, having nodded to his host, who was glaring at him from the head of the table, as much as to say that all would be explained in God's good time, he shot his cuffs and started to make sparkling conversation to Lady Prenderby.

'Charming place you have here, what?'

Lady Prenderby said that the local scenery was generally admired. She was one of those tall, rangy, Queen Elizabeth sort of women, with tight lips and cold, blancmangey eyes. Freddie didn't like her looks much, but he was feeling, as I say, fairly fizzy, so he carried on with a bright zip.

'Pretty good hunting country, I should think.'

'I believe there is a good deal of hunting near here, yes.'

'I thought as much,' said Freddie. 'Ah, that's the stuff, is it not? A cracking gallop across good country with a jolly fine kill at the end of it, what, what? Hark for'ard, yoicks, tally-ho, I mean to say, and all that sort of thing.'

Lady Prenderby shivered austerely.

'I fear I cannot share your enthusiasm,' she said. 'I have the strongest possible objection to hunting. I have always set my face against it, as against all similar brutalizing blood sports.'

This was a nasty jar for poor old Freddie, who had been relying on the topic to carry him nicely through at least a couple of courses. It silenced him for the nonce. And as he paused to collect his faculties, his host, who had now been glowering for six and a half minutes practically without cessation, put a hand in front of his mouth and addressed the girl Dahlia across the table. Freddie thinks he was under the impression that he was speaking in a guarded whisper, but, as a matter of fact, the words boomed through the air as if he had been a costermonger calling attention to his Brussels sprouts.

'Dahlia!'

'Yes, Father?'

'Who's that ugly feller?'

'Hush!'

'What do you mean, hush? Who is he?'

'Mr Widgeon.'

'Mr Who?'

'Widgeon.'

'I wish you would articulate clearly and not mumble,' said Sir Mortimer fretfully. 'It sounds to me just like "Widgeon". Who asked him here?'

'I did.'

'Why?'

'He's a friend of mine.'

'Well, he looks a pretty frightful young slab of damnation to me. What I'd call a criminal face.'

'Hush!'

'Why do you keep saying "Hush"? Must be a lunatic, too. Throws cats at people.'

'Please, Father!'

'Don't say "Please Father!" No sense in it. I tell you he does throw cats at people. He threw one at me. Halfwitted, I'd call him – if that. Besides being the most offensive-looking young toad I've ever seen on the premises. How long's he staying?'

'Till Monday.'

'My God! And today's only Friday!' bellowed Sir Mortimer Prenderby.

It was an unpleasant situation for Freddie, of course, and I'm bound to admit he didn't carry it off particularly well. What he ought to have done, obviously, was to have plunged into an easy flow of small talk: but all he could think of was to ask Lady Prenderby if she was fond of shooting. Lady Prenderby having replied that, owing to being deficient in the savage instincts and wanton blood-lust that went to make up a callous and cold-hearted murderess, she was not, he relapsed into silence with his lower jaw hanging down.

All in all, he wasn't so dashed sorry when dinner came to an end.

As he and Sir Mortimer were the only men at the table, most of the seats having been filled by a covey of mildewed females whom he had classified under the general heading of aunts, it seemed to Freddie that the moment had now arrived when they would be able to get together once more, under happier conditions than those of their last meeting, and start to learn to appreciate one another's true worth. He looked forward to a cosy tête-à-tête over the port, in the course of which he would smooth over that cat incident and generally do all that lay within his power to revise the unfavourable opinion of him which the other must have formed.

But apparently Sir Mortimer had his own idea of the duties and obligations of a host. Instead of clustering round Freddie with decanters, he simply gave him a long, lingering look of distaste and shot out of the french window into the garden. A moment later, his head reappeared and he uttered the words: 'You and your dam' cats!' Then the night swallowed him again.

Freddie was a good deal perplexed. All this was new stuff to him. He had been in and out of a number of country houses in his time, but this was the first occasion on which he had ever been left flat at the conclusion of the evening meal, and he wasn't quite sure how to handle the situation. He was still wondering, when Sir Mortimer's head came into view again and its owner, after giving him another of those long, lingering looks, said: 'Cats, forsooth!' and disappeared once more.

Freddie was now definitely piqued. It was all very well, he felt, Dahlia Prenderby telling him to make himself solid with her father, but how can you make yourself solid with a fellow who doesn't stay put for a couple of consecutive seconds? If it was Sir Mortimer's intention to spend the remainder of the night flashing past like a merry-go-round, there seemed little hope of anything amounting to a genuine *rapprochement*. It was a relief to his feelings when there suddenly appeared from nowhere his old acquaintance the tortoiseshell cat. It seemed to offer to him a means of working off his spleen.

Taking from Lady Prenderby's plate, accordingly, the remains of a banana, he plugged the animal neatly at a range of two yards. It yowled and withdrew. And a moment later, there was Sir Mortimer again.

'Did you kick that cat?' said Sir Mortimer.

Freddie had half a mind to ask this old disease if he thought he was a man or a jack-in-the-box, but the breeding of the Widgeons restrained him.

'No,' he said, 'I did not kick that cat.'

'You must have done something to it to make it come charging out at forty miles an hour.'

'I merely offered the animal a piece of fruit.'

'Do it again and see what happens to you.'

'Lovely evening,' said Freddie, changing the subject.

'No, it's not, you silly ass,' said Sir Mortimer. Freddie rose. His nerve, I fancy, was a little shaken.

'I shall join the ladies,' he said, with dignity.

'God help them!' replied Sir Mortimer Prenderby in a voice instinct with the deepest feeling, and vanished once more.

Freddie's mood, as he made for the drawing room, was thoughtful. I don't say he has much sense, but he's got enough to know when he is and when he isn't going with a bang. Tonight, he realized, he had been very far from going in such a manner. It was not, that is to say, as the Idol of Matcham Scratchings that he would enter the drawing room, but rather as a young fellow who had made an unfortunate first impression and would have to do a lot of heavy ingratiating before he could regard himself as really popular in the home.

He must bustle about, he felt, and make up leeway. And, knowing that what counts with these old-style females who have lived in the country all their lives is the exhibition of those little politenesses and attentions which were all the go in Queen Victoria's time, his first action, on entering, was to make a dive for one of the aunts who seemed to be trying to find a place to put her coffee cup.

'Permit me,' said Freddie, suave to the eyebrows.

And bounding forward with the feeling that this was the stuff to give them, he barged right into a cat.

'Oh, sorry,' he said, backing and bringing down his heel on another cat.

'I say, most frightfully sorry,' he said.

And, tottering to a chair, he sank heavily on to a third cat.

Well, he was up and about again in a jiffy, of course, but it was too late. There was the usual not-at-all-ing and don't-mention-it-ing, but he could read between the lines. Lady Prenderby's eyes had rested on his for only a brief instant, but it had been enough. His standing with her, he perceived, was now approximately what King Herod's would have been at an Israelite Mothers Social Saturday Afternoon.

The girl Dahlia during these exchanges had been sitting on a sofa at the end of the room, turning the pages of a weekly paper, and the sight of her drew Freddie like a magnet. Her womanly sympathy was just what he felt he could do with at this juncture. Treading with infinite caution, he crossed to where she sat: and, having scanned the terrain narrowly for cats, sank down on the sofa at her side. And conceive his agony of spirit when he discovered that womanly sympathy had been turned off at the main. The girl was like a chunk of ice cream with spikes all over it.

'Please do not trouble to explain,' she said coldly, in answer to his opening words. 'I quite understand that there are people who have this odd dislike of animals.'

'But, dash it . . .' cried Freddie, waving his arm in a frenzied sort of way. 'Oh, I say, sorry,' he added, as his fist sloshed another of the menagerie in the short ribs.

Dahlia caught the animal as it flew through the air.

'I think perhaps you had better take Augustus, Mother,' she said. 'He seems to be annoying Mr Widgeon.'

'Quite,' said Lady Prenderby. 'He will be safer with me.'

'But, dash it . . .' bleated Freddie.

Dahlia Prenderby drew in her breath sharply.

'How true it is,' she said, 'that one never really knows a man till after one has seen him in one's own home.'

'What do you mean by that?'

'Oh, nothing,' said Dahlia Prenderby.

She rose and moved to the piano, where she proceeded to sing old Breton folk songs in a distant manner, leaving Freddie to make out as best he could with a family album containing faded photographs with 'Aunt Emily bathing at Llandudno, 1893', and 'This is Cousin George at the fancy-dress ball' written under them.

And so the long, quiet, peaceful home evening wore on, till eventually Lady Prenderby mercifully blew the whistle and he was at liberty to sneak off to his bedroom.

You might have supposed that Freddie's thoughts, as he toddled upstairs with his candle, would have dwelt exclusively on the girl Dahlia. This, however, was not so. He did give her obvious shirtiness a certain measure of attention, of course, but what really filled his mind was the soothing reflection that at long last his path and that of the animal kingdom of Matcham Scratchings had now divided. He, so to speak, was taking the high road while they, as it were, would take the low road. For whatever might be the conditions prevailing in the dining room, the drawing room, and the rest of the house, his bedroom, he felt, must surely be a haven totally free from cats of all descriptions.

Remembering, however, that unfortunate episode before dinner, he went down on all fours and subjected the various nooks and crannies to a close examination. His eye could detect no cats. Relieved, he rose to his feet with a gay song on his lips: and he hadn't got much beyond the first couple of bars when a voice behind him suddenly started taking the bass: and, turning, he perceived on the bed a fine Alsatian dog.

Freddie looked at the dog. The dog looked at Freddie. The situation was one fraught with embarrassment. A glance at the animal was enough to convince him that it had got an entirely wrong angle on the position of affairs and was regarding him purely in the light of an intrusive stranger who had muscled in on its private sleeping quarters. Its manner was plainly resentful. It fixed Freddie with a cold, yellow eye and curled its upper lip slightly, the better to display a long, white tooth. It also twitched its nose and gave a sotto voce imitation of distant thunder.

Freddie did not know quite what avenue to explore. It was impossible to climb between the sheets with a thing like that on the counterpane. To spend the night in a chair, on the other hand, would have been foreign to his policy. He did what I consider the most statesmanlike thing by sidling out on to the balcony and squinting along the wall of the house to see if there wasn't a lighted window hard by, behind which might lurk somebody who would rally round with aid and comfort.

There was a lighted window only a short distance away, so he shoved his head out as far as it would stretch, and said:

'I say!'

There being no response, he repeated:

'I say!'

And, finally, to drive his point home, he added:

'I say! I say! I say!'

This time he got results. The head of Lady Prenderby suddenly protruded from the window.

'Who,' she enquired, 'is making that abominable noise?'

It was not precisely the attitude Freddie had hoped for, but he could take the rough with the smooth.

'It's me. Widgeon, Frederick.'

'Must you sing on your balcony, Mr Widgeon?'

'I wasn't singing. I was saying "I say".'

'What were you saying?'

' "I say".'

'You say what?'

'I say I was saying "I say". Kind of a heart-cry, if you know what I mean. The fact is, there's a dog in my room.'

'What sort of dog?'

'A whacking great Alsatian.'

'Ah, that would be Wilhelm. Good night, Mr Widgeon.'

The window closed. Freddie let out a heart-stricken yip.

'But I say!'

The window reopened.

'Really, Mr Widgeon!'

'But what am I to do?'

'Do?'

'About this whacking great Alsatian!'

Lady Prenderby seemed to consider.

'No sweet biscuits,' she said. 'And when the maid brings you your tea in the morning please do not give him sugar. Simply a little milk in the saucer. He is on a diet. Good night, Mr Widgeon.'

Freddie was now pretty well nonplussed. No matter what his hostess might say about this beastly dog being on a diet, he was convinced from its manner that its medical adviser had not forbidden it Widgeons, and once more he bent his brain to the task of ascertaining what to do next.

There were several possible methods of procedure. His balcony being not so very far from the ground, he could, if he pleased, jump down and pass a health-giving night in the nasturtium bed. Or he might curl up on the floor. Or he might get out of the room and doss downstairs somewhere.

This last scheme seemed about the best. The only obstacle in the way of its fulfilment was the fact that, when he started for the door, his room mate would probably think he was a burglar about to loot silver from a lonely country house and pin him. Still, it had to be risked, and a moment later he might have been observed tiptoeing across the carpet with all the caution of a slack-wire artist who isn't any too sure he remembers the correct steps.

Well, it was a near thing. At the instant when he started, the dog seemed occupied with something that looked like a cushion on the bed. It was licking this object in a thoughtful way, and paid no attention to Freddie till he was halfway across No Man's Land. Then it suddenly did a sort of sitting high jump in his direction, and two seconds later Freddie, with a draughty feeling about the seat of his trouserings, was on top of a wardrobe, with the dog underneath looking up. He tells me that if he ever moved quicker in his life it was only on the occasion when, a lad of fourteen, he was discovered by his uncle, Lord Blicester, smoking one of the latter's cigars in the library: and he rather thinks he must have clipped at least a fifth of a second off the record then set up.

It looked to him now as if his sleeping arrangements for the night had been settled for him. And the thought of having to roost on top of a wardrobe at the whim of a dog was pretty dashed offensive to his proud spirit, as you may well imagine. However, as you cannot reason with Alsatians, it seemed the only thing to be done: and he was trying to make himself as comfortable as a sharp piece of wood sticking into the fleshy part of his leg would permit, when there was a snuffling noise in the passage and through the door came an object which in the dim light he was at first not able to identify. It looked something like a pen wiper and something like a piece of a hearthrug. A second and keener inspection revealed it as a Pekingese puppy.

The uncertainty which Freddie had felt as to the newcomer's status was shared, it appeared, by the Alsatian: for after raising its eyebrows in a puzzled manner it rose and advanced enquiringly. In a tentative way it put out a paw and rolled the intruder over. Then, advancing again, it lowered its nose and sniffed.

It was a course of action against which its best friend would have advised it. These Pekes are tough eggs, especially when, as in this case, female. They look the world in the eye, and are swift to resent familiarity. There was a sort of explosion, and the next moment the Alsatian was shooting out of the room with its tail between its legs, hotly pursued. Freddie could hear the noise of battle rolling away along the passage, and it was music to his ears. Something on these lines was precisely what that Alsatian had been asking for, and now it had got it.

Presently, the Peke returned, dashing the beads of perspiration from its forehead, and came and sat down under the wardrobe, wagging a stumpy tail. And Freddie, feeling that the All Clear had been blown and that he was now at liberty to descend, did so.

His first move was to shut the door, his second to fraternize with his preserver. Freddie is a chap who believes in giving credit where credit is due, and it seemed to him that this Peke had shown itself an ornament of its species. He spared no effort, accordingly, to entertain it. He lay down on the floor and let it lick his face two hundred and thirty-three times. He tickled it under the left ear, the right ear, and at the base of the tail, in the order named. He also scratched its stomach.

All these attentions the animal received with cordiality and marked gratification: and as it seemed still in pleasure-seeking mood and had plainly come to look upon him as the official Master of the Revels, Freddie, feeling that he could not disappoint it but must play the host no matter what the cost to himself, took off his tie and handed it over. He could not have done it for everybody, he says, but where this life-saving Peke was concerned the sky was the limit.

Well, the tie went like a breeze. It was a success from the start. The Peke chewed it and chased it and got entangled in it and dragged it about the room, and was just starting to shake it from side to side when an unfortunate thing happened. Misjudging its distance, it banged its head a nasty wallop against the leg of the bed.

There is nothing of the Red Indian at the stake about a puppy in circumstances like this. A moment later, Freddie's blood was chilled by a series of fearful shrieks that seemed to ring through the night like the dying cries of the party of the second part to a first-class murder. It amazed him that a mere Peke, and a juvenile Peke at that, should have been capable of producing such an uproar. He says that a Baronet, stabbed in the back with a paper-knife in his library, could not have made half such a row.

Eventually, the agony seemed to abate. Quite suddenly as if nothing had happened, the Peke stopped yelling and with an amused smile started to play with the tie again. And at the same moment there was a sound of whispering outside, and then a knock at the door.

'Hullo?' said Freddie.

'It is I, sir. Biggleswade.'

'Who's Biggleswade?'

'The butler, sir.'

'What do you want?'

'Her ladyship wishes me to remove the dog which you are torturing.'

There was more whispering.

'Her ladyship also desires me to say that she will be reporting the affair in the morning to the Society for the Prevention of Cruelty to Animals.'

There was another spot of whispering.

'Her ladyship further instructs me to add that, should you prove recalcitrant, I am to strike you over the head with the poker.'

Well, you can't say this was pleasant for poor old Freddie, and he didn't think so himself. He opened the door, to perceive without, a group consisting of Lady Prenderby, her daughter Dahlia, a few assorted aunts, and the butler, with poker. And he says he met Dahlia's eyes and they went through him like a knife.

'Let me explain . . .' he began.

'Spare us the details,' said Lady Prenderby with a shiver. She scooped up the Peke and felt it for broken bones.

'But listen . . .'

'Good night, Mr Widgeon.'

The aunts said good night, too, and so did the butler. The girl Dahlia preserved a revolted silence.

'But, honestly, it was nothing, really. It banged its head against the bed . . .'

'What did he say?' asked one of the aunts, who was a little hard of hearing.

'He says he banged the poor creature's head against the bed,' said Lady Prenderby.

'Dreadful!' said the aunt.

'Hideous!' said a second aunt.

A third aunt opened up another line of thought. She said that with men like Freddie in the house, was anyone safe? She mooted the possibility of them all being murdered in their beds. And though Freddie offered to give her a written guarantee that he hadn't the slightest intention of going anywhere near her bed, the idea seemed to make a deep impression.

'Biggleswade,' said Lady Prenderby.

'M'lady?'

'You will remain in this passage for the remainder of the night with your poker.'

'Very good, m'lady.'

'Should this young man attempt to leave his room, you will strike him smartly over the head.'

'Just so, m'lady.'

'But, listen . . .' said Freddie.

'Good night, Mr Widgeon.'

The mob scene broke up. Soon the passage was empty save for Biggleswade the butler, who had begun to pace up and down, halting every now and then to flick the air with his poker as if testing the lissomness of his wrist muscles and satisfying himself that they were in a condition to ensure the right amount of follow-through.

The spectacle he presented was so unpleasant that Freddie withdrew into his room and shut the door. His bosom, as you may imagine, was surging with distressing emotions. That look which Dahlia Prenderby had given him had churned him up to no little extent. He realized that he had a lot of tense thinking to do, and to assist thought he sat down on the bed.

Or, rather, to be accurate, on the dead cat which was lying on the bed. It was this cat which the Alsatian had been licking just before the final breach in his relations with Freddie – the object, if you remember, which the latter had supposed to be a cushion.

He leaped up as if the corpse, instead of being cold, had been piping hot. He stared down, hoping against hope that the animal was merely in some sort of coma. But a glance told him that it had made the great change. He had never seen a deader cat. After life's fitful fever it slept well.

You wouldn't be far out in saying that poor old Freddie was now appalled. Already his reputation in this house was at zero, his name mud. On all sides he was looked upon as Widgeon the Amateur Vivisectionist. This final disaster could not but put the tin hat on it. Before, he had had a faint hope that in the morning, when calmer moods would prevail, he might be able to explain that matter of the Peke. But who was going to listen to him if he were discovered with a dead cat on his person?

And then the thought came to him that it might be possible not to be discovered with it on his person. He had only to nip downstairs and deposit the remains in the drawing room or somewhere and suspicion might not fall upon him. After all, in a super-catted house like this, cats must always be dying like flies all over the place. A housemaid would find the animal in the morning and report to GHQ that the cat strength of the establishment had been reduced by one, and there would be a bit of tut-tutting and perhaps a silent tear or two, and then the thing would be forgotten.

The thought gave him new life. All briskness and efficiency, he picked up the body by the tail and was just about to dash out of the room when, with a silent groan, he remembered Biggleswade.

He peeped out. It might be that the butler, once the eye of authority had been removed, had departed to get the remainder of his beauty sleep. But no. Service and Fidelity were evidently the watchwords at Matcham Scratchings. There the fellow was, still practising half-arm shots with the poker. Freddie closed the door.

And, as he did so, he suddenly thought of the window. There lay the solution. Here he had been, fooling about with doors and thinking in terms of drawing rooms, and all the while there was the balcony staring him in the face. All he had to do was to shoot the body out into the silent night, and let gardeners, not housemaids, discover it.

He hurried out. It was a moment for swift action. He raised his burden. He swung it to and fro, working up steam. Then he let it go, and from the dark garden there came suddenly the cry of a strong man in his anger.

'Who threw that cat?'

It was the voice of his host, Sir Mortimer Prenderby.

'Show me the man who threw that cat!' he thundered.

Windows flew up. Heads came out. Freddie sank to the floor of the balcony and rolled against the wall.

'Whatever is the matter, Mortimer?'

'Let me get at the man who hit me in the eye with a cat.'

'A cat?' Lady Prenderby's voice sounded perplexed. 'Are you sure?'

'Sure? What do you mean sure? Of course I'm sure. I was just dropping off to sleep in my hammock, when suddenly a great beastly cat came whizzing through the air and caught me properly in the eyeball. It's a nice thing. A man can't sleep in hammocks in his own garden without people pelting him with cats. I insist on the blood of the man who threw that cat.'

'Where did it come from?'

'Must have come from that balcony there.'

'Mr Widgeon's balcony,' said Lady Prenderby in an acid voice. 'As I might have guessed.'

Sir Mortimer uttered a cry.

'So might I have guessed! Widgeon, of course! That ugly feller. He's been throwing cats all the evening. I've got a nasty sore place on the back of my neck where he hit me with one before dinner. Somebody come and open the front door. I want my heavy cane, the one with the carved ivory handle. Or a horsewhip will do.'

'Wait, Mortimer,' said Lady Prenderby. 'Do nothing rash. The man is evidently a very dangerous lunatic. I will send Biggleswade to overpower him. He has the kitchen poker.'

Little (said the Crumpet) remains to be told. At two-fifteen that morning a sombre figure in dress clothes without a tie limped into the little railway station of Lower Smattering on the Wissel, some six miles from Matcham Scratchings. At three-forty-seven it departed Londonwards on the up milk train. It was Frederick Widgeon. He had a broken heart and blisters on both heels. And in that broken heart was that loathing for all cats of which you recently saw so signal a manifestation. I am revealing no secrets when I tell you that Freddie Widgeon is permanently through with cats. From now on, they cross his path at their peril.

What I Did on My Holidays

☆★☆

KEITH WATERHOUSE

For my holiday this year we went to the town of Venice. There, many canals are to be found, together with a big square, and, much ice-cream is to be had. But, there are no Dodgems. It not as good as Woburn Abbey.

Leaving home at 10 past 7 we arrived in the town of Venice later. Our taxi driver was Mr Briggs. He vouchsafed, (I wish I coming with you) to which my erstwhile Father reply, (You can take my place if you like). The meaning of this Mysterious Remark was to be revealed ere an enchanting holiday was over.

Arriving in the town of Venice, we had Veal and Beetroot Salad followed by Cake, also as much Coca-Cola as you wanted. This on the plane before we got there, it was the Concorde. Arriving at our destination we travelled by Water Taxi to Journey's End, from whence our weary footsteps took us to our hotel. (What a dump) cried My Father, upon espying the Imposing Pile. The Water Taxi is not like an ordinary Taxi, it like a Boat. (I thought we supposed to overlook a Canal) he added for good measure, (This remind me of a Doss-house in the Caledonian Road).

(You were one who wanted to come Venice so stop moaning) maintained My Mother sturdily, adding as an afterthought, (I would have been just as happy in Frinton, at least it not smell).

(If left to me I would have stayed at home and played Golf) snorted My Father by way of reply, adding with a Meaning Glance towards the Writer of this narrative, (And if he fall in Canal after all I have told him, I not fish him out). Thus the scene was set for a Holiday I shall never forget.

Came the Dawn. In the town of Venice, as I was to discover to my cost, they only have Bread for their breakfast, eggs and Bacon being unknown in this backward land. But, if, you go to the Shops, they always give you Sweets, if, you are on Holiday and, you buy something. This because these primitive people do not have money. They, the Holidaymakers, have money, but They, the shopkeepers, do not. Therefore, when you buy something, they do not give you change, they give you Sweets. Some of the aforesaid Sweets are red, some are blue, and others are purple, they like bubble-gum. Thus, I was able with God's Grace to survive that Fateful morning.

Little was said about the Matter until, My Parents came into my room, to see if I washed my hands before Lunch. I had not, but, I did not tell them, rather the reverse. Espying the Things I had bought upon my Bed, That Worthy sneered, (What all this junk?) Upon hearing my calm explanation, that, they were Presents, the Latter bellowed in voice stentorian (How much money you got left?) Upon hearing me boldly declare (Nothing) he go Purple. He same colour as my Sweets. (We been here only 10 mins and, he has got through 5000 lire, it supposed to last him fortnight!) exploded the comical figure. His face a mask of evil he snarled (Look at all this rubbish, why he buy castanets? I suppose if we go to Spain next year he spend every penny on blessed toy gondolas!!!)

(Leave boy alone, for goodness sake, you always picking on him, pick pick pick) My Mother quavered staunchly, the blood draining from her lips.

(I will pick on him all right, I will pick him up and throw him out of bedroom window before I finished) swore My Father. So saying, he led the way to, the restaurant where we were destined to have lunch, but, I not hungry.

(By all means leave your canelloni if it not to your taste, it only costing the best part of a day's earnings) observed My Relentless Father, whereupon he turned to His Spouse with the rejoinder (Or perhaps he'd prefer some spaghetti hoops?) This proved to be a cruel jest. I was Fated to have nothing to break my fast but fizzy water, a Morsel of bread and Profiteroles, also a Peach.

After our frugal meal My Mother vouchsafed that she would like to sit on the Big Square and, listen to the Band, but, My Father would have none of it. (You do not catch me paying £1 for thimble of coffee) declared the Miserly Fellow. After much discussion a compromise was reached, and, we went to see the Doge's Palace, where, many interesting dungeons are to be found, as well as the Torture Chamber, also many big drawings. Descending the golden staircase I meekly asked My Father if, I could have a pizza for supper. At this he gave a Hollow Laugh and groan (That bloody fantastic. You cart him all this way, you plonk him down in most beautiful city on God's earth, and all he can think about is Stomach). (We can't all be intellectuals) interjected My Mother with Dry humour. But, this not enough to stem My Father's Fury. Baring his teeth, he continue (At least he could use his eyes. When he came along Grand Canal yesterday, he not even look up, he just slouch in Water Taxi poking his finger through a Knothole). At this My Mother volunteered that, her Feet had swollen, also, that she wanted to spend Penny, so, we went back to the Hotel to be received by our Genial Host. After simple repast, I had Diarrhoea. So ended another Memorable Day.

On Monday we went to an Island, to see, them Blowing Glass, it like balloons but it is not, it is glass. I burn my Hand on furnace and, it was bandaged by, a Nun. On Tuesday, we went round many Churches, they have much painting, but not on the wall, it is on the ceiling. My Father keep saying (Look up, lad! Look up, lad!) Also (Is he mentally deficient?) On Wednesday, My Mother had a Blister, we sat in the big square at her request, pigeons being seen in large numbers. She had a Red Drink, whilst I had a Coke, and My Father had Whiskey. He go white when he get bill. (This cannot be the total, it the date) ran his statement.

On Thursday we went to, the Sands. Many ignorant people do not know that there are Sands in, the town of Venice, but, there are. It is called the Lido. The Lido is reached by boat, it pass an Island which is a Graveyard. In the town of Venice, when you are dead, the funeral is done by boats, strange to relate. Likewise, the fire brigade and, emptying the dustbins, but, we did not see any of this.

Our fruitful expedition to the Lido was uneventful, except, My Father offered me 1000 lire if, I could swim to Yugoslavia, but, I did not, and also, My Mother turn Bright Red all over. (I told you not to overdo it First Day) My Father crowed with scant sympathy for the Former, (You look like Lobster). (Oh shut up, Miseryguts) My Mother riposted. They did not Speak again until Dinnertime when, I had Melon, a Plate of Chips and Mela Stragata, together with eighteen grapes. There are Dodgems at the Lido, but, My Father would not let me go on them. (This the Byzantine jewel of the Adriatic, not Battersea Fun Fair) quoth he darkly, with little meaning to my Good Self.

On Saturday, after tasting the Many Delights of the town of Venice the previous day, I ill. My Mother gasp shrewdly (This not just Diarrhoea, this Dysentry). My Father retort (With muck he been shovelling down, I surprised it not Bubonic Plague. Anyway, you not Fit to look after him, you are like a Lobster and also you are peeling like an Old Door, stuff this for game of candles, I am going to see if can get on tomorrow flight for Heathrow). With which he turned on his heel and Stormed Out.

My Mother said I could play quietly in my Room but, I did not. I went for Walk. Suffice to say that, My Father found me in Railway Station at, 9 p.m. My Mother was also among those present, saying (He wet through, he will catch Pneumonia). His Temples throbbing, My Father said monosyllabically (He been in Canal, he has probably got Every Disease Known To Man by now. We are going, to take the Next Train to Milan, and, we will take Pot Luck from there. If, there are only two cancellations on plane, we will leave him Behind.) Thus our Idyllic Holiday came to an auspicious end, and we said farewell to the town of Venice.

Here Come the Tigers

☆★☆

JAMES THURBER

It was after midnight and I had got up to turn off the radio and go to bed when a baritone began to sing 'Bye-Bye, Blackbird' with the rueful reverence the song deserves. I sat down again, and I was lost. If I had shut off the radio, turned out the lights, and locked the door, Jordan and Hayes would have driven up to a dark house and gone away, or if they had hammered on the door, I would have let them hammer till they got discouraged and drove off. The lights were on, though, and the door was unlocked. The tyres of a car swashed over the gravel of the driveway and came to a sudden, complaining stop. My door opened and they tumbled in without knocking, like a pair of comics taking an encore. I turned off the radio and reached for the light switch.

'Hold!' Jordan cried. 'Stay that naughty hand!'

I took my hand off the switch. 'I'm tired,' I said, 'and Alice is asleep.'

'Sleep! Sleep – on a night of wild discovery!' Jordan moaned. He went over to the bar in a corner of the living room and began mixing a bourbon-and-soda. Hayes took Jordan's place at the bar when his companion flopped into a chair and swung one leg over an arm. 'We have discovered a new dimension of meaning,' Jordan said. He took a great gulp of his drink. 'And a new plane of beauty.'

'You want a drink?' Hayes asked me.

'It's late,' I said, 'and I'm tired.'

Jordan snorted, choked on his whisky, and coughed for a full minute. 'The man wants torpor,' he spluttered finally. 'On a night like this, the man wants torpor.'

'Torpor is a good word,' Hayes said. He sat on the arm of a chair. 'Shall we take it apart for him?'

'You guys are stiff,' I said.

Jordan frowned, finished his drink, and went back to the bar. 'Stiff is better,' he said. 'I think stiff is probably perfect. Let me get at it.' He dropped into the chair again, with a new highball.

I stared at the ceiling. If I didn't humour them, they might go away.

'We're starting too high,' Jordan said. 'We're the hell too high. He won't get it. Look at him.'

'Nuts,' I said coldly.

'Let me unwrap stiff for you,' Jordan said. 'God knows that ought to be simple enough. Listen to this. It's perfect. Stiff, tiff, fists, fits.'

'He means that the mood and tone and colour of a word are echoed in its component parts,' Hayes said. 'Tiff is argument, fist is fight, fits – fits – '

'Don't make it glare,' Jordan said. 'You're making it glare. Let him feel it. You got to feel it.'

'Look – ' I began wanly.

Jordan regarded me sorrowfully and shook his head. 'He's going to compare it to Joyce or Dada or Gertrude Stein,' he said. 'He is an enemy of the new dimension. Oh, no, he can't be,' he added. 'Not in *this* house, he can't be.' He had some trouble getting up, but he made the bar.

'It's *his* house,' Hayes said.

I was glad he was soberer than Jordan, who after a moment of deep thought said, 'Last place in the world a man should make an ass of himself. Host, you know, and all that.'

'Where have you guys been?' I asked.

Jordan looked at Hayes and shrugged, splashing a dollop of his new drink on the carpet. 'We have been in a new dimension of meaning and beauty,' he said, 'but I doubt if you could understand it.'

'Well, what the hell is it?' I demanded. I went to the bar and poured myself a short drink. 'Are you going to crawl around it all night, or are you coming out with it?'

'Tell him the quatrain,' Jordan said. 'I want him to hear the quatrain.'

Hayes studied the floor for a while. Then he recited the quatrain:

'There are lips in pistol
And mist in times,
Cats in crystal,
and mice in chimes.'

I stared coldly at Jordan's transfigured face. 'Is this the spearhead of the New Beauty?' I asked.

Jordan globbered his drink down, ran his hand through his hair, and glared at me demoniacally. 'Shows what What's-his-name of

"Christabel" and Keats of "Eve of St Agnes" could have done if the goddam fairy casements had opened on this lovely dimension!' he shouted.

'Coleridge,' Hayes said. He was nursing his drink along, and seemed to be getting sober.

Jordan went to the bar and sloshed out more bourbon. 'Well?' he demanded, but he didn't wait for me to answer. 'We were unlocking animals from almost every word you can think of when we got to cats in crystal and mice in chimes. Tell him some of 'em, Tom. You got 'em all written down.'

Hayes put his drink on the floor and pulled a piece of folded cardboard out of his pocket. I saw that it was a dinner menu with pencil scribblings on the back. 'There's the wolf in the flower, the gander in danger, and the frog in forget,' he said. 'There's the emu in summer, the ant in autumn, the wren in winter, and the pig in spring.' He turned the cardboard upside down and scowled at it. 'There's the gnu in jungle,' he went on, 'the swan in answer, and the toad in toward.' He put the menu down, and I thought he looked a little unhappy, as if the whisky and the spell of the new dimension were wearing off at the same time.

Jordan kept snapping his fingers, trying to remember other beasts in other words.

'Try to find the tiger in a six-letter word,' Hayes said to me. 'It isn't easy. There are three six-letter words with tiger, but it isn't easy.'

'It's not a game, it's more than a game,' Jordan said severely. 'Let's not get back to the game.'

'It began as a game,' Hayes said to me. 'It's an old word game. You try to see how many words you can make out of another word.'

'We played it a million times before,' Jordan said, 'but tonight, for the first time, I see what we got, like Emily What's-her-name hearing the river in the trees. You might hear the wind in the trees all your life and never hear the river. Give me that thing, Tom.' He reached out and took the menu from Hayes, and began turning it slowly in his big hands. The writing on the back apparently ran in all directions. He sighed dolefully and handed it back to Hayes. 'There's practically a sentence in woman,' he said. 'It's perfect in mood and tone. In mood and tone it's practically perfect. See if you can find the sentence, Tom.'

Hayes patted away an incipient yawn. 'Woman: moan now won wan man,' he chanted, and then the yawn got the best of him.

'What'd I say it had in it, Tom?'

Hayes consulted the back of the menu. 'The thunder of Genesis,' he announced finally, 'it says here.'

'It's practically Biblical,' Jordan said, 'with only five letters.' He went to the bar again. 'Who wants a drink?' he asked. Neither of us said anything. Hayes had slumped a little in his chair. I leaned back, gazed at the ceiling, and hunted the tiger. For the next five minutes, I heard the sound of Jordan's voice but I didn't take in the sense. I found the roach in orchard, the horse in shore, the owl in wobble, the stag in ghastly, and the bear and zebra in brazen, but no glimmer of a tiger anywhere.

'It's like little boxes, one inside each other,' Jordan was saying when I came out of my own jungle of words. 'You lift out concentric meanings of practically identical mood and tone. Yet people have let the component parts of words go for a thousand years. They lose the depth and the roundness and the whole quality.' He turned to Hayes. 'Take pistol apart for Jim,' he begged. 'Take pistol apart.' I got up and went to the bar and poured out a stiff rye. 'Go ahead,' I said.

'It kind of rips and squirts and goes all to hell, the way pistol should,' Jordan said by way of foreword.

'Shoot,' I said.

'No gags,' Jordan implored me. 'For God's sake, no gags.'

'Pistol,' Hayes began. 'Slip, spit, split, spilt, spoil, spoilt, slop, slot, tips, tops, spot, pots, stop.'

'You see what I mean?' Jordan asked. I visualized the word and studied it for a while.

'He left out oils and soil,' I said finally, 'and what are Lois and silo doing in pistol?'

Jordan turned to Hayes, who had shut his eyes. 'Didn't I tell you we'd be up against that?' he demanded. 'What'd I say we'd be up against, Tom?'

'The obscurantism of the explicit,' Hayes brought out after frowning over it.

'That's it! That's what I said we'd be up against, like in chalice.'

Hayes decided to try another drink, and he went over and poured himself a short one. 'You get lace and hail and ice and Alice in chalice,' he said, 'but you got lice to account for.'

'So what?' said Jordan. 'So what the hell?' He spread his hands.

'What about the rats in crystal, with the cats?' I asked.

'Jordan hasn't got the technic and ethic worked out yet,' Hayes told me.

'I can handle the rats,' Jordan said.

'And the salt and the slat and the cyst and the cart?' I asked.

'Yeh, and the star and the cry and the satyr. They all mix into crystal.'

Hayes yawned openly. He was drinking slowly. 'It seems a little thin, somehow,' he said. 'I mean the whole thing, in times like these.'

'What does?' Jordan stared at him blankly.

I saved an argument by suddenly running across Roget in forget. 'If there were no forget,' I said to Jordan, 'it would not be necessary to create Roget.'

'I don't think you get the idea,' he said. 'I don't think he gets the idea, Tom. What was it I said earlier this evening? I said, "Tom, he'll never get it in a million years." I said, "Tom, the obscurantism of the explicit is what's going to louse up this lovely thing." Didn't I say that, Tom?'

'Yes,' Hayes said, tapping another yawn.

'Do hotels for him, Tom. Maybe that'll give him the idea.'

'Hotels,' Hayes read. 'Sot, lost, hose, stole, shoe. Hotel so hot she shot host. . . . I'm tired.' He sagged in his chair.

'A lost mood, see?' Jordan tried to express it with a gesture of his hands. 'You got to feel it like a child. Do you feel it?'

'I certainly do,' I said.

'What are you tired for, Tom?' Jordan gave his friend a worried glance.

'I don't know,' Hayes said. 'It just seems a little thin, somehow.'

'What does?'

'Mice in chimes. It seems a little thin.'

'What's he talking about?' Jordan asked me.

'I mean when you get to thinking of the hare twisting in the frozen grass and the mastiff bitch in the moonshine cold,' Hayes said.

'What the *hell's* he talking about?' Jordan almost wailed.

'What's-his-name and Keats,' I said.

Jordan made a small, despairing gesture. 'Do phrase,' he pleaded.

'Oh, for God sake!' Hayes got up and went to the radio.

'Don't wake Alice,' I said.

'Do phrase and then we'll get the hell out,' Jordan said.

'Do phrase,' I insisted quickly.

'Explain about it first in its own words,' Jordan said. 'You know.'

'OK, OK' Hayes sighed and sat down. 'You don't have to dwell on the parse phase, the sharp rasp, the rape shape,' he droned.

'Now show him where Tenniel and What's-his-name, the *douanier*, come in,' Jordan said eagerly.

'In the apes and the asp and the hares,' Hayes went on. 'In the peas and the pears and the tea, in the seraph and the harp.'

Jordan's eyes glowed, like a cat's in a barn. 'Tenniel and What's-his-name, the *douanier*,' he said in a throaty voice.

'Come on, let's go, I got to go,' Hayes said, getting up.

'You didn't have a hat,' I told him.

'Take the oranges and gibbons of What's-his-name,' Jordan went on, in a rapt croak.

'Rousseau, for God sake,' Hayes said. 'Come on.'

Jordan got to his feet. His eyes moved slowly around the room.

'You didn't have a hat,' Hayes said. 'Come on.'

He got Jordan just outside the living-room door. Four more steps would have taken them through the hall to the front door.

'Where do you get the tea in phrase?' I asked suddenly. 'There isn't any "t" in phrase.'

Jordan turned and loped back to his chair and sat down hard, like a tired setter. 'A posset for the highway!' he bawled.

'You asked for this,' Hayes told me wearily.

'Mix him a short one,' I said.

Hayes went slowly back into the living room and I closed the door behind him. I knew Alice was standing at the head of the stairs in the dark. 'What *is* it?' she whispered.

'A posset for the highway,' I told her.

'Jink Jordan? Oh, no!' She went back to her room.

I lingered in the hall, hoping they would come out, but Jordan's voice was loud and argumentative. 'Will you stop saying it's thin, for God sake?' he shouted.

'All right, all right, it's exiguous, then,' Hayes said.

'It's exiguous because it's undeveloped, that's why,' Jordan replied. 'You can't develop a thing like this in one night.'

I went back into the room and shut the door behind me. Jordan was sitting in the chair I had been in, pulling some papers out of his inside coat pocket.

'Put that stuff away,' Hayes commanded him sharply.

'Just a second,' Jordan said. 'I knew we'd left something out. How in the hell could you let me leave Blake out?' He began to pore over a pencilled scrawl on the back of a typewritten page. 'We proved Blake had it,' he said loudly. 'We proved Blake knew all about it, and here it is!'

Hayes grabbed the sheet of paper away from him. 'If I read it, will you get up and go home?' he asked. 'And don't drink that so fast.'

'Read it,' Jordan said, waving his glass. 'Wait a minute!' He pointed a finger at me. 'How many tigers are there in – what's the line, Tom?'

' "Tiger! Tiger! burning bright in the forests of the night",' Tom recited.

'One tiger,' I said. 'How many Toms are there in "Tom, Tom, the piper's son"?'

Jordan set his drink down and waved his arms despairingly. 'Journalist!' he said bleakly.

'This is kind of interesting,' Hayes said hurriedly. 'There are actually five tigers in the first two lines of the poem – that is, the necessary letters are repeated often enough to spell the word five times, three times in addition to "tiger, tiger," with a couple of "t"s and an "i" left over.'

Jordan finished his drink in a gulp. 'Nursery rhymes!' he said bitterly.

'In those two lines,' Hayes cut in, 'Blake used only twelve letters of the alphabet, so Jink thinks he was on to the new dimension.'

'Thinks!' Jordan cried.

'Wordsworth, who was not on to it,' Hayes continued, 'used nineteen letters in "She dwelt among the untrodden ways, beside the springs of Dove." '

Jordan shook his head at me slowly. 'It'll take me ten years to work this thing out,' he snarled, 'and you giggle at it like a girl. Tell him about Planters Peanuts, Tom.'

Hayes handed the sheet of paper back to Jordan and ran his hand over his forehead. 'There are nine letters in Planters Peanuts, or only three fewer than Blake used in those two lines. Come on, let's go.'

'One more, maybe?' Jordan said, holding out his glass.

'I'm going,' Hayes snapped. 'I'll wait just two minutes for you in the car.' He walked over and opened the door, closed it behind him, went out the front door, got in the car, and slammed the car door shut.

'There goes one of the sweetest characters in the whole world,' Jordan said.

I started turning out the table lamps, and Jordan got to his feet. 'So long, Jink,' I said. He walked slowly to the door, opened it, and said over his shoulder, 'Not in a million years.' The only light left on now was the one in the hall. Jordan closed the front door after him with great care. After a moment, the engine started and the car drove off.

Half an hour later, in bed, I had almost dropped off when, in the narrow strip of lucidity between the bright compound of consciousness and the dark jungle of sleep, I remembered, with a start like a gunshot, the tiger in the three six-letter words. I tried all the permutations I could think of, using one consonant after another, from 'b' to 'z'. I couldn't fit the tiger into any six-letter word except tigers, and that obviously didn't count. I began all over again: tibger, bitger, grebit, trebig, briget, ticger, grecit, gercit, tidger, gertid, dregit.

The dawn was fluttering at the window when I finally found the three words, one after another, with tiger in them.

Alice woke up. 'Haven't you been to sleep *yet?*' she asked.

'Gaiter, goitre, aigret,' I said. 'Avoid the consonants. It's as simple as that.'

'Go to sleep,' she said.

I managed it finally. It wasn't easy.

Eng. Lit.

☆★☆★☆★☆★☆★☆★☆★☆★☆

JOYCE GRENFELL

The scene is a book-lined study with stone-framed Gothic windows. A row of small painted shields are ranged along the shelves above the bookcases. There are group photographs about the room, and over the door is a pair of crossed oars. The linen chair- and sofa-covers are made from a cloth designed by William Morris. It is just possible they are original. The speaker is the wife of the Vice-Chancellor of an Oxbridge University. She wears an elderly cardigan of which she is fond. Her speech is Educated-English, well articulated, but she cannot pwonounce her Rs.

Interview

It's really very difficult to describe my grandmother. She wasn't particularly patrician but she did look very like the great Duke of Wellington, only rather prettier. Just as well, really. You know, there is a picture of her in the front of my new book. I don't know – have you read my book, Mr Wimble? No, I know it is so difficult to find time to read what one really wants to. No, it was only since you have so very kindly invited me to come on to your television programme in order to discuss my book I thought – you know – that you might just possibly have read it. But I do know how it is.

Were you up at this university, Mr Wimble? Oh, how very interesting. No, I've never been there, but now I shall make a point of going . . .

No, this is *not* my first book. I've written several. Lives. They're all Lives. And the reason I have written the Life of my grandmother is because she was a remarkable woman and I liked her. She lived a very long time you know – and she never lost interest. She was what you might call *consumed* with interest till the very last gasp. And I think ninety-four is a goodly span and that is why I have called my book *The Long Result of Time* and I don't have to tell you that is Tennyson. I expect you have 'Locksley Hall' by heart, and I very much wish I had.

Yes, she was very eccentric. Very. And I think we ought to celebrate our eccentrics. It seems to me they are getting rarer and rarer. No, I don't know where they've all gone, Mr Wimble. I suppose they have been ironed out. I must say there's one thing about my grandmother: you could not have ironed her out! Oh, no – she was far too hilly.

Oh, yes, indeed, she was intellectual. Very. She came from a long line of intellectuals – father, grandfather, etcetera. I suppose the nearest parallel to my grandmother's family was the great clan of Darwins and Huxleys, and like the Darwin–Huxley lot my grandmother's family were all very much concerned with Natural Science and Genetics. And my grandmother's own particular area of interest was in the world of very small mammals.

Yes, isn't it interesting.

She had a long and very close relationship with a small red squirrel – yes, indeed, with a bushy tail! No, I've never known a squirrel at all well, but my grandmother did. And I must tell you that as well as her very strong scientific side, she was also very much concerned with reincarnation, and she was convinced that this small red squirrel was in fact the reincarnation of a much-loved cousin, who had been gathered at an earlier date. Indeed she always called the squirrel Edwin after this much-loved cousin, and I think you will agree Edwin is not a very squirrel-like name. I don't know what you should call a squirrel – Charlie, perhaps? Or if one had Greek one might call him Skyouros! I expect you have Greek. I've only got a little bread-and-butter Greek – just enough to go through Greece, but alas, in no way classical Greek.

Oh, hello, Mrs Finley. What have you got there? The evening paper? Kindly conceal it from me, dear woman, until I feel stronger and can surprise it later. Thank you. Oh, Mrs Finley – is there a favourable chance of your finding yourself in close proximity to a kettle? I think Mr Wimble and I are both very well disposed towards the idea of some tea. And something crunchy? Lovely.

Yes, my grandmother was a great dazzler.

Oh, no, don't let's talk about me. I'd far rather talk about my grandmother. Oh dear, what sort of things do television viewers want to know about one? Likes and dislikes – yes, I've got some of those. Oh, yes, I'm *very* passionate.

Well now, which do I like best – men or women? I think it rather depends what for. I am more *familiar* with men. You see, both my father and my husband were Masters of Colleges in this University, and now my husband is Vice-Chancellor, and we have four very agreeable sons, so you see, it's men, really, men all the way along the line.

I don't know what I'd have done if I'd had a daughter, but the question never arose. I do have a very frilly little grand-daughter about whom I am prejudiced. I think she's rather too aware of her appearance and her clothes for one of only six, but I find her very fetching – very.

Clothes? Oh, yes, I like clothes – on other people. Well, somehow they seem to suffer a sea-change when they get on to me. They look quite promising in the shop; and not entirely without hope when I get them back into my wardrobe. But then, when I put them on they tend to deteriorate with a very strange rapidity and one feels so sorry for them.

I tell you what I do like – *hats*! Could I, perhaps, wear a hat if I come on to your television programme? Alas, one of the things of which I am not possessed is an *in*formal hat. I fear my hats tend to be rather purposeful. Oh, well, I'll have to ask my adviser. My adviser? Oh, that's my grandson, Edward. He's only eleven, but he is *very* wise and he knows far more about the world of today than do I, and I abide by his judgment quite considerably.

I may say, Mr Wimble, that when I told him you had so very kindly invited me to appear on your television programme he said, 'Go ahead, Gaga.' (With a certain deadly accuracy he calls me Gaga!) 'Go ahead, Gaga. Live dangerously!'

I must confess this advice has somewhat unnerved me, and it prompts me to put a question to you: Mr Wimble, are you very cruel to the people who come on to your programme?

I see. And do they *like* that?

Oh, it's the *viewers* who like it. . . . I wonder if I should.

Oh, thank you, Mrs Finley, we'll come and consume it instantly. In the dining-room? Right.

Tea.

Well, now I do very much appreciate your kindness in asking me to do this programme. I shall certainly consider it. . . . A thought has just crossed my mind. Mr Wimble, what would happen if I were to come on to your programme and I were to be very cruel to you?

An event

Mrs Finley dear, we are out of the dining-room at long last, thank you so very much. And that was a most triumphant repast. Oh, Mrs Finley, when the time is ripe for you, we are in the market for some coffee – in here if you can manage it, thank you so much.

Now, my dear nephew, sit you down somewhere comfortable.

Yes, that really was a *very* triumphant meal.

Oh well, you see Mrs Finley has only just come to terms and made friends with our new electric cooker. It has rather a number of knobs, and it really is rather daunting. One feels one is piloting a spacecraft. And for a while Mrs Finley only dared to be a Daniel about a knob called Simmer, so we had to make do with rather many meals of a tepid nature. But, now, if you see what I mean, things are hotting up, as it were.

If you are in the mood for a peppermint they are in the tin marked Edinburgh Rock. No, thank you very much. I shall try to resist.

It's very good to see you in our midst again, my dear John. How is progress doing in Africa? Oh good. One hardly dares to ask that question, for I so rarely like the answer. Progress everywhere today does seem to come so *very* heavily disguised as Chaos.

Oh John, do me a kindness and keep your eye on the time for me. There is a programme on the television that I *would* rather like you to see. It's not in the least important and we need not let it distract us unless we want it to. Perhaps you'd rather not? It's at 8.30, I think.

Oh, it's just a programme to which I faintly contribute.

Didn't you know I'd taken to going on the telly? Well that's an overstatement. I've been on it *once*. Yes, when my book about my grandmother won a literary prize. Yes, it was rather fun. This is my second venture.

There is no doubt about it, flattery does get one somewhere, and it got me on to the television. And for a while I was in grave peril owing to the great size of my head. Well, because everyone was so very nice to me and the young man who did the interview was very encouraging and so pretty. He had lovely clean hair, and he had on a psychedelic tie and, what's more, he treated me almost as if I were his equal. So you see it was very over-exciting.

Oh the programme? It's a sort of discussion programme between so-called 'intelligent people' – they get you together and then they throw you a topic.

Oh, such as 'Infidelity'. Always very popular they tell me. And 'Is Happiness Wrong?'. I don't think it is, do you? No, I rather like it.

Now and again I did find myself a little out of my depth. Well, I know so little about Elementary Sex in Schools – or was it Sex in Elementary Schools? I can't remember now, but I thought it rather a bore.

Yes, I did enjoy doing the programme; only afterwards the producer said to me, 'You are *so* natural,' as if there was a possible alternative. I felt as if I must have erred in some way; and I now feel a little self-conscious about the whole thing and I do rather dread seeing it. And I may tell you that is why I accidentally-on-purpose forgot to tell my husband, the dear Vice-Chancellor, this morning that his exhibitionist wife was going to be on the telly tonight. Because I do *not* wish to shame him in any way.

No, he won't remember. He only remembers Events if they are written down on his little Memory Jogger Pad by his remarkable secretary, Mrs Brittle. She does all his Event-remembering for him, so he doesn't have to bother.

He's dining with the Bursar – did I tell you? They've got some university business on hand. Protest, no doubt. It usually is.

The other people on the programme were tolerably agreeable. I think they were all very well known – except to me. You know there has to be something called a Fair Balance, so if you have a Labour then you have to have a Tory – and we had one of each; one thick and one thin. And then if you have a man of Science, say, for special knowledge, then you have to have a Light Relief in the shape of a TV personality, and we had rather a crack-pot charmer of Scottish origin, dressed a little unusually, I thought, for one so deeply wedded to Caledonia.

Well, he was wearing an Arab burnous. No, it was never explained; nor was his relief *all* that light, come to think of it. And if you will forgive a Laurentian joke – he wasn't much of a Pillar of Wisdom either!

Oh, I was there as a *woman*. There always has to be a woman for reasons of provocation and/or commonsense and, alas, I think I know which I was there to represent.

But, of course, *the* star of the whole thing was Dr Barstin. He's always on the programme, and you know all about him.

My dear John, where have you been? Oh yes, of course, Africa.

Well, he is a tremendous egg-head and vastly knowledgeable about a number of things without which I have managed, through a long and happy marriage, to do.

Such as the High Density of Infra-Radiation of Contra Ballic Span.

Exactly.

He is also a very, very devout agnostic, than which there are few things more bigoted. (He's a little under privileged in a number of ways.)

Oh yes, I got on with him all right until I thought he got mildly out of control on the subject of animals. People do, you know.

Mark you, I like animals – in their right place. But I do not find them as much fun as people, do you? We have our dear old hearth-rug of a dog, Hengist – or Horsa – he answers to both. I prefer people for talking to and inventing safety-pins and playing Mozart.

But Dr Barstin could not, or would not, agree. He looked at the panel very carefully and then he said that in his opinion people were always *much* less beautiful than horses.

I quite saw his point. But I did think it was a trifle rude, and I couldn't resist saying: 'What about Greta Garbo?'

And you won't believe the depths to which he descended. He said: 'What *is* a Greta Garbo?' Laughter in court.

Can you believe it? I said: 'What a very sheltered life you must have led, Dr Barstin! You sound just like a comic magistrate in an old Ealing comedy.'

Yes, it did go down very well. There was considerable mirth. But Dr Barstin didn't like it, and he made a very cross face at me. I'm rather looking forward to seeing his cross face. Oh, is it time? Yes, turn it on. There is a knob at the side. It takes a moment to warm up, before it bursts into flower.

I think you may not recognize me when I come on because I am most unnaturally tidy. They sprayed me with some grassy substance that reduced my hair to the exact consistency of a dried loofah. I am uncannily wispless, and it stayed rigid for days.

Yes, Mrs Finley? The telephone? Oh, how tiresome. Who? My husband? To remind me to watch the programme! *Dear* man. How very nice of him. Will you please tell him I had *entirely* forgotten about it and thank him very much for reminding me. Come back and see it if you would like to, Mrs Finley, when you bring the coffee.

He is a *dear* man.

You realize, John, that Mrs Brittle must have put me down on his little Memory Jogger Pad as an Event!

Miss Mapp

☆★☆★☆★☆★☆★☆★☆★☆★☆★☆★☆★☆

E. F. BENSON

Diva was sitting at the open drawing-room window of her house in the High Street, cutting with a pair of sharp nail scissors into the old chintz curtains which her maid had told her no longer 'paid for the mending'. So, since they refused to pay for their mending any more she was preparing to make them pay, pretty smartly too, in other ways. The pattern was of little bunches of pink roses peeping out through trellis work, and it was these which she had just begun to cut out. Though Tilling was noted for the ingenuity with which its more fashionable ladies devised novel and quaint effects in the dress in an economical manner, Diva felt sure, ransack her memory though she might, that nobody had thought of *this* before.

The hot weather had continued late into September and showed no signs of breaking yet, and it would be agreeable to her and acutely painful to others that just at the end of the summer she should appear in a perfectly new costume, before the days of jumpers and heavy skirts and large woollen scarves came in. She was preparing, therefore, to take the light white jacket which she wore over her blouse, and cover the broad collar and cuffs of it with these pretty roses. The belt of the skirt would be similarly decorated, and so would the edge of it, if there were enough clean ones. The jacket and skirt had already gone to the dyer's, and would be back in a day or two, white no longer, but of a rich purple hue, and by that time she would have hundreds of these little pink roses ready to be tacked on. Perhaps a piece of the chintz, trellis and all, could be sewn over the belt, but she was determined to have single little bunches of roses peppered all over the collar and cuffs of the jacket, and, if possible, round the edge of the skirt. She had already tried the effect, and was of the opinion that nobody could possibly guess what the origin of these roses was. When carefully sewn on they looked as if they were a design in the stuff.

She let the circumcised roses fall on to the window-seat, and from time to time, when they grew numerous, swept them into a cardboard box. Though she worked with zealous diligence, she had an eye to the movements in the street outside, for it was shopping-hour, and there were many observations to be made. She had not anything like Miss Mapp's genius for conjecture, but her memory was appallingly good, and this was the third morning running on which Elizabeth had gone into the grocer's. It was odd to go to your grocer's every day like that: groceries twice a week was sufficient for most people. From here on the floor above the street she could easily look into Elizabeth's basket, and she certainly was carrying nothing away with her from the grocer's, for the only thing there was a small bottle done up in white paper with sealing wax, which, Diva had no need to be told, certainly came from the chemist's, and was no doubt connected with too many plums.

Miss Mapp crossed the street to the pavement below Diva's house, and precisely as she reached it, Diva's maid opened the door into the drawing-room, bringing in the second post, or rather not bringing in the second post, but the announcement that there wasn't any second post. This opening of the door caused a draught, and the bunches of roses which littered the window-seat rose brightly in the air. Diva managed to beat most of them down again, but two fluttered out of the window. Precisely then, and at no other time, Miss Mapp looked up, and one settled on her face, the other fell into her basket. Her trained faculties were all on the alert, and she thrust them both inside her glove for future consideration, without stopping to examine them just then. She only knew that they were little pink roses, and that they had fluttered out of Diva's window . . .

She paused on the pavement, and remembered that Diva had not yet expressed regret about the worsted, and that she still 'popped' as much as ever. Thus Diva deserved a punishment of some sort, and happily, at that very moment she thought of a subject on which she might be able to make her uncomfortable. The street was full, and it would be pretty to call up to her, instead of ringing her bell, in order to save trouble to poor overworked Janet. (Diva only kept two servants, though of course poverty was no crime.)

'Diva darling!' she cooed.

Diva's head looked out like a cuckoo in a clock preparing to chime the hour.

'Hullo!' she said. 'Want me?'

'May I pop up for a moment, dear?' said Miss Mapp. 'That's to say if you're not very busy.'

'Pop away,' said Diva. She was quite aware that Miss Mapp said 'pop' in crude inverted commas, so to speak, for purposes of mockery, and so she said it herself more than ever 'I'll tell my maid to pop down and open the door.'

While this was being done, Diva bundled her chintz curtains together and stored them and the roses she had cut out into her work-cupboard, for secrecy was an essential to the construction of these decorations. But in order to appear naturally employed, she pulled out the woollen scarf she was knitting for the autumn and winter, forgetting for the moment that the rose-madder stripe at the end on which she was now engaged was made of that fatal worsted which Miss Mapp considered to have been feloniously appropriated. That was the sort of thing Miss Mapp never forgot. Even among her sweet flowers. Her eye fell on it the moment she entered the room, and she tucked the two chintz roses more securely into her glove.

'I thought I would just pop across from the grocer's,' she said. 'What a pretty scarf, dear! That's a lovely shade of rose-madder. Where can I have seen something like it before?'

This was clearly ironical, and had best be answered by irony. Diva was no coward.

'Couldn't say, I'm sure,' she said.

Miss Mapp appeared to recollect, and smiled as far back as her wisdom teeth. (Diva couldn't do that.)

'I have it,' she said. 'It was the wool I ordered at Heynes's, and then he sold it you, and I couldn't get any more.'

'So it was,' said Diva. 'Upset you a bit. There was the wool in the shop. I bought it.'

'Yes, dear; I see you did. But that wasn't what I popped in about. This coal-strike, you know.'

'Got a cellar-full,' said Diva.

'Diva, you've not been hoarding, have you?' asked Miss Mapp with great anxiety. 'They can take away every atom of coal you've got, if so, and fine you I don't know what for every hundredweight of it.'

'Pooh!' said Diva, rather forcing the indifference of this rude interjection.

'Yes, love, pooh by all means, if you like poohing!' said Miss Mapp. 'But I should have felt very unfriendly if one morning I found you were fined – found you were fined – quite a play upon words – and I hadn't warned you.'

Diva felt a little less poohish.

'But how much do they allow you to have?' she asked.

'Oh, quite a little: enough to go on with. But I daresay they won't discover you. I just took the trouble to come and warn you.'

Diva did remember something about hoarding; there had surely been dreadful exposures of prudent house-keepers in the papers which were very uncomfortable reading.

'But all these orders were only for the period of the war,' she said.

'No doubt you're right, dear,' said Miss Mapp brightly. 'I'm sure I hope you are. Only if the coal-strike comes on, I think you'll find that the regulations against hoarding are quite as severe as they ever were. Food hoarding, too. Twemlow – such a civil man – tells me that he thinks we shall have plenty of food, or anyhow sufficient for everybody for quite a long time, provided that there's no hoarding. Not been hoarding food, too, dear Diva? You naughty thing: I believe that great cupboard is full of sardines and biscuits and Bovril.'

'Nothing of the kind,' said Diva indignantly. 'You shall see for yourself – ' and then she suddenly remembered that the cupboard was full of chintz curtains and little bunches of pink roses, neatly cut out of them, and a pair of nail scissors.

There was a perfectly perceptible pause, during which Miss Mapp noticed that there were no curtains over the window. There certainly used to be, and they matched with the chintz cover of the window-seat, which was decorated with little bunches of pink roses peeping through trellis. This was in the nature of a bonus: she had not up till then connected the chintz curtains with the little things that had fluttered down upon her and were now safe in her glove; her only real object in this call had been to instill a general uneasiness into Diva's mind about the coal-strike and the danger of being well provided with fuel. That she humbly hoped that she had accomplished. She got up.

'Must be going,' she said. 'Such a lovely little chat! But what has happened to your pretty curtains?'

'Gone to the wash,' said Diva firmly.

'Liar,' thought Miss Mapp, as she tripped downstairs. 'Diva would have sent the cover of the window-seat too, if that was the case. Liar,' she thought again as she kissed her hand to Diva, who was looking gloomily out of the window.

As soon as Miss Mapp had gained her garden-room, she examined the mysterious treasures in her left-hand glove. Without the smallest doubt Diva had taken down her curtains (and high time too, for they were sadly shabby), and was cutting the roses out of them. But what on earth was she doing that for? For what garish purpose could she want to use bunches of roses cut out of chintz curtains?

Miss Mapp had put the two specimens of which she had so providentially become possessed in her lap, and they looked very pretty against the navy-blue of her skirt. Diva was very ingenious: she used up all sorts of odds and ends in a way that did credit to her undoubtedly parsimonious qualities. She could trim a hat with a tooth-brush and a banana in such a way that it looked quite Parisian till you firmly analysed its component parts, and most of her ingenuity was devoted to dress: the more was the pity that she had such a round-about figure that her waistband always reminded you of the equator . . .

'Eureka!' said Miss Mapp aloud, and, though the telephone-bell was ringing, and the postulant might be one of the servants' friends ringing them up at an hour when their mistress was usually in the High Street, she glided swiftly to the large cupboard underneath the stairs which was full of the things which no right-minded person could bear to throw away: broken basket-chairs, pieces of brown paper, cardboard boxes without lids, and cardboard lids without boxes, old bags with holes in them, keys without locks and locks without keys and worn chintz covers. There was one – it had once adorned the sofa in the garden-room – covered with red poppies (very easy to cut out), and Miss Mapp dragged it dustily from its corner, setting in motion a perfect cascade of cardboard lids and some door-handles.

Withers had answered the telephone, and came to announce that Twemlow the grocer regretted he had only two large tins of corned beef, but –

'Then say I will have the tongue as well, Withers,' said Miss Mapp. 'Just a tongue – and then I shall want you and Mary to do some cutting out for me.'

The three went to work with feverish energy, for Diva had got a start, and by four o'clock that afternoon there were enough poppies cut out to furnish, when in seed, a whole street of opium dens. The dress selected for decoration was, apart from a few mildew-spots, the colour of ripe corn, which was superbly appropriate for September. 'Poppies in the corn,' said Miss Mapp over and over to herself, remembering some sweet verses she had once read by Bernard Shaw or Clement Shorter or somebody like that about a garden of sleep somewhere in Norfolk . . .

'No one can work as neatly as you, Withers,' she said gaily, 'and I shall ask you to do the most difficult part. I want you to sew my lovely poppies over the collar and facings of the jacket, just spacing them a little and making a dainty irregularity. And then Mary – won't you, Mary? – will do the same with the waistband while I put a border of them round the skirt, and my dear old dress will look quite new and lovely. I shall be at home to nobody, Withers, this afternoon, even if the Prince of Wales came and sat on my doorstep again. We'll all work together in the garden, shall we, and you and Mary must scold me if you think I'm not working hard enough. It will be delicious in the garden.'

Thanks to this pleasant plan, there was not much opportunity for Withers and Mary to be idle. . . .

It was not to be supposed that Diva would act on Miss Mapp's alarming hints that morning as to the fate of coal-hoarders, and give, say, a ton of fuel to the hospital at once, in lieu of her usual smaller Christmas contribution, without making further inquiries in the proper quarters as to the legal liabilities of having, so she ascertained, three tons in her cellar, and as soon as her visitor had left her this morning, she popped out to see Mr Wootten, her coal-merchant. She returned in a state of fury, for there were no regulations whatever in existence with regard to the amount of coal that any householder might choose to amass, and Mr Wootten complimented her on her prudence in having got in a reasonable supply, for he thought it quite probable that, if the coal-strike took place, there would be some difficulty in a month's time from now in replenishing cellars. 'But we've had a good supply all the summer,' added agreeable Mr Wootten, 'and all my customers have got their cellars well stocked.'

Diva rapidly recollected that the perfidious Elizabeth was among them.

'Oh, but, Mr Wootten,' she said, 'Miss Mapp popped – dropped in to see me just now. Told me she had hardly got any.'

Mr Wootten turned up his ledger. It was not etiquette to disclose the affairs of one client to another, but if there was a cantankerous customer, one who was never satisfied with prices and quality, that client was Miss Mapp . . .

He allowed a broad grin to overspread his agreeable face.

'Well, ma'am, if in a month's time I'm short of coal, there are friends of yours in Tilling who can let you have plenty,' he permitted himself to say . . .

It was idle to attempt to cut out bunches of roses while her hand was so feverish, and she trundled up and down the High Street to cool off. Had she not been so prudent as to make inquiries, as likely as not she would have sent a ton of coal that very day to the hospital, so strongly had Elizabeth's perfidious warning inflamed her imagination as to the fate of hoarders, and all the time Elizabeth's own cellars were glutted, though she had asserted that she was almost fuelless. Why, she must have in her possession more coal than Diva herself, since Mr Wootten had clearly implied that it was Elizabeth who could be borrowed from! And all because of a wretched piece of rose-madder worsted . . .

By degrees she calmed down, for it was no use attempting to plan revenge with a brain at fever-heat. She must be calm and icily ingenious. As the cooling process went on she began to wonder whether it was worsted alone that had prompted her friend's diabolical suggestion. It seemed more likely that another motive (one strangely Elizabethan) was the cause of it. Elizabeth might be taken for certain as being a coal-hoarder herself, and it was ever so like her to divert suspicion by pretending her cellar was next to empty. She had been equally severe on any who might happen to be hoarding food, in case transport was dis-arranged and supplies fell short, and with a sudden flare of authentic intuition, Diva's mind blazed with the conjecture that Elizabeth was hoarding food as well.

Luck ever attends the bold and constructive thinker: the apple, for instance, fell from the tree precisely when Newton's mind was groping after the law of gravity, and as Diva stepped into her grocer's to begin her morning's shopping (for she had been occupied with roses ever since breakfast) the attendant was at the telephone at the back of the shop. He spoke in a lucid telephone-voice.

'We've only two of the big tins of corned beef,' he said; and there was a pause, during which, to a psychic, Diva's ears might have seemed to grow as pointed with attention as a satyr's. But she could only hear little hollow quacks from the other end.

'Tongue as well. Very good. I'll send them up at once,' he added, and came forward into the shop.

'Good morning,' said Diva. Her voice was tremulous with anxiety and investigation. 'Got any big tins of corned beef? The ones that contain six pounds.'

'Very sorry, ma'am. We've only got two, and they've just been or-dered.'

'A small pot of ginger then, please,' said Diva recklessly. 'Will you send it round immediately?'

'Yes, ma'am. The boy's just going out.'

That was luck. Diva hurried into the street, and was absorbed by the headlines of the news outside the stationer's. This was a favourite place for observation, for you appeared to be quite taken up by the topics of the day, and kept an oblique eye on the true object of your scrutiny . . . She had not got to wait long, for almost immediately the grocer's boy came out of the shop with a heavy basket on his arm, delivered the small pot of ginger at her own door, and proceeded along the street. He was, unfortunately, a popular and a conversational youth, who had a great deal to say to his friends, and the period of waiting to see if he would turn up the steep street that led to Miss Mapp's house was very protracted. At the corner he deliberately put down the basket altogether and lit a cigarette, and never had Diva so acutely deplored the spread of the tobacco-habit among the juvenile population.

Having refreshed himself he turned up the steep street. He passed the fishmonger's and the fruiterer's; he did not take the turn down to the dentist's and Mr Wyse's. He had no errand to the Major's house or to the Captain's. Then, oh then, he rang the bell at Miss Mapp's back-door. All the time Diva had been following him, keeping her head well down so as to avert the possibility of observation from the window of the garden-room, and walking so slowly that the motion of her feet seemed not circular at all . . . Then the bell was answered, and he delivered into Wither's hands one, two tins of corned beef and a round ox-tongue. He put the basket on his head and came down the street again, shrilly whistling. If Diva had had any reasonably small change in her pocket, she would assuredly have given him some small share in it. Lacking this, she trundled home with all speed, and began cutting out roses with swift and certain strokes of the nail scissors.

Now she had already noticed that Elizabeth had paid visits to the grocer's on three consecutive days (three consecutive days: think of it!), and given that her purchases on other occasions had been on the same substantial scale as today, it became a matter of thrilling interest as to where she kept these stores. She could not keep them in the coal-cellar, for that was already bursting with coal, and Diva, who had assisted her (the base one) in making a prodigious quantity of jam that year from her well-stocked garden, was aware that the kitchen cupboards were like to be as replete as the coal-cellar, before those hoardings of dead oxen began. Then there was the big cupboard under the stairs, but that could scarcely be the site of this prodigious cache, for it was full of cardboard and curtains and carpets and all the rubbishy accumulations which Elizabeth could not bear to part with. Then she had large cupboards in her bedroom and spare-rooms full to overflowing of mouldy clothes, but there was positively not another cupboard in the house that Diva knew of, and she crushed her temples in her hands in the attempt to locate the hiding-place of the hoard.

Diva suddenly jumped up with a happy squeal of discovery, and in her excitement snapped her scissors with so random a stroke that she completely cut in half the bunch of roses that she was engaged on. There was another cupboard, the best and biggest of all and the most secret and the most discreet. It lay embedded in the wall of the garden-room, cloaked and concealed behind the shelves of a false bookcase, which contained no more than the simulacra of books, just books with titles that had never yet appeared on any honest book. There were twelve volumes of 'The Beauties of Nature', a shelf full of 'Elegant Extracts', there were volumes simply called 'Poems', there were 'Commentaries', there were 'Travels' and 'Astronomy' and the lowest and tallest shelf was full of 'Music'. A card-table habitually stood in front of this false repository of learning, and it was only last week that Diva, prying casually round the room while Elizabeth had gone to take off her gardening-gloves, had noticed a modest catch let into the woodwork. Without doubt, then, the bookcase was the door of the cupboard, and with a stroke of intuition, too sure to be called a guess, Diva was aware that she had correctly inferred the storage of this nefarious hoard. It only remained to verify her conclusion, and, if possible, expose it with every circumstance of public ignominy. She was in no hurry: she could bide her time, aware that, in all probability, every day that passed would see an addition to its damning contents. Some day, when she was playing bridge and the card-table had been moved out, in some rubber when she herself was dummy and Elizabeth greedily playing the hand, she would secretly and accidentally press the catch which her acute vision had so providentially revealed to her . . .

She attacked her chintz curtains again with her appetite for the pink roses agreeably whetted. Another hour's work would give her sufficient bunches for her purpose, and unless the dyer was as perfidious as Elizabeth, her now purple jacket and skirt would arrive that afternoon. Two days' hard work would be sufficient for so accomplished a needle-woman as herself to make these original decorations.

In the meantime, for Diva was never idle, and was chiefly occupied with dress, she got out a certain American fashion paper. There was in it the description of a tea-gown worn by Mrs Titus W. Trout which she believed was within her dressmaking capacity. She would attempt it, anyhow, and if it proved to be beyond her, she could entrust the more difficult parts to that little dressmaker whom Elizabeth employed, and who was certainly very capable. But the costume was of so daring and splendid a nature that she feared to take anyone into her confidence about it, lest some hint or gossip – for Tilling was a gossipy place – might leak out. Kingfisher-blue! It made her mouth water to dwell on the sumptuous syllables!

Miss Mapp was so feverishly occupied all next morning with the application of poppies to the corn-coloured skirt that she paid very little attention to the opening gambits of the day, either as regards the world in general, or, more particularly, Major Benjy. After his early retirement last night he was probably up with the lark this morning, and when between half-past ten and eleven his sonorous 'Qui-hi!' sounded through her open window, the shock she experienced interrupted for a moment her floral industry. It was certainly very odd that, having gone to bed at so respectable an hour last night, he should be calling for his porridge only now, but with an impulse of unusual optimism, she figured him as having been at work on his diaries before breakfast, and in that absorbing occupation having forgotten how late it was growing. That, no doubt, was the explanation, though it would be nice to know for certain, if the information positively forced itself on her notice . . . As she worked (framing her lips with elaborate motions to the syllables) she dumbly practised the phrase 'Major Benjy'. Sometimes in moments of gallantry he called her 'Miss Elizabeth', and she meant, when she had got accustomed to it by practice, to say 'Major Benjy' to him by accident, and he would, no doubt, beg her to make a habit of that friendly slip of the tongue . . . 'Tongue' led to a new train of thought, and presently she paused in her work, and pulling the card-table away from the deceptive bookcase, she pressed the concealed catch of the door, and peeped in.

There was still room for further small precautions against starvation owing to the impending coal-strike, and she took stock of her provisions. Even if the strike lasted quite a long time, there would now be no immediate lack of the necessaries of life, for the cupboard glistened with tinned meats, and the flour-merchant had sent a very sensible sack. This with considerable exertion she transferred to a high shelf in the cupboard, instead of allowing it to remain standing on the floor, for Withers had informed her of an unpleasant rumour about a mouse, which Mary had observed, lost in thought in front of the cupboard. 'So mousie shall only find tins on the floor now,' thought Miss Mapp. 'Mousie shall try his teeth on tins.'. . . There was tea and coffee in abundance, jars of jam filled the kitchen shelves, and if this morning she laid in a moderate supply of dried fruits, there was no reason to face the future with anything but fortitude. She would see about that now, for, busy though she was, she could not miss the shopping-parade. Would Diva, she wondered, be at her window, snipping roses out of chintz curtains? The careful, thrifty soul. Perhaps this time tomorrow, Diva, looking out of her window, would see that somebody else had been quicker about being thrifty than she. That would be fun!

The Major's dining-room window was open, and as Miss Mapp passed it, she could not help hearing loud, angry remarks about eggs coming from inside. That made it clear that he was still at breakfast, and that if he had been working at his diaries in the fresh morning hours and forgetting the time, early rising, in spite of his early retirement last night, could not be supposed to suit his Oriental temper. But a change of habits was invariably known to be upsetting, and Miss Mapp was hopeful that in a day or two he would feel quite a different man. Farther down the street was quaint Irene lounging at the door of her new studio (a converted coach-house), smoking a cigarette and dressed like a jockey.

'Hullo, Mapp,' she said. 'Come and have a look round my new studio. You haven't seen it yet. I shall give a house-warming next week. Bridge-party!'

Miss Mapp tried to steel herself for the hundredth time to appear quite unconscious that she was being addressed when Irene said 'Mapp' in that odious manner. But she never could summon up sufficient nerve to be rude to so awful a mimic . . .

'Good morning, dear one,' she said sycophantically. 'Shall I peep in for a moment?'

The decoration of the studio was even more appalling than might have been expected. There was a German stove in the corner made of pink porcelain, the rafters and roof were painted scarlet, the walls were of magenta distemper and the floor was blue. In the corner was a very large orange-coloured screen. The walls were hung with specimens of Irene's art, there was a stout female with no clothes on at all, whom it was impossible not to recognize as being Lucy; there were studies of fat legs and ample bosoms, and on the easel was a picture, evidently in process of completion, which represented a man. From this Miss Mapp instantly averted her eyes.

'Eve,' said Irene, pointing to Lucy.

Miss Mapp naturally guessed that the gentleman who was almost in the same costume was Adam, and turned completely away from him.

'And what a lovely idea to have a blue floor, dear,' she said. 'How original you are. And that pretty scarlet ceiling. But don't you find when you're painting that all these bright colours disturb you?'

'Not a bit: they stimulate your sense of colour.'

Miss Mapp moved towards the screen.

'What a delicious big screen,' she said.

'Yes, but don't go behind it, Mapp,' said Irene, 'or you'll see my model undressing.'

Miss Mapp retreated from it precipitately, as from a wasp's nest, and examined some of the studies on the wall, for it was more than probable from the unfinished picture on the easel that Adam lurked behind the delicious screen. Terrible though it all was, she was conscious of an unbridled curiosity to know who Adam was. It was dreadful to think that there could be any man in Tilling so depraved as to stand to be looked at with so little on . . .

Irene strolled round the walls with her.

'Studies of Lucy,' she said.

'I see, dear,' said Miss Mapp. 'How clever! Legs and things! But when you have your bridge-party, won't you perhaps cover some of them up, or turn them to the wall? We should all be looking at your pictures instead of attending to our cards. And if you were thinking of asking the Padre, you know . . .'

They were approaching the corner of the room where the screen stood, when a movement there as if Adam had hit it with his elbow made Miss Mapp turn round. The screen fell flat on the ground and within a yard of her stood Mr Hopkins, the proprietor of the fish shop just up the street. Often and often had Miss Mapp had pleasant little conversations with him, with a view to bringing down the price of flounders. He had little bathing-drawers on . . .

'Hullo, Hopkins, are you ready?' said Irene. 'You know Miss Mapp, don't you?'

Miss Mapp had not imagined that Time and Eternity combined could hold so embarrassing a moment. She did not know where to look, but wherever she looked, it should not be at Hopkins. But (wherever she looked) she could not be unaware that Hopkins raised his large bare arm and touched the place where his cap would have been, if he had had one.

'Good morning, Hopkins,' she said. 'Well, Irene darling, I must be trotting, and leave you to your – ' she hardly knew what to call it – 'to your work.'

She tripped from the room, which seemed to be entirely full of unclothed limbs, and redder than one of Mr Hopkins's boiled lobsters hurried down the street. She felt that she could never face him again, but would be obliged to go to the establishment in the High Street where Irene dealt, when it was fish she wanted from a fish shop . . . Her head was in a whirl at the brazenness of mankind, especially womankind. How had Irene started the overtures that led to this? Had she just said to Hopkins one morning: 'Will you come to my studio and take off all your clothes?' If Irene had not been such a wonderful mimic, she would certainly have felt it her duty to go straight to the Padre, and, pulling down her veil, confide to him the whole sad story. But as that was out of the question, she went into Twemlow's and ordered four pounds of dried apricots.

The dyer, as Diva had feared, proved perfidious, and it was not till the next morning that her maid brought her the parcel containing the coat and skirt of the projected costume. Diva had already done her marketing, so that she might have no other calls on her time to interfere with the tacking on of the bunches of pink roses, and she hoped to have the dress finished in time for Elizabeth's afternoon bridge-party next day, an invitation to which had just reached her. She had also settled to have a cold lunch today, so that her cook as well as her parlourmaid could devote themselves to the job.

She herself had taken the jacket for decoration, and was just tacking the first rose on to the collar, when she looked out of the window, and what she saw caused her needle to fall from her nerveless hand. Tripping along the opposite pavement was Elizabeth. She had on a dress, the material of which, after a moment's gaze, Diva identified: it was that corn-coloured coat and skirt which she had worn so much last spring. But the collar, the cuffs, the waistband and the hem of the skirt were covered with staring red poppies. Next moment, she called to remembrance the chintz that had once covered Elizabeth's sofa in the garden-room.

Diva wasted no time, but rang the bell. She had to make certain.

'Janet,' she said, 'go straight out into the High Street, and walk close behind Miss Mapp. Look very carefully at her dress; see if the poppies on it are of chintz.'

Janet's face fell.

'Why, ma'am, she's never gone and – ' she began.

'Quick!' said Diva in a strangled voice.

Diva watched from her window. Janet went out, looked this way and that, spied the quarry, and skimmed up the High Street on feet that twinkled as fast as her mistress's. She came back much out of breath with speed and indignation.

'Yes, ma'am,' she said. 'They're chintz sure enough. Tacked on, too, just as you were meaning to do. Oh, ma'am – '

Janet quite appreciated the magnitude of the calamity and her voice failed.

'What are we to do, ma'am?' she added.

Diva did not reply for a moment, but sat with eyes closed in profound and concentrated thought. It required no reflection to decide how impossible it was to appear herself tomorrow in a dress which seemed to ape the costume which all Tilling had seen Elizabeth wearing today, and at first it looked as if there was nothing to be done with all those laboriously acquired bunches of rosebuds; for it was clearly out of the question to use them as the decoration for any costume, and idle to think of sewing them back into the snipped and gashed curtains. She looked at the purple skirt and coat that hungered for their flowers, and then she looked at Janet. Janet was a short, roundabout person; it was ill-naturedly supposed that she had much the same figure as her mistress . . .

Then the light broke, dazzling and diabolical, and Diva bounced to her feet, blinded by its splendour.

'My coat and skirt are yours, Janet,' she said. 'Get on with the work both of you. Bustle. Cover it with roses. Have it finished tonight. Wear it tomorrow. Wear it always.'

She gave a loud cackle of laughter and threaded her needle.

'Lor, ma'am!' said Janet, admiringly. 'That's a teaser! And thank you, ma'am!'

'It was roses, roses all the way.' Diva had quite miscalculated the number required, and there were sufficient not only to cover collar, cuffs and border of the skirt with them but to make another line of them six inches above the hem. Original and gorgeous as the dress would be, it was yet a sort of parody of Elizabeth's costume which was attracting so much interest and attention as she popped in and out of shops today. Tomorrow that would be worn by Janet, and Janet (or Diva was much mistaken) should encourage her friends to get permission to use up old bits of chintz. Very likely chintz decoration would become quite a vogue among the servant maids of Tilling . . . How Elizabeth had got hold of the idea mattered nothing, but anyhow she would be surfeited with the idea before Diva had finished with her. It was possible, of course (anything was possible), that it had occurred to her independently, but Diva was loath to give so innocent an ancestry to her adoption of it. It was far more sensible to take for granted that she had got wind of Diva's invention by some odious, underhand piece of spying. What that might be must be investigated (and probably determined) later, but at present the business of Janet's roses eclipsed every other interest.

Miss Mapp's shopping that morning was unusually prolonged, for it was important that every woman in Tilling should see the poppies on the corn-coloured ground, and know that she had worn that dress before Diva appeared in some mean adaptation of it. Though the total cost of her entire purchases hardly amounted to a shilling, she went in and out of an amazing number of shops, and made a prodigious series of inquiries into the price of commodities that ranged from motor-cars to sealing-wax, and often entered a shop twice because (wreathed in smiling apologies for her stupidity) she had forgotten what she was told the first time. By twelve o'clock she was satisfied that practically everybody, with one exception, had seen her, and that her costume had aroused a deep sense of jealousy and angry admiration. So cunning was the handiwork of herself, Withers and Mary that she felt fairly sure that no one had the slightest notion of how this decoration of poppies was accomplished, for Evie had run round her in small mouse-like circles, murmuring to herself: 'Very effective idea; is it woven into the cloth, Elizabeth? Dear me, I wonder where I could get some like it,' and Mrs Poppit had followed her all up the street, with eyes glued to the hem of her skirt, and a completely puzzled face: 'but then,' so thought Elizabeth sweetly, 'even Members of the Order of the British Empire can't have everything their own way.' As for the Major, he had simply come to a dead stop when he bounced out of his house as she passed, and said something very gallant and appropriate. Even the absence of that one inhabitant of Tilling, dear Diva, did not strike a jarring note in this paean of triumph, for Miss Mapp was quite satisfied that Diva was busy indoors, working her fingers to the bone over the application of bunches of roses, and, as usual, she was perfectly correct in her conjecture. But dear Diva would have to see the new frock tomorrow afternoon, at the latest, when she came to the bridge-party. Perhaps she would then, for the first time, be wearing the roses herself, and everybody would very pleasantly pity her. This was so rapturous a thought, that when Miss Mapp, after her prolonged shopping and with her almost empty basket, passed Mr Hopkins standing outside his shop on her return home again, she gave him her usual smile, though without meeting his eye, and tried to forget how much of him she had seen yesterday. Perhaps she might speak to him tomorrow and gradually resume ordinary relations, for the prices at the other fish shop were as high as the quality of the fish was low . . . She told herself that there was nothing actually immoral in the human skin, however embarrassing it was.

Miss Mapp had experienced a cruel disappointment last night, though the triumph of this morning had done something to soothe it, for Major Benjy's window had certainly been lit up to a very late hour, and so it was clear that he had not been able, twice in succession, to tear himself away from his diaries, or whatever else detained him, and go to bed at a proper time. Captain Puffin, however, had not sat up late; indeed he must have gone to bed quite unusually early, for his window was dark by half-past nine. Tonight, again the position was reversed, and it seemed that Major Benjy was 'good' and Captain Puffin was 'bad'. On the whole, then, there was cause for thankfulness, and as she added a tin of biscuits and two jars of Bovril to her prudent stores, she found herself a conscious sceptic about those Roman roads. Diaries (perhaps) were a little different, for egoism was a more potent force than archaeology, and for her part she now definitely believed that Roman roads spelt some form of drink. She was sorry to believe it, but it was her duty to believe something of the kind, and she really did not know what else to believe. She did not go so far as mentally to accuse him of drunkenness, but considering the way he absorbed red-currant fool, it was clear that he was no foe to alcohol and probably watered the Roman roads with it. With her vivid imagination she pictured him –

Miss Mapp recalled herself from this melancholy reflection and put up her hand just in time to save a bottle of Bovril which she had put on the top shelf in front of the sack of flour from tumbling to the ground. With the latest additions she had made to her larder, it required considerable ingenuity to fit all the tins and packages in, and for a while she diverted her mind from Captain Puffin's drinking to her own eating. But by careful packing and balancing she managed to stow everything away with sufficient economy of space to allow her to shut the door, and then put the card-table in place again. It was then late, and with a fond look at her sweet flowers sleeping in the moonlight, she went to bed. Captain Puffin's sitting-room was still alight, and even as she deplored this, his shadow in profile crossed the blind. Shadows were queer things – she could make a beautiful shadow-rabbit on the wall by a dexterous interlacement of fingers and thumbs – and certainly this shadow, in the momentary glance she had of it, appeared to have a large moustache. She could make nothing whatever out of that, except to suppose that just as fingers and thumbs became a rabbit, so his nose became a moustache, for he could not have grown one since he came back from golf . . .

She was out early for her shopping next morning, for there were some delicacies to be purchased for her bridge-party, more particularly some little chocolate cakes she had lately discovered which looked very small and innocent, but were in reality of so cloying and substantial a nature, that the partaker thereof would probably not feel capable of making any serious inroads into other provisions. Naturally she was much on the alert today, for it was more than possible that Diva's dress was finished and in evidence. What colour it would be she did not know, but a large quantity of rosebuds would, even at a distance, make identification easy. Diva was certainly not at her window this morning, so it seemed more than probable that they would soon meet.

Far away, just crossing the High Street at the farther end, she caught sight of a bright patch of purple, very much of the required shape. There was surely a pink border round the skirt and a pink panel on the collar, and just as surely Mrs Bartlett, recognizable for her gliding mouselike walk, was moving in its fascinating wake. Then the purple patch vanished into a shop, and Miss Mapp, all smiles and poppies, went with her basket up the street. Presently she encountered Evie, who, also all smiles, seemed to have some communication to make, but only got as far as 'Have you seen –' when she gave a little squeal of laughter, quite inexplicable, and glided into some dark entry. A minute afterwards, the purple patch suddenly appeared from a shop and almost collided with her. It was not Diva at all, but Diva's Janet.

The shock was so indescribably severe that Miss Mapp's smile was frozen, so to speak, as by some sudden congealment on to her face, and did not thaw off it till she had reached the sharp turn at the end of the street, where she leaned heavily on the railing and breathed through her nose. A light autumnal mist overlay the miles of marsh, but the sun was already drinking it up, promising the Tillingites another golden day. The tidal river was at the flood, and the bright water lapped the bases of the turf-covered banks that kept it within its course. Beyond that was the tram-station towards which presently Major Benjy and Captain Puffin would be hurrying to catch the tram that would take them out to the golf-links. The straight road across the marsh was visible, and the railway bridge. All these things were pitilessly unchanged, and Miss Mapp noted them blankly, until rage began to restore the numbed current of her mental processes.

If the records of history contained any similar instance of such treachery and low cunning as was involved in this plot of Diva's to dress Janet in the rosebud chintz, Miss Mapp would have liked to be told clearly and distinctly what it was. She could trace the workings of Diva's base mind with absolute accuracy, and if all the archangels in the hierarchy of heaven had assured her that Diva had originally intended the rosebuds for Janet, she would have scorned them for their clumsy perjury. Diva had designed and executed that dress for herself, and just because Miss Mapp's ingenuity (inspired by the two rosebuds that had fluttered out of the window) had forestalled her, she had taken this fiendish revenge. It was impossible to pervade the High Street covered with chintz poppies when a parlourmaid was being equally pervasive in chintz rosebuds, and what was to be done with this frock executed with such mirth and malice by Withers, Mary and herself she had no idea. She might just as well give it Withers, for she could no longer wear it herself, or tear the poppies from the hem and bestrew the High Street with them . . . Miss Mapp's face froze into immobility again, for here, trundling swiftly towards her, was Diva herself.

Diva appeared not to see her till she got quite close.

'Morning, Elizabeth,' she said. 'Seen my Janet anywhere?'

'No,' said Miss Mapp.

Janet (no doubt according to instructions received) popped out of a shop, and came towards her mistress.

'Here she is,' said Diva. 'All right, Janet. You can go home. I'll see to the other things.'

'It's a lovely day,' said Miss Mapp, beginning to lash her tail. 'So bright.'

'Yes. Pretty trimming of poppies,' said Diva. 'Janet's got rosebuds.'

This was too much.

'Diva, I didn't think it of you,' said Miss Mapp in a shaking voice. 'You saw my new frock yesterday, and you were filled with malice and envy, Diva, just because I had thought of using flowers off an old chintz as well as you, and came out first with it. You had meant to wear that purple frock yourself – though I must say it fits Janet perfectly – and just because I was first in the field you did this. You gave Janet that frock, so that I should be dressed in the same style as your parlourmaid, and you've got a black heart, Diva!'

'That's nonsense,' said Diva firmly. 'Heart's as red as anybody's, and talking of black hearts doesn't become *you*, Elizabeth. You knew I was cutting out roses from my curtains –'

Miss Mapp laughed shrilly.

'Well, if I happen to notice that you've taken your chintz curtains down,' she said with an awful distinctness that showed the wisdom teeth of which Diva had got three at the most, 'and pink bunches of roses come flying out of your window into the High Street, even my poor wits, small as they are, are equal to drawing the conclusion that you are cutting roses out of curtains. Your well-known fondness for dress did the rest. With your permission, Diva, I intend to draw exactly what conclusions I please on every occasion, including this one.'

'Ho! That's how you got the idea then,' said Diva. 'I knew you had cribbed it from me.'

'Cribbed?' asked Miss Mapp, in ironical ignorance of what so vulgar and slangy an expression meant.

'Cribbed means taking what isn't yours,' said Diva. 'Even then, if you had only acted in a straightforward manner –'

Miss Mapp, shaken as with palsy, regretted that she had let slip, out of pure childlike joy, in irony, the manner in which she had obtained the poppy-notion, but in a quarrel regrets are useless, and she went on again.

'And would you very kindly explain how or when I have acted in a manner that was not straightforward,' she asked with laborious politeness. 'Or do I understand that a monopoly of cutting up chintz for personal adornment has been bestowed on you by Act of Parliament?'

'You knew I was meaning to make a frock with chintz roses on it,' said Diva. 'You stole my idea. Worked night and day to be first. Just like you. Mean behaviour.'

'It was meaner to give that frock to Janet,' said Miss Mapp.

'You can give yours to Withers,' snapped Diva.

'Much obliged, Mrs Plaistow,' said Miss Mapp.

Diva had been watching Janet's retreating figure, and feeling that though revenge was sweet, revenge was also strangely expensive, for she had sacrificed one of the most strikingly successful frocks she had ever made on that smoking altar. Now her revenge was gratified, and deeply she regretted the frock. Miss Mapp's heart was similarly wrung by torture: revenge too had been hers (general revenge on Diva for existing), but this dreadful counter-stroke had made it quite impossible for her to enjoy the use of this frock any more, for she could not habit herself like a housemaid. Each, in fact, had, as matters at present stood, completely wrecked the other, like two express trains meeting in top-speed collision, and, since the quarrel had clearly risen to its utmost height, there was no further joy of battle to be anticipated, but only the melancholy task of counting the corpses. So they paused, breathing very quickly and trembling, while both sought for some way out. Besides Miss Mapp had a bridge-party this afternoon, and if they parted now in this extreme state of tension, Diva might conceivably not come, thereby robbing herself of her bridge and spoiling her hostess's table. Naturally any permanent quarrel was not contemplated by either of them, for if quarrels were permanent in Tilling, nobody would be on speaking terms any more with anyone else in a day or two, and (hardly less disastrous) there could be no fresh quarrels with anybody, since you could not quarrel without words. There might be songs without words, as Mendelssohn had proved, but not rows without words. By what formula could this deadly antagonism be bridged without delay?

Diva gazed out over the marsh. She wanted desperately to regain her rosebud frock, and she knew that Elizabeth was starving for further wearing of her poppies. Perhaps the wide, serene plain below inspired her with a hatred of littleness. There would be no loss of dignity in making a proposal that her enemy, she felt sure, would accept: it merely showed a Christian spirit, and set an example to Elizabeth, to make the first move. Janet she did not consider.

'If you are in a fit state to listen to reason, Elizabeth,' she began.

Miss Mapp heaved a sigh of relief. Diva had thought of something. She swallowed the insult at a gulp.

'Yes, dear,' she said.

'Got an idea. Take away Janet's frock, and wear it myself. Then you can wear yours. Too pretty for parlourmaids. Eh?'

A heavenly brightness spread over Miss Mapp's face.

'Oh, how wonderful of you to have thought of that, Diva,' she said. 'But how shall we explain it all to everybody?'

Diva clung to her rights. Though clearly Christian, she was human.

'Say I thought of tacking chintz on and told you,' she said.

'Yes, darling,' said Elizabeth. 'That's beautiful, I agree. But poor Janet!'

'I'll give her some other old thing,' said Diva. 'Good sort, Janet. Wants me to win.'

'And about her having been seen wearing it?'

'Say she hasn't ever worn it. Say they're mad,' said Diva.

Miss Mapp felt it better to tear herself away before she began distilling all sorts of acidities that welled up in her fruitful mind. She could, for instance, easily have agreed that nothing was more probable than that Janet had been mistaken for her mistress . . .

'*Au reservoir* then, dear,' she said tenderly. 'See you at about four? And will you wear your pretty rosebud frock?'

This was agreed to, and Diva went home to take it away from Janet.

Polyurethane

(A synthetic resin used in varnishes)

☆★☆

FRANK MUIR AND DENIS NORDEN

There is something splendidly British about a village pageant. It is so Christian in its aim to bring pleasure to the community, so unselfish in the amount of time and energy freely given by the participants, and so certain to disintegrate into malevolent vendettas which split happy families into warring factions and cause a sharp upward swing in the cottage hospital's intake of found-drunk-and-incapables, nervous collapses and victims of assault and battery perpetrated after rehearsals by loved ones. The effect on a village community of staging a pageant is equal to a visitation of the Black Death.

Black Death – in the shape of 'THORPE DOWN THE AGES. Our Village Through the Centuries, tickets 30p and 45p from the Post Office Stores or, if closed, Mrs Rumbold' – visited my village about twelve years ago.

The guilty men, towards whom the chicken bone should be pointed, were my son Jamie and Vicar, The Revd. Nicholas Menon (known to all as Nick the Vic).

Jamie was going to direct the pageant, which was to take place in the church, using the aisles and the chancel and the apse as the stage in the modern manner. Nick the Vic was to co-write the pageant with Jamie. They were aiming for a working partnership along the lines of Burbage and Shakespeare. Nick the Vic was a gifted writer but his skills ran mainly to writing metaphysical verse of a high quality in the manner of John Donne or fairly fruity, black farce in the style of Evelyn Waugh's *Vile Bodies*, neither of which styles was wholly suited to 'THORPE DOWN THE ÁGES'.

It was their inexperience as producers of pageants which was the basic snag, but then *all* producers of pageants are inexperienced. Nobody – but nobody – ever produces a village pageant twice.

Now, twelve years later, angers have more or less cooled and I'm able to reveal that it was the last-minute appearance of my dear wife, Polly, which saved the evening. Because of Polly, the pageant is now remembered as being a sickening disappointment but not a total disaster.

It all began to go wrong before it had properly started. Nick the Vic announced plans for the pageant in the pulpit one Sunday, pointing out that it was a project to involve the entire village, not only the Dramatic Society.

'If you want to be in it you *shall* be in it!' cried Nick the Vic (Shakespeare) recklessly. 'I shall write each and every one of you a special part.' Carried away in his boyish enthusiasm Nick had forgotten the Golden Rule of amateur dramatics which states: those who *can* act, won't; those who volunteer are entirely without any kind of talent whatsoever.

The first get-together and casting session was organized to take place in the village hall. Some sixty bright-eyed, pitifully keen and totally ungifted souls turned up. Some of them, even if in an emergency, were unable to speak louder than a whisper and were inaudible six feet away. Others could project their voices in a thrilling wall of sound which was audible in the Red Lion half a mile away but it was not possible to distinguish one word from another. A number were afflicted with speech impediments. Three of the volunteers were newcomers to the village and their turbans presented a casting problem. One lady spoke only in French.

Jamie (Burbage) got to work organizing them. He first divided them into two groups, a few to each century, with instructions to devote all their spare time during the coming weeks to making their costumes. One group was to be assorted gentry and the other to be humble villagers.

All those appointed to be gentry entered into the spirit of the thing and pranced about the hall going: 'Fie, milady', 'pshaw!', and 'Bring wine, varlet!' Those cast as humble villagers went very quiet, left the hall shortly afterwards and subsequently sent in letters of resignation.

Nick the Vic and Jamie spread charm and affability and lies and got most of the humble villagers back but it was clear that the swineherds and maidservants were going to be up-market or nothing. The peasant costumes they knocked up, which historically were sacking and odd rags, were amazing. The lady playing old Mrs Toft, the eighteenth-century crone in Guildford who pretended she had given birth to a litter of rabbits, prinked on stage looking like Barbara Cartland, bejewelled, in rosy-beige.

Jamie and Nick, having got the cast sorted out and – however unsuitably – clad, then turned to compiling the script. They borrowed *The History of Chertsey and Thorpe* from the Chertsey Museum and bore it off home with a view to selecting the very best events, the most dramatic items, to make for a really gripping pageant.

This is when the second blow fell. The history of Thorpe took up a page and a half of the book. Nothing had happened in Thorpe. Not just nothing – *absolutely* nothing had *ever* happened, either in, about, or near Thorpe. It had just squatted, a smallish village, in the shadow of the great medieval abbey of Chertsey with nothing happening in it for century after century.

Eventually Burbage and Shakespeare saved the day. On the night of the pageant they put me into clergyman's clothes and I stood in the pulpit (ill with fatigue having been filming all day) reading out the non-story of Thorpe while the villagers illustrated the passing years with mimes of various activities. The script was a masterpiece of speciousness and audience manipulation.

Highlights, I recall, included:

> ME (*half-asleep, reading from script*): '1543, the year of the Great Freeze. The Thames froze over. So would have done the duckpond in Coldharbour Lane, where Thorpe villagers would have enjoyed themselves in traditional village winter sports:'
>
> ENTER prosperous-looking serfs who pretend to skate and fall over amusingly.
>
> ME: 'In 1603 All England celebrated the crowning of its new monarch, James I. And the villagers of Thorpe, poor though they were, would not have been left out of the patriotic revelry:'
>
> ENTER richly-dressed poor villagers who sit in a circle while Charlene Legg (aged 9, daughter of Councillor Legg, Independent Rate-Payers) obliges with her tap dance to the music of *West Side Story*.

Then real disaster struck. Our big finish was King John signing the Magna Carta (Runnymede is only a few miles away). King John (Mrs Dean), surrounded by Knights and Earls, will not sign. Suddenly a vast, hairy Thane from the Scottish delegation springs forward with his claymore upraised. King John screams in fear and signs. The whole cast cheers, we fade up the music and the whole cast links arms and sings 'You'll Never Walk Alone', swaying.

Curtain.

The trouble was that our Thane, the enormous Pete, had developed stage fright and during the first half had popped over to the Red Lion for a stiffener. By halfway through the second half he was so stiff that they had to take him home in a hired car.

I was the first to notice he was missing from the final scene. I slipped out of the pulpit and went backstage. There was his costume lying in a heap but no him. And there was my wife Polly, prompting through a gap in the curtain.

In a flash I had flung the great Scottish cloak over Polly's frail shoulders – it drooped along the ground like Dopey's – put the mighty claymore in her hand and pushed her towards the stage entrance.

'You're our big, glossy finish!' I said. 'On you go!'

'How do you mean? Who am I supposed to *be*, dressed in all this stuff?'

I explained. Quietly, simply:

'Polly – you're a Thane'.

Mr Prendergast's Story

☆★☆

EVELYN WAUGH

Paul was awakened next morning by a loud bang on his door, and Beste-Chetwynde looked in. He was wearing a very expensive-looking Charvet dressing-gown.

'Good morning, sir,' he said. 'I thought I'd come and tell you, as you wouldn't know: there's only one bathroom for the masters. If you want to get there before Mr Prendergast, you ought to go now. Captain Grimes doesn't wash much,' he added, and then disappeared.

Paul went to the bath and was rewarded some minutes later by hearing the shuffling of slippers down the passage and the door furiously rattled.

As he was dressing Philbrick appeared.

'Oh, I forgot to call you. Breakfast is in ten minutes.'

After breakfast Paul went up to the Common Room. Mr Prendergast was there polishing his pipes, one by one, with a chamois leather. He looked reproachfully at Paul.

'We must come to some arrangement about the bathroom,' he said. 'Grimes very rarely has a bath. I have one before breakfast.'

'So do I,' said Paul defiantly.

'Then I suppose I shall have to find some other time,' said Mr Prendergast, and he gave a deep sigh as he returned his attention to his pipes. 'After ten years, too,' he added, 'but everything's like that. I might have known you'd want the bath. It was so easy when there was only Grimes and that other young man. He was never down in time for breakfast. Oh dear! oh dear! I can see that things are going to be very difficult.'

'But surely we could both have one?'

'No, no, that's out of the question. It's all part of the same thing. Everything has been like this since I left the ministry.'

Paul made no answer, and Mr Prendergast went on breathing and rubbing.

'I expect you wonder how I came to be here?'

'No, no,' said Paul soothingly. 'I think it's very natural.'

'It's not natural at all; it's most unnatural. If things had happened a little differently I should be a rector with my own house and bathroom. I might even have been a rural dean, only' – and Mr Prendergast dropped his voice to a whisper – 'only I had *Doubts*.

'I don't know why I'm telling you all this; nobody else knows. I somehow feel you'll understand.

'Ten years ago I was a clergyman of the Church of England. I had just been presented to a living in Worthing. It was such an attractive church, not old, but *very* beautifully decorated, six candles on the altar, Reservation in the Lady Chapel, and an excellent heating apparatus which burned coke in a little shed by the sacristy door; no graveyard, just a hedge of golden privet between the church and the rectory.

'As soon as I moved in my mother came to keep house for me. She bought some chintz, out of her own money, for the drawing-room curtains. She used to be "at home" once a week to the ladies of the congregation. One of them, the dentist's wife, gave me a set of the *Encyclopaedia Britannica* for my study. It was all very pleasant until my *Doubts* began.'

'Were they as bad as all that?' asked Paul.

'They were insuperable,' said Mr Prendergast; 'that is why I am here now. But I expect I am boring you?'

'No, do go on. That's to say, unless you find it painful to think about.'

'I think about it all the time. It happened like this, quite suddenly. We had been there about three months, and my mother had made great friends with some people called Bundle – rather a curious name. I think he was an insurance agent until he retired. Mrs Bundle used very kindly to ask us in to supper on Sundays after Evensong. They were pleasant, informal gatherings, and I used quite to look forward to them. I can see them now as they sat there on this particular evening; there was my mother and Mr and Mrs Bundle, and their son, rather a spotty boy, I remember, who used to go in to Brighton College by train every day, and Mrs Bundle's mother, a Mrs Round, rather deaf, but a very good Churchwoman, and Mrs Abel – that was the name of the dentist's wife who gave me the *Encyclopaedia Britannica* – and old Major Ending, the people's warden. I had preached two sermons that day besides taking the children's Bible-class in the afternoon, and I had rather dropped out of the conversation. They were all talking away quite happily about the preparations that were being made on the pier for the summer season, when suddenly, for no reason at all, my *Doubts* began.' He paused, and Paul felt constrained to offer some expression of sympathy.

'What a terrible thing!' he said.

'Yes, I've not known an hour's real happiness since. You see, it wasn't the ordinary sort of Doubt about Cain's wife or the Old Testament miracles or the consecration of Archbishop Parker. I'd been taught how to explain all those while I was at college. No, it was something deeper than all that. *I couldn't understand why God had made the world at all.* There was my mother and the Bundles and Mrs Round talking away quite unconcernedly while I sat there wrestling with this sudden assault of doubt. You see how fundamental that is. Once granted the first step, I can see that everything else follows – Tower of Babel, Babylonian captivity, Incarnation, Church, bishops, incense, everything – but what I couldn't see, and what I can't see now, is, *why* did it all begin?

'I asked my bishop; he didn't know. He said that he didn't think the point really arose as far as my practical duties as a parish priest were concerned. I discussed it with my mother. At first she was inclined to regard it as a passing phase. But it didn't pass, so finally she agreed with me that the only honourable thing to do was to resign my living; she never really recovered from the shock, poor old lady! It was a great blow after she had bought the chintz and got so friendly with the Bundles.'

A bell began ringing down a distant passage.

'Well, well, we must go to prayers, and I haven't finished my pipes.' He took his gown from the peg behind the door and slipped it over his shoulders.

'Perhaps one day I shall see Light,' he said, 'and then I shall go back to the ministry. Meanwhile – '

Clutterbuck ran past the door, whistling hideously.

'That's a nasty little boy,' said Mr Prendergast, 'if ever there was one.'

Prayers were held downstairs in the main hall of the Castle. The boys stood ranged along the panelled walls, each holding in his hands a little pile of books. Grimes sat on one of the chairs beside the baronial chimney-piece.

''Morning,' he said to Paul; 'only just down, I'm afraid. Do I smell of drink?'

'Yes,' said Paul.

'Comes of missing breakfast. Prendy been telling you about his Doubts?'

'Yes,' said Paul.

'Funny thing,' said Grimes, 'but I've never been worried in that way. I don't pretend to be a particularly pious sort of chap, but I've never had any Doubts. When you've been in the soup as often as I have, it gives you a sort of feeling that everything's for the best, really. You know, God's in His heaven; all's right with the world. I can't quite explain it, but I don't believe one can ever be unhappy for long provided one does just exactly what one wants to and when one wants to. The last chap who put me on my feet said I was "singularly in harmony with the primitive promptings of humanity". I've remembered that phrase because somehow it seemed to fit me. Here comes the old man. This is where we stand up.'

As the bell stopped ringing Dr Fagan swept into the hall, the robes of a Doctor of Philosophy swelling and billowing about him. He wore an orchid in his button-hole.

'Good morning, gentlemen,' he said.

'Good morning, sir,' chorused the boys.

The Doctor advanced to the table at the end of the room, picked up a Bible, and opening it at random, read a chapter of blood-curdling military history without any evident relish. From that he plunged into the Lord's Prayer, which the boys took up in a quiet chatter. Mr Prendergast's voice led them in tones that testified to his ecclesiastical past.

Then the Doctor glanced at a sheet of notes he held in his hand. 'Boys,' he said, 'I have some announcements to make. The Fagan cross-country running challenge cup will not be competed for this year on account of the floods.'

'I expect the old boy has popped it,' said Grimes in Paul's ear.

'Nor will the Llanabba Essay Prize.'

'On account of the floods,' said Grimes.

'I have received my account for the telephone,' proceeded Dr Fagan, 'and I find that during the past quarter there have been no less than twenty-three trunk calls to London, none of which was sent by me or by members of my family. I look to the prefects to stop this, unless of course they are themselves responsible, in which case I must urge them in my own interests to make use of the village post-office, to which they have access.

'I think that is everything, isn't it, Mr Prendergast?'

'*Cigars*,' said Mr Prendergast in a stage whisper.

'Ah, yes, cigars. Boys, I have been deeply distressed to learn that several cigar ends have been found – where have they been found?'

'Downstair lavatory.'

'In the downstair lavatory. I regard this as reprehensible. What boy has been smoking cigars in the downstair lavatory?'

There was a prolonged silence, during which the Doctor's eye travelled down the line of boys.

'I will give the culprit until luncheon to give himself up. If I do not hear from him by then the whole school will be heavily punished.'

'Damn!' said Grimes. 'I gave those cigars to Clutterbuck. I hope the little beast has the sense to keep quiet.'

'Go to your classes,' said the Doctor.

The boys filed out.

'I should think, by the look of them, they were exceedingly cheap cigars,' added Mr Prendergast sadly. 'They were a pale yellow colour.'

'That makes it worse,' said the Doctor. 'To think of any boy under my charge smoking pale yellow cigars in a lavatory! It is *not* a gentlemanly fault.'

The masters went upstairs.

'That's your little mob in there,' said Grimes; 'you let them out at eleven.'

'But what am I to teach them?' said Paul in sudden panic.

'Oh, I shouldn't try to *teach* them anything, not just yet, anyway. Just keep them quiet.'

'Now that's a thing I've never learned to do,' sighed Mr Prendergast.

Paul watched him amble into his class-room at the end of the passage, where a burst of applause greeted his arrival. Dumb with terror, he went into his own class-room.

Ten boys sat before him, their hands folded, their eyes bright with expectation.

'Good morning, sir,' said the one nearest him.

'Good morning,' said Paul;

'Good morning, sir,' said the next.

'Good morning,' said Paul.

'Good morning, sir', said the next.

'Oh, shut up,' said Paul.

At this the boy took out a handkerchief and began to cry quietly.

'Oh, sir,' came a chorus of reproach, 'you've hurt his feelings. He's very sensitive; it's his Welsh blood, you know: it makes people very emotional. Say "Good morning" to him, sir, or he won't be happy all day. After all, it is a good morning, isn't it, sir?'

'Silence!' shouted Paul above the uproar, and for a few moments things were quieter.

'Please, sir,' said a small voice – Paul turned and saw a grave-looking youth holding up his hand – 'please, sir, perhaps he's been smoking cigars and doesn't feel well.'

'Silence!' said Paul again.

The ten boys stopped talking and sat perfectly still, staring at him. He felt himself getting hot and red under their scrutiny.

'I suppose the first thing I ought to do is to get your names clear. What is your name?' he asked, turning to the first boy.

'Tangent, sir.'

'And yours?'

'Tangent, sir,' said the next boy. Paul's heart sank.

'But you can't both be called Tangent.'

'No, sir, *I'm* Tangent. He's just trying to be funny.'

'I like that. *Me* trying to be funny! Please, sir, I'm Tangent, sir; really I am.'

'If it comes to that,' said Clutterbuck from the back of the room 'there is only one Tangent here, and that is me. Anyone else can jolly well go to blazes.'

Paul felt desperate.

'Well, is there anyone who isn't Tangent?'

Four or five voices instantly arose.

'I'm not, sir; I'm not Tangent. I wouldn't be called Tangent, not on the end of a barge-pole.'

In a few seconds the room had become divided into two parties: those who were Tangent and those who were not. Blows were already being exchanged, when the door opened and Grimes came in. There was a slight hush.

'I thought you might want this,' he said, handing Paul a walking stick. 'And if you take my advice, you'll set them something to do.'

He went out; and Paul, firmly grasping the walking stick, faced his form.

'Listen,' he said. 'I don't care a damn what any of you are called, but if there's another word from anyone I shall keep you all in this afternoon.'

'You can't keep me in,' said Clutterbuck; 'I'm going for a walk with Captain Grimes.'

'Then I shall very nearly kill you with this stick. Meanwhile you will all write an essay on "Self-indulgence". There will be a prize of half a crown for the longest essay, irrespective of any possible merit.'

From then onwards all was silence until break. Paul, still holding the stick, gazed despondently out of the window. Now and then there rose from below the shrill voices of the servants scolding each other in Welsh. By the time the bell rang Clutterbuck had covered sixteen pages, and was awarded the half-crown.

'Did you find those boys difficult to manage?' asked Mr Prendergast, filling his pipe.

'Not at all,' said Paul.

'Ah, you're lucky. I find all boys utterly intractable. I don't know why it is. Of course my wig has a lot to do with it. Have you noticed that I wear a wig?'

'No, no, of course not.'

'Well, the boys did as soon as they saw it. It was a great mistake my ever getting one. I thought when I left Worthing that I looked too old to get a job easily. I was only forty-one. It was very expensive, even though I chose the cheapest quality. Perhaps that's why it looks so like a wig. I don't know. I knew from the first that it was a mistake, but once they had seen it, it was too late to go back. They make all sorts of jokes about it.'

'I expect they'd laugh at something else if it wasn't that.'

'Yes, no doubt they would. I dare say it's a good thing to localize their ridicule as far as possible. Oh dear! oh dear! If it wasn't for my pipes, I don't know how I should manage to keep on. What made you come here?'

'I was sent down from Scone for indecent behaviour.'

'Oh, yes, like Grimes?'

'No,' said Paul firmly, 'not like Grimes.'

'Oh, well, it's all much the same really. And there's the bell. Oh dear! oh dear! I believe that loathsome little man's taken my gown.'

Porterhouse Blue

☆★☆★☆★☆★☆★☆★☆★☆★☆★☆★☆★☆★☆★☆★☆

TOM SHARPE

Zipser stirred on the floor of his room. His face in contact with the carpet felt sore and his head throbbed. Above all he was cold and stiff. He turned on his side and stared at the window, where an orange glow from the sky over Cambridge shone dimly through the falling snow. Slowly he gathered himself together and got to his feet. Feeling distinctly weak and sick he went to the door and turned on the light and stood blinking at the two large cartons on the floor. Then he sat down hurriedly in a chair and tried to remember what had happened to him and why he was the possessor of two gross of guaranteed electronically tested 3-teat vending machine pack contraceptives. The details of the day's events slowly returned to him and with them the remembrance of his misunderstanding with the Dean. 'Gated for a week,' he murmured and realized the implications of his predicament. He couldn't deliver the beastly things to the Unicorn now and he had signed the slip at the wholesale office. Enquiries would be made. The barman at the Unicorn would identify him. So would the wretched clerk at the wholesale office. The police would be informed. There would be a search. He'd be arrested. Charged with being in felonious possession of two gross of . . . Zipser clutched his head in his hands and tried to think what to do. He'd have to get rid of the things. He looked at his watch. Eleven o'clock. Got to hurry. Burn them? He looked at the gas fire and gave up the idea. Out of the question. Flush them down the lavatory? Better idea. He threw himself at the cartons and began to open them. First the outer carton, then the inner one, then the packet itself and finally the foil wrapper. It was a laborious job. He'd never do it. He'd got to do it.

Beside him on the carpet a pile of empty packets slowly grew and with it a pile of foil and a grotesque arrangement of latex rings looking like flattened and translucent button mushrooms. Lubricated with sensitol, his hands were sticky, which made it even more difficult to tear the foil. Finally after an hour he had emptied one carton. It was twelve o'clock. He gathered the contraceptives up and took a handful out on to the landing and into the lavatory. He dropped them into the pan and pulled the chain. A rush of water, swirls, bubbles, gone? The water subsided and he stared down at two dozen rubber rings floating defiantly in the pan. 'For God's sake,' said Zipser desperately and waited until the cistern had filled again. He waited a minute after the water had stopped running and pulled the chain again. Two dozen contraceptives smiled up at him. One or two had partially unfurled and were filled with air. Zipser stared at the things frantically. Got to get them to go down somehow. He reached behind the pan and grabbed the cleaning brush and shoved it down on them. One or two disappeared round the U bend but for the most part they resisted his efforts. Three even had the audacity to adhere to the brush itself. Zipser picked them off with fastidious disgust and dropped them back into the water. By this time the cistern had filled again, gurgling gently and ending with a final swish. Zipser tried to think what to do. If buying the damned things had been fraught with appalling difficulties, getting rid of them was a nightmare.

He sat down on the lavatory seat and considered the intractability of the matter. A tin of lavatory cleanser caught his attention. He picked it up and wondered if it would dissolve rubber. Then he got off the seat and emptied the contents on to the rings floating into the water. Whatever chemical action the cleanser promised failed altogether. The contraceptives remained unaffected. Zipser grabbed the brush again and plunged it into the pan. Wafts of disinfectant powder irritated his nose. He sneezed loudly and clutched the chain. For the third time the cistern flushed and Zipser was just studying the subsidence and counting the six contraceptives which remained immune to chemistry and the rush of water when someone knocked on the door.

'What the hell's going on in there?' a voice asked. It was Foxton, who lived in the room next door.

Zipser looked hauntedly at the door. 'Got diarrhoea,' he said weakly.

'Well, must you pull the bloody chain so often?' Foxton asked. 'Making a bloody awful noise and I'm trying to sleep.' He went back to his room and Zipser turned back to the pan and began fishing for the six contraceptives with the lavatory brush.

Twenty minutes later he was still searching for some method of disposing of his incriminating evidence. He had visited six lavatories on neighbouring staircases and had found a method of getting the things to disappear by first filling them with water from a tap and tying the ends. It was slow and cumbersome and above all noisy and when he had tried six at a time on J staircase he had had to spend some time unblocking the U pipe. He went back to his room and sat shivering with cold and anxiety. It was one o'clock and so far he had managed to rid himself of thirty-eight. At this rate he would still be flushing lavatories all over the College when Mrs Biggs arrived in the morning. He stared at the pile of foil and the packets. Got to get rid of them too. Put them behind the gas fire and burn them he thought and he was just wrestling with the gas fire and trying to make space behind it when the howling draught in the chimney gave him a better idea. He went to the window and looked out into the night. In the darkness outside snowflakes whirled and scattered while the wind battered at the window pane. Zipser opened the window and poked his head out into the storm before wetting his finger and holding it up to the wind. 'Blowing from the East,' he muttered and shut the window with a smile of intense satisfaction. A moment later he was kneeling beside the gas fire and undoing the hose of his gas ring and five minutes afterwards the first of 250 inflated contraceptives bounced buoyantly against the sooty sides of the medieval chimney and disappeared into the night sky above. Zipser rushed to the window and gazed up for a glimpse of the winsome thing as it whirled away carrying its message of abstinence far away into the world, but the sky was too dark and there was nothing to see. He went back and fetched a torch and shone it up the chimney but apart from one or two errant snowflakes the chimney was clear. Zipser turned cheerfully back to the gas ring and inflated five more. Once again the experiment was entirely successful. Up the chimney they floated, up and away. Zipser inflated twenty and popped them up the chimney with equal success. He was just filling his hundredth when the gas gave out, with a hideous wheeze the thing deflated. Zipser rummaged in his pockets for a shilling and finally found one. He put it into the meter and the contraceptive assumed a new and satisfactory shape. He tied the end and stuffed it up the chimney. The night wore on and Zipser acquired a wonderful dexterity. On to the tube, gas on, gas off, a knot in the end and up the chimney. Beside him on the floor the cartons filled with discarded foil and Zipser was just wondering if there were schoolchildren who collected used contraceptive containers like milk-bottle tops when he became aware that something had gone wrong in the chimney. The bloated and strangulated rear of his last contraceptive was hanging suspended in the fireplace. Zipser gave it a shove of encouragement but the poor thing merely bulged dangerously.

Zipser pulled it out and peered up the chimney. He couldn't peer very far. The chimney was crowded with eager contraceptives. He extracted another, smeared with soot, and put it down on the floor. He extracted a third and thrust it behind him. Then a fourth and a fifth, both deeply encrusted with soot. After that he gave up. The rest were too high to reach. He clambered out of the fireplace and sat on the floor wondering what to do. At least he had disposed of all two gross, even if some were lodged in the chimney stack. They were well hidden there – or would be once he had put the gas fire back in place. He would think of some way of disposing of them in the morning. He was too tired to think of anything now. He turned to reach for the five he had managed to extract only to find that they had disappeared. 'I put them down on the carpet. I'm sure I did,' he muttered lightheadedly to himself and was about to look under the bookcase when his eye caught sight of a movement on the ceiling. Zipser looked up. Five sooty contraceptives had lodged themselves in a corner by the door. Little bits of soot marked the ceiling where they had touched.

Zipser got wearily to his feet and climbed on to a chair and reached up. He could just manage to get his fingers on to the belly of one of the things but the sensitol made it impossible to get a grip. Zipser squeezed and with a coy squeak the contraceptive evaded his grasp and lumbered away across the room, leaving a track of soot behind it. Zipser tried again on another with the same result. He moved the chair across the room and reached up. The contraceptive waddled gently into the corner by the window. Zipser moved the chair again but the contraceptive rolled away. Zipser climbed down and stared manically at his ceiling. It was covered in delicate black trails as if some enormous snail had called after a stint of coal-heaving. The self-control Zipser had been exercising began to slip. He picked up a book and lobbed it at a particularly offensive-looking contraceptive, but apart from driving it across the room to join the flock in the corner by the door the gesture was futile. Zipser crossed to the desk and pushed it over to the door. Then he fetched the chair and stood it on the desk and climbed precariously up and seized a contraceptive by its knotted tail. He climbed down and thrust it up the chimney. Five minutes later all five were back in place and although the last one still protruded below the lintel, when he pushed the gas fire back into position it was invisible. Zipser collapsed on to his sofa and stared at the ceiling. All that remained was to clean the soot off the plaster. He went out into the gyp room and fetched a duster and spent the next half hour pushing his desk round the room and climbing on to it to dust the ceiling. Traces of soot still remained but they were less noticeable now. He pushed the desk back into its corner and looked round the room. Apart from a noticeable smell of gas and the more intransigent stains on the ceiling there was nothing to connect him with two gross of contraceptives fraudulently obtained from the wholesalers. Zipser opened the window to clear the room of gas and went through to his bedroom and went to bed. In the eastern sky the first light of dawn was beginning to appear, but Zipser had no eyes for the beauties of nature. He fell into a restless sleep haunted by the thought that the logjam in his chimney might break during the coming day to issue with shocking ebullience above the unsuspecting College. He need not have worried. Porterhouse was already infested. The falling snow had seen to that. As each porcine sensitol-lubricated protective had emerged from the chimney stack the melting snow had ended its night flight almost abruptly. Zipser had not foreseen the dangers of icing.

Children: Pro or Con?

☆★☆★☆★☆★☆★☆★☆★☆★☆★☆★☆★☆★☆★☆★☆★☆★☆

FRAN LEBOWITZ

Moving, as I do, in what would kindly be called artistic circles, children are an infrequent occurrence. But even the most artistic of circles includes within its periphery a limited edition of the tenaciously domestic.

As I am generally quite fond of children I accept this condition with far less displeasure than do my more rarefied acquaintances. That is not to imply that I am a total fool for a little grin but simply that I consider myself to be in a position of unquestionable objectivity and therefore eminently qualified to deal with the subject in an authoritative manner.

From the number of children in evidence it appears that people have them at the drop of a hat – for surely were they to give this matter its due attention they would act with greater decorum. Of course, until now prospective parents have not had the opportunity to see the facts spelled out in black and white and therefore cannot reasonably be held accountable for their actions. To this end I have carefully set down all pertinent information in the fervent hope that it will result in a future populated by a more attractive array of children than I have thus far encountered.

Pro

I must take issue with the term 'a mere child,' for it has been my invariable experience that the company of a mere child is infinitely preferable to that of a mere adult.

Children are usually small in stature, which makes them quite useful for getting at those hard-to-reach places.

Children do not sit next to one in restaurants and discuss their preposterous hopes for the future in loud tones of voice.

Children ask better questions than do adults. 'May I have a cookie?' 'Why is the sky blue?' and 'What does a cow say?' are far more likely to elicit a cheerful response than 'Where's your manuscript?' 'Why haven't you called?' and 'Who's your lawyer?'

Children give life to the concept of immaturity.

Children make the most desirable opponents in Scrabble as they are both easy to beat and fun to cheat.

It is still quite possible to stand in a throng of children without once detecting even the faintest whiff of an exciting, rugged after-shave or cologne.

Not a single member of the under-age set has yet to propose the word *chairchild*.

Children sleep either alone or with small toy animals. The wisdom of such behavior is unquestionable, as it frees them from the immeasurable tedium of being privy to the whispered confessions of others. I have yet to run across a teddy bear who was harboring the secret desire to wear a maid's uniform.

Con

Even when freshly washed and relieved of all obvious confections, children tend to be sticky. One can only assume that this has something to do with not smoking enough.

Children have decidedly little fashion sense and if left to their own devices will more often than not be drawn to garments of unfortunate cut. In this respect they do not differ greatly from the majority of their elders, but somehow one blames them more.

Children respond inadequately to sardonic humor and veiled threats.

Notoriously insensitive to subtle shifts in mood, children will persist in discussing the color of a recently sighted cement-mixer long after one's own interest in the topic has waned.

Children are rarely in the position to lend one a truly interesting sum of money. There are, however, exceptions, and such children are an excellent addition to any party.

Children arise at an unseemly hour and are oft times in the habit of putting food on an empty stomach.

Children do not look well in evening clothes.

All too often children are accompanied by adults.

The Silent Brothers

☆★☆★☆★☆★☆★☆★☆★☆★☆★☆★☆★☆★☆★☆★☆★☆★☆★☆

ARNOLD BENNETT

I

John and Robert Hessian, brothers, bachelors, and dressed in mourning, sat together after supper in the parlour of their house at the bottom of Oldcastle Street, Bursley. Maggie, the middleaged servant, was clearing the table.

'Leave the cloth and the coffee,' said John, the elder, 'Mr Liversage is coming in.'

'Yes, Mr John,' said Maggie.

'Slate, Maggie,' Robert ordered laconically, with a gesture towards the mantelpiece behind him.

'Yes, Mr Robert,' said Maggie.

She gave him a slate with slate-pencil attached, which hung on a nail near the mantelpiece.

Robert took the slate and wrote on it: *'What is Liversage coming about?'*

And he pushed the slate across the table to John.

Whereupon John wrote on the slate: *'Don't know. He telephoned me he wanted to see us tonight.'*

And he pushed back the slate to Robert.

This singular procedure was not in the least attributable to deafness on the part of the brothers; they were in the prime of life, aged forty-two and thirty-nine respectively, and in complete possession of all their faculties. It was due simply to the fact that they had quarrelled, and would not speak to each other. The history of their quarrel would be incredible were it not full of that ridiculous pathetic quality known as human nature, and did not similar things happen frequently in the manufacturing Midlands, where the general temperament is a fearful and strange compound of pride, obstinacy, unconquerableness, romance, and stupidity. Yes, stupidity.

No single word had passed between the brothers in that house for ten years. On the morning after the historical quarrel Robert had not replied when John spoke to him. 'Well,' said John's secret heart – and John's secret heart ought to have known better, as it was older than its brother heart – 'I'll teach him a lesson. I won't speak until he does.' And Robert's secret heart had somehow divined this idiotic resolution, and had said: 'We shall see.' Maggie had been the first to notice the stubborn silence. Then their friends noticed it, especially Mr Liversage, the solicitor, their most intimate friend. But you are not to suppose that anybody protested very strongly. For John and Robert were not the kind of men with whom liberties may be taken; and, moreover, Bursley was slightly amused – at the beginning. It assumed the attitude of a disinterested spectator at a fight. It wondered who would win. Of course, it called both the brothers fools, yet in a tone somewhat sympathetic, because such a thing as had occurred to the Hessians might well occur to any man gifted with the true Bursley spirit. There is this to be said for Bursley man: Having made his bed, he will lie on it, and he will not complain.

The Hessians suffered severely by their self-imposed dumbness, but they suffered like Stoics. Maggie also suffered, and Maggie would not stand it. Maggie it was who had invented the slate. Indeed, they had heard some plain truths from that stout, bustling woman. They had not yielded, but they had accepted the slate in order to minimize the inconvenience to Maggie, and afterwards they deigned to make use of it for their own purposes. As for friends – friends accustomed themselves to the *status quo*. There came a time when the spectacle of two men chattering to everybody else in a company, and not saying a word to each other, no longer appealed to Bursley's sense of humour. The silent scenes at which Maggie assisted every day did not, either, appeal to Maggie's sense of humour, because she had none. So the famous feud grew into a sort of elemental fact of Nature. It was tolerated as the weather is tolerated. The brothers acquired pride in it; even Bursley regarded it as an interesting municipal curiosity. The sole imperfection in a lovely and otherwise perfect quarrel was that John and Robert, being both employed at Roycroft's Majolica Manufactory, the one as works manager and the other as commercial traveller, were obliged to speak to each other occasionally in the way of business. Artistically, this was a pity, though they did speak very sternly and distantly. The partial truce necessitated by Roycroft's was confined strictly to Roycroft's. And when Robert was not on his journeys, these two tall, strong, dark, bearded men might often be seen of a night walking separately and doggedly down Oldcastle Street from the works, within five yards of each other.

And no one suggested the lunatic asylum. Such is the force of pride, of rank stupidity, and of habit.

The slate-scratching was scarcely over that evening when Mr Powell Liversage appeared. He was a golden-haired man, with a jolly face, lighter and shorter in structure than the two brothers. His friendship with them dated from school-days, and it had survived even the entrance of Liversage into a learned profession. Liversage, who, being a bachelor like the Hessians, had many unoccupied evenings, came to see the brothers regularly every Saturday night, and one or other of them dropped in upon him most Wednesdays; but this particular night was a Thursday.

'How do?' John greeted him succinctly between two puffs of a pipe.

'How do?' replied Liversage.

'How do, Pow?' Robert greeted him in turn, also between two puffs of a pipe.

And 'How do, little 'un?' replied Liversage.

A chair was indicated to him, and he sat down, and Robert poured out some coffee into a third cup which Maggie had brought. John pushed away the extra special of the *Staffordshire Signal*, which he had been reading.

'What's up these days?' John demanded.

'Well,' said Liversage, and both brothers noticed that he was rather ill at ease, instead of being humorous and lightly caustic as usual, 'the will's turned up.'

'The devil it has!' John exclaimed. 'When?'

'This afternoon.'

And then, as there was a pause, Liversage added: 'Yes, my sons, the will's turned up.'

'But where, you cuckoo, sitting there like that?' asked Robert. 'Where?'

'It was in the registered letter addressed to your sister that the Post Office people wouldn't hand over until we'd taken out letters of administration.'

'Well, I'm dashed!' muttered John. 'Who'd have thought of that? You've got the will, then?'

Liversage nodded.

The Hessians had an elder sister, Mrs Bott, widow of a colour merchant, and Mrs Bott had died suddenly three months ago, the night after a journey to Manchester. (Even at the funeral the brothers had scandalized the town by not speaking to each other.) Mrs Bott had wealth, wit, and wisdom, together with certain peculiarities, of which one was an excessive secrecy. It was known that she had made a will, because she had more than once notified the fact, in a tone suggestive of highly important issues, but the will had refused to be found. So Mr Liversage had been instructed to take out letters of administration of the estate, which, in the continued absence of the will, would be divided equally between the brothers. And twelve or thirteen thousand pounds may be compared to a financial beef-steak that cuts up very handsomely for two persons. The carving-knife was about to descend on its succulence, when, lo! the will!

'How came the will to be in the post?' asked Robert.

'The handwriting on the envelope was your sister's,' said Liversage. 'And the package was posted in Manchester. Very probably she had taken the will to Manchester to show it to a lawyer or something of that sort, and then she was afraid of losing it on the journey back, and so she sent it to herself by registered post. But before it arrived, of course, she was dead.'

'That wasn't a bad scheme of poor Mary Ann's!' John commented.

'It was just like her!' said Robert, speaking pointedly to Liversage. 'But what an odd thing!'

Now, both these men were, no doubt excusably, agonized by curiosity to learn the contents of the will. But would either of them be the first to express that curiosity? Never in this world! Not for the fortune itself! To do so would scarcely have been Bursleyish. It would certainly not have been Hessianlike. So Liversage was obliged at length to say –

'I reckon I'd better read you the will, eh?'

The brothers nodded.

'Mind you,' said Liversage, 'It's not my will. I've had nothing to do with it; so kindly keep your hair on. As a matter of fact, she must have drawn it up herself. It's not drawn properly at all, but it's witnessed all right, and it'll hold water, just as well as if the blooming Lord Chancellor had fixed it up for her in person.'

He produced the document and read, awkwardly and self-consciously –

' "This is my will. You are both of you extremely foolish, John and Robert, and I've often told you so. Nobody has ever understood, and nobody ever will understand, why you quarrelled like that over Annie Emery. You are punishing yourselves, but you are punishing her as well, and it isn't fair her waiting all these years. So I give all my estate, no matter what it is, to whichever of you marries Annie. And I hope this will teach you a lesson. You need it more than you need my money. But you must be married within a year of my death. And if the one that marries cares to give five thousand pounds or so to the other, of course there's nothing to prevent him. This is just a hint. And if you don't either of you marry Annie within a year, then I just leave everything I have to Miss Annie Emery (spinster), stationer and fancy-goods dealer, Duck Bank, Bursley. She deserves something for her disappointment, and she shall have it. Mr Liversage, solicitor, must kindly be my executor. And I commit my soul to God, hoping for a blessed resurrection. 20th January, 1896. Signed Mary Ann Bott, widow." As I told you, the witnessing is in order,' Liversage finished.

'Give it here,' said John shortly, and scanned the sheet of paper.

And Robert actually walked round the table and looked over his brother's shoulder – ample proof that he was terrifically moved.

'And do you mean to tell me that a will like that is good in law?' exclaimed John.

'Of course it's good in law!' Liversage replied. 'Legal phraseology is a useful thing, and it often saves trouble in the end; but it ain't indispensable, you know.'

'Humph!' was Robert's comment as he resumed his seat and relighted his pipe.

All three men were nervous. Each was afraid to speak, afraid even to meet the eyes of the other two. An unmajestic silence followed.

'Well, I'll be off, I think,' Liversage remarked at length with difficulty.

He rose.

'I say,' Robert stopped him. 'Better not say anything about this to Miss – to Annie, eh?'

'I will say nothing,' agreed Liversage (infamously and unprofessionally concealing the fact that he had already said something).

And he departed.

The brothers sat in flustered meditation over the past and the future.

Ten years before, Annie Emery had been an orphan of twenty-three, bravely starting in business for herself amid the plaudits of the admiring town; and John had fallen in love with her courage and her sense and her feminine charm. But alas, as Ovid points out, how difficult it is for a woman to please only one man! Robert also had fallen in love with Annie. Each brother had accused the other of underhand and unbrotherly practices in the pursuit of Annie. Each was profoundly hurt by the accusations, and each, in the immense fatuity of his pride, had privately sworn to prove his innocence by having nothing more to do with Annie. Such is life! Such is man! Such is the terrible egoism of man! And thus it was that, for the sake of wounded pride, John and Robert not only did not speak to one another for ten years, but they spoilt at least one of their lives; and they behaved ignobly to Annie, who would certainly have married either one or the other of them.

At two o'clock in the morning John pulled a coin out of his pocket and made the gesture of tossing.

'Who shall go first!' he explained.

Robert had a queer sensation in his spine as his elder brother spoke to him for the first time in ten years. He wanted to reply vocally. He had a most imperious desire to reply vocally. But he could not. Something stronger even than the desire prevented his tongue from moving.

John tossed the coin – it was a sovereign – and covered it with his hands.

'Tail!' Robert murmured, somewhat hoarsely.

But it was head.

Then they went to bed.

II

The side door of Miss Emery's shop was in Brick Passage, and not in the main street, so that a man, even a man of commanding stature and formidable appearance, might by insinuating himself into Brick Street, off King Street, and then taking the passage from the quieter end, arrive at it without attracting too much attention. This course was adopted by John Hessian. From the moment when he quitted his own house that Friday evening in June he had been subject to the delusion that the collective eye of Bursley was upon him. As a matter of fact, the collective eye of Bursley is much too large and important to occupy itself exclusively with a single individual. Bursley is not a village, and let no one think it. Nevertheless, John was subject to the delusion.

The shop was shut, as he knew it would be. But the curtained window of the parlour, between the side-door and the small shuttered side-window of the shop, gave a strange suggestion of interesting virgin spotless domesticity within. John cast a fearful eye on the main thoroughfare. Nobody seemed to be passing. The chapel-keeper of the Wesleyan Chapel on the opposite side of Trafalgar Road was refreshing the massive Corinthian portico of that fane, and paying no regard whatever to the temple of Eros which Miss Emery's shop had suddenly become.

So John knocked.

'I am a fool!' his thought ran as he knocked.

Because he did not know what he was about. He had won the toss, and with it the right to approach Annie Emery before his brother. But what then? Well, he did desire to marry her, quite as much for herself as for his sister's fortune. But what then? How was he going to explain the tepidity, the desertion, the long sin against love of ten years? In short, how was he going to explain the inexplicable? He could decidedly do nothing that evening except make a blundering ass of himself. And how soon would Robert have the right to come along and say *his* say? That point had not been settled. Points so extremely delicate cannot be settled on a slate, and he had not dared to broach it *viva voce* to his younger brother. He had been too afraid of a rebuff.

He then hoped that Annie's servant would tell him that Annie was out.

Annie, however, took him at a disadvantage by opening the door herself.

'Well, *Mr Hessian*!' she exclaimed, her face bursting into a swift and welcoming smile.

'I was just passing,' the donkey in him blundered forth. 'And I thought – '

However, in fifteen seconds he was on the domestic side of the sitting-room window, and seated in the antimacassared armchair between the fire-place and the piano, and Annie had taken his hat and told him that her servant was out for the evening.

'But I'm disturbing your supper, Miss Emery,' he said. Flurried though he was, he could not fail to notice the white embroidered cloth spread diagonally on the table, and the cold meat and the pastry and the glittering cutlery and crystal thereon.

'Not at all,' she replied. 'You haven't had supper yet, I expect?'

'No,' he said, not thinking.

'It will be nice of you to help me to eat mine,' said she.

'Oh! But really – '

But she got plates and things out of the cupboard below the bookcase – and there he was! She would take no refusal. It was wondrous.

'I'm awfully glad I came now,' his thought ran; 'I'm managing it rather well.'

And –

'Poor Bob!'

His sole discomfort was that he could not invent a sufficiently ingenious explanation of his call. You can't tell a woman you've called to make love to her, and when your previous call happens to have been ten years ago, some kind of an explanation does seem to be demanded. Ultimately, as Annie was so very pleased to see him, so friendly, so feminine, so equal to the occasion, he decided to let his presence in her abode that night stand as one of those central facts in existence that need no explanation. And they went on talking and eating till the dusk deepened and Annie lit the gas and drew the blind.

He watched her on the sly as she moved about the room. He decided that she did not appear a day older. There was the same plump, erect figure, the same neatness, the same fair skin and fair hair, the same little nose, the same twinkle in the eye – only perhaps the twinkle in the eye was a trifle less cruel than it used to be. She was not a day older. (In this he was of course utterly mistaken; she was ten years older, she was thirty-three, with ten years of successful commercial experience behind her; she would never be twenty-three again. Still she was a most desirable woman, and a woman infinitely beyond his deserts.) Her air of general capability impressed him. And with that there was mingled a strange softness, a marvellous hint of a concealed wish to surrender. . . . Well, she made him feel big and masculine – in brief, a man.

He regretted the lost ten years. His present way of life seemed intolerable to him. The new heaven opened its gate and gave glimpses of paradise. After all, he felt himself well qualified for that paradise. He felt that he had all along been a woman's man, without knowing it.

'By Jove!' his thought ran. 'At this rate I might propose to her in a week or two.'

And again –

'Poor old Bobbie!'

A quarter of an hour later, in some miraculous manner, they were more intimate than they had ever been, much more intimate. He revised his estimate of the time that must elapse before he might propose to her. In another five minutes he was fighting hard against a mad impulse to propose to her on the spot. And then the fight was over, and he had lost. He proposed to her under the rose-coloured shade of the Welsbach light.

She drew away, as though shot.

And with the rapidity of lightning, in the silence which followed, he went back to his original criticism of himself, that he was a fool. Naturally she would request him to leave. She would accuse him of effrontery.

Her lips trembled. He prepared to rise.

'It's so sudden!' she said.

Bliss! Glory! Celestial joy! Her words were at least equivalent to an absolution of his effrontery! She would accept! She would accept! He jumped up and approached her. But she jumped up too and retreated. He was not to win his prize so easily.

'Please sit down,' she murmured. 'I must think it over,' she said, apparently mastering herself. 'Shall you be at chapel next Sunday morning?'

'Yes,' he answered.

'If I am there, and if I am wearing white roses in my hat, it will mean –' She dropped her eyes.

'Yes?' he queried.

And she nodded.

'And supposing you aren't there?'

'Then the Sunday after,' she said.

He thanked her in his Hessian style.

'I prefer that way of telling you,' she smiled demurely. 'It will avoid the necessity for another – so much – you understand? . . .'

'Quite so, quite so!' he agreed. 'I quite understand.'

'And if I *do* see those roses,' he went on, 'I shall take upon myself to drop in for tea, may I?'

She paused.

'In any case, you mustn't speak to me coming out of chapel, *please*.'

As he walked home down Oldcastle Street he said to himself that the age of miracles was not past; also that, after all, he was not so old as the tale of his years would mathematically indicate.

III

Her absence from chapel on the next Sunday disagreed with him. However, Robert was away nearly all the week, and he had the house to himself to dream in. It frequently happened to him to pass by Miss Emery's shop, but he caught no glimpse of her, and though he really was in serious need of writing-paper and envelopes, he dared not enter. Robert returned on the Friday.

On the morning of the second Sunday, John got up early, in order to cope with a new necktie that he had purchased in Hanbridge. Nevertheless he found Robert afoot before him, and Robert, by some unlucky chance, was wearing not merely a new necktie, but a new suit of clothes. They breakfasted in their usual august silence, and John gathered from a remark of Robert's to Maggie when she brought in the boots that Robert meant to go to chapel. Now, Robert, being a commercial traveller and therefore a bit of a caution, did not attend chapel with any remarkable assiduity. And John, in the privacy of his own mind, blamed him for having been so clumsy as to choose that particular morning for breaking the habits of a lifetime. Still, the presence of Robert in the pew could not prejudicially affect John, and so there was no genuine cause for gloominess.

After a time it became apparent that each was waiting for the other to go. John began to get annoyed. At last he made the plunge and went. Turning his head halfway up Oldcastle Street, opposite the mansion which is called 'Miss Peel's', he perceived Robert fifty yards behind. It was a glorious June day.

He blushed as he entered chapel. If he was nervous, it may be accorded to him as excuse that the happiness of his life depended on what he should see within the next few minutes. However, he felt pretty sure, though it was exciting all the same.

To reach the Hessian pew he was obliged to pass Miss Emery's. And it was empty! Robert arrived.

The organist finished the voluntary. The leading tenor of the choir put up the number of the first hymn. The minister ascended the staircase of the great mahogany pulpit, and prayed silently, and arranged his papers in the leaves of the hymn-book, and glanced about to see who was there and who was presumably still in bed, and coughed; and then Miss Annie Emery sailed in with that air of false calm which is worn by the experienced traveller who catches a train by the fifth of a second. The service commenced.

John looked.

She was wearing white roses. There could be no mistake as to that. There were about a hundred and fifty-five white roses in the garden of her hat.

What a thrill ran through John's heart! He had won Annie, and he had won the fortune. Yes, he would give Robert the odd five thousand pounds. His state of mind might even lead him to make it guineas. He heard not a word of the sermon, and throughout the service he rose up and sat down several instants after the rest of the congregation, because he was so absent-minded.

After service he waited for everybody else to leave, in order not to break his promise to the divine Annie. So did Robert. This ill-timed rudeness on Robert's part somewhat retarded the growth of a young desire in John's heart to make friends with poor Bob. Then he got up and left, and Robert followed.

They dined in silence, John deciding that he would begin his overtures of friendship after he had seen Annie, and could tell Robert that he was formally engaged. The brothers ate little. They both improved their minds during their repast – John with the *Christian Commonwealth*, and Robert with the Saturday cricket edition of the *Signal* (I regret it).

Then, after pipes, they both went out for a walk, naturally not in the same direction. The magnificence of the weather filled them both with the joy of life. As for John, he went out for a walk simply because he could not contain himself within the house. He could not wait immovable till four-thirty, the hour at which he meant to call on Annie for tea and the betrothal kiss. Therefore he ascended to Hillport and wandered as far as Oldcastle, all in a silk hat and a frock-coat.

It was precisely half-past four as he turned, unassumingly, from Brick Street into Brick Passage, and so approached the side door of Annie Emery's. And his astonishment and anger were immense when he saw Robert, likewise in silk hat and frock-coat, penetrating into Brick Passage from the other end.

They met, and their inflamed spirits collided.

'What's the meaning of this?' John demanded, furious; and, simultaneously, Robert demanded: 'What in Hades are *you* doing here?'

Only Sunday and the fine clothes and the proximity to Annie prevented actual warfare.

'I'm calling on Annie,' said John.

'So am I,' said Robert.

'Well, you're too late,' said John.

'Oh, I'm too late, am I?' said Robert, with a disdainful laugh. 'Thanks!'

'I tell you you're too late,' said John. 'You may as well know at once that I've proposed to Annie and she's accepted me.'

'I like that! I like that!' said Robert.

'Don't shout!' said John.

'I'm not shouting,' said Robert. 'But you may as well know that you're mistaken, my boy. It's me that's proposed to Annie and been accepted. You must be off your chump.'

'When did you propose to her?' said John.

'On Friday, if you must know,' said Robert.

'And she accepted you at once?' said John.

'No. She said that if she was wearing white roses in her hat this morning at chapel, that would mean she accepted,' said Robert.

'Liar!' said John.

'I suppose you'll admit she *was* wearing white roses in her hat?' said Robert, controlling himself.

'Liar!' said John, and continued breathless: 'That was what she said to *me*. She must have told you that white roses meant a refusal.'

'Oh no, she didn't!' said Robert, quailing secretly, but keeping up a formidable show of courage. 'You're an old fool!' he added vindictively.

They were both breathing hard, and staring hard at each other.

'Come away,' said John. 'Come away! We can't talk here. She may look out of the window.'

So they went away. They walked very quickly home, and, once in the parlour, they began to have it out. And, before they had done, the reading of cricket news on Sunday was as nothing compared to the desecrating iniquity which they committed. The scene was not such as can be decently recounted. But about six o'clock Maggie entered, and, at considerable personal risk, brought them back to a sense of what was due to their name, the town, and the day. She then stated that she would not remain in such a house, and she departed.

IV

'But whatever made you do it, dearest?'

These words were addressed to Annie Emery on the glorious summer evening which closed that glorious summer day, and they were addressed to her by no other person than Powell Liversage. The pair were in the garden of the house in Trafalgar Road occupied by Mr Liversage and his mother, and they looked westwards over the distant ridge of Hillport, where the moon was setting.

'Whatever made me do it!' repeated Annie, and the twinkle in her eye had that charming cruelty which John had missed. 'Did they not deserve it? Of course, I can talk to you now with perfect freedom, can't I? Well, what do you *think* of it? Here for ten years neither one nor the other does more than recognize me in the street, and then all of a sudden they come down on me like that – simply because there's a question of money. I couldn't have believed men could be so stupid – no, I really couldn't! They're friends of yours, Powell, I know, but – however, that's no matter. But it was too ridiculously easy to lead them on! They'd swallow any flattery. I just did it to see what they'd do, and I think I arranged it pretty well. I quite expected they would call about the same time, and then shouldn't I have given them my mind! Unfortunately they met outside, and got very hot – I saw them from the bedroom window – and went away.'

'You mustn't forget, my dear girl,' said Liversage, 'that it was you they quarrelled about. I don't want to defend 'em for a minute, but it wasn't altogether the money that sent them to you; it was more that the money gave them an excuse for coming!'

'It was a very bad excuse, then!' said Annie.

'Agreed!' Liversage murmured.

The moon was extremely lovely and romantic against the distant spire of Hillport Church, and its effect on the couple was just what might have been anticipated.

'Perhaps I'm sorry,' Annie admitted at length, with a charming grimace.

'Oh! I don't think there's anything to be *sorry* about,' said Liversage. 'But of course they'll think I've had a hand in it. You see, I've never breathed a word to them about – about my feelings towards you.'

'No?'

'No. It would have been rather a delicate subject, you see, with them. And I'm sure they'll be staggered when they know that we got engaged last night. They'll certainly say I've – er – been after you for the – No, they won't. They're decent chaps, really; very decent.'

'Anyhow, you may be sure, dear,' said Annie stiffly, 'that *I* shan't rob them of their vile money! Nothing would induce me to touch it!'

'Of course not, dearest!' said Liversage – or, rather the finer part of him said it; the baser part somewhat regretted that vile twelve thousand or so. (I must be truthful.)

He took her hand again.

At the same moment old Mrs Liversage came hastening down the garden, and Liversage dropped the hand.

'Powell,' she said. 'Here's John Hessian, and he wants to see you!'

'The dickens!' exclaimed Liversage, glancing at Annie.

'I must go,' said Annie. 'I shall go by the fields. Good night, dear Mrs Liversage.'

'Wait ten seconds,' Liversage pleaded, 'and I'll be with you.' And he ran off.

John, haggard and undone, was awaiting him in the drawing-room.

'Pow,' said he, 'I've had a fearful row with Bob, and I can't possibly sleep in our house tonight. Don't talk to me. But let me have one of the beds in your spare room, will you? There's a good chap.'

'Why, of course, Johnnie,' said Liversage. 'Of course.'

'And I'll go right to bed now,' said John.

An hour later, after Powell Liversage had seen his affianced to her abode and returned home, and after his mother had gone to bed, there was a knock at the front door, and Liversage opened to Robert Hessian.

'Look here, Pow,' said Robert, whose condition was deplorable, 'I want to sleep here tonight. Do you mind? Fact is, I've had a devil of a shindy with Jack, and Maggie's run off, and, anyhow, I couldn't possibly stop in the same house with Jack tonight.'

'But what – ?'

'See here,' said Robert. 'I can't talk. Just let me have a bed in your spare room. I'm sure your mother won't mind.'

'Why, certainly,' said Liversage.

He lit a candle, escorted Robert upstairs, opened the door of the spare room, gave the candle to Robert, pushed him in, said 'Good night,' and shut the door.

What a night!

Doctor in the Soup

☆★☆★☆★☆★☆★☆★☆★☆★☆★☆★☆★☆★☆★☆★☆

RICHARD GORDON

The Old Tyme Inne was 1930s Tudor, a 'roadhouse', an ancient monument from the era when driving a car was as romantic as flying your own plane.

The food was choking. The wine was poisonous. The waiters were unintelligible.

The evening was delicious.

And the candlelight was as good as you would get anywhere.

'You really are the most wonderful person I've ever met, doctor,' said Mrs Osgood huskily, dropping her eyes over her coffee with *crème de menthe* and After Eight.

I said tut.

'So helpful,' she breathed. 'So kind. So considerate.'

I said tut tut.

'So understanding, so gentle, so courteous, so chivalrous.'

I said tut tut tut.

Mrs Osgood sighed deeply.

'I never imagined, after that perfectly disgusting divorce, that I'd find . . .' Her eyes held mine. 'Such a lovely boss.'

I asked pressingly, 'Not pompous?'

'Oh, no, doctor! Your conversation twinkles like bubbles in a glass.'

I held her hand across the paper marigolds.

'Mrs Osgood,' I suggested modestly. 'You are so refreshing you must find parts of me which other people cannot reach.'

She left her hand *in situ*. She dropped her eyes. She said huskily, 'Oh, I do, I do, doctor.'

I added another hand to her hand.

'I'd love you to come to my flat, doctor,' she murmured.

I jumped up. 'Now?'

'Oh, no.' She seemed surprised. 'Not at this moment.'

I gathered the scattered marigolds.

'When, Mrs Osgood?' I implored.

She nibbled her After Eight. 'Perhaps after the weekend, doctor?'

'Fine!' I exclaimed. I sat down again. 'Monday? Tuesday?'

'Wednesday?'

'Lovely!'

She smiled slowly. 'There! You are so nice. You didn't need inviting twice.'

'What a delightful modesty you display about your overwhelming sexual attraction,' I meant to say, but it came out urk.

Her eyes dropped as beautifully as butterflies alighting on roses.

'Come early after surgery, doctor. We can make a night of it.'

'Splendid!' I cried. I gathered up the marigolds again.

I arrived home towards midnight. I had qualms. But even Mr Pickwick had his amorous adventures. He found himself in the bedroom of the middle-aged lady in the yellow curl-papers at the Great White Horse in Ipswich. He was looking for his watch. A likely story!

I softly opened the front door. The lights were still on. I was surprised. Sandra was sitting beside the hearth, embroidering a tea cosy.

I said jovially, 'Staying up late, dear?'

'It was a long lecture at the General?'

'Dreadfully. Hours and hours. You know Basil Barty-Howells. Absolutely brilliant, of course, electrolyte balance at his finger tips, but as wordy as an unheckled politician.' I added with satisfaction, 'However, now I know absolutely everything about electrolyte balance.'

I poured myself an Old Fettercairn.

'Since when were you an electrolyte balance buff?' enquired Sandra, stitching.

'Oh, years. Fascinating corner of medicine, electrolyte balance.'

'Come to think of it, when did you last attend a lecture on anything, since you were in medical school and had to?'

'One has the urge,' I enlightened her. 'One must grasp the latest advances before it's too late. *Torschlusspanik!* You know.'

I took a gulp.

'It's a funny thing,' she observed quietly, snipping a stitch. 'That your own partner Elaine Spondek didn't see you there.'

'What the bloody hell was Elaine doing at an electrolyte balance lecture?' I demanded hotly. 'That stuff's far above her head.'

Sandra concentrated on threading a needle. 'She thought it would be a nice gesture towards Basil Barty-Howells.'

I silently poured myself another Old Fettercairn.

'Darling!' Sandra looked at me. 'I'm not cross. Not a little bit.'

'I'm sorry,' I mumbled humbly. 'Dreadfully, dreadfully sorry.'

'You enjoyed yourself?'

I shrugged. 'Not at all. How could I? I was laden with disgrace, remorse, shame.'

She smiled wanly. 'I'm sure you did, really. Didn't you?'

'Perhaps it wasn't too bad,' I admitted.

'There!'

'I deserve absolutely anything you say to me.'

'But I'm touched! You took such trouble, cooking up an excuse.'

'I'm a duplicitous worm,' I conceded.

'Because you know how terribly upset I am at your leaving me alone night after night to go out and play that damfool game snooker.'

She set aside her sewing things. 'I hope you won, darling? Coming to bed?'

I stared after her. I poured myself another Old Fettercairn.

Monday morning.

'What amazing tenderness!' laughed Sandra.

I looked puzzled.

'Richard, you've been biting my ear lobes steadily all weekend, and now you're boiling me an egg. Is it another woman? Oh, dear! You've dropped the toast butter side down. An affair's the usual cause of an unexpected outbreak of affection in a mature marriage,' she informed me. 'Everyone says so.'

I murmured something unconvincing about redeeming forgetfulness of her birthday.

My partner motherly Elaine Spondek greeted me in the small, square, mustard-walled, plastic-floored hall of our surgery.

'Sandra seemed to think you were attending that horribly boring lecture on Friday,' she announced cheerfully.

'Can't think what gave her the idea. It was keen of you to go.'

'Only because I'm hoping that Basil Barty-Howells is going to buy my old car. I want to talk to you about Judy Osgood.'

I jumped. 'You mean, the Old Tyme Inne?'

She frowned.

I asked falteringly, 'You know all about it?'

'Well, it's in Yellow Pages.'

'Ah! Then you don't.'

She stared at me. 'Richard, are you suffering from a confusional state?'

'It's the *Torschlusspanik!*' I explained hastily.

'I do hope you know how to treat it. Listen, I was going to ask about Judy Osgood.'

I slapped my hands. 'We are just good friends.'

'I should hope so! You're working together all day long.'

'But not that good friends.'

She pursed her lips.

'Richard, this is Monday morning, when even the Marx Brothers with performing seals on ice would not be so funny.' She said as to a difficult child, 'I only want to know your assessment of Judy Osgood.'

'A treasure.'

'If she wants to stay, do you want to keep her?'

'I'd love to keep her.'

'That's all right, then. I can't understand your making such a fuss. What was the name of that German disease again?'

'*Torschlusspanik!* There's a lot of it about.'

I strode into my consulting room. Mrs Osgood was laying patients' cards on the desk.

'Har!' I greeted her.

She dropped her eyes.

'Last night was utterly wonderful, doctor.'

'Har!'

'I shall always remember it, doctor.'

'But it won't be anything compared to next Wednesday night.'

She looked up, fluttering her lashes, smiling coyly. 'I'll do my best,' she promised.

'Then you're not going to forget that one, either.'

I rattled cheerfully through my patients.

I ended the morning hoping I had given them all the appropriate prescriptions. Though I suppose with most patients a GP sees, it does not much matter.

'*No* snooker with Jack Windrush this evening,' Sandra reproved me at lunch. 'Have you forgotten that Jilly and Peter are coming for dinner? They've still no more idea of their wedding day than the end of the world.'

I suppose I should have been proud of regular humiliation by someone as brainy as Peter pretending I knew more medicine than he did. Over the roast leg of pork I asked about the latest in gynaecological research.

'Oh, even more dangers in sex,' he replied, smiling. 'We've been through the statistics of men dying from coronaries in bed, and discovered that a high proportion occurred during intercourse.'

'Tut,' I said.

'How dreadful for the poor wife,' observed Jilly.

Peter laughed. 'Be your age, darling. It's generally *not* the poor wife. Most deaths occur during extramarital sex. The excitement, you know.'

'Yes, the excitement,' I muttered.

'I suppose it puts up the blood pressure far higher than the mundane marital sort?' enquired Jilly. 'Mum, you haven't lost your touch with the apple sauce.'

'A squeeze of orange-juice, darling.'

Peter continued informatively, 'Let's take a typical case. Some middle-aged professional or businessman with his twenty-year-old secretary. Probably overweight and under-exercised, blood pressure already a bit up, gets breathless running for a cab. He throws himself into it like trying to win the 100 metres in the Olympics, not a care in the world, then zingo.'

'Horribly embarrassing for the corpse,' Jilly remarked. 'He never knows where he might be found.'

I stared at Peter. 'Rare cases, surely?'

'Really quite frequent, Richard, you'd be surprised. A nasty experience for the girl. I suppose it's like being rolled on by your dead mount in the Grand National.'

'Is your pork all right?' Sandra asked me anxiously.

'I'm not very hungry.'

Wednesday.

I arrived home from evening surgery.

'Darling, I must dash,' I apologized to Sandra. 'I've got Monday's postponed snooker game with Jack Windrush.'

She looked up from arranging a bowl of roses.

'Oh, Jack just rang. Reminding you that if you happened to be thinking of going to the club tonight, the snooker table's booked for the match against the cricket club. Stay at home, dear, and I'll cook you a nice dinner.' She stared at me. 'But what's the matter? It isn't a disaster.'

'I must go out,' I muttered.

She looked concerned. 'Not another attack of that foreign thing, is it?'

'Must go and see some patients,' I croaked.

'But you're not on call, darling! Elaine is.'

'Still must see some patients.'

'You've been seeing patients all day.'

'Must see some more.'

'Surely you can't have any of today's left?'

'Well, I'm going out,' I said.

I went.

Mrs Osgood's flat was in a ten-storey modern block overlooking the Churchill Memorial Park. I had three patients there. I hoped they were out.

I went up in the lift. I had racing pulse, short breath, nausea and dryness of the mouth. The onset of a heart attack? I saw myself coming down again on a stretcher, transported with flashing blue lights to the coronary care unit at the General, and faced with Basil Barty-Howells, who I knew to be as unreliable in the practice of medicine that evening as I was.

I rang the bell. I decided they were all symptoms of *Torschlusspanik!*

Mrs Osgood, radiant in wispy dress.

She gave a lovely smile.

'Hello, doctor,' she said huskily, dropping her eyes. 'This is the moment I've been waiting for.'

I said urk.

'Receiving you in my own home. Do come in.'

I went in.

I could not decide whether I was going to enjoy myself or drop dead.

'You must meet my mother,' said Mrs Osgood.

A good-looking, smartly-dressed, curly-haired lady held out a delicate hand, also with a lovely smile.

'My daughter's told me all about you, doctor.'

I said urk again.

'Thank you so much for looking after Judy. Her life was utterly shattered after that cruel divorce, but she very sensibly didn't want to start rebuilding it the wrong way. Did you, dear? But from all the encouraging things you've said to her in the practice, she's absolutely convinced she's the right type to join.'

'Join what?' I muttered.

'The Samaritans,' said Mrs Osgood proudly. 'Then I can *really* help unfortunate people. Of course it's voluntary, but I've been offered this wonderfully well paid job at the estate agents and I'm starting on Monday. I'm sure you'll overlook the short notice, doctor.' She turned to her mother. 'He's such a good sort.'

Clang!

The *Tor* was *schlussed.*

'You're soon back.' Sandra looked up in surprise from making an omelette. 'You couldn't have seen many patients.'

I poured myself half a tumbler of Glenmorangie.

'I haven't seen any patients,' I confessed.

'You left the house as though the Black Death had broken out again.'

'I've been to the Old Tyme Inne. You know, five miles along the Dover Road.'

'But what for? Have you gone off my cooking?'

I drank Glenmorangie and nibbled her earlobe. 'It's as tasty as ever, but you deserve an evening off. On your birthday. I'm standing dinner for fifty. George, Dilys, ask all your family, all our friends in Churchford. It'll be by candlelight.'

'Richard!' She glowed. 'You really are a wonderful husband.'

'Thank you. Also, I've given up snooker.'

That Friday evening, Jack Windrush was the first to arrive at the Old Tyme Inne.

'Sorry I'm early,' he apologized. 'But I thought Daphne could join me here, as I was called urgently to the General. Had to organize a full blood count for Basil Barty-Howells.'

'But he's coming to the dinner party,' I objected.

'He isn't,' said Jack with relish. 'He's going to the theatre with a perforated duodenal ulcer. Jilly says she'll be late, as she's assisting Bill Igtham with the cutting. Though personally, I think Bill's made the wrong diagnosis. It's labour pains, giving birth to a knight. Do I see a bottle of Bruichladdich you've craftily hidden for yourself behind the gladioli? No need to wait for your other guests, surely? Wouldn't it be bloody funny if it comes out at midnight that the Queen has changed her mind about Basil? I hear Margaret's been seen in Asprey's trying on tiaras.'

Basic Training

☆★☆★☆★☆★☆★☆★☆★☆★☆★☆★☆★☆★☆★☆★☆★☆

CLIVE JAMES

National Service was designed to turn boys into men and make the Yellow Peril think twice about moving south. It was universally known as Nasho – a typically Australian diminutive. Once you were in it, four years went by before you were out of it: there was a three-week camp every year, plus numerous parades. But the most brutal fact about Nasho was the initial 77-day period of basic training, most of which took place at Ingleburn. Each new intake of gormless youth was delivered into the hands of regular army instructors who knew everything about licking unpromising material into shape. When we stepped off the bus at Ingleburn, they were already screaming at us. Screaming sergeants and corporals appeared suddenly out of huts. I stood clutching my Globite suitcase and wondered what had gone wrong with my life. While I goggled at a screaming sergeant, I was abruptly blown sideways by a bellow originating from somewhere behind my right ear. Recovering, I turned to face Ronnie the One.

His real name was Warrant Officer First Class Ronald McDonald, but he was known throughout the army as Ronnie the One. Responsible for battalion discipline, he had powers of life and death over all non-commissioned personnel and could even bring charges against officers up to the rank of captain. His appearance was almost inconceivably unpleasant. A pig born looking like him would have demanded plastic surgery. His brass gleamed like gold and his leather like mahogany, but the effect was undone by his khaki drills, which despite being ironed glass smooth were perpetually soaked with sweat. Ronnie the One dripped sweat even on a cold day. It was not just because he was fat, although he had a behind like an old sofa. It was because he was always screaming so hard. At that moment he was screaming directly at me. 'GEDYAHAYAHCARD!' Later on a translator told me that this meant

'Get your hair cut' and could generally be taken as a friendly greeting, especially if you could still see his eyes. When Ronnie was really annoyed his face swelled up and turned purple like the rear end of an amorous baboon.

For the next eleven weeks, I was running flat out, but no matter how fast my feet moved, my mind was moving even faster. It was instantly plain to me that only cunning could ensure survival. Among the university students in our intake, Wokka Clark was undoubtedly the golden boy. Already amateur middleweight champion of NSW, he was gorgeous to behold. But he couldn't take the bullshit. What happened to him was like a chapter out of *From Here to Eternity*. They applauded him in the boxing ring at night and screamed at him all day. That summer the noon temperature was a hundred plus. Ronnie the One would take Wokka out on the parade ground and drill him till he dropped. The reason Wokka dropped before Ronnie did was simple. All Ronnie had on his head was a cap. Wokka had on a steel helmet. The pack on his back was full of bricks. After a few weeks of that, plus guard duty every night that he wasn't boxing, even Wokka was obeying orders.

You couldn't fight them. Even the conscientious objectors ended up looking after the regimental mascot – a bulldog called Onslow who looked like Ronnie's handsome younger brother. It was like one of Kenny Mears's games of marbles: nobody was allowed not to play. I could appreciate the psychology of it. The first task when training new recruits is to disabuse them of the notion that life is fair. Otherwise they will stand rooted to the spot when they first come up against people who are trying to kill them. But my abstract understanding of what was going on impinged only tangentially on the concrete problem of getting through the day without landing myself in the kind of trouble that would make the next day even more impossibly difficult than it was going to be anyway.

Something about my general appearance annoyed Ronnie. There were a thousand trainees in the intake but I was among the select handful of those whose aspect he couldn't abide. I could be standing in a mess queue, Ronnie would be a dot in the distance, and suddenly his voice would arrive like incoming artillery. 'GEDDABIGGAHAD!' He meant that I should get a bigger hat. He didn't like the way it sat on top of my head. Perhaps he just didn't like my head, and wanted the whole thing covered up. The drill that I had learned in Boys' Brigade saved my life. When it came to square-bashing, it turned out that the years I had spent interpreting Captain Andrews's commands had given me a useful insight into what Ronnie was likely to mean by his shouts and screams. When Ronnie yelled 'ABARD HARGH!' I knew almost straight away that it must mean 'about turn'. Thus I was able to turn decisively with the many, instead of dithering with the few.

On the parade ground Peebles drew most of the lightning. So unco-ordinated that he was to all intents and purposes a spastic, Peebles should not have been passed medically fit. But since he had been, the Army was stuck with him. After a month of training, when Ronnie shouted 'ABARD HARGH!' 999 soldiers would smartly present their backs and Peebles would be writhing on the ground, strangled by the sling of his rifle. For Peebles the day of reckoning came when he obeyed an order to fix bayonets. This was one of Ronnie's most frightening orders. It had the verb at the end, as in German or Latin. In English the order would have sounded something like: 'Bayonets . . . fix!' Bellowed by Ronnie, it came out as: 'BAHAYONED . . . *FEE*!' The last word was delivered as a high-pitched, almost supersonic, scream. It was succeeded on this occasion by another scream, since Peebles's bayonet, instead of appearing at the end of his rifle, was to be seen protruding from the back of the soldier standing in front of him. After that, they used to mark Peebles present at company parade every morning but lose him behind a tree on the way to battalion parade, where he was marked absent.

My kit, not my drill, was what got me into trouble. For once in my life I had to make my own bed every morning, without fail, and lay out for inspection my neatly polished and folded belongings. Since the penalty for not doing this properly was to have the whole lot thrown on the floor and be obliged to start again, I gradually got better at it, but I never became brilliant. National Servicemen had to wax and polish their webbing instead of just powdering it with blanco. It was a long process which bored me, and the same fingers which had been so tacky at woodwork were still likely to gum up the job. The problem became acute when it was my platoon's turn to mount guard. Throughout the entire twenty-four hours it was on duty, the guard was inspected, supervised, harassed and haunted by Ronnie the One. The initial inspection of kit, dress and rifle lasted a full hour. Ronnie snorted at my brass, retched at my webbing, and turned puce when he looked down the barrel of my rifle. 'THASSNODDAGHARDRIVAL!' he yelled. He meant that it was not a guard rifle. 'ISSFULLAPADAYDAHS!' He meant that it was full of potatoes. I looked down the barrel. I had spent half a day pulling it through until it glowed like El Dorado's gullet. Now I saw that a single speck of grit had crept into it.

In the guard-house we had to scrub the floors and tables, whitewash the walls and polish the undersides of the drawing pins on the notice board. When we went out on picket we could not afford to relax for a moment, since Ronnie could be somewhere in the vicinity preparing to do his famous Banzai charge. At two o'clock in the morning I was guarding the transport park. It was raining. Sitting down in the sentry box, I had the brim of my hat unbuttoned and was hanging from the collar of my groundsheet, praying for death. I had my rifle inside my groundsheet with me, so that I could fold my hands on its muzzle, lean my chin on the cushion formed by my hands under the cape, and gently nod off while still looking reasonably alert. I had calculated that Ronnie would not come out in the rain. This proved to be a bad guess. I thought the sentry box had been struck by lightning, but it was merely Ronnie's face going off like a purple grenade about a foot in front of mine. I came to attention as if electrocuted and tried to shoulder arms. Since the rifle was still inside my groundsheet, merely to attempt this manoeuvre was bound to yield Peebles-like results. Ronnie informed me, in a tirade which sounded and felt like an atomic attack, that he had never seen anything like it in his life.

The inevitable consequence was extra kitchen duty. I can safely say that I did more of this than anybody else in the battalion. While everybody else was out in the donga learning to disguise themselves as ant-hills and sneak up on the enemy, I was in the kitchen heading a crack team of cleaners composed of no-hopers like Peebles. The kitchen was as big as an aircraft hangar. All the utensils were on an enormous scale. The smallest dixies would be four feet long, two feet across and three feet deep. Lined with congealed custard and rhubarb, they took half an hour each to clean. The biggest dixie was the size of a Bessemer converter and mounted on gimbals. I was lowered into it on a rope. When I hit the bottom it rang like a temple gong. After the kitchen sergeant was satisfied that the dixie was shining like silver he pulled a crank and I was tipped out, smothered in mashed potato.

It must have been while I was inside the dixie that I missed out on the chance to volunteer for Infantry. That was how I found myself in the Assault Pioneers – the one specialist course that nobody sane wanted to be on, since it involved land mines, booby traps and detonators. In the long run the lethality of the subject proved to be a boon. National Service was winding to an end by that stage – ours was to be the last intake – and the government didn't want any mother's son getting killed at the eleventh hour. So instead of burying mines for us to dig up, they buried rocks. While our backs were turned, they would bury a hundred rocks in a careful pattern. We would move through the area, probing the earth with our bayonets, and dig up two hundred. It wasn't as glamorous as being in, say, the mortar platoon, but I came to appreciate the lack of excitement, especially after we were all marched out to the range and given a demonstration of what the mortar specialists had learned.

The mortars in question were the full three inches across the barrel – not the two-inch pipes that had little more than nuisance value, but really effective weapons which could throw a bomb over a mountain and kill everything within a wide radius at the point of impact. A thousand of us, including the colonel and all his officers, sat around the rim of a natural amphitheatre while the mortar teams fired their weapons. All looked downwards at the mortars with fascination, except for Ronnie the One, who was down with the mortars looking upwards, tirelessly searching for anyone with too small a hat. Team after team loaded and fired. The bomb was dropped into the mortar and immediately departed towards the stratosphere, where it could be heard – and even, momentarily, seen – before it dived towards its target, which was a large cross on a nearby hill. You saw the blast, then you heard the sound. It was a bit like watching Ronnie having a heart attack on the horizon.

Every team did its job perfectly until the last. The last team was Wokka Clark and Peebles. They had to do *something* with Peebles. If they had put him in the Pioneers he probably would have bitten the detonator instead of the fuse. It went without saying that he could not be allowed to drive a truck or fire a Vickers machine gun, especially after the way he had distinguished himself on the day everyone in the battalion had had to throw a grenade. (One at a time we entered the throwing pit. The sergeant handed you a grenade, from which you removed the pin. You then threw the grenade. When he handed Peebles a grenade, Peebles removed the pin and handed the grenade back to him.) The safest thing to do with Peebles was team him up with Wokka, who was so strong that he could throw the base plate of a three-inch mortar twenty yards. All Peebles had to do was wait until Wokka had done the calibrations and then drop in the bomb. He must have done it successfully scores of times in practice. He did it quite smoothly this time too, except that the bomb went in upside down.

If you were to rig a vacuum cleaner to blow instead of suck and then point it at a pile of dust, you would get some idea of what those thousand supposedly disciplined men did a split second after they noticed the bomb going into the mortar with its fins sticking up instead of down.

They just melted away. Some tried to dig themselves into the earth. Some started climbing trees. But most of us ran. I was running flat out when an officer went past me at head height, flapping his arms like a swan. Ronnie stopped the panic by shouting 'HARD!', meaning 'halt'. The noise could have been the bomb going off, but since it was unaccompanied by shrapnel it seemed safe to pay attention. Everyone turned and looked down. Ronnie picked up the whole mortar, base plate included, shook out the bomb and handed it to Peebles. Silence. Wokka still had his hands over his eyes. Peebles dropped the bomb in the right way up. The mortar coughed. There was a crackle in the sky and a blast on the hill. Then we all marched thoughtfully back to camp.

By now I had made a career out of being a private. Having made the mistake of supplying all the right answers in the intelligence test (since it was exactly the same test that I had been studying in Psychology I, this was no great feat) I was at first put under some pressure to become an officer, or failing that an NCO. But it soon became clear to all concerned that I was a born private. I had revived my joker persona as a means of ingratiating myself with my fellow conscripts. I had no wish to lose their approval by being raised above them. Nor was I morally equipped to accept responsibility for others. But I did manage to get better at being the lowest form of life in the army. I was a digger. I learned the tricks of looking neat without expending too much energy. And although it would have been heresy to say so, I actually enjoyed weapons training. I had the eyes to be good at firing the .303 rifle, but not the hands. Yet I relished being instructed on it. And the Bren was such a perfect machine that there was avid competition to specialize. I never got to the stage of wanting to sleep with one, but must admit that there were times when, as I eyed the Bren's sleek lines, I discovered in myself a strong urge to fiddle with its gas escape regulator.

The weapons sergeants were all regular soldiers with combat experience, usually in Korea. There was virtue, it seemed to me, in listening when they talked. They were wise in their craft. Every few intakes one of them got shot by a National Serviceman. None of them wanted to be the one. After surviving a long encounter with half a million glory-hungry Chinese it makes no sense to be finished off by some adolescent pointing his rifle at you and saying, 'Sergeant, it's stuck.' They were particularly careful when it came to instructing us on the Owen machine carbine. This was the same gun I had once carted around Jannali. The Owen cocked itself if you dropped it and shot you when you picked it up. It disgorged fat, 9mm. slugs at a very high rate of fire and the barrel clawed up to the right during the burst. If due precautions were not taken, the man on the left of the line would mow down everyone else; including the instructor. The sergeants were very cautious about whom they put on the left, and always stood well to the left themselves. Some of them stood so far to the left they were out of sight. Without exception they refused to let Peebles fire the thing at all. They parked him behind his usual tree on the way to the range and faked his score.

I also enjoyed drill. Einstein once said that any man who liked marching had been given his brain for nothing: just the spinal column would have done. But I wasn't Einstein. Since most of one's time in the army is wasted anyway, I preferred to waste it by moving about in a precise manner. It was better than blueing my pay-packet at a pontoon game in the lavatories. As fit as I would ever be in my life, I could fling a Lee-Enfield .303 rifle around like a baton. When I was ordered to volunteer as Right Front Marker for the exhibition drill squad, I sensibly said yes. Saying no would have immediately entailed being lowered into the big dixie, so it was scarcely a courageous decision.

The drill squad was one of the star items on the big day. Visiting brass and proud parents lined the parade ground. Dressed in white singlets, khaki drill trousers, gaiters and boots, ninety-nine strapping examples of bronzed young Australian manhood all took their time from me. We looked like an erotic dream by Leni Riefenstahl. Ronnie gave the orders in his usual mixture of Urdu and epilepsy, but by now I could read his mind. Miraculously dry-handed in the heat, I put the .303 through its paces. It was all a matter of not worrying. Just let the body remember. It wasn't until the routine was over and we were marching off to a storm of applause that the thought occurred to me: they had done it. They had got what they wanted out of me. But on the other hand I had got what I wanted out of them. I had acquired my first real measure of self-sufficiency, which is something other, and quieter, than mere self-assertion, and probably the opposite of being self-absorbed.

Ash, No Sackcloth

☆★☆★☆★☆★☆★☆★☆★☆★☆★☆★☆★☆★☆★☆

ALICE THOMAS ELLIS

The telephone continues to baffle me. I came home the other day to find a message from Maureen. She had been dusting the drawing room when the lunatic thing rang and told her to tell me that my brother in Australia was returning my call and would ring again that evening. 'Oh good,' I thought, and it took me a moment to remember that I don't have a brother – in Australia or anywhere else. I am an only child, although my mother occasionally appears to forget this too. Sometimes when I ring her I say, 'Hullo Mummy', and she says, 'Is that you darling?'

Being so solitary I was enchanted to discover the other day that my cousin Jeffrey (no relation, if you follow me – I wondered for a while whether it was my fate to dote on men called Jeffrey, and then I remembered Mrs Thatcher's one) and I are exactly alike – well, not exactly. You could tell us apart, but he and I are very similar. For one thing he smokes and drinks, and when told by people shaking their heads mournfully that he will not reach a ripe old age he says he doesn't give a toot: my sentiments entirely. I often think, when it's raining and the telephone doesn't stop ringing, that if the Grim Reaper were to lean over the garden wall beckoning with a bony digit, I would slip my tiny hand trustfully in his and go off with him without a backward glance. In passing: I was told recently by an economist, who presumably has a good grasp of numbers, that there are now more people alive than there are dead – that the great majority is now the minority. Can this be true? How does he know? How many angels can dance on the point of a pin?

But to return to my cousin Jeffrey. He loves cooking. He spends hours in the kitchen smoking and drinking and making elaborate Chinese meals for his wife and children, and then he doesn't eat any of it himself. I do that too. I like everyone to sit down at the table out of my way while I hover about in the back kitchen with the fags. Guests, of course, find this rather disconcerting, and I can see why. It is not reassuring to reflect that the *patron* doesn't *mange ici*, but I promise everyone the food is perfectly wholesome and there isn't even any fag ash in it, because us confirmed smokers are adept at holding the left, fag-bearing, hand well out of the way. My cousin smokes in the bath and can wash his hair with one hand, and I have developed a method of flicking the ash down my sleeve when I find myself marooned in the middle of a room surrounded by people with the ashtray miles out of reach on a corner table. The butt presents a problem, though; now so many people are straining after Health, a lot of them leave their drinks half drunk, and a glass with a bit of white wine in it offers a safe means of disposal and is less offensive to the host than burn-holes in the Axminster, I think. I was once asked to a party by some Americans who wrote on the invitation: 'This is a non-smoking household.' I didn't bother to reply. Could they have imagined that I would prefer to be with them rather than sitting in my kitchen, smoking?

I find some people's thought-processes awfully difficult to follow. Not least those of my friend the analyst, who has just telephoned me because he wanted somebody to shout at. He was mad with three other people, but they were all out; so he went prowling round to find a legitimate cause of complaint and was grimly delighted to discover what he describes as a burn-hole in a plastic thing in his garden. He accused me of causing it by dropping a lighted cigarette-end off his flat roof, and when I indignantly denied it he said I was only making it worse by telling lies. If he will go out on to his flat roof he will find, in the wall flanking it, a hole in the pointing; and if he will look in this hole he will find that I have stuffed all the fag-ends in there.

I love most of my friends and some of my relations, but the ones I love best are visible in the dark because they have a glowing fag in their face.

How To Borrow Money

☆★☆★☆★☆★☆★☆★☆★☆★☆★☆★☆★☆★☆★☆★☆★☆★☆★☆

STEPHEN LEACOCK

The process is quite easy, provided you borrow enough

Have you ever, my dear readers, had occasion to borrow money? Have you ever borrowed ten dollars under a rigorous promise of your word of honour as a Christian to pay it back on your next salary day? Have you ever borrowed as much as a million at a time?

If you have done these things, you cannot have failed to notice how much easier it is to borrow ten thousand dollars than ten, how much easier still to borrow a hundred thousand, and that when you come at last to raising an international loan of a hundred million the thing loses all difficulty.

Here below are the little things that take place on the occasion of an ascending series of loans.

Tableau No. I

The scene in which Hardup Jones borrows ten dollars till the first of next month from his friend, Canny Smith

'Say, look here, old man, I was wondering whether perhaps you wouldn't mind letting me have ten dollars till the end of the month – '

'Ten dollars!!'

'Oh, I could give it back all right, for dead sure, just the minute I get my salary.'

'Ten dollars!!!'

'You see, I've got into an awful tangle – I owe seven and a half on my board, and she said yesterday she'd have to have it. I couldn't pay my laundry last week, so he said he wouldn't leave it, and I got this cursed suit on the instalment plan and they said they'd seize my trunk, and – '

'Say, but Gol darn it, I lent you five dollars, don't you remember, last

November, and you swore you'd pay it back on the first and I never got it till away after New Year's – '

'I know, I know. But this is absolutely sure. So help me, I'll pay it right on the first, the minute I get my cheque.'

'Yes, but you won't – '

'No, I swear I will – '

And after about half an hour of expostulations and protests of this sort, having pledged his soul, his body, and his honour, the borrower at last gets his ten dollars.

Tableau No. II

The scene in which Mr. McDuff of the McDuff Hardware Store in Central City (pop. 3,862) borrows $1,000 from the local bank

The second degree in borrowing is represented by this scene in which Mr John McDuff, of McDuff Bros. Hardware Store (Everything in Hardware), calls on the local bank manager with a view to getting $1,000 to carry the business forward for one month till the farmers' spring payments begin to come in.

Mr McDuff is told by one of the (two) juniors in the bank to wait – the manager is engaged for the moment.

The manager in reality is in his inner office, sorting out trout flies. But he knows what McDuff wants and he means to make him wait for it and suffer for it.

When at last McDuff does get in, the manager is very cold and formal.

'Sit down, Mr McDuff,' he says.

When they go fishing together, the manager always calls McDuff 'John.' But this is different. McDuff is here to borrow money. And borrowing money in Central City is a criminal act.

'I came in about that loan,' says McDuff.

The manager looks into a ledger.

'You're overdrawn $17.00 right now,' he says.

'I know, but I'll be getting my accounts in any time after the first.'

Then follows a string of severe questions. What are McDuff's daily receipts? What is his overhead? What is his underfoot? Is he a churchgoer? Does he believe in a future life?

And at last even when the manager finally consents to lend the thousand dollars (he always meant to do it), he begins tagging on conditions:

'You'll have to get your partner to sign.'

'All right.'

'And you'd better get your wife to sign.'

'All right.'

'And your mother, she might as well sign too –'

There are more signatures on a county bank note for one month than on a Locarno treaty.

And at last McDuff, of Everything in Hardware, having pledged his receipts, his premises, his credit, his honour, his wife, and his mother – gets away with the thousand dollars.

Tableau No. III

How Mr P. Q. Pingpoint, of the great financial House of Pingpoint, Pingpong and Company, New York and London, borrows a million dollars before lunch

Here the scene is laid in a fitting setting. Mr Pingpoint is shown into the sumptuous head office of the president of the First National Bank.

'Ah, good morning,' says the president as he rises to greet Mr Pingpoint, 'I was expecting you. Our general manager told me that you were going to be good enough to call in. Won't you take this larger chair – you'll find it easier?'

'Ah, thank you. You're very comfortable here.'

'Yes, we rather think this is a pleasant room. And our board room, we think, is even better. Won't you let me show you our board room?'

'Oh, thanks, I'm afraid I hardly have the time. I just came in for a minute to complete our loan of a million dollars.'

'Yes, our executive vice-president said that you are good enough to come to us. It is very kind of you, I'm sure.'

'Oh, not at all.'

'And you are quite sure that a million is all that you care to take? We shall be delighted, you know, if you will take a million and a half.'

'Oh, scarcely. A million, I think, will be ample just now; we can come back, of course, if we want more.'

'Oh, certainly, certainly.'

'And do you want us to give any security, or anything of that sort?'

'Oh no, quite unnecessary.'

'And is there anything you want me to sign while I am here?'

'Oh no, nothing, the clerks will attend to all that.'

'Well, thanks, then, I needn't keep you any longer.'

'But won't you let me drive you up-town? My car is just outside. Or, better still, if you are free, won't you come and eat some lunch with me at the club?'

'Well, thanks, yes, you're really extremely kind.'

And with this, quite painlessly and easily, the million dollars has changed hands.

But even that is not the last degree. Eclipsing that sort of thing, both in ease and in splendour, is the international loan, as seen in –

Tableau No. IV

The scenes which accompany the flotation of an Anglo-French loan, in the American market, of a hundred million dollars, by the Right Hon. Samuel Rothstein of England and the Vicomte Baton Rouge de Chauve Souris of France

This occurrence is best followed as it appears in its triumphant progress in the American press.

NEW YORK, *Friday.* – An enthusiastic reception was given yesterday to the Right Hon. Mr Samuel Rothstein, of the British Cabinet, and to the Vicomte de Chauve Souris, French plenipotentiary, on their landing from the Stacquitania. It is understood that they will borrow $100,000,000. The distinguished visitors expect to stay only a few days.

NEW YORK, *Saturday.* – An elaborate reception was given last evening in the home of Mrs Bildermont to the Right Hon. Samuel Rothstein and the Baron de Chauve Souris. It is understood that they are borrowing a hundred million dollars.

NEW YORK, *Monday.* – The Baron de Chauve Souris and the Right Hon. Samuel Rothstein were notable figures in the Fifth Avenue church parade yesterday. It is understood that they will borrow a hundred million dollars.

NEW YORK, *Tuesday.* – The Baron de Chauve Souris and the Right Hon. Samuel Rothstein attended a baseball game at the Polo Grounds. It is understood that they will borrow a hundred million dollars.

NEW YORK, *Wednesday.* – At a ball given by Mr and Mrs Ashcoop-Vandermore for the distinguished English and French plenipotentiaries, Mr Samuel Rothstein and the Baron de Chauve Souris, it was definitely stated that the loan which they are financing will be limited to a hundred million dollars.

NEW YORK (WALL STREET), *Thursday.* – The loan of $100,000,000 was subscribed this morning at eleven o'clock in five minutes. The Right Hon. Mr Rothstein and the Baron Baton Rouge de Chauve Souris left America at twelve noon, taking the money with them. Both plenipotentiaries expressed their delight with America.

'It is,' said the Baron – 'how do you call it? – a cinch.'

Epilogue

And yet, six months later, what had happened? Who paid and who didn't?

Hardup Jones paid $5.40 within a month, $3.00 the next month and the remaining one dollar and sixty cents two weeks later.

McDuff Bros. met their note and went fishing with the manager like old friends.

The Pingpoint Syndicate blew up and failed for ten million dollars.

And the international loan got mixed up with a lot of others, was funded, equated, spread out over fifty years, capitalized, funded again – in short, it passed beyond all recognition.

And, the moral is, when you borrow, borrow a whole lot.

That Certain Smile

☆★☆★☆★☆★☆★☆★☆★☆★☆★☆★☆★☆★☆★☆★☆★☆★☆

MILES KINGTON

I wasn't really going to write about my four-week-old son just yet. Not, I thought, until he was nearing 21 years old and able to fight back, but something has just happened which can't wait for 20 years and needs discussing right now. The health visitor has told his mother and me that within a week or so we can expect him to give us a 'social smile'.

This worries me a lot. I think I know what she means, mark you. She means that for the first few weeks a baby produces false smiles caused by wind, or rain, or plummeting shares, and that real, person-to-person smiles only come after that. That's what she means by 'a social smile'. But it still worries me.

I've been mixing with adults for more than 20 years, after all, and I have come to fear and distrust the social smile. There are so many kinds, especially at parties. There's the kind that says: 'I remember your name, but I bet you don't remember mine.' There's the kind that says: 'Excuse me, I want to squeeze past you, but I don't want to talk to you.'

Other messages conveyed by the social smile are:

'I have a much funnier story than yours, which I will tell as soon as you've finished.'

'I know the people you're talking about rather better than you do.'

'I am smiling and looking over your shoulder in case someone more interesting than you comes in the room.'

There are even people who go through the whole of life with a faint social smile playing round their lips, as if they are in line for a Sainthood. They worry me most, because nobody can have a reason to smile all the time. What I want to know is: when he produces his first social smile, which will it be?

At the moment, I am getting a great variety of expressions from him, all except the social smile. I am getting the social frown, the social yawn, the social burp, the social pursed lips and raising of the eyebrows, and the social stare into the distance which pretends I'm not even there. That's very disconcerting. I am holding him and he is staring past my eyeline at someone more interesting behind me. But there's no one behind me. That's very odd. It's even more disconcerting, of course, when he stares straight at me and through me. Only four weeks old, and he's cutting me dead already.

What I want is just a plain old smile. I have a fantasy daydream of meeting him at a party, where he flashes me a smile and we move into conversation together . . .

'Hello! We've met somewhere, haven't we?'

'That's right. I'm your father.'

'Right! I didn't recognize you. Normally, when you're leaning over me, you've got that great damned light behind you, and I can't see a thing, so I just stare into space.'

'I'm sorry, I hadn't realized. I thought you were cutting me dead.'

'Not at all! Good heavens, you're one of the very few people I know in this world. You and the one who thinks I look like you.'

'Your mother.'

'That's the one! Dreary old party this, isn't it? Do you know anyone here?'

'No, not really. Can I get you anything to drink, by the way?'

'Yes, please. Mother's milk would be fine.'

That would be nice, a straightforward social smile. But I suspect it won't be like that at all – I suspect that the very first time he gives me a social smile, as opposed to a wind-aided smile, it will be in code, like a real adult social smile . . .

'You think you change nappies as well as Mum does, but you don't . . .'

'If you say "Who's a lovely baby, then?" once more, I'll throw up . . .'

'Is that the only song you know?'

'You haven't really gone and bought those BP shares, have you?'

'As you've been reading so much about getting the parent-child bonding going, I suppose the least I can do is flash you a smile . . .'

Maybe I'm worrying about this unnecessarily. Maybe if I just keep handing the peanuts round, and filling his glass up again, and emptying the ashtrays, as it were, he'll give me a social smile of his own accord one day, with no strings attached. But it's a long time coming. I mean, it's melancholy to think that, at the age of four weeks, my son may have gone off me already. Never smiled at me in his entire life, when I come to think of it.

On the other hand, I think I may have solved the mystery of those people who go through life with a faint, saintly smile hovering on their beatific faces 24 hours a day.

They have got wind.

Love in a Cold Climate

☆★☆★☆★☆★☆★☆★☆★☆★☆★☆★☆★☆★☆★☆★☆★☆★☆

NANCY MITFORD

When I was ready I went down to the Long Gallery, where Lord and Lady Montdore were sitting in their usual chairs one each side of the chimney-piece, but not at all in their usual frame of mind. They were both, and especially Lady Montdore, in a twitter of nerves, and looked up quite startled when I came into the room, relaxing again when they saw that it was only me. I thought that from the point of view of a stranger, a backwoodsman from the American continent, they struck exactly the right note. Lord Montdore, in an informal green velvet smoking-jacket, was impressive with his white hair and carved unchanging face, while Lady Montdore's very dowdiness was an indication that she was too grand to bother about clothes, and this too would surely impress. She wore printed black-and-white crêpe-de-chine, her only jewels the enormous half-hoop rings which flashed from her strong old woman's fingers, and sat as she always did, her knees well apart, her feet in their large buckled shoes firmly planted on the ground, her hands folded in her lap.

'We lit this little fire,' she said, 'thinking that he may feel cold after the journey.' It was unusual for her to refer to any arrangement in her house, people being expected to like what they found there, or else to lump it. 'Do you think we shall hear the motor when it comes up the drive? We generally can if the wind is in the west.'

'I expect I shall,' I said, tactlessly. 'I hear everything.'

'Oh, we're not stone deaf ourselves. Show Fanny what you have got for Cedric, Montdore.'

He held out a little book in green Morocco, Gray's Poems.

'If you look at the fly-leaf,' he said, 'you will see that it was given to my grandfather by the late Lord Palmerston the day that Cedric's grandfather was born. They evidently happened to be dining together. We think that it should please him.'

I did so hope it would. I suddenly felt very sorry for these two old people, and longed for Cedric's visit to be a success and cheer them up. 'Canadians,' he went on, 'should know all about the poet Gray, because General Wolfe, at the taking of Quebec — '

There were footsteps now in the drawing-room, so we had not heard the motor after all. Lord and Lady Montdore got up and stood together in front of the fireplace as the butler opened the door and announced 'Mr Cedric Hampton'.

A glitter of blue and gold crossed the parquet, and a human dragonfly was kneeling on the fur rug in front of the Montdores, one long white hand extended towards each. He was a tall, thin young man, supple as a girl, dressed in rather a bright blue suit; his hair was the gold of a brass bed-knob, and his insect appearance came from the fact that the upper part of the face was concealed by blue goggles set in gold rims quite an inch thick.

He was flashing a smile of unearthly perfection, relaxed and happy he knelt there bestowing this smile upon each Montdore in turn.

'Don't speak,' he said, 'just for a moment. Just let me go on looking at you – wonderful, wonderful people!'

I could see at once that Lady Montdore was very highly gratified. She beamed with pleasure. Lord Montdore gave her a hasty glance to see how she was taking it, and when he saw that beaming was the note, he beamed too.

'Welcome,' she said, 'to Hampton.'

'The beauty,' Cedric went on, floating jointlessly to his feet. 'I can only say that I am drunk with it. England, so much more beautiful than I had imagined (I have never had very good accounts of England, somehow), this house, so romantic, such a repository of treasures, and above all, you – the two most beautiful people I have ever seen!'

He spoke with rather a curious accent, neither French nor Canadian, but peculiar to himself, in which every syllable received rather more emphasis than is given by the ordinary Englishman. Also he spoke, as it were, through his smile, which would fade a little, then flash out again, but which never altogether left his face.

'Won't you take off your spectacles?' said Lady Montdore. 'I should like to see your eyes.'

'Later, dear Lady Montdore, later. When my dreadful, paralysing shyness (a disease with me) has quite worn off. They give me confidence, you see, when I am dreadfully nervous, just as a mask would. In a mask one can face anything – I should like my life to be a perpetual *bal masqué*, Lady Montdore, don't you agree? I long to know who the Man in the Iron Mask was, don't you, Lord Montdore? Do you remember when Louis XVIII first saw the Duchesse d'Angoulême after the Restoration? Before saying anything else you know – wasn't it all awful or anything, he asked if poor Louis XVI had ever told her who the Man in the Iron Mask was? I love Louis XVIII for that – so like *One*.'

Lady Montdore indicated me. 'This is our cousin – and a distant relation of yours, Cedric – Fanny Wincham.'

He took my hand and looked long into my face, saying, 'I am enchanted to meet you' as if he really was. He turned again to the Montdores, and said, 'I am so happy to be here.'

'My dear boy, we are so happy to have you. You should have come before – we had no idea – we thought you were always in Nova Scotia, you see.'

Cedric was gazing at the big French map table. 'Riesener,' he said, 'this is a very strange thing, Lady Montdore, and you will hardly believe it, but where I live in France we have its pair – is that not a coincidence. Only this morning, at Chèvres, I was leaning upon that very table.'

'What is Chèvres?'

'Chèvres – Fontaine, where I live, in the Seine et Oise.'

'But it must be quite a large house,' said Lady Montdore, 'if that table is in it?'

'A little larger, in every dimension, than the central block at Versailles, and with much more water. At Versailles there only remain seven hundred *bouches* (how is *bouche* in English? Jets?). At Chèvres we have one thousand five hundred, and they play all the time.'

Dinner was announced. As we moved towards the dining-room Cedric stopped to examine various objects, touched them lovingly, and murmured:

'Weisweiller – Boulle – Caffieri – Jacob. How is it you come to have these marvels, Lord Montdore, such important pieces?'

'My great-grandfather (your great-great-grandfather), who was himself half French, collected it all his life. Some of it he bought during the sales of royal furniture after the Revolution and some came to him through his mother's family, the Montdores.'

'And the boiseries!' said Cedric, 'first quality Louis XV. There is nothing to equal this at Chèvres, it's like jewellery when it is so fine.'

We were now in the little dining-room.

'He brought them over too, and built the house round them.' Lord Montdore was evidently much pleased by Cedric's enthusiasm, he loved

French furniture himself but seldom found anybody in England to share his taste.

'Porcelain with Marie-Antoinette's cypher, delightful. At Chèvres we have the Meissen service she brought with her from Vienna. We have many relics of Marie-Antoinette, poor dear, at Chèvres.'

'Who lives there?' asked Lady Montdore.

'I do,' he replied carelessly, 'when I wish to be in the country. In Paris I have an apartment of all beauty, *One's* idea of heaven.' Cedric made great use of the word one, which he pronounced with peculiar emphasis. Lady Montdore had always been a one for one, but she said it quite differently, 'w'n'. 'The first floor of the Hotel Pomponne – you see that? Purest Louis XIV. Tiny, you know, but all one needs, that is to say a bedroom and a bed-ballroom. You must come and stay with me there, dear Lady Montdore, you will live in my bedroom, which has comfort, and I in the bed-ballroom. Promise me that you will come.'

'We shall have to see. Personally, I have never been very fond of France, the people are so frivolous, I greatly prefer the Germans.'

'Germans!' said Cedric earnestly, leaning across the table and gazing at her through his goggles. 'The frivolity of the Germans terrifies even *One*. I have a German friend in Paris and a more frivolous creature, Lady Montdore, does not exist. This frivolity has caused me many a heart-ache, I must tell you.'

'I hope you will make some suitable English friends now, Cedric.'

'Yes, yes, that is what I long for. But please can my chief English friend be you, dear dearest Lady Montdore?'

'I think you should call us Aunt Sonia and Uncle Montdore.'

'May I really? How charming you are to me, how happy I am to be here – you seem, Aunt Sonia, to shower happiness around you.'

'Yes, I do. I live for others, I suppose that's why. The sad thing is that people have not always appreciated it, they are so selfish themselves.'

'Oh, yes, aren't they selfish? I too have been victim to the selfishness of people all my life. This German friend I mentioned just now, his selfishness passes comprehension. How one does suffer!'

'It's a he, is it?' Lady Montdore seemed glad of this.

'A boy called Klugg. I hope to forget all about him while I am here. Now, Lady Montdore – dearest Aunt Sonia – after dinner I want you to do me a great great favour. Will you put on your jewels so that I can see you sparkling in them? I do so long for that.'

'Really, my dear boy, they are down in the strong-room. I don't think they've been cleaned for ages.'

'Oh, don't say no, don't shake your head! Ever since I set eyes on you I have been thinking of nothing else, you must look so truly glorious in them. Mrs Wincham (you are Mrs I hope, aren't you, yes yes, I can tell that you are not a spinster), when did you last see Aunt Sonia laden with jewels?'

'It was at the ball for— ' I stopped awkwardly, jibbing at the name, which was never now mentioned, but Cedric saved me from embarrassment by exclaiming:

'A ball! Aunt Sonia, how I would love to see you at a ball, I can so well imagine you at all the great English functions, coronations, Lords, balls, Ascot, Henley. What is Henley? No matter – and I can see you, above all, in India, riding on your elephant like a goddess. How they must have worshipped you there.'

'Well, you know, they did,' said Lady Montdore, delighted, 'they really worshipped us, it was quite touching. And of course, we deserved it, we did a very great deal for them, I think I may say we put India on the map. Hardly any of one's friends in England had ever even heard of India before we went there, you know.'

'I'm sure. What a wonderful and fascinating life you lead, Aunt Sonia. Did you keep a journal when you were in the East? Oh! please say yes, I would so love to read it.'

This was a very lucky shot. They had indeed filled a huge folio, whose morocco label, surmounted by an earl's coronet, announced 'Pages from our Indian Diary. M. and S. M.'

'It's really a sort of scrap-book,' Lord Montdore said, 'accounts of our journeys up-country, photographs, sketches by Sonia and our brother-in – that is to say a brother-in-law we had then, letters of appreciation from rajahs— '

'And Indian poetry translated by Montdore – "Prayer of a Widow before Suttee", "Death of an old Mahout", and so on, touching, it makes you cry.'

'Oh, I must read it all, every word, I can hardly wait.'

Lady Montdore was radiant. How many and many a time had she led her guests to 'Pages from Our Indian Diary', like horses to water, and watched them straying off after one half-hearted sip. Never before, I guess, had anybody so eagerly demanded to read it.

'Now you must tell us about your life, my dear boy,' said Lady Montdore. 'When did you leave Canada? Your home is in Nova Scotia, is it not?'

'I lived there until I was eighteen.'

'Montdore and I have never been in Canada – the States, of course, we spent a month once in New York and Washington and we saw Niagara Falls, but then we were obliged to come home, I only wish we could have gone on, they were quite touchingly anxious to have us, but Montdore and I cannot always do as we should like, we have our duties. Of course, that was a long time ago, twenty-five years I should think, but I daresay Nova Scotia doesn't alter much?'

'I am very very happy to say that kindly Nature has allowed a great sea-fog of oblivion to rise between me and Nova Scotia so that I hardly remember one single thing about it.'

'What a strange boy you are,' she said indulgently, but she was very well suited by the fact of the sea-fog, since the last thing she wanted would have been long-winded reminiscences of Cedric's family life in Canada; it was all no doubt much better forgotten, and especially the fact that Cedric had a mother. 'So you came to Europe when you were eighteen?'

'Paris. Yes, I was sent to Paris by my guardian, a banker, to learn some horrid sort of job, I quite forget what, as I never had to go near it. It is not necessary to have jobs in Paris, one's friends are so very very kind.'

'Really, how funny. I always thought the French were so mean.'

'Certainly not to *One*. My needs are simple, admittedly, but such as they are they have all been satisfied over and over again.'

'What are your needs?'

'I need a very great deal of beauty round me, beautiful objects wherever I look and beautiful people who see the point of *One*. And speaking of beautiful people, Aunt Sonia, after dinner the jewels? Don't, don't, please say no!'

'Very well, then,' she said, 'but now, Cedric, won't you take off your glasses?'

'Perhaps I could. Yes, I really think the last vestige of my shyness has gone.'

He took them off, and the eyes which were now disclosed, blinking in the light, were the eyes of Polly, large, blue, and rather blank. They quite startled me, but I do not think the Montdores were specially struck by the resemblance, though Lady Montdore said:

'Anybody can tell that you are a Hampton, Cedric. Please never let's see those horrid spectacles again.'

'My goggles? Specially designed by Van Cleef for me?'

'I hate spectacles,' said Lady Montdore firmly.

Lady Montdore's maid was now sent for, given the key of the safe from Lord Montdore's key-ring and told to bring up all the jewel cases. When dinner was over and we got back to the Long Gallery, leaving Lord

Montdore to his port, but accompanied by Cedric, who was evidently unaware of the English custom which keeps the men in the dining-room after dinner and who followed Lady Montdore like a dog, we found the map-table covered with blue velvet trays each of which contained a parure of large and beautiful jewels. Cedric gave a cry of happiness and got down to work at once.

'In the first place, dear Aunt Sonia,' he said, 'this dress won't do. Let me see – ah, yes' – he took a piece of red brocade off the piano and draped her in it very cleverly, pinning it in place on one shoulder with a huge diamond brooch. 'Have you some maquillage in this bag, dear? And a comb?'

Lady Montdore rummaged about and produced a cheap lipstick and a small green comb with a tooth out.

'Naughty, naughty you,' he said, carefully painting her face, 'it cakes! Never mind, that will do for now. Not pulling your hair, am I? We've got to show the bone structure, so beautiful on you. I think you'll have to find a new coiffeur, Aunt Sonia – we'll see about that – anyway, it must go up – up – like this. Do you realize what a difference that makes? Now, Mrs Wincham, will you please put out the top lights for me, and bring the lamp from that bureau over here. Thank you.'

He placed the lamp on the floor at Lady Montdore's feet and began to hang her with diamonds, so that the brocade was covered with them to her waist, finally poising the crown of pink diamonds on the top of her head.

'Now,' he said. 'Look!' and he led her to a looking-glass on the wall. She was entranced by the effect, which was indeed very splendid.

'My turn,' he said.

Although Lady Montdore seemed to be almost solid with diamonds the cases on the table still held many huge jewels. He took off his coat, his collar and tie, pulled open his shirt and clasped a great necklace of diamonds and sapphires round his neck, wound up another piece of silk into a turban, stuck a diamond feather in it and put it on his head. He went on talking all the time.

'You really must pat your face more, Aunt Sonia.'

'Pat?'

'With nourishing creams. I'll show you. Such a wonderful face, but uncultivated, neglected and starved. We must feed it up, exercise it and look after it better from now on. You'll soon see what a lot can be done. Twice a week you must sleep in a mask.'

'A mask?'

'Yes, back to masks, but this time I mean the sort you paint on at night. It goes quite hard, so that you look like the Commandeur in *Don*

Juan, and in the morning you can't smile, not a glimmer, so you mustn't telephone until you've removed it with the remover, because you know how if you telephone smilelessly you sound cross, and if it happened to be *One* at the other end, *One* couldn't bear that.'

'Oh, my dear boy, I don't know about this mask. What would Griffith say?'

'If Griffith is your maid she won't notice a thing, they never do. We shall notice, though, your great new beauty. Those cruel lines!'

They were absorbed in each other and themselves, and when Lord Montdore came in from the dining-room they did not even notice. He sat for a while in his usual attitude, the fingers of both hands pressed together, looking into the fire, and very soon crept off to bed. In the months which had passed since Polly's marriage he had turned into an old man, he was smaller, his clothes hung sadly on him, his voice quavered and complained. Before he went he gave the little book of poems to Cedric, who took it with a charming show of appreciation and looked at it until Lord Montdore was out of sight, when he quickly turned back to the jewels.

I was pregnant at this time and began to feel sleepy very soon after dinner. I had a look at the picture papers and then followed Lord Montdore's example.

'Good night,' I said, making for the door. They hardly bothered to answer. They were now standing each in front of a looking-glass, a lamp at their feet, happily gazing at their own images.

'Do you think it is better like that?' one would say.

'Much better,' the other would reply, without looking.

From time to time they exchanged a jewel ('Give me the rubies, dear boy.' 'May I have the emeralds if you've finished with them?') and he was now wearing the pink tiara, jewels lay all around them, tumbled on to the chairs and tables, even on the floor.

'I have a confession to make to you, Cedric,' she said, as I was leaving the room. 'I really rather like amethysts.'

'Oh, but I love amethysts,' he replied, 'so long as they are nice large dark stones set in diamonds. They suit *One* so well.'

The next morning when I went to Lady Montdore's room to say good-bye I found Cedric, in a pale mauve silk dressing-gown, sitting on her bed. They were both rubbing cream into their faces out of a large pink pot, it smelt delicious, and certainly belonged to him.

'And after that,' he was saying, 'until the end of her life (she only died just the other day), she wore a thick black veil.'

'And what did he do?'

'He left cards on all Paris, on which he had written "*mille regrets*".'

Experience of the McWilliamses with Membranous Croup

As related to the author of this book by Mr McWilliams, a pleasant New York gentleman whom the said author met by chance on a journey.

☆★☆

MARK TWAIN

Well, to go back to where I was before I digressed to explain to you how that frightful and incurable disease, membranous croup, was ravaging the town and driving all mothers mad with terror, I called Mrs McWilliam's attention to little Penelope and said:

'Darling, I wouldn't let that child be chewing that pine stick if I were you.'

'Precious, where is the harm in it?' said she, but at the same time preparing to take away the stick – for women cannot receive even the most palpably judicious suggestion without arguing it; that is, married women.

I replied:

'Love, it is notorious that pine is the least nutritious wood that a child can eat.'

My wife's hand paused, in the act of taking the stick, and returned itself to her lap. She bridled perceptibly, and said:

'Hubby, you know better than that. You know you do. Doctors *all* say that the turpentine in pine wood is good for weak back and the kidneys.'

'Ah – I was under a misapprehension. I did not know that the child's kidneys and spine were affected, and that the family physician had recommended – '

'Who said the child's spine and kidneys were affected?'

'My love, you intimated it.'

'The idea! I never intimated anything of the kind.'

'Why my dear, it hasn't been two minutes since you said – '

'Bother what I said! I don't care what I did say. There isn't any harm in the child's chewing a bit of pine stick if she wants to, and you know it perfectly well. And she *shall* chew it, too. So there, now!'

'Say no more, my dear. I now see the force of your reasoning, and I will go and order two or three cords of the best pine wood today. No child of mine shall want while I – '

'O *please* go along to your office and let me have some peace. A body can never make the simplest remark but you must take it up and go to arguing and arguing and arguing till you don't know what you are talking about, and you *never* do.'

'Very well, it shall be as you say. But there is a want of logic in your last remark which – '

However, she was gone with a flourish before I could finish, and had taken the child with her. That night at dinner she confronted me with a face as white as a sheet:

'O, Mortimer, there's another! Little Georgie Gordon is taken.'

'Membranous croup?'

'Membranous croup.'

'Is there any hope for him?'

'None in the wide world. O, what is to become of us!'

By and by a nurse brought in our Penelope to say good-night and offer the customary prayer at the mother's knee. In the midst of 'Now I lay me down to sleep,' she gave a slight cough! My wife fell back like one stricken with death. But the next moment she was up and brimming with the activities which terror inspires.

She commanded that the child's crib be removed from the nursery to our bedroom; and she went along to see the order executed. She took me with her, of course. We got matters arranged with speed. A cot bed was put up in my wife's dressing room for the nurse. But now Mrs McWilliams said we were too far away from the other baby, and what if *he* were to have the symptoms in the night – and she blanched again, poor thing.

We then restored the crib and the nurse to the nursery and put up a bed for ourselves in a room adjoining.

Presently, however, Mrs McWilliams said suppose the baby should catch it from Penelope? This thought struck a new panic to her heart, and the tribe of us could not get the crib out of the nursery again fast enough to satisfy my wife, though she assisted in her own person and well nigh pulled the crib to pieces in her frantic hurry.

We moved down stairs; but there was no place there to stow the nurse, and Mrs McWilliams said the nurse's experience would be an inestimable help. So we returned, bag and baggage, to our own bedroom once more, and felt a great gladness, like storm-buffeted birds that have found their nest again.

Mrs McWilliams sped to the nursery to see how things were going on there. She was back in a moment with a new dread. She said:

'What *can* make Baby sleep so?'

I said:

'Why, my darling, Baby *always* sleeps like a graven image.'

'I know. I know; but there's something peculiar about his sleep, now. He seems to – to – he seems to breathe so *regularly*. O, this is dreadful.'

'But my dear he always breathes regularly.'

'Oh, I know it, but there's something frightful about it now. His nurse is too young and inexperienced. Maria shall stay there with her, and be on hand if anything happens.'

'That is a good idea, but who will help *you*?'

'You can help me all I want. I wouldn't allow anybody to do anything but myself, any how, at such a time as this.'

I said I would feel mean to lie abed and sleep, and leave her to watch and toil over our little patient all the weary night. – But she reconciled me to it. So old Maria departed and took up her ancient quarters in the nursery.

Penelope coughed twice in her sleep.

'Oh, why *don't* that doctor come! Mortimer, this room is too warm. This room is certainly too warm. Turn off the register – quick!'

I shut it off, glancing at the thermometer at the same time, and wondering to myself if 70 *was* too warm for a sick child.

The coachman arrived from down town, now, with the news that our physician was ill and confined to his bed. – Mrs McWilliams turned a dead eye upon me, and said in a dead voice:

'There is a Providence in it. It is foreordained. He never was sick before. – Never. We have not been living as we ought to live, Mortimer. Time and time again I have told you so. Now you see the result. Our child will never get well. Be thankful if you can forgive yourself; I never can forgive *my*self.'

I said, without intent to hurt, but with heedless choice of words, that I could not see that we had been living such an abandoned life.

'*Mortimer!* Do you want to bring the judgment upon Baby, too!'

Then she began to cry, but suddenly exclaimed:

'The doctor must have sent medicines!'

I said:

'Certainly. They are here. I was only waiting for you to give me a chance.'

'Well do give them to me! Don't you know that every moment is precious now? But what was the use in sending medicines, when he *knows* that the disease is incurable?'

I said that while there was life there was hope.

'Hope! Mortimer, you know no more what you are talking about than the child unborn. If you would – . As I live, the directions say give one teaspoonful once an hour! Once an hour! – as if we had a whole year before us to save the child in! Mortimer, please hurry. Give the poor perishing thing a tablespoonful, and *try* to be quick!'

'Why, my dear, a tablespoonful might – '

'*Don't* drive me frantic! . . . There, there, there, my precious, my own; it's nasty bitter stuff, but it's good for Nelly – good for Mother's precious darling; and it will make her well. There, there, there, put the little head on Mamma's breast and go to sleep, and pretty soon – Oh, I know she can't live till morning! Mortimer, a tablespoonful every half hour will – . Oh, the child needs belladonna too; I know she does – and aconite. Get them, Mortimer. Now do let me have my way. You know nothing about these things.'

We now went to bed, placing the crib close to my wife's pillow. All this turmoil had worn upon me, and within two minutes I was something more than half asleep. Mrs McWilliams roused me:

'Darling, is that register turned on?'

'No.'

'I thought as much. Please turn it on at once. This room is cold.'

I turned it on, and presently fell asleep again. I was aroused once more:

'Dearie, would you mind moving the crib to your side of the bed? It is nearer the register.'

I moved it, but had a collision with the rug and woke up the child. I dozed off once more, while my wife quieted the sufferer. But in a little while these words came murmuring remotely through the fog of my drowsiness.

'Mortimer, if we only had some goose-grease – will you ring?'

I climbed dreamily out, and stepped on a cat, which responded with a protest and would have got a convincing kick for it if a chair had not got it instead.

'Now, Mortimer, why do you want to turn up the gas and wake up the child again?'

'Because I want to see how much I am hurt, Caroline.'

'Well look at the chair, too – I have no doubt it is ruined. Poor cat, suppose you had – '

'Now I am not going to suppose anything about the cat. It never would have occurred if Maria had been allowed to remain here and attend to these duties, which are in her line and are not in mine.'

'Now Mortimer, I should think you would be ashamed to make a remark like that. It is a pity if you cannot do the few little things I ask of you at such an awful time as this when our child – '

'There, there, I will do anything you want. But I can't raise anybody with this bell. They're all gone to bed. Where is the goose-grease?'

'On the mantelpiece in the nursery. If you'll step there and speak to Maria – '

I fetched the goose-grease and went to sleep again: Once more I was called:

'Mortimer, I so hate to disturb you, but the room is still too cold for me to try to apply this stuff. Would you mind lighting the fire? It is all ready to touch a match to.'

I dragged myself out and lit the fire, and then sat down disconsolate.

'Mortimer, don't sit there and catch your death of cold. Come to bed.'

As I was stepping in, she said:

'But wait a moment. Please give the child some more of the medicine.'

Which I did. It was a medicine which made a child more or less lively; so my wife made use of its waking interval to strip it and grease it all over with the goose-oil. I was soon asleep once more, but once more I had to get up.

'Mortimer, I feel a draft. I feel it distinctly. There is nothing so bad for this disease as a draft. Please move the crib in front of the fire.'

I did it; and collided with the rug again, which I threw in the fire. Mrs McWilliams sprang out of bed and rescued it and we had some words. I had another trifling interval of sleep, and then got up, by request, and constructed a flax-seed poultice. This was placed upon the child's breast and left there to do its healing work.

A wood fire is not a permanent thing. I got up every twenty minutes and renewed ours, and this gave Mrs McWilliams the opportunity to shorten the times of giving the medicines by ten minutes, which was a great satisfaction to her. Now and then, between times, I reorganized the flax-seed poultices, and applied sinapisms and other sorts of blisters where unoccupied places could be found upon the child. Well, toward morning the wood gave out and my wife wanted me to go down cellar and get some more. I said:

'My dear, it is a laborious job, and the child must be nearly warm enough, with her extra clothing. Now mightn't we put on another layer of poultices and – '

I did not finish, because I was interrupted. I lugged wood up from below for some little time, and then turned in and fell to snoring as only a man can whose strength is all gone and whose soul is worn out. Just at broad daylight I felt a grip on my shoulder that brought me to my senses suddenly. – My wife was glaring down upon me and gasping. As soon as she could command her tongue she said:

'It is all over! All over! The child's perspiring! What *shall* we do?'

'Mercy, how you terrify me! *I* don't know what we ought to do. Maybe if we scraped her and put her in the draft again – '

'O, idiot! There is not a moment to lose! Go for the doctor. Go yourself. Tell him he *must* come, dead or alive.'

I dragged that poor sick man from his bed and brought him. He looked at the child and said she was not dying. This was joy unspeakable to me, but it made my wife as mad as if he had offered her a personal affront. Then he said the child's cough was only caused by some trifling irritation or other in the throat. At this I thought my wife had a mind to show him the door. – Now the doctor said he would make the child cough harder and dislodge the trouble. So he gave her something that sent her into a spasm of coughing, and presently up came a little wood splinter or so.

'This child has no membranous croup,' said he. 'She has been chewing a bit of pine shingle or something of the kind, and got some little slivers in her throat. They won't do her any hurt.'

'No,' said I, 'I can well believe that. Indeed the turpentine that is in them is very good for certain sorts of diseases that are peculiar to children. My wife will tell you so.'

But she did not. She turned away in disdain and left the room; and since that time there is one episode in our life which we never refer to. Hence the tide of our days flows by in deep and untroubled serenity.

A Bushel of Learning

☆★☆★☆★☆★☆★☆★☆★☆★☆★☆★☆★☆★☆★☆★☆★☆

GERALD DURRELL

Scarcely had we settled into the Strawberry-pink Villa before Mother decided that I was running wild, and that it was necessary for me to have some sort of education. But where to find this on a remote Greek island? As usual when a problem arose, the entire family flung itself with enthusiasm into the task of solving it. Each member had his or her own idea of what was best for me, and each argued with such fervour that any discussion about my future generally resulted in an uproar.

'Plenty of time for him to learn,' said Leslie; 'after all, he can read, can't he? I can teach him to shoot, and if we bought a boat I could teach him to sail.'

'But, dear, that wouldn't *really* be much use to him later on,' Mother pointed out, adding vaguely, 'unless he was going into the Merchant Navy or something.'

'I think it's essential that he learns to dance,' said Margo, 'or else he'll grow up into one of these awful tongue-tied hobbledehoys.'

'Yes, dear; but that sort of thing can come *later*. He should be getting some sort of grounding in things like mathematics and French . . . and his spelling's appalling.'

'Literature,' said Larry, with conviction, 'that's what he wants, a good solid grounding in literature. The rest will follow naturally. I've been encouraging him to read some good stuff.'

'But don't you think Rabelais is a little *old* for him?' asked Mother doubtfully.

'Good, clean fun,' said Larry airily; 'it's important that he gets sex in its right perspective now.'

'You've got a mania about sex,' said Margo primly; 'it doesn't matter what we're discussing, you always have to drag it in.'

'What he wants is a healthy, outdoor life; if he learnt to shoot and sail . . .' began Leslie.

'Oh, stop talking like a bishop . . . you'll be advocating cold baths next.'

'The trouble with you is you get in one of these damned supercilious moods where you think you know best, and you won't even listen to anyone else's point of view.'

'With a point of view as limited as yours, you can hardly expect me to listen to it.'

'Now, now, there's no sense in fighting,' said Mother.

'Well, Larry's so bloody unreasonable.'

'I like that!' said Larry indignantly; 'I'm far and away the most reasonable member of the family.'

'Yes, dear, but fighting doesn't solve the problem. What we want is someone who can teach Gerry and who'll encourage him in his interests.'

'He appears to have only one interest,' said Larry bitterly, 'and that's this awful urge to fill things with animal life. I don't think he ought to be encouraged in *that*. Life is fraught with danger as it is . . . I went to light a cigarette only this morning and a damn' great bumble-bee flew out of the box.'

'It was a grasshopper with me,' said Leslie gloomily.

'Yes, I think that sort of thing ought to be stopped,' said Margo. 'I found the *most revolting* jar of wriggling things on the dressing-table, of all places.'

'He doesn't mean any harm, poor little chap,' said Mother pacifically; 'he's so interested in all these things.'

'I wouldn't mind being attacked by bumble-bees, if it *led* anywhere,' Larry pointed out. 'But it's just a phase . . . he'll grow out of it by the time he's fourteen.'

'He's been in this phase from the age of two,' said Mother, 'and he's showing no signs of growing out of it.'

'Well, if you insist on stuffing him full of useless information, I suppose George would have a shot at teaching him,' said Larry.

'*That's* a brain-wave,' said Mother delightedly. 'Will you go over and see him? I think the sooner he starts the better.'

Sitting under the open window in the twilight, with my arm round Roger's shaggy neck, I had listened with interest, not unmixed with indignation, to the family discussion on my fate. Now it was settled, I wondered vaguely who George was, and why it was so necessary for me to have lessons. But the dusk was thick with flower-scents, and the olive-groves were dark, mysterious and fascinating. I forgot about the imminent danger of being educated, and went off with Roger to hunt for glow-worms in the sprawling brambles.

I discovered that George was an old friend of Larry's, who had come to Corfu to write. There was nothing very unusual about this, for all Larry's acquaintances in those days were either authors, poets or painters. It was George, moreover, who was really responsible for our presence in Corfu, for he had written such eulogistic letters about the place that Larry had become convinced we could live nowhere else. Now George was to pay the penalty for his rashness. He came over to the villa to discuss my education with Mother, and we were introduced. We regarded each other with suspicion. George was a very tall and extremely thin man who moved with the odd disjointed grace of a puppet. His lean, skull-like face was partially concealed by a finely pointed brown beard and a pair of large tortoise-shell spectacles. He had a deep, melancholy voice, a dry and sarcastic sense of humour. Having made a joke, he would smile in his beard with a sort of vulpine pleasure which was quite unaffected by anyone else's reactions.

Gravely George set about the task of teaching me. He was undeterred by the fact that there were no school-books available on the island; he simply ransacked his own library and appeared on the appointed day armed with a most unorthodox selection of tomes. Sombrely and patiently he taught me the rudiments of geography from the maps in the back of an ancient copy of *Pears Cyclopœdia*, English from books that ranged from Wilde to Gibbon, French from a fat and exciting book called *Le Petit Larousse*, and mathematics from memory. From my point of view, however, the most important thing was that we devoted some of our time to natural history, and George meticulously and carefully taught me how to observe and how to note down observations in a diary. At once my enthusiastic but haphazard interest in nature became focused, for I found that by writing things down I could learn and remember much more. The only mornings that I was ever on time for my lessons were those which were given up to natural history.

Every morning at nine George would come stalking through the olive-trees, clad in shorts, sandals and an enormous straw hat with a frayed brim, clutching a wedge of books under one arm, swinging a walking-stick vigorously.

'Good morning. The disciple awaits the master agog with anticipation, I trust?' he would greet me, with a saturnine smile.

In the little dining-room of the villa the shutters would be closed against the sun, and in the green twilight George would loom over the table, methodically arranging the books. Flies, heat-drugged, would crawl slowly on the walls or fly drunkenly about the room, buzzing sleepily. Outside the cicadas were greeting the new day with shrill enthusiasm.

'Let me see, let me see,' George would murmur, running a long forefinger down our carefully prepared time-table; 'yes, yes, mathematics. If I remember rightly, we were involved in the Herculean task of discovering how long it would take six men to build a wall if three of them took a week. I seem to recall that we have spent almost as much time on this problem as the men spent on the wall. Ah, well, let us gird our loins and do battle once again. Perhaps it's the *shape* of the problem that worries you, eh? Let us see if we can make it more exciting.'

He would droop over the exercise-book pensively, pulling at his beard. Then in his large, clear writing he would set the problem out in a fresh way.

'If it took two caterpillars a week to eat eight leaves, how long would four caterpillars take to eat the same number? Now, apply yourself to that.'

While I struggled with the apparently insoluble problem of the caterpillars' appetites, George would be otherwise occupied. He was an expert fencer, and was at that time engaged in learning some of the local peasant dances, for which he had a passion. So, while waiting for me to finish the sum, he would drift about in the gloom of the room, practising fencing stances or complicated dancing-steps, a habit that I found disconcerting, to say the least, and to which I shall always attribute my inability to do mathematics. Place any simple sum before me, even now, and it immediately conjures up a vision of George's lanky body swaying and jerking round the dimly lit dining-room. He would accompany the dancing sequences with a deep and tuneless humming, like a hive of distraught bees.

'Tum-ti-tum-ti-tum . . . tiddle tiddle tumty *dee* . . . left leg over . . . three steps right . . . tum-ti-tum-ti-tum-ti-*dum* . . . back, round, down and up . . . tiddle iddle umpty *dee* . . .,' he would drone, as he paced and pirouetted like a dismal crane. Then, suddenly, the humming would stop, a steely look would creep into his eyes and he would throw himself into an attitude of defence, pointing an imaginary foil at an imaginary enemy. His eyes narrowed, his spectacles a-glitter, he would drive his adversary back across the room, skilfully avoiding the furniture. When his enemy was backed into the corner, George would dodge and twist round him with the agility of a wasp, stabbing, thrusting, guarding. I could almost see the gleam of steel. Then came the final moment, the upward and outward flick that would catch his opponent's weapon and twist it harmlessly to one side, the swift withdrawal, followed by the long, straight lunge that drove the point of his foil right through the adversary's heart. Through all this I would be watching him, fascinated, the exercise-book lying forgotten in front of me. Mathematics was not one of our more successful subjects.

In geography we made better progress, for George was able to give a more zoological tinge to the lesson. We would draw giant maps, wrinkled with mountains, and then fill in the various places of interest, together with drawings of the more exciting fauna to be found there. Thus for me the chief products of Ceylon were tapirs and tea; of India tigers and rice; of Australia kangaroos and sheep, while the blue curves of currents we drew across the oceans carried whales, albatross, penguins and walrus, as well as hurricanes, trade winds, fair weather and foul. Our maps were works of art. The principal volcanoes belched such flames and sparks one feared they would set the paper continents alight; the mountain ranges of the world were so blue and white with ice and snow that it made one chilly to look at them. Our brown, sun-drenched deserts were lumpy with camel-humps and pyramids, and our tropical forests so tangled and luxuriant that it was only with difficulty that the slouching jaguars, lithe snakes and morose gorillas managed to get through them, while on their outskirts emaciated natives hacked wearily at the painted trees, forming little clearings apparently for the purpose of writing 'coffee' or perhaps 'cereals' across them in unsteady capitals. Our rivers were wide, and blue as forget-me-nots, freckled with canoes and crocodiles. Our oceans were anything but empty, for where they had not frothed themselves into a fury of storms or drawn themselves up into an awe-inspiring tidal wave that hung over some remote, palm-shaggy island, they were full of life. Good-natured whales allowed unseaworthy galleons, armed with a forest of harpoons, to pursue them relentlessly; bland and innocent-looking octopi tenderly engulfed small boats in their arms; Chinese junks, with jaundiced crews, were followed by shoals of well-dentured sharks, while fur-clad Eskimos pursued obese herds of walrus through ice-fields thickly populated by polar bears and penguins. They were maps that lived, maps that one could study, frown over and add to; maps, in short, that really *meant* something.

Our attempts at history were not, at first, conspicuously successful, until George discovered that by seasoning a series of unpalatable facts with a sprig of zoology and a sprinkle of completely irrelevant detail, he could get me interested. Thus I became conversant with some historical data which, to the best of my knowledge, have never been recorded before. Breathlessly, history lesson by history lesson, I followed Hannibal's progress over the Alps. His reason for attempting such a feat, and what he intended to do on the other side were details that scarcely worried me. No, my interest in what I considered to be a very badly planned expedition lay in the fact that *I knew the name of each and every elephant*. I also knew that Hannibal had appointed a special man not only to feed and look after the elephants, *but to give them hot-water bottles when the weather got cold*. This interesting fact seems to have escaped most serious historians. Another thing that most history books never seem to mention is that Columbus's first words on setting foot ashore in America were: 'Great heavens, look . . . a jaguar!' With such an introduction, how could one fail to take an interest in the continent's subsequent history? So George, hampered by inadequate books and a reluctant pupil, would strive to make his teaching interesting, so that the lessons did not drag.

Roger, of course, thought that I was simply wasting my mornings. However, he did not desert me, but lay under the table asleep while I wrestled with my work. Occasionally, if I had to fetch a book, he would wake, get up, shake himself, yawn loudly and wag his tail. Then, when he saw me returning to the table, his ears would droop, and he would walk heavily back to his private corner and flop down with a sigh of resignation. George did not mind Roger being in the room, for he behaved himself well, and did not distract my attention. Occasionally, if he was sleeping very heavily and heard a peasant dog barking, Roger would wake up with a start and utter a raucous roar of rage before realizing where he was. Then he would give an embarrassed look at our disapproving faces, his tail would twitch and he would glance round the room sheepishly.

For a short time Quasimodo also joined us for lessons, and behaved very well as long as he was allowed to sit in my lap. He would drowse there, cooing to himself, the entire morning. It was I who banished him, in fact, for one day he upset a bottle of green ink in the exact centre of a large and very beautiful map that we had just completed. I realized, of course, that this vandalism was not intentional, but even so I was annoyed. Quasimodo tried for a week to get back into favour by sitting outside the door and cooing seductively through the crack, but each time I weakened I would catch a glimpse of his tail-feathers, a bright and horrible green, and harden my heart again.

Achilles also attended one lesson, but he did not approve of being inside the house. He spent the morning wandering about the room and scratching at the skirting-boards and door. Then he kept getting wedged under bits of furniture and scrabbling frantically until we lifted the object and rescued him. The room being small, it meant that in order to move one bit of furniture we had to move practically everything else. After a third upheaval George said that as he had never worked with Carter Paterson and was unused to such exertions, he thought Achilles would be happier in the garden.

So there was only Roger left to keep me company. It was comforting, it's true, to be able to rest my feet on his woolly bulk while I grappled with a problem, but even then it was hard to concentrate, for the sun would pour through the shutters, tiger-striping the table and floor, reminding me of all the things I might be doing.

There around me were the vast, empty olive-groves echoing with cicadas; the moss-grown stone walls that made the vineyards into steps where the painted lizards ran; the thickets of myrtle alive with insects, and the rough headland where the flocks of garish goldfinches fluttered with excited pipings from thistle-head to thistle-head.

Realizing this, George wisely instituted the novel system of outdoor lessons. Some mornings he arrived carrying a large furry towel, and together we would make our way down through the olive-groves and along the road that was like a carpet of white velvet under its layer of dust. Then we branched off on to a goat-track that ran along the top of miniature cliffs, until it led us to a bay, secluded and small, with a crescent-shaped fringe of white sand running round it. A grove of stunted olives grew there, providing a pleasant shade. From the top of the little cliff the water in the bay looked so still and transparent that it was hard to believe there was any at all. Fishes seemed to drift over the wave-wrinkled sand as though suspended in mid-air; while through six feet of clear water you could see rocks on which anemones lifted frail, coloured arms, and hermit crabs moved, dragging their top-shaped homes.

We would strip beneath the olives and walk out into the warm, bright water, to drift, face down, over the rocks and clumps of seaweed, occasionally diving to bring up something that caught our eye: a shell more brightly coloured than the rest; or a hermit crab of massive proportions, wearing an anemone on his shell, like a bonnet with a pink flower on it. Here and there on the sandy bottom grew rib-shaped beds of black ribbon-weed, and it was among these beds that the sea-slugs lived. Treading water and peering down, we could see below the shining, narrow fronds of green and black weeds growing close and tangled, over which we hung like hawks suspended in air above a strange woodland. In the clearing among the weed-bed lay the sea-slugs, perhaps the ugliest of the sea fauna. Some six inches long, they looked exactly like overgrown sausages made out of thick, brown, carunculated leather; dim, primitive beasts that just lie in one spot, rolling gently with the sea's swing, sucking in sea-water at one end of their bodies and passing it out at the other. The minute vegetable and animal life in the water is filtered off somewhere inside the sausage, and passed to the simple mechanism of the sea-slug's stomach. No one could say that the sea-slugs led interesting lives. Dully they rolled on the sand, sucking in the sea with monotonous regularity. It was hard to believe that these obese creatures could defend themselves in any way, or that they would ever need to, but in fact they had an unusual method of showing their displeasure. Pick them up out of the water, and they would squirt a jet of sea-water out of either end of their bodies, apparently without any muscular effort. It was this water-pistol habit of theirs that led us to invent a game. Each armed with a sea-slug we would make our weapon squirt, noting how and where the water struck the sea. Then we moved over to that spot, and the one who discovered the greatest amount of sea fauna in his area won a point. Occasionally, as in any game, feeling would run high, indignant accusations of cheating would be made and denied. It was then we found our sea-slugs useful for turning on our opponent. Whenever we had made use of the sea-slugs' services we always swam out and returned them to their forest of weed. Next time we came down they would still be there, probably in exactly the same position as we had left them, rolling quietly to and fro.

Having exhausted the possibilities of the slugs, we would hunt for new shells for my collection, or hold long discussions on the other fauna we had found; George would suddenly realize that all this, though most enjoyable, could hardly be described as education in the strictest sense of the word, so we would drift back to the shallows and lie there. The lesson then proceeded, while the shoals of little fish would gather about us and nibble gently at our legs.

'So the French and British fleets were slowly drawing together for what was to be the decisive sea battle of the war. When the enemy was sighted, Nelson was on the bridge bird-watching through his telescope . . . he had already been warned of the Frenchmen's approach by a friendly gull . . . eh? . . . oh, a greater black-backed gull I think it was . . . well, the ships manœuvred round each other . . . of course they couldn't move so fast in those days, for they did everything by sail . . . no engines . . . no, not even outboard engines . . . The British sailors were a bit worried because the French seemed so strong, but when they saw that Nelson was so little affected by the whole thing that he was sitting on the bridge labelling his birds'-egg collection, they decided that there was really nothing to be scared about . . .'

The sea was like a warm, silky coverlet that moved my body gently to and fro. There were no waves, only this gentle underwater movement, the pulse of the sea, rocking me softly. Around my legs the coloured fish flicked and trembled, and stood on their heads while they mumbled at me with toothless gums. In the drooping clusters of olives a cicada whispered gently to itself.

'. . . and so they carried Nelson down below as quickly as possible, so that none of the crew would know he had been hit . . . He was mortally wounded, and lying below decks with the battle still raging above, he murmured his last words: "Kiss me, Hardy," and then he died . . . What? Oh yes. Well, he had already told Hardy that if anything happened to him he could have his birds' eggs . . . so, though England had lost her finest seaman, the battle had been won, and it had far-reaching effects in Europe . . .'

Across the mouth of the bay a sun-bleached boat would pass, rowed by a brown fisherman in tattered trousers, standing in the stern and twisting an oar in the water like a fish's tail. He would raise one hand in lazy salute, and across the still, blue water you could hear the plaintive squeak of the oar as it twisted, and the soft clop as it dug into the sea.

Fish Royal

☆★☆★☆★☆★☆★☆★☆★☆★☆★☆★☆★☆

A. P. HERBERT

TINRIB, RUMBLE, AND OTHERS *v.* THE KING AND QUEEN
(*Before Mr Justice Wool*)

In this unusual action, the hearing of which was begun today, an interesting point is raised concerning the rights and duties of the Crown in connexion with a dead whale.

Sir Ethelred Rutt, K. C. (*for the plaintiffs*): May it please your Lordship, this action is brought by Mr Tinrib, Mr Rumble, and the other plaintiffs on behalf of the inhabitants of Pudding Magna, situated, milord, in the county of Dorset—

The Court: Where is Dorset?

Sir Ethelred: Milord, I have a map here. Dorset, milord, if your Lordship will glance at the bottom left-hand corner – Dorset, milord, is, milord, Dorset—

The Court: Quite – quite. Get on, please, Sir Ethelred.

Sir Ethelred: I am greatly obliged to your Lordship. Pudding Magna, milord, is situated in the north-east corner of Pudding Bay, or the Devil's Entry. The inhabitants are mainly fisher-folk of lowly origin and modest means, and, so far as can be ascertained, the place is not referred to in any of the works of Mr Thomas Hardy, Mr William Wordsworth, or any other writer—

The Court: O si sic omnes!

Sir Ethelred: Ha! Milord, in the night of June 21st last a dead whale was washed up on the shore of Pudding Bay, at a point south-west by south from the township of Pudding Magna. Now, the whale, milord, together with the sturgeon and the swan, is Fish Royal, and belongs to the King; or, to be precise, the head of the whale belongs to His Majesty the King and the tail to Her Majesty the Queen. Your Lordship will recall the case of *Rex* v. *Monday* (1841) 3 A. C., which decided the latter point.

The Court: I recall nothing of the kind.

Sir Ethelred: Your Lordship is very good. The loyal inhabitants of Pudding Magna, milord, made haste to extract from the carcass of the whale the whalebone, the blubber, and other valuable and perishable portions, with the intention, I am instructed, of holding them in trust for the Crown. And I may say at once that any other construction of their motives will be most strenuously resisted, if necessary, by sworn evidence. Three days later, milord, the wind, which had been northerly, shifted to the prevailing quarter, which is south-east—

Sir Wilfred Knocknee, K. C.: You mean south-west.

Sir Ethelred: I am very greatly obliged to me learned friend. Me learned friend is perfectly right, milord; the prevailing wind is south-west, milord; and, milord, on the fifth day the presence of the whale began to be offensive to the inhabitants of Pudding Magna. They therefore looked with confidence to the Crown to remove to a more convenient place the remnant of the Crown's property—

Sir Wilfred (aside): For which they had no use.

Sir Ethelred: Really, milord, me learned friend must not whisper insinuations of that kind under his breath; really, milord, I am entitled to resent, milord—

The Court: Go on, Sir Ethelred.

Sir Ethelred: Your Lordship is extraordinarily handsome and good. Accordingly, milord, the Mayor of Pudding Magna addressed a humble petition to the Home Secretary, milord, begging him to acquaint His Majesty with the arrival of his property and praying for its instant removal. And by a happy afterthought, milord, a copy of this petition was sent to the Minister of Agriculture and Fisheries.

Happy, milord, for this reason, that the original communication appears to have escaped the notice of the Home Secretary entirely. At the Ministry of Agriculture and Fisheries, however, the Mayor's letter was handed to a public servant named Sleep, a newcomer to the Service, and one, it seems, who combined with a fertile imagination an unusual incapacity for the conduct of practical affairs. This gentleman has now left the public service, milord, and will be called.

It appears, milord, that, when the Mayor's letter had been lying unconsidered on Mr Sleep's desk for several days, the following telegram was handed to him:

> *'To the King London whale referred to in previous communications now in advanced stages decomposition humbly petition prompt action*
>
> *Tinrib'*

Mr Sleep, milord, according to his own account, turning the matter over in his sagacious mind, at once hit upon a solution which would be likely to satisfy the requirements of His Majesty's Treasury with regard to public economy. Two days later, therefore, a letter was addressed to the Director of the Natural History Museum informing him that an unusually fine specimen of *Balaena Biscayensis* was now lying in Pudding Bay and that the Minister was authorized by His Majesty to offer the whale to the Museum in trust for the nation, the Museum to bear the charges of collection and transport.

On July 3rd, milord, the Secretary to the Natural History Museum replied that he was desired by the Director to express his regret that, owing to lack of space, the Museum was unable to accept His Majesty's gracious offer. He was to add that the Museum was already in possession of three fine specimens of *Balaena Biscayensis.*

Milord, for some days, it appears, Mr Sleep took no further action. Meanwhile, milord, the whale had passed from the advanced to the penultimate stages of decomposition, and had begun to poison the sea at high water, thereby gravely impairing the fishermen's livelihood. Mr Tinrib, milord, was in constant, but one-sided, correspondence with Mr Sleep; and on the 12th of July, milord, Mr Sleep lunched with a friend and colleague at the Admiralty, Mr Sloe. While they were engaged, milord, upon the discussion of fish, the topic of whales naturally arose, and Mr. Sleep, milord, unofficially, milord, expressed to Mr Sloe the opinion that the Ministry of Agriculture and Fisheries would be willing to grant to the Admiralty the use of the whale for the purpose of target-practice; and he suggested that one of His Majesty's ships should be immediately detailed to tow His Majesty's whale out to sea. He also pointed out the peculiar advantages of such a target for the exercise of such vessels as were called upon to fire at submarines. Mr Sloe, milord, undertook to explore the opinion of the Admiralty on the proposal, and the conference broke up.

That was on the 12th. On the 17th, milord, Mr Sloe unofficially, milord, at a further lunch, intimated to Mr Sleep that he could find no support among their Lordships of the Admiralty for the proposal of the Ministry of Agriculture and Fisheries; for, while excellent practice was to be had from a disappearing target, their Lordships could not sanction the expenditure of ammunition on a target which must, at most ranges, be quite invisible. Further, it was their opinion that by the date of the autumn firing-practices the whale would have suffered dissolution by the ordinary processes of nature.

The inhabitants of Pudding Magna, milord, did not share this view. On the 20th, milord, Mr Tinrib and a deputation waited upon Mr Sleep. They pointed out to Mr Sleep that all fishing was suspended in Pudding Bay; that Pudding Magna was now scarcely habitable except on the rare occasions of a northerly wind; that the majority of the citizens had fled to the hills and were living in huts and caves. They further inquired, milord, whether it would be lawful for the fishermen themselves to destroy the whale, so far as that could be done, with explosives, and, if so, whether the Crown would refund the cost of the explosives, which might be considerable. As to this, milord, Mr Sleep was unable to accept the responsibility of expressing an opinion; but the whale was undoubtedly Crown property, and he questioned gravely whether the Treasury would sanction the expenditure of public money on the destruction of Crown property by private citizens. He also pointed out that the Treasury, if approached, would be likely to require a strict account of any whalebone, blubber, and other material extracted from the whale's carcass. Mention of explosives, however, had suggested to his mind that possibly the War Office might be interested in the whale, and he undertook to inquire. The deputation agreed, milord, that this perhaps would be the better course, and withdrew.

On the 24th, milord, a letter was dispatched to the War Office pointing out that the whale now lying in Pudding Bay offered excellent opportunities for the training of engineers in the removal of obstacles, and could well be made the centre of any amphibious operations, landing-parties, invasions, etc., which might form part of the forthcoming manœuvres. The War Office would doubtless take note of the convenient proximity of the whale to the Tank Corps Depot at Lulworth.

On the 31st, milord, the War Office replied that the destruction of whales by tanks was no longer considered a practicable operation of war, and that no part of the forthcoming manœuvres would be amphibious.

From this date, milord, Mr Sleep seems to have abandoned his efforts. At any rate, on the 4th of August, Mr Tinrib received the following evasive and disgraceful communication:

'WHALE, CARCASS OF

'Dear Sir,

'I am desired by the Minister of Agriculture and Fisheries to observe that your representations to this Department appear to have been made under a misapprehension. It should hardly be necessary to state that the whale is not a fish but a mammal. I am therefore to express regret that the Ministry of Agriculture and Fisheries can accept no responsibility in the matter.'

In these circumstances, milord, the inhabitants, or I should say the *late* inhabitants, of Pudding Magna have been compelled to institute these proceedings, and humbly pray—

The case was adjourned.

Moving to New Hampshire

☆★☆

P. J. O'ROURKE

Not long ago I moved from New York City to a small town in New Hampshire. I didn't know much about country life, but I was in love with New England scenery. I wanted to do my writing in an atmosphere of pastoral serenity. And I felt a need for a healthier life. Also, I'd never had a roof repaired so I thought New York was the most expensive place on earth to live. Since many other city people are moving into the countryside, I feel an obligation to pass along what I've learned. I also feel an obligation to pay for my new roof.

When moving to rural New England, the first consideration is choice of a town. There are three kinds of town in New England: towns that know they're cute, towns that don't know they're cute, and towns determined to become cute no matter what.

Towns that know they're cute are characterized by high real-estate prices, frequent arts-and-crafts fairs, and numerous Volvos with 'Save the Whales' bumper stickers. It's Vermont, really, that specializes in this kind of town. You don't want to live in one of these. The 'shoppe' signs are all misspelled, the arts-and-crafts fairs tie up traffic, and (it hurts to tell this to the people in the Volvos) Vermont doesn't *have* any whales.

Towns that don't know they're cute are even worse. Most seem to have zoning regulations requiring lawn ornaments and house trailers in every yard. You'll buy a beautiful home on Main Street and wake up the next morning to find someone else has bought the beautiful home directly across from you, torn it down, and built a gas station. And the teenage natives use the Meeting House's 1690 weather vane for rifle practice. This is painful to those of us with finer aesthetic sensibilities who'd like to make it into a lamp.

The right kind of town is the one determined to become cute. My own town, Jaffrey, is one of these. We're taking up a collection to repair the weather vane, and there's an effort under way to have our Main Street gas station spell Shell with an extra 'e.' Towns like Jaffrey have civic pride and local spirit, but they have their drawbacks too. Civic pride means committees. And there's always the danger of getting drafted. Last year we had an infestation of gypsy moths. My committee spent three weeks cutting oak leaves out of yellow construction paper and gluing them to tree limbs so sightseers wouldn't be disappointed during the autumn foliage season.

Once you've chosen a town, the next step is to choose a house. There is a general rule about houses in New England: the worse the architecture, the more authentically Colonial the house. If a house has a grand appearance, handsome layout, and large airy rooms, it's Victorian junk. But if you can't, at first glance, tell it from a mobile home, it was built before 1700. Of course, it isn't fair to say that. Very few mobile homes have five-foot ceilings, basements full of water, or sill rot. Anyway, when checking for authenticity, make sure the rooms are the size of bath mats and that the electrical system looks horrid. Our colonial forebears seem to have been notably poor electricians.

One thing you will not have to worry about is your view. Every authentic Colonial house in New England has a splendid view. Just ask the real-estate agent. 'View?' said mine. 'Of course there's a view! Climb out this window onto the porch roof, Mr O'Rourke, and shinny up that chimney – absolutely breathtaking.'

Actually buying the house will be no different from buying a house anywhere else, except for the title search. New England deed records go back 350 years, and in every one of those years somebody made a mistake. This results in unusual deeds. One property I looked at had fifteen acres. Two acres were in front of the house and the remaining land ran in a three-inch-wide strip fifty-five miles north to Lake Winnipesaukee. Be prepared to pay a large legal fee. 'You know,' said the local lawyer doing my title search, 'that land originally belonged to the Indians. I had to go looking all over for them. I looked in Aspen, Vail, and Sun Valley. They weren't there, so . . .'

And even after you've cleared the title and paid for the house, it won't be called yours. My house is 'the Yateman place.' There hasn't been a Yateman in Jaffrey for fifty years. And I don't think a Yateman ever owned my house anyway. 'The Yateman place' is just a device to rag newcomers. Though I have been assured that my house will eventually be called 'the O'Rourke place.'

'Everybody'll call it that,' said a neighbor, 'just as soon as you die there.'

Another thing, no matter how stately the home or how much land or how many outbuildings, the only thing the natives will ever say about it is, 'You know that place sold for eight thousand in 1976.'

It will take time for you to get used to these country ways, not to mention getting used to the country itself. The climate, for instance – we have two seasons in New England, winter and getting-ready-for-winter. I was used to banging on my apartment building's pipes when I wanted more heat in the middle of the night. I've found this doesn't work with my own wood furnace. Nor are municipal services exactly like the city's. I was putting trash out at the end of my driveway for three months before I noticed . . . well, I noticed three months' worth of trash out at the end of my driveway.

Just running simple errands is a problem for transplanted New Yorkers. We are brusque, fast-moving people. But there's an unwritten law in New England: Anytime you go anywhere to conduct any type of business, first you have to have a little talk.

When you go to the butcher shop, you're not going there to buy meat. It's a social call. Even if you've never seen the butcher before, you say, 'How's it going?' and 'Come on by sometime' and 'Give my regards to your wife if you're married.'

He'll say, 'Black flies bad up at your place this year?'

You'll say, 'Getting any wood in?'

And so on. Anything to do with pot roast is strictly incidental, and the subject cannot be raised politely for at least thirty minutes.

This frightens me. I know people do it to be friendly. I try to talk for hours with everyone I see. But I'm scared that if I call the fire department and yell 'Help! My house is on fire!' I'll get someone on the other end of the line saying, 'Ah-yep, fellow down at Antrim had his house on fire too. Must have been just about this time, 1981. Black flies bad up at your place this year?'

The local newspapers are a great help in catching the spirit of country life. These publications show that rural New Englanders live in a different world than New Yorkers, possibly on a different planet.

I've been collecting items from the papers in my area. This headline was printed large on page one of the *Monadnock Ledger*: 'Spaghetti Supper Set for Friday.' It's the sort of headline we could do with more of in the *New York Post*. 'Motorist Damages Yard in Hit and Run Accident' – that appeared on the front page of the *Peterborough Transcript*. And here, from the *Keene Sentinel*, is my personal favorite: 'Maine Legislature Goes Home.'

A story about the planning board in Jaffrey read, in part, 'The planners did not decide on the subdivision last week. By the time the public hearings were over . . . it was after 11:00 P.M. The planners did not think they should be making decisions when they were tired.' It's hard to imagine Congress being that downright. I'd like to see a story in the *New York Times* saying, 'Congressmen did not decide on the defense budget last night. The members of Congress did not think they should be making decisions when they were half-witted, corrupt, and drunk.' But the most telling item I've found in my local papers read simply, 'Money was found on Middle Hancock Road on Sunday, June 5.' Eleven words which paint a picture of almost baffling decency.

Things like that will make you want to get to know your neighbors. Believe me, they'll already know you. New Englanders are not nosy. They pride themselves on respecting the privacy of others. All the same, they manage to know everything about you, and sometimes they'll let it slip. You'll be on the phone, making a long-distance call. 'Operator,' you'll say, 'I'm having trouble getting through to my mother in Florida.'

The operator will say, 'You really ought to call her more often, and you haven't written her a real letter since Christmas.'

Or you'll be shopping in a local store and the salesclerk, a total stranger to you, will say, 'But that's not the kind of undershirt you usually wear.'

The first of these neighbors you should get to know is the plumber. Marry him if you can. In some rural places the most prominent citizen is the doctor or the reverend at the church; not so in New England. It's the plumber, and for good reason. When your water pipes freeze and burst at 3:00 A.M., try calling an M.D. or a priest.

It will be easier to get to know the plumber, and everyone else, if you understand local values. One local value is early rising. Don't let on that you sleep until 10:00. It's considered hilarious. Personally, I sleep in my clothes with a coffee mug beside my bed. That way, when someone rings the doorbell at 5:00 A.M. to see if I'd like help stacking cordwood, I can run downstairs with cup in hand and pretend to have been awake for hours. Getting up early means going to bed early, and it worries people if you don't. When I first moved to Jaffrey, I was having a 1:00 A.M. nightcap when I heard a knock on the door. It was a concerned-looking native in a bathrobe. 'We saw your lights on,' he said. 'Is anything wrong?'

The two most important New England values, however, are honesty and thrift. Honesty you've already seen exampled in Middle Hancock Road where someone found money and did what only a born and bred small-town Yankee would do and called the newspapers. This honesty is a great thing but dangerously habit-forming. On visits to New York I have found myself telling people, 'Just charge me what you think is fair.' And there is no polite way to express what people in New York think is fair.

More important even than honesty is thrift, not to say outright tight-fistedness. Money in the city is like money in Weimar Germany. You go to the Citibank cash machine, get a wheelbarrowful of the stuff, and shovel it out whenever you're told. Then you cross your fingers and hope to die before the Visa Card people process your change of address. But Yankees are serious about spending money. And they give advice at length on the subject.

'Drive over to Portland, Maine,' they'll say, 'and you can get two cents off paper towels.' Or 'There's a special on five-gallon cans of margarine at the A&P. Limit, six to a customer.' And they're especially forthcoming with advice about what you should have paid for your house. 'You know that place sold for eight thousand in 1976.'

Besides changes in values, country life means changes in all your activities. Many city pursuits are inappropriate to the new venue. If you go jogging in Jaffrey, people will stop and offer you a ride. And having dinner at 9:00 is considered as bizarre as sunbathing on a roof. Do not, however, adopt local customs wholesale.

Fishing, for example, turns out to be less serene than it looks on calendars. It is a sport invented by insects and you are the bait.

Hunting is as uncomfortable and much more hazardous. Deer hunting, particularly, attracts Visigothic types from places like Worcester, Massachusetts. I spend all of deer-hunting season indoors trying not to do anything deerlike.

Gardening is better. Everyone in New England will be eager to give you advice about a flower garden – too eager, in fact. By the time I'd spent a month listening to gardening advice, I was so confused the only thing I could remember was that you shouldn't plant bulbs upside down. This is nonsense, and I have a septic tank full of daffodil blooms to prove it.

Vegetable gardening is even more frustrating. The last hard frost in New England comes about July 10 and the first autumn frost comes about two weeks later. Then there are the raccoons. If anything does grow, the raccoons will take it and you'll have to call the Pentagon Rapid Deployment Force to get it back. What I do is just *say* I have a vegetable garden. I dig up some of the lawn, put on a raccoon suit, make tracks in the dirt, and go buy my vegetables at the local garden stand.

I've adopted similar techniques for home renovation. At first I thought it would be relaxing and a fine hobby to fix up my own house. But visits to the hardware store proved too embarrassing. Whatever it is you need, you don't know what it's called. And they'll laugh at you when you ask for 'a large metal thing which is heavy at one end but a good deal heavier at the other.'

While being careful not to fix up your own house, be especially careful not to fix it up in real Colonial antiques. There's one place where the honesty of rural New Englanders breaks down in a woeful fashion. This is the antique store. New England antique stores are dens of iniquity. If you ever do go into one, keep repeating this to yourself: 'It's *not* an authentic milk-paint pre-Revolutionary hanging cupboard. It's a dirty old box out of somebody's garage.'

Moving to the country is, in general, a splendid way of finding out how ignorant and unhandy you are. I knew I didn't know much about gardening or fixing things around the house, but I thought even I could burn a pile of brush. It's worth noting that practically everything in rural areas is flammable. So much for the lovely scenery.

Indeed, by the time I'd lived six months in New England, all my good reasons for moving there had disappeared. Pastoral serenity is elusive in a town where every man, woman, and child over five owns a chain saw and starts it promptly at dawn each day. And as for healthy living, the state motto of New Hampshire seems to be 'Can I freshen that up for you?'

I was feeling quite glum about all this one day while I was helping another ex-city fellow pull stumps out of his pasture. My friend George, a former resident of San Diego, had rented a backhoe, and he and I had spent all morning cutting, digging, and yanking at tree roots while I wondered why I'd ever left Murray Hill. George and I were down in a trench hacking at one particularly recalcitrant oak carcass when a local farmer pulled up in his truck. The farmer stared out across the pasture, surveyed the dozen holes with uprooted stumps sitting next to each, looked down in the hole where George and I were, and said, 'George, you'll never make any money planting those.'

Then I realized why I'd moved to the country. Neighbors gather from miles around to see me try to light a wood stove. My sojourns at the town dump with my Volkswagen convertible buried to its hubs in mud are local legend. And the residents of Jaffrey consider it a better show than *Return of the Jedi* to see a New Yorker try to get a porcupine out of the barn with two oven mitts and a broom handle.

You move to the country for the same reason that underlies many great artistic endeavors. It's done for the sake of entertainment. And what better thing is there in life than bringing mirth and merriment to the people all around you?

Acknowledgements

The publishers wish to thank the following for their permission to use the following material: David Higham Associates for 'Funny Turns' from *Every Living Thing* by James Herriot; Alberto and Carlotta Guareschi for 'On the Trail' from *The Little World of Don Camillo* by Giovanni Guareschi; David Higham Associates for 'Confessions of a TV Playwright' from *An Unnatural Pursuit* by Simon Gray; Aurum Press for 'December' from *Letter from New York* by Helene Hanff; Penguin Books Ltd for an extract from *A Year in Provence* by Peter Mayle; Reed Consumer Books for 'The Futility of Life' from *The Dagenham Dialogues* by Peter Cook and Dudley Moore (Methuen London); Constable Publishers for 'My Father' from *Runyon from First to Last* by Damon Runyon; Reed Consumer Books for an extract from *The Queen and I* by Sue Townsend (Methuen London); HarperCollins Publishers for an extract from *The Dalkey Archive* by Flann O'Brien; Reed Consumer Books for an extract from *The Long Dark Tea-Time of the Soul* by Douglas Adams (William Heinemann); Random House UK Ltd for 'A Sunday Kind of Love' from *The Kandy-Kolored Tangerine-Flake Streamline Baby* by Tom Wolfe; Reed Consumer Books for 'Cleaning' from *Up to You Porky* by Victoria Wood (Methuen London); Reed Consumer Books and Michael Imison Playwrights Ltd for 'Stop Me if You've Heard It' from *The Short Stories* by Noël Coward (Methuen London); Penguin Books Ltd for 'A Country Christmas' from *Great Meadow* by Dirk Bogarde; Random House UK Ltd for 'The Metropolitan Touch' from *The Inimitable Jeeves* and 'Goodbye to all Cats' from *Young Men in Spats* by P.G. Wodehouse; Penguin Books Ltd for an extract from *The Moon's a Balloon* by David Niven; Aitken, Stone and Wylie Ltd for 'Loser Wins' from *The Consul's File* by Paul Theroux; Pan Macmillan Children's Books for 'William and Photography' from *William the Fourth* by Richmal Crompton; Reed Consumer Books for 'A White Wedding' from *A Bit of a Do* by David Nobbs (Methuen London); Gerald Duckworth and Co Ltd for 'The Sexes' from *The Best of Dorothy Parker* by Dorothy Parker; Reed Consumer Books for an extract from *1066 and All That* by

W.C. Sellar and R.J. Yeatman (Methuen London); Faber and Faber Ltd and Macmillan Publishers Inc for 'Shy Rights' from *Happy to Be Here* by Garrison Keillor; David Campbell Publishers Ltd for 'Philippa's Fox-Hunt' from *Further Experiences of an Irish RM* by Edith Somerville and Martin Ross; Little, Brown for 'The Man They Tried to Kill' from *Gridlock* by Ben Elton; Reed Consumer Books for 'The Wash-Tub' from *65 Short Stories* by W. Somerset Maugham (William Heinemann) and for an extract from *The Lost Continent* by Bill Bryson (Martin Secker and Warburg); Robson Books Ltd for 'Deflowered but not For-Lawn' from *Something to Fall Back On* by Maureen Lipman, and for 'Smiling Through' from *Bin Ends* by Alan Coren; Laurence Pollinger Ltd and the Estate of H.E. Bates for an extract from *The Darling Buds of May* by H.E. Bates; Bernard Geis Associates (New York), the original publisher, for 'On Thrift', excerpted from *Memoirs of a Mangy Lover* by Groucho Marx, © 1963 Groucho Marx; Macmillan London for 'The Royal Me' from *My Gorgeous Life* by Dame Edna Everage; David Higham Associates for 'Trefusis and Rosina' from *The Paperweight* by Stephen Fry; Faber and Faber Ltd for an extract from 'Green Forms' from *Office Suite* by Alan Bennett; Reed Consumer Books for 'Hunting with the Hoorays' from *Turn Right at the Spotted Dog* by Jilly Cooper (Methuen London); David Higham Associates for 'What I Did on My Holidays' from *Fanny Peculiar* by Keith Waterhouse; Penguin Books Ltd for 'Here Come the Tigers' from *The Beast in Me and Other Animals* by James Thurber; Richard Scott Simon Ltd for 'Eng. Lit.' from *Stately as a Galleon* by Joyce Grenfell; Reed Consumer Books for 'Polyurethane' from *You Have My Word* by Frank Muir and Denis Norden (Methuen London); Peters Fraser and Dunlop Group for 'Mr Prendergast's Story' from *Decline and Fall* by Evelyn Waugh, 'Basic Training' from *Unreliable Memoirs* by Clive James, and an extract from *Love in a Cold Climate* by Nancy Mitford; Reed Consumer Books for an extract from *Porterhouse Blue* by Tom Sharpe (Martin Secker and Warburg); Random House UK Ltd for an extract from *Doctor in the Soup* by Richard Gordon; Gerald Duckworth and Co Ltd for 'Ash, no Sackcloth' from *More Home Life* by Alice Thomas Ellis; Random House UK Ltd on behalf of the Estate of Stephen Leacock for 'How to Borrow Money' from *The Bodley Head Leacock*; Robson Books Ltd for 'That Certain Smile' from *Welcome to Kington* by Miles Kington; HarperCollins Publishers for 'A Bushel of Learning' from *My Family and Other Animals* by Gerald Durrell; A.P. Watt Ltd on behalf of Jocelyn Herbert and Crystal Hale for 'Fish Royal' from *Uncommon Law* by A.P. Herbert; Pan Macmillan Ltd and Grove Atlantic (Atlantic Monthly Press) for 'Moving to New Hampshire' from *Republican Party Reptile* by P.J.

O'Rourke. The Publishers have made every effort to trace copyright-holders, and trust that their apologies will be accepted for any errors or omissions.